Comparative Politics Today
A World View

Advanced Placement* Edition

Gabriel A. Almond
Stanford University

Russell J. Dalton
University of California, Irvine

G. Bingham Powell, Jr.
University of Rochester

Kaare Strøm
University of California, San Diego

PEARSON
Longman

New York   San Francisco   Boston
London   Toronto   Sydney   Tokyo   Singapore   Madrid
Mexico City   Munich   Paris   Cape Town   Hong Kong   Montreal

The editors and co-authors of *Comparative Politics Today*
dedicate this book to the memory of Gabriel A. Almond,
a giant in the field of comparative politics and a friend,
colleague, and leader, who passed away at the age of 91.

Editor-in-Chief: Eric Stano
Senior Marketing Manager: Elizabeth Fogarty
Supplements and Media Editor: Kristi Olson
Production Manager: Eric Jorgensen
Project Coordination, Text Design, and Electronic Page Makeup: GGS Book Services
Cover Design/Manager: John Callahan
Cover Photo: Courtesy of PhotoDisc, Inc.
Photo Research: Jody Potter
Senior Manufacturing Buyer: Dennis J. Para
Printer and Binder: The Hamilton Printing Co.
Cover Printer: Phoenix Color Corp.

Library of Congress Cataloging-in-Publication Data

Comparative politics today: a world view / [edited by] Gabriel A. Almond, Russell J. Dalton, G.
Bingham Powell, and Kaare Strøm.—Advanced Placement ed.
    p. cm.
  Includes bibliographical references and index.
  ISBN 0-13-194568-8
  1. Comparative government—Textbooks. I. Almond, Gabriel A. (Gabriel Abraham). II. Dalton,
Russel J. III. Powell, G. Bingham. IV. Strøm, Kaare.
  JF51.C62 2007
  320.3—dc22

                                        2006008317

Visit us at www.ablongman.com

ISBN 0-13-194568-8

  3 4 5 6 7 8 9 10—HT—09 08 07

BRIEF CONTENTS

DETAILED CONTENTS

CHAPTER 10

Politics in Mexico   254

Wayne A. Cornelius and Jeffrey A. Weldon

CHAPTER 11

Politics in Nigeria   310

Robert J. Mundt and Oladimeji Aborisade

PREFACE TO THE ADVANCED PLACEMENT * EDITION OF *COMPARATIVE POLITICS TODAY*

It is a pleasure to be able to offer this special AP* edition of *Comparative Politics Today* for use in high school Advanced Placement Program* courses. The first seven chapters of this edition offer the general introduction to the field of comparative politics. The country chapters, written by distinguished specialists on the politics of each country, include the countries that are in the AP* program: Great Britain, Russia, China, Mexico, and Nigeria. We have a new chapter on politics in Iran, written especially for the AP* edition. We have also included our chapter on the United States, which we think helps students to understand some new concepts by presenting them in a familiar context.

Comparative Politics Today has long been used in AP* courses, as well as in introductory college courses in comparative politics. We introduce the fundamental concepts of political system, political culture, political functions and structures, and policymaking that allow us to compare very different kinds of political systems. We discuss how governments try to achieve such goals as building community, providing security, promoting economic development, protecting rights, and enhancing social justice. We explain how sometimes government becomes part of the problem, rather than the solution. We describe the social, economic, and international conditions that make government more difficult. We also discuss the roles of different kinds of political organizations—interest groups, political parties—and political institutions—legislatures, executives, courts—in the policymaking process. All these concepts are applied and illustrated in the chapters on specific countries.

It may be helpful to indicate more specifically where the topics that are designated in the **AP* Comparative Government and Politics Course Description Outline** can be found in the Introductory and System, Process, Policy chapters in this text. These topics are also covered, as appropriate, in the country chapters. We recommend that users follow the logic of the book itself, taking the introductory chapters in order, taking special note of AP* content area topics when these arise. However, it is also possible to address them in the order of the AP* curriculum. The correlation between the **AP* Course Description Outline** and the presentation in our theoretical chapters is provided in a table on page xv.

Each of the country chapters is organized following a common framework, making them easy to compare with each other, with the themes in the introductory and theoretical chapters and with the AP* curriculum. That common framework begins with current policy challenges and then discusses the unique historical origins of politics in that political system, as well as relevant features of the social and economic environment. The constitutional arrangements and main political institutions are introduced, usually followed by a discussion of the political culture and citizen participation. Interest groups and interest articulation are usually described next, followed by electoral system, parties, and party system. The policymaking process and the roles played by various institutions, emphasizing the ones most important in the specific country, are the next section. The chapter generally concludes with an overview of

* AP, Advanced Placement, and Advanced Placement Program are registered trademarks of The College Board, which was not involved in the production of, and does not endorse, this product.

public policy and policy performance, domestic and international.

The country chapters were revised in 2005 to include such recent events as the May 2005 election in Britain that returned Tony Blair as Prime Minister for a third consecutive time, and the American election that reelected George W. Bush as president in 2004. The Russia chapter includes the 2003 Duma election, which produced a majority for the United Party linked to President Putin, as well as Putin's own reelection in 2004 and his increasing domination of Russia. The China chapter covers the dramatic changes sweeping Chinese economy and society, in the context of continuing domination by the communist party-state. In Mexico we see the consequences of the remarkable election of 2000, which brought Vincente Fox into office as the first president from an opposition political party, signifying Mexico's transition to democracy. Nigeria demonstrates the terribly difficult struggle to sustain a constitutional, elected government in a context of great poverty, human hardship, ethnic division, and

corruption. The new chapter on Iran describes the complex, multiple centers of power in the world's only large theocratic state, one engaged in challenging interactions with the rest of the world.

We live in a dynamic and increasingly connected world, with important changes occurring across the globe. This makes it an interesting time to be a student of comparative politics. Events in far-flung capitals affect our own lives in many ways. At the same time, seeing the many different ways of running political systems and the impacts of different cultural and economic environments helps us understand the nature of our own political system. We hope that this special AP* edition will be helpful to AP* teachers of comparative politics, who have our greatest respect as they challenge their outstanding students to step outside the familiar bounds of American politics.

RUSSELL J. DALTON
G. BINGHAM POWELL
KAARE STRØM

COMPARATIVE POLITICS TODAY SUPPLEMENTS

Longman Publishers is pleased to be able to offer qualified adopters of this text, and their students, several ancillaries that will make teaching and learning from this text even more effective and enjoyable.

AP* Test Prep
ISBN: 0-13-229866-X

Specifically created to accompany *Comparative Politics Today*, this student guide contains an overview of the AP* program and the AP* Comparative Politics and Government exam. It also provides test-taking strategies, correlations between key AP* test topics and the textbook, practice study questions, guidelines for mastering multiple-choice and free-response questions, and practice tests.

AP* Instructor's Manual & Tests
ISBN: 0-13-195999-9

This supplement provides chapter overviews, chapter outlines, learning objectives, teaching suggestions, key terms, discussion and essay questions, and AP*-style multiple-choice questions for each chapter.

AP* TestGen
ISBN: 0-13-196046-6

This easy-to-customize test generation software package contains all of the AP*-style multiple-choice questions from the printed Test Bank. This fully net-workable, user-friendly program enables instructors to view and edit questions, and print tests in a variety of formats.

ACKNOWLEDGMENTS

We are pleased to acknowledge the contributions of some of the many people who helped us prepare *Comparative Politics Today*. In particular, we are grateful to Carl LeVan, who made a most valuable and timely contribution to the updating of the Nigeria chapter. We would also like to thank the following individuals for their careful review and analysis of the book: Maria Hsia Chang at the University of Nevada, Reno; James Sperling at the University of Akron; James Warhola at the University of Maine.

The co-authors want to make a number of specific acknowledgments for help on their contributions to *Comparative Politics Today*.

Melanie Manion wishes to thank Russ Dalton for his helpful comments and to thank Michel Oksenberg and Nina Halpern for their comments on an earlier version of the China chapter.

Wayne Cornelius and Jeffery Weldon wish to thank Claudia Y. Carmona and Luis Estrada for research assistance on the Mexico chapter.

Oladimeji Aborisade thanks Robert LaGamma, Curtis Huff, Arlene Jacquerre, and Charlotte Peterson for bringing together himself and Robert Mundt under the auspices of the U.S. Information Agency, and colleagues John A. Ayoade, Cecil Brown, Roger Brown, Charles Coe, Chukwuemeka Ebo, Alex Gboyega, Jim Mean, Aladosu Oyelakin, Gary Rassel, Jim Svara, and Deil Wright for help in comparing the United States and Nigeria in the earlier version of the Nigeria chapter.

Arang Keshavarzian thanks Adrian Dumitru, Nicola Gaye, and Katayon Kholdi-Haghighi for their research assistance.

CONTRIBUTORS

OLADIMEJI ABORISADE
*Obafemi Awolowa University,
Nigeria*

GABRIEL A. ALMOND
Stanford University

H.E. CHEHABI
Boston University

WAYNE A. CORNELIUS
University of California, San Diego

RUSSELL J. DALTON
University of California, Irvine

ARANG KESHAVARZIAN
Connecticut College

MELANIE MANION
University of Wisconsin

ROBERT J. MUNDT
University of North Carolina at Charlotte

G. BINGHAM POWELL, JR.
University of Rochester

AUSTIN RANNEY
University of California, Berkeley

THOMAS F. REMINGTON
Emory University

RICHARD ROSE
University of Aberdeen

KAARE STRØM
University of California, San Diego

JEFFREY A. WELDON
*Instituto Technologico Autónomo de Mexíco
(ITAM)*

CORRELATION GUIDE

AP∗ COMPARATIVE GOVERNMENT AND POLITICS COURSE DESCRIPTION OUTLINE CORRELATED TO *COMPARATIVE POLITICS TODAY*, ADVANCED PLACEMENT∗ EDITION

AP∗ Topics	*Comparative Politics Today*, AP∗ Edition
I. Introduction to Comparative Politics	Chapters 1 & 2
Purpose and methods of comparison and classification	13–16, 31–44
Why/ways to organize government	34–44
Normative and empirical questions	13–16, 31–34
Concepts (state, nation, regime, government)	2, 11–13, 16–17
Process and policy (what is politics; purpose of government; what is political science/comparative; common policy challenges)	1, 3–11, 16–29, 31–32, 129–150
II. Sovereignty, Authority, and Power	Chapters 1, 3, 6, Country studies
Political culture, communication, and socialization	46–60, 177–178, 180–183, 226–230, 266–269, 326–332, 379–383, 420–423, 474–483
Nations and states	11–13
Supranational governance (e.g., European Union)	12–13, 356
Sources of power	3, 11
Constitutions (forms, purposes, application)	27–28, 101–103, 167–168, 334–335, 416–417, 460–461, 467–468
Regime types	48–50, 103–110, 240
Types of economic systems	150–153
State building, legitimacy, and stability	3–6, 11, 47–48, 177–178
Belief systems as sources of legitimacy	1–3, 19–21, 36, 47–50, 54–55, 215–216, 365–366, 457, 480–482
Religion	19–21, 54–55, 365–366, 457, 480–482
Ideology (liberalism, communism, socialism, conservatism, fascism)	1–3, 36, 47–50, 215–216
Governance and accountability	110–111
III. Political Institutions	Chapters 4–6, Country studies
Levels of government	Chapter 6, Country studies
Supranational/national/ regional/local	217, 374–379, 474
Unitary/federal	107–108, 162–165, 335–338, 373–374, 417-418
Centralization/decentralization	194–197
Executives (head of state, head of government, cabinets)	115–122, 168–173, 218, 370–372, 464–466
Single or dual	115–118
President	370–371, 465–466
Prime minister	168–171

AP* Topics	*Comparative Politics Today,* AP* Edition
Consequences	24–25, 59, 160–162, 197, 209, 317–318
Relationship between political and economic change	10–11, 59, 211–214, 363–365, 398–401
Globalization and fragmentation: interlinked economies, global culture, reactions against globalization, regionalism	29, 69, 75, 344, 498–499
VI. Public Policy	Chapter 7, Country studies
Common policy issues	38, 108–111, 171, 218–219, 224–226, 277, 302–304, 339–340, 374, 401–403, 420, 465–467, 488
Economic performance	22–23, 199–200, 243–245, 412, 414–416, 458–459
Social welfare (e.g., education, health, poverty)	135–137, 350–352, 412, 443–446, 492–494
Civil liberties, rights, and freedoms	27–29, 354, 494–496
Environment	25–27, 151, 446–447
Population and migration	17–18, 25–27, 214, 245–248, 318
Economic development	22–27, 248, 349–350, 357–358, 490–492
Factors influencing public policymaking and implementation	158–159, 180, 188, 200–202, 238, 241, 248–249, 257–258, 320–321, 324, 349, 353, 405–406, 429–432, 441–446, 496–498
Domestic	158–159, 180, 188, 238, 324, 349, 429–432, 441–446
International	248–249, 257–258, 353, 496–498

A BRIEF GUIDE TO ANALYZING VISUALS

We are used to thinking about reading written texts critically—for example, reading a textbook carefully for information, sometimes highlighting or underlining as we go along—but we do not always think about "reading" visuals in this way. We should, for images and informational graphics can tell us a lot if we read and consider them carefully. Especially in the so-called information age, in which we are exposed to a constant stream of images on TV and the Internet, it is important for you to be able to analyze and understand their meanings. This brief guide will provide some information about the types of visuals you will encounter in *Comparative Politics Today: A World View*, and will offer some questions to help you analyze everything from charts and graphs to news photographs.

Tables

Tables are the least "visual" of the visuals we explore. They consist of textual information and/or numerical data arranged in columns and rows. Tables are frequently used when exact information is required and when orderly arrangement is necessary to locate, and, in many cases, to compare the information. For example, Table 1.4 makes data on the income distribution of many nations organized and easy to compare. Here are a few questions to guide your analysis:

- What is the purpose of this table? What information does it show? There is usually a title that offers a sense of the table's purpose.
- What information is provided in the column headings (provided in the top row)? How are the rows labeled? Are there any clarifying notes at the bottom of the table?
- Is there a time period indicated, such as July to December 2005? Or, are the data as of a specific date, such as January 1, 2006? Are the data shown at multiple intervals over a fixed period or at one particular point in time?
- If the table shows numerical data, what do these data represent? In what units? Dollars spent on social service programs? Percentage of voters who support the British Labour Party? Projected population increases?
- What is the source of the information presented in the table? Is it government information? Private polling information? A newspaper? A corporation? The United Nations? An individual? Is the source trustworthy? Current? Does the source have a vested interest in the data expressed in the table?

Charts and Graphs

Charts and graphs depict numerical data in visual forms. The most common kinds of graphs plot data in two dimensions along horizontal and vertical axes. Examples that you will encounter throughout this text are line graphs, pie charts, bar graphs, and timelines. These kinds of visuals emphasize data relationships: at a particular point in time, at regular intervals over a fixed period of time, or, sometimes, as parts of a whole. Line graphs show a progression, usually over time [as in Crimes Reported in Mexico's Federal District (Mexico City), 1993–2002 (daily average)]. Pie charts (such as 2004 Russian State Budget) demonstrate how a whole (total government spending) is divided into its parts (different types of government programs). Bar graphs compare values across categories, showing how proportions are related to each other (as in the male and female populations in China by age bracket). Bar graphs can

T A B L E   1 . 4   Income Distribution for Selected Nations

Country	Year	Wealthiest 10%	Poorest 40%	Per Capita GNP (1998)
Japan	1979	22.4	21.9	32,380
United States	1994	28.5	15.3	29,340
Germany	1989	22.6	22.5	25,850
France	1989	24.9	19.9	24,940
Britain	1986	24.7	19.9	21,400
Brazil	1995	47.9	8.2	4,570
Mexico	1992	39.2	11.9	3,970
Russia	1993	22.2	20.0	2,300
Egypt	1991	26.7	21.2	1,290
China	1995	30.9	15.3	750
India	1994	25.0	22.2	430
Nigeria	1992	31.4	12.9	300

Source: World Bank, *World Development Report, 1999-2000* (New York: Oxford University Press, 2000), table 5. pp. 238-39.

F I G U R E   1 0 . 8   Crimes Reported in Mexico's Federal District (Mexico City), 1993–2002 (daily average)

Note: Reported crimes include robberies of passerby, on public transport, of vehicle, of house, of business, violent homicide, aggravated assault and rape. Information is updated until May 1, 2002.

Source: Procuraduría de Justicia del Distrito Federal's website: www.pgjdf.gob.mx

present data either horizontally or vertically. Timelines show events and changes over a defined period of time (such as the list of Prime Ministers of Britain over time). You will also encounter charts that map out processes and hierarchies throughout this text (as in the structure of the government of Nigeria).

Many of the same questions you ask about tables are important when analyzing graphs and charts as well (see above). Here are more questions to help you:

- In the case of line and bar graphs, how are the axes labeled? Are symbols or colors used to represent different groups or units?

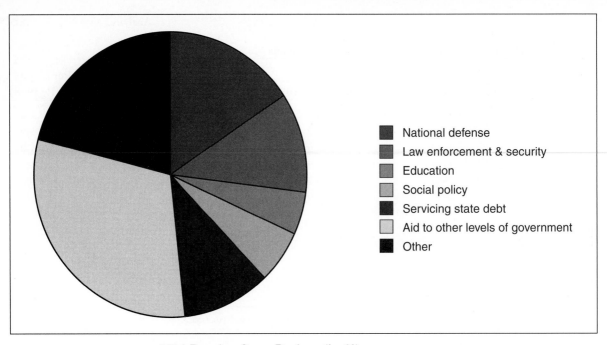

FIGURE 12.5   2004 Russian State Budget (in %)

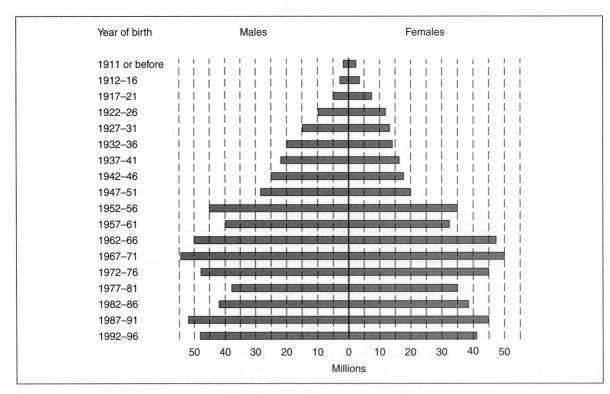

FIGURE 9.5   Estimated Midyear Population Structure, 1996

Source: Projections by the U.S. Bureau of the Census, based on birth rates from the Chinese State Statistical Bureau and preliminary results from the 1995 1 percent sample census. From Judith Banister, "China: Population Dynamics and Economic Implications," edited by the Joint Economic Committee, U.S. Congress in *China's Economic Future: Challenges to U.S. Policy* (Armonk, NY: M. E. Sharpe, 1997), p. 347.

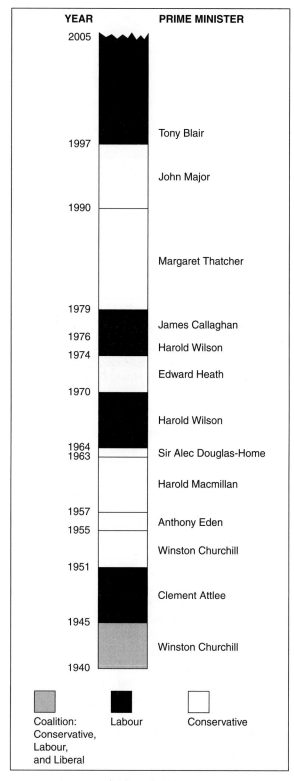

YEAR	PRIME MINISTER
2005	
1997	Tony Blair
1990	John Major
1979	Margaret Thatcher
1976	James Callaghan
1974	Harold Wilson
1970	Edward Heath
1964	Harold Wilson
1963	Sir Alec Douglas-Home
1957	Harold Macmillan
1955	Anthony Eden
1951	Winston Churchill
1945	Clement Attlee
1940	Winston Churchill

Coalition: Conservative, Labour, and Liberal   Labour   Conservative

FIGURE 8.2   Prime Minister and Governments Since 1940

- Are the data shown at multiple intervals over a fixed period or at one particular point in time?
- If there are two or more sets of figures, what are the relationships among them?
- Is there distortion in the visual representation of the information? Are the intervals equal? Does the area shown distort the actual amount or the proportion? Distortion can lead you to draw an inaccurate conclusion on first sight, so it's important to look for it.

Maps

Maps of countries, regions, and the world are often used in political analysis to illustrate demographic, social, economic, and political issues and trends. See, for example, Levels of Social Well-Being by State, in 2000 (page xxiii). Though tables and graphs might be able to give more precise information in some cases, maps help us to understand data in a geographic context that is more difficult to express in words or numbers alone. Here are a few more questions to add to those in the above sections:

- What does the map key/legend show? What are the factors that the map is analyzing? Are symbols or colors used to differentiate sections of the map? Maps can express information on political boundaries, natural resources, ethnic groups, and many other topics, so it is important to know what exactly is being shown.
- What is the region being shown? How detailed is the map?
- Maps usually depict a specific point in time. What is the point in time being shown on the map?

News Photographs

Photos can have a dramatic—and often immediate—impact on politics and government. Think about some photos that have political significance. For example, do you remember the photos from the

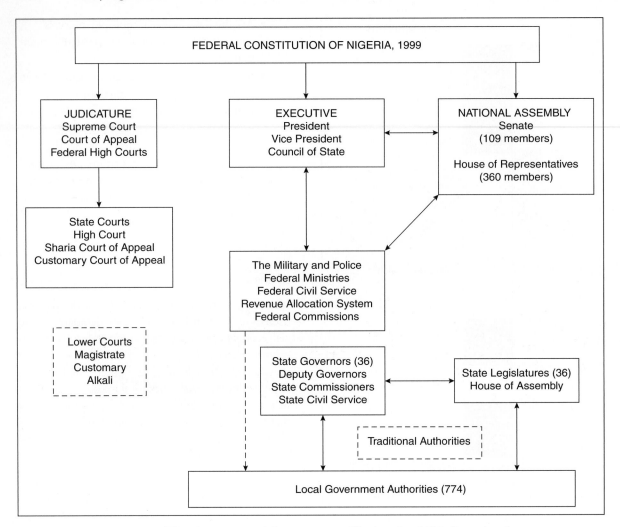

FEDERAL CONSTITUTION OF NIGERIA, 1999

JUDICATURE
Supreme Court
Court of Appeal
Federal High Courts

EXECUTIVE
President
Vice President
Council of State

NATIONAL ASSEMBLY
Senate
(109 members)

House of Representatives
(360 members)

State Courts
High Court
Sharia Court of Appeal
Customary Court of Appeal

The Military and Police
Federal Ministries
Federal Civil Service
Revenue Allocation System
Federal Commissions

Lower Courts
Magistrate
Customary
Alkali

State Governors (36)
Deputy Governors
State Commissioners
State Civil Service

State Legislatures (36)
House of Assembly

Traditional Authorities

Local Government Authorities (774)

F I G U R E   1 1 . 4   The Structure of Government Under the 1999 Constitution

September 11, 2001, terrorist attacks? Visual images usually evoke a stronger emotional response from people than do written descriptions. For this reason, individuals and organizations have learned to use photographs as a means to document events, make arguments, offer evidence, and even in some cases to manipulate the viewer into having a particular response. The photo of a student protester confronting tanks in Tiananmen Square (page xxiv) captured the attention of the world and drew attention to the violent response of the Chinese government to the protesters. Here are a few questions to guide your analysis:

- When was the photograph taken? (If there is no date given for the photograph in its credit line or caption, you may be able to

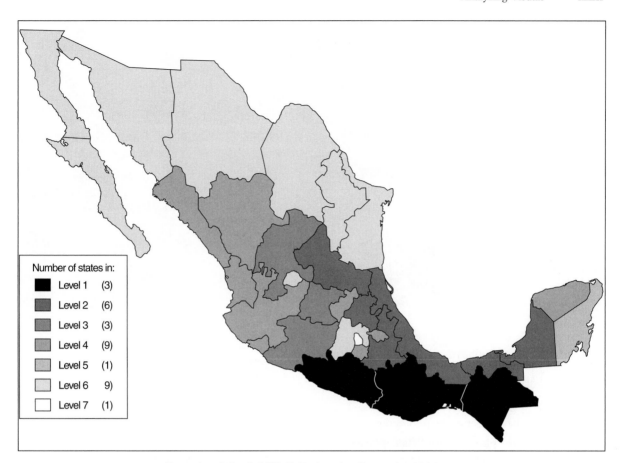

F I G U R E   1 0 . 7   Levels of Social Well-Being by State, in 2000

Level 1: Chiapas, Guerrero, Oaxaca.
Level 2: Campeche, Hidalgo, Puebla, San Luis Potosí, Tabasco, Veracruz.
Level 3: Guanajuato, Michoacán, Zacatecas.
Level 4: Colima, Durango, Jalisco, Morelos, Nayarit, Querétaro, Sinaloa, Tlaxcala, Yucatán.
Level 5: Quintana Roo.
Level 6: Aguascalientes, Baja California, Baja California Sur, Coahuila, Chihuahua, México, Nuevo León, Sonora, Tamaulipas.
Level 7: Distrito Federal.

Note: Level of social well-being is measured by characteristics of dwellings (have electricity, refrigerator, television, concrete vs. dirt floors, sewerage connection, private bathroom; number of rooms; use something other than firewood or coal for cooking) and population characteristics (percentage economically active; literate; 6–19-year-olds who attend school; receive health care; live in urban area; average number of children born to women over 12 years of age).

Source: Instituto Nacional de Estadística, Geografía e Informática, www.inegi.gob.mx

In 1989, ordinary Chinese participated in the largest spontaneous protest movement the communists had ever faced. A lone protester shows defiance of regime violence in his intransigent confrontation with a Chinese tank.

AP/Wide World Photos

approximate the date according to the people or events depicted in the photo.)

- What is the subject of the photograph?
- Why was the photo taken? What appears to be the purpose of the photograph?
- Is it spontaneous or posed? Did the subject know he or she was being photographed?

- Who was responsible for the photo? (An individual, an agency, or an organization?) Can you discern the photographer's attitude toward the subject?
- Is there a caption? If so, what kind of information does it provide? Does it identify the subject of the photo? Does it provide an interpretation of the subject?

Issues in Comparative Politics

WHAT IS POLITICS?

Some people love politics. They may relish the excitement of political events, such as elections, as they would an exciting athletic contest (a World Series or SuperBowl, perhaps). Others are fascinated with politics because they care about the issues and their consequences for people in their own communities or around the world. On the other hand, there are those who hate politics, either because it sets groups and individuals against each other, or because it involves abuse of power, deceit, manipulation, treachery, and violence. Finally, there are those who are indifferent to politics, who perhaps find it boring because it has little to do with the things that matter most to them. Most of us react to politics with a mixture of these sentiments, which may change with time and events. Politics has many faces and can be a force for good as well as evil. This book is about the comparative study of politics. In order to make political comparisons, we need to understand what is meant by politics as well as what it means to study it comparatively. The former is the task of this chapter, whereas Chapter 2 will discuss the latter.

Politics has to do with human decisions, and political science is the study of such decisions. Yet, not all decisions are political, and many of the social sciences are concerned with decisions that are of little interest to political scientists. For example, consider a situation in which you go with a friend (a date, perhaps) to an event such as a concert or a soccer match. You have a certain amount of money at your disposal. You can spend this money on your tickets (to get the best seats possible) or on food and drink, or you can save it. Economists might be interested in

what sorts of spending decisions you make. Psychologists might wish to know why you were going with this friend and not with someone else, or in how you and your friend decided what to do. Political scientists are not likely to want to study any of these questions, unless perhaps the event you attended turned into a riot (both soccer matches and concerts occasionally do), or the experience somehow changed your political outlook (which may occasionally happen at soccer matches and concerts, too, though you probably should not hold your breath).

The main point here is that not all choices or decisions are political. Specifically, political decisions are *public* and *authoritative*. To say that politics has to do with public decisions is to say that politics is inherently social. Politics always involves and has consequences for multiple human beings. There is no such thing as political solitaire, playing politics by yourself. Political decisions always take place within some community that we may call a *political system*. We shall discuss that concept later.

Yet, not all social decisions are public. Most of what happens within families, among friends, or within voluntary associations belongs to the *private* sphere. Actions within this sphere are voluntary, not regulated, and do not bind anyone outside the group involved. In most societies, with whom you go to concerts and what food you buy are private decisions. When many people are indifferent to politics, it is largely because they value this private sphere, in which they may place their family life, friendships, faith, and nature, more highly than they regard the public domain. Societies vary greatly in the scope of the public versus the private sphere. In totalitarian societies, the public sphere is very large and private life very limited. In other societies, the private domain may almost crowd out the public one. To complicate things even more, the boundaries between the public and private spheres get redrawn all the time. A couple of decades ago, the sex lives of U.S. presidents or members of the British royal family were considered private matters, not to be discussed in public and certainly not by politicians. In recent years, this seems to have changed, although in other countries the traditional standards remain. On the other hand, there was a time in British history when certain religious beliefs were in themselves considered treasonous. People who held such beliefs could be executed, as was Thomas More under King Henry VIII. Nowadays, most modern democracies consider religious beliefs to be private matters, though other societies may not. Yet, all societies maintain some distinction between public and private affairs. And although politics may be influenced by what happens in the private domain, it has directly to do only with those decisions that are public.

Also, politics is authoritative. Authority means formal power that is vested in individuals or groups with the expectation that their decisions will be carried out and respected. That is to say that the choices in which we are interested are designed to be binding (compulsory) for those individuals or groups to whom they apply. In some cases, force (coercion) may be applied to ensure that they are implemented. Those who have political authority typically have access to force and to monetary resources so that they can enforce their decisions. We call such resources means of coercion. Authority does not have to be backed up by coercion, but in politics it often is. Nowadays, in most advanced democracies religious authorities, such as the Pope, have few coercive powers. They can only persuade, but rarely compel, their followers. On the other hand, tax authorities, such as the Internal Revenue Service in the United States, can typically not only exhort but also compel.

By politics we thus refer to the activities associated with the control of public decisions among a given people and in a given territory, where this control may be backed up by authoritative and coercive means. Politics refers to the use of these authoritative and coercive means—who gets to employ them and for what purposes.

GOVERNMENTS AND THE STATE OF NATURE

Authority and coercive control are typically exercised by governments. **Governments** are organizations of individuals who are legally empowered to make binding decisions on behalf of a particular community. Governments thus have authoritative and coercive powers. Governments do many things. They wage war or encourage peace, cultivate or restrict international trade, open their borders to the exchange of ideas and art or close them, tax their populations heavily or lightly and through different means, allocate resources for education, health, and welfare, or leave such matters to others.

Governments may take many different forms, and they may be more or less ambitious or expansive. In the nineteenth century, most Western countries had very limited governments built on the model of the **night watchman state:** governments that provided basic law and order, defense, and protection of property rights, but little else (though education was also becoming a major government concern). Twentieth-century political development has produced two much more expansive types of governments. One is the **police state** seen in many authoritarian societies, particularly under communism or fascism. The second is the **welfare state** with programs of social welfare assistance, unemployment benefits, accident and sickness insurance, old age pensions, public education, and the like. German Chancellor Otto von Bismarck's government first began developing such programs in the 1880s in response to Germany's rapid industrialization and urbanization, which had caused widespread social displacement and distress. His programs were soon copied by governments in many other countries and especially democratic ones. The scope and cost of welfare state programs have since grown enormously, particularly from the Great Depression of the 1930s until the 1970s. Yet, welfare state policies differ greatly from country to country. Welfare policies in the United States stress equality of opportunity through public education. In contrast, many Western European countries have given priority to social security and health programs over education.

As government expenditures have grown to between one-third and one-half of the national product in most industrialized democracies, problems have arisen. In some countries the increasing cost and alleged inefficiencies of the welfare state have brought about efforts to prevent further increases in programs and to impose limits on public expenditures. The size of the government budget and its effects on savings, investment, inflation, and employment have become central issues. In effect, the government's role in providing welfare services has become more contested. The **regulatory state** that had developed alongside the welfare state has also come in for criticism and reassessment, and many economic sectors have been deregulated. We shall return to these issues in Chapter 7.

This debate over the welfare state and the regulatory state is far from new. On the contrary, it calls to mind a classic polemic in political philosophy. For centuries, political philosophers have debated whether government is a force for good or evil. In the seventeenth and eighteenth centuries—the time of the English, French, and American revolutions—much of this debate was couched in arguments concerning the **state of nature**. Philosophers thought about the state of nature as the condition that would obtain if no government existed. In some cases, they may have thought that such a state had actually existed before the advent of the first governments. At any rate, these philosophers used their ideas of a state of nature to identify some ideal social contract (agreement) on which societies could build. We therefore often refer to them as social contract theorists. The age of exploration, the discovery of previously unknown continents, and encounters with unfamiliar societies and cultures fed their imaginations. Even today, many political philosophers find it useful to make such a mental experiment to consider the consequences of political intervention.

Among the social contract philosophers whose reflections on the state of nature have become highly influential are Britons Thomas Hobbes and John Locke, and the Frenchman Jean-Jacques Rousseau. Though the state of nature had a similarly critical place in their respective political philosophies, their ideas about this condition varied dramatically. The contrast between Hobbes and Rousseau is most striking. Hobbes thought of the state of nature as mercilessly inhospitable, a situation of eternal conflict of all against all, and a source of barbarism and continuous fear. Referring to the state of nature, he pessimistically argued that "In such condition, there is no place

for Industry; because the fruit thereof is uncertain: and consequently no Culture of the Earth; no Navigation, nor use of the commodities that may be imported by Sea; no commodious Building, . . . no Arts; no Letters; no Society; and which is worst of all, continuall feare, and danger of violent death; And the life of man, solitary, poor, nasty, brutish, and short."[1]

For Rousseau, on the other hand, the state of nature represented humanity before its fall from grace, without all the corruptions that governments have introduced. "Man is born free," Rousseau observed in *The Social Contract*, "and yet everywhere he is in chains." Rousseau saw governments as the source of power and inequality, and these conditions in turn as the causes of human alienation and corruption. "The extreme inequality in our way of life," he argued, "excess of idleness in some, excess of labor in others; . . . late nights, excesses of all kinds, immoderate ecstasies of all the passions; fatigues and exhaustion of mind, numberless sorrows and afflictions . . . that most of our ills are our own work; that we would have avoided almost all of them by preserving the simple, uniform, and solitary way of life prescribed to us by nature."[2]

Finally, John Locke, whose ideas have been particularly important for the development of Western democracies, took a position in between those of Hobbes and Rousseau. Locke did not share Hobbes's dire view of the state of nature. Compared with Hobbes, Locke thought of human beings as more businesslike and less war prone. Yet, like Hobbes he proposed a social contract to replace the state of nature with a system of government. But whereas for Hobbes, the main task for government was to quell disorder and protect against violence and war, Locke saw the state's main role as protecting property and commerce and promoting economic growth. This it would do, in his view, by establishing and enforcing property rights and rules of economic exchange. And whereas Hobbes thought government needed to be a Leviathan, a benevolent dictator to whom the citizens would yield all their power, Locke promoted a limited government.

WHY GOVERNMENTS?

As the social contract philosophers have pointed out, there are many reasons why human beings create governments and prefer to live under such a social order. Later social theorists and politicians have come to add many items to their catalog of useful functions that governments serve. We shall discuss some of these, beginning with activities that help generate a stable community in the first place and proceeding to those that help this community prosper.

Community- and Nation-Building

One of the first purposes that governments can serve is to help create and maintain a stable and peaceful community. While humans are social beings, it is not always easy to build a community in which large numbers of individuals can communicate, feel at home, and engage in constructive interaction such as settled family life or trade. It is a particular challenge to foster such a common identity among large numbers of people living in an extended area without regular interaction with one another. We commonly call such large-scale communities based on a common perceived identity nations. Governments can help generate such communities in many different ways, for example by teaching a common language, instilling common norms and values, creating common myths and symbols, supporting a national identity, and so forth. Nation-building activities help instill common world views, values, and expectations. Using a concept discussed at greater length in Chapter 3, we can say that such government activities can help homogenize the **political cultures** of their citizens. And the more homogeneous the political culture, the easier it is to live in peaceful coexistence and engage in activities for mutual gain, such as commerce.

Security and Order

Thomas Hobbes believed that governments, and only strong governments, could make society safe for its inhabitants. Providing security, law, and order are indeed among the most essential tasks that governments are called upon to perform. We often distinguish between external and internal security, both of which were important concerns to Hobbes. External security means protection against attacks from other political systems. National defense forces, such as armies, navies, and air forces, are typically created to perform this function. Internal security means protection against theft, aggression, and violence from members of one's own society. In most societies this

is the function of the police. The provision of security and order still plays a critical role in modern states, most of which employ military as well as police forces. The German social scientist Max Weber saw a monopoly on the use of force as the defining property of the modern state. Consider this issue for a moment. While governments across the world have privatized many of the services they used to perform—for example, post offices, railroads, telecommunications, health care, and pensions—it is hard to think of governments that have privatized their police or defense forces (though some U.S. states have privatized prisons).

Protecting Property and Other Rights

John Locke saw the establishment and protection of economic and political rights as the most essential purpose of government. Though Locke's greatest concern may have been with economic property rights, there are many other social and political rights that governments, and perhaps only governments, can provide. Among them are freedoms of speech and association and protection against various forms of discrimination and harassment. Nonetheless, Locke considered property rights to be particularly critical to the sustained development of nations and other communities. Without effective protection of property rights, people will not invest much of their goods or energies in productive processes. Also, unless property rights exist and credible contracts can be negotiated and enforced, people will not trust their neighbors enough to engage in much trade and commerce. Therefore, anything beyond the mere subsistence economy requires effective property rights and contracts. Effective property rights must clearly allocate ownership and use and protect against trespass and violations. Such rights must also make the buying and selling ("alienation") of property relatively inexpensive and painless. Finally, citizens must have faith that their property rights will persist and be defended (long-term credibility). The more effective the property rights, the more people will trade, invest, and enter into other long-term agreements that generate sustained economic growth.

Promoting Economic Efficiency and Growth

Governments can thus help promote economic development by establishing and enforcing effective property rights and by facilitating trade. Particularly in the twentieth century, however, economists have come to see many other ways in which government can promote economic development. These are related to market failures in capitalist economies. Neoclassical economics shows that market economies are efficient when property rights are defined and protected, competition rigorous, and information freely available. When one or several of these conditions do not hold, however, market failures may result, and supply may not efficiently meet demand.

Public goods are particularly susceptible to market failure. Public goods have two defining characteristics. One is that if they are provided to one consumer, they cannot be withheld from anyone else. The second is that one person's enjoyment or consumption of the good does not detract from anyone else's. Consider clean air or national defense. It is, for most practical purposes, impossible to provide one person with clean air or defense without also giving it to his or her neighbors. Moreover, my enjoyment of clean air or national security does not mean that my neighbors have any less of it. It is often argued that for these reasons, in a market economy people will not pay for public goods which will therefore be undersupplied. If anyone can benefit from such goods as public parks and lighthouses, why should I (or anyone else) voluntarily pay for them? Only government, it is argued, can by taxing its citizens step in and provide such public goods as parks, roads, lighthouses, national defense, and environmental protection.

A second and related type of market failure is **externalities**, which occur when some economic activity produces costs that are not borne or taken into account by any of the parties. Though externalities need not be bad, some certainly are. Many forms of environmental degradation occur when neither those who produce the goods nor those who consume them bear all the production costs. Polluting factories, waste dumps, prisons, pornographic shops, or major highways can impose large uncompensated costs on those who live near them, and recent years have witnessed a major rise in protest activity among so-called NIMBY ("not-in-my-backyard") groups. Governments can help protect against the imposition of obnoxious externalities or ensure that burdens are fairly shared.

So-called natural monopolies represent yet another role governments can play in promoting economic growth and efficiency. There are some goods, it is commonly held, for which efficiency dictates that there should be only one supplier. This typically occurs because there are very large start-up costs or because of the prohibitive costs of coordination between different suppliers. The government may then step in and become the monopolist, or it may tightly control a private or semipublic monopolist. In the nineteenth century, for example, many countries created railroad monopolies, which were frequently run by the government. Similarly, telecommunications have commonly been a government monopoly, as have mail services and in many countries strategic defense industries.

Social Justice

Governments can play a role not only in promoting economic growth but also in dividing the fruits of such growth equitably. Many people argue that governments are needed to promote social justice by redistributing wealth and other resources. In many countries the distribution of income is highly uneven. Land and other wealth are typically even more unequally distributed than income. Moreover, in many societies income and wealth inequalities have been getting worse over time. Brazil, for example, has one of the most severe income inequalities in the world, an inequality that grew in every decade from the 1930s to the 1990s.

Under such circumstances, social justice may dictate a "new deal," especially if existing inequalities deprive many individuals of education, adequate health care, and other basic needs. Government intervention may be needed to redistribute resources from the better-off to the poor. Some theorists of distributive justice argue that such transfers should attempt to equalize the conditions of all citizens. Others would instead prefer governments to redistribute enough to "create a level playing field" and thus equalize opportunities but then let individuals be responsible for their own fortunes. Either way, citizens in many societies would agree that there should be efforts to make the distribution of wealth and income more even. Though many private individuals, organizations, and foundations participate in voluntary efforts to help the poor, they generally do not have the capacity or authority to effect large-scale redistribution. Governments can, at least under some circumstances. Many tax and welfare policies are indeed designed to do just that, though how successful they are, or how far such redistribution should go, is often hotly disputed. But even many individuals who do not think that governments have a general responsibility to redistribute wealth would agree that they should at least provide certain minimum standards of living, a social safety net, for all citizens.

Protecting the Weak

We commonly rely on the government to protect individuals and groups, such as future generations, that are not able to speak for themselves. Such groups obviously cannot act to protect their own interests. Governments, however, can protect the interests of the unborn and prevent them from getting saddled with economic debts or environmental degradation. And in recent decades, governments have become much more involved in protecting groups that for various reasons are politically weak or unenfranchised, such as children, the old, and the infirm or disabled, as well as nonhuman parts of the creation—from whales and birds to trees and other parts of our natural environment.

WHEN DOES GOVERNMENT BECOME THE PROBLEM?

Although there are many reasons that governments may be called upon to intervene in and regulate human affairs, such intervention is not always welcomed by all. Whether and when government intervention is necessary and desirable has been one of the greatest issues in twentieth-century politics. Over the course of this century, the role of governments has expanded enormously. At the same time, criticisms of many government policies have persisted and in some cases intensified. Such skepticism has been directed at virtually all government activities. Yet, the critics of governments have been particularly insistent and influential when they have criticized the economic roles that many governments have taken on.

Critics of Government: Anarchists and Libertarians

Critics of government intervention come in many camps and political shades, but two groups are especially outspoken: anarchists and libertarians. Both groups believe that governments do many things that

---

B O X 1 . 1 Tage Erlander and the "People's Home"

In much of Europe, social democratic parties have been a main force behind the expansion of government that has taken place in the twentieth century, and particularly from the Great Depression of the 1930s to the 1970s. The Swedish Social Democratic Party, for example, ruled virtually without interruption from 1932 to 1976. For most of that time Tage Erlander was the party leader and Sweden's prime minister (1946–1969). Under his leadership, Sweden developed one of the most extensive welfare states in the world and virtually eradicated most forms of poverty, though at the cost of the highest tax rates in the Western world.

Tage Erlander referred to the Swedish welfare state as the "people's home" and a "strong society," by which he meant a powerful government guided by a sense of solidarity and community spirit. In a 1954 parliamentary speech, Erlander presented this argument:

> It is a mistake to think that the freedom of human beings, whether in the economic area or the political

one, will diminish if they agree to join forces to do such things as they cannot manage by themselves. What is . . . the main part of our political activity other than attempts to organize such cooperation? We want health insurance, but nobody can manage that on his own. We must therefore create the opportunity for a collective solution. The same is true with respect to our wish to provide social security, to improve our roads, schools, defense, etc. All our political activities are filled with our striving to secure community cooperation to solve such tasks, which we can accomplish together, but which we cannot solve by ourselves. For us social democrats, it has been important to try to create a society in which the citizens consider the government's activities as an expression of their own efforts.

Source: Riksdagens Protokoll, January 20, 1954, p. 169. Translation by the editors.

are unnecessary or even harmful. Both see excessive government intervention and regulation as a serious threat to basic human values. They differ, however, in the threats they see as most serious, as well as in their favored alternatives to government intervention. **Libertarians** are *individualists* who see society as composed of individual human beings with fundamental rights that must be protected. Among these are property rights and the freedoms of speech and association. The main problem with government, libertarians argue, is that the more tasks it takes on, the more prone it is to violate such basic rights. While **anarchists** agree that governments impose undesirable effects, they see the ills of governments somewhat differently. Anarchists are *communitarians*. They see societies not as collections of individuals but as naturally close-knit and egalitarian communities. Governments and power corrupt such communities and lead to oppression and alienation. Anarchists see the alternative to government in voluntary cooperation and natural communities. Libertarians, on the other hand, promote a society of unfettered individuals, free to make their own choices and to seek out the groups to which they want to belong. Their differences aside, both libertarians and anarchists find much to criticize in the activities of contemporary governments. Many of these concerns are shared by individuals that are neither anarchists nor libertarians.

Destruction of Community

Whereas some see governments as a way to build community, anarchists argue with Rousseau that governments destroy natural communities. Government, they hold, implies power and inequality between human beings. And power corrupts. In Lord Acton's famous words, "power corrupts, and absolute power corrupts absolutely." While those who have power are corrupted, those without it are degraded and alienated. According to Rousseau, only human beings unfettered by government can form bonds that allow them to develop their full human potential. By imposing an order based on coercion, hierarchy, and the threat of force, governments therefore destroy natural communities. The stronger government becomes, the more it creates inequalities of power that have such pernicious consequences. In more contemporary terms, some would argue that governments create a "client society," in which people learn to be subservient to authorities and to rely on governments to meet their needs, and in which governments patronize and pacify their citizens.

Violations of Basic Rights

At the same time that power allows governments to destroy communities, it also enables them to

---

BOX 1.2 The Anarchist Kropotkin

Prince Petr Alekseevich Kropotkin (1842–1921), a Russian geographer and philosophical anarchist, believed that cooperation rather than competition is the norm in both animal and human life. In such a society based on cooperative norms, government would be replaced by voluntary groups. The economy would be based on need, which would leave citizens much time for leisure and creative activity. Kropotkin was imprisoned under the czars for preaching this philosophy and spent much of his later life in exile in England. His ideas are developed in a book entitled *Mutual Aid*, which was published in 1902.

> The State was established for the precise purpose of imposing the rule of landowners, the employers of industry, the warrior class, and the clergy upon the peasants on the land and the artisans in the city. And the rich perfectly well know that if the machinery of

the State ceased to protect them, their power over the laboring classes would be gone immediately. Socialism, we have said—whatever form it may take in its evolution toward communism—must find *its own form* of political organization. . . . This is why socialism *cannot* utilize representative government as a weapon for liberating labor. . . . A new form of political organization has to be worked out the moment that socialist principles shall enter into our life. And it is self-evident that this new form will have to be *more popular, more decentralized, and nearer to the folkmote self-government* than representative government can ever be.

Source: Petr Alekseevich Kropotkin, "Modern Science and Anarchism," in Emile Capouya and Keitha Tompkins, eds., *The Essential Kropotkin* (New York: Liveright, 1975, pp. 85–86). Emphases in the original.

B O X 1 . 3   The Libertarian Barry Goldwater

Some might call Barry Goldwater (1909–1998) a libertarian. A businessman and an Air Force officer, he won a seat in the U.S. Senate for Arizona (1953–1965, 1969–1987) and ran for the presidency on the Republican ticket in 1964. In his nomination acceptance address he insisted, "extremism in the defense of liberty is no vice . . . and moderation in the pursuit of justice is no virtue." He is viewed as the founder of modern Republican conservatism, though his libertarian beliefs often put him at odds with other members of his party.

> For the American Conservative, there is no difficulty in identifying the day's overriding political challenge: it is *to preserve and extend freedom.* . . . Throughout history, government has proved to be the chief instrument for thwarting man's liberty. . . . The *legitimate*

functions of government are actually conducive to freedom. Maintaining internal order, keeping foreign foes at bay, administering justice, removing obstacles to the free interchange of goods—the exercise of these powers makes it possible for men to follow their chosen pursuits with maximum freedom. But note that the very instruments by which these desirable ends are achieved *can* be the instrument for achieving undesirable ends—that government can, instead of extending freedom, restrict freedom. And note, secondly, that the "can" quickly becomes "will" the moment the holders of government power are left to their own devices.

Source: Barry M. Goldwater, *The Conscience of a Conservative*, Shepherdsville, KY: Victor Publishing, 1960, pp. 14–17. Emphases in the original.

---

infringe on the rights of citizens. This is the main concern of many libertarians. Just as governments can help establish and defend many essential rights, they can also use their powers to violate these rights in the most serious manner. The twentieth century has witnessed enormous progress in the extension of political, economic, and social rights in societies all around the world. At the same time, however, basic human rights have probably never before been violated on such a gross scale. The loss of millions of lives to political persecution is only the most serious manifestation of these violations. Such horrors have happened not only in Nazi extermination camps and during Stalin's Great Terror in the Soviet Union, but also on a huge scale in China and Cambodia, and on a smaller scale in such countries as Iraq, Argentina, Guatemala, Haiti, and Rwanda. These extreme abuses of government power illustrate a dilemma that troubled James Madison and other founding fathers of the American Revolution: the problem of creating a government strong enough to govern effectively but not so strong that it could destroy the rights of those whom it was designed to serve.

Economic Inefficiency

Many of the most important criticisms of modern governments have come from economists. And the objec-

tions that arise out of economic scholarship and research have convinced the citizens of many countries to restrict the role of governments in the economy. Economic problems might arise even if government officials do not actively abuse their power. Critics of government regulation of the economy point out that it may distort the terms of trade and lower people's incentives to produce, thus hurting overall economic performance. When governments not only regulate the economy, but also act as producers in their own right, they may generate further inefficiencies. This is particularly likely if the government is a monopoly producer of an important good, since monopolies generally cause goods to be undersupplied and overpriced. Moreover, government industries may be especially prone to inefficiency and complacency because management and workers often have far better job protection than those in the private sector. Therefore, they may not have to worry about losing their jobs or benefits even if their enterprises perform poorly.

Government for Private Gain

What happens if public officials are neither benevolent nor tyrannical, but simply self-interested? This is a question that economists and other social scientists increasingly raise. If politicians are rational and self-interested, they may be inclined to make decisions from which they would personally profit, re-

BOX 1.4   Rent Seeking and the Case of Mobutu Sese Seko

The problem of rent seeking has been the particular concern of economists and political scientists in the public choice tradition, founded in the 1960s by James Buchanan and Gordon Tullock. Until that time, economists had generally assumed that governments intervene only when markets fail. They further assumed that once the government intervenes, it will do so to benefit the economy as a whole. Public choice scholars ask instead, "what if government officials acted in the same ways that economics assumes that other producers and consumers behave?" That is to say, what happens if politicians use their power in their own self-interest, or to benefit individuals or groups that support them? Public choice analysts tend to see the competition of political parties and interest groups over government policy as driven by a pursuit of rents (private benefits generated through government intervention). Once in power, they argue, politicians and organizations seek to benefit themselves and their followers at the expense of their competitors.

President Mobutu Sese Seko (1930–1997) of Zaire offers a tragic example of the costs that rent-seeking politicians can impose on their societies. After seizing power in a 1965 coup, Mobutu ruled the large African state of Congo (which he renamed Zaire) for more than 30 years. Mobutu banned opposition parties and ruled his country as a dictator until he was finally deposed by rebel forces in 1997. During his long rule, President Mobutu used government funds, including aid from Western states such as the United States, to amass a huge personal fortune which he invested abroad. In addition to large sums of money, he is reported to have owned about 30 luxury residences abroad, including a number of palatial estates on the French Riviera. Meanwhile, living standards in Zaire, a poor country with large natural resources, plummeted, and the country was racked with epidemic disease and civil war. Mobutu died of natural causes shortly after his ouster.

---

gardless of whether this would be the best choice for society as a whole. Such self-interested political pursuit of private gain has become known as **rent seeking**. *Rents* are benefits created through government intervention in the economy—for example, tax revenue or profits created because the government has restricted competition. Rent seeking refers to efforts that individuals, groups, firms, or organizations exert in order to reap such benefits. While the terminology may sound unfamiliar, the idea behind it is really quite simple. Rent seeking occurs when people seek to use governments for their private gain.

Rent seeking is at best a game in which one person's gain is another person's loss. At worst, however, rent seeking can impose large net costs on society, because each party or group is willing to expend large resources in order to control the spoils of government. It may turn into outright corruption, in which influence is traded for money or other advantage. We discuss the problem of corruption at greater length in Chapter 6. Rent seeking may be a particularly serious problem in poor societies, where politics is often the surest or most effective way to get rich, and where the courts and mass media may be too weak to constrain government officials from abusing their power. Besides, many developing societies do not have strong norms against using government for private gain. On the contrary, people often expect those in government to use their power to benefit themselves, their families, kin, and neighbors. Remember also that even in many advanced democratic societies—for example, in Britain—the line between the private property of the monarch and that of the government was not clearly drawn even in the recent past.

Vested Interests and Inertia

The fact that governments create rents also means that they are difficult to change or abolish once established. We speak of individuals, groups, or firms that benefit from specific government jobs, contracts, or policies as having *vested interests* in the existing government. The larger the government and the more attractive the benefits it provides, the more likely it is that those who have such vested interests will resist change (unless change means making their benefits even larger). Therefore, any government will foster a class of people with a vested interest in maintaining or enlarging government benefits. Such groups may become a powerful force against change and in favor of the status quo. This makes it difficult to change government policies or make them more efficient. Instead, once established, agencies and policies tend to live on far beyond their usefulness. When, for example, the Spanish Armada in 1588 threatened to invade, the English government posted a military observation post at Land's End in southwest England. This observation post remained in place in the late twentieth century, long after the Spanish navy had ceased to be a threat. In the United States, many federal programs created during the New Deal of the 1930s remained in place toward the end of the millennium, even though the need for them might have changed dramatically. One example is the Rural Electrification Administration, which was created in 1935 and persisted for almost 60 years, until it was finally merged into the Rural Utilities Service in 1994. Similarly, the U.S. Senate maintained and staffed a Committee on Revolutionary War Claims until well into the twentieth century.

Vested interests are particularly likely to prevail in political systems that contain a lot of safeguards against rapid political change. While the checks and balances in such political systems as the United States are designed to safeguard the rights of individuals, groups, and local communities, they may also end up protecting the privileges of vested interests. Yet, even political systems that contain far fewer such checks may be slow to change. Britain is an excellent example. Until the Blair government came to power in 1997, for example, the majority of the members of the House of Lords (noblemen, bishops, and judges) represented the social groups (the "estates") that dominated British society before the Industrial Revolution more than 200 years ago.

Alternatives to Government: Markets and Voluntary Coordination

To the extent that governments cannot always be trusted to solve social problems, what can take their place? Here, the answers vary substantially between different camps of government critics. Anarchists and communitarians suggest that many central government functions can instead be performed either through much more local and decentralized governments, or through voluntary cooperation without formal political authority. Radical anarchists reject all forms of private property as well as all formal au-

thority. To the extent that governments have to exist, anarchists argue, they should be as close to the people as possible. That is to say that office holders should have limited terms and few privileges, that decision making should be as transparent as possible, and that ordinary citizens should be given the opportunity to participate extensively in political decision making. Of course, many people who are not anarchists may support such causes. For example, "Green" (environmentalist) political parties, particularly in European countries such as Germany, seek to promote political reforms of these kinds.

While libertarians and market-oriented economists (such as the so-called "Chicago school") support some of these causes (for example, government decentralization), they tend to focus on a different set of reforms. Most libertarians accept the role of governments in protecting security, individual rights, and commerce. Yet, they are sharply critical of government economic regulation and production. A few libertarians go further in their critique of governments and advocate draft resistance, tax resistance, and legalization of all drugs. Building on strands in modern economics, including the influential work of Ronald H. Coase, libertarians argue that much of what appears to be market failure can be solved without government intervention, by strengthening ownership. Their preferred alternative is to rely on free markets and individual property rights.

The debate between the proponents and critics of strong governments continues and is likely to be a key political controversy for a long time. In the past 20 years or so, there has been a clear trend away from extensive government regulation of many economic sectors. Yet, the overall size of governments in advanced industrial countries has not changed very much. Measured as a proportion of the total economy (for example, gross domestic product), the government's share has declined in some countries (e.g., Britain and New Zealand), increased in others (e.g., Japan), and stayed fairly constant in yet others (e.g., the United States). In the former Communist countries and in some developing countries, however, the government's size has shrunk much more dramatically. Since the 1970s especially, there has been a movement in many societies to privatize many economic sectors and to deregulate others, such as telecommunications, transportation (e.g., the airline industry), and banking, which many governments had previously strictly regulated.

But whereas government regulation has become less extensive in some areas, it has grown in others—for example, in passing laws protecting the environment or the rights of children.

POLITICAL SYSTEMS

Politics takes place within and between political systems. Since the term **political system** is the main organizing concept of this book, we shall elaborate its meaning below. Any system must necessarily have two properties: (1) a set of interdependent parts, and (2) boundaries towards the outside environment. There are many kinds of systems: mechanical systems such as automobiles, ecological systems (ecosystems) such as the plants and animals coexisting in a single habitat, and social systems such as a family. All have interdependent parts and boundaries. Political systems are a particular type of social system—namely, one involved in the making of authoritative public decisions. To put it slightly differently, the political system is a set of institutions, such as parliaments, bureaucracies, and courts, that formulate and implement the collective goals of a society or of groups within it.

Governments typically require obedience from their citizens, and their authoritative decisions can normally be backed up by coercion (force) if necessary. Yet, most governments much prefer that citizens comply because of legitimacy than due to the threat of force. By legitimacy we mean that those who are ruled believe that the rulers have a "right" (whether by law or by custom) to implement their decisions. The legitimacy of a political system may vary over time. The legitimacy of the U.S. political system was high just after World War II; it declined substantially during and after the Vietnam War but has since then recovered at least somewhat. In Germany, on the other hand, the new democratic system had little support just after World War II but has gradually gained in legitimacy since then. Low legitimacy may result in breakdowns in political organization and public policy failures. Policy failures in turn can cause declining legitimacy. The Soviet system collapsed in 1991 after its legitimacy had been undermined by a failed and costly war in Afghanistan, a nuclear power disaster in Chernobyl, corruption, and declining economic productivity. We discuss legitimacy at greater length in Chapter 3.

Political systems feature governments at their core, but they also encompass important parts of the environment in which governments operate. There is more to politics than authoritative and coercive activities—for example, political organizations such as political parties or interest groups. Such organizations do not have coercive authority, unless they control the government. Likewise, the mass media only indirectly affect elections, legislation, and law enforcement. Then there is a whole host of institutions beginning with the family and including communities, churches, schools, universities, corporations, foundations, and think-tanks, which influence political attitudes and public policy. The term *political system* refers to this whole collection of related, interacting institutions and agencies.

Political systems mold and are molded by a domestic and an international environment. The system receives inputs from these environments and shapes them through its outputs. The boundaries of political systems are defined in terms of persons, territory, and property. Most human beings belong to, and have citizenship rights in, only one country. Similarly, territory is divided between states in ways that are meant to be mutually exclusive. A given piece of land is supposed to belong to one and only one country. Much the same is true with respect to other property rights. Of course, disputes over citizenship, territory, and property are by no means uncommon and have indeed been among the most frequent causes of international conflict all through history.

Comparative politics is the study of political systems, not as isolated cases but through generalizations and comparisons. Chapter 2 discusses how and why we make such comparisons. There are many kinds of political systems, such as cities, states, international organizations, klans, or even influential families. In principle, comparative politics could compare any or all of these types of political systems. In practice, however comparative politics focuses on comparisons of *states*, or what we commonly refer to as countries. We shall therefore discuss states and their role in the contemporary world next.

STATES

The twelve political systems that we compare in this book are all *states*. A **state** is a political system that has **sovereignty**—independent legal authority over a population in a particular territory, based on the recognized right to self-determination. Sovereignty rests with those who have the ultimate right to make political decisions. We distinguish between internal and external sovereignty. *Internal sovereignty* means the right, without external intervention, to determine matters having to do with one's own citizens. *External sovereignty* means the right to conclude binding agreements (treaties) with other states. For example, the British government has internal sovereignty in the sense that it can impose whatever taxes it wants on British citizens. Similarly, its external sovereignty means that it can enter into treaties with other states. The city of Edinburgh does not have these rights. Nor does the county of Kent or the principality of Wales. All of them are dependent on the central British government in tax matters and foreign policy. Yet, sovereignty is never absolute, and every state in the real world faces constraints on its internal and external sovereignty. With the increasing integration of the United Kingdom (Britain) into the European Union (EU), the British government has in fact had to give up parts of its sovereignty to the EU, and this loss of sovereignty has been a major topic of political debate.

In the United States we confuse things a bit by calling the 50 constituent units "states," even though they enjoy much less sovereignty than Britain. The states of the United States share the power and authority of the "state" with the central government in Washington, DC. However confusing this usage is today, it does reflect what American government was once like, under the Articles of Confederation. Since then, however, much authority has been shifted from the states to the central (federal) government.

We often think of the world as a patchwork quilt of states with sizable and contiguous territories and a common national identity. We call such cases, in which national identification and the scope of legal authority largely coincide, **nation-states**. In the twentieth century, we have come to think of nation-states as the natural way to organize states, and often as an ideal. The national right to self-determination, the idea that every nation had a right to form its own state if it so wished, was enshrined in the Treaty of Versailles signed at the end of World War I.

But even though this may seem the natural way to organize world politics, it has not always been so. Un-til about 500 years ago, Europe was comprised of many very small states and a few very large ones, whose territorial possessions were not always very stable or contiguous. Nor did states always consist of people with the same national identity. Most probably knew next to nothing about the political system to which they belonged. Gradually, a set of European nation-states evolved, and the 1648 Treaty of Westphalia established that principle for the political organization of Europe. The eighteenth and nineteenth centuries were the main era during which the concentration of power in the nation-state occurred. Since then, Europe has transformed itself into something approximating a set of nation-states, each of which contains a people with a common identity. This did not happen accidentally—the governments of the emerging nation-states consciously strove to instill a sense of community, a common national identity, among the peoples they controlled. They did so, often heavy-handedly and with massive doses of coercion, by promoting a common language, a common educational system, and often a common religion. While we may in retrospect find many aspects of this *nation-building* process deplorable, it has produced a Europe in which the inhabitants of most states have a strong sense of community.

Many societies in the developing world today face similar challenges. Especially in Africa, the former colonial powers (particularly Britain and France) left the newly independent states with very weak national identities. In many parts of Africa, large-scale national communities simply did not exist before colonization. Even where they did exist, they were rarely reflected in the boundaries that the colonial powers drew between their possessions. These boundaries were frequently drawn according to the strategic and military interests of the colonizers, who often knew and cared little about local identities among the populations they ruled. After independence, many new states have therefore been left with huge nation-building tasks.

There are additional challenges to contemporary states. After World War II, power began shifting from the state downward to local governments, and upward to supranational organizations. The European Union (EU) and the North American Free Trade Agreement (NAFTA) are examples of the latter development. Most of the countries of Western Europe have, after centuries of costly and destructive wars, gradually created a common market econ-

The United Nations is the most inclusive organization of states. As of 2005, the United Nations had 191 member states, represented by the flags flying outside its headquarters in New York City.

omy and in 1999 many of them adopted a common currency, the Euro. Originally consisting of six countries—France, Germany, Italy, Belgium, the Netherlands, and Luxembourg—the European Union has expanded to 25. 10 of these countries, mostly from Eastern and Central Europe, were admitted in 2004.

The **United Nations (UN)**, formed at the end of World War II in 1945, is the most important organization that encompasses almost all the world's states. With the accession of Switzerland and East Timor, the United Nations in 2002 reached a membership of 191 states. There is only a small number of countries (such as Taiwan and the Vatican) that are not members of the UN.[3] The United Nations has acquired new responsibilities since the collapse of the Soviet Union in 1991. Most dramatically, UN forces have been deployed as peacekeepers in a large number of countries. Many of these are areas stricken by

civil war and lawlessness. The UN has acquired increased authority over world security, constraining, supporting, and replacing the unilateral actions of individual states. But while the sovereignty of states may thus be slipping away, they are still the most important political systems around. That, of course, is the main reason that they are the subject of this, and most other, texts on comparative politics.

Old and New States

Just about the entire surface of the world today is covered by close to 200 independent states, and there are some secessionary movements that, if successful, would make our figures obsolete. When the United States declared its independence in 1776, most independent states were European (see Figure 1.1). Much of the rest of the world had been parceled out as colonies to some European

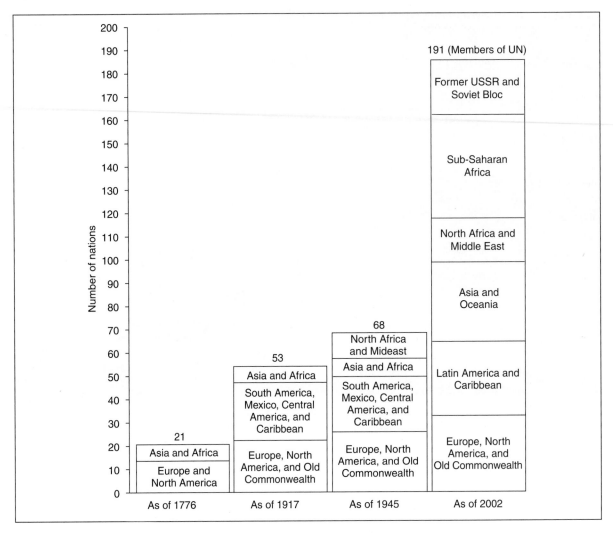

Source: For contemporary members, Information Office, United Nations. Data to 1945 from Charles Taylor and Michael Hudson, *World Handbook of Political and Social Indicators* (New Haven, CT: Yale University Press, 1972), pp. 26 ff.

FIGURE 1.1 Formation of States Since 1776

empire. In the nineteenth and early twentieth centuries, the number of states increased, principally in Latin America where the Spanish and Portuguese empires broke up into 20 independent states. In Europe, newly independent countries emerged in the Balkans, Scandinavia, and the Low Countries. Between the two world wars, national proliferation extended to North Africa and the Middle East; and Europe continued to fragment as Poland, Finland, Czechoslovakia, and Yugoslavia gained their independence. At the same time, the

three Baltic countries—Lithuania, Latvia, and Estonia—briefly experienced independence but were again swallowed by the Soviet Union from 1939 until its collapse in 1991. Since World War II, the development of new states has really taken off. By 2005, 125 new countries had joined the 68 states that existed in 1945. The largest group of new states is in Sub-Saharan Africa. The 1990s alone witnessed more than 20 new countries— mostly the successor states of the Soviet Union, Yugoslavia, and Czechoslovakia.

TABLE 1.1   Area and Population of Selected Countries

Country	Population (millions in 2000)	Average Annual Growth of Population, 1990–2000	Area 1995 (thousands of square km)
China	1,261	1.1	9,326
India	1,016	1.8	2,973
United States	282	1.2	9,159
Brazil	170	1.4	8,457
Russia	146	−0.2	16,889
Japan	127	0.3	377
Nigeria	127	2.8	911
Mexico	98	1.6	1,909
Germany	82	0.3	349
Egypt	64	2.0	995
Britain	60	0.4	242
France	59	0.4	550

Source: World Bank, *World Development Report: 2002.* (New York, Oxford University Press), 2002, tables 1 and 3, pp. 232–33, and previous editions.

First, Second, and Third World, North and South

From the 1950s on, it became customary to divide the states of the world into three categories: the first, second, and third world. The first world consisted of the advanced capitalist democracies; the second world encompassed the communist bloc of countries, at that time led by the Soviet Union; the third world made up the remaining states of the world, those that were neither rich and Western nor communist. Indeed, most of the world's states and population fell into this third category. With the collapse of most communist states and the increasing differences between developing societies, these categories are no longer as useful as they once were. Today, it is common to refer to the developing states collectively as the South and the rich, capitalist democracies as the North. Not all southern states are poor (e.g., Australia), and not all northern states are rich or democratic (e.g., North Korea), but there is still a strong tendency for these characteristics to go together.

Big and Small States

Russia is the largest country in area, encompassing more than 17 million square kilometers. China has the most people, approximately 1.3 billion. There are many countries at the other extreme, but the

smallest legally independent political entity in both respects is Vatican City, the headquarters of the Catholic Church, with less than half a square kilometer of turf and under a thousand residents. Table 1.1 reports the widely differing populations and areas of 12 countries we cover in detail in this book.[4] The political implications of these striking contrasts in population size and geographic area are not always obvious. Big countries are not always the most important and do not always prevail over the small ones. Cuba has challenged the United States for 40 years; Israel stands off the Arab world; and tiny Vatican City has great cultural power and influence.

Nor do area and population size determine a country's political system. Both Luxembourg and the United States are democracies. Authoritarian regimes can be found in small, medium, or large countries. These enormous contrasts in size show only that the countries now making up the world differ greatly in their physical and human resources. Yet, area and population do affect economic development, foreign policy and defense problems, and many other issues of political significance. For example, with population growth rates double those of the industrialized countries, developing countries have to grow twice as fast economically just to avoid falling further behind.

A state's geographic location has important strategic implications. In the sixteenth through nineteenth centuries, a state located in the center of Europe could not avoid building a large land army to protect itself from its neighbors. It would have difficulty developing free political institutions, since it needed a strong government to extract resources and keep its population under control. Britain has historically been protected by the English Channel and could defend itself through its navy. It could do with a smaller army, lower taxation, and less centralization of power. The United States was a similar case. The Atlantic Ocean and the relatively open continent critically shaped U.S. political institutions. Most peoples of Asia, Africa, and Latin America were dominated, and in most cases colonized, by the more powerful Western nations. Those that had the richest natural resources and the most benign climates tended to attract the largest numbers of settlers.

Whether they are old or new, large or small, most of the world's states face a number of common challenges. The first is building community. Most of the world's states do not have a homogeneous population, and instilling a sense of shared identity and interest can be a serious problem. So can creating a sense of allegiance to the government. The second is the ability to foster economic, social, and political development now and in the future, a challenge that confronts even the wealthiest states. Finally, most states face significant challenges in securing and furthering democracy and civil liberties. These challenges should be familiar from our discussion of the purposes and dangers of governments. In the remainder of this chapter, we shall discuss these challenges successively.

BUILDING COMMUNITY

One of the most important challenges facing political systems all over the world is to build a common identity and a sense of community among their citizens. The absence of such a sense of common identity can have the most severe political consequences. Conflicts over national, ethnic, or religious identities are among the most explosive causes of political turmoil, as we have recently witnessed in Northern Ireland, the former Yugoslavia, Rwanda, Indonesia, the Middle East and elsewhere. But while building community is a pervasive challenge, some countries are in a much more favorable situation than others. Japan, for example, has relatively little to worry about. Its population is ethnically quite homogeneous and shares a language and a long political history. Large majorities of the Japanese share the faiths of Buddhism and Shintoism, and the country is separated by hundreds or thousands of miles of ocean from its most important neighbors. Nigeria, on the other hand, has an extremely diverse population of more than 100 million. The country itself is an accidental and artificial creation of British colonial rule and has no common precolonial history. The population is sharply divided between Muslims and Christians; the Christians are divided equally into Catholics and Protestants. There are some 250 different ethnic groups, speaking a variety of local languages, in addition to English. Obviously, the challenges of building community are much greater in Nigeria than they are in Japan. But although few countries face problems as complicated as those of the Nigerians, the community-building challenge is one of the most serious issues facing many states today.

States and Nations

The word *nation* is sometimes used to mean almost the same as a state, as in the name the United Nations. Strictly speaking, however, we wish to use the term **nation** to refer to a group of people with a common identity. When we speak of a "nation," we thus refer to the self-identification of a people. That common identity may be built upon a common language, history, race, or culture, or simply upon the fact that this group has occupied the same territory. Nations may or may not have their own state or independent government. In some cases, such as Japan, France, or Sweden, there is a close correspondence between the memberships of the state and the nation. Most people who identify themselves as Japanese do in fact live in the state of Japan, and most people who live in Japan identify themselves as Japanese. As mentioned above, we call such states nation-states.

But in the case of most states today or in the past, the correspondence between the nation and the state is not so neat. Nor is it obvious that it should be. In some cases, states are *multinational*—consisting of a multitude of different nations. The Soviet Union,

Yugoslavia, and Czechoslovakia were multinational states that have now broken apart. On the other hand, there are some nations that are much larger than the corresponding states, such as the Germans for most of their history, or the Chinese. Some nations have been divided into two or more states for political reasons, such as Koreans today and the Germans between 1949 and 1990. Some nations have no state at all, such as the Kurds, the Basques, the Jews in the past, and the Palestinians today. When states and nations do not coincide, it can cause explosive political conflict. On the other hand, the presence of several nations within the same state can also be a source of cultural enrichment.

Nationality and Ethnicity

There is a fine line between nations and *ethnic groups*, which may also have common physical traits, languages, cultures, or history. But whereas we think of nationality as a form of primary identification, **ethnicity** may be of lesser importance to the group involved. Like nationality, ethnicity need not have any objective basis in genetics, culture, or history. In his classic introduction to sociological theory, the German sociologist Max Weber defined ethnic groups as "those human groups that entertain a subjective belief in their common descent because of similarities of physical type or of customs or both, or because of memories of colonization and migration. . . . [I]t does not matter whether or not an objective blood relationship exists."[5] Similarly, groups that are physically quite similar, but differ by language, religion, customs, marriage patterns, and historical memories (for example, the Serbs, Croats, and Muslim Bosnians) may believe themselves to be descended from different ancestors and hence insist on their separate identities. Over centuries, originally homogeneous populations may become substantially intermixed genetically with other populations, even though the culture may continue. This is true, for example, of the Jewish population of Israel, which has come together after more than two millennia of global dispersion.

Ethnic differences have been the source of a large number of political conflicts around the world. Even before the end of the Cold War, ethnic autonomy movements in parts of old countries—such as the United Kingdom (the Scots and Welsh) and Canada (the Quebecois)—sought to break free or achieve greater autonomy. And since the end of the Cold War, many states of the former Soviet bloc have been coming apart at their ethnic and religious seams. In the former Yugoslavia, secession by a number of provinces triggered several wars. The most brutal of these has taken place in Bosnia-Herzegovina, where a new Muslim regime faced rebellion and murderous "ethnic cleansing" by the large Serbian minority, backed by their fellow Serb majority in the remaining Yugoslavian state. Intervention by the UN, NATO, and the United States to contain Serbian aggression has led to an uneasy settlement, but considerable tension remains. Later the Serbs in Yugoslavia undertook to "cleanse" Albanians from the province of Kosovo, even though they were the ethnic majority there. After thousands of Albanians were killed and hundreds of thousands driven from their homes, NATO intervened with a bombing campaign, forcing the Serbs to withdraw their forces and permit the Kosovans to return.

In many developing countries, boundaries established by former colonial powers cut across ethnic lines. In 1947 the British withdrew from India and divided the subcontinent into a northern Muslim area—Pakistan—and a southern Hindu area—India. The immediate consequence was a terrible civil conflict and "ethno-religious" cleansing incidental to the exchange of populations. There still are almost 100 million Muslims in India. Similarly, 30 years ago the Ibo "tribe" of Nigeria fought an unsuccessful separatist war against the rest of Nigeria, resulting in the deaths of millions of people. The Tutsi and Hutu peoples of the small African state of Rwanda have been engaged in a civil war of extermination, with hundreds of thousands of people slaughtered, and millions fleeing the country in fear of their lives.

Vestiges of imperial conquest (by Russia, Britain, France, Spain, Portugal, or the Netherlands) are one source of contemporary division. The migration of labor, forced or voluntary, across state boundaries, is another. The North and South American descendants of Africans forcibly enslaved between the seventeenth and the nineteenth centuries remind us of the largest coercive labor migration in world history. Voluntary migration takes the form, for example, of the many Indians, Bangladeshi, Egyptians, and Palestinians seeking better lives in the oil

These are starved Muslim refugees released from a Croatian prison where they had been confined in the course of the "ethnic cleansing" after the breakup of the old multinational country of Yugoslavia.

Yannis Behrakis/Reuters Bettmann/ Corbis

sheikhdoms around the Persian Gulf; of Mexican and Caribbean migrant workers in the United States; and of Turkish and Algerian migrants in Germany, France, and other European countries. Some migration is politically motivated, triggered by civil war or repression. A recent book refers to the contemporary world as living through an "Age of Migration,"[6] comparable in scale to that of the late nineteenth and early twentieth centuries.

Table 1.2 provides examples of politically significant "ethnicity," broadly defined, in our twelve selected countries. Five sets of traits are included, beginning with physical differences, then language, norms against intermarriage, religion, and negative historical memories. The table illustrates the importance of each distinction to ethnic identity and shows that ethnicity may or may not be based on objective differences. The most important bases of distinction lie in intermarriage, religion, and historical memories. Language differences are of great importance in three cases and of some importance in five; and finally, and perhaps surprisingly, physical differences are of great importance in only two cases.

Recent migration has made such previously homogeneous states as France, Japan, and Germany more multiethnic. Other countries such as the United States, Britain, and Canada have long been multiethnic and have become even more so. The political problems resulting from ethnic diversity range

from demands for recognition, civil rights, and equality of treatment, through struggles for autonomy or national independence, to ethnocentric demands for ethnic cleansing.

Language

Language can be source of social division that may or may not be associated with ethnicity. There are approximately 5,000 different languages in use in the world today, and a much smaller number of language families. Most of these languages are spoken by relatively small tribal groups in North and South America, Asia, Africa, or Oceania. Only 200 languages have a million or more speakers, and only eight may be classified as world languages. English is the most truly international language. There are approximately 350 million people who speak English at home, and 1.8 billion who live in countries where it is an official language. Other international languages include Spanish (more than 300 million home speakers), Arabic (200 million), Russian (165 million), Portuguese (165 million), French (100 million), and German (100 million). The language with the largest number of speakers, though in several varieties, is Chinese (1.2 billion). The major languages with the greatest international spread are those of the former colonial powers—Great Britain, France, Spain, and Portugal.[7]

TABLE 1.2   Examples of Ethnicity: Its Bases and Their Salience*

	Physical Differences	Language	Norms Against Intermarriage	Religion	Negative Historical Memories
Brazil: Blacks	XX	O	XX	X	X
Britain: Scots	O	O	O	X	X
China: Tibetans	X	XX	XX	XX	XX
Egypt: Copts	O	O	XX	XX	X
France: Algerians	X	X	XX	XX	XX
Germany: Turks	X	XX	XX	XX	O
India: Muslims	O	X	XX	XX	XX
Japan: Buraku-min	O	O	XX	O	XX
Mexico: Mayan	X	X	XX	X	XX
Nigeria: Ibo	O	X	XX	XX	XX
Russia: Chechens	X	XX	XX	XX	XX
United States: African-Americans	XX	X	XX	O	XX

*Salience is estimated at the following levels: O = none or almost none; X = some; XX = much importance in affecting political differences.

Linguistic divisions can create particularly thorny political problems. It has been said that "constitutions can be blind but not dumb." That is to say that while political systems can choose to ignore racial, ethnic, or religious differences among their citizens, they cannot avoid committing themselves to one or several languages. Linguistic conflicts typically show up in controversies over educational policies, or over language use in the government. Occasionally, language regulation is more intrusive, as in Quebec, where English-only street signs are prohibited and larger corporations are required to conduct their business in French.

Religious Beliefs and Fundamentalism

States vary in their religious characteristics. In some such as Israel, the Irish Republic, and Pakistan, a common faith can be a basis of national identity for a majority of the population. In other societies, such as Poland under communism, religious authorities can serve as rallying points for opponents of authoritarian regimes. In many Latin American countries clergy have spoken out as advocates of the poor and critics of government brutality. But religious beliefs can also be more directly woven into the fabric of government. Iran is an example of a theocratic regime, in which religious authorities directly govern and religious law is part of the country's legal code.

In Afghanistan the Taliban had installed an Islamic theocracy that was serving as a base for the terrorist organization Al Qaeda. But the Taliban were ousted from power by a U.S.-led alliance of forces in late 2001. (See Box 1.5.)

Christianity is the largest and most widely spread religion, with about 2 billion believers worldwide, whereas the Muslims, the next most numerous group, muster a little more than half that number (see Table 1.3). There are about 800 million Hindus. The Christians are in turn divided into three major groups—Roman Catholics, Protestants (of many denominations), and Orthodox (e.g., Greek and Russian). The Catholics are dominant in Europe and Latin America; there is a more equal distribution of Catholics and Protestants elsewhere. While the traditional Protestant denominations have been on the decline in North America, Pentecostalism and Evangelical Protestantism have been on the rise. The Muslims are the most rapidly growing religion, primarily concentrated in Asia and Africa, though they are present in substantial numbers even in Europe and North America, and becoming revitalized in the Asian successor states of the Soviet Union. Muslims have been particularly successful in missionary activities in Sub-Saharan Africa.

Religious beliefs can be a powerful motivation for political involvement in causes ranging from the abolition of slavery, through efforts to bring about

BOX 1.5   Osama Bin Laden, Al Qaeda, and the Taliban

Osama bin Laden was born in Riyadh, Saudi Arabia in 1957, the scion of a powerful and wealthy Saudi family. In his early twenties, he recruited a group of Arab volunteers to fight against the Soviet occupation of Afghanistan. Later, when Egypt, Algeria, and Yemen accused him of supporting subversive activities in their countries, the Saudi authorities deprived him of his passport. He ultimately fled to Afghanistan and to the protection of the Taliban. It was in this struggle in the 1980s and 1990s, and in opposition to the Saudi-American alliance and stationing of American air bases and troops in Saudi Arabia, that he developed his anti-American, radical Islamic ideology. He is believed to have been the master mind behind the World Trade Center bombing in February 1993, the Riyadh bombing of a Saudi-American training facility in November 1995, and the Dhahran, Al-Khobar bombing of U.S. Air Force housing in June 1998. Yet, the evidence for bin Laden's role in these bombings, as well as in the later bombings of American embassies in Kenya and Tanzania, is sketchy and indirect. He presumably commanded the operations resulting in the September 11,

2001 World Trade Center and Pentagon atrocities. (See Box 19.1.)

Al Qaeda, meaning "the base," refers to the organization that bin Laden employs in carrying out his program. It began as an organization to provide information to concerned family members about their sons who were in the Mujahideen. Later this organization was converted into a Jihad action organization. Until fall 2001, its central command apparatus was in Afghanistan, and under the protection of the Taliban.

The Taliban, (the students), are a radical Islamic militia primarily recruited from the refugees to Pakistan from Afghanistan during the Soviet occupation. In Pakistan these young men were educated in the religious schools (hence the "students"). In September 2001 they controlled two-thirds of Afghanistan and provided the cover for Al Qaeda. An international coalition removed the Taliban from power early in 2002, and restored the government to moderates, who are still battling Taliban insurgents. Afghanistan had democratic elections for president in October 2004, electing Hanid Karzai; the new government is now trying to rebuild the nation.

TABLE 1.3   Adherents of All Religions by Six Continental Areas (mid-1999, in millions)*

Religion	Africa	Asia	Europe	Latin America	North America	Oceania	Total	Percentage
Christian	351.3	306.4	559.2	473.7	258.8	24.8	1974.2	33.0
Muslims	310.5	807.0	31.2	1.6	4.4	.3	1155.1	19.3
Nonreligious and Atheists	5.3	724.5	130.6	18.5	29.8	3.7	912.3	15.3
Hindus	2.3	792.9	1.4	.8	1.3	.3	799.0	13.4
Buddhists	.1	351.0	1.5	.6	2.6	.3	356.3	6.0
Folk and Ethnic	94.6	507.6	1.6	1.5	1.2	.4	607.0	10.2
Sikhs	.1	22.0	.2	0	.5	.0	22.8	.4
Jews	.2	4.3	2.5	1.1	6.0	.1	14.3	.2
Other	2.5	118.6	.7	13.5	2.6	.8	137.4	2.2
Total	766.6	3634.3	728.9	511.3	307.2	30.0	5978.4	100

*Adherents as defined in *World Christian Encyclopedia* (1982).

world peace, to the banning of secular textbooks in schools. Such beliefs can be a source of intense antagonism since they often form deep personal convictions on which it is difficult or impossible to compromise. Religious groups are often embattled over such issues as education, marriage, divorce, child-rearing, freedom of speech and press, sexual moral-

ity, abortion and euthanasia, the emancipation of women, and the regulation of religious observances such as the Sabbath. Religious communities commonly take a special interest in education in order to transmit their ideas of nature and humankind. On such issues and others religious groups may clash with one another as well as with more secular groups. Although religious groups can coexist peacefully, indeed are often the source of exemplary acts of pacifism, compassion and reconciliation, they may also be the source of acts of violence, cruelty, and terrorism.[8]

Even societies in which most people ostensibly belong to the same community of faith may be riven by conflicts between "fundamentalists" and those who are either more mainstream or secular in their beliefs. **Religious fundamentalism** is a relatively recent development, world wide, but has emerged in some form in all major faiths as they reassert themselves against expressions of modernity. Fundamentalism got its name in the decades before World War I when some Protestant clergymen in the United States banded together to defend the "fundamentals" of religious belief against the secularizing inroads of science, and against biblical scholarship which questioned the divine inspiration and authorship of the Bible. The "fundamentalists" affirmed the inerrancy (the absolute truth) of the Bible and formed enclaves to protect themselves from error and sin. Fundamentalists have frequently been technologically adaptive, even while militantly rejecting some elements of modernity.[9]

Christianity, Judaism, and Islam are all "religions of the book," although not exactly the same book. The Jews believe only in the Old Testament; the Christians add the New Testament; and the Muslims add the Koran to these two. While each religion has experienced serious disagreement over the interpretation of these texts, Christian, Muslim, and Jewish fundamentalists all believe in the inerrancy of their respective sacred books and criticize their own "mainstream" clergy for lukewarm defense of the truth of these sacred texts. There are also Hindu and Buddhist Fundamentalists. The rise of fundamentalism has affected the entire world.

Some extremist wings of fundamentalist movements have employed violence in many forms: from threats and property destruction to assassination and destructive suicide, as among Palestinian protesters in Israel. In most countries with substantial Muslim populations, fundamentalist Islamic movements have appeared, frequently employing violence and terrorism in their efforts to gain power. The September 11, 2001, attack on the World Trade Center and the Pentagon was an act of mega-terrorism, involving not only suicide pilot-hijackers, but aircraft filled with volatile fuel and innocent passengers, converted into immense projectiles. (See Box 19.1 in chapter 19). This act of mega-terrorism required three elements—leadership, organization, and cover. Osama bin Laden provided the first; Al Qaeda provided the second; and the Taliban along with other governments and institutions, the third (See Box 1.5). The massive bombings of tourist spots in Bali in October 2002 appear to have been similarly motivated. The terrorism of these acts lies in their enormity. They stagger the imagination and are intended to lame the will.

Cumulative and Cross-Cutting Cleavages

National, ethnic, linguistic, and religious divisions can interact in a variety of ways. When they systematically affect political allegiances and policies, we refer to such divisions as **political cleavages**. When a political system is affected by more than one such cleavage, it matters whether the different cleavages are *cumulative* or *cross-cutting*. If cleavages are cumulative, they pit the same people against each other on many different issues. If, on the other hand, cleavages cross-cut, it means that groups that share a common interest on one issue are likely to be on opposite sides of a different issue. Consider the cases of Northern Ireland and the Netherlands. Both countries have traditionally had class divisions, and both are divided between Catholics and Protestants. The interaction between these cleavages is different, though. In Northern Ireland, class and religion are cumulative cleavages. If you are Catholic, you are also more likely to be poor, and you may have suffered a history of discrimination. In the Netherlands, on the other hand, class and religion tend to cross-cut. Catholics and Protestants are about equally likely to be poor or rich, and discrimination against Catholics is a thing of the past.

Where the cleavage lines within a country are cumulative, and especially where they coincide with economic inequalities, they often fuel violence and intractable political struggles (as, for example, in Lebanon). Political conflicts and divisions based on language, ethnicity, and religion once were thought to have been subordinated or even eliminated by "modern" differences between social classes, interests, and ideologies. In the post—Cold War world though, ideological differences have often been overshadowed by ethnic and religious ones.

FOSTERING DEVELOPMENT

As important as the task of building community is, political systems cannot generally expect to satisfy their citizens unless they can foster social and economic development. Thus, as significant as nation-building may be, such factors as the availability of natural resources, the level of economic and social development, and the rate of economic growth and social change are of equal, if not greater, importance. Economic development implies that citizens can enjoy new resources. On the other hand, it can often have a devastating impact on nature. For better or worse, the social changes that result from economic development transform the politics of developing countries.

Rich and Poor Countries

Figure 1.2 gives the per capita **gross national product (GNP)**—the total economic output per person—for our twelve nations. There are two ways to compare the economies of countries that use different currencies. The standard measure is computed according to the exchange rates of the national currencies. An alternative and newer measure instead uses **purchasing power parity (PPP)**, which takes into account differences in price levels from one country to another. Figure 1.2 shows that the income of developing countries turns out to be substantially higher in purchasing power parity than when we use currency exchange rates. Thus, in U.S. dollar equivalents, Mexican per capita PPP is almost twice its per capita GNP, whereas China's and India's are about five times as high. At the opposite extreme, the Japanese economy is less impressive in actual purchasing power. Thus the gap in economic wealth between the rich and the poor countries is not as great if we take into account what money actually buys. In per capita output, the Brazilian economy is more than one-fourth that of the Japanese economy according to purchasing powers, as opposed to one-tenth according to exchange rates. The Chinese per capita product turns out to be about one-seventh that of Japan, instead of less than one-fortieth.

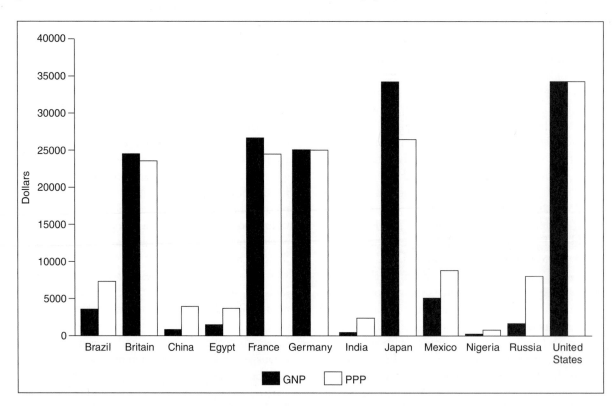

F I G U R E   1 . 2   Per Capita GNP and PPP in Selected Nations, 2000 (in U.S. Dollars)

Source: World Bank, *World Development Report: 2002.* (New York, Oxford University Press), 2002, table 1, pp. 232–33.

Traditional official statistics have exaggerated the income inequality among nations in other respects, too. Our statistics tend to underestimate goods and services produced and consumed in subsistence agriculture, or in household production for family use. Similarly, national product estimates are not corrected for differences in the "cost of living" under different environmental conditions. As the World Development Report points out, "GNP is higher in colder countries, where people spend more money on heating and warm clothing, than in balmy climates, where people are comfortable wearing light clothing in the open air."[10]

Figure 1.3 compares the percentages of the economically active populations employed in agriculture. In comparing Figures 1.2 and 1.3 we see that the smaller the per capita GNP (or PPP), the larger

is the proportion of the labor force in agriculture. The five advanced industrial countries all have agricultural labor forces in the single digits, with the United States and Britain at 2 percent each. The three poorest countries—China, India, and Nigeria—have more than two-thirds of their labor forces employed in agriculture. The middle-income countries—Mexico and Brazil—have around a third to a fifth of their labor forces in agriculture. Thus, the economies of the rich countries are predominantly industrial, commercial, and professional, while those of the poor countries are predominantly agricultural. Countries that are rich and industrialized, with a large professional service sector, also tend to have healthy, literate, and educated populations. In highly industrialized countries, practically everyone over the age of 15 can read and write. In India, Nigeria, and Egypt, on the other hand, almost one-half the adult population is illiterate. Moreover, the countries with the fewest literate citizens also have the fewest radios and television sets—devices that do not require literacy.

Industrialization, education, and exposure to the communications media are associated with better nutrition and medical care. In the economically advanced countries, fewer children die in infancy, and the average citizen has a life expectancy at birth of more than 75 years (81 in Japan). The average Mexican has a life expectancy of 72 years; the Egyptian, 67 years; the Indian, 63 years; and the Nigerian only 47 years. Material productivity, education, exposure to communications media, and longer and healthier lives are closely interconnected. Only economically productive countries can afford good education, communications media, and good nutrition and health care. In order to become more productive, a country needs to develop a skilled and healthy labor force and build its infrastructure, but doing so requires significant resources. Preindustrial nations face urgent issues of economic development: how to improve the immediate welfare of their citizens yet also build and invest for the future. Typically, these are newer nations that also face the challenges of building community and effective political institutions.

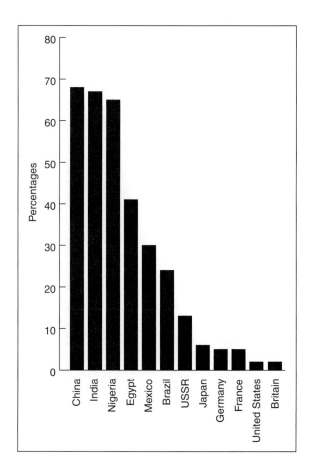

FIGURE 1.3 Percentage of Economically Active Population in Agriculture for Selected Nations (1990)

Source: FAO, United Nations, *FAO Production Yearbook 1990* (Rome: UN, 1991), table 3.

Economic Inequality

It may be misleading to refer to states only on the basis of average economic measures such as per capita income, gross national product, and so on. Wealth,

Poverty in third world cities is illustrated by this scene of a back street in Calcutta, in India, where the poor make their beds in the street. Similar scenes, though on a lesser scale, are to be encountered in modern American cities where homeless people sleep on the sidewalks and in doorways.

Jehangir Gazdar/Woodfin Camp & Associates

income, and opportunity are not evenly distributed domestically, and such inequalities are among the most serious causes of political conflict. A large gross national product may conceal significant differences in the distribution of economic and social amenities and opportunities. A high rate of national growth may benefit only particular regions or social groups, leaving large parts of the population even less well off than before. The "inner cities" of the United States; the older parts of such Indian cities as Delhi and Calcutta; the peripheral ramshackle settlements around the cities of Latin America; such regions as Appalachia in the United States, the Mezzogiorno (south) of Italy, and the arid northeast of Brazil—all suffer from poverty and hopelessness, while other parts of their countries experience growth and improved welfare.

A country's politics may be sharply affected by internal divisions of income, wealth, and other resources. Table 1.4 compares income distribution for our 12 countries. Clearly, there is a positive association between economic development and equality of income, at least past a certain stage of economic growth. Wealthy nations like Japan, the United States, or Germany tend to have more egalitarian income distributions than middle-income countries such as Brazil and Mexico. In Japan, the rich receive

a little over four times the income going to the poor. In Mexico, a middle-income country, the ratio is closer to 10 to 1; and in Brazil it is more than 20 to 1. Yet the table also suggests that ideological and political characteristics make a difference. Particularly surprising is the inequality of income in China, the only Communist nation, where the poorest 40 percent get less of the total (15.3 percent), than the poorest 40 percent in Japan (21.9 percent).

Industrialization and high productivity have historically gone along with more equal distribution of income. This tends to be true today, too. Yet, the first stages of industrialization and modernization may actually increase income inequality by creating a dual economy—a rural sector and an urban industrial and commercial sector, both with inequalities of their own. This pattern is apparent if we contrast inequality in India with the even greater inequalities in the somewhat richer countries of Mexico and Brazil. These inequalities tend to increase as education and communication spread. This pattern helps explain the political instability of many developing countries, since income inequality grows at the same time that awareness of it is increasing. Even though inequality may tend to diminish in later stages of development, this trend cannot be taken for granted. In Brazil, income inequality has increased for decades,

TABLE 1.4   Income Distribution for Selected Nations

Country	Year	Wealthiest 10%	Poorest 40%	Per Capita GNP (1998)
Japan	1979	22.4	21.9	32,380
United States	1994	28.5	15.3	29,340
Germany	1989	22.6	22.5	25,850
France	1989	24.9	19.9	24,940
Britain	1986	24.7	19.9	21,400
Brazil	1995	47.9	8.2	4,570
Mexico	1992	39.2	11.9	3,970
Russia	1993	22.2	20.0	2,300
Egypt	1991	26.7	21.2	1,290
China	1995	30.9	15.3	750
India	1994	25.0	22.2	430
Nigeria	1992	31.4	12.9	300

Source: World Bank, *World Development Report, 1999–2000* (New York: Oxford University Press, 2000), table 5, pp. 238–39.

even as the economy developed. Nor does inequality disappear in the most economically advanced nations. In the United States, income inequality increased substantially from the 1970s to the mid-1990s as a consequence of changes in economic structure, the increase in single-parent families, immigration, and a lowering of income taxes in the 1980s. Similar trends are evident in Britain and in many other advanced states, driven by the same factors as well as by high unemployment, and rapid salary gains among highly educated people. These developments are most dramatic in Russia and other post-communist societies. Inequality is an issue that all nations must face.

Economic inequality has a very important international side. A series of studies sponsored by the World Bank in the 1970s and 1980s, with the title "Redistribution with Growth," proposed a variety of policy solutions to mitigate the hardships economic inequality causes in developing societies and specifically to avoid the extreme cases of "unequal development," such as in Brazil and Mexico.[11] Instead, the economists involved in these studies pointed to Taiwan and South Korea, which had combined rapid economic growth with greater social equality. In these countries early land reforms had equalized opportunity at the outset of the developmental process. Investment in education, in agricultural inputs and rural infrastructure (principally roads and water), and in labor-intensive in-

dustries, and an emphasis on export-oriented growth, produced remarkable results for several decades. Their comparative advantage in cheap and skilled labor enabled these countries to compete effectively in international markets. Thus it is possible to identify growth policies with lesser inequalities, but it can be very difficult to put them into practice, especially where substantial inequalities already exist.

Population Growth, Economic Development, and the Environment

While the goal of economic growth for the world's lower-income economies is generally accepted and fostered by such international agencies as the UN, the World Bank, and the International Monetary Fund, as well as the by the foreign aid programs of advanced industrial nations, it has an ominous "downside." The advanced economies have only begun to pay for the environmental costs of their industrial development. Despoiled forests, depleted soils and fisheries, polluted air and water, nuclear waste, endangered species, and a threatened ozone layer now burden their legislative dockets. Some of these environmental problems—for example, deforestation—are even more acute in developing countries. With increasing industrialization and urbanization in the developing world, many environmental problems could get dramatically worse.

The world's increasing energy use is causing serious environmental challenges. Nuclear power plants, such as this one in Northern Bohemia, pose the risk of nuclear radiation.

Sean Sprague/Panos Pictures

Thus economic development can impose serious environmental costs. The book *The Population Explosion* drew attention to the great environmental burden that had resulted from the population growth and industrial development of the nineteenth and twentieth centuries.[12] Our arable soil, our forests, the quality of our air and water, the welfare of our plant and animal life, and the continuity of our climate have been seriously damaged by the combination of economic and demographic growth. In addition to the challenge of combining economic growth with equity, we must now find a way to counteract the environmental degradation caused by the combined growth of the economy and the population.

Table 1.5 puts the second dilemma in sharp relief. The table divides world population into three strata: low-income economies, middle-income economies, and high-income economies. In 1992 the low-income countries had a population total of more than 3 billion, or 60 percent of the total world population; the middle-income group had roughly one-fourth of the total population, and the high-income population had 15 percent. Projections are that world population in 2025 will increase to 8 billion and that the poorer countries will still see a more rapid growth of population. Rapid economic growth in the developing world would result in great burdens on the environment indeed.

These frightening prospects have produced a mixed literature of both light and heat. Economist Amartya Sen warns of a "danger that in the confrontation between apocalyptic pessimism on one hand, and a dismissive smugness, on the other, a genuine understanding of the nature of the population problem may be lost."[13] The first impact of "modernization" on population is to increase it rapidly, as new sanitation measures and modern pharmaceuticals reduce the death rate. As an economy develops, however, public policies and changing incentives tend to reduce fertility. With improved education (particularly of women), health, and welfare, the advantages of lower fertility become clear, and population growth declines. This happened in Europe and North America as they underwent industrialization and appears to be taking place in the developing world. Thus annual population growth in the world has in the last two decades declined from 2.2 percent to 1.4 percent. The rate of population growth in India, for example, rose to 2.2 percent in the 1970s and has since declined. Latin America peaked at a higher rate and then came down sharply. The great problem area is Sub-Saharan Africa with an average growth rate of more than 2.7 percent each year during the 1990s.[14] Tragically, the fertility rate in Africa has most potently been counteracted by a rising death rate from the epidemic spread of AIDS.

T A B L E   1 . 5   Population by Economic Development Level in 1992 and Projected to 2025 (in millions US $)

Economic Development Level	In 1992		Projected to 2025	
	Number	Percentage	Number	Percentage
Low-income economies	3,191	59	5,062	62
Middle-income economies	1,416	26	2,139	27
High-income economies	828	15	922	11
Total	5,437	100	8,123	100

Source: World Bank, World Development Report 1994 (New York: Oxford University Press, 1994), tables 1 and 25.

But while the trend is in the desired direction, population growth is still a very serious problem. China has confronted this problem with a coercive policy of abortion and contraception, which in urban areas has produced dramatic results at great costs. India and other countries have had some success with what Sen calls a "collaborative" approach, involving governmental intervention in influencing family choices, as well as counting on the market and education to affect family choices.[15] Kerala in southern India is a dramatic example of what can be accomplished by this approach. Expanding education, particularly among women, and otherwise improving living conditions, has reduced fertility more than in China, or even Sweden, the United States, or Canada. To avoid the irreversible catastrophes prophesied by the "apocalyptic pessimists," however, requires sacrifices and foresight.

SECURING DEMOCRACY, HUMAN RIGHTS, AND CIVIL LIBERTIES

Democracy is the form of government to which most contemporary states, more or less sincerely and successfully, aspire. A **democracy**, briefly defined, is a political system in which citizens enjoy a number of basic civil and political rights, and in which their most important political leaders are elected in free and fair elections and accountable under a rule of law. Democracy literally means "government by the people." In small political systems, such as local communities, it may be possible for "the people" to share directly in debating, deciding, and implementing public policy. In large political systems, such as contemporary states, democracy must be achieved largely through indirect participation in policymaking. Elections, competitive political parties, free mass media, and representative assemblies make some degree of democracy possible. This indirect, or representative, democracy is not complete or ideal. But the more citizens are involved and the more influential their choices, the more democratic the system.

The most important general distinction in classifying political systems is between democratic systems and others. Nondemocracies, which we usually speak of as *authoritarian*, lack one or several of the defining features of democracy. In democracies, competitive elections give citizens the chance to shape the entire policymaking process through their selection and rejection of key policymakers. In authoritarian systems the policymakers are typically chosen by military councils, hereditary families, or dominant political parties. Citizens are either ignored or pressed into symbolic assent to the government's choices. In **oligarchies**, literally "rule by the few," important political rights are withheld from the majority of the population. South Africa until the abolition of apartheid in the early 1990s was a good example. In **totalitarian systems,** such as Nazi Germany or the Soviet Union under Stalin, the government constricts the rights and privacy of its citizens in a particularly severe and intrusive manner. All totalitarian systems are authoritarian, but most authoritarian systems are not totalitarian.

Democracy is not an all-or-nothing question. No democracy is perfect, and we can speak of shades or gradations of democracy. Nor does democracy typically come about overnight. It often takes time to establish democratic institutions and to have citizens recognize them and comply with the rules of the democratic process. One of the most hopeful developments of the past couple of decades is the large number of countries that have undergone or are undergoing a transition to democracy. Transitions toward democracy have been a major feature of world politics in the last 20 or 30 years. Many transitions have been relatively peaceful, as authoritarian rulers have negotiated a solution in response to citizen pressures. Military forces have frequently stood aside or even supported the citizens against the dictators. Authoritarian regimes have lost legitimacy everywhere, especially since the model (and support) of the Soviet Union has collapsed.

As political systems become more complex, richer, and more technologically advanced, the probability of citizen involvement increases. At the same time this participation may become less freely chosen. In the past century most Western states have been transformed from authoritarian regimes, or oligarchies with limited voting rights, to democracies. And during the past century, the power of the state has increasingly been used to meet popular needs and demands. Yet, in a modern society the government can try to control and manipulate the flow of information and communication, the formation of attitudes and culture, and the choices—if any—offered to citizens. Thus more developed political systems, especially in industrial societies, have greater potential for authoritarian control of citizens on a mass scale. On the other hand, independent social and political groups and organizations can exert autonomous political influence. High levels of education and information can contribute to a participant political culture.

Samuel P. Huntington speaks of the recent move toward democracy as a "Third Wave" of worldwide **democratization**. The first of these waves began in the nineteenth century and culminated with the establishment of many new democracies after World War I. But this wave reversed itself in the next 20 years, when many democracies collapsed or were conquered by authoritarian states. After World War II a second democratic wave, which lasted from 1943 until the early 1960s, saw both newly independent states (such as India and Nigeria) and defeated authoritarian powers (such as Germany and Japan) set up the formal institutions of democracy. While quite a number of countries became formally democratic in these years, most quickly lapsed into authoritarianism. Many of these would-be democracies failed in their first decade; another "reverse wave" in the 1960s and early 1970s swept away some older democracies (Chile, Greece, and Uruguay, for example) as well. The third wave of democratization, beginning in 1974, has involved Southern Europe, East Asia, Latin America, and recently Eastern Europe, the successor states to the Soviet Union, and a number of African states.

It can be difficult to consolidate democracies, especially in less economically developed societies. Not all of the newly democratizing countries are succeeding beyond the first few years. In some, democratic processes fail to produce stable institutions and effective public policies and give way to some form of authoritarianism. In Nigeria, a democratic-leaning regime installed in 1979 was overthrown by a military coup in 1983, and a precarious civilian regime was only reestablished in 1999. Nigeria is by no means unique. Transition can move in either direction, toward or away from democracy. While today's Third Wave of democratization is supported by the more favorable environments of more modernized societies and the very fact that there are now more democracies in the world, we cannot be sure how long the democratic gains will last.

Even when states democratize, there is no guarantee that they will grant human rights and civil liberties to all their people. In some countries, majority rule turns into a "tyranny of the majority" against ethnic or religious minorities. Therefore, democracies always have to find a balance between respecting the will of the majority and protecting the rights of the minority. But even when political rulers sincerely try to promote human rights and civil liberties (which is by no means always the case), they do not always agree what those rights should be. Although the United Nations has tried to secure agreement on a range of rights and liberties that all individuals should enjoy, different governments and cultures seriously disagree about the implementation of such protections. Some societies believe that freedom of speech should not be protected when it is used for blasphemy, or to denigrate particular social groups. Governments in Western industrial societies tend to want gender equality policies that are sometimes considered religiously unacceptable in Muslim countries. In most developing societies and most states in the United States, capital punishment is considered an acceptable penalty for particularly heinous crimes. Most Western European societies, however, do not permit such punishment and consider it inhumane.

Community-building, development, and democratization cannot be dealt with in isolation from one another. On the contrary, progress in one of these areas can create new opportunities, but also new problems, in another. Economic development, for example, can reinforce (but also ameliorate) ethnic strife and destabilize political institutions. While development has obvious positive consequences for productivity and welfare, it can disrupt social life. The growth of technology and the service economy coupled with the spread of market economies results in growing wealth and income inequality. This trend has in recent decades become quite noticeable in advanced industrial societies, and it tends to affect the developing economies even more sharply. Increasing inequality of income and wealth can sharpen class antagonisms and partisanship.

The political effects of these developments vary from country to country, depending on economic resources, demography, geography, historical experience, and the like. Environmental deterioration, growing economic inequality, economic dislocation, and migration as well as ethnic and religious mobilization can cause political fragmentation and polarization and make it more difficult to form stable governments. A more affluent and information-driven citizenry impairs the effectiveness of political parties, interest groups, parliaments, and political executives. It is more difficult to structure political alternatives when party and interest group leaders can no longer effectively muster and discipline their followers, and when political leaders are losing control of the political agenda to such new forces as the electronic media. In subsequent chapters, we examine in more detail the ways in which these challenges affect the political choices of citizens and policymakers.

KEY TERMS

anarchists
civil liberties
democracy
democratization
ethnicity
European Union (EU)
externalities
governments
gross national product (GNP)

human rights
income and wealth inequality
libertarians
nations
nation-states
night watchman state
oligarchies

police state
political cleavages
political cultures
political system
public goods
purchasing power parity (PPP)
regulatory state

religious fundamentalism
rent seeking
sovereignty
state
state of nature
totalitarian systems
United Nations (UN)
welfare state

SUGGESTED READINGS

Chenery, Hollis, et al. *Redistribution with Growth.* New York: Oxford University Press, 1981.

Cornelius, Wayne, et al., eds. *Controlling Immigration: A Global Perspective.* Stanford, CA: Stanford University Press, 1995.

Dahl, Robert A. *Democracy and Its Critics.* New Haven: Yale University Press, 1989.

Diamond, Larry, ed. *Developing Democracy: Towards Consolidation.* Baltimore: Johns Hopkins, 1999.

Ehrlich, Paul and Anne Ehrlich. *The Population Explosion.* New York: Simon and Schuster, 1990.

Hoffman, Stanley and Robert Keohane, eds. *The New European Community.* Boulder, CO: Westview, 1991.

Horowitz, Donald. *Ethnic Groups in Conflict.* Berkeley: University of California Press, 1985.

Huntington, Samuel. *The Third Wave: Democratization in the Late Twentieth Century.* Norman, OK: University of Oklahoma Press, 1991.

Lijphart, Arend. *Patterns of Democracy.* New Haven: Yale University Press, 1999.

Linz, Juan and Alfred Stepan, eds. *Problems of Democratic Transitions and Consolidation.* Baltimore: Johns Hopkins, 1996.

Marty, Martin and Scott Appleby. *Fundamentalism Observed.* Chicago: University of Chicago Press, 1991.

Putnam, Robert. *Making Democracy Work: Civic Traditions in Modern Italy.* Princeton, NJ: Princeton University Press, 1993.

Weiner, Myron. *The Global Migration Crisis: Challenge to States and to Human Rights.* New York: HarperCollins, 1995.

World Bank. *World Development Report.* New York: Oxford University Press, annual editions.

ENDNOTES

1. Thomas Hobbes, *Leviathan*, ed. C. B. Macpherson (New York: Penguin, 1968, p. 186).

2. J. J. Rousseau, *Second Discourse On Inequality, The First And Second Discourses* (New York: St. Martin's, 1964), pp.109–10.

3. The Vatican is not a member but maintains a permanent observer mission at the UN headquarters. Taiwan was expelled from the UN in 1971 to accommodate mainland China (the People's Republic).

4. More detailed discussions of the politics of each of these 12 countries are found in chapters 8–19 below.

5. Max Weber, *Economy and Society*, ed. Guenther Roth and Claus Wittich (Berkeley: University of California Press, 1978), p. 389.

6. Stephen Castles and Mark J. Miller, *The Age of Migration: International Population Movements in The Modern World* (New York: Guilford, 1994).

7. Erik V. Gunnemark, *Countries, Peoples, and Their Languages: The Geolinguistic Handbook* (Gothenburg, Sweden: Lanstryckeriet, 1991).

8. A recent book dealing with this theme bears the title *The Ambivalence of the Sacred* by R. Scott Appleby, (Rowman & Littlefield, 2000).

9. See, among others, Martin Marty and Scott Appleby, *Fundamentalism Observed* (Chicago, IL: University of Chicago Press, 1991).

10. World Bank, *World Development Report* (New York: Oxford University Press, 1994), p. 230.

11. Hollis Chenery et al., *Redistribution with Growth* (New York: Oxford University Press, 1981).

12. Paul and Anne Ehrlich, *The Population Explosion* (New York: Simon and Schuster, 1990).

13. Amartya Sen, "Population: Delusion and Reality," *New York Review of Books,* Sept. 22, 1994, pp. 62ff.

14. World Bank, *World Development Report, 1998–1999* (New York: Oxford University Press, 1999).

15. Sen, "Population: Delusion and Reality."

2

Comparing Political Systems

WHY WE COMPARE

The great French interpreter of American democracy, Alexis de Tocqueville, while on his travels in America in the 1830s, wrote to a friend about how his ideas about French institutions and culture entered into the writing of *Democracy in America*. Tocqueville wrote "Although I very rarely spoke of France in my book, I did not write one page of it without having her, so to speak, before my eyes."[1] On a more general note about the comparative method, he offered this comment: "Without comparisons to make, the mind does not know how to proceed."[2]

Tocqueville was telling us that comparison is fundamental to all human thought. We add that it is the methodological core of the humanistic and scientific methods as well. It is the only way we can fully understand our own political system. Comparing the past and present of our nation and comparing our experience with that of other nations deepen our understanding of our own institutions. Examining politics in other societies permits us to see a wider range of political alternatives and illuminates the virtues and shortcomings of our own political life. By taking us beyond our familiar arrangements and assumptions, comparative analysis helps expand our awareness of the possibilities of politics.

Comparison is the methodological core of the scientific study of politics. Comparative analysis helps us develop explanations and test theories of the ways in which political processes work and in which political change occurs. Here the logic and the intention of the comparative methods used by political scientists are similar to those used in more exact sciences. Political scientists cannot normally design experiments to control and manipulate political arrangements and observe the consequences, especially when dealing with large-scale events that drastically affect many people. For example, researchers cannot and would not want to start a social revolution to see its effects. Nor would they want to initiate military escalation to see if it leads to war. It is possible, however, to use the comparative method to describe and explain the different combinations of political events and institutions found in different societies. More than two thousand years ago, Aristotle in his *Politics* contrasted the economies and social structures of the many Greek city-states in an effort to determine how the social and economic environment affected political institutions and policies. (See Box 2.1.)

A contemporary political scientist, Robert Dahl, in his studies of democracy, compares the economic characteristics, cultures, and historical experiences of many contemporary nations in an effort to discover the combinations of conditions and characteristics that are associated with that form of government.[3] Other theorists, in their attempt to explain differences between the processes and performance of political systems, have compared constitutional **regimes** with tyrannies, two-party democracies with multiparty democracies, parliamentary with presidential regimes, and stable governments with unstable ones.

The end of the Cold War left a world engaged in vast experiments in different approaches to economic growth, different strategies for transition to democracy, differing ways of controlling and using the powers of government. Governments today are grappling with new issues of preserving our environment, old issues of opportunity and economic security for citizens, and ancient issues of conflicts of ethnic identities and religious beliefs. In a world made ever smaller by instantaneous **communication** and

B O X   2 . 1   Aristotle's Library

There is historical evidence that Aristotle had accumulated a library of more than 150 studies of the political systems of the Mediterranean world of 400–300 B.C. Many of these had probably been researched and written by his disciples.

While only the Athenian constitution survives of this library of Aristotelian polities, it is evident from the references to such studies that do survive, that Aristotle was concerned with sampling the variety of political systems then in existence, including the "barbarian" (Third World?) countries such as Libya, Etruria, and Rome: "the references in ancient authorities give us the names of some 70 or more of the states

described in the compilation of 'polities.' They range from Sinope, on the Black Sea, to Cyrene in North Africa; they extend from Marseilles in the Western Mediterranean to Crete, Rhodes, and Cyprus in the East. Aristotle thus included colonial constitutions as well as those of metropolitan states. His descriptions embraced states on the Aegean, Ionian, and the Tyrrhenian Seas, and the three continents of Europe, Asia, and Africa."

Source: Ernest Barker, ed., *The Politics of Aristotle* (London: Oxford University Press, 1977), p. 386.

interdependent economies, these problems and achievements spill across national boundaries. Comparative analysis is a powerful and versatile tool. It enhances our ability to describe and understand political processes and political change in any country by offering concepts and reference points from a broader perspective. The comparative approach also stimulates us to form general theories of political relationships. It encourages and enables us to test our political theories by confronting them with the experience of many institutions and settings. A primary goal of this book is to provide access to this powerful tool for thought and analysis.

HOW WE COMPARE

We study politics in several different ways: we describe it; we seek to explain it; and sometimes we try to predict it. These are all parts of the scientific process, and in each of them we may use the comparative method. The first stage in the study of politics is description. If we cannot describe a political process or event, we cannot really hope to understand or explain, much less predict what might happen next, or in similar situations. In order to describe politics, we need a set of concepts that are clearly defined and well understood. We speak of this as a conceptual framework. The easier this set of concepts is to understand, and the more generally it can be applied, the more helpful it is to the study of politics. Conceptual frameworks are not generally right or wrong, but they may be more or less useful to the task at hand.

Once we are able to describe politics with the help of the conceptual framework that we choose, the next task is to explain it. What we mean by explaining political phenomena is seeking to identify relationships between them. For example, we might be interested in the relationship between democracy and international peace (Box 2.2). Are democratic states more peaceful than others? If so, are they peaceful because they are democratic, are they democratic because they are peaceful, or are they perhaps both peaceful and democratic because they are more prosperous than other states?

These questions show that we often want explanations to go beyond associating one thing with another. Ideally we want to put many political relationships in causal terms, so that we can say that one political feature is the cause of another, and the latter is the effect of the former. For example, a theory may state that countries are peaceful because they are democratic. There are different kinds of causal statements that we can make about this relationship between war and form of government. One such statement might be "only authoritarian governments start wars"; in other words, authoritarianism is necessary to starting wars. Another statement might be, "all democracies are peaceful"; in other words, democracy is sufficient to guarantee peacefulness. A third statement might express only a tendency or probability, such as "authoritarian governments tend to be more warlike than democracies."

Theories are statements about causal relationships between general classes of events—for exam-

B O X 2 . 2   Statistical Methods

A popular contemporary research program known as *democratic peace research* illustrates the pros and cons of statistical and case study research. It has been of primary interest to international relations scholars, who took the diplomatic history of the Cold War period and asked whether democratic countries are more peaceful in their foreign policy than authoritarian and nondemocratic ones. Many scholars in the democratic peace research group took the statistical route. They counted each year of interaction between two states as one case, and with roughly half a century of diplomatic history involving a state system of 100 countries or more, they had a very large number of cases, even after eliminating the many irrelevant cases of countries that never, or rarely, had any relations with one another. Political scientists Andrew Bennett and Alexander George drew these conclusions after surveying the statistical research:

> Statistical methods achieved important advances on the issue of whether a nonspurious inter-democratic peace exists. A fairly strong though not unanimous consensus emerged that: (1) democracies are not less war-prone in general; (2) they have very rarely if ever fought one another; (3) this pattern of an inter-democratic peace applies to both war and conflicts short of war; (4) states in transition to democracy are more war prone than established democracies; and (5) these correlations were not spuriously brought about by the most obvious alternative explanations.

There is a consensus now that statistical studies are not as good as are case studies at answering "why" questions. Case studies make clinical depth possible, revealing causal interconnections in individual cases. Careful repetition of these causal tracings from case to case strengthens confidence in these relationships. Thus Bennett and George concluded that the best research strategy to follow is to use statistical and case study methods together, with each one of the methods having its own strengths.

Source: Andrew Bennett and Alexander George, "An Alliance of Statistical and Case Study Methods: Research on the Interdemocratic Peace," APSA-CP: *Newsletter of the APSA Organized Section in Comparative Politics* 9, no. 1: 6.

ple, about what causes democracy, war, or political development. Theories are always tentative; they are always subject to modification or falsification as our knowledge improves. And theories need to be testable. A good theory is one that holds up after continued trials and experiments, that can be confirmed or modified as we test the theory again and again. The number of cases that political scientists have to generalize about varies from problem to problem. Similarly, the number of cases that are examined when we test theories can vary dramatically.

Researchers in political science distinguish between studies based on large numbers (large "n") and small numbers (small "n"). Large "n" studies are usually referred to as *statistical studies*, small "n" as *case studies*. Large "n" studies have a sufficient number and variety of cases to enable the researcher to examine the relation among the variables (variables being the dimensions or the parameters on which our cases differ—for example, "form of government: democracy or dictatorship," or "income per capita"). Small "n" studies permit investigators to go deeply into a case, identify the particularities of it, get the clinical details, and examine each link in the causal process.

In this manner, political scientists may come to know not only whether democracies are more peaceful than dictatorships, but more precisely why democratic leaders behave in the way that they do.

It is now generally recognized that these methods are complementary. Large "n" statistical studies allow us to be more certain and precise in our explanations. On the other hand, we need the depth that case studies provide in order to formulate insightful hypotheses for statistical testing in the first place. Also, case study methods can be used to examine in detail some aspects of cause-and-effect relations better than large "n" studies.

An example may suggest how you might go about theorizing in comparative politics, going beyond "just mastering the facts." It is well known that rich countries are more likely to be democracies than are poor countries; democracy and economic development are strongly associated. But there are many possible reasons for this association. Some have suggested that comes about because democracy encourages education and economic development. Others have argued that as countries develop economically, their new middle classes or better organized working class are more likely to demand democratization. Yet others have seen that both democracy and economic development are commonly found in some regions of the world, such as Western Europe, while both tend to be scarce in the Middle East and Africa, suggesting that certain cultures may encourage or discourage both of them. We want to understand the causal nature of this association, for reasons of both science and policy. The recent work of Przeworski and his associates examines the full experience of democracies, nondemocracies, and transitions between them in all parts of the world between 1950 and 1990.[4] Their statistical analysis leads them to conclude that the explanation for the association does not lie in regional effects or superior economic growth in democracy. Moreover, nations at any level of development seem able to introduce democracy. The key to the relationship lies rather in the consistently greater fragility of democracies in societies at lower levels of economic development; democracy can easily be introduced in poor societies with less educated populations, but in these social conditions it is relatively more likely to be replaced by some kind of dictatorship. We still need to understand just why democracy is more precarious in less developed societies, but we have made progress in understanding the causal element in the relationship.

We can also generate and test hypotheses about the causes and consequences of political change by comparing countries at different historical periods, just as we can compare the institutions of different countries in our search for political theories. Tocqueville's study of the French Revolution contributed to a general theory of revolution by comparing pre- and post-revolutionary France.[5] Theda Skocpol based her theories of the causes of revolution on a comparison of the "old regimes" of France, Russia, and China with their revolutionary and post-revolutionary regimes.[6]

SYSTEMS: ENVIRONMENT AND INTERDEPENDENCE

Comparative Politics Today suggests that we approach the comparison of political systems with a structural-functional system framework. To do so, we need to discuss in some detail these three general concepts that we use throughout this book: (1) system, (2) structure, and (3) function. **System,** as we defined it in Chapter 1, suggests an object having moving parts, interacting with a setting or an **environment**. The **political system** is a set of institutions and agencies concerned with formulating and implementing the collective goals of a society or of groups within it. **Governments** or **states** are the **policymaking** parts of political systems. The decisions of governments are normally backed up by legitimate coercion, and obedience may be compelled. We discuss legitimacy at greater length in Chapter 3.

Figure 2.1 tells us that a political system exists in both a domestic and an international environment, molding these environments and being molded by them. The system receives **inputs** from these environments and attempts to shape them through its outputs. In the figure, which is quite schematic and simple, we use the United States as the central actor, and we include some other countries as our environmental examples—Russia, China, Britain, Germany, Japan, Mexico, and Egypt. Exchanges among countries may vary in many ways. For example, they may be "dense" or "sparse"; United States–Canadian relations exemplify the dense end of the continuum, while United States–Nepalese relations would be at the sparse end. Relationships between political systems may be of many different kinds. The United States has substantial trade relations with some nations and relatively little trade with others. Some countries have an excess of imports over exports, whereas others have an excess of exports over imports. With such countries as the NATO nations, Japan, South Korea, Israel, and Saudi Arabia, military exchanges and support have been of great importance to the United States. The interdependence of nations—the volume and value of imports and exports, transfers of capital, the extent of foreign travel and international communication—has increased enormously in the last decades. We might represent this process as a thickening of the input and output arrows between the United States and other countries in Figure 2.1. Fluctuations in this flow of international transactions and traffic attributable to depression, inflation, protective tariffs, international terrorism, war, and the like may wreak havoc with the economies of the nations affected.

The interaction of the political system with its domestic environment—the economic and social systems and the culture of its citizens—may be illustrated in the American case by the rise of the "high-

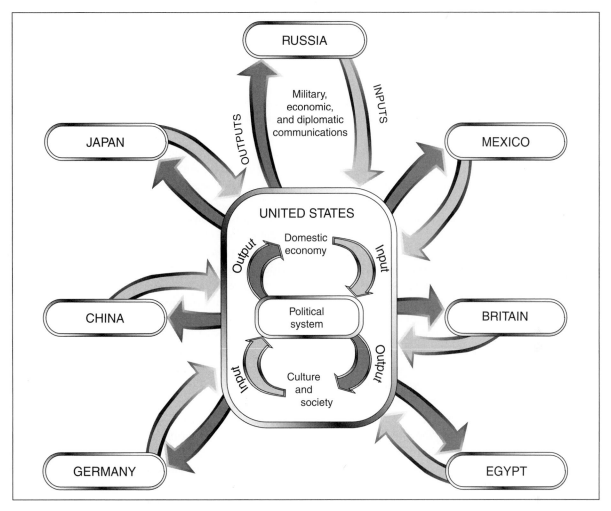

FIGURE 2.1 The Political System and Its Environments

tech information-based economy." The composition of the American labor force, and consequently its citizenry, has changed dramatically in the last century. Agriculture has declined to under 3 percent of the gainfully employed. Employment in heavy extractive and manufacturing industries has decreased substantially, and the newer, high-technology occupations, the professions, and the service occupations have increased sharply as a proportion of the labor force. The last half-century has also witnessed significant improvements in the educational level of the American population, although the quality of education particularly at the primary and secondary levels has come in for very serious criticism in recent years. These and other changes in American social structure have transformed the social bases of the party

system. There are now as many independents among American voters as loyal Democrats and Republicans. Workers of the older, primarily European, ethnic stocks have ceased being a solid support for the Democratic Party; they now tend to divide their votes almost equally between the two parties. On the whole, these changes in the labor force have been associated with a more conservative trend in economic policy and with efforts to cut back welfare and other expenditures. A more educated and culturally sophisticated society has become more concerned with the quality of life, the beauty and healthfulness of the environment, and similar issues. In input-output terms, socioeconomic changes have transformed the political demands of the electorate and the kinds of policies that it supports.

Thus a new pattern of society results in different policy outputs, different kinds and levels of taxation, changes in regulatory patterns, and changes in welfare expenditures. The advantage of the system-environment approach is that it directs our attention to the **interdependence** of what happens within and between nations, and it provides us with a vocabulary to describe, compare, and explain these interacting events. If we are to make sound judgments in politics, we need to be able to place political systems in their domestic and international environments, recognizing how these environments both set limits on and provide opportunities for political choices. This approach keeps us from reaching quick and biased political judgments. If a country is poor in natural resources and lacks the skills necessary to exploit what it has, we cannot fault it for having a low industrial output or poor educational and social services. Similarly, a country dominated and exploited by another country with a conservative policy cannot be condemned for failing to introduce social reforms.

The policies that leaders and political activists can follow are limited by the interdependence of the system and its institutions, as well as by the environment. However, in this era of rapid change, if the goals of the leadership and the political activists change, one set of political institutions may quickly be replaced by another. One of the most dramatic illustrations of such an institutional transformation was the breakdown of control by the Communist parties in Eastern Europe, and their replacement by multiparty systems when the leadership of the Soviet Union lost its confidence in the Soviet system and the future of socialism. Once the Soviet leadership lost confidence in the legitimacy of the Soviet Communist Party, it had no choice but to adopt a permissive and conciliatory policy toward its former satellites.

The notion of interdependence goes even further than this relationship between policy and institutions. The various structural parts of a political system are also interdependent. If a government is based on popularly elected representatives in legislative bodies, then a system of election must be instituted. If many people enjoy the right to vote, then the politicians seeking office will have to mobilize the electorate and organize political parties to carry on election campaigns. As the policymaking agencies of the political system enact laws, they will need administrators and civil servants to implement these laws, and they will need judges to determine whether the laws have been violated and to decide what punishments to impose on the violators.

STRUCTURES AND FUNCTIONS

Governments do many things—from establishing and operating school systems, to maintaining public order, to fighting wars. In order to carry on these many activities, governments have specialized agencies, or **structures**, such as parliaments, bureaucracies, administrative agencies, and courts, which perform **functions**, which in turn enable the government to formulate, implement, and enforce its policies. The policies reflect the goals; the agencies provide the means.

Figure 2.2 locates within the political system six types of political structures—political parties, interest groups, legislatures, executives, bureaucracies, and courts. Such structures are found in almost all modern political systems. One might therefore think that if we understand how such structures work in one political system, we can apply this insight to any other system. Unfortunately that is not always the case, and this sixfold classification will not carry us very far in comparing political systems with each other. The problem is that similar structures may have very different functions across political systems. Britain and China have all six types of political institutions, at least in name; however, these institutions are organized differently in the two countries, and they function in dramatically different ways. Britain has a monarch—currently Elizabeth II—who performs ceremonial functions, like opening Parliament and conferring knighthoods and other honors. China does not have a specialized ceremonial executive. There is, however, a president, elected by the National People's Congress, who performs the ceremonial functions as well as some political functions. The political executive in Britain consists of the prime minister, the ministers assigned to the Cabinet, and the larger ministry, which consists of all the heads of departments and agencies. All these officials are usually selected from Parliament. There is a similar structure in China, called the State Council, headed by a premier and consisting of the various ministers and ministerial commissions. But while the British prime minister and Cabinet have substantial policymaking power, the State Council in China is

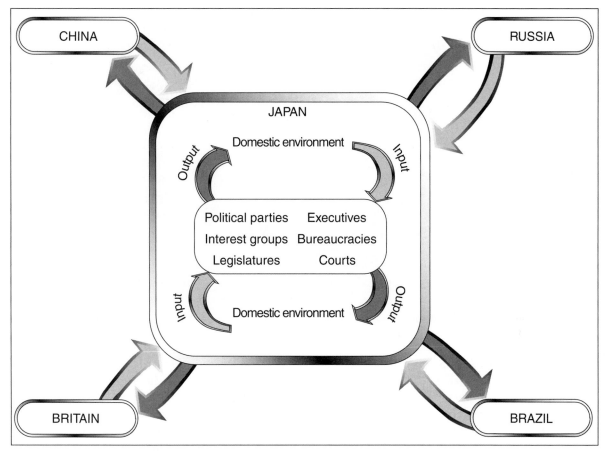

FIGURE 2.2 The Political System and Its Structures

closely supervised by the general secretary of the Communist Party, the Politburo, and the Central Committee of the party. Both Britain and China have legislative bodies—the House of Commons in Britain and the National People's Congress in China. But while the House of Commons is a key institution in the policymaking process, the Chinese Congress meets for only brief periods, ratifying decisions made mainly by the Communist Party authorities.

There are even larger differences between political parties in the two countries. Britain has a competitive party system. The majority in the House of Commons and the Cabinet are constantly confronted by an opposition party or parties, competing for public support and looking forward to the next election when they may unseat the incumbent majority, as happened most recently in 1997, when the Labour Party replaced the Conservatives in government. In China the Communist Party controls the whole polit-

ical process. There are no other political parties. The principal decisions are taken in the Politburo and to some extent in the Central Committee of the Communist Party. The governmental agencies implement the policies, which have to be initiated and/or approved by the top Communist Party leaders.

British interest groups are autonomous organizations that play important roles in the polity and the economy. Chinese trade unions and other professional organizations have to be viewed as parts of the official apparatus, dominated by the Communist Party, that perform mobilizing, socializing, and facilitating functions. Thus an institution-by-institution comparison of British and Chinese politics that did not spell out functions in detail would not bring us far toward understanding the important differences in the politics of these countries.

Figure 2.3 shows how we relate structure to function and process to policy and performance.

This meeting of the National Assembly of the People's Republic of China in the Great Hall of the People in Beijing illustrates the importance of structural functionalism. While this is called the "National People's Congress" and the delegates are raising their hands in a vote, the vote is purely formal, since there is no real choice between alternatives.

Mark Avery/AP/Wide World Photos

(The functions and processes shown in the figure are discussed in greater detail in Chapter 3 through Chapter 6.) In the center of Figure 2.3 under the heading "**Process functions**" are listed the distinctive activities necessary for policy to be made and implemented in any kind of political system: **interest articulation, interest aggregation,** policymaking, and policy **implementation** and **adjudication.** We call these process functions because they play a direct and necessary role in the process of making policy. Before policy can be decided, some individuals and groups in the government or the society must decide what they want and hope to get from politics. The political process begins as these interests are expressed or articulated. The many arrows on the left of the figure show these initial expressions.

To be effective, however, these demands must be combined (aggregated) into policy alternatives—such as higher or lower taxes or more or less social security benefits—for which substantial political support can be mobilized. Thus the arrows on the left are consolidated as the process moves from interest articulation to interest aggregation. Alternative policies are then considered. Whoever controls the government backs one of them, and authoritative policymaking takes place. The policy must be enforced and implemented, and if it is challenged or violated, there must be some process of adjudication.

Each policy may affect several different aspects of a society, as reflected in the many arrows for the implementation phase. These process functions that we have been describing are performed by such political structures as parties, legislatures, political executives, bureaucracies, and courts. The structural-functional approach stresses the point that while a particular institution such as a legislature may have a special relationship to a particular function such as law-making or rule-making, it does not have a monopoly on this function. Presidents and governors may share in the legislative function (veto powers), as do the higher courts (judicial review of statutes for their constitutionality).

The three functions listed at the top of the figure—socialization, recruitment, and communication—are not directly involved in making and implementing public policy but are of fundamental importance to the political system. We refer to these three functions as **system functions,** because they determine whether or not the system will be maintained or changed—for example—whether policymaking will continue to be dominated by a single authoritarian party or military council, or whether competitive parties and a legislature will replace them. The arrows leading from these three functions to all parts of the political process suggest their crucial role in underpinning and permeating the political process.

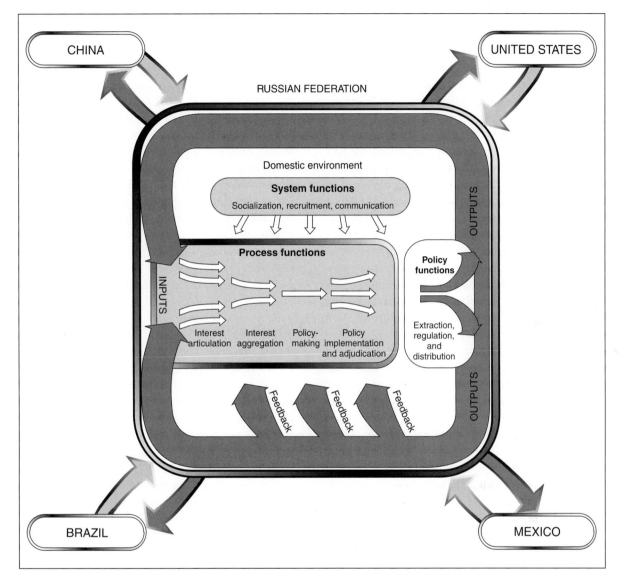

FIGURE 2 . 3 The Political System and Its Functions

Political socialization involves families, schools, communications media, churches, and all the various political structures that develop, reinforce, and transform attitudes of political significance in the society. **Political recruitment** refers to the selection of people for political activity and government offices. **Political communication** refers to the flow of information through the society and through the various structures that make up the political system. Understanding the performance of the system functions is essential to understanding how political systems respond to the great contemporary challenges of building community, fostering economic development and securing democracy that we discussed in Chapter 1.

The third set of functions, listed at the right of the figure, treats the **outputs**—the implementations of the political process. We call these the **policy functions,** the substantive impacts on the society, the economy, and the culture. These functions include the various forms of **regulation** of behavior, **extractions** of resources in the form of taxes and the like, and **distribution** of benefits and services to various groups in the population. The **outcomes** of all these political activities, in a cyclical fashion, result in new inputs, in new demands for legislation or for administrative action, and in increases or decreases in the amount of support given to the political system and incumbent officeholders. These functional concepts describe the activities carried on in any society regardless of how its political system is organized, or what kinds of policies it produces. Using these functional categories, we can determine how institutions in different countries combine in making and implementing different kinds of public policy. The term **political regime** is often used to describe the structural-functional-policy configuration governments take on at different times.

Some writers have argued that structural functionalism is an approach to politics that is conservative in its methodology, that it is biased in favor of the status quo, since it describes a set of institutions at a particular time. However, to describe political institutions precisely and comprehensively at some particular time is not to praise or defend them but to try to comprehend them. We would use the structural-functional approach to compare Nazi Germany, which we reject with horror, with democratic, peaceful, and prosperous states such as Sweden and Switzerland, which many of us may admire. Moreover, we recognize the need to supplement the structural-functional approach with a dynamic developmental approach, since we want to know not only how a political system functions, but why as well. A structural-functional approach does not in itself tell us why Germany or France developed as they did in the 1930s and 1940s. It tells us what changes occurred in these regimes. The explanation of why they changed requires that we bring in the economic, social, cultural, and international context in a historical way. We may speak of the structural-functional mapping of government and politics that we do in the theoretical chapters that follow, as a "comparative statics," a way to understand how different political processes interact at any one time, and of the analysis of political development and change as a "political dynamics."

AN ILLUSTRATIVE COMPARISON: RUSSIA IN 1985 AND 2002[7]

Figures 2.4 and 2.5 offer a simplified graphic comparison of structures and functions in Russia before and after the breakdown of communist rule in the Soviet Union. They illustrate the use of the comparative method to assess the way a political regime changed significantly in a short period of time. The point here is to illustrate how we can use the tools of political analysis, rather than provide the details of the Russian case (which are discussed in depth in Chapter 12). The figures depict the changes in the functioning of the major structures of the political system brought about by the collapse of communism. These include two revolutionary changes: the end of the single-party political system dominated by the Communist Party of the Soviet Union, which held together the vast, multinational Soviet state, and the dissolution of the Soviet Union itself as a state into its 15 member republics. As a result of these two remarkable events, Russia, the republic that was the core republic of the old union, became an independent noncommunist state.

In June 1991, Boris Yeltsin, a bitter rival to the Soviet president, Mikhail Gorbachev, was elected President of Russia. Six months later, the Soviet Union collapsed and Gorbachev gave up his office. In December 1993, Russian voters were called upon to ratify a new Constitution, which provided for a powerful executive presidency and at the same time elected a new parliament dominated by a diverse range of political parties.

In the new Russia, democratic tendencies competed with pressures for authoritarian rule. Overall the system was a mixture of pluralism with vestiges of the old, bureaucratically run, state socialist order. The major political parties were represented in Parliament and were developing national political bases of support for the next elections, while the reborn Communist Party—called the Communist Party of the Russian Federation—regularly denounced Yeltsin and called for the restoration of a strong state and more social protection. Parliament, now called the Federal Assembly, had become a meaningful site for policy debate and decision making. The mass media were no longer tightly controlled by the Communist Party. New organized interest groups, such as business associations and labor unions, were actively involved in policymaking. The bureaucracy remained a powerful central player in the political process, however, with substantial continued control over the economy.

These and subsequent changes are reflected in the differences between the two figures. In 1985 (the

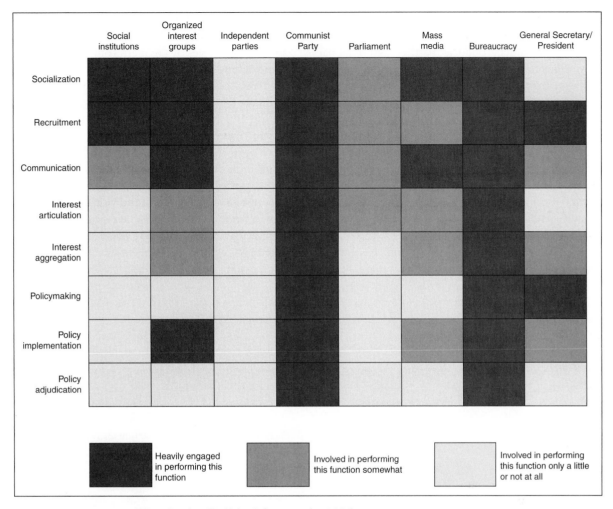

F I G U R E   2 . 4   The Soviet Political System in 1985

year that the reform leader Mikhail Gorbachev came to power), the Soviet Union was a communist regime. Its Communist Party ruled the country. The top leader of the country was the General Secretary of the Communist Party. Although the country had the formal trappings of democracy, power actually flowed downward from the decisionmakers at the top to government and society. Figure 2.4 therefore shows how the basic functions of the political system were performed in 1985, when the Communist Party was the dominant political institution of the country, overseeing schools and media, the arts and public organizations, the economy and the courts. For this reason, all the cells of the chart in the column marked "Communist Party" are shaded dark, as are the cells under the column marked "Bureaucracy." Although social institutions such as the family, work-

place, arts, and hobby groups exercised some influence over such system-level functions as socialization, recruitment, and communication, it was the Communist Party and state bureaucracy that dominated process-level functions. Under their tutelage, the mass media in 1985 were a key agent of communist political socialization and communication, while Parliament was a compliant instrument for ratifying decisions made by the party and bureaucracy. No other parties could exist beside the Communist Party, and the only organized interest groups were those authorized by the party. The party's General Secretary was the most powerful official in the country, since there was no state presidency.

By 2002 the political system had undergone fundamental change, as shown in Figure 2.5. Many more structures played a role in the political process, as is immediately evident by the larger number of cells that are heavily shaded. In particular, Parliament, independent political parties, and regional governments all acquired important new powers in policymaking. The freedom enjoyed by ordinary citizens to articulate their interests and to organize to advance them had expanded enormously. The Communist Party, no longer an official or monopolistic party, had declined substantially in power and was playing by the rules of the parliamentary game. The state bureaucracy remained an important element in the political system, although adapting itself to the new trend of movement toward a market economy by adopting quasi-commercial forms. The presidency, now occupied by Vladimar Putin, was a dominant policymaking institution. The Parliament, al-

though fairly representative of the diversity of opinion in the country, was frustrated in its policymaking and oversight roles by the inertia of the vast state bureaucracy, its inability to compel compliance with its laws, its weak links with the electorate, and by the president's power to make policy by decree. Nevertheless, it played a crucial role in aggregating interests and making policy.

The brief comparisons presented here are meant to illustrate the use of the structural-functional approach, an approach that enables us to examine how the same functions are performed in different countries, or in the same country, at two different points in time. Similarly, we may examine changes in the functions performed by the same structures over time or across different political systems. In a coun-

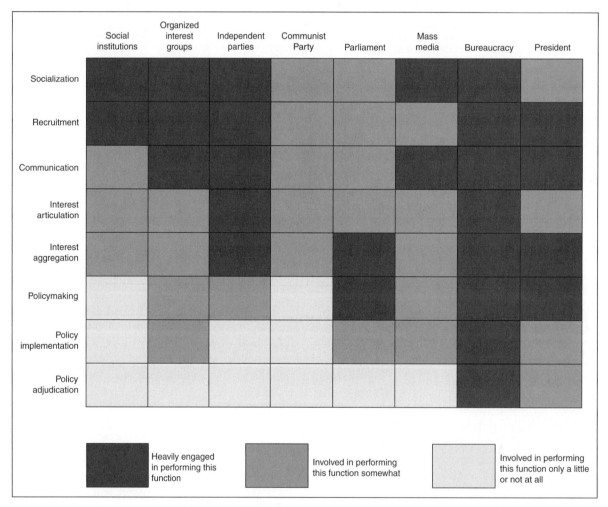

FIGURE 2.5 The Russian Political System in 2002

try undergoing as rapid and dramatic transition as Russia in the 1990s, this framework helps us to analyze changes in the distribution of power among the major institutions making up the political system. Neither the analysis of structures nor that of functions is complete without the other. A structural analysis tells us the number of political parties, or the organization of the legislature, and how the executive branch, the courts, the bureaucracy, the mass media, interest groups, and other elements of the political system are set up and by what rules or standards they operate. A functional analysis tells us how these institutions and organizations interact to produce and implement policies. In Part 2 of this book we deal more specifically with the functions of the various political institutions, with the variety of interest groups and their functions, and with the structural-functional properties of party systems, legislatures, executives, and cabinets. Here we have only illustrated the method and its advantages.

THE POLICY LEVEL: PERFORMANCE, OUTCOME, AND EVALUATION

The important question is what these differences in structure and function do for the interests, needs, and aspirations of people. Looking again at Figures 2.1 and 2.3, we see a reflection of the relationship between what happens in politics and in the society, and between what happens in the society and the international environment. The structural-functional differences determine the give-and-take between politics and environment, and the importance of that give-and-take for such goals and objectives as welfare, justice, freedom, equality, peace, and prosperity. At the left of Figure 2.3 are arrows signifying inputs of demands and supports from the society and the international system and inputs from the independent initiatives of political leaders and bureaucrats. At the right are arrows signifying outputs and outcomes, the end products of the political process, the things a government does for and to its people.

We have to distinguish between the efforts—the things a government does—and the actual outcome of these efforts. Governments may spend equal amounts on education and health, or defense, but with different consequences. Not only government efficiency or corruption but the underlying cultural, economic, and technological level, as well as changes in its environment, play a role in the effectiveness of politics. Americans spend more per capita on education than any other people in the world, but their children perform less well in important subjects such as mathematics than do children in some other countries that spend substantially less. The United States and the Soviet Union spent enormous sums on defense in the 1970s and 1980s, and

The wall dividing California from Mexico illustrates the input-output model of comparative politics. The two men are trying to escape from the poverty of the Mexican economy. The wall is part of the output of the American political system, intended to frustrate illegal immigrants. The two figures illustrate the point that outputs do not necessarily produce the intended outcomes.

Les Stone/Sygma

yet both countries were held at bay by small countries resolved to resist at all costs, and because of these failed efforts, they were weakened internally. The outcome of public policy is never wholly in the hands of the people and their leaders in the various nations of the world. Conditions in the internal environment, conditions and events in the larger external world, and simple chance may frustrate the most thoughtfully crafted programs and plans. We call the outputs of a political system—its extractions, distributions, regulations, and symbolic acts—its performance.

Finally, we must step even further back to consider the whole situation of political system, process, and policy, and the environment, to evaluate what political systems are doing. Evaluation is complex because people value different things and put different emphasis on what they value. We will refer to the different things people may value as political "goods."

In Chapter 7 we discuss goods associated with the system level, such as the stability or adaptability of political institutions; goods associated with the process level, such as citizen participation in politics; and goods associated with the policy level, such as welfare, security, and liberty. To evaluate what a political system is doing, we must look at each of these areas and assess performance and outcomes. We must also be aware of how outcomes affect individuals and subgroups in the society, of specific changes that may often be overlooked in presenting averages, and of the continuing problem of building for the future as well as living today. This last problem affects both poor nations, which wish to survive and alleviate suffering today but also to improve their children's lot tomorrow, and rich nations, which must deal with the costs to their children of polluted and depleted natural resources as the result of the thoughtless environmental policies of the past.

KEY TERMS

adjudication

communication

distribution

environment

extraction

functions

government

implementation

inputs

interdependence

interest aggregation

interest articulation

outcomes

outputs

policy functions

policymaking

political communication

political performance

political recruitment

political regime

political socialization

political system

process functions

regime

regulation

states

structural functional approach

structures

system

system functions

SUGGESTED READINGS

Collier, David. "The Comparative Method," in Ada W. Finifter, ed., *Political Science: The State of the Discipline II.* Washington: American Political Science Association, 1993.

Dogan, Mattei and Dominique Pelassy. *How to Compare Nations: Strategies in Comparative Politics.* Chatham, NJ: Chatham House, 1990.

Goodin, Robert E. and Hans-Dieter Klingemann. *A New Handbook of Political Science.* New York: Oxford University Press, 1996, chs. 2 and 3, and part 4.

King, Gary, Robert O. Keohane, and Sidney Verba. *Scientific Inference in Qualitative Research.* New York: Cambridge University Press, 1993.

Lichbach, Mark and Alan Zuckerman. *Comparing Nations: Rationality, Culture, and Structure.* New York: Cambridge University Press, 1997.

Przeworski, Adam and Henry Teune. *The Logic of Comparative Social Inquiry.* New York: Wiley, 1970.

ENDNOTES

1. Alexis de Tocqueville to Ernest de Chabrol, October 7, 1831, and Louis de Kergolay, October 18, 1847, in *Alexis de Tocqueville: Selected Letters on Politics and Society*, ed. Roger Boesche (Berkeley: University of California Press, 1985), pp. 59 and 191.

2. See also George Wilson Pierson, *Tocqueville and Beaumont in America* (New York: Oxford University Press, 1938).

3. Robert A. Dahl, *Polyarchy: Participation and Opposition* (New Haven, Ct.: Yale University Press, 1971); Robert A. Dahl, *Democracy and Its Critics* (New Haven, Ct.: Yale University Press, 1989.)

4. Adam Przeworski, Michael E. Alvarez, Jose Antonio Cheibub, Fernando Limongi, *Democracy and Development* (Cambridge: Cambridge University Press, 2000).

5. Alexis de Tocqueville, *The Old Regime and the French Revolution,* trans. Stuart Gilbert (New York: Doubleday, 1955).

6. Theda Skocpol, *States and Social Revolutions* (New York: Cambridge University Press, 1979).

7. Figures 2.4 and 2.5 and the text of "An Illustrative Comparison: Russia in 1985 and 2002" were contributed by Thomas Remington.

CHAPTER 3

Political Culture
and Political Socialization

POLITICAL CULTURE

Americans' strong feelings of patriotism, the Japanese deference toward political elites, and French proclivity toward protest are all examples of how cultural norms shape politics. Our attitudes and values inevitably affect how we act, and it is the same with politics. The functioning of political institutions at least partially reflects the attitudes, norms, and expectations of the citizenry. Thus the English use their constitutional arrangements to sustain their liberty, while the same institutions were once used as instruments of repression in South Africa and Northern Ireland. In times of systemic change a supportive public can facilitate the development of a new political system, while the lack of public support may erode the foundations of a political system. To understand the tendencies for present and future behavior in a nation, we must begin with public attitudes toward politics and their role within the political system—what we call a nation's **political culture.**

Political culture does not explain everything about politics. Even people with similar values and skills will behave differently when they face different opportunities or problems. Nor is political culture unchangeable. New experiences can alter the attitudes of individuals; for example, peasants who migrate to the city learn new ways of urban life. But cultural norms typically change slowly and reflect enduring patterns of political action. This means that political culture is a critical element in understanding politics across countries or across time. If we do not take it into account, we will not understand how politics really functions.

This chapter begins by mapping the important parts of political culture. Then, we discuss **political socialization:** how individuals form their political attitudes and thus, collectively, how citizens form their political culture. We conclude with observations about the trends in political culture in world politics today.

MAPPING THE THREE LEVELS OF POLITICAL CULTURE

A nation's political culture includes its citizens' orientations toward three levels: the political system, the political and policymaking process, and policy outputs and outcomes (Table 3.1). The *system* level involves the citizens' and leaders' views of the values and organizations that comprise the political system. Do citizens identify with the nation and accept the general system of government? The *process* level includes expectations of how politics should function, and individuals' relationship to the political process. The *policy* level deals with citizens' and leaders' policy expectations from the government. What are the government's policy goals and how are they to be achieved?

TABLE 3.1   The Aspects of Political Culture

Aspects of Political Culture	Examples
System	Pride in nation
	National identity
	Legitimacy of government
Process	Role of citizens
	Perceptions of political rights
Policy	Role of government
	Government policy priorities

The System Level

Orientations toward the political system are important because they tap basic commitments to the polity and the nation. Feelings of national pride are a revealing example of this aspect of the political culture (Figure 3.1). National pride seems strongest in nations with a long history that has emphasized feelings of patriotism—the United States is a prime example. Such a common sense of identity and national history is often what binds a people together in times of political strain. The figure indicates that high levels of pride exist in nations with much different political and economic systems, such as the United States and Poland. In contrast, national pride is low in Japan and Germany, two nations that have avoided nationalist sentiments in reaction to the pre–World War II regimes and their excesses. In other cases, ethnicity, language, or history divide the public, which may strain national identities and ultimately lead to conflict and division.

The **legitimacy** of the political system also provides a foundation for a successful political process. When citizens believe that they ought to obey the laws, then legitimacy is high. If they see no reason to obey, or if they comply only from fear, then legitimacy is low. Because it is much easier for government to function when citizens believe in the legitimacy of the political system, virtually all governments, even the most brutal and coercive, try to make their citizens believe that the laws ought to be obeyed. A political system and a government with high legitimacy will be more effective in making and carrying out policies and more likely to overcome hardships and reversals.

Citizens may grant legitimacy to a government for different reasons. In a traditional society, legitimacy may depend on the ruler's inheriting the throne or on the ruler's obedience to religious customs, such as making sacrifices and performing rituals. In a modern democracy, the legitimacy of the authorities will depend on their selection by voters in competitive elections and on their following constitutional procedures in their actions. In other political cultures, the leaders may base their claim to legitimacy on their special grace, wisdom, or ideology, which they claim will transform citizens' lives for the better, even though the government does not respond to specific demands or follow prescribed procedures.[1]

Whether legitimacy is based on tradition, ideology, citizen participation, or specific policies, the basis of legitimacy defines the fundamental understanding between citizens and political authorities. Citizens obey the laws—and in return the government meets the obligations set by the terms of its legitimacy. As long as the government meets its obligations, the public is supposed to comply, be supportive, and act appropriately. If legitimacy is violated—the line of succession is broken, the constitution is subverted, or the ruling ideology is ignored—then the government may expect resistance and perhaps rebellion.

In systems with low legitimacy or where the claimed bases for legitimacy are not accepted, people often resort to violence to solve political disagreement. Legitimacy may be undermined where

100	
	Egypt
	United States/Poland
	Mexico/Canada/ Tanzania
	Peru/Finland
	India/Argentina
90	Nigeria
	France
	Britain/Hungary/Turkey
	Sweden/Italy
	Israel
	China
80	Latvia/Czech Republic
	Netherlands
	Germany (East)
70	
	Russia
	Estonia
	Germany (West)
60	
	Japan/Lithuania

F I G U R E   3 . 1   Feelings of National Pride (in percent)

Source: Selected nations from the 2000–2002 *World Values Survey* and the 1999 *European Values Survey.* Figure entries are the percent "proud" and "very proud"; missing data are excluded from the calculation of percentages.

the public disputes the boundaries of the political system (as in Northern Ireland or East Timor) rejects the current arrangements for recruiting leaders and making policies (as when Filipinos took to the streets and demanded the ouster of Ferdinand Marcos and free elections) or loses confidence that the leaders are fulfilling their part of the political bargain in making the right kinds of laws or following the right procedures (as when Indonesians protested deteriorating of living conditions under Sukarno).

The Soviet Union disintegrated in the early 1990s because all three kinds of legitimacy problems appeared. After Communist ideology failed as a legitimizing force, there was no basis for a national political community in the absence of common language or ethnicity. Similarly, the general loss of confidence in the Communist Party as the dominating political structure led many people to call for new arrangements. Finally, shortages of food and consumer goods caused people to lose faith in the government's short-term economic and political policies. Soviet President Mikhail Gorbachev failed in his efforts to deal with all three problems at the same time.

Another systemic orientation involves regime norms. In the early twentieth century a variety of political systems divided the world. Fascism was on the rise in Europe, communism was establishing itself in the Soviet Union, colonial administrations governed large parts of the world, monarchical or authoritarian governments ruled other parts of the world, and Western Europe and North America strained to maintain democracy in this sea of conflicting currents.

Today, many of these forms of governance are no longer widely accepted. Communism still has strongholds in China and Cuba, but it has lost its image as a progressive force for global change. Some nations of the world still accept autocratic or religiously based systems of government. However, the global wave of democratization in the 1990s has raised democratic principles to a position of prominence. Most of the people in the world today seem to favor democratic principles even if they differ in how those principles should be applied.[2]

The Process Level

The second level of the political culture involves what the public expects of the political process. If you are English or Nigerian, what do you think about the institutions of your political system and what is expected of you as a citizen?

Broadly speaking, three different patterns describe the citizens' role in the political process.[3] **Participants** are involved as actual or potential participants in the political process. They are informed about politics and make demands on the polity, granting their support to political leaders based on performance. **Subjects** passively obey government officials and the law, but they do not vote or actively involve themselves in politics. **Parochials** are hardly aware of government and politics. They may be illiterates, rural people living in remote areas, or simply people who ignore politics and its impact on their lives.

As shown in Figure 3.2, in a hypothetical modern industrial democracy a sizable proportion (for instance, 60 percent) are participants, another third are simply subjects, and a small group are parochials. Such a distribution provides enough political activists to ensure competition between political parties and sizable voter turnout, as well as critical audiences for debate on public issues by parties, candidates, and pressure groups. At the same time, not all citizens feel the need to be active or concerned about the political system.

The second column in Figure 3.2 depicts the pattern we expect in a industrialized authoritarian society, such as the former communist nations of Eastern Europe. A small minority of citizens are involved in a one-party system, which penetrates and oversees the society, as well as decides government policies. Most other citizens are mobilized as subjects by political institutions: political parties, the bureaucracy, and government-controlled mass media. People are encouraged and even forced to cast a symbolic vote of support in elections and to pay taxes, obey regulations, and accept assigned jobs. Because of the effectiveness of modern social organization and mass communications and the efforts of the authoritarian power structure, few citizens are unaware of the government and its influence on their lives. If such a society suddenly attempts to democratize its politics, many citizens must learn to become participants as well as democrats.

The third column shows an authoritarian society that is partly traditional and partly modern, such as in Egypt or China. In spite of an authoritarian political organization, some participants—students and intellectuals, for example—oppose the system and

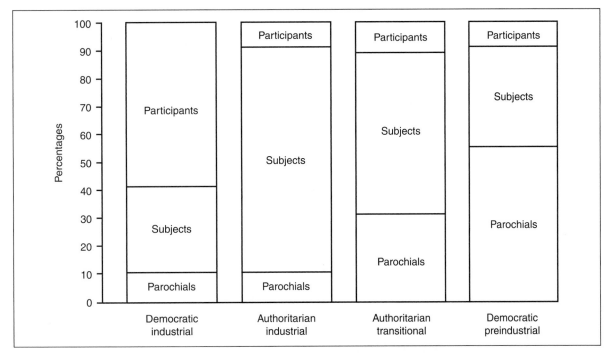

F I G U R E   3 . 2   Models of Political Culture: Orientations Toward Involvement
in the Political Process

try to change it by persuasion or more aggressive acts of protest. Favored groups, like business people and landowners, discuss public issues and engage in lobbying. Most people in such systems are passive subjects, aware of government and complying with the law but not otherwise involved in public affairs. The parochials—poor and illiterate urban dwellers, peasants, or farm laborers—have little conscious contact with the political system.

Our fourth example is the democratic preindustrial system, perhaps one like India, which has a predominantly rural, illiterate population. In such a country there are few political participants, chiefly educated professionals, business people, and landowners. A much larger number of employees, workers, and perhaps independent farmers are directly affected by government taxation and other official policies. The largest group of citizens are illiterate farmworkers and peasants, whose knowledge of and involvement with national politics is minimal. In such a society it is a great challenge to create a more aware citizenry that can participate meaningfully and shape public policies through democratic means.

In summary, the distribution of these cultural patterns is related to the type of political process that

citizens expect and support. For instance, we normally identify democracy with a more participatory political culture. Authoritarian states are more likely to endure when the public is characterized by subjects and parochials—although authoritarian states can come in many forms, ranging from communism, to dictatorships, to religion-based regimes.

Another critical feature of the process culture involves beliefs about other groups and oneself as a group member. Do individuals trust their fellow citizens? Do they see the society as divided into social classes, regional groups, or ethnic communities? Do they identify themselves with particular factions or parties? How do they feel about groups of which they are not members? When people trust others they will be more willing to work together for political goals, and group leaders may be more willing to form coalitions.[4] Governing a large nation requires forming large coalitions, and there must be substantial amounts of trust in other leaders to keep bargains and ensure honesty in negotiations.

The opposite of trust is hostility, which can destroy intergroup and interpersonal relations. The tragic examples of ethnic, religious, and ideological conflict in many nations—such as the conflicts in

Cubans wave flags at pro-government rally organized by the Castro government.

AP/Wide World Photos

Rwanda, Lebanon, Northern Ireland, and Chechnya—show how easily hostility can be converted into violence and aggressive action. Respect for human life and dignity is sometimes in too short supply in the contemporary world.

The Policy Level

The politics of a country are also influenced by public images of what constitutes the good society and how to achieve it. At one level, the political culture includes expectations of the government's overall involvement in society and the economy. Should government manage the economy, or should private property rights and market forces guide economic activity? Should the state be interventionist in addressing societal issues, or follow a minimalist strategy? The ongoing debates over "big government" versus "small government" in democratic states, and between socialist and market-based economies reflect these different images of the scope of government (see Chapter 1).

Figure 3.3 illustrates the extent of cross-national differences in public expectations about whether it is the government's role to ensure that everyone is provided for. The range in opinions is considerable,

from around three-quarters believing this is a government responsibility in Israel and Nigeria, to only a quarter of the French. In general, such sentiments are more common in developing nations and in the formerly communist nations in Eastern Europe—reflecting both the socioeconomic context and political ideologies. There are some Western nations, such as Sweden and Finland, where traditions also include a large role for the government. In general, however, it appears that public support for government action decreases as national affluence increases.[5] When the public expects a larger role for government, it is likely that the policies of the government will grow to meet the public's expectations.

Policy expectations also involve specific policy demands.[6] Some policy goals, such as material welfare, are valued by nearly everyone. Concern about other policy goals may vary widely across nations because of the nation's circumstances and because of cultural traditions. People in developing countries are more likely to focus on the government's provision of basic services to ensure public well-being. Advanced industrial societies provide for basic needs, and in these nations people may be more concerned with quality of life goals, such as preservation of nature and even government support for

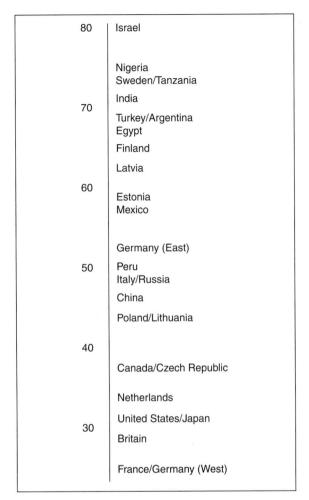

80	Israel
	Nigeria
	Sweden/Tanzania
70	India
	Turkey/Argentina
	Egypt
	Finland
	Latvia
60	
	Estonia
	Mexico
	Germany (East)
50	Peru
	Italy/Russia
	China
	Poland/Lithuania
40	
	Canada/Czech Republic
	Netherlands
30	United States/Japan
	Britain
	France/Germany (West)

FIGURE 3.3 The Government Should Ensure Everyone Is Provided For (percent agreeing)

Source: Selected nations from the 2000–2002 *World Values Survey* and 1999 *European Values Survey*; missing data are excluded from the calculation of percentages.

the arts. One of the basic measures of government performance is its ability to meet the policy expectations of its citizens.

Another set of expectations involves the functioning of government. Some cultures put more weight on the policy outputs of government, such as providing welfare and security. Other cultures also emphasize how the process functions, which involves values such as the rule of law and procedural justice. Among Germans, for example, the rule of law is given great importance; in many developing nations political relations are personally based, and there is less willingness to rely on legalistic frameworks.

Cultural Congruence

At the heart of our discussion of political culture is the belief that political structures and political cultures are mutually reinforcing in stable political systems. It is difficult to sustain democracy in a nation lacking participatory democrats, just as it is difficult to sustain an authoritarian state if the citizens are politically sophisticated and want to participate. Indeed, one of the major political issues in the world today is whether the democratic transitions in Eastern Europe, Latin America, and East Asia that began in the 1990s can be sustained. The political culture in these nations will provide a significant part of the answer.

Figure 3.4 illustrates the relationship between history and political culture. The figure displays public satisfaction with the functioning of democracy for three groups of nations; each oval in the figure represents a separate nation. One can readily see that satisfaction with democracy is higher in the first group of stable and very democratic nations; these are largely the established democracies of Western Europe and North America. Political satisfaction is lower in the second group of nations that have recently developed strong democratic structures—several Latin American and East European nations fall into this category. Finally, political satisfaction is lowest in the third group—nations with new political systems having weak democratic structures, such as the states of the former Soviet Union. Structure and culture do overlap in these nations.[7]

One may ask whether democracies create a satisfied and democratic public, or whether such a political culture leads to a democratic political system. Obviously it works both ways. For example, immediately after World War II Germans were less supportive of democracy, but the political culture was transformed by political institutions and political experiences over the generation.[8] At the same time, democracy endured in Britain during the strains of the Great Depression and World War II at least in part because the British public was supportive of the democratic process. The important conclusion is that there is normally a relationship between political culture and political structures.

Consensual or Conflictual Political Cultures

We have described political culture as a characteristic of a nation, but values and beliefs also vary within

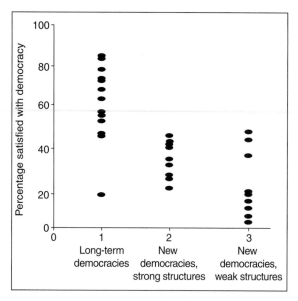

FIGURE 3.4 The Relationship Between Democratic Experience and Political Support

Source: Calculated from data on system age from Ted Gurr, *Polity III* dataset; the 1996 democracy rating from the Freedom House; satisfaction with the functioning of democracy is from Hans-Dieter Klingemann, "Mapping Political Support in the 1990s: A Global Analysis," in Pippa Norris, ed. *Critical Citizens: Global Support for Democratic Government* (Oxford, England: Oxford University Press, 1999), table 2.10.

nations. Political cultures may be consensual or conflictual on issues of public policy and, more fundamentally, on views of legitimate governmental and political arrangements. In a **consensual political culture,** citizens tend to agree on the appropriate means of making political decisions and to agree on the major problems facing the society and how to solve them. In a **conflictual political culture,** the citizens are sharply divided, often on both the legitimacy of the regime and solutions to major problems.

When a country is deeply divided in political attitudes and these differences persist over time, distinctive **political subcultures** may develop. The citizens in these subcultures may have sharply different points of view on at least some critical political matters, such as the boundaries of the nation, the nature of the regime, or the correct ideology. Typically, they affiliate with different political parties and interest groups, read different newspapers, and even have separate social clubs and sporting groups. Thus they are exposed to quite distinctive

patterns of learning about politics. Such organized differences characterize the publics in India, Nigeria, and Russia today.

Where political subcultures coincide with ethnic, national, or religious differences, as in Northern Ireland, Bosnia, and Lebanon, the divisions can be enduring and threatening. The fragmentation of the Soviet empire, the breakup of Yugoslavia, and the impulses toward autonomy and secession among ethnically distinct regions (such as in Scotland or separatist movements in Africa) all reflect the lasting power of language, culture, and historical memory to create and sustain the sense of ethnic and national identity among parts of contemporary states. Samuel Huntington has predicted that the places in the world where the major traditional cultures collide will be major sources of political conflict in the next century.[9]

POLITICAL SOCIALIZATION

Political cultures are sustained or changed as people acquire their attitudes and values. We use the term *socialization* to refer to the way in which political values are formed and the political culture is transmitted from one generation to the next. Most children acquire their basic political orientations and behavior patterns at a relatively early age.[10] Some of these attitudes will evolve and change through life, but others may remain part of the political self throughout life.

At any specific time, an individual's political self will be a combination of several feelings and attitudes. At the deepest level, there are general identifications and beliefs such as nationalism, ethnic or class self-images, religious and ideological commitments, and a fundamental sense of rights and duties in the society. Divisions between ethnic or religious groups often generate such attachments because they are based on such self-images. At an intermediate level, individuals acquire less intense emotional attitudes toward politics and governmental institutions. Finally, there are more immediate views of current events, policies, issues, and personalities. All these attitudes can change, but those in the first group usually were acquired earliest, have been most frequently reinforced, and tend to be the most durable.

Three general points about political socialization and learning need to be emphasized. First, there can be either **direct** or **indirect socialization.** Socialization is direct when it involves the explicit communication of information, values, or feelings toward politics. Civics courses in public schools are direct political socialization, as are the efforts of Islamic fundamentalist movements to indoctrinate children in such countries as Iran and Pakistan. Communist political systems also heavily use indoctrination programs. Political socialization is indirect when political views are inadvertently molded by our experiences. Such indirect political socialization may have particular force in a child's early years. For example, the child's relationships to parents, teachers, and friends are likely to affect the adult's posture toward political leaders and fellow citizens in later life. Or, growing up in a time of deprivation and hardship may leave the future adult more concerned about economic well-being.

Second, socialization continues throughout an individual's life. Early family influences can create an individual's initial values, but subsequent life experiences—becoming involved in new social groups and roles, moving from one part of the country to another, shifting up or down the social ladder, becoming a parent, finding or losing a job—may change one's political perspectives. More dramatic experiences, such as immigration to a new country or suffering through an economic depression or a war, can alter even quite basic political attitudes. Such events seem to have their greatest impact on young people just becoming involved in politics, such as first-time voters, but most people are affected to some degree.

Third, patterns of socialization in a society can either be *unifying* or *divisive*. Some events, such as international conflict or the loss of a popular public figure, can affect nearly the entire nation similarly. In contrast, subcultures in a society can have their own distinctive patterns of socialization. Social groups that provide their members with their own newspapers, their own neighborhood groups, and perhaps their own schools can create distinctive subcultural attitudes. Divisive patterns of socialization can lead to civil strife or social hostility within a nation.

AGENTS OF POLITICAL SOCIALIZATION

Individuals in all societies are affected by **agents of political socialization:** institutions and organizations that influence political attitudes. Some, like

civics courses in schools, are direct and deliberate sources of political learning. Others, like play and work groups, are likely to affect political socialization indirectly.

The Family

The direct and indirect influences of the family—the first socialization source that an individual encounters—are powerful and lasting. The family has distinctive influences on attitudes toward authority. Participation in family decision making can increase a child's sense of political competence, providing skills for political interaction and encouraging active participation in the political system as an adult. By the same token, unquestioning obedience to parental decisions may predispose the child to a role as a political subject. The family also shapes future political attitudes by locating the individual in a vast social world; establishing ethnic, linguistic, class, and religious ties, affirming cultural values, and directing occupational and economic aspirations.

The family is also changing in some societies. A revolution in women's resources and expectations in recent decades has profoundly affected the advanced industrial nations. Greater gender equality in education, occupation, and profession has transformed the structure of the family. The lessening of gender differences in self-images, in parental roles, and in relations to the economy and the political system is significantly affecting patterns of political recruitment, political participation, and public policy. A more open family, equality of parenting, and the early exposure of children to child care and preschool group experiences have modified the impact of the family in the socialization process in ways that are still being assessed. Especially in the developing world, the changing role of women may have profound influences in modernizing the society.[11]

Schools

Schools provide children and adolescents with knowledge about the political world and their role in it and with more concrete information on political institutions and relationships. Schools also transmit the values and attitudes of the society. They can play an important role in shaping attitudes about the unwritten rules of the political game, instilling the values of public duty, and developing informal political

BOX 3.1   Socializing Values

Communist East Germany had a special ceremony for eighth graders that marked their passage to adulthood. The heart of the ceremony was the endorsement of the following four pledges:

- As young citizens of our German Democratic Republic, are you prepared to work and fight loyally for the great and honorable goals of socialism, and to honor the revolutionary inheritance of the people?

- As sons and daughters of the worker-and-peasant state, are you prepared to pursue higher education, to cultivate your mind, to become a master of your trade, to learn permanently, and to use your knowledge to pursue our great humanist ideals?

- As honorable members of the socialist community, are you ready to cooperate as comrades, to respect and support each other, and to always merge the pursuit of your personal happiness with the happiness of all the people?

- As true patriots, are you ready to deepen the friendship with the Soviet Union, to strengthen our brotherhood with socialist countries, to struggle in the spirit of proletarian internationalism, to protect peace and to defend socialism against every imperialist aggression?

relations. Schools can reinforce affection for the political system and provide common symbols, such as the flag and pledge of allegiance, that encourage emotional attachments to the system. When a new nation comes into being, or a revolutionary regime comes to power in an old nation, it usually turns immediately to the schools as a means to supplant "outdated" values and symbols with new ones more congruent with the new ideology.

In some nations educational systems do not provide unifying political socialization but send starkly different messages to different groups. For instance, some Muslim states segregate girls and boys within the school system. Even if educational experiences are intended to be equivalent, such segregation begins to create different experiences and expectations. And often the content of education differs between boys and girls. Perhaps the worst example occurred under the Taliban in Afghanistan, where for several years young girls were prohibited from attending school. Such treatment of young girls severely limits their life changes, and ensures they will have limited roles in society and the economy—which was the intent of the Taliban system. One of the new programs of the post-Taliban government was to reverse this policy, and now young Afghani girls are being included in the education system, and their future life prospects are improving as a result.

Education also affects the political skills and resources of the public. Educated persons are more aware of the impact of government on their lives and pay more attention to politics. The better-educated have mental skills that improve their ability to interpret and act on new information. They also have more information about political processes and undertake a wider range of political activities. These effects of education appear in studies of political attitudes in many nations.[12]

Religious Institutions

The religions of the world are carriers of cultural and moral values, which often have political implications. The great religious leaders have seen themselves as teachers, and their followers have usually attempted to shape the socialization of children through schooling, preaching, and religious services. In contrast to the pattern in the United States, in most nations there are formal ties between the dominant religion and the government. In these instances, religious values and public policy inevitably overlap. Catholic nations, for instance, are less likely to have liberal abortion policies, just as Islamic governments enforce strict moral codes.

Where the churches systematically teach values that may be at odds with the controlling political system—as in the conflict between Islamic fundamentalists and secular governments in Algeria and Egypt, or in the efforts of American fundamentalists to introduce prayer in the schools—the struggle over socialization can be of the greatest significance in the society. In these nations religious subcultures may oppose the policies of the state, or even the state itself.

The emergence of aggressive religious fundamentalism in recent decades has had a major impact on the society and politics of countries as diverse as the United States, India, Israel, Lebanon, Iran, Pakistan, Algeria, and Nigeria. Such **fundamentalism** is often a defensive reaction against the spread of scientific views of nature and human behavior, and the libertarian values and attitudes that accompany these views. Fundamentalism usually defines a world in which believers must engage in the great struggle between the forces of spiritual goodness and evil.[13] While the influence of fundamentalism has been most visible in the Middle East and among Muslim countries, it is important in Christian countries as well. There are both Protestant and Catholic versions of fundamentalism in the United States, Europe, and Latin America. Versions of fundamentalism are also to be found, combined with ethnic and nationalist tendencies, among the Confucian, Buddhist, and Hindu countries of Asia. Broadly speaking, fundamentalism seeks to raise conservative social, moral, and religious issues to the top of the contemporary policy agenda.

Of course, religious institutions of many kinds offer valuable moral and ethical guidance that individuals often need to make choices in complex societies. Religious affiliations are often important sources of partisan preferences and can guide people in making other political choices. Thus even though the frequency of church attendance is declining in many nations, the political relevance of religion continues.

Peer Groups

Peer groups are important social units that shape political attitudes. They include childhood play groups, friendship cliques, school and college fraternities, and small work groups, in which members share relatively equal status and close ties. They can be as varied as a group of Russian mothers who meet regularly at the park, a street gang in Brazil, or a group of Wall Street executives who are members of a social club.

A peer group socializes its members by motivating or pressuring them to conform to the attitudes or behavior accepted by the group. Individuals often adopt the views of their peers because they like or respect them or because they want to be like them. An individual may become interested in politics or attend a political demonstration because close friends do so.[14] In such cases, the individual modifies his or her interests and behavior to reflect those of the group in an effort to be accepted by its members. The international youth culture symbolized by rock music, T-shirts, and blue jeans may have played a major role in the failure of communist officials to mold Soviet and Eastern European youth to the "socialist personality" that was the Marxist-Leninist ideal. Likewise, the "skinheads" groups that have sprouted up among lower-class youth in many Western countries have adopted political views that are based on peer interactions.

Social Class and Gender

Most societies have significant social divisions based on class or occupation. Individuals live in different social worlds defined by their class position. For instance, industrialization created a working class in Britain that was concentrated in particular neighborhoods and developed its own forms of speech, dress, recreation, and entertainment and its own organizations, including trade unions and political parties. Similarly, in many less-developed nations the life experience of the rural peasantry is radically different from urban dwellers. In many instances these social divisions are politically relevant: identifying oneself as a member of the working class or the peasantry leads to distinct political views about what issues are important and which political groups best represent one's interest.

Gender is another important pattern of social and political learning. From birth, nature and society ascribe different patterns of behavior to males and females. Traditionally these social divisions have carried over to politics, defining politics as a male activity and focusing the interests of women on social and family issues. In many less-developed nations these gender roles still exist today. In many industrial nations, however, gender roles are changing.[15] The rise of the women's movement and self-help groups have encouraged women to become active and provided social cues about how women should relate to politics.

Mass Media

Much of the world has become a single audience, exposed to the same information and moved by the same events. There is virtually no part so remote that its inhabitants lack the means to be informed almost simultaneously about events elsewhere: mass-produced and inexpensive transistor radios are omnipresent, even in Third World villages far removed from political power centers. The mass media—newspapers, radio, television, magazines—play an important part in internationalizing attitudes and values around the globe.

Television, enlisting the senses of both sight and sound, can have a powerful emotional impact on large public audiences. Watching war on television—such as the live broadcasts provided by CNN during the war in Iraq—gives a reality to the news, just as people's feelings were touched by media coverage of Princess Diana's death in 1997. The mass media can also transcend national boundaries and ideological divides. The movements for democracy throughout Eastern Europe were partially created by the image of another way of life that came through the international media. As these democratic revolutions spread in the late 1980s, they fed on the knowledge of the tactics and successes of others, given extra impact through newspapers, television, and radio newly free to report these exciting events. Today the internet is providing a new source of news for those who live in closed societies.

In addition to providing specific and immediate information about political events, the mass media also convey, directly or indirectly, the major values on which a society agrees. The media can portray certain events as symbolizing the nation—for example, national holidays or traditional government activities—and the events take on a specific emotional color. Mass media controlled by an authoritarian government can shape political beliefs. However, citizens eventually will ignore reports that are inconsistent with their personal experiences, and word-of-mouth transmission of inconsistent attitudes is often a powerful antidote to the effectiveness of government-controlled mass media.

Interest Groups

Interest groups, associations, economic groups, and similar organizations also shape political attitudes. Among economic groups, trade unions may have had the most important consequences for politics. In most industrial countries, the rise of trade unions transformed political culture and politics, created new political parties, and ushered in new social benefit programs. Other occupational and professional associations, such as groups of peasants and farmers, manufacturers, wholesalers and retailers, medical societies, and lawyers can

The international press cover emergency summit of the Organization of the Islamic Conference (OIC) called to discuss the Iraqi crisis in March 2003.

AP/Wide World Photos

also influence political attitudes in modern and modernizing societies. These groups ensure the loyalty of their members by defending their economic and professional interests. They can also provide valuable political cues to nonmembers, who might identify with a group's interests or political ideology.

Also important in political socialization are the public groups that define a civil society; this might include ethnic organizations, fraternal associations, civic associations (such as parent-teacher associations), and policy groups (such as taxpayers' associations, women's groups, or environmental groups). Such groups provide valuable political cues to their members and try to reinforce distinct social and political orientations. In addition, these groups—using the media and other sources—send out large quantities of information on political, social, and economic issues to the public and elites.

Political Parties

As specialized political structures that exist in democratic and nondemocratic systems, political parties play an important role in political socialization. Political parties attempt to mold issue preferences, arouse the apathetic, and find new issues to mobilize support. Party leaders and party spokespersons provide the public with a steady flow of information on the political issues of the day. Party organizations regularly contact voters by mail or phone, and in many nations party activists visit voters at home. And every few years there is an election in democratic systems, in which parties present their past accomplishments and discuss the nation's political future. Elections can serve as national civics lessons, and parties are the teachers.

In competitive party systems, partisan socialization can be also a divisive force. In their efforts to gain support, leaders may appeal to class, language, religion, and ethnic divisions and make citizens more aware of these differences. The Labour and Conservative parties in Britain, for example, draw heavily on traditional symbols of class to attract supporters. Similarly, the Congress Party in India tries to develop a national program and appeal, but other parties emphasize the ethnic and religious divisions. Leaders of preindustrial nations often oppose competitive parties because they fear such divisiveness. Although this is sometimes a sincere concern, it is also self-serving to government leaders, and is becoming increasingly difficult to justify against widespread contemporary demands for multiparty systems.

Authoritarian governments often use a single party to attempt to inculcate common attitudes of national unity, support for the government, and ideological agreement. The combination of a single party and controlled mass media is potent: The media present a single point of view, and the party activities reinforce that perspective by directly involving the citizen. Yet, as demonstrated in Eastern Europe in 1989, years of directed socialization by media and the government cannot compete with citizens' personal experiences in shaping basic attitudes.

Direct Contact with Governmental Structures

In modern societies, the wide scope of governmental activities brings citizens into frequent contact with various bureaucratic agencies. One study found that 72 percent of adult Americans had interacted with at least one government agency in the preceding year; about a third had interacted with more. The most frequent contacts were with tax authorities, school officials, and the police.[16] The degree of government intervention in daily life, and hence the necessity for contacts with government, is greater in many Western European nations than in the United States, and it is greater yet in the remaining communist countries.

These personal experiences are powerful agents of socialization, strengthening or undercutting the images presented by other agents. No matter how positive the view of the political system that has been taught in school, citizens who face a different reality in everyday life are likely to change their early-learned views. Indeed, the contradictions between ideology and reality proved to be one of the weaknesses of the communist systems in Eastern Europe.

In their study of citizen attitudes in five nations, Almond and Verba found marked differences across countries in the expectations that citizens had of their treatment by police and bureaucrats.[17] Italians, and particularly Mexicans, had quite dismal expectations as to equality and

---

BOX 3.2 Becoming Modern

Inkeles and Smith report how one Nigerian worker replied to a question about how his new job in a factory made him feel. "Sometimes like 9 feet tall with arms a yard wide. Here in the factory I alone with my machine can twist any way I want a piece of steel that all the men in my home village together could not be-

gin to bend at all." Such experiences, and the parallel changes in educational levels and access to information can create a more modern political culture.

Source: Alex Inkeles and David Smith, *Becoming Modern* (Cambridge, MA: Harvard University Press, 1974), p. 158.

---

responsiveness of treatment. African Americans also reported quite negative expectations in these 1960 interviews. It is likely that these expectations were in large measure a response to actual patterns of treatment by government.

TRENDS IN CONTEMPORARY POLITICAL CULTURES

A political culture exists uniquely in its own time and place. Citizens' attitudes and beliefs are shaped by personal experiences and by the agents of political socialization. Yet, in any historical period there may be trends that change the culture in many nations. The major social trends of our time—modernity and secularism, postmaterial values, fundamentalism and ethnic awareness, democratization, and marketization—reflect both general societal developments and specific historic events.

The major cultural trend that has transformed the world and public values has been **modernization.** For almost two centuries now, the secularizing influences of science and control over nature have altered economic and social systems and shaped political cultures, first in the West and increasingly throughout the world. This trend toward cultural modernization continues to have powerful effects as it penetrates societies (or parts of societies) that have been shielded from it. Exposure to modernity through work, education, and the media shapes an individual's personal experiences and sends messages about modernity in other societies. It encourages citizen participation, a sense of individual equality, the desire for improved living standards and increased life expectancy, and government legitimacy based on policy performance. It also frequently disrupts familiar ways of life, traditional bases of le-

gitimacy, and political arrangements that depend on citizens remaining predominantly parochials or subjects. Alex Inkeles and David Smith's study of the development of modern attitudes emphasized how factory experience can create an awareness of the possibilities of organization, change, and control over nature (see Box 3.2).

A by-product of socioeconomic modernization appears in the nations of North America, Western Europe, and Japan that have developed the characteristics of a postindustrial society. Younger generations who grew up under conditions of economic prosperity and international peace are now less concerned with material well-being and personal security than their parents.[18] Instead, the young are more likely to emphasize **postmaterial values:** social equality, environmental protection, cultural pluralism, and self-expression. Postmaterial values have spawned new citizen groups, such as the environmental movement, the women's movement, and other public interest associations. These changing values have also reshaped the policy agenda of industrial democracies; more citizens are asking government to restore the environment, expand social and political freedoms, and emphasize policies to ensure social equality. Politicians in these democracies are struggling to balance these new policy demands against the continuing policy needs of the past.

A much different response to modernization has been the resurgence of **ethnicity,** or ethnic identities, in many parts of the world.[19] As citizen skills and self-confidence have increased, formerly suppressed ethnic groups are expressing their identities and demanding equal treatment. Development of education and communication skills may encourage a flourishing of literature in a local language whose previous tradition has been informal and oral. This development can further intensify awareness of common symbols and history. While resurgence of distinctive local cultures enriches the global society, clashes between cultures and subcultures can also be particularly deadly bases of political conflict. Moreover, the migration of peoples into new areas, made possible by easier transportation and encouraged by wars, political conflicts, and the desire for economic betterment, can seem to threaten the way of life of the host society. The exposure to values from other cultures may intensify one's own self-image, which may increase cultural tensions. Although such exposure may eventually lead to greater tolerance, there is no guarantee of this outcome.

In the last decade the major new development is the trend toward democracy in Eastern Europe, East Asia, and other parts of the developing world. This **democratization** trend reflects long-term responses to modernity as well as immediate reactions to current events. Modernization gradually eroded the legitimacy of nondemocratic ideologies, while the development of citizens' skills and political resources made their claim to equal participation in policy-making (at least indirectly) more plausible. Thus many studies of political culture in Eastern Europe and the former Soviet Union uncovered surprising support for democratic norms and processes among the citizenry as the new democratic system formed.[20]

Ironically, as democratic values have begun to take root in Eastern Europe, citizens in many Western democracies have become increasingly skeptical about politicians and political institutions. In 1964, three-quarters of Americans said they trusted the government; today only a third of the public say as much—and the malaise is spreading to Western Europe and Japan.[21] Recent research shows that citizen support for democratic norms has not waned; in fact, democratic norms and values have strengthened over time as democracy has developed in the West. Instead, people are critical about how democracy functions. Western citizens expect democracy to fulfill its ideals and are critical of politicians and political parties when they fall short of these ideals. Although this cynicism is a strain on democratic politicians, it presses democracy to continue to improve and adapt, which is ultimately democracy's greatest strength.

Another cultural trend in recent years has been a shift toward **marketization**—that is, a greater public acceptance of free markets and private profit incentives, rather than a government-managed economy. The movement appeared in the United States and many Western European nations in the 1980s, where economies had experienced serious problems of inefficiency and economic stagnation. Margaret Thatcher in Britain and Ronald Reagan in the United States rode to power on waves of public support for reducing the scale of government. Public opinion surveys show that people in these nations feel that government had grown too large (see again Figure 3.3). The political victories of Reagan and Thatcher gave further prestige to efforts to roll back government involvement.

Just as Western Europeans began to question the government's role in the economy, the political changes in Eastern Europe and the Soviet Union added a new feature to the discussion. The command economies of Eastern Europe were almost exclusively controlled by state corporations and government agencies. The government set both wages and prices and directed the economy. Today, the collapse of these systems raises new questions about public support for marketization. Public opinion surveys generally find that Eastern Europeans support a capitalist market system.[22]

Support for market economies has also apparently grown in the developing world. In the past decade, many developing nations had difficulties in modernizing their economies through government-controlled economic development; this made freer markets a plausible alternative. The successes of the Asian "tigers" of South Korea, Taiwan, and Singapore in achieving rapid economic growth encouraged this movement, which has even affected policy directions in the People's Republic of China. It is difficult to disentangle the fundamental political economy issues here from the effects of contemporary events. The trend toward marketization is a response to a long period of increased government intervention in economies. At the moment, no particular mixture of free market and government intervention seems ideal. We expect much further experimentation; the current trend to marketization may also encounter reversals or countertrends in the future.

Clearly, political culture is not a static phenomenon. Our understanding of political culture must be dynamic. It must encompass how the agents of political socialization communicate and interpret historic events and traditional values. It must juxtapose these with the exposure of citizens and leaders to new experiences and new ideas. We must understand also that the gradual change of generations means continuing modification of the political culture as new groups of citizens have different experiences on which to draw.

KEY TERMS

agents of political
  socialization
conflictual political culture
consensual political
  culture
democratization

direct and indirect
  socialization
ethnicity
fundamentalism
legitimacy

marketization
modernization
parochials
participants
political culture

political socialization
political subcultures
postmaterial values
subjects

SUGGESTED READINGS

Aberbach, Joel D., Robert D. Putnam, and Bert A. Rockman. *Bureaucrats and Politicians in Western Democracies.* Cambridge, MA: Harvard University Press, 1981.

Abramson, Paul and Ronald Inglehart. *Value Change in Global Perspective.* Ann Arbor: University of Michigan Press, 1995.

Almond, Gabriel A. and Sidney Verba. *The Civic Culture.* Princeton, NJ: Princeton University Press, 1963.

———, eds. *The Civic Culture Revisited.* Boston: Little Brown, 1980.

Barnes, Samuel and Janos Simon, eds. *The Postcommunist Citizen.* Budapest: Erasmus Foundation, 1998.

Dalton, Russell. *Democratic Challenges, Democratic Choices: The Erosion of Political Support in Advanced Industrial Democracy.* Oxford: Oxford University Press, 2004.

Eckstein, Harry. "A Culturalist Theory of Political Change." *American Political Science Review* 82 (Sept. 1988): 789–804.

Harrison, Lawrence and Samuel P. Huntington, eds. *Culture Matters: How Values Shape Human Progress.* New York: Basic Books, 2000.

Horowitz, Donald. *Ethnic Groups in Conflict.* Berkeley: University of California Press, 1985.

Huntington, Samuel. *The Clash of Civilizations and the Remaking of World Order.* New York: Simon & Schuster, 1996.

Inglehart, Ronald and Christian Welzel. *Modernization, Cultural Change and Democracy: The Human Development Sequence.* New York: Cambridge University Press, 2005.

Inkeles, Alex and David H. Smith. *Becoming Modern.* Cambridge, MA: Harvard University Press, 1974.

Jennings, M. Kent and Richard Niemi. *Generations and Politics: A Panel Study of Young Adults and their Parents.* Princeton, NJ: Princeton University Press, 1981.

Klingemann, Hans Dieter and Dieter Fuchs. *Citizens and the State.* Oxford, England: Oxford University Press, 1995.

Norris, Pippa, ed. *Critical Citizens: Global Support for Democratic Government.* Oxford, England: Oxford University Press, 1999.

Norris, Pippa and Ronald Inglehart. *Rising Tide: Gender Equality and Cultural Change around the World.* New York: Cambridge University Press, 2003.

Pharr, Susan and Robert Putnam. *Disaffected Democracies: What's Troubling the Trilateral Democracies.* Princeton: Princeton University Press, 2000.

Putnam, Robert. *The Beliefs of Politicians.* New Haven, CT: Yale University Press, 1973.

———. *Making Democracy Work: Civic Traditions in Modern Italy.* Princeton, NJ: Princeton University Press, 1993.

Pye, Lucian W. and Sidney Verba, eds. *Political Culture and Political Development.* Princeton, NJ: Princeton University Press, 1965.

Rochon, Thomas. *Culture Moves: Ideas, Activism and Changing Values.* Princeton, NJ: Princeton University Press, 1998.

Rose, Richard, Christian Haerpfer, and William Mishler. *Testing the Churchill Hypothesis: Democracy and its Alternatives in Post-communist Societies.* Cambridge, UK: Polity/Baltimore: Johns Hopkins University Press, 2000.

Sears, David O. "Political Socialization." In F. I. Greenstein and N. W. Polsby, *Handbook of Political Science,* vol. 2, ch. 2. Reading, MA: Addison-Wesley, 1975.

ENDNOTES

1. This concept of legitimacy and its bases in different societies draws upon the work of Max Weber. For example, see Max Weber, *Basic Concepts in Sociology,* trans. H. P. Secher (New York: Citadel Press, 1964), chs. 5–7.

2. Pippa Norris, ed., *Critical Citizens: Global Support for Democratic Government* (Oxford, England: Oxford University Press, 1999).

3. These terms were developed in Gabriel A. Almond and Sidney Verba, *The Civic Culture: Political Attitudes and Democracy in Five Nations* (Princeton, NJ: Princeton University Press, 1963).

4. On the importance of trust, see Almond and Verba, *Civic Culture,* ch. 10; Ronald Inglehart, *Culture Shift in Advanced Industrial Society* (Princeton, NJ: Princeton University Press, 1990), ch. 1; and Robert D. Putnam, *Making Democracy Work: Civic Traditions in Modern Italy* (Princeton, NJ: Princeton University Press, 1993), especially chs. 4 and 6.

5. Ronald Inglehart, *Modernization and Postmodernization* (Princeton: Princeton University Press, 1997), chs. 6–7.

6. Ole Borre and Elinor Scarbrough, eds., *The Scope of Government* (Oxford, England: Oxford University Press, 1995).

7. Also see, Putnam, *Making Democracy Work.*

8. Kendall Baker, Russell Dalton, and Kai Hildebrandt, *Germany Transformed* (Cambridge, MA: Harvard University Press, 1981).

9. Samuel P. Huntington, *The Clash of Civilizations and the Remaking of World Order* (New York: Simon and Schuster, 1996).

10. See Almond and Verba, *Civic Culture,* ch. 12; M. Kent Jennings, Klaus R. Allerbeck, and Leopold Rosenmayr, "Generations and Families," in Samuel H. Barnes, Max Kaase, et al., *Political Action* (Beverly Hills, CA: Sage, 1979), chs. 15 and 16.

11. Martha Nussbaum and Jonathan Glover, eds., *Women, Culture, and Development: A Study of Human Capabilities* (New York: Oxford University Press, 1995).

12. For example, see Sidney Verba, Norman H. Nie, and Jae-on Kim, *Participation and Political Equality: A Seven-Nation Study* (New York: Cambridge University Press, 1978); Barnes, Kaase, et al., *Political Action,* ch. 4.

13. See, among others, Martin Marty and Scott Appleby, *Fundamentalism Observed* (Chicago: University of Chicago Press, 1991).

14. Richard E. Dawson, Kenneth Prewitt, and Karen Dawson, *Political Socialization,* 2nd ed. (Boston: Little, Brown, 1977), ch. 9.

15. Pippa Norris and Ronald Inglehart, *Rising Tide: Gender Equality and Cultural Change around the World* (New York: Cambridge University Press, 2003).

16. Robert G. Lehnen, *American Institutions: Political Opinion and Public Policy* (Hinsdale, IL: Holt, Rinehart, and Winston, 1976), p. 183; see also Charles Goodsell, *The Case for Bureaucracy,* 3rd ed. (Chatham, NJ: Chatham House, 1994), ch. 2.

17. Almond and Verba, *Civic Culture,* pp. 108–09.

18. Ronald Inglehart, *Culture Shift in Advanced Industrial Society*; Ronald Inglehart, *The Silent Revolution: Changing Values and Political Styles among Western Publics* (Princeton, NJ: Princeton University Press, 1977).

19. Donald Horowitz, *Ethnic Groups in Conflict* (Berkeley: University of California Press, 1985).

20. Arthur Miller, William Reisinger, and Vicki Hesli, eds., *Public Opinion and Regime Change* (Boulder, CO: Westview Press, 1993); William Mishler and Richard Rose, "Trajectories of Fear and Hope: Support for Democracy in Post-communist Europe," *Comparative Political Studies* 28 (1995): 553–81. Compare to Robert Rohrschneider, "Institutional Learning Versus Value Diffusion," *Journal of Politics* 58 (1996): 442–66.

21. Norris, *Critical Citizens*; Russell Dalton, *Democratic Challenges, Democratic Choices* (Oxford: Oxford University Press, 2003).

22. See William Zimmerman, *The Russian People and Foreign Policy: Russian Elite and Mass Perspectives* (Princeton: Princeton University Press, 2002), ch. 2; Raymond Duch, "Tolerating Economic Reform," *American Political Science Review* 87 (1993): 590–608. Russian support for marketization noticeably lags behind that of most Eastern Europeans.

4

Interest Articulation

Every political system has some way for citizens and social groups to express their needs and demands to the government. This process of **interest articulation** can take many forms. The most basic might be an individual making a request to a city council member or other government official, or, in a more traditional system, to the village head or tribal chieftain. Collective action by groups of citizens is also an essential part of the articulation process. In larger political systems, individuals working together as a formal interest group are a prime tool in promoting political interests.

During the last hundred years or so, as societies have become internally more complex and the scope of government activity has widened, the quantity and variety of different forms of interest articulation have grown proportionately. Citizens work together to address local and national needs, ranging from the provision of clean water in a village to the passage of national clean water standards. Social movements involve the public in issues as diverse as protecting the rights of indigenous people in the Amazon to debating nuclear power. Interest group headquarters, in large numbers, are found in capitals like London, Washington, Tokyo, and Rome. Some of these headquarters are in buildings as imposing as those housing major governmental agencies. In countries with powerful local governments, interest groups are active at the provincial or local level as well.

This chapter considers the multiple ways that political interests might be expressed and represented in political systems. We discuss both the informal and direct forms of citizen action, as well as more institutionalized forms of articulation. For example, in most countries that allow them, labor unions, manufacturers' associations, farm groups,

and associations of doctors, lawyers, engineers, and teachers form to represent these interests. And in the end, most political systems rely on all of these forms of interest articulation to determine what the public and social groups desire of their government.

CITIZEN ACTION

Before political institutions and political processes come into play, we are first members of a society. We interact with family and friends throughout our lives, we express our interests and needs, and we work with others to achieve our goals. These human patterns of social interaction carry over to politics.

In interest articulation, individual citizens can use a variety of methods to make requests, demands, and pleas for policies (Table 4.1). The most common form of citizen participation is voting in an election—something found even in many authoritarian political systems. Elections provide a basis for the public to express their interests and to make a collective choice about the government's past progress and the future policies for the nation. Even though elections select political elites, they often have a blunt policy impact because elections involve many different issues, and between elections officeholders may stray from the voters' preferences.

Another form of interest articulation occurs when people work with others in their community to address common social or political needs, as when parents work to better the local schools or residents express a concern about how the community is developing. These activities tend to be very policy focused and to exert direct pressure on decision-makers. Such group activity can be found in democratic and authoritarian systems, although nondemocracies

TABLE 4.1   Forms of Citizen Interest Articulation

Form	Scope of Interests	Degree of Pressure on Elites
Voting, participation in elections	Broad, collective decision on government leaders and their programs	Modest pressure, but unfocused
Informal group, social movement	Collective action focused on a common interest	High pressure
Personal interest contact	Normally deals with specific, personal problem	Low pressure
Protest activity	Highly expressive support for specific interests	High pressure

may limit the methods of expression to ones that do not openly confront authorities.

Some interest articulation involves only an individual and his or her family, as when a veteran writes to his legislator for help in getting benefits approved, or when a homeowner asks the local party precinct leader to get her driveway snowplowed regularly. These are **personal interest contacts,** and they are universal in all kinds of political systems including the authoritarian ones. However, the interests being expressed tend to be limited to those of a specific individual or a small group of people.

The expression of interests and political demands also may extend beyond the bounds of conventional politics to involve protests or other forms of direct action. The spontaneous gathering of outraged ghetto dwellers, the public **protests** that overthrew the communist governments of Eastern Europe, and the environmental protests of Greenpeace are all examples of how political protest can focus political interests and influence. Protests and other direct actions tend to be high-pressure activities that can both mobilize the public and directly pressure elites; these activities can also be very focused in their political content.

In summary, citizens have many routes available to them in expressing their political interests, and each of these routes has particular characteristics associated with it.

How Citizens Participate

The amount of citizen participation in politics varies greatly according to the type of activity and the type of political system. Table 4.2 shows some examples of different types of citizen participation in several nations examined in this book. The table reveals that common forms of political participation revolve around elections: turning out to vote, trying to convince others how to vote, or working with political

parties. Because elections are the most common form of public involvement in the political process, they are important in the interest articulation process. During elections, citizens speak their minds on current issues through conversations, attending meetings, contributing to campaigns, and even expressing their opinions to pollsters. Ultimately, individuals decide their preferences in their ballot choices. At the same time, however, elections perform many other functions: the aggregation of political interests (see Chapter 5), the recruitment of political elites, and even the socialization of political values and preferences through the campaign process.

Democracies are remarkable in that competitive elections offer important political resources to all citizens. Among the democracies, the United States stands out for its rather low levels of national voting participation: both West Europeans (with their long democratic experience) and Russians (who are new to democratic elections) vote more frequently than Americans. However, as the table shows, Americans' low level of election turnout does not simply reflect apathy. Americans are much more likely to try to discuss politics with others than are their British counterparts, and they are much more likely to work for a party or candidate than either Britons or Germans.

Public efforts to express political interests and influence public policy extend beyond elections. Grassroots politics, people working together to address a common problem, represents a very direct method for articulating political interests and attempting policy influence. Alexis de Tocqueville considered such grassroots community action as the foundation of democratic politics. Today such activities are often identified with middle-class participation in affluent societies—PTA groups, community associations, public interest groups—but group activity can be a form of political participation in any nation.[1] Indian villagers working together to build a

T A B L E   4 . 2   Citizen Participation in Eight Nations (percentage)

Type of Participation	United States	Britain	France	Germany	Japan	Russia	Mexico	Nigeria
Voter turnout in most recent national elections	49%	59%	72%	82%	63%	62%	64%	41%
Discussed politics with others	74	46	65	84	64	75	58	74
Participated in political party activities	18	3	2	3	4	1	5	—
Participated in citizen interest group	36	7	6	7	9	2	11	—
Signed a petition	81	81	68	52	63	12	19	7
Participated in lawful protest demonstration	21	13	39	28	13	24	4	17

Sources: Election turnout data for most recent national election from Elections in the World, downloaded Oct. 30, 2002 from www.electionworld.org; 2000–2002 *World Values Survey* and the 1999 *European Values Survey* for other participation statistics. We would like to thank Ronald Inglehart for granting access to these data.

communal latrine or to develop rural electricity, or indigenous people protecting their land rights are other examples of community action.

Table 4.2 also indicates that group activity has become a frequent form of political expression in the advanced industrial democracies. Nearly a third of Americans are members of a citizen interest group, and significant numbers are active in European polities as well.[2] Such activity is high in Mexico, perhaps because this survey overlaps with the politicization of Vincente Fox's election. However, surveys from the developing world suggests that these activities are regularly used, albeit less frequently than in more developed nations.

Perhaps the most expressive and visible form of citizen action involves participation in protests, demonstrations, or other direct actions. What better way to articulate one's interest in preventing pollution than to hang an environmental banner from a polluting smokestack, stage a mass demonstration outside of parliament, or boycott polluters? Participation in political protests can arise for quite different reasons. On the one hand, protest and direct action is often used by individuals and groups that feel they lack access to legitimate political channels. The mass demonstrations in Eastern Europe in the late 1980s and the public rallies and marches of black South Africans against apartheid illustrate protests as the last resort of the disadvantaged. On the other hand, peaceful protests are also increasingly used by the young and better-educated citizens in Western democracies. To many democratic citizens, protest is the continuation of "normal" politics by other means.

A majority in most nations have signed a petition, a form of political action that has become so common that it no longer can be described as unconventional (see again Table 4.2). Roughly a fifth of Americans and Germans have at some time participated in a legal demonstration. Protests are now used by many sectors of society.[3] The French have far more protest involvement than the other established democracies, with nearly two-fifths of the population reporting participation at some point. These numbers reflect both French traditions of popular protest and the difficulties citizens often find in getting the attention of government. The Russian patterns are also striking, in 1990 only 4 percent of citizens reported participating in a protest, reflecting the communist government's repression of such activities. A decade later, nearly a quarter of Russians now say they have participated in a legal demonstration—they are learning to express their grievances in a more democratic setting. The table also indicates that challenging activities are relatively less frequent in developing societies such as Mexico and Nigeria.

Citizen participation thus reflects the way that people with various participant attitudes utilize the opportunities existing within a political system. In nations with active political parties and competitive elections, many citizens may be mobilized to participate in the electoral process; in nations where such activities are limited, people may turn to group-based activity or protest in order to express their preferences.

Cross-national research shows that the better-educated and higher social status individuals are

---

BOX 4.1   The Velvet Revolution

On November 17, 1989, a large group of students staged a sit-in in the center of Prague to urge democratic reform. They placed lighted candles on the ground, and sang the Czech version of "We Shall Overcome." Confronted by this civil disobedience, the police beat the students and several bystanders. This was the spark that set the Czech democracy movement on fire. The students went on strike and called for a general strike by the workforce. The public demonstrations grew day by day, and the government entered into negotiations with Vaclav Havel and representatives of the Civic Forum reform movement. By November 25, half a million protestors assembled in a demonstration against the regime, and the government was struggling under the weight of the general strike. A television broadcast showing tapes of the November 17 protest mobilized further support for the reformers. By mid-December the regime capitulated: communism had come to an end, its demise marked by large celebrations in the city center. In less than a month, people had seized power in order to establish democracy in Czechoslovakia.

Source: Timothy Garton Ash, *The Magic Lantern: The Revolution of 1989* (New York: Random House, 1990), ch. 5.

---

more likely to use the various opportunities for participation. These individuals tend to develop attitudes that encourage participation, such as feelings of efficacy and a sense of civic duty,[4] and they possess the personal resources and skills that are easily converted into political involvement when duty calls or need arises. Skill and confidence are especially important in complicated activities like organizing new groups or becoming a leader in an organization. This pattern is less pronounced for easier activities, such as voting participation and personal contacting. The tendency for the better-off to dominate in the arenas of participation is also more evident in societies, such as the United States, with weak party organizations, weak working-class groups (such as labor unions), and a lack of parties appealing distinctively to the interests of the lower classes. In nations with stronger working-class parties and labor unions, organizational networks encourage the relative awareness and participation of less affluent citizens.

INTEREST GROUPS

A more institutionalized form of interest articulation occurs through the activities of social or political groups that represent the interests of their constituents. In contrast to individual citizen action, interest groups normally have an enduring organizational base, and they often have professional staffs to provide the group with expertise and representation. In addition, interest groups often participate within the political process, serving on government advisory bodies and testifying at parliamentary hearings. Interest groups vary in structure, style, financing, and support base, and these differences may influence a nation's politics, its economics, and its social life.

Anomic Groups

Anomic groups are generally spontaneous groups that form suddenly when many individuals respond similarly to frustration, disappointment, or other strong emotions. They are flash affairs, rising and subsiding suddenly. Without previous organization or planning, frustrated individuals may suddenly take to the streets to vent their anger as news of a government action touches deep emotions or as a rumor of new injustice sweeps the community. Their actions may lead to violence, although not necessarily. Particularly where organized groups are absent or where they have failed to obtain adequate representation in the political system, smoldering discontent may be sparked by an incident or by the emergence of a leader. It may then suddenly explode in relatively unpredictable and uncontrollable ways.

Some political systems, including those of the United States, France, Italy, India, and some Arab nations, report a rather high frequency of violent and spontaneous anomic behavior.[5] This often involves spontaneous public demonstrations or acts of violence, rather than the planned and orchestrated protests of institutionalized political groups. Other countries are notable for the infrequency of such

The British Society of Civil Servants, a well-organized and unusually effective associational interest group, assembles for an orderly meeting in a London hall to plan a 24-hour work stoppage.

Les Wilson/Photri

disturbances. Traditions and models of anomic behavior help turn frustration into action.

In France, for example, protests have become part of the tradition of politics (see Table 4.2). In the late 1960s, the French government nearly collapsed as the result of protests that began when university students were not allowed to have members of the opposite sex visit their dorm rooms. Soon other disenchanted French men and women joined the students' protest. In a typical year Paris might experience protests by students, shopkeepers, farmers, housewives, government employees, environmentalists, women's groups, and a host of other interests. Protest is almost a national political sport in France.

Anger over the assassination of a popular political leader or other catastrophic event can also stimulate a public outburst. For instance, one commonly sees relatively spontaneous public demonstrations when one nation makes a hostile action toward another nation. Wildcat strikes (spontaneous strike actions by local workers, not organized actions by national unions), long a feature of the British trade union scene, also occur frequently in such European countries as France, Italy, and Sweden.

Sometimes anomic groups are a subset of autonomous individuals drawn from a larger social grouping, such as a racial or ethnic group. For instance, in 1992 there was rioting and looting by some residents in minority neighborhoods of Los Angeles following the acquittal of police officers accused of

excessive violence in the beating of an African-American suspect. Similarly, in 1992, riots broke out in Algeria when some Muslim fundamentalists protested the government's invalidation of the recent election. We treat these as anomic group actions because there is no structure or planning to the event, and the individuals involved disperse after the protest ends.

We must be cautious, however, about characterizing as anomic political behavior what is really the result of detailed planning by organized groups. For instance, the demonstrations against the World Trade Organization in Seattle and Geneva have owed much to indignation but little to spontaneity.

Nonassociational Groups

Like anomic groups, **nonassociational groups** rarely are well organized, and their activity is episodic. They differ from anomic groups because they are based on common interests and identities of ethnicity, region, religion, occupation, or perhaps kinship. Because of these continuing economic or cultural ties, nonassociational groups have more continuity than anomic groups. Subgroups within a large nonassociational group (such as blacks or workers) may act as an anomic group, as in the 1992 Los Angeles riots or the riots in East Timor in the late 1990s. Throughout the world, ethnicity and religion, like occupation, are powerful identities that can be a basis for collective activity.

There are two especially interesting kinds of nonassociational groups. One is the very large group that has not become formally organized, although its members perceive, perhaps dimly, their common interests. Many ethnic, regional, and occupational groups fit into this category. It can be very difficult to organize such groups. Members may share a common problem, but none of them may find it sufficiently rewarding to commit the effort and time needed to organize other group members. Moreover, if large collective benefits—for example, ending discriminatory legislation or cleaning up water pollution—are achieved, they will be shared even by those who did not work to achieve them, the so-called "free riders." Thus many may prefer to wait for the rewards without sharing the cost or risk of action. The study of such **collective action problems** is valuable in understanding why some groups (including governments and revolutionary challengers) become organized and others do not, and why and under what circumstances the obstacles to collective action can be overcome.[6]

A second type of nonassociational group is the small village or economic or ethnic subgroup whose members know each other personally. The small, face-to-face group has some important advantages and may be highly effective in some political situations. If its members are well connected or its goals unpopular or illegal, the group may prefer to remain informal or even inconspicuous. Examples of the action of such groups include work stoppages and petitions demanding better support and training by students, requests made by large landowners asking a bureaucrat to continue a grain tariff, and the appeal by relatives of a government tax collector for favored treatment for the family business. As the last two examples suggest, personal interest articulation may often have more legitimacy and be put on a more permanent basis by invoking group ties and interests.

Institutional Groups

Political parties, business corporations, legislatures, armies, bureaucracies, and churches often support separate political groups or have members with special responsibility for representing a group's interests. **Institutional groups** are formal and have other political or social functions in addition to interest articulation. Either as corporate bodies or as smaller groups within these bodies (legislative blocs, officer cliques, groups in the clergy, or ideological cliques in bureaucracies), such groups express their own interests or represent the interest of other groups in the society. The influence of institutional interest groups is usually derived from the strength of their primary organizational base—for instance, the size of their membership or their income. A group based on a governmental institution has direct access to policymakers.

In industrial democracies, bureaucratic and corporate interests use their resources and special information to affect policy. In the United States the military-industrial complex consists of the combination of personnel in the Defense Department and defense industries who join in support of military expenditures. Similarly, the farm lobby and the Department of Agriculture often unite in advocating agricultural policies. Political parties represent one of the most active institutional participants in the policy process of most democracies. And as in most societies, government bureaucracies do not simply react to pressures from the outside; in the absence of political directives they often act as independent forces of interest representation.

Nonpolitical institutional groups can also become involved in the political process. In Italy, for example, the Roman Catholic Church has been an institutional interest group with great influence in Italian politics. A major form of intervention has been religious education. In electoral politics, the Church used to admonish Catholics to use their votes to defeat the Communists. Less overtly, the Church seeks influence by having members of the clergy call on officeholders to express opinions on matters of concern to the Church. In Islamic countries fundamentalist clergy pursue a similar role, prescribing what morals public policy should follow, actively lobbying governmental officials, and sometimes participating in the governing process.

In authoritarian regimes, which prohibit or at least control explicit political groups, institutional groups can still play a large role. Educational officials, party officials, jurists, factory managers, officers in the military services, and government bodies representing other social units had significant roles in interest articulation in Communist regimes.[7] In preindustrial societies, which usually have fewer associational groups and where such groups usually fail to mobilize much support, military groups, corporations, party factions, and bureaucrats often play prominent political roles. Even where the military does not seize power directly, the possibility of such action often forces close government attention to military requests.

Associational Groups

Associational groups are formed explicitly to represent the interests of a particular group. This includes trade unions, chambers of commerce and manufacturers' associations, ethnic associations, and religious associations. These organizations have orderly procedures for formulating interests and demands, and they usually employ a full-time professional staff. Associational groups are often very active in representing the interests of their members in the policy process. For instance, in recurring debates about health care in the United States there is an enormous mobilization of pressure groups and lobbyists—from representatives of doctors and health insurance organizations to consumer groups and the like—in efforts to influence legislation.

Associational interest groups—where they are allowed to flourish—affect the development of other types of groups. Their organizational base gives them an advantage over nonassociational groups, and their tactics and goals are often recognized as legitimate in society. Labor unions, for example, are often central political actors because they represent the mass of the working class; in the same way, business associations often speak for the corporate interests of the nation. By representing a broad range of interests, these groups may limit the influence of anomic, nonassociational, and institutional groups.

A special subset of associational group is composed of citizens who are united not by a common economic or individual self-interest but by a common belief in a political ideology or a policy goal.[8] The environmental movement, many women's groups, and other civic groups are examples of this kind of associational group. In some of these issue groups the members may seldom interact directly and not even share common social characteristics (such as employment or ethnicity), but are bound together by their support of a political organization, such as Greenpeace or Amnesty International. On the organizational side, many of these new social groups have more fluid and dynamic organizations, with frequent turnover in both leadership and membership. On the tactical side, they use a wide range of approaches, often discounting the value of partisan campaigning and conventional lobbying in favor of unconventional protests and direct actions.

Civic associations represent another way for citizens to directly and explicitly articulate their policy goals by supporting groups that advocate their preferred policy positions. Such groups have proliferated in most advanced industrial democracies in the past generation, and they are now spreading to the developing world.

In summary, a social interest can manifest itself in many different groups. We can illustrate this point with examples of different groups that might involve members of the working class:

> *Anomic group:* a spontaneous group of working-class individuals living in the same neighborhood
>
> *Nonassociational group:* the working class as a collective
>
> *Institutional group:* the labor department within the government
>
> *Associational group:* a labor union

Civil Society

In recent years there has been increasing attention to whether an extensive network of interest groups and public participation in these groups creates a **civil society**—a society in which people are involved in social and political interactions free of state control or regulation. Community groups, voluntary associations, and even religious groups, as well as access to free communication and information through the mass media and (now) the Internet, are important parts of a civil society.[9] Participation in associational and institutional groups socializes individuals into the types of political skills and cooperative relations that are part of a well-functioning society. People learn how to organize, how to express their interests, and how to work with others to achieve common goals. They also learn the important lesson that the political process itself is as important as the immediate results. Thus a system of active associational groups can lessen the development of anomic or nonassociational activity. Group involvement can also be an important route into politics for citizens with fewer individual resources. Group activity can help citizens to develop and clarify their own prefer-

Striking Romanian coal-
miners confront riot police.
The miners went on strike
demanding a 35 percent
wage increase.

Robert Ghement/Corbis/AFP

ences, provide important information about political events, and articulate the interests of citizens more clearly and precisely than parties and elections.[10] Thus, an active public involved in a diversity of interest groups provides a fertile ground for the development of democratic politics.

As political and economic conditions become interdependent across nations, there is also increasing attention directed toward the development of a global civil society to parallel these political and economic developments. Individuals and groups in one nation are connected to groups with similar concerns in other nations, and jointly reinforce their individual efforts. Environmental groups in the developed democracies, for example, assist environmental groups in developing nations with the expertise and organizational resources to address the issues facing their country. National groups meet at international conferences and policy forums, and the network of social relations, as well as Internet connections, extends across national borders.[11] This is another sign of how the international context of domestic politics is growing throughout the world.

One of the problems faced by the nations of Eastern Europe and other newly democratizing nations is building a rich associational group life in societies where organized groups have long been suppressed or controlled. The Communist Party and the government bureaucracy dominated these nations for over 40 years, and the government controlled associational life to pursue its goals. The process of building new, independent associational groups to articulate the specialized interests of different citizens is underway and will be important to the democratic process. Similarly, many less economically developed nations face an urgent need to develop a civil society of associational groups to involve citizens in the political process and represent their interests if democratization is to have a chance for success.

Interest Group Systems

Another characteristic of politics is the systematic connection between interest groups and government policymaking institutions. Differences in the types of connections create different interest group systems. All modern societies have large numbers of interest groups, but the patterns of relationships differ. Interest group systems are classified into three major groupings: (1) pluralist, (2) democratic corporatist, and (3) controlled.[12]

Pluralist interest group systems are characterized by several features that involve both how interests are organized and how they participate in the political process:

- Multiple groups may represent a single societal interest.

- Group membership is voluntary and limited.
- Groups often have a loose or decentralized organizational structure.
- There is a clear separation between interest groups and the government.

For instance, not only are there different groups for different social sectors, such as labor business, and professional interests, but there may be many multiple labor unions or business associations within each sector. These groups compete among themselves for membership and influence, and all simultaneously press their demands on policymakers and the bureaucracies. The United States is the best-known example of a strongly pluralist interest group system; Canada and New Zealand are also typically cited as examples. Despite its greater labor union membership and somewhat greater coordination of economic associations, Britain tends to fall on the pluralist side in most analyses, as do France and Japan.

Democratic corporatist interest group systems are characterized by a much more organized representation of interests:

- A single peak association normally represents each societal interest.
- Membership in the peak association is often compulsory and nearly universal.
- Peak associations are centrally organized and direct the actions of their members.
- Groups are often systematically involved in making and implementing policy.

For instance, in a corporatist system there may be a single peak association that represents all the major business or industrial interests; a pluralist system may have a wide diversity of business groups that act autonomously. Equally important, interest groups in corporatist systems often regularly and legitimately work with the government agencies and/or political parties as partners in negotiating solutions to policy problems. The best-studied democratic corporatist arrangements have been in the area of economic problems. Countries with large and unified peak associations of business and labor that negotiate with each other and the government have better records than more pluralist countries in sustaining employment, restraining inflation, and increasing social spend-

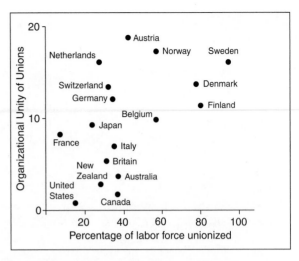

F I G U R E   4 . 1   Interest Group Systems of Labor Unions

Sources: Data for the percentage of the labor force unionized is from Organization for Economic Cooperation and Development, *Employment Outlook, July 1997* (Paris: OECD, 1997), p. 71; the unity of unions is from Arend Lijphart and Marcus Crepaz, "Corporatism and Consensus Democracy in Eighteen Countries," *British Journal of Political Science* 21 (1991): pp. 235–56.

ing.[13] The most thoroughly corporatist interest group systems are in Austria, the Netherlands, Norway, and Sweden. Substantial democratic corporatist tendencies are also found in Germany and Denmark. Some developing nations also follow a corporatist pattern.

Because different sectors of a society may vary in their organized interest groups and in their government relations, we must be cautious about generalizing too much about interest group systems. Figure 4.1, however, describes the striking differences in organization of the labor movements in some industrialized societies. The countries are arrayed along the horizontal axis in terms of the percentage of the total labor force that belongs to a labor union. The vertical axis displays the degree or organizational unity within the labor union movement.

In Sweden, for example, about 90 percent of the nonagricultural workforce is organized into unions, and the movement is highly centralized and united on most labor-related issues. This is an example of a highly corporatist system of labor union interests.

Examples of more pluralist systems can be seen in Britain and the United States. Less than half the

British labor force is unionized, but these unions are not as highly coordinated as those in corporatist countries. The member unions in the British Trades Union Congress have strong traditions of individual autonomy and are themselves relatively decentralized. Moreover, the influence of the labor unions on government policymakers has waned over the past two decades. The Thatcher government moved away from direct negotiation with labor, and thus away from corporatism in the 1980s, and even the Labour Party distanced itself from the labor unions in the 1990s. The United States is the polar opposite to Sweden; only about a sixth of the labor force is unionized, and the unions maintain a great deal of independence.

Figure 4.1 also shows that union membership in Japan and France is relatively low, with only about one worker in four or fewer belonging to a union. Moreover, the union movements themselves are relatively fragmented and decentralized. In these countries there are few traditions of "social partnership" between government, unions, and employer associations. In the area of labor policy, at least, these are highly pluralist, not corporatist, interest group systems. However, corporatist-type arrangements among individual industries, trade associations, and governmental bureaucracies (without organized labor involvement) exist in Japan.

In some democratic systems—for example, in Latin America—some interest groups such as trade unions and peasant associations are controlled by political parties or religious interests. Usually, these groups mobilize support for the political parties or social institutions that dominate them. This lack of autonomy can have serious consequences for politics. Restricting the independent expression of interest groups may lead to outbreaks of violence, and the subordination of interest group interests may limit the adaptability of the political process.

Finally, the pattern of interest groups is completely different in **controlled interest group systems:**

- There is a single group for each social sector.
- Membership is often compulsory.
- Each group is normally hierarchically organized.
- Groups are controlled by the government or its agents in order to mobilize support for government policy.

The most important factor is the last: Groups exist to facilitate government control of society. The best examples are the traditional Communist systems in which the dominating party organizations penetrate all levels of society and exercise close control over all the associational groups that are permitted to exist. Unions and youth associations, for example, are completely subordinated to the Communist Party, and they are only rarely permitted to articulate the interests of their members. This control was exercised in the Soviet Union and Eastern Europe; it continues today in North Korea, Vietnam, and Cuba. The political systems of several non-Communist nations, such as Brazil and Mexico, also encourage highly controlled interest groups. These nations limit interest articulation to leaders of institutional groups, who can use their positions in political institutions as a base for expressing their demands. As we have already noted, numerous institutional interest groups do emerge in these societies, especially from parts of the party and bureaucracy, such as the military, as do informal nonassociational groups.

ACCESS TO THE INFLUENTIAL

To be effective, interest groups must be able to reach key policymakers through **channels of political access.** Groups may express the interests of their members and yet fail to have an impact on policymakers. Political systems vary in the ways they respond to political interests. Interest groups vary in the tactics used to gain access to policy makers. Their tactics are shaped in part by the opportunities offered by the structure of policymaking, as well as by their own values and preferences.

It is useful to distinguish between legitimate and constitutional channels of political access (such as the mass media, parties, and legislatures) and illegitimate, coercive access channels. These channels correspond to the two major types of political resources that can be used to influence elites. The first type is established by the legitimate structures of the government, which designate the resources to be used in policymaking. In a democratic political system, an appropriate resource may be votes in the national assembly. Various groups may attempt to control legislative votes by influencing the parties that win elections, or the voters who choose them, or through bargaining, persuasion, or promises of support to incumbents. However, direct action remains as a second type of resource, a coercive channel of influence for individuals and groups who feel that they are otherwise ineffective.

If only one major legitimate channel of political access is available, as in a political system dominated by a single party, it is difficult for all groups to have access. Demands transmitted through that channel may be distorted as they work their way to key decision-makers. The leadership thus may not get information about the needs and demands of important groups. Over the long run, such misperceptions can easily lead to miscalculations by the leadership and to unrest among the dissatisfied groups, who may turn to violence. Thus a system with multiple channels of access is often more efficient in responding to societal interests.

Legitimate Access Channels

An important means of reaching political elites in all societies is through personal connections—the use of family, school, local, or other social ties. An excellent example is the information network among the British elite based on old school ties originating at Eton, Harrow, or other "public" schools, or in the colleges at Oxford and Cambridge universities. Similarly, in Japan many alumni of the University of Tokyo Law School hold top positions among the political and bureaucratic elites who interact because of these personal ties. Although personal connections are commonly used by nonassociational groups representing family or regional interests, they serve other groups as well. Face-to-face contact is one of the most effective means of shaping attitudes and conveying messages. Demands communicated by a friend or neighbor carry much more weight than a formal letter from a stranger. In modern nations personal connections are usually cultivated with special care. In Washington, the business of advising interest groups and individuals on access to politicians has become an increasingly lucrative profession (and, increasingly a target of government regulation). These activities are often carried on by former officeholders who use their personal governmental contacts for their lobbyist clients.

The **mass media**—television, radio, newspapers, and magazines—are another important access channel in democratic societies. The mass media can also mobilize support for interest group efforts, leading to donations of time and money, as well as stimulating similar demands from sympathizers. Many interest groups thus spend a great deal of effort hiring skillful public relations specialists, purchasing direct advertising, trying to see that their interests receive favorable attention in the media. Interest groups, such as senior citizens organizations, encourage media reports on their needs as well as coverage of their views on specific policies. When a cause receives national media attention, the message to policymakers carries added weight because they know that millions of voters have been sensitized to the issue. Moreover, groups believe that in an open society, "objective" news coverage has more credibility than sponsored messages. However, the confusion created by multiple messages and by their lack of specific focus can limit the effectiveness of the mass media for many less important groups.

The loosening of government control from the media in the communist regimes of Eastern Europe and the former Soviet Union gave a huge boost to democracy movements. When asked what caused the democratic revolution in Poland in the 1990s, Lech Walesa pointed to a television and said "that did." Media reports on the failures in communist government policy and the lifestyles in the West undermined the legitimacy of the regimes. As democratic protests spread across Eastern Europe in 1989 and 1990, stories of successful protests in other parts of the country, or in other countries, enhanced the confidence of demonstrators. Citizen protest encouraged by mass media reports helped convince the ruling groups that their support had vanished.

Political parties are another important legitimate channel of access. Democratic political parties often rely on interest groups for financial and voter support, and serve as institutional representatives of these interests within government. In a nation like Germany, the various components of the party organization, particularly parliamentary committees, are important channels for transmitting demands to the cabinet and the party in power. In some cases, other factors may limit the role of parties as interest representatives. For instance, highly ideological parties with a hierarchical structure, such as most Communist parties, are more likely to control affiliated interest groups than to communicate the interest groups' demands. Decentralized party organizations, like those in the United States, whether inside or outside the legislative organization, may be less helpful than individual legislators in providing access.

Legislatures are another common target of interest group activities. Standard lobbying tactics include appearances before legislative committees, providing information to individual legislators, and similar activities. In the United States political action committees raise campaign contributions for individual members of Congress and can usually be sure of some political attention in exchange. In Britain and France the strong party discipline in the legislature lessens the importance of individual members of Parliament (MPs) as access channels for interest groups. In Germany and many other European democracies, the presence of strong committees and/or power divided among multiple parties encourage interest groups to use them as access channels. The combination of loose party discipline and decentralized committees as a source of much legislation makes the members of the U.S. Congress major targets of group efforts.

Government bureaucracies are major access channels in most political systems. Contacts with the bureaucratic agencies may be particularly important where the bureaucracy has been delegated policy-making authority, or where interests are narrow and directly involve few citizens. A bureaucrat sympathetic to a group may try to respond to its demands without leaving bureaucratic channels, by exercising administrative discretion. A government official may also help to gain consideration of a problem, or may help to frame an issue in a way more likely to receive a sympathetic hearing by policymakers. Thus a study of access channels used by groups in Birmingham, England, showed that on broad issues involving class, ethnic, or consumer groups, interest groups tended to work through the political parties. On narrower issues, involving few other groups and less political conflict, the groups tended to turn to the appropriate administrative department.[14]

Protest demonstrations, strikes, and other forms of dramatic and direct pressure on government may be regarded by authorities as legitimate or illegitimate tactics, depending on the political system. Demonstrations may be either spontaneous actions of an anomic group or a planned use of unconventional channels by an organized group. In democratic societies, demonstrations may attempt to mobilize popular support—eventually electoral support—for the group's cause. The gay rights and environmental demonstrations in the United States are examples of such activity, as are the continuing pro-life and pro-choice rallies on the Mall in Washington. In nondemocratic societies, such demonstrations are more hazardous and represent perhaps more extreme dissatisfaction with alternative channels.

Lawful protest can be a tactic of society's powerless, those who do not have access or resources to influence policymakers through conventional channels. As a tactic of the powerless, protest activity is especially attractive to young people and minority groups, who are not among the elite. Protests have also been a favored tactic of groups whose ideological commitments focus on challenging the established social and political order.[15] Yet, since the 1970s protest demonstrations have increasingly been used as a channel for interest articulation by organized and accepted interests who feel that disciplined parties and bureaucratic agencies are deaf to their complaints. Protests can supplement other channels, especially in gaining the attention of the mass media in an age when television comes to every household. Thus we find doctors in Paris, civil servants in Sweden, and "gray panthers" (the elderly) in Germany using a tactic once limited to the poor and minorities.

Coercive Access Channels and Tactics

Most scholars see acts of collective violence as closely associated with the character of a society and the circumstances that prevail there. In his studies of civil strife, Ted Robert Gurr developed the concept of relative deprivation to explain the frustration or discontent that motivates people to act aggressively. Gurr defines relative deprivation as a "discrepancy between people's expectations about the goods and conditions of life to which they are entitled, on the one hand, and, on the other, their value capabilities—the degree to which they think they can attain these goods and conditions."[16] The sense of relative deprivation leads to frustration and anger; aggressive violence releases those feelings.

Feelings of relative deprivation are a source of frustration, discontent, and anger. The more such discontent and anger persist, the greater the chance

Protestors march in opposition to Venezuelan President Chavez in Carcas in January 2003.

of collective violence. Other conditions are important as well. People will tend to turn to violence if they believe it is justified and if they believe it will lead to success. If they think that their government is illegitimate and that the cause of their discontent is justified, they will more readily turn to political violence if there are no other means of bringing about change. To this end, it is the responsibility of the government and its institutions to provide peaceful alternatives to violence as a means of change.

This general analysis of violence should not blind us to the differences between types of violent political activity. A riot, for example, involves the spontaneous expression of collective anger and dissatisfaction by a group of citizens. Though riots have long been dismissed as aberrant and irrational action by social riffraff, modern studies have shown that rioters vary greatly in their motivation, behavior, and social background.[17] Most riots in fact seem to follow some fairly clear-cut patterns, such as confining destruction or violence to particular areas or targets. Relative deprivation seems to be a major cause of riots, but the release of the frustrations is not as aimless as is often supposed.

In the 1992 riots in Los Angeles, although the destruction began within hours of the acquittal of Rodney King's assailants, there was consensus among

those involved that the trial outcome was only a proximate cause, a "spark" that ignited already volatile ingredients. Violence against the property of Korean shopowners during the riots reflected widely felt ethnic hostility unrelated to Rodney King. At least a few individuals justified looting through comparison with the massive thefts from savings and loans and insider trading in the previous few years. Many more simply felt that society had moved on and left them in poverty and decay; clear examples of relative deprivation abounded. The immediate results made matters worse: more than 50 people dead, mostly African Americans; thousands of businesses destroyed, with a loss of 14,000 jobs; and thousands of people left without access to necessary retail outlets. Although much of the mayhem seems poorly related to effective political action, it was a poignant cry for attention; and the slogan that emerged—"no peace without justice"—was a clear political message.

While deprivation may help fuel the discontent, strikes and obstructions—such as the recent efforts in the United States to block or prevent the blocking of entry into abortion clinics—are typically carried out by well-organized associational or institutional groups. Many violent demonstrations are called "riots" but should not be. For instance, recent violent protests in Seattle and Genoa against the World Trade

BOX 4.2   Attacks on Globalization

In July 2001 tens of thousands of protestors arrived in Genoa to demonstrate at the G8 Summit Meeting. Hundreds of different groups came to protest at the meetings, and several of the more radical groups engaged in running battles with the police. Many of the most violent clashes involved what became known as the "Black Block". The Block was comprised of several loosely organized anarchist and radical groups, wearing trademark black clothing, black hoods, and gas masks. Confrontations with police often appeared choreographed in advance, coordinated by cell phones, and videotaped by sympathetic activists—and subsequently distributed through the Internet. Many other protest groups in Genoa were worried that the radical anarchist goals of the Block detracted attention from their policy concerns about the economic and social impacts of globalization. After two days of violent clashes the summit ended. Damage ran into the tens of millions of dollars, 200 protestors were arrested, and one protestor was shot in a clash with police. In the end, the violence in the streets overshadowed both the elected politicians at the summit and the policy goals of the non-violent groups in Genoa.

Source: BBC World News.

Organization and "globalization" involved highly organized activities among some of the more radical groups participating in the protests (see Box 4.2).

Historically, labor unions used the general strike to pressure the government or employers on fundamental issues. However, the influence of strikes and obstructions has varied, depending on the legitimacy of the government and coercive pressure from other groups. A massive truckers' strike helped bring down the government in Chile in 1972 and 1973, but student-inspired boycotts in Korea in the 1980s had only a modest impact on the government. Most spectacularly, the strikes, obstructions, and demonstrations in Eastern Europe in 1989 and 1990, like the earlier people's power movement in the Philippines, had massive success against regimes that had lost legitimacy.

Finally, **political terror tactics,** including deliberate assassination, armed attacks on other groups or government officials, and provocation of bloodshed have been used to articulate interests in some societies. The use of terrorism typically reflects the desire of some group to change the rules of the political game. The tragedies in Northern Ireland, the frequent suicide bombings and attacks by groups in the Middle East seeking to dramatize the situation of the Palestinians, and the assassinations carried out by the Sendero Luminoso (Shining Path) guerrillas in Peru in the 1980s demonstrate the use of such tactics.

The use of political terror tactics has seldom been successful without large-scale backing of terrorist groups, the public or an international sponsor.

Massive deadly violence may destroy a democratic regime, leading to curtailment of civil rights or even military intervention when many people and leaders feel that any alternative is preferable to more violence. President Fujimori and military leaders in Peru justified their suppression of democratic institutions in April 1992 as necessary to their battle against the Shining Path and cocaine lords. An authoritarian, repressive response often promises quick results against terrorists; however, small-group terrorism usually fails when confronted by united democratic leadership.[18] In a democratic society, violence often forfeits the sympathy that a group needs if its cause is to receive a responsive hearing.

POLICY PERSPECTIVES ON INTEREST ARTICULATION

As we pointed out in Chapter 2, we need to look at the structures performing political functions from both a process and a policy perspective. If we are to understand the formation of policies, we need to know which groups articulate interests, and what policy preferences they express. Many associational interest groups specialize in certain policy areas. The concerns of other interest groups, such as anomic or institutional groups, may be less easily discerned, but they are equally important for the policy process.

Table 4.3 provides examples of interest articulation for different types of interest groups and different policy areas: extractive, distributive, and regulative policies in the domestic arena, and international

TABLE 4.3   Process and Policy Perspectives on Interest Articulation

Examples of Interest Articulation in Various Policy Areas

Types of Interest Groups	Domestic Extractive Policy	Domestic Distributive Policy	Domestic Regulative Policy	International Policy
Anomic groups	Nigerian women riot over rumor of taxes (1950s).[a]	Russian workers strike to protest price increases.	Indonesians demonstrate against dictatorship (1997).[a]	Germans demonstrate against war in Iraq.
Nonassociational groups	Mexican business leaders discuss taxes with president.	U.S. Black Caucus Congress calls for minority jobs.	Foreign workers in Germany protest citizenship law.	Saudi royal family faction favors oil price increase.
Institutional groups	American universities urge that charitable contributions remain tax deductible.	U.S. Department of Agriculture proposes price supports for honey production.	Church leaders ask for an end to apartheid in South Africa.	Chinese politburo faction favors liberal international trade.
Associational groups	French student groups protest government-imposed tuition increases.[b]	British Medical Association negotiates salaries under Health Services.	National Rifle Association lobbies against gun control.	Palestinian Hamas launch terror attacks on Israel.[a]

[a] Use of coercive, unconstitutional access channels and tactics.

[b] Use of coercion by some elements or subgroups.

policies. The table footnotes indicate when coercive or illegitimate channels were used. Careful examination of each case provides a more precise illustration of the access channels, such as elite representation by African-American members of Congress, Mexican business leaders lobbying their government, Hamas using terror tactics on the West Bank. One can also use this framework to think about how a single interest might pursue their goals through multiple channels, including protests, representation by institutional groups, and lobbying by associational groups. U.S. honeybee farmers, for instance, have lobbied their representatives in Congress to maintain federal price supports, but also used their allies in the Department of Agriculture to lobby in their behalf (will honeybee protests be next?). This table uses examples from many nations in order to suggest the varied possibilities, as well as to fill in all the categories with reasonably obvious cases. If we were studying interest articulation patterns in one nation, of course, we could build a table showing the structures, policies, and channels involved during a particular period.

INTEREST GROUP DEVELOPMENT

One of the consequences of modernization is a widespread belief that the conditions of life can be altered through human action. Modernization normally involves education, urbanization, rapid growth in public communication, and in most cases improvement in the physical conditions of life. These changes are closely related to increases in political awareness, participation, and feelings of political competence. Such participant attitudes encourage more diverse and citizen-based interest articulation.

At the same time that participant attitudes emerge in the political culture of modernizing countries, there is a specialization of labor as people work in many types of jobs—a process that leads to the formation of large numbers of special interests. The interdependence of modern life, the exposure provided by mass communications, and the wide-ranging role of government further multiply political interests. Complex processes organize these interests and attitudes into associational interest groups. The barriers to coordination and cooperation are overcome in many different ways. The emergent interest group systems, pluralist or corporatist, autonomous or controlled, dominated by the better-off or more equally mobilized, are shaped by the history of interest group development during modernization.

Successful democratic development requires that complex interest group systems emerge to express the needs of groups and individuals in the so-

French environmentalists
protect the government's
nuclear power program.

J.M. Turpin/Gamma Liaison

ciety. Yet, this process is by no means automatic. The problems of organizing large groups for collective action are very large. Societies vary widely in the extent to which people engage in associational activity. One factor explaining participation is the level of trust shared among members of the society. Robert Putnam and his colleagues found that an active associational life in Northern Italian communities was associated with widespread trust in others and that these qualities of political culture were related to economic growth and a participant political life.[19] Ronald Inglehart has shown similar continuity in social trust across nations.[20] Thus modernization may weaken traditional structures in some societies but fail to foster the development of effective associational groups in others because of the inhibition of social attitudes. A nation's ability to achieve either stability or democracy will be hindered as a result.

In other cases, as we have noted, authoritarian parties and bureaucracies may control and penetrate associational groups and choke off the channels of political access. Eastern Europe offers a situation in which 40 years or more of authoritarian domination suppressed autonomous interest groups. Eventually, the processes of economic modernization put great pressure on these authoritarian systems to allow more open organization and expression of political interests. In addition, social change led to an expansion of interest articulation activity and a need for associational groups to provide regular and organized expression for citizens' interests. Associational groups are also needed to counterbalance the demands from institutional groups in the civilian and military bureaucracies.

The recent development of organized interest groups in Eastern Europe should not, however, lead us to conclude that every conceivable group now has equal standing. Using the American experience as an example, the articulation of interests is frequently biased toward the goals of the better-off, who are also often better organized.[21] It is often pointed out that the American Association of Retired Persons (AARP) is an effective group that is not counterbalanced by a "Young Taxpayers Group," and that the traditional labor-management competition leaves consumers under represented.

We might test this notion more broadly by evaluating systems in terms of their inclusiveness: What proportion of the population is represented to what degree in national-level politics? In South Africa under apartheid, we had the extreme case where the majority were prevented outright from forming associational groups. In the Third World competing interests in the capital rarely involve the interests of rural peasants;

sometimes peasant organizations are brutally suppressed, while urban middle- and upper-class groups are able to petition authorities. It seems to be no coincidence that the bias in group inclusion appears greatest where the gap in income and education is widest. We have suggested above that, pushed to the extreme, those excluded from the process will engage in anomic activity or resort to violence, a conclusion supported by statistical studies of inequality and violence.[22] Even in less extreme cases, the presence of different levels of political awareness means that every interest group system is somewhat biased. Democratization involves not only the provision of competitive elections but also the reduction of the bias in interest representation.

Another challenge faces the patterns of interest articulation and representation in advanced industrial democracies. Turnout in national elections has gradually declined over the last few decades. In the United States, for example, turnout in presidential elections averaged 61 percent during the 1950s and was only 51 percent in 2000. Fewer citizens in the established democracies attend a campaign rally or display their partisan support during a campaign than participated a generation ago. There is evidence that participation in associa-

tional groups is also decreasing in the United States, and perhaps in other established democracies.[23] Some scholars argue that it represents a growing social isolation in developed nations, as people forsake social and political involvement for the comfort of their favorite chair and their favorite TV program. If elections are the celebration of democratic politics, fewer individuals seem to be joining in.

Political analysts worry that decreasing political involvement and group activity signal the erosion in the democratic, participatory spirit in the established democracies. This presents a basic puzzle. Why are citizens in established democracies voting *less often* and participating less frequently in democratic elections? At the same time, other peoples around the world are struggling to win their political freedom and the opportunity to participate in democratic politics.

The one thing that can be certain is that democratic politics rests upon a participatory public that uses individual and group methods to express and represent their interests. Thus the development of an active social and political life is an important standard for measuring the political development of a nation.

KEY TERMS

anomic groups

associational groups

channels of political access

civil society

collective action problems

controlled interest group
  systems

democratic corporatist
  interest group systems

institutional groups

interest articulation

mass media

nonassociational group

personal interest contacts

pluralist interest group
  systems

political terror tactics

protests

SUGGESTED READINGS

Barnes, Samuel H., Max Kaase, et al. *Political Action: Mass Participation in Five Western Democracies.* Beverly Hills, CA: Sage, 1979.

Dahl, Robert A. *Polyarchy: Participation and Opposition.* New Haven, CT: Yale University Press, 1971.

———. *Democracy and Its Critics.* New Haven, CT: Yale University Press, 1989.

Dalton, Russell J. *Citizen Politics: Public Opinion and Political Parties in Advanced Industrial Democracies,* 4th ed. Washington: CQ Press, 2005.

Denardo, James. *Power in Numbers: The Political Strategy of Protest and Rebellion.* Princeton, NJ: Princeton University Press, 1985.

Grant, Wyn, ed. *The Political Economy of Corporatism.* New York: St. Martin's, 1985.

Hirschman, Albert. *Exit, Voice, and Loyalty.* Cambridge, MA: Harvard University Press, 1970.

Keck, Margaret and Kathryn Sikkink. *Activists Beyond Borders: Advocacy Networks in International Politics.* Ithaca: Cornell University Press, 1998.

Lichbach, Mark. *The Rebel's Dilemma.* Ann Arbor: University of Michigan Press, 1994.

Meyer, David and Sidney Tarrow, eds. *The Social Movement Society: Contentious Politics for a New Century.* Lanham, MD: Rowman and Littlefield, 1998.

Norris, Pippa. *Democratic Phoenix: Reinventing Political Activism.* New York: Cambridge University Press, 2003.

Olson, Mancur. *The Logic of Collective Action.* Cambridge, MA: Harvard University Press, 1965.

Putnam, Robert. *Making Democracy Work: Civic Traditions in Modern Italy.* Princeton, NJ: Princeton University Press, 1993.

Putnam, Robert. *Bowling Alone: The Collapse and Revival of American Community.* New York: Simon and Schuster, 2000.

Putnam, Robert D. ed. *Democracies in Flux: The Evolution of Social Capital in Contemporary Society.* Oxford: Oxford University Press, 2002

Richardson, Jeremy J., ed. *Pressure Groups.* New York: Oxford University Press, 1993.

Rootes, Christopher. *Environmental Movements: Local, National, and Global.* London: Frank Cass, 1999.

Shi, Tianjian. *Political Participation in Beijing.* Cambridge, MA: Harvard University Press, 1997.

Thomas, Clive. *Political Parties and Interest Groups: Shaping Democratic Governance.* Boulder, CO: L. Rienner, 2001.

Van Deth, Jan, et al. *Social Capital and European Democracy.* New York: Routledge, 1999.

Verba, Sidney, Norman H. Nie, and Jae-on Kim. *Participation and Political Equality.* Cambridge, England: Cambridge University Press, 1978.

Verba, Sidney, Kay Schlozman, and Henry Brady. *Voice and Equality.* Cambridge, MA: Harvard University Press, 1996.

Wattenberg, Martin. *Where Have all the Voters Gone?* Cambridge, MA: Harvard University Press, 2003.

Wiarda, Howard J. *Corporatism and Comparative Politics: The Other Great "ism."* Armonk, NY: Sharpe, 1997.

ENDNOTES

1. International Studies of Values in Politics Project, *Values and the Active Community: A Cross-national Study of the Influence of Local Leadership* (New York: Free Press, 1971); Sidney Verba, Norman N. Nie, and Jae-on Kim, *Participation and Political Equality* (Cambridge, England: Cambridge University Press, 1978).

2. Citizen interest group activity includes membership in groups working on local community issues, environmental interests, humans rights issues, women's issues, or the peace movement. For additional analyses, see Russell Dalton and Robert Rohrschneider, "Political Action and the Political Context: A Multi-level Model of Environmental Activism," in Dieter Fuchs, et al., eds. *Citizens and Democracy in East and West: Studies in Political Culture and Political Process* (Opladen: Westdeutscher Verlag, 2002).

3. Russell Dalton, *Citizen Politics,* 3rd ed. (Chatham, NJ: Chatham House, 2002), ch. 4; M. Kent Jennings, Jan W. van Deth, et al., *Continuities in Political Action* (New York: de Gruyter, 1990); Richard Topf, "Beyond Electoral Participation," in Hans D. Klingemann and Dieter Fuchs, eds., *Citizens and the State* (Oxford, England: Oxford University Press, 1995), pp. 27–51.

4. See Verba, Nie, and Kim, *Participation and Political Equality;* and Barnes, Kaase, et al., *Political Action.*

5. See the data on riots in Charles Taylor and David Jodice, *World Handbook of Political and Social Indicators,* vol. 1, 3rd ed. (New Haven, CT: Yale University Press, 1983), chs. 2–4.

6. Studies of these problems were stimulated by the now classic work of Mancur Olson, *The Logic of Collective Action* (Cambridge, MA: Harvard University Press, 1965). See also Mark Lichbach, *The Rebel's Dilemma* (Ann Arbor: University of Michigan Press, 1994); Mancur Olson, "Dictatorship, Democracy, and Development" *American Political Science Review* 87, no. 3 (Sept. 1993): 567–76; Todd Sandler, ed., *Collective Action: Theory and Applications* (Ann Arbor: University of Michigan Press, 1992).

7. See G. F. Skilling and F. Griffiths, eds., *Interest Groups in Soviet Politics* (Princeton, NJ: Princeton University Press, 1971); the essays by Frederick C. Barghoorn and Skilling in

Robert A. Dahl, *Regimes and Oppositions* (New Haven, CT: Yale University Press, 1973); and Roman Kolkowicz, "Interest Groups in Soviet Politics," *Comparative Politics* 2, no. 3 (April 1970): 445–72.

8. Christopher Rootes, ed. *Environmental Movements: Local, National, and Global.* (London: Frank Cass, 1999); Amrita Basu, ed., *The Challenges of Local Feminism: Women's Movements in Global Perspective* (Boulder, CO: Westview, 1995).

9. Jean Cohen and A. Arato, *Civil Society and Political Theory* (Cambridge, MA: MIT Press, 1992); M. Walzer, ed., *Toward a Global Civil Society* (Oxford, England: Berghahn Books, 1995).

10. Gabriel A. Almond and Sidney Verba, *The Civic Culture* (Princeton, NJ: Princeton University Press, 1963), pp. 300–22; John Pierce et al., *Citizens, Political Communication, and Interest Groups: Environmental Organizations in Canada and the United States* (Westport, CT: Praeger, 1992).

11. Keck, Margaret and Kathryn Sikkink. *Activists Beyond Borders: Advocacy Networks in International Politics.* (Ithaca: Cornell University Press, 1998).

12. Philippe Schmitter, "Interest Intermediation and Regime Governability," in Suzanne Berger, ed., *Organizing Interests in Western Europe* (New York: Cambridge University Press, 1981), ch. 12; Arend Lijphart and Markus Crepaz, "Corporatism and Consensus Democracy in 18 Countries," *British Journal of Political Science* 21, no. 2 (April 1991): 235–46; Wyn Grant, ed., *The Political Economy of Corporatism* (New York: St. Martin's Press, 1985).

13. On the relative success of the corporatist systems in economic performance, see Miriam Golden, "The Dynamics of Trade Unionism and National Economic Performance," *American Political Science Review* 87, no. 2 (June 1993): 439–54; Arend Lijphart, Ronald Rogowski, and R. Kent Weaver, "Separation of Powers and Cleavage Management," in R. Kent Weaver and Bert A. Rockman, *Do Institutions Matter? Government Capabilities in the United States and Abroad* (Washington: Brookings Institution, 1993), pp. 302–44.

14. Kenneth Newton and D. S. Morris, "British Interest Group Theory Reexamined," *Comparative Politics* 7 (July 1975): 577–95.

15. See the essays in Russell J. Dalton and Manfred Kuechler, *Challenging the Political Order: New Social and Political Movements in Western Democracies* (New York: Oxford University Press, 1990).

16. Ted Robert Gurr, "A Comparative Study of Civil Strife," in Hugh David Graham and Ted Robert Gurr, eds., *The History of Violence in America* (New York: Bantam Press, 1969), pp. 462–63.

17. See Mark Baldassare, ed., *The Los Angeles Riots: Lessons for the Urban Future* (Boulder, CO: Westview, 1994); James F. Short and Marvin E. Wolfgang, eds., *Collective Violence* (Chicago: Aldine-Atherton, 1972).

18. On violence and democratic survival, see G. Bingham Powell, Jr., *Contemporary Democracies: Participation, Stability and Violence* (Cambridge, MA: Harvard University Press, 1982), ch. 8; see also the contributions to Juan J. Linz and Alfred Stepan, eds., *The Breakdown of Democratic Regimes* (Baltimore: Johns Hopkins University Press, 1978).

19. Robert D. Putnam, *Making Democracy Work: Civic Traditions in Modern Italy* (Princeton, NJ: Princeton University Press, 1993).

20. Ronald Inglehart, *Culture Shift in Advanced Industrial Societies* (Princeton, NJ: Princeton University Press, 1990), pp. 34–36; see also Almond and Verba, *Civic Culture,* ch. 11.

21. Sidney Verba, Kay Schlozman, and Henry Brady, *Voice and Equality* (Cambridge, MA: Harvard University Press, 1996); Frances Piven and Richard Cloward, *Why Americans Don't Vote* (New York: Pantheon, 1989).

22. Many of these studies are reviewed by Mark I. Lichbach, "An Evaluation of 'Does Economic Inequality Breed Political Conflict' Studies," *World Politics* 41 (1989): 431–70. More recent references and analysis appear in T. Y. Wang, William Dixon, Edward N. Muller, and Mitchell A. Seligson, "Inequality and Political Violence Revisited," *American Political Science Review* 87, no. 4 (Dec. 1993): 979–93.

23. Putnam, Robert. *Bowling Alone: The Collapse and Revival of American Community.* New York: Simon and Schuster, 2000; Eva Cox and Robert D. Putnam, eds. *Democracies in Flux: The Evolution of Social Capital in Contemporary Society.* (Oxford: Oxford University Press, 2002).

5

Interest Aggregation
and Political Parties

Interest aggregation is the activity in which the political demands of individuals and groups are combined into policy programs. For example, farmers' desires for higher crop prices, public preferences for lower taxes, environmentalists' demands for natural resource quality, and the interests of businesses often have to be balanced together in determining an economic policy program. A specific program becomes politically significant when it is backed up by substantial political resources, such as popular votes, commitments of campaign funds, seats in the legislature, positions of executive influence, media access, or even armed force.

How interests are aggregated is a key feature of the political process. The nature of the aggregation process inevitably has major implications for which interests are heard, and what individuals and groups are allowed to participate in the process. Interest aggregation also helps create a balanced government program, as competing policy goals must be compromised to produce a single governing program. The pattern of interest aggregation also is linked to the stability of governments and their ability to function and adapt.

Interest aggregation can occur in many ways. If an influential party leader or military dictator controls substantial political resources, his or her personal impact on interest aggregation may be considerable. Large nations usually develop more specialized organizations for aggregating interests and resources behind a policy. Political parties are just such organizations.

Political parties are important in interest aggregation in democratic and in many nondemocratic systems. Each party (or its candidates) stands for a set of policies and tries to build a coalition of support for this program. In a democratic system two or more parties compete to gain support for their alternative policy programs. In authoritarian systems a single party or institution may try to mobilize citizens' support for its policies. In both systems interest aggregation may take place within a political party; for example, party leaders hear the demands of different groups—unions, consumers, party factions, business organizations—and create policy alternatives. In authoritarian systems the process is frequently covert and controlled, and interests are often mobilized to support the government, rather than the government responding to public interests.

The structural-functional approach highlights the point that political parties may perform many different functions and that different structures may perform the interest aggregation function. For instance, in addition to aggregating interests, parties frequently shape the political culture as they organize thought about political issues and strive to build support for their ideologies, issue positions, and candidates. Parties are involved in political recruitment as they mobilize voters and select would-be officeholders. They articulate interests of their own and transmit the demands of others. Governing parties are also involved in making public policy and even overseeing its implementation and adjudication. The distinctive and defining goal of a political party, its mobilization of support for policies and candidates, is especially related to interest aggregation. In this chapter we compare the role of parties to other structures in interest aggregation.

PERSONAL INTEREST AGGREGATION

One way to bring political interests together in the governing processes is through personal connections. A nearly universal political connection is the

During the 1998 referendum to resolve the conflict in Northern Ireland, one wall banner calls out for people to "Vote for Peace."

Peter Turnley/Corbis

patron-client network—a structure in which a central officeholder, authority figure, or group provides benefits to supporters in exchange for their loyalty. It was the defining principle of feudalism. The king and his lords, the lord and his knights, the knight and his serfs and tenants—all were bound by ties of personal dependence and loyalty. The American political machines of Boss Tweed of New York or Richard Daley, Sr., of Chicago were similarly bound together by patronage and loyalty. Such networks are not confined to relationships cemented by patronage only. The president of the United States, for instance, usually has a circle of personal confidants, a "brain trust" or "kitchen cabinet," bound to their chief by ideological and policy propensities as well as by ties of friendship.

The patron-client network is so common in politics that it seems to be like the cell in biology or the atom in physics—the primitive structure of all politics, the human interactions out of which larger and more complicated political structures are composed. Students of politics in all countries report such networks.

Contemporary patron-client theory was pioneered in studies of Asian politics, where this structure runs through the political processes of countries such as the Philippines, Indonesia, Thailand, Japan, and India.[1] Once these networks were discussed as part of the political process, parallels were found in Europe, Latin America, and most regions of the world. The political processes in the kingdom of Saudi Arabia or the Brunei Sultanate conform to many aspects of the patron-client model. Patron-client relationships involve the recruitment to political office, interest aggregation, policymaking, and policy implementing. As we see in Table 5.1, the extensive reliance upon patron-client networks as a means of aggregating political interests is confined mainly to the less economically developed countries.

When interest aggregation is predominately performed by patron-client ties, this affects the style of the political process. In such a system it is difficult to mobilize political resources behind unified policies of social change or to respond to crises, because taking action depends on ever-shifting agreements between many factional leaders (patrons). Patron-client politics thus typically means a static political system.

TABLE 5.1   Structures Performing Interest Aggregation
in Selected Contemporary Nations*

| Country | *Extensiveness of Interest Aggregation by Actor* | | | | |
	Patron-Client Networks	Associational Groups	Competitive Parties	Authoritarian Parties	Military Forces
Britain	Low	High	High		Low
Brazil	Moderate	Moderate	Moderate		Moderate
China	Moderate	Low		High	High
Egypt	High	Low		Moderate	High
France	Low	Moderate	High		Low
Germany	Low	High	High		Low
India	High	Moderate	Moderate		Low
Japan	Moderate	High	High		Low
Mexico	Moderate	Moderate	Moderate		Low
Nigeria	High	Low	Moderate		Moderate
Russia	Moderate	Low	Moderate		Moderate
United States	Low	Moderate	High		Low

*Extensiveness of interest aggregation rated as low, moderate, or high. Rating refers to broad-level performance and may vary in different issue areas and at different times. Blank implies not appropriate.

INSTITUTIONAL INTEREST AGGREGATION

In modern societies, as citizens become aware of larger collective interests and have the resources and skills to work for them, personal networks tend to be regulated, limited, and incorporated within broader organizations.

The subtle dividing line between interest articulation and aggregation can easily be crossed by organizations with powerful resources. **Associational groups** operate to express demands and support political contenders such as political parties. But they can occasionally wield sufficient resources to become contenders in their own right. For instance, the political power of the labor unions within the British Labour Party historically rested on the unions' ability to develop coherent policy positions and mobilize the votes of their members (who were formally represented in the party) to support those positions. As we discussed in Chapter 4, a system of democratic corporatism can effectively aggregate the interests of both labor and business groups into economic policies. These arrangements include continuous political bargaining among organized labor, official representatives of business interests, political parties, and state bureaucracies. Such corporatist systems inter-

connect organizations that in other political systems play very different, often antagonistic, roles.

Institutional groups like bureaucratic and military factions can also be important interest aggregators. Indeed, the bureaucracy acts as an interest aggregator in most societies. Although established primarily to implement policies set by higher authorities, the bureaucracy may negotiate with various groups to identify their preferences or to mobilize their support. Government agencies may even be "captured" by interest groups and used to support their demands. The desire of bureaucrats to expand their organizations by discovering new problems and policies, as well as increasing their ability to solve problems in their areas of expertise, often leads them to create client support networks.

Military organizations, with their special control of physical force, have great potential power as interest aggregators. If the legitimacy of the government breaks down and all groups feel free to use coercion and violence to shape policies, then a united military can usually be decisive. By one account, around two-fifths of the world's nations have confronted military coup attempts at some time, and these were at least partially successful in changing leaders or policy in about a third of the nations. Less than half of these coup attempts, however, focused on general political issues and public policy. Most coups seemed motivated by grievances and fear that the professional interests of the military would be slighted by civil authorities.[2]

Table 5.1 illustrates how associational groups tend to play a larger role in democratic politics that accept the independence of interest groups and their attempts to influence government policy. Conversely, the military generally plays a role in non-democratic states, often providing the leadership of government or supporting an authoritarian regime.

COMPETITIVE PARTY SYSTEMS AND INTEREST AGGREGATION

In many contemporary political systems, parties are the primary structures of interest aggregation. However, we must keep in mind the critical distinction between **competitive party systems,** which primarily try to build electoral support, and noncompetitive or **authoritarian party systems,** which seek to direct society. This distinction does not depend on the closeness of electoral victory, or even on the number of parties. It depends on the ability of political parties to freely form and to compete for citizen support, and their winning citizen support as a prerequisite for controlling government. Thus a party can win most of the votes in a certain area, or even one national election, but nonetheless still be a competitive party. Its goals involve winning elections, either as a primary objective or as a means for policymaking; its dominance at the polls can be challenged by other parties.

The role of competitive parties in interest aggregation depends not only on the individual party but also the structure of parties, electorates, electoral laws, and policymaking bodies that interact together. Typically, interest aggregation in a competitive party system takes place at several stages: within the individual parties, as the party chooses candidates and adopts policy proposals; through electoral competition, as voters give varying amounts of support to different parties; and through bargaining and coalition building in the legislature or executive.

Competitive Parties and Elections

At the first step, individual parties develop policy positions. Typically, a party believes that its positions are backed by a large or cohesive group of voters. In systems with only two parties, it is important for a party to win a majority, so targeting the "center" of the electorate is often strategically necessary to win the enough votes.[3] In systems with many political parties, where no one group has much chance of winning a majority, parties may seek a distinctive and cohesive electoral base. Party policies may reflect the preferences of specific groups, such as labor unions, business associations, or religious and ethnic groups. Historical issue commitments and ideological traditions also play a role.[4]

In developing their policy proposals parties anticipate the way that election competition brings together party offerings and voter choices. One important element is the election law that determines how voter choices are translated into election outcomes.[5] In the United States, Britain, and many countries once influenced by Britain (such as India, Jamaica, and Canada), the legislative election rules divide the country into many election districts. In each district, the candidate who has more votes than any other—a *plurality*—wins the election in the district. This simple, **single-member district plurality election rule** is often called "first past the post," a horse racing term, because the winner need only finish ahead of the others but not win a majority of the votes. (See Box 5.1: Duverger's Law.) This system seems obvious and natural to Americans, but it is rarely used in the democracies in Europe or in Latin America.

In contrast to the single-member district system, most democracies use some form of **proportional representation.** In these systems the country is divided into a few, large districts (or kept as a single national district). The competing parties offer lists of candidates, rather than a single candidate. The number of legislative representatives a party wins depends on the overall proportion of the votes it receives. If the entire country were a single legislative district, as in the Netherlands and Israel, a party receiving 4 percent of the vote would be awarded 4 percent of the seats in the national legislature. Sometimes parties must achieve a minimum threshold of votes, usually 3–5%, to receive any seats at all. (If so many parties compete that a lot of them fall below the threshold, many voters may be left unrepresented, as happened in Russia in 1995 and in some other early elections in the new Eastern European democracies.)

The procedure that parties use to develop policy positions varies greatly from country to country and

BOX 5.1   Duverger's Law

Duverger's Law is one of the best-known phenomena in political science. It reflects the tendency for plurality single-member district election rules to create "two-party" systems in the legislature, while proportional representation electoral systems generate multiple party systems. In single-member district systems, smaller parties that receive a minority of the vote across many districts receive little or no representation in Parliament. This discourages politicians from forming more parties and greatly underrepresents small parties that do compete. In Britain in the 2001 election, for example, 18 percent of the electorate voted for the Liberal Democratic Party, but it received only 8 percent of the seats in Parliament. Duverger's Law is named after the French political scientist Maurice Duverger, who recognized and analyzed it as a general rule.

Source: Maurice Duverger, *Political Parties: Their Organization and Activity in the Modern State,* [1954] trans. Barbara and Robert North, New York: John Wiley, 1963.

from party to party. In the United States the national party conventions held at each presidential election formalize the party's policy positions, both through the development of party platforms and through the selection of candidates committed to certain policies. In other countries, parties have more regular congresses, centralized party organizations issue party programs, and the parties develop manifestos for each national election.[6] Whatever the system, the final party position is usually a mixture of strategic electioneering and the aggregation of interests existing within the party.

The parties then offer their chosen candidates and policies to the electorate. They not only present candidates, but they also attempt to publicize them and mobilize electoral support through rallies, media advertising, door-to-door campaigning, and other activities. The act of voting by the individual citizen is one of the simplest and most frequently performed political actions. The citizen enters a voting booth and indicates support for a political candidate, party, or policy proposal. Elections are one of the few devices where diverse interests can be expressed equally and comprehensively. By casting ballots and aggregating these votes the citizens can make a collective decision about their future leaders and public policies.[7]

Figure 5.1 shows levels of voter turnout in a variety of nations in recent years.[8] In Britain, Germany, and the United States, as in most of the world's democracies, most citizens are eligible to participate, and they may choose between competing political parties and candidates. In Western Europe about three-quarters of the citizens usually vote; in the United States about half the electorate goes to the polls in presidential elections, which was about the same level as in Nigeria in 1999. Voter turnout in Russia, Japan and Mexico fell between these. The lowest turnout in Figure 5.1 appears in Egypt, where government control made elections distinctly noncompetitive.

Despite the simplicity and limitations of the vote, its implications can be profound. The voters' choice between competing parties or candidates is one of the few ways that a nation can make a collective choice on government goals—thus this is a prime method of aggregating specific interests. Electoral outcomes determine who manages the affairs of government and who makes public policy. Shifts in citizen support can bring to power new coalitions committed to new policies. Citizens thus can influence interest aggregation and policymaking through their role in selecting elites.

In other countries, however, elections have other functions. Elections have been used to legitimate the government, even though the electoral outcome was predetermined, as in Egypt, or to select a government, even while excluding many citizens. Nearly all the communist nations of Eastern Europe utilized some form of elections to legitimize their governments. In these nations reported turnout routinely exceeded 98 percent of the electorate. At the same time, the government guaranteed the outcome in advance. Until 1990, voters in the Soviet Union could only vote for one candidate, who was always a nominee of the Communist Party. In some other communist nations, the voters could endorse a government slate of candidates or parties, but the parties had agreed upon the division of seats before the

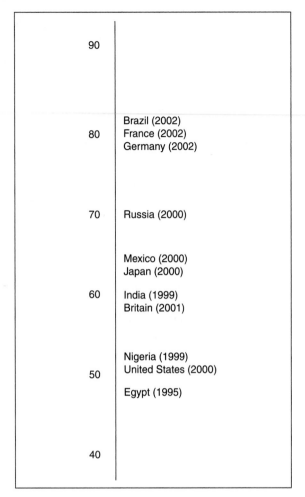

90	
80	Brazil (2002) France (2002) Germany (2002)
70	Russia (2000)
60	Mexico (2000) Japan (2000) India (1999) Britain (2001)
50	Nigeria (1999) United States (2000) Egypt (1995)
40	

FIGURE 5.1   Turnout in Most Recent National Elections

Source: Elections in the World, downloaded October 30, 2002 from www.electionworld.org. Voter turnout is percent of registered voters except in the USA, where it is percent of voting age population. Egypt 2000, not available.

votes were counted. The very high levels of voter participation in these nations reflected government pressure on the public to express their symbolic support for the regime. Elections and voting in these systems, as in national elections in Egypt and China today, played a role in socializing and shaping citizens' attitudes, but had little to do with interest articulation or aggregation.[9]

Political scientists have shown that voting choices reflect a mix of motivations.[10] Many citizens evaluate past government policies or the future policy promises of the parties; issue-based

voting enables the public to express their policy preferences. For other individuals, elections are a simple referendum on government performance; vote the rascals out if times are bad, and reelect them if times are good. In other cases, the charisma of a strong leader, or the incompetence of a weak one, can dominate an election. In each case, however, elections aggregate these diverse concerns to make a collective decision on the composition of government.

Figure 5.2 offers a comparative "snapshot" of interest aggregation by parties and voters in several democratic countries. It uses the device of the left-right scale, which in many countries acts as a summary of the issues that voters find most important. The figure shows where party supporters in each country placed themselves on a scale of numbers, with 1 identified as Left (or liberal in the United States) and 10 identified as Right (or conservative in the United States) in public opinion surveys in the late 1990s. It's important to realize that the left-right placements reflect the relative positions of party supporters in the national issues within the society; the meaning of the "center" is substantively different in different societies (see Table 3.3 in Chapter 3, for example.) The height of the columns above the scale shows what percentage of the electorate voted for each party.

In the countries at the top of Figure 5.2, especially in the United States, most voters support only a few parties. Moreover, the parties are fairly close to the center of the continuum, where the bulk of voters place themselves. Democrats are somewhat to the left and Republicans somewhat to the right, with a lot of overlap. The left-right "gap" between the average party supporters, although larger than it was 20 years ago, is still fairly small. Thus aggregation implies concentration of political resources behind the fairly "centrist" policies of both parties.

In France, toward the bottom of the figure, many parties received voter support. Leftist voters divided themselves between the Communist, Socialist, and Green parties, (and several other smaller leftist parties not shown.) The rightist vote was split between the Gaullist RPR and the more moderate UDF. In addition, there was significant support for an extreme right-wing party, the National Front. There is a very large distance between the left-most party (the Communists) and right-most party (the National Front), and even between

B O X   5 . 2   Election Upset!

Elections can often show that the public's preferences are much different from what political leaders expect. After the Khomeini revolution in 1979, Iran was governed by a conservative religious establishment and its political allies. The regime rolled back civil liberties and followed repressive policies in several areas, while claiming popular legitimacy for its actions. In 1997 Iranians went to the polls to select a president. The choices were between the conservative speaker of parliament and a moderate who few thought would do well. In a stunning upset the moderate, Mohammed Katami, won 69 percent of the vote. Katami has attempted to expand the freedoms enjoyed by Iranians, but he is constrained by the strong conservative and religious forces in Iran.

the two largest parties (Socialists and RPR.) The dispersed aggregation of the party-electoral outcomes means that a much more diverse range of ideological interests may be represented in the electoral debates.

Britain and Germany fell between these more extreme cases. Britain looked more like the United States in its pattern of voter support, but the parties were further apart and the smaller Liberal Democratic Party fell between them. The major German political parties were the SPD on the left and the CDU/CSU on the right, a small centrist party between them, an environmentally oriented Green party, and a reformed communist party (the PDS) on the left.

Mexico in 2000 shows the intense competition that emerged between the long-dominant, previously-authoritarian PRI and its challengers as transition to a real democracy took place. In the legislative election the PAN, which competed in an alliance with the Green Party in the Alliance for Change, was neck and neck with the newly democratic PRI, and drew voters from across the left-right spectrum. Cardenas's PRD, competing in a coalition called Alliance for Mexico, posed a leftist challenge to both major parties. The exciting presidential election was won by PAN's Vincente Fox, who became the first non-PRI president in three-quarters of a century.

Competitive Parties in Government

If a competitive party wins control of the legislature and the executive, it will (if unified) be able to pass and implement its policies. Sometimes this control emerges directly from the electoral process, as a single party wins a majority of the vote. In many countries the election laws are designed to benefit the largest party to help it gain the votes to govern. If these distortions are sufficient, less than 50 percent of the vote may be converted into more than 50 percent of the legislative seats. Such "artificial" legislative majorities have been the rule in countries with "first past the post" electoral systems, such as Britain.[11]

For example, since 1974 none of the legislature majorities won by either the Conservative Party or the Labour Party in Britain were based on support of a majority of voters. Margaret Thatcher's Conservative Party won a solid majority of legislative seats in 1983 and 1987 with the backing of only about 42 percent of the voters. With almost exactly the same level of support in the 1997 and 2001 elections, Tony Blair and the Labour Party won nearly two-thirds of the seats in Parliament. In all these elections, the quarter of the electorate supporting the smaller parties received only a handful of legislative seats.

In other countries, multiparty elections do not yield single-party majorities, but party coalitions formed before the election may still offer the voters a direct choice of future governments. During the election, a group of parties may encourage mutual support from their voters, agree to run candidates in different districts in order to maximize their combined vote, or agree to govern together if they jointly win a majority of legislative seats. Such agreements have appeared in many (but not all) elections in France and Germany. Preelection coalition governments are similar to majoritarian governments because they can provide voters with clear targets if they choose to reward or punish the incumbents of government. Voters thus have the ability to choose the direction of government policy through their party choice.

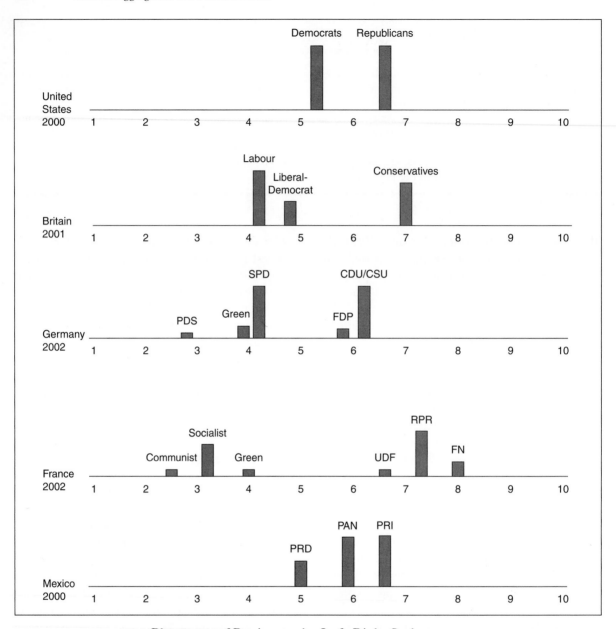

FIGURE 5.2 Placement of Parties on the Left-Right Scale and Their Voter Support in Election

The aggregation of policy preferences through elections is important because parties generally fulfill their electoral promises when they gain control of government.[12] For example, British parties take pride in carrying out their promises while in office. When Socialist and Social Democratic governments have come to power in Europe, they have tended to expand the size and efforts of the governmental sector; conservative parties have generally retarded the growth of government programs. Republicans and Democrats in the United States also have been fairly responsible in keeping their promises. However, parties that have been out of office a long time or that have developed radical programs often find it diffi-

The 1999 presidential elections in Nigeria returned democratic institutions to this nation; the former military dictator Obasanjo was elected president.

Ochoko/Sipa Press

cult to implement their programs when they eventually come to power. After coming to power as part of a coalition government in 1998, the Green Party had to modify its promise to shut down Germany's nuclear power plants immediately, negotiating instead a phase out over many years.

When elections do not create a majority party (or preelection coalition), then a new government is formed by postelection negotiations among political parties and their leaders. This is a common aspect of politics in many party systems, such as those in the Netherlands and Belgium.[13] In these nations interests are not aggregated at the level of elections, because the election does not determine the government. Instead, the aggregation of interests occurs at the governmental level when a coalition is negotiated. (Also see the discussion in Chapter 6, and Figure 6.2.)

The aggregation of interests at the governmental level, rather than the electoral level, can have both costs and benefits. On the one hand, when coalitions formed at the elite level determine government policy, voters may be frustrated and disillusioned, feeling that elections do not directly define government outcomes. In addition, because interest aggregation occurs among political elites this means that new

elite coalitions can form on different issues. This can be confusing to citizens (and even informed observers). It is difficult for people to assign clear responsibility for government policy when power is shifting and widely shared. This situation lessens the value of the vote as an instrument to shape future governments or to punish parties held responsible for undesirable policy.[14]

On the other hand, the aggregation of interests at the governmental level can mean that voters for all parties, not just the election winners, are represented in policymaking. Such representation can be especially important for minority interests. All citizens hold minority opinions on some issues, and some are minorities on many issues. If the rules of election and representation are fair, the possibility that their representatives can influence policy between elections is a valuable protection for minority interests. Finally, even elected governments that win a majority of votes typically lack majority support for all of their policy proposals. So a flexible pattern of interest aggregation at the legislative level, if based on fair representation, may benefit the nation as a whole. Bargaining between fairly represented groups may even increase the possibility that policies reflect different majorities on different issues.

The role of elections as instruments of representation may increase through a system of aggregating interests within the government, even though the role of elections as instruments of accountability may diminish.[15]

Classifying Competitive Party Systems

Figure 5.3 classifies examples of each type of competitive party system. Majoritarian and multiparty systems are distinguished by the number of political parties. The **majoritarian two-party systems** are either dominated by just two parties, as in the United States, or they have two substantial parties and election laws that usually create legislative majorities for one of them, as in Britain. **Majority-coalition systems** are those where parties establish open pre-electoral coalitions so voters know which parties will attempt to work together to form a government. The purely **multiparty systems** have combinations of parties, voter support, and election laws that virtually ensure that no single party wins a legislative majority. Interest aggregation by party bargaining after the election is critical for shaping policy directions. Germany and

France, as we have already mentioned, are among the multiparty systems in which voter support of party coalitions at the electoral level has often had a major impact on forming governments and policies.

The degree of antagonism or polarization among the parties is another important characteristic of party systems. In a **consensual party system** the parties commanding most of the legislative seats are not too far apart on policies and have a reasonable amount of trust in each other and in the political system.[16] These are typically party systems like those shown toward the top of Figure 5.2 Bargaining may be intense and politics exciting in these systems, but it seldom threatens the system itself.

In a **conflictual party system,** the legislature is dominated by parties that are far apart on issues or are highly antagonistic toward each other and the political system, such as the Russian party system. If a party system has mixed characteristics of a certain kind—that is, both consensual and conflictual—we classify it as **accommodative.** Arend Lijphart has used those terms to describe party systems in which political leaders are able to bridge the intense differences between antagonistic voters.[17]

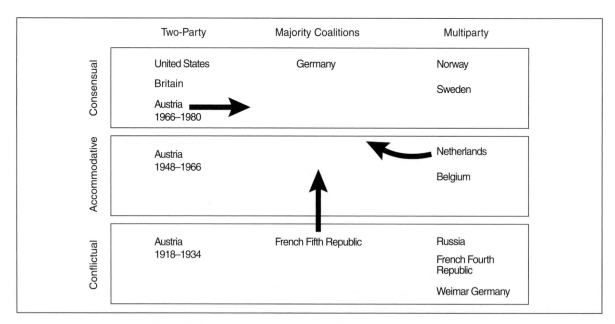

FIGURE 5.3   Classifying Party Systems by Number of Parties and Antagonism Between Parties

The United States and Britain are contemporary examples of relatively consensual majoritarian party systems. They are not perfect two-party systems because minor parties exist in both nations. However, in Britain a single party usually wins a legislative majority and controls the legislature and the executive with disciplined party voting. In the Unites States, the shifting programs of presidential party candidates alter the degree of consensus from election to election. Moreover, the looser cohesion of American parties and the frequently divided control of legislature and executive lead to post-election bargaining that is similar to consensual multiparty systems.

Good examples of consensual multiparty systems are found in Norway and Sweden. In these countries there are four or five parties—socialists, agrarian/center, liberals, conservatives, and small communist movements. A subset of these parties has usually been able to construct long-lived governments, singly or in coalition.

Austria between 1918 and 1934 is the best example of a majoritarian conflictual party system. Antagonism between the Socialist Party and the other parties was so intense that in the mid-1930s it produced a brief civil war. The Austrian experience also illustrates how party systems can change over time. After World War II, the leaders of the two major parties negotiated an elaborate coalition agreement of mutual power sharing—checks and balances—to control its conflicts. After some 20 years of the consociational "Grand Coalition," party antagonism had declined to the point that more normal majority politics could be tolerated, although some consociational elements remained. Later the Austrian party system moved toward a consensual system, with some single-party majorities and some coalitions. Most recently, the Freedom Party, a controversial populist party of the far right, won substantial support by attacking the consensual style of the party system. The party's entry into a coalition government after the 1999 election damaged Austria's relations with other members of the European Union, because of the party's extreme political views.

France, Italy, and Weimar Germany are good historical examples of conflictual multiparty systems, with powerful Communist parties on the left and conservative or Fascist movements on the right. Cab-

inets had to form out of centrist movements, which were themselves divided on many issues, thus making for instability, poor government performance, and loss of citizen confidence in democracy. These factors contributed to the overthrow of democracy in Weimar Germany, the collapse of the French Fourth Republic, and government instability and citizen alienation from politics in Italy.

More recently, some of the emerging party systems in Central and Eastern Europe have tended to follow this pattern of conflictual, multiparty competition. For instance, in the 1995 parliamentary elections in Russia, 43 parties appeared on the ballot—ranging from unreformed communists on the left to nationalist parties on the right—and seven parties won representation in Parliament. The hope is that this is a transitional period as a new party system is established, not a precursor to the instability that has haunted other polarized party systems.[18]

The mixed consociational system can enable a deeply divided nation to find a way to peaceful democratic development. In the Netherlands, for example, the leaderships of competing movements found bases of accommodation that provide mutual guarantees to the various groups. In Austria and Lebanon after World War II, suspicious and hostile groups—the socialists and Catholics in Austria, and the Christians and Muslims in Lebanon—worked out a set of consociational understandings making it possible for stable governments to be formed. Austria's accommodation was based on a two-party system and Lebanon's on many small, personalistic religious parties. After 1975, however, Lebanon was penetrated and fragmented by the Middle Eastern conflict and fell victim to civil war.

South Africa adopted consociational practices in its transition to democracy. Leaders of the major political parties of the white minority and two major segments of the black majority negotiated (with great difficulty) arrangements for a democratic election and a multiparty coalition government to follow it. A typically consociational feature of the "Interim Constitution" of the transition guaranteed a share in power and government—cabinet posts—to all parties winning over 5 percent of the vote in the election. Later, this feature was abandoned. As the contrasting examples of Austria and Lebanon suggest, such practices (and the ability even to agree to attempt them) offer hope but no guarantees of long-term success to deeply divided democracies.

All this suggests that, although the number of parties affects the degree of political stability, the degree of antagonism among parties is more important. Where multiparty systems consist of relatively moderate antagonists, stability and effective performance seem possible. Where systems consist of highly antagonistic elements, collapse and civil war are ever-present possibilities, regardless of the number of parties. When crises develop, the commitment of party leaders to work together to defend democracy can be critical for its survival. It may be easier, however, to arrange such commitments in a multiparty, representational setting.[19] Some of the new democracies of Eastern Europe and Latin America and Asia, especially those divided by language or ethnicity, face similar challenges.

AUTHORITARIAN PARTY SYSTEMS

Authoritarian party systems are also specialized interest aggregation structures. They deliberately attempt to develop policy proposals and to mobilize support for them, but they do so in a completely different way from competitive party systems. With authoritarian party systems, aggregation takes place within the ranks of the party or in interactions with business groups, landowners, and institutional groups in the bureaucracy or military. The citizens have no real opportunity to shape aggregation by choosing between party alternatives, although controlled elections are often organized.

Authoritarian party systems can be distinguished among themselves according to the degree of top-down control within the party and the degree of the party's control over other groups in society. At one extreme is the **exclusive governing party,** which insists on control over political resources by the party leadership. It recognizes no legitimate interest aggregation by groups within the party nor does it permit any free activity by social groups, citizens, or other government agencies. In its most intensive form, sometimes called totalitarianism, it penetrates the entire society and mobilizes support for policies developed at the top. Its policies are legitimated by an encompassing political ideology that claims to know the true interests of the citizens, whatever their immediate preferences.[20] At the other extreme is the **inclusive governing party** that recognizes and attempts to coordinate various social groups in the society. It accepts and aggregates certain autonomous interests, while repressing others and forbidding any serious challenges to its own control.

Exclusive Governing Parties

Few parties have long maintained the absolute central control, penetration, and ideological mobilization of the most intensive (totalitarian) form of the exclusive government party. However, the ruling Communist parties of the USSR before 1985, of Eastern Europe before 1989, of North Korea, Vietnam, and Cuba today fall toward the controlling end of the authoritarian party scale. Today, while withdrawing from direct administration of much of the economy, the Chinese regime, for example, still does not recognize the legitimacy of any other large political groups within Chinese society. Interest articulation by individuals, within bounds, may be permitted; the mobilization of wide support before the top elite has decided on policy is not permitted.[21]

The penetrating and controlling single-party systems can play important roles in mobilizing support for policies. An unchallenged ideological focus provides legitimacy and coherence; the party penetrates and organizes most social structures in the name of that ideology and in accordance with centralized policies. As a tool designed for unified mobilization, the exclusive governing party has been used by many leaders who were committed to massive social change. A party that successfully mobilized a colonial people behind independence, for example, might be used to change an underdeveloped society.

Even at the stage of ideological mobilization, the exclusive governing party may experience more internal aggregation than is commonly recognized or legitimately permitted. Internally, various groups may unite around such interests as region or industry, or behind leaders of policy factions. Either openly or covertly, beneath the supposedly united front, power struggles may erupt in times of crisis, with different leaders mobilizing backing for themselves and their positions. Succession crises are particularly likely to generate such power struggles, as demonstrated at the death of Stalin in the Soviet Union and Mao Zedong in China.

In addition, the Chinese Communist Party several times has had to rely on the army, even on coalitions of regional army commanders, to sustain its control.

As the experiences of many new nations show, moreover, the creation of an exclusive governing party as an agent for social transformation is extremely difficult. The seduction of power regularly leads to political excesses that are not checked by competitive democratic politics and may distort ideological objectives. The exclusive governing parties in some African states also had limited capacity to control society. Furthermore, the loss of confidence in Marxist-Leninist ideology and in the Soviet model of authoritarian development led all eight of the African regimes that had once invoked it to abandon that approach by the early 1990s.[22]

As exclusive governing parties age, many enter a stage of more "mature" exclusive authoritarianism that maintains control but places less emphasis on mobilization. Some may degenerate into vehicles for personal rule and exploitation by the family and supporters of the ruler.[23] Finally, as shown by the collapse of communism in the former Soviet Union and Eastern Europe, if and when the party leaders lose faith in the unifying ideology, it may be difficult to maintain party coherence.

Inclusive Governing Parties

Among the preindustrial nations, especially in nations with notable ethnic and tribal divisions, the more successful authoritarian systems have seemed to have inclusive party systems. These systems recognize the autonomy of social, cultural, and economic groups and try to incorporate them or bargain with them, rather than control and remake them. In the more successful African one-party systems, such as Kenya and Tanzania, aggregation around personalistic, factional, and ethnic-based groups was permitted within decentralized organizations of the party.

Inclusive party systems have sometimes been labeled authoritarian corporatist systems. Like the democratic corporatist systems (see Chapter 4), some of these systems encourage the formation of large organized interest groups that can bargain with each other and the state. Unlike the democratic corporatist systems, however, these authoritarian systems provide no political resources directly to the populace. Independent protest and political activity outside of offi-cial channels are suppressed. The party leaders permit only limited autonomous demands within the ranks of the party and by groups associated with it.

The degree of legitimate aggregation permitted in the inclusive authoritarian systems may be substantial and take many forms. The party typically tries to gather various social groups under the general party umbrella and negotiate with social groups and institutions outside the party. Some of these inclusive parties have attempted aggressive programs of social change. Others have been primarily arenas for aggregating various social interests. Many inclusive party governments permit other parties to offer candidates in elections, as long as they have no real chance of winning. Indeed, one of the interesting features of politics in the last twenty-five years, along with the increasing number of liberal democracies, has been the growth of "electoral authoritarianism," in which a facade of democracy provides "some space for political opposition, independent media, and social organizations that do not seriously criticize or challenge the regime."[24] The PRI in Mexico was long a successful example of an inclusive governing party featuring electoral authoritarianism until its recent transition.

The relative stability of some inclusive authoritarian party systems should not obscure their frequent failures to build a stable governing structure. In many countries these parties coexist in uneasy and unstable coalitions with the armed forces and the civilian bureaucracy. In some countries the party has become relatively unimportant window dressing for a military regime or personal tyranny. Seldom have these parties been able to solve the economic or ethnic problems that face their nation.

These political systems were often created by unifying struggle against colonialism, and their viability has declined as colonialism has become more distant. As memories of the independence struggle have faded and the leaders of independence movements have departed, the ties of ideology and experience that held these parties together have weakened. These events, in conjunction with the world-wide expansion of democracy, have led to a general loss of legitimacy for the single-party model. In some cases the failure of authoritarian parties has permitted the emergence of some real party competition. More frequently, electoral authoritarianism with varying

---

BOX 5.3   Mexico's PRI

One of the oldest and the most elaborately inclusive authoritarian parties was the Partido Revolucionario Institucional (PRI) in Mexico. The PRI dominated the political process and gave other parties no realistic chances of winning elections for more than 50 years. The PRI maintained popular support after the creation of a broad coalition within the party by Lázaro Cárdenas in the 1930s; it was also careful to control the counting of the ballots. Its actions were not shaped by electoral competition, at least until the 1990s. However, the party incorporated many social groups within it, with separate sectors for labor, agrarian, and popular interests. While some discontent was suppressed, other dissatisfied individuals were deliberately enticed into the party. The party also gave informal recognition to rather distinct and well-organized political factions grouped behind such figures as former presidents. Various Mexican leaders mobilized their factions within the PRI and in other important groups not directly affiliated with it, such as big business interests. Bargaining was particularly important every six years when the party chose a new presidential nominee. The legal provision that the incumbent president could not succeed himself guaranteed some turnover of elites and may have facilitated more legitimate and open internal bargaining. In recent decades, however, rising discontent illustrated the difficulties in coordinating all interests through a single party. The urban and rural poor who had not shared in Mexico's general growth joined with others who want a more fully democratic system. An armed uprising of peasant guerrillas in early 1994 shocked the political establishment and led to more promises of genuine democratic competition. Legislative elections in 1997 were more open than earlier contests, and ended the 70-year rule of the PRI, which then lost the presidency in the 2000 election. The PRI seeks to play a new role as a competitive democratic party.

---

degrees of manipulation and control has been introduced to provide a veneer of legitimacy for internal and external consumption. In more than a few, the outcome has been a resort to naked coercion by government agencies or private forces, with the military serving as final arbiter.[25]

THE MILITARY AND INTEREST AGGREGATION

After World War II, parliamentary and democratic governments were instituted among most of the nations of the Third World. In many countries the lack of effectiveness and authority of these civil governments led to their breakdown and their replacement by **military governments.** With its control of instruments of force, and in the absence of a strong constitutional tradition, the military was an effective contender for power. Even in those regimes where civilian authority was reestablished, the military generally constituted a significant power contender, and exercised influence in the political process. In Brazil, for example, the military played a crucial interest aggregation role in the democratic processes before 1964 and was the dominant aggregating and policymaking actor for the next 20 years. In many other nations, including Syria, Pakistan, Guinea, Zaire,

Paraguay, and Haiti, the military has long been the dominant, or at least a major, interest aggregator. Nonetheless, a striking development in recent years has been the decline of military regimes as an official form of government, with Pakistan and Myanmar the outstanding exceptions.

The military's virtual monopoly of coercive resources gives it great potential power, even if it chooses to exercise it behind the scenes. Thus, when agreement fails on aggregation either through democratic or authoritarian party systems, the military may emerge by default as the only force able to maintain orderly government. The soldiers then remain the basic force underpinning the personal tyranny of a civilian president or a dominant party. Or the armed forces may use their power to further institutional or ideological objectives. Military rulers may try to create military and/or bureaucratic versions of authoritarian corporatism, linking organized groups and the state bureaucracy with the military as final arbiter of disagreement. They may undertake "defensive" modernization in alliance with business groups or even undertake more radical modernization. In Latin America almost all the corporatist versions of authoritarian aggregation have had a strong military component and only rarely a dominating role for the authoritarian party.

Rebel soldiers (on right), who staged an uprising against the Ivory Coast government and took over large areas of the country, meet with French troops monitoring a cease fire in 2002.

Pascal Le Segretain/Getty Images

BOX 5.4   Trying to Make Democracy Work

The military government in Nigeria responded to the democratization wave of the 1990s by initiating state-level elections in 1991, and federal legislative elections in 1992. However, the military mandated a restricted process under which politicians from former civilian regimes were disqualified (as tainted by corruption). Voters were thus left with a choice of only two parties, both created by the government. Turnout was adversely affected by a spreading cynicism about the meaningfulness of the vote. Citizens' doubts were confirmed when the military annulled the presidential election of June 1993, even before the votes were announced, and appointed an Interim National Government to organize new elections. In November 1993 a military coup by Defense Minister General Sani Abacha overturned the Interim National Government, banned all political activity, dissolved the legislature, dismissed the 30 elected state governments, and thus ended even a limited role of elections in interest representation. In spring 1999 the military government allowed an election for president. The victor was a former army general, who is now trying to implement democratic reforms. But continuing ethnic violence and political murders threaten to destabilize democracy again. (See Chapter 18.)

The major limitation of the military in interest aggregation is that their internal structures are not designed to mobilize support across a range of issues or outside their coercive control. The military is primarily organized for the downward processing of commands under threat of coercion. It is not set up to aggregate internal differences, to build a compromise, to mobilize wide support of government policy, or even to communicate with social groups outside the command hierarchy. Nor does the military regime have the surface claim of legitimacy that elec-

tions provide for the international community. Thus the military lacks many of the advantages in mobilizing voluntary support held by party systems. These internal limitations may be less serious when the military is dealing with common grievances and putting pressure on—or seizing power from—incumbent authorities. These limitations become a major problem, however, when a military government needs to mobilize backing for economic development or other broad government programs. For these reasons military governments frequently prove unstable, are forced to share power with other institutions, or encourage the formation of cooperating authoritarian parties.

TRENDS IN INTEREST AGGREGATION

As we have previously noted, the democratic trend in the world gained momentum with the collapse of authoritarian regimes in Eastern Europe at the end of the 1980s. Figure 5.4 classifies the world's regimes by the predominant interest aggregation structure at three points: the end of the 1970s, the end of the 1980s, and the late 1990s. The percentages should be viewed as estimates, often based on limited information. But the figure provides a rough idea of the frequency of the three major forms: competitive parties, single-party, and military-dominated regimes. The "residual" category of traditional governments con-

sists mostly of small kingdoms in the Middle East, South Asia, and the Pacific.

In 1978 about one-third of the world's 150-plus independent countries had competitive party and electoral systems as their predominant interest aggregation structures. These regimes were the main form in Western Europe and North America (including the Caribbean), not uncommon in Latin America and Asia, but rare in Africa and the Middle East. Nearly as many countries had some versions of a single-party regime. Single-party systems were the main form in Eastern Europe and relatively common in Africa and Asia. In slightly less than a quarter of the countries the military dominated interest aggregation, either formally (military governments) or in practice (military-dominated civilian governments). The military-dominated regimes accounted for about a third or more of the countries in Africa and Latin America.

A decade later, the trend is obviously away from single-party governments. Across the world they decline from 30 to 24 percent of the world's nations, although still accounting for nearly 40 percent of African nations. As we already know, the decline of exclusive governing party regimes is even more striking. The democratic trend toward competitive party and electoral systems is also notable, with an increase from 36 to 41 percent of the world's political systems (and more experimenting with some competition). The proportion of military governments actually increases slightly, from 23 to 26 percent of the world's countries.

The trend toward democracy took off beginning in 1989 with the dramatic changes occurring in Eastern Europe, and new pressures for democracy in the developing world. The proportion of competitive regimes is now well over 50 percent, with decline in the proportions of all other forms. The majority of the remaining single-party systems are loosely corporatist, with a few exceptions such as China and Cuba. The decline of ideological underpinnings for authoritarian governments, as well as the withdrawal of support from the Soviet Union, has contributed to this trend, especially in Africa.

Many African nations moved toward a more democratic and free system during the 1990s. This trend has continued, as has a notable decline in formally military regimes. Larry Diamond classified about a third of the African states as electoral democracies at the end of 2001.[26] However, the bulk of African nations fall into one of the varieties of "elec-

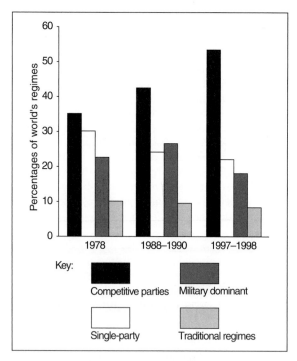

FIGURE 5.4   Change in Predominant Interest Aggregation Structure—Moving Toward Democracy in the World?

Source: Adapted from Raymond D. Gastil, *Freedom in the World 1979, 1988–1989, 1997–1998* (New York: Freedom House, 1979, 1989, 1998).

toral authoritarianism" discussed above, with severe constraints on civil freedom and electoral opposition. A few remain unabashed authoritarian systems or mired in deadly civil war (as in Sudan and Zaire).

Perhaps in deference to the decline in the legitimacy of authoritarianism, the military throughout the world is now more likely to dominate from behind the scenes than through direct rule. Latin America also has experienced the genuine replacement of military regimes by competitive party regimes in such important countries as Argentina, Brazil, Chile, and Uruguay. Although the era of confidence in the military as a solution to development seems to have passed, military domination remains a likely outcome when other types of government are unable to solve internal conflicts.

Where there has been "backsliding" on the road to democracy, such as the assaults on democratic competition by Peru's President Fujimori in the 1990s, or the overthrow of Pakistan's elected president by the army in 1999, the military has usually been at least part of the antidemocratic movement. With such examples in mind, we cannot assume that the democratizing trend will continue relentlessly. Multiparty regimes that seem unable to cope with economic and social problems often lose their legitimacy. Such is now the challenge facing the new competitive regimes of Eastern Europe and the former Soviet Union, as well as the Third World.

SIGNIFICANCE OF INTEREST AGGREGATION

How interests are aggregated is an important determinant of what a country's government does for and to its citizens. The factors that most interest us about government and politics—stability, revolution, participation, welfare, equality, liberty, security—are very much consequences of the pattern of interest aggregation.

One importance outcome of the aggregation process is the narrowing of policy options. Through interest aggregation, the desires and demands of citizens are converted into a few policy alternatives. The consequence is that many possible policies have been eliminated and only a few remain. In addition, this means that political resources have been accumulated in the hands of the relatively few political

actors who decide policy. The policy alternatives that reach this stage are serious matters for political consideration because they have the backing of significant sectors of society. For instance, a policy alternative such as the United States government taking over the steel production industry has never been "serious," because no group with major political resources has favored it, even though this policy has been implemented in other nations.

Narrowing and combining policy preferences are easily seen in the working of competitive party systems. Of the many possible policy preferences, only a few are promoted by parties after the parties choose leaders and establish election platforms. In the elections, voters support some of these parties and thus shape the strength of party representation in the legislature. Even at the legislative stage, some further consolidation and coalition building takes place between party factions or party groups. At some point, however, most policy options have been eliminated from consideration. Either they were never backed by parties or the parties supporting them did badly in the elections.

In noncompetitive party systems, military governments, and monarchies, aggregation works differently, but with the similar effect of narrowing policy options. It may be that on some issues, aggregation will virtually determine policy, as when a military government or a faction of an authoritarian party can decide the government's program. In other cases the legislative assembly, military council, or party politburo may contain several factions of similar strength that negotiate to determine policy outcomes. The narrowing of policy choices also implies that the influence and access of certain social interests are determined by the process of interest aggregation.

Another consequence of interest aggregation is that the pattern of polarization in the political culture often carries over to the policy making body. In a relatively consensual society like Germany, the parliament is made up of mainly moderate and tolerant parties. Thus the policy making style of the legislature tends to encourage cooperation and consensus building. In more conflictual Italy, the stalemated Parliament was long dominated by two parties very distant from each other—the Communists and the Christian Democrats. Thus, the workings of the government are often a reflection of the patterns of interests within the society.

But politics shapes its environment as well as reflecting it. Interest aggregation often alters the amount of polarization that the political culture projects into policymaking. That is one reason why politics is so fascinating. Well-organized and well-led political parties might, at least for a while, be able to dominate politics and limit the strength of extremist groups in the legislature, as in the accommodative model that we mentioned earlier. Conversely, well-organized extremists might be able to appeal to the fears and prejudices of some groups and get their support at the polls, thus gaining more legislative strength in an otherwise consensual country.

The ultimate implication of aggregation processes may be in the representativeness and adaptability of the government, and thus its stability. Authoritarian interest aggregation tends to create political power structures that do not reflect popular opinion. In a highly divided and conflict-ridden society, such unrepresentativeness may be proposed as a great virtue. Leaders of military coups often justify their overthrow of party governments by claiming to depolarize politics and rid the nation of conflict it cannot afford. Similarly, heads of authoritarian parties typically claim that their nation must concentrate all its energies and resources on common purposes and that party competition would be too polarizing.

In contrast, proponents of democratic interest aggregation argue that the best hope for mutual accommodation of conflicting social and political interests lies in free expression and participation in fair electoral competition, followed by negotiation using constitutional resources. Without such democratic aggregation, suppression of dissent leads to injustice and the frustration of the excluded, the corruption of the included, and eventually to violence and greater instability.

Democracy thus leads policy makers to act as the people wish. In a polarized political culture, the cost of interest aggregation that reflects division and uncertainty may be seen as a price to pay for citizen control. As the frequent instability in authoritarian and military governments indicates, however, it may be easier to do away with the appearance of polarization than the reality. Cultural divisions may end up being reflected through military factions or intraparty groups, instead of through party competition, and the citizens may end up without either freedom and participation or stability.

KEY TERMS

accommodative party systems

associational groups

authoritarian party systems

competitive party systems

conflictual party systems

consensual party systems

exclusive governing party

inclusive governing party

institutional groups

interest aggregation

majoritarian two-party systems

majority-coalition systems

military government

multiparty systems

patron-client network

plurality election rules

proportional representation

single-member districts

SUGGESTED READINGS

Converse, Philip E. and Roy Pierce. *Political Representation in France.* Cambridge, MA: Harvard University Press, 1986.

Cox, Gary. *Making Votes Count: Strategic Coordination in the World's Electoral Systems.* Cambridge: Cambridge University Press, 1997.

Dalton, Russell J. and Martin P. Wattenberg. *Parties Without Partisans: Political Change in Advanced Industrial Democracies.* New York: Oxford University Press, 2000.

Downs, Anthony. *An Economic Theory of Democracy.* New York: Harper and Row, 1957.

Farrell, David. *Electoral Systems: A Comparative Introduction.* New York: St. Martin's Press, 2001.

Farrell, David, Ian Holliday, and Paul Webb, eds. *Political Parties in Democratic States,* Oxford: Oxford University Press, 2002.

Gallagher, Michael, Michael Laver, and Peter Mair. *Representative Government in Modern Europe,* 3rd ed. New York: McGraw-Hill, 1995.

Jackson, Robert H. and Carl G. Rosberg. *Personal Rule in Black Africa.* Berkeley: University of California Press, 1982.

Kitschelt, Herbert. *The Transformation of European Social Democracy.* New York: Cambridge University Press, 1994.

Klingemann, Hans-Dieter, Richard Hofferbert, and Ian Budge. *Parties, Policy and Democracy.* Boulder, CO: Westview Press, 1994.

Laver, Michael and Norman Schofield. *Multiparty Government.* New York: Oxford University Press, 1990.

Lijphart, Arend. *Electoral Systems and Party Systems.* New York: Oxford University Press, 1994.

———. *Patterns of Democracy.* New Haven, CT: Yale University Press, 1999.

Linz, Juan J. *Totalitarian and Authoritarian Regimes.* Baltimore, MD: Johns Hopkins University Press, 2002.

——— and Alfred Stepan, eds. *The Breakdown of Democratic Regimes.* Baltimore, MD: Johns Hopkins University Press, 1978.

Mainwaring, Scott. *Rethinking Party Systems in the Third Wave of Democratization.* Stanford: Stanford University Press, 1999.

Nordlinger, Eric A. *Soldiers in Politics: Military Coups and Governments.* Englewood Cliffs, NJ: Prentice-Hall, 1976.

O'Donnell, Guillermo, Philippe C. Schmitter, and Laurence Whitehead. *Transitions from Authoritarian Rule: Prospects for Democracy.* Baltimore, MD: Johns Hopkins University Press, 1986.

Powell, G. Bingham, Jr. *Contemporary Democracies: Participation, Stability and Violence.* Cambridge, MA: Harvard University Press, 1982.

———. *Elections as Instruments of Democracy.* New Haven, CT: Yale University Press, 2000.

Riker, William H. *Liberalism Against Populism.* San Francisco, CA: W. H. Freeman, 1982.

Sartori, Giovanni. *Parties and Party Systems.* Cambridge, England: Cambridge University Press, 1976.

Ware, Alan. *Citizens, Parties, and the State.* Princeton, NJ: Princeton University Press, 1988.

ENDNOTES

1. Luis Roniger and Ayse Gunes-Ayata, eds., *Democracy, Clientelism, and Civil Society* (Boulder, CO: Lynne Rienner, 1994); S. Eisenstadt and L. Roniger, *Patrons, Clients and Friends* (Cambridge, England: Cambridge University Press, 1984); Lucian W. Pye, *Asian Power and Politics* (Cambridge, MA: Harvard University Press, 1985); Martin Shefter, "Patronage and Its Opponents," in *Political Parties and the State* (Princeton, NJ: Princeton University Press, 1994); see also the studies of the personal networks of leaders in the politics of the former Soviet Union, such as T. H. Rigby and Rokdan Harasimin, *Leadership Selection and Patron Client Relations in the USSR and Yugoslavia* (Beverly Hills, CA: Sage, 1981).

2. William Thompson, *The Grievances of Military Coup-Makers* (Beverly Hills, CA: Sage, 1973).

3. The extensive literature on party strategies owes its largest debt to Anthony Downs, *An Economic Theory of Democracy* (New York: Harper and Row, 1957). More generally, see Dennis C. Mueller, *Public Choice II* (Cambridge, England: Cambridge University Press, 1989) and Gary Cox, *Making Votes Count* (New York: Cambridge University Press, 1997.)

4. Russell J. Dalton, Scott C. Flanagan, and Paul Allen Beck, eds., *Electoral Change in Advanced Industrial Societies* (Princeton, NJ: Princeton University Press, 1984); Mark Franklin et al., *Electoral Change* (Cambridge, England: Cambridge University Press, 1992); Herbert Kitschelt, *The Transformation of European Social Democracy* (New York: Cambridge University Press, 1994); Wolfgang C. Mueller and Kaare Strom, *Policy, Office or Votes? How Political Parties in Western Europe Make Hard Decisions* (New York: Cambridge University Press, 1999).

5. Maurice Duverger, *Political Parties: Their Organization and Activity in the Modern State*, [1954] trans. Barbara and Robert North (New York: Wiley, 1963). For more recent discussions of electoral systems and consequences, see Rein Taagepera and Matthew Shugart, *Seats and Votes* (New Haven, CT: Yale University Press, 1989); Cox, *Making Votes Count;* and the references in Note 11 below.

6. Ian Budge, David Robertson, and Derek Hearl, *Ideology, Strategy and Party Change: Spatial Analyses of Post-War Election Programmes in 19 Democracies* (New York: Cambridge University Press, 1987); Richard Katz and Peter Mair, eds., *How Parties Organize: Change and Adaptation in Party Organizations in Western Democracies* (Thousand Oaks: Sage Publications, 1994).

7. Despite their virtues, elections cannot solve perfectly all the complex problems in fairly aggregating interests. For example, giving each citizen one vote does not take account of the varying intensities with which different people may hold their opinions. Moreover, a very large literature in economics and political science has demonstrated various problems, notably that for some distributions of preferences about three or more alternatives, there is no fair rule for aggregating the votes to select a single, unequivocally best, outcome ("Arrow's Paradox"). Important original works in this literature were Duncan Black, "On the Rationale of Group Decision Making," *Journal of Political Economy* 56 (1948) 23–34; and Kenneth Arrow, *Social Choice and Individual Values* (New Haven, CT: Yale University Press, 1951). For an accessible, although controversial, discussion of some implications for political science, see William H. Riker, *Liberalism Against Populism* (San Francisco: W. H. Freeman, 1982). More recently, see Kenneth A. Shepsle and Mark S. Bonchek, *Analyzing Politics: Rationality, Behavior and Institutions* (New York: W. W. Norton, 1997), Part II.

8. Richard Topf, "Electoral Participation," in H. Klingemann and D. Fuchs, eds., *Citizens and the State* (Oxford, England: Oxford University Press, 1995); Mark Franklin, "Electoral Participation," in Lawrence LeDuc, Richard Niemi, and Pippa Norris, eds, *Comparing Democracies 2: Elections and Voting in Global Perspective* (Beverly Hills: Sage Publications, 2002), pp. 216–35.

9. However, the initiation of semi-competitive elections for Chinese village leadership positions since 1987 has in some areas had significant impact on the correspondence of opinions between citizens and local leaders. See Melanie Manion, "The Electoral Connection in the Chinese Countryside," *American Political Science Review* 90 (1996): 736–48.

10. Russell J. Dalton, *Citizen Politics: Public Opinion and Political Parties in Advanced Industrial Democracies*, 3rd ed. (Chatham, NJ: Chatham House, 2002; Philip E. Converse

and Roy Pierce, *Representation in France* (Cambridge, MA: Harvard University Press, 1986); Michael Lewis-Beck, *Economics and Elections: The Major Western Democracies* (Ann Arbor: University of Michigan Press, 1988).

11. For analyses of the implications of election laws for party representation and government majorities, see Douglas Rae, *The Political Consequences of Election Laws* (New Haven, CT: Yale University Press, 1967); Taagepera and Shugart, *Seats and Votes*, 1989; Arend Lijphart, *Electoral Systems and Party Systems: A Study of Twenty-seven Democracies, 1945–1990* (Oxford, England: Oxford University Press, 1994).

12. Hans-Dieter Klingemann, Richard Hofferbert, and Ian Budge, *Parties, Policy and Democracy* (Boulder, CO: Westview, 1995); Gallagher, Michael, Michael Laver, and Peter Mair, *Representative Government in Western Europe*, 2nd ed. New York: McGraw-Hill, 1995, Ch. 13. See also Richard Rose, *Do Parties Make a Difference?* (Chatham, NJ: Chatham House, 1984), ch. 5.

13. The literature on coalitions, their formation and durability, has now become very large. See especially Michael Laver and Norman Schofield, *Multiparty Government: The Politics of Coalition in Europe* (New York: Oxford University Press 1990); and Wolfgang C. Mueller and Kaare Strom, *Coalition Governments in Western Europe* (New York: Oxford University Press, 2000).

14. Generally, see G. Bingham Powell, Jr., *Elections as Instruments of Democracy* (New Haven, CT: Yale University Press, 2000), Chs. 3, 4.

15. On elections and the representation of votes and preferences, as well as the trade-off with accountability, see Powell, *Elections as Instruments of Democracy*, Chs. 5–10.

16. This classification is adapted from Arend Lijphart, *Democracy in Plural Societies* (New Haven, CT: Yale University Press, 1977); and Arend Lijphart, *Patterns of Democracy* (New Haven, CT: Yale University Press, 1999).

17. Lijphart, *Democracy in Plural Societies*.

18. There is a burgeoning literature on the new party systems of Eastern and Central Europe; see especially Herbert Kitschelt, Zdenka Mansfeldova, and Radoslaw Markowski, *Post-Communist Party Systems: Competition, Representation and Inter-party Cooperation* (Cambridge, England: Cambridge University Press, 1999).

19. See Lijphart, *Patterns of Democracy*, 1999; G. Bingham Powell, Jr., *Contemporary Democracies* (Cambridge, MA: Harvard University Press, 1982), chs. 8 and 10; and Juan J. Linz and Alfred Stepan, eds., *The Breakdown of Democratic Regimes* (Baltimore, MD: Johns Hopkins University Press, 1978).

20. Juan Linz, *Totalitarian and Authoritarian Regimes* (Boulder, CO: Lynne Rienner, 2000; Amos Perlmutter, *Modern Authoritarianism: A Comparative Institutional Analysis* (New Haven, CT: Yale University Press, 1981), especially pp. 62–114.

21. See Melanie Manion, "Politics in China", Chapter 13 below; for the earlier period, see, for example, Franz Schurman, *Ideology and Organization in Communist China* (Berkeley: University of California Press, 1966).

22. On the efforts in Africa, see Crawford Young, *Ideology and Development in Africa* (New Haven, CT: Yale University Press, 1982), ch. 2.

23. Juan Linz calls these "sultanistic" regimes, see *Authoritarian and Totalitarian Regimes* 2000, 151–157; Houchang Chehabi and Juan Linz, eds, *Sultanistic Regimes* (Baltimore: Johns Hopkins, 1998; and Robert H. Jackson and Carl G. Rosberg, *Personal Rule in Black Africa* (Berkeley: University of California Press, 1982).

24. Larry Diamond, "Thinking About Hybrid Regimes," *Journal of Democracy* 13 (2002): 26. In general see the articles by Diamond; Andreas Schedler; Steven Levitsky and Lucian Way; and Nicolas van der Valle in a section of this issue of *Journal of Democracy* devoted to "Elections without Democracy," pp. 21–80.

25. See the references in notes 22–24

26. Diamond, "Thinking About Hybrid Regimes," 30–31.

6

Government and Policymaking

Policymaking is the pivotal stage in the political process, the point at which bills become law, or edicts are issued by the rulers. Later, policies are implemented and enforced. To understand public policy, we must know how decisions are made. Where is power effectively located in different political systems? What does it take to change public policy: a simple majority vote in the legislature or approval also by an independently elected executive? Or is it a decree issued by the monarch, a signed agreement by military commanders, or a decision by the party central committee? Or is it merely the whim of the personal dictator?

This chapter focuses on decision rules and on the policymaking role of government agencies such as legislatures, chief executives, bureaucracies, and courts. Government agencies are at the core of policymaking. While parties, interest groups, and other actors may be very active in articulating and aggregating interests, government officials, legislators, and their staffs do most of the actual initiation and formulation of policy proposals. Interest group demands for tax relief or for the protection of endangered species cannot succeed unless they are transformed into law or policy by government officials according to some accepted decision rules. They cannot be effective until these policies are appropriately implemented by other officials. Yet, government action does not flow in one direction only. The interaction between government and citizens is a two-way process, including an upward flow of influence and demands from the society, as well as a downward flow of decisions from the government.

CONSTITUTIONS AND DECISION RULES

A constitution is the basic rules concerning decision making, rights, and the distribution of authority in a political system. We sometimes use this word to refer to a specific document laying out such principles—for example, the one adopted by the founding fathers of the United States in 1787. But a constitution need not be embodied in a single document and in fact rarely is. We should therefore think of a constitution as a set of rules and principles, whether it is a specific written document, a set of customs or practices, or, as is usually the case, both. Even a military or other dictatorship typically attempts to have set procedures for having decrees proposed, considered, and adopted. Written, or codified, constitutions are particularly important in political systems based on the *rule of law*. This means that government can take no action that has not been authorized by law and that citizens can be punished only for actions that violate an existing law. Under a codified constitution, the constitution is the supreme body of laws.

A constitution contains a set of **decision rules**—the basic rules governing how decisions are made, setting up agencies and offices with specific powers, assigning them territorial and functional jurisdiction, and the like. All governments have decision rules. Decision rules may be simple or complex, and any given political system may have many such rules, or a smaller repertoire of rules that they use in many different circumstances. For example, the U.S. Congress has many different decision rules that apply under different circumstances, such as a simple majority in each house to pass a bill initially, but a two-thirds majority to override a presidential veto. The British House of Commons uses a much smaller set of rules (mainly simple majority rule). Decision rules may be more or less formal and precise. Most legislatures have formal and precise decision rules, whereas cabinets at the head of the executive branch often have informal and flexible rules.

Perhaps the most important rules that constitutions establish are those that govern the policymaking process. Policymaking is the conversion of social interests and demands into authoritative public decisions. Constitutions establish the rules by which this happens. They confer the power to propose policies on specific groups or institutions, and they give others the right to amend, reject, or approve such proposals, or to implement, police, or adjudicate them. The branches of government in modern democracies are largely known by the formal functions they play in this policy process. The legislative branch makes public policies; the executive branch implements and executes them; and the judicial branch adjudicates disputes that arise from them. In reality, however, the functions that different branches of government play are not so easily identified and distinguished from one another. For example, the executive branch is often accountable for most of the policy formulation and initiation (especially in parliamentary democracies), even though officially this function belongs to the legislature.

Knowing what policymaking function a political institution (such as a legislature) plays, however, may still leave us with a very rudimentary understanding of how policies get made. We also need to know how decisions are made within that institution. Within any given branch of government or other political institution, there are numerous rules that affect the policymaking process. The most important of these may be voting rules. In most modern legislative chambers, and in many courts, voting rules are *egalitarian*, which is to say that each member has the same voting power (though presiding officers, such as the Speaker of the British House of Commons, may have the power to break a tie vote). Simply speaking: one person, one vote. That is hardly ever true in government departments (ministries), however. There, decision making is *hierarchical*, and everybody is supposed to defer to his or her superior. In a pure hierarchy, only the vote of a person at the very top (for example, the minister) counts.

When decisions are made through voting, rules are still needed to determine the outcome. Many institutions operate through simple majority voting, which means that in a choice between two options, whichever option gets the larger number of votes wins. An absolute majority means that a winning proposal (for example, a legislative bill) must have the support of a majority of those eligible to vote, including those that might choose to abstain. Qualified majorities of three-fifths, two-thirds, or even three-fourths, are sometimes required for particularly consequential decisions. For example, the U.S. Constitution requires two-thirds majorities in both houses of Congress in order to amend the constitution or override a presidential veto. The most extreme voting rule is unanimity, which means that any one member can block any decision. Different voting rules have different attractions. Qualified majority rules, requiring over 50 percent, can protect against hasty decisions, or against decisions that disadvantage large proportions (perhaps close to half) of the voters. On the other hand, qualified majority rules can give a small minority the power to block proposals favored by a large majority, and the more restrictive voting rules are (as the percentage to approve approaches unanimity,) the less likely it is that any decision can be made at all.

Decision rules affect political activity because they determine what political resources to seek and how to acquire and use them. Individuals and groups seeking to influence policy have to operate within the framework of these rules. In a federal and decentralized system such as the United States, a pressure group may have to approach both the legislative and the executive branch, and it may have to be active both at the state and the federal level. If instead decisions are made by decree from the commander of the armed forces or the central committee of a single party state, groups will need to influence these crucial policymakers.

It is important that decision rules be transparent and stable. If they are not, citizens will not know what to expect from government. That may in turn cause them to be less trusting and less willing to invest or make other commitments. It may also lead to serious conflicts, and ultimately government may break down and issues be decided by force. The importance of having predictable decision rules was suggested by Thomas Jefferson in his introduction to the first Manual of the House of Representatives: "A bad set of rules is better than no rules at all."

Making Constitutions

Constitution making is a fundamental political act: It creates or transforms decision rules. Most of the constitutions that are in force today were formed as the result of some break, often violent, with the past—war, revolution, or rebellion against colonial rule. New decision rules have to accommodate new internal or external powers. Thus, the defeated powers and the successor states of World Wars I and II all adopted new constitutions or had new constitutions imposed on them. Britain is unusual in having not a formal written constitution but only a long-accepted and highly developed set of customs and conventions, buttressed by important ordinary statutes. This reflects the British record of gradual, incremental, and, on the whole, peaceful political change. Nevertheless, the major changes in British decision rules, such as the shift of power from the Crown to Parliament in the seventeenth century, and the Reform Acts of 1832 and 1867, which established party and cabinet government and vastly extended the right to vote, followed on periods of civil war or unrest.

Perhaps the greatest exception to the association between disruptive upheavals and constitution creation is the peaceful development over the last 40 years of the constitution of the European Union, whose growing powers are altering the decision rules affecting almost 400 million Europeans in 15 countries. But while there has been no violence associated with the formation and growth of the European Union, its origins lie in the bitter lessons of World Wars I and II.

The decades since World War II have seen much constitutional experimentation. Not only the defeated powers, but many new states, such as India and Nigeria, that achieved independence with the break up of colonial empires of Britain, France, and Portugal, introduced new political arrangements. Some of the new states in the developing areas, such as Nigeria, have subsequently changed their form of government several times. France has had two constitutions in this period, the second of which—the Fifth Republic of 1958—appears more stable than previous French constitutions. In the last two decades the worldwide trend toward democracy, the end of the Cold War, and the dissolution of the Soviet Union have precipitated a new round of constitutional design. The recent constitutional crafting in Eastern Europe, Russia, and the other Soviet successor states as well as in South Africa and elsewhere, have reignited old polemics about the virtues and faults of different constitutional arrangements, or about the very wisdom of constitutional engineering.[1]

DEMOCRACY AND AUTHORITARIANISM

The most important distinction in policymaking functions is between democratic and authoritarian systems. **Democracy** means "government by the people." In small political systems, such as local communities, "the people" may be able to share directly in debating, deciding, and implementing public policy. In large political systems, such as contemporary states, democracy must be achieved largely through indirect participation in policymaking. Policymaking power is delegated to officials chosen by the people. Elections, competitive political parties, free mass media, and representative assemblies are political structures that make some degree of democracy, some "government by the people," possible in large political systems. Such indirect democracy is not complete or ideal. Moreover, the democratic opportunities in less economically developed societies are often meaningful to educated elites or to those living near the centers of government, but less relevant to the average citizen in the countryside. But the more citizens are involved and the more influential their choices, the more democratic the system.

In democratic systems, competitive elections give citizens the chance to shape policy through their selection and rejection of key policymakers. In large societies, competitive elections with full adult suffrage are a necessary condition for meaningful "government by the people." In **authoritarian regimes,** on the other hand, the policymakers are chosen by military councils, hereditary families, dominant political parties, and the like. Citizens are either ignored or pressed into symbolic assent to the government's choices.

Transitions toward democracy have been a major feature of world politics in the last 25 years, beginning in Southern Europe, extending to Latin America and Asia, and more recently to Eastern Europe and the former Soviet Union. This movement toward democracy is a "Third Wave" of worldwide democratization.[2] Both of the previous waves have been followed by reversals, though the overall number of democracies has grown over time. The first wave began in the nineteenth century and culminated with the establishment of many new democracies after the Allied victory in World War I. After World War II, a second democratic wave included many newly independent ex-colonial states, as well as the defeated authoritarian powers. Since about 1975, a third wave has undermined the legitimacy of authoritarian regimes everywhere, especially since the collapse of the Soviet Union in 1991. But note the case of Nigeria, where attempts to establish civilian and democratic regimes have fallen twice to military coups (1966 and 1983), and where a transition toward democracy was again aborted by the military in 1993 before being restored in 1999. Nigeria is not unique. It can be difficult to consolidate stable democratic regimes, especially in poor societies.[3] Today's Third Wave of democratization may well experience many reversals. In such systems as China and Egypt democracy has not yet taken hold.

SEPARATION OF GOVERNMENT POWERS

The basic decision rules of democratic political systems differ along three important dimensions: (1) the separation of powers between different branches of government; (2) the geographic distribution of authority between the central (national) government and lower levels, such as states, provinces, or municipalities; and (3) limitations on government authority. We shall discuss these dimensions in order, beginning with the separation of authority between executive and legislative institutions.

The theory of **separation of powers** has a long and venerable history going back at least to the work of Locke and Montesquieu.[4] Separation of power, they argued, has the virtue of preventing the injustices that might result from an unchecked executive or legislature. Madison and Hamilton elaborated this theory in *The Federalist*,[5] which described and defended the institutional arrangements proposed by the U.S. Constitutional Convention of 1787. Political theorists in the course of the nineteenth and first part of the twentieth centuries reflecting on the two successful historical cases of representative democracy—Britain

and the United States—gradually codified what we may call the "classic" separation of powers theory that dominated the political science of the pre–World War II period. This theory argued that there are essentially two forms of representative democratic government—the presidential and the parliamentary.

The **democratic presidential regime** provides two separate agencies of government—the executive and the legislative—separately elected and authorized by the people. Each branch is elected for a fixed term; no one branch can by ordinary means unseat the other; and each has specific powers under the constitution. Ultimate power to authorize legislation and approve budgets in modern democracies resides with the legislature, whose relationships with the executive are then critical for concentration or dispersal of power. Different presidential regimes provide their presidents with a variety of different powers over government appointments and policymaking, such as the authority to veto legislation or to make policy by executive decree under some conditions.[6] In a country such as the United States, both legislature and executive (Congress and the Presidency) have large and significant roles in policymaking. In some other democratic presidential systems, such as Brazil, the president may have such a variety of constitutional powers, including the power to make laws through "emergency" decrees, that he or she can reduce the role of the legislature. But coordination between the separate institutions of executive and legislature must somehow be achieved to make policy.

The **parliamentary regimes,** on the other hand, make the executive and legislative branches interdependent. First of all, only the legislative branch is directly elected, whereas the prime minister and his or her cabinet (the collective leadership of the executive branch) emerge from the legislature. The cabinet is chaired by the prime minister who is the head of government and selects the other cabinet members.[7] Typically, neither branch has a fixed term of office. The cabinet can be voted out of office at any time, and most often this is true of the legislature (the parliament) as well.

The critical feature that makes this possible is the **confidence relationship** between the prime minister and the parliamentary majority. (See Box 6.1.) In a parliamentary system, the prime minister and his or her cabinet must at all times enjoy the confidence of the parliamentary majority. Whenever the

BOX 6.1   The Confidence Vote in Parliamentary Democracies

Prime ministers in parliamentary democracies lead precarious political lives. Unlike presidents in presidential systems, prime ministers can be voted out of office at any time, and for any reason, by a parliamentary majority. There are two ways in which this can happen. One is when parliament passes a motion expressing a lack of confidence in the prime minister—a no-confidence motion. The other possibility is when parliament defeats a motion expressing confidence in the prime minister—a confidence motion. No-confidence motions are typically introduced by the parliamentary opposition in the hope of bringing down the prime minister. Confidence motions, on the other hand, are normally introduced by prime ministers themselves, and it is not at all self-evident why they would do so. Since one possible result of a confidence motion is being kicked out of office, it may seem like a form of Russian roulette.

In reality, however, the confidence vote can be a powerful weapon in the hands of the prime minister. It is typically attached to a bill (a policy proposal) that is favored by the prime minister but not by the parliamentary majority. By attaching a confidence motion to the bill, the prime minister forces the members of parliament to choose between the bill and the fall of the cabinet. This can be a particularly painful choice for dissident members of the prime minister's own party. If they vote for the bill, they may bring down their own government, and perhaps immediately have to face the voters to boot. British prime ministers have often resorted to the confidence motion in order to bring rebellious party members into line. In 1993, Conservative Prime Minister John Major faced a parliamentary crisis over the ratification of the Maastricht Treaty, which expanded the powers of the European Union. Major had only a slim majority in the House of Commons, and many "Euro-skeptics" in his own party were opposed to the Maastricht Treaty. About 20 of these Conservative dissidents voted with the opposition and helped defeat the Maastricht Treaty in the House of Commons. Immediately after this embarrassing defeat, however, Major introduced a confidence motion on his Maastricht policy and announced that if he lost this vote, he would dissolve the House of Commons and hold new elections. Many of the Conservative dissidents feared that their party would do poorly in such an election and that they might personally lose their seats. Major's confidence motion passed by a vote of 339 to 299, and the House of Commons approved the Maastricht Treaty. Thus, the confidence vote actually helps explain why party discipline tends to be stronger in parliamentary than in presidential systems.

---

parliamentary majority for whatever reason expresses its lack of confidence (through a no-confidence vote), the prime minister and all the other cabinet members have to resign. On the other hand, the prime minister typically has the power to dissolve parliament and call new elections at any time. These two powers, the parliamentary majority's dismissal power and the prime minister's dissolution power, make the two branches mutually dependent. It induces agreement between them by forcing the executive branch to be acceptable to the parliamentary majority. Thus parliamentary democracies do not experience the form of divided government that is common under presidentialism, when the party that controls the presidency does not control the legislature, or vice versa. Instead, the chief executive (prime minister and cabinet) becomes the agent of the parliamentary majority, and in most parliamentary systems consists largely of members of parliament. Conflicts between parliament and the executive are less likely to occur, and decision making tends to be more efficient than under presidentialism. Since the same party (or parties) controls both branches of government, the cabinet tends to dominate policymaking, and the legislature may be less influential than under a presidential constitution.

Not all democracies fit neatly into the presidential or parliamentary category. Some, such as France, are often characterized as mixed or **"semi-presidential."** In some of these mixed types, the president and the legislature are separately elected (as in presidential systems), but the president then has the power to dissolve the legislature (as in parliamentary systems). In such systems, the cabinet may be appointed by the president (as under presidentialism), but subject to dismissal by the legislature (as under parliamentarism). Shugart and Carey identify several kinds of mixed systems with independently elected presidents who have substantial policymaking power but must share control over the executive branch with the legislature. A variety of arrangements exist for such shared control; their consequences are often sharply affected by which party or coalition controls the presidency and legislature. Many of the new constitutions of the emergent democracies of Eastern Europe and Asia are of this mixed type.

Reading across Figure 6.1, we see political systems classified by the separation of policymaking powers between executive and legislative institutions, from concentrated to dispersed. The vertical dimension of the table shows geographic division of power, which is discussed in the next section. In authoritarian governments on the left, executive, legislative, and judicial power are typically concentrated. Two of the twelve countries discussed in this book—China and Egypt—have authoritarian governments not chosen in competitive elections. Britain, Germany, Japan, and India are parliamentary systems in which executive and legislative powers are concentrated in cabinets responsible to the popularly elected lower houses of parliament. At the extreme right of Figure 6.1 are pure presidential systems such as Brazil, Mexico, and the United States. Nigeria seems to be in transition to a presidential democracy. In between, we find mixed systems such as France and Russia.

In the debate over the best system of representative democracy, many political theorists traditionally favored the British-style parliamentary system. This version of parliamentarism, coupling plurality voting rules that usually create clear single party majorities in Parliament with a Cabinet and prime minister responsible to Parliament, can result in fairly stable governments responsible to the public will. Parliamentarism coupled with proportional representation—as in Germany and France between the two world wars—seemed more crisis prone. Such crises occurred because of the emergence of large extremist political parties, which resulted in cabinet instability and even breakdown. On the other hand, the Scandinavian countries demonstrated that parliamentary systems with proportional representation can be quite stable when ideological conflict between the political parties remains moderate, whereas dominating parliamentary majorities, as in Northern Ireland, can sometimes threaten minority groups and intensify conflict.[8] In comparison to both versions of parliamentary government, the U.S. presidential system has often been criticized for periodically producing divided government, which could result in stalemate or "gridlock."

The Third Wave of democratization has reopened these parliamentary-presidential debates. Advocates of parliamentarism, particularly of the pro-

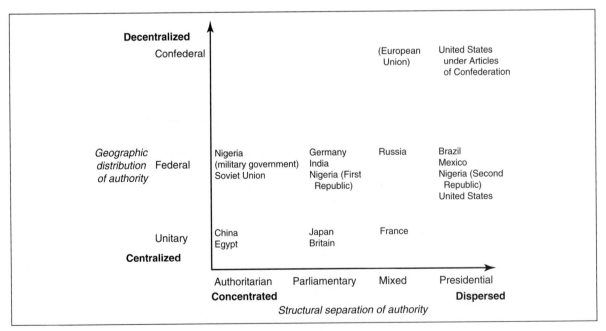

FIGURE 6 . 1   Division of Governmental Authority

portional variety, argue that it provides a consensual framework in which different economic, ethnic and religious groups can find representation and negotiate their differences. Parliamentary systems also have the flexibility to change governments between elections if the people disapprove of actions of the executive. Since many of the current transitional democracies are deeply divided, a parliamentary, proportional representation system may be particularly suitable. Presidentialism, they argue, is more susceptible to social conflict and democratic breakdown.[9] Under conditions of divided government, a confrontation between the two legitimately elected institutions representing the people can tear a political system apart. Or, a strong president can use executive powers to repress competition. Other scholars point out that while many scholars prefer the parliamentary solution, practical politics is coming out on the side of elected presidents with some political power.[10] Even in the domain of the former British empire (such as in Nigeria) and in most of Eastern Europe and the Soviet successor states, the constitutions provide for powerful presidents. Latin America has been dominated by presidential regimes for more than a century, and a 1993 referendum in Brazil reaffirmed its commitment to presidentialism. Presidentialism also offers the citizens a more direct choice of chief executive, and it puts more effective checks on the power of the majority in the legislature.

The relationships between executives and legislatures are not the only important non-geographic choices about dividing or sharing policymaking powers. In some smaller European democracies—such as Austria or Sweden—we find a form of "corporatist" democracy.[11] These are arrangements where the "class struggle" between workers and management, so threatening to democratic stability, could be abated by a social partnership. Through deliberation and bargaining over wages, benefits, prices, and social policy, top leaders from labor, management, and government would attempt to set economic policy (see Chapter 4). Thus often severe and disruptive conflicts could become technical rather than ideological questions, resolvable by deliberation and compromise.

A major trend in the division of policymaking powers in recent years has been the growth of **independent central banks.** Central banks, such as the Federal Reserve in the United States, have the critical task of regulating the supply of money and the interest rates, as well as many financial transactions for government and society. In most countries such bank policy was long controlled by the chief executive as part of the government bureaucracy. But in the last twenty years, and especially since the early 1990s, many countries have given their central banks substantial independence and set for them the primary task of using monetary policy to maintain price stability and limit inflation. Their independence from the executive is encouraged by giving bank governors long terms of office free from the possibility of dismissal, as well as stipulated policy objectives and responsibilities.[12] Such independence reassures investors, domestic and foreign, and seems to constrain inflation, but it limits the economic policy alternatives of the chief executive and cabinet.

GEOGRAPHIC DISTRIBUTION OF GOVERNMENT POWER

According to the geographic division of power, we have confederal systems at one extreme, unitary systems at the other extreme, and **federal systems** in the middle. (See the vertical dimension of Figure 6.1.) The United States under the Articles of Confederation was confederal. Ultimate power rested with the states. The central government had authority over foreign affairs and defense but depended on financial and other support from the states. Under the Constitution of 1787, the American government changed from confederal to federal, which is to say that both central and state governments had separate spheres of authority and the means to implement their power. Today, the United States, Germany, Russia, India, Nigeria, Mexico, and Brazil are federal systems in which central and local units each have autonomy in particular spheres of public policy. These policy areas and powers are, however, divided among central and local units in varying ways. Britain, France, China, Japan, and Egypt are unitary systems with power and authority concentrated in the central government. Regional and local units have only those powers specifically delegated to them by the central government, which may change or withdraw these powers at will.

Most of the world's states are unitary. In fact, only 18 states are federal, or fewer than one in ten. But whereas the federal states are relatively few in number, they tend to be large and politically important. Thus, federal states account for more than one-third of the world's population and 41 percent of its land area. Generally speaking, the larger and the more diverse a state is, the more likely it is to be federal. Federalism is commonly thought to have a number of advantages. In multinational or otherwise divided societies, it may help protect ethnic, linguistic, or religious minorities, particularly if they are geographically concentrated. It may generally serve as a check on overly ambitious rulers and thus protect markets and citizen freedoms. Moreover, federalism may allow subunits (such as states) to experiment with different policy programs. Governments may thus learn from the experiences of others. In addition, citizens may be free to "vote with their feet" and choose the policy environment that best fits their preferences. However, while federalism promotes choice and diversity, it does so at the expense of equality. Since federalism allows local governments to pursue different policies, the implication is that citizens may get systematically different treatments and benefits from different local governments. Unitary governments may also be in a better position to redistribute resources from richer regions to poorer regions, if that is desirable.

In comparing confederal, federal, and unitary systems, however, we must keep in mind the distinction between formal and actual distribution of power. In unitary systems, in spite of the formal concentration of authority at the center, regional and local units may acquire power that the central government rarely challenges. In the American federal system over the last century, power has steadily moved from the states toward the center. In recent years there has been an effort, under the slogan of a new federalism, to move power from the federal government back to the states. Even in unitary systems there have been efforts to shift some power to provincial and local governments. This has been a response to democratic pressures, demands for greater grassroots influence. Thus, the real differences between federal and unitary systems may be considerably less significant than their formal arrangements suggest. Mexico is an example of the discrepancy between formal and actual federalism. Until recently the Partido Revolucionario Institucional (PRI) had centralized control in this formally federal system. Recent developments in Mexico, with oppositional parties winning ground in some states and the PRI power monopoly under challenge, have produced some "real" federalism to go along with the formalities.

LIMITATIONS ON GOVERNMENT POWER

Unlike authoritarian regimes, democracies are characterized by some legal or customary limitation on the exercise of power. Systems in which the powers of various government units are defined and limited by a written constitution, statutes, and custom are called **constitutional regimes.** Civil rights—such as the right to a fair trial and freedom to speak, petition, publish, and assemble—are protected against government interference except under specified circumstances.

The courts are crucial to the limitations on governmental power. As illustrated in Table 6.1, governments may be divided into those, at one extreme, in which the power to coerce citizens is relatively unlimited by the courts, and those, at the other extreme, in which the courts not only protect the rights of citizens but also police other parts of the government to see that their powers are properly exercised. The United States and India are examples of systems in which high courts rule effectively on challenges that other parts of the government have exceeded the powers allocated by the constitution. This practice of **judicial review** is authorized to various degrees in about half of the world's democracies and seems to be growing in popularity. But judicial review is often weakened by lack of independence of the appointment or tenure of judges, as in Japan, or by their ineffectiveness in overcoming executive power. Some other constitutional regimes have inde-

T A B L E 6 . 1   Judicial Limitation of Governmental Authority

Unlimited		Limited
Nonindependent Courts	Independent Courts	Judicial Review
China	Britain	United States
Egypt	Finland	India
Nigeria		Germany
		France
		Japan
		Russia

pendent courts that protect persons against the improper implementation of laws and regulations, but cannot legally overrule the assembly or the political executive, as in Britain. The substantive rights of persons in these systems are protected by statute, custom, self-restraint, and political pressure—which are also essential to the effectiveness of courts even where judicial review is authorized. In authoritarian systems policymakers do not usually allow courts to constrain their use and abuse of power, even where brave judges attempt to rule against them.

Arend Lijphart characterizes only four of the 36 democratic systems he examines as having "strong" judicial review: Germany, India, the United States, and Canada after 1982.[13] The Supreme Court of India has been singled out as most similar to the United States Supreme Court, having successfully overruled the Prime Minister and assembly by declaring over 100 national laws and ordinances unconstitutional.[14] The German Constitutional Court has also had a substantial impact on national and state policymaking, both through its rulings and through government's anticipation of those rulings. About a quarter of Lijphart's democracies had either strong or medium strength judicial review. In both France and Germany new legislation may be challenged in court by opposition members of parliament even before it takes effect, a process called "abstract" judicial review. Lijphart classified a little over half of his democracies as having "weak judicial review," with the powers of courts constrained by very limited constitutional authority, as in Sweden, or limited independence of government-appointed judges, as in Japan. In the remaining democracies, including Britain, courts enjoyed no power of judicial review of legislation, although, as suggested in Table 6.1, they may still protect individuals from government abuse not specifically authorized by law.

In many of the new democracies of Eastern Europe judicial review was proclaimed in the constitution, but proved harder to implement in practice. There have been striking successes in constraining governments in some countries, as in Bulgaria, but failures in others, such as Albania and Belarus. In Nigeria the courts long retained a striking degree of judicial independence under a succession of otherwise undemocratic military regimes, but were shown little respect under the Abacha regime of the mid-1990s, which established special military tri-

bunals to prosecute its perceived enemies. Similarly, the president has used military and security courts, as well as executive decrees and a long-standing State of Emergency to limit efforts by courts to exert judicial independence in Egypt. China, on the other hand, after explicit rejection of any limits on "mass justice" from the late-1950s to 1970s, has gradually attempted to introduce a very limited "rule by law," as a way of encouraging stability and economic growth and controlling corruption. But the practice falls far short of the promise of even partial limitation on governmental authority.

All written constitutions provide for amending procedures. Most framers of constitutions have recognized that basic decision rules must be adaptable, because of potential ambiguities, inefficiencies, changes in citizen values, or unforeseen circumstances. On the other hand, if amendments are too easy to make, then important constitutional protections may be jeopardized. Therefore, many constitutions provide that certain arrangements may not be amended—for example, the provision in the U.S. Constitution granting each state equal representation in the Senate. Amending procedures vary widely, ranging from the complex to the simple. Perhaps the simplest case is that of the United Kingdom, where an ordinary parliamentary statute may alter the constitution. Thus the Parliament Act of 1911 reduced the power of the House of Lords to that of proposing amendments and delaying legislation for one parliamentary session. The current effort to eliminate the power of the hereditary peers is similarly taking place through ordinary legislation. Due to the Lords' power to delay legislation, the new reforms may require enactment in two successive parliamentary sessions.

Some constitutions prescribe qualified majorities, such as a two-thirds majority, for constitutional amendments. Others require that an amendment be approved twice with an interval of time between passages. Brazil requires its legislature to vote an amendment in two separate occasions with a three-fourths vote each time. In some cases, constitutional amendments must be approved by a popular vote. The U.S. Constitution has the most difficult formal procedure, requiring initiation by two-thirds of both houses of the Congress (or by the never-employed procedure of a national convention called by two-thirds of the states), and approval by three-fourths of the state legislatures, or three-fourths of specially elected states' conventions. Constitutions that have complicated amending procedures, such as the American one, are called "rigid." On average, they tend to be amended less frequently than their "flexible" counterparts.[15]

One of the main points of Figure 6.1 and Table 6.1 is that constitutions may concentrate or disperse government power along several dimensions. There are necessary trade-offs involved in making such constitutional choices. Probably no one who favors democracy and individual liberties would argue for extreme centralization of power in an omnipotent dictator, as in Thomas Hobbes's *Leviathan* (Chapter 1). However, constitutional democracies that concentrate power to a somewhat lesser degree, such as the British system, have some important advantages. Their governments tend to be effective and efficient, and by relying on majority rule, they tend to treat all citizens equally. No small group can hold up a decision favored by a solid majority. On the other hand, constitutions that disperse power have their own advantages. They are more likely to check potential abuses of power, such as the tyranny of a majority, and policies will tend to be more stable over time.

CHECKING THE TOP POLICYMAKERS

In many authoritarian systems, there is no legal and institutionalized way to remove the top political leaders if they become unpopular or overstep whatever bounds they may face. Moreover, authoritarian leaders can usually change or simply ignore the constitution itself, when it restricts their desires. Democracies have various procedures for keeping the leaders in check, but the procedures vary between types of systems. In parliamentary systems, chief executives can be removed virtually at any time through a vote of no confidence if they lose the support of a parliamentary majority. In Germany, Social Democratic Chancellor Helmut Schmidt was ousted by Helmut Kohl of the Christian Democratic Party in October 1982. In Britain Prime Minister Margaret Thatcher's own Conservative Party replaced her with John Major in 1990.

Democratic presidential systems fall somewhere in between. Unlike prime ministers under parliamentary constitutions, presidents have fixed terms of office. Most presidential systems do allow presidents to be removed before their term is up, but typically

only if they are guilty of serious criminal or other wrongdoing. The procedure through which this is done is called **impeachment.** Impeachment typically involves three components: (1) impeachable offenses are usually identified as presenting unusual danger to the public good or safety; (2) the penalty is removal from office (sometimes with separate criminal penalties); (3) impeachment cases are decided by the legislature, but require more than ordinary majorities and may also involve the judiciary in some way. In the American system, impeachment procedures can be used against the incumbents in top offices, even the president (as in the cases of Presidents Nixon and Clinton) or a Supreme Court justice, if their activities stray too far beyond legal bounds.

The establishment of the impeachment power has been associated with the rise of presidential separation-of-powers systems, and with the need in such systems for an extraordinary check against abuse of power on the part of high executive officers. (However, its modern origin was in eighteenth century Britain; see Box 6.2.) The framers of the American constitution viewed the normal checks and balances as insufficient protection against serious corruptions of power. Impeachment typically combines legislative and judicial powers against an executive out of control. The positive value of impeachment is that it provides a way of legally mobilizing political power against a threat to the constitutional or legal order. On the other hand, the danger is that it can be used for less pressing purposes. It can be tempting under a separation-of-powers system, when the executive and legislative are controlled by different political parties, and particularly when these parties are hostile to one another, to employ the institution out of primarily partisan motives. To prevent abuse of the impeachment procedure, the odds are typically stacked in favor of the defendant. Impeachment is often a cumbersome procedure, and it typically takes a large majority to convict—in the United States, a two-thirds majority in the Senate. No U.S. president has yet been convicted by the Senate and removed from office, although that fate has befallen other federal officials, such as judges.

Brazil, Mexico, and many other Latin American nations with strong presidents have impeachment traditions imbibed from the United States. In Mexico, the president, the state governors, and federal

BOX 6.2   Impeachment

Impeachment is often thought of as a procedure that is typical of presidential rather than parliamentary systems. Nevertheless, its modern origins lie in Britain. The framers of the American constitution adopted impeachment from their British institutional heritage. In English constitutional tradition, impeachment was a process affecting top executive and civil officers accused of "high crimes and misdemeanors," for which the penalty was removal from office. Impeachment was quite separate from judicial control over criminal behavior.

An illustrative impeachment case was in process in the British Parliament at the very time that the U.S. Federal Constitution was being drafted, while the *Federalist Papers* were written, and while the states

were engaged in ratification. Warren Hastings, Governor General of India (1774–1784), was accused and impeached for "high crimes and misdemeanors" by the Whig Party, which then controlled the House of Commons. The House of Lords tried the case over a seven-year period (1787–1795) but failed to convict Hastings. The institution then fell into disuse in Britain as her system of parliamentary government evolved. In a parliamentary system, cabinet members and ministers hold office only when they have the confidence of a parliamentary majority. A no-confidence vote can bring them down at any time and for any reason. Parliament can therefore much more easily hold the top political elite accountable through the threat of a no-confidence vote rather than impeachment.

judges are subject to impeachment. Brazil also has an impeachment process similar to that of the United States, except that it takes a two-thirds vote to charge the president and other high civil officers with impeachable offenses. A two-thirds vote is also required in the Senate to convict. The clause was invoked in 1992 when President Collor was impeached on charges of large-scale corruption. He resigned before trial in the Senate. While impeachment is associated with constitutions having powerful presidencies with fixed terms of office, it has also been adopted in semi-presidential regimes, and even in purely parliamentary regimes.

In the long run the ultimate control of democratic order is periodic and competitive elections. This need to achieve and regularly renew their mandates is the fundamental device that leads politicians to respond to the needs and demands of citizens. It is deeply imperfect. It may be difficult to tell when elected officials are incompetent, deceitful, or just unlucky. The complexities of policymaking may baffle the attempt of even trained observers to assign responsibility for successes or failures. The multiplicity of political issues may leave citizens torn between their candidate choices. Or, none of the choices may seem very palatable. Yet, deeply imperfect as it is, this remarkable recruitment structure, through its effects on information, group activity, and party competition, gives every citizen some influence on the policymaking process.

For this reason we consider it the most significant democratic structure.

ASSEMBLIES

Three important types of government institutions are frequently involved in policymaking: (1) the legislative assembly; (2) the chief executive; and (3) the higher levels of bureaucracy. The distribution of policymaking predominance among these three institutions varies from country to country and from issue area to issue area. Legislative **assemblies** have existed for thousands of years. Ancient Greece and Rome had them, as did many other ancient societies, and indeed the Roman Senate has given its name to modern assemblies in the United States and many other countries. The Icelandic Althingi, first assembled in A.D. 930, is the oldest existing assembly. The British Parliament dates back to the Model Parliament of 1295 and beyond. Almost all contemporary political systems have assemblies, variously called senates, chambers, diets, houses, and the like. Assemblies may also be known as "legislatures" (regardless of what role they actually play in legislating) or as "parliaments" (mainly in parliamentary systems). Their formal approval is usually required for major public policies. They are generally elected by popular vote, and hence are at least formally accountable to the citizenry. Today more than 80 percent of the countries belonging to the United Nations have such governmental bodies. The almost universal adoption of legislative assemblies suggests that in the modern world a legitimate government must formally include a representative popular component.

Assembly Structure

Assemblies vary in their size—from less than 100 to more than 1000—and their organization. Legislatures may consist of one (in which case they are called unicameral) or two (bicameral) chambers. Most democracies, and some authoritarian systems, have bicameral (two-chamber) assemblies. Federal systems normally provide simultaneously for two forms of representation: often one chamber in which representation is based on population, and a second in which representation is based on geographic units. Even in unitary systems (such as France), **bicameralism** is common, but the purpose of the second chamber is to provide a check on policymaking rather than to represent subnational units. The bicameral U.S. Congress grew out of both federalism and the desire to separate the power of the federal government. The House of Representatives directly represents the citizens, with districts roughly equal in population size. In the Senate, on the other hand, the 50 U.S. states are equally represented. The U.S. congressional chambers check and balance one another as well as the other branches of government. Thus the Senate must approve treaties and executive appointments made by the president; both the Senate and the House must consent to a declaration of war; and the House must initiate all measures involving taxation and appropriations.

The American system, in which the two chambers have roughly equal powers, is unusual. In most bicameral systems one chamber is dominant, and the second (such as the Russian Council of the Federation or the French Senate) has more limited powers that are often designed to protect regional interests. While representatives in the dominant chamber are popularly elected, those in the second chamber are sometimes chosen by the regional governments (as in Germany) or in other indirect ways. The prime minister in most parliamentary systems is responsible only to the more popularly elected chamber, which therefore has a more important position in policymaking than the second chamber. (See the discussion of the vote of confidence procedure above and in Box 6.1.) In such systems members of the prime minister's cabinet are usually chosen from the majority party or parties' leadership in this chamber.

Assemblies also differ in their internal organization, in ways that have major consequences for policymaking. There are two kinds of internal legislative organization: party groups and formal assembly subunits (presiding officers, committees, and the like). There is often an inverse relationship between the strength of parties versus other subunits (such as committees). The stronger parties are, the weaker are committees, and vice versa. British members of Parliament vote strictly along party lines much more consistently than members of the U.S. Congress. As in most parliamentary systems, British members of Parliament rarely vote against the instructions of their party leaders. Because cabinets generally hold office as long as they can command a parliamentary majority, deviating from the party line means risking the fall of the government and new elections. (See Box 6.1 on the Confidence Vote.) In presidential systems, the president and the legislators are independently elected for fixed terms of office. Thus the fate of the governing party is less directly tied up with voting on legislative measures. In American legislatures, party discipline operates principally on procedural questions, such as committee assignments or the selection of a presiding officer. On substantive policy issues, Democratic and Republican legislators are freer to decide whether or not to vote with their party leaders.

All assemblies have a committee structure, some organized arrangement that permits legislators to divide up their labor and to specialize in particular issue areas. Without such a sublegislative organization, it would be impossible to handle the large flow of legislative business. As we have seen, however, the importance of committees varies. In some legislatures, such as the United States, committees are very influential. This is at least in part because they are highly specialized, have jurisdictions that match those of the executive departments, and have large staff resources. Strong committees tend to have a clear legislative division of labor that matches the executive branch, and they are often arenas in which the opposition can be influential. British committees are much weaker than their opposite numbers in the United States, since they have small staffs, are dominated by the governing party, and get appointed for one bill at a time. Hence, they cannot accumulate expertise in a particular policy area. German and Japanese committees are stronger than those of Britain but weaker than their American counterparts.[16]

Assembly Functions

Assembly members deliberate, debate, and vote on policies that come before them. Most important policies and rules must be considered and at least formally approved by these bodies before they have the force of law. Assemblies typically also control public spending decisions, so that control of the purse strings (budgeting) is one of their major functions. In addition, some assemblies have important appointment powers, and some (like the British House of Lords in criminal cases) may serve as a court of appeals. Although laws typically need assembly approval, in most countries legislation is actually formulated elsewhere, usually by the political executive and the upper levels of the bureaucracy. When we compare the importance of assemblies as policymaking agencies, the U.S. Congress, which plays a very active role in the formulation and enactment of legislation, is at one extreme. The other extreme is represented by the National People's Congress of the People's Republic of China, which meets infrequently and does little more than listen to statements by party leaders and rubberstamp decisions made elsewhere. Roughly midway between the two is the House of Commons in Britain. There, legislative proposals are sometimes initiated or modified by ordinary members of Parliament, but public policy is usually initiated and proposed by members of the Cabinet (who are, to be sure, chosen from the members of the parliamentary body). The typical assembly provides a deliberating forum, formally enacts legislation, and sometimes amends it.

Assemblies should not be viewed only as legislative bodies. All assemblies in democratic systems have an important relationship to legislation, but not necessarily a dominant role. Their political importance is based not just on this function, but also on the great variety of other political functions they perform. Assemblies can play a major role in elite recruitment, especially in parliamentary systems where prime ministers and cabinet members typically serve their apprenticeships in parliament. Legislative committee hearings and floor debates may be important sites for interest articulation and interest aggregation, especially if there is no cohesive majority party. Debates in assemblies can be a source of public information about politics and thus contribute to the socialization of citizens generally and elites in particular. However, as in policymaking, the assemblies of different nations play very different roles in their respective political systems. The British House of Commons ordinarily does not make much of an independent impact on policymaking, because it is controlled by the ruling party's majority. The Commons and its debates are, however, central to public debate, and one of its chief functions is to prepare politicians for executive office. Through its committees, the U.S. Congress plays a major role in making laws and budgets, but must share other functions with many other institutions in the decentralized American system. The People's Congress in China plays only a limited socialization role.

Representation: Mirroring and Representational Biases

Contemporary legislative assemblies, especially in democratic systems, are valued particularly because they represent the citizens in the national policymaking process. It is not obvious, however, what the ideal linkage between citizens and government officials should be. One body of thought holds that government officials should mirror the characteristics of the citizens as far as possible. This principle, also known as *descriptive representation*, is held to be particularly important with respect to potentially conflictual divisions such as race, class, ethnicity, gender, language, and perhaps age.

However, descriptive representation is not the only concern in recruiting public officials. The limits of mirroring were inadvertently expressed by a U.S. senator. In defending a Supreme Court nominee that was accused of mediocrity, the senator lamely contended, "even if he were mediocre, there are a lot of mediocre judges and people and lawyers. They are entitled to a little representation, aren't they?" Most people would probably not go as far as to argue that government officials should mirror the general population in their abilities to do their jobs. Instead, we generally want political elites to be the best possible *agents* for their constituents. In this view, government officials should be selected for their ability to serve the interests of the citizens, whether or not they share the voters' background characteristics.

For politicians to be good agents, they need to have similar *preferences* to the citizens they represent and they need the appropriate *skills* to do their jobs. In democracies, political parties are the most important mechanism by which the preferences of citizens and leaders get aligned. As far as skills are concerned, education and experience are the most important factors. Political and governmental leadership, particularly in modern, technologically advanced societies, requires knowledge and skills that are hard to acquire except through education and training. Natural intelligence or experience may, to a limited degree, take the place of formal education.

Hence, it might be a good thing for government officials to be better informed, more intelligent, more experienced, and perhaps better educated than the people they serve. Just as medical patients tend to look for the most capable physician, rather than the one that is most like themselves, so, one could argue, citizens should look for the best qualified officeholder. In this view, selecting government officials, including representative policymakers, is like delegating to experts. It may be a hopeful sign that citizens in many modern democracies are increasingly willing to select leaders who do not share their background characteristics.

As in the case of so many other political choices, there is no obvious or perfect way to choose between mirroring and expert delegation. This is an old debate, and in many situations it is necessary to make a trade-off between the two. And different offices may require different considerations. Most people would, for example, probably put a higher emphasis on mirroring in their local assembly than in a regulatory agency overseeing nuclear technology.

The bad news is that political elites, even democratically elected members of legislative assemblies, hardly ever mirror the citizens they represent on any of the ascriptive characteristics. Even in democracies such as the United States, Britain, and France, political leaders tend to be of middle- or upper-class background or unusually well-educated and upwardly mobile individuals from the lower classes. There are exceptions. In some countries trade unions or leftist political parties may serve as channels of political advancement for people with modest economic or educational backgrounds.

These representatives acquire political skills and experience by holding offices in working class organizations. Thus the Labour Party delegation in the British House of Commons and the Communist delegation in the French National Assembly have included substantial numbers of workers. And during the long domination of the executive by the Norwegian Labor Party, which held the prime ministership for all but seven years between 1935 and 1981, none of its prime ministers had even completed secondary school. But these are rare and vanishing examples. In most contemporary states, the number of working-class people in high office is small and declining.

Women have traditionally also been poorly represented in political leadership positions in most countries. History certainly offers examples of strong and influential female rulers, such as Queen Elizabeth I of England (who ruled from 1558 to 1603). Yet in most countries women did not have the right to vote until well into the twentieth century and have not held many political leadership positions. That has changed significantly in the last twenty-five years. In 1980, women on average held fewer than 10 percent of the parliamentary seats in the advanced industrial democracies. By 1990, that figure was up to about 15 percent, and by 1997 women had surpassed 20 percent. Women have also held the chief executive office in a growing number of countries, particularly in Europe and Asia. (See Box 6.3.) The most famous female chief executive is probably Margaret Thatcher, who was Britain's longest-serving prime minister (1979–1990) in modern times and a highly effective and influential political leader. But women's advancement has been uneven, and their representation remains low in the developing world. In many Northern European countries, such as Sweden, women by the late 1990s accounted for 30 to 40 percent of the legislators and a similar proportion of cabinet members. In the United States, they had made similar gains in some states—most notably in Arizona, where women held five out of six statewide elective offices after the 1998 elections. But in Russia, Mexico, Brazil, and Japan, women still accounted for fewer than one legislator in ten in the 1990s.[17]

Political elites also tend to be unrepresentative with respect to age. In many countries, legislators (much less chief executives) under 40 are a rarity,

BOX 6.3   Women as Chief Executives

From about 1970 on, women have gained chief executive office in a growing number of countries. Interestingly, many of them have been from Asian and Middle Eastern countries, where women's roles in public life traditionally have been limited. Sinmavo Bandaranaike of Sri Lanka (1960–1965 and 1970–1977), Indira Gandhi of India (1966–1977 and 1980–1984), and Golda Meir of Israel (1969–1974) were among the pioneers. In the 1980s and 1990s, women also came to power in the Philippines, Pakistan, and Bangladesh, and again in Sri Lanka. In Burma, Nobel Peace Prize winner Aung San Suu Kyi won the elections of 1990 but the military prevented her from taking office.

Women have also made inroads in leadership positions in Europe and North America, though they are still few and far between in Africa and Latin America. The first female leader in a major European country was Prime Minister Margaret Thatcher of Britain (1979–1990). Her strong and decisive leadership made her one of Europe's most influential politicians in the

1980s. Thatcher, who now serves in Britain's House of Lords, was not a conventional feminist, however. She showed little interest in gender issues and appointed very few women to her cabinets. Women have come to power in other western countries as well. Both Ireland and Iceland have had female presidents. Canada, France, and Switzerland have had brief stints with female prime ministers. In Norway, Gro Harlem Brundtland held the prime ministership for a total of about ten years between 1981 and 1996. Brundtland, a physician and environmentalist, later headed the World Health Organization.

The career paths of Asian women leaders have tended to differ from those in Europe. Many of the former have come from prominent political families, such as the Gandhi family in India and the Bhuttos in Pakistan. In several cases, they have been the widows or daughters of important political leaders. In Europe, women leaders are more likely to have made independent political careers, and they can rely on stronger women's interest groups.

---

whereas a large proportion of leading politicians are past normal retirement age. Japan is an extreme example. In 1990, there were about eight legislators over the age of 60 for every one member under 40. In many countries, university graduates—and often lawyers and civil servants in particular—are vastly overrepresented, whereas ethnic, linguistic, and religious minorities are often underrepresented. Representational biases are thus numerous and pervasive. And while women's representation is increasing, class biases are getting worse.

POLITICAL EXECUTIVES

In modern states, the executive branch is by far the largest, the most complex, and typically the most powerful branch of government. It is not easy to describe executives in simple ways, but it is sensible to start at the top. Governments typically have a small number of **chief executives,** officials who sit at the very top of the often-colossal executive branch. Such executives have various names, titles, duties, and powers. Some are called presidents, others prime ministers, chancellors, premiers, or secretaries general, and still others are chairmen or chairs. There are even a few kings who still have

genuine power. Titles may mislead us as to what functions these officials perform, but they tend to be the main formulators and executors of public policy. We shall discuss the chief executives, including their cabinets, which are an important part of the policymaking process, especially in parliamentary systems, before turning to the subordinate parts of the executive, called the bureaucracy.

Structure of the Chief Executive

Democratic governments typically feature either a single chief executive (in presidential systems), or a split chief executive of two offices: a largely ceremonial head of state, who represents the nation on formal occasions, and a more powerful head of government, who determines public policies. Table 6.2 distinguishes among executives according to the bases of their power to affect policymaking. In the left column we see the chief executives in authoritarian systems, whose power ultimately rests on coercion. The middle and right columns show the chief executives in democratic countries. The middle column shows executives whose power rests primarily on their partisan influence in the legislature, which is the case of the prime ministers in most parliamentary

T A B L E 6 . 2 Bases of Legislative Power of Chief Executives

Authoritarian	Democratic: Partisan Influence	Democratic: Constitutional Powers
Effective		
General Secretary, China	British Prime Minister	
	French Prime Minister	
	German Chancellor	
	Indian Prime Minister	
	Japanese Prime Minister	
	(Russian Prime Minister)	
Ceremonial		
Chinese President		British Queen
		German President
		Indian President
		Japanese Emperor
Ceremonial and Effective		
Egyptian President	French President	Brazilian President
		Mexican President
		Nigerian President
		Russian President
		U.S. President

systems. The right column includes chief executives whose ability to influence legislation resides in powers directly granted them by the constitution, rather than partisan connection alone. Strong presidents may have the ability to veto legislation, for example, or to issue decrees that have the force of law, or to introduce the budget. They usually have the power to appoint and dismiss members of the cabinet

Reading down the table, we see the distinction between executives with effective power over policy, purely ceremonial roles, or both effective and ceremonial power. Political executives are effective only if they have genuine discretion in the enactment and implementation of laws and regulations, in budgetary matters, or in important government appointments. Where they do not have these powers, they are symbolic or ceremonial. In presidential systems the ceremonial and effective roles are almost always held by the same person, the president, as we see in both authoritarian and democratic systems at the bottom of Table 6.2. In parliamentary democratic systems, and in some authoritarian systems, the two roles are separated between the "head of state," who is primarily a ceremonial official, and a "head of government," who

makes and implements the decisions. The British, German, Indian and Japanese prime ministers appear in column two at the top right of the table, while their ceremonial counterparts appear at the center right. These distinctions are not absolute. Some constitutions, such as the German, give substantial formal powers to their prime ministers, while even largely ceremonial presidents can exert important influence if the parties are divided or by exercising special constitutional powers (or both, as has recently happened in India.) Moreover, partisan influence in the legislature is useful even to the strongest democratic presidents. Still, it is usually easy to determine the primary sources of legislative power, even where the formal names may be misleading.

As noted earlier, a few countries, such as France and Russia have both significant presidents and prime ministers. The balance of power between them depends on the constitutional powers of the president and on the partisan division in the legislature. In Russia the constitutional powers of veto and decree of the President are very great, and the legislature has seldom been unified against him; the Prime Minister has been mostly just another admin-

Chief executives of the leading economic nations and the European Union pose in the shadow of the Kananaskis mountains in Alberta, Canada in June 2002: (left to right) Italian Prime Minister Berlusconi, German Chancellor Schroeder, U.S. President Bush, French President Chirac, Canadian Prime Minister Chretien, Russian President Putin, British Prime Minister Blair, Japanese Prime Minister Koizumi, Spanish Prime Minister Aznar, European Commission President Prodi.

Getty Images

istrator, with little effective power. In France, however, the President's formal powers are much weaker; when the legislature has been unified under opposition parties it has elected a Prime Minister who has effectively dominated policymaking, reducing the President to a largely ceremonial role.

The Chairman of China's Communist Party is the most powerful political figure and the effective chief executive; the president is the head of state, which is a purely ceremonial role, without associated powers. However, in recent years the same individual (Jiang Zemin and now Yu Jintao) has held both offices, and also a key role as chairman of the party military commission. A third role was the premier, or head of government, which was a largely administrative position.

Monarchies are much more rare at the end of the twentieth century than they were at its beginning. Some monarchs, such as the king of Saudi Arabia and some other Arab monarchs, still exercise real power. Most contemporary monarchs, however, have little or no actual political influence. Monarchs like the British queen or the Scandinavian kings are principally ceremonial and symbolic officers with very occasional political powers. They are living symbols of the state and nation and of their historical continuity. Britain's queen may bestow honors or peerages (appointments to the nobility) with a stroke of her wand, but these are recommended by the prime

minister. When there is an election, or when a government falls, the queen formally appoints a new prime minister. Normally she has no discretion in selecting a prime minister, however, but is required by convention to pick the leader of the majority party in the House of Commons. The Japanese monarchy has also traditionally been dignified and exalted and played an important role as a national symbol. In contrast, the Scandinavian and Low Country monarchies are more humdrum. Because members of these royal families occasionally use more humble means of transportation, these dynasties are sometimes called "bicycle monarchies" (see Box 6.4).

In republican democracies with parliamentary systems, presidents perform the functions that fall to kings and queens in parliamentary monarchies. Thus German presidents give speeches on important anniversaries and designate prime ministers after elections or when a government has resigned. Like parliamentary systems, communist countries have tended to separate the ceremonial and the effective executives. The president of the People's Republic of China, for example, has usually been a ceremonial officer. He greeted distinguished visitors and opened and presided over meetings of the People's Congress.

A system in which the ceremonial executive is separated from the effective executive has a number of advantages. The ceremonial executive symbolizes

BOX 6.4   Pomp and Circumstance Versus Bicycle Monarchies

Monarchies may be a dying breed, but Western Europe still has more of them than any other region of the world. Britain and Spain are monarchies, as are six of the smaller European democracies (the Netherlands, Belgium, Luxembourg, Denmark, Norway, and Sweden), plus a few microstates such as Monaco. Most of these monarchies have a long history, but two were created in the twentieth century: the Norwegian monarchy in 1905, and the Spanish one in 1975, as Spain transited from the Franco dictatorship to democracy. Monarchies are not all the same. The Spanish king may have more influence than any other European monarch, but few of them have any real power. The Swedish king was even stripped of all his remaining formal powers in a constitutional reform in the 1970s.

Monarchies vary more in style than in power. The British tend toward pomp and ceremony, with decorated horses carrying the Queen to Parliament in a gilded carriage. The Scandinavian and Low Country monarchies are often called "bicycle monarchies." The late King Olav V of Norway (who reigned 1957–1991) was a particularly folksy monarch. An Olympic ski jumper in his youth, he could even in later years often be seen cross-country skiing in the woods around Oslo (the capital of Norway), accompanied only by his dog. During the oil crisis of the 1970s, he insisted on taking public transportation from the royal palace to the ski trails (and on paying for his ticket). When he was still crown prince, he once gave an interview to an American journalist who showed up at the royal cottage without an appointment. While the journalist was interviewing him, the Crown Prince proceeded to do the family dishes.

Queen Beatrix of the Netherlands rides her bicycle on a visit in East Holland, thus illustrating why the Scandinavian and Low Country monarchies are called "bicycle monarchies."

Hulton-Deutsch/Hulton-Getty

---

unity and continuity and can be above politics. The U.S. presidency, which combines both effective and ceremonial functions, runs the risk that the president will use his ceremonial and symbolic authority to enhance his political power or that his involvement in politics may make him a less effective symbolic or unifying figure.

Recruitment of Chief Executives

Historically, finding generally acceptable ways to select the individuals to fill the top policymaking roles has been critical to political order and stability. A major accomplishment of stable democracies has been to regulate the potential conflict involved in leadership succession and confine it to the mobilization of votes instead of weapons. When we refer generally to "recruitment structures," we are thinking of how nations choose their top policymakers and executives. Table 6.3 shows the recruitment structures in the countries selected for this book. The most familiar structures are the presidential and parliamentary forms of competitive party systems. In presidential systems, as in Brazil and the United States, parties select candidates for nomination,

T A B L E   6 . 3   Recruitment of Chief Executive

Country	Chief Executive Structure	Recruitment Structures	How Often Has This Type of Government Survived Succession?[b]
Brazil	President	Party and voters	Often
Britain	Prime minister	Party, House of Commons, voters	Very often
China	Party secretary[a]	Party and military	Often
Egypt	President	Party and military	Twice
France	President/Prime minister	Party, (Assembly,) voters	Often
Germany	Chancellor	Party, Bundestag, voters	Often
India	Prime minister	Party, Lok Sabha, voters	Often (one interruption)
Japan	Prime minister	Party, Diet, voters	Often
Mexico	President	Party and voters	Once
Nigeria	President	Military, party, voters	Never
Russia	President	Party and voters	Once
United States	President	Party and voters	Very often

[a]"Party secretary" refers to that position or a similar one as head of party in communist regime.

[b]"Often" means that at least three successions have taken place under that type of government.

and the electorate chooses between these. Russia and France have directly elected presidents but also give an important role to the prime minister, who is appointed by the president but can be removed by the legislature.

Mexico appears similar to other presidential systems, but the Partido Revolucionario Institucional (PRI) had such control over the electoral process that for half a century the voters merely ratified the party's presidential nominee. That nomination itself was announced by the outgoing president after complex bargaining between party factions and other powerful groups. Mexico seemed to be moving to give the voters an honest role in choosing between alternative candidates, but until the remarkable July 2000 election many voters remained skeptical that a non-PRI president could really come to power. As the table shows, Mexico now seems a newly democratic presidential system, with parties nominating candidates and voters genuinely choosing between them.

In both presidential and parliamentary democracies the tenure of the chief executive is limited, directly or indirectly. In the presidential system this happens directly, through fixed terms of office for the chief executive. In the parliamentary system there is a maximum term for the parliament, which then indirectly also limits the life of the cabinet, since the prime minister is accountable to the new parliamentary majority and can be removed by it.

Table 6.3 also illustrates the role of noncompetitive parties and military organizations in China and Egypt. The important role played by political parties illustrates the great need to mobilize broad political support behind the selection of chief executives. The frequent appearance of parties also reflects, no doubt, the modern legitimacy of popular sovereignty: the promise that the rulers' actions will be in the interest of the ruled.

Authoritarian systems rarely have effective procedures for leadership succession. The more power is concentrated at the top, the riskier it is to transfer it from one person to the next. Very often, authoritarian leaders do not dare to relinquish their power, and leadership succession occurs only when they die. In Communist regimes, the Communist Party selected the general secretary (or equivalent), who was the controlling executive force. Individual succession was not a simple matter. These systems did not limit the terms of incumbents, who were difficult to oust once they had consolidated their supporters into key party positions. Nonetheless, they always had to be aware of the possibility of a party coup of the type that ousted Nikita Khrushchev from the Soviet leadership in 1964. As a system, however, the Soviet leadership structure seemed quite stable until the dramatic 1991 coup attempt against Gorbachev. Although he was briefly restored to power, the events surrounding the coup stripped the Soviet presidency of power, and legitimacy passed to the presidencies and legislatures of the 15 constituent republics, most importantly to President Boris Yeltsin of Russia. Russia managed its first democratic transition surprisingly smoothly, from Yeltsin to his chosen successor Vladimar Putin, who was elected as the new president in April 2000.

The poorer nations show substantially less stability, and the regimes have usually had less experience at surviving succession crises. Nigeria is typical. It experienced a succession of military coups and governments from 1966 until 1979, then introduced a competitive presidential system, which was overthrown by a military coup shortly after its second election in 1983. The military government again moved toward civilian rule in the early 1990s but then annulled the 1993 presidential election before the results were announced. The military rulers finally allowed a return to civilian rule in 1999.

Many African nations are under military governments; some of them have experienced repeated coups. Military governments, stable or unstable, have also been common in Latin America and the Middle East. The Chinese Communist Party has remained in power for 50 years but has suffered several periods of internal strife, and the army has been involved in recruitment at all levels. India's democracy, having persisted through assassinations and other crises, has been an exception to the rule among poorer nations. It has provided a number of democratic successions with a single interruption (authoritarian emergency rule that postponed elections for several years) in the 1970s.

The Cabinet

In many political systems, the **Cabinet** is the most important collective decision-making body. Its power can be particularly great in parliamentary systems, where its formation is closely linked to selection of the prime minister. It typically contains the leaders (often called "ministers" or "secretaries of state") of all the major departments (sometimes called "ministries") into which the executive branch is divided. The Cabinet meets frequently—often several times per week—and it is typically selected and led by the head of government: the president in presidential systems and the prime minister in parliamentary ones. In some parliamentary systems the entire cabinet is collectively responsible to the legislature

and the prime minister may be little more than "first among equals," especially under conditions of multiparty coalition governments. In other parliamentary systems, such as Germany, the constitution confers much more authority on the prime minister.[18] Confidence motions (Box 6.1) are usually introduced by the prime minister. In all cases the entire cabinet must resign when the government loses a vote of confidence or no-confidence.

How does the Cabinet get selected? In presidential systems, selecting Cabinet members is typically a presidential prerogative, though sometimes (as with the U.S. Senate), the legislature has to give its approval. The president can typically also dismiss Cabinet members at will, whereas the legislature's ability to do so is most often severely limited.

Coalition partners emphasize their solidarity before the German Bundestag in February 2003: Chancellor Gerhard Schroeder of the Social Democratic Party (right) welcomes Foreign Minister Joschka Fischer of the Green Party. Their two parties had campaigned together in a pre-election coalition in the 2002 parliamentary election and formed a majority coalition cabinet afterwards.

AP/Wide World Photos

In parliamentary systems, on the other hand, the process is very different, since the prime minister and his or her cabinet need to maintain the confidence of the parliamentary majority. Therefore, Cabinet formation depends on the result of parliamentary elections and on the composition of Parliament. If a competitive party wins a parliamentary majority by itself, it will (if unified) be able to form a Cabinet of its own members and can then pass and implement its policies. Sometimes who controls the majority is determined directly by the elections. This will always be the case in pure two-party systems, where one party or the other will always have a parliamentary majority. It can also happen in multiparty systems, whenever one party gets more seats than all its competitors combined. But the more parties there are, the less likely it is that one of them will have a majority on its own. We call the outcome in which one party controls a parliamentary majority by itself a majority situation. Whenever majority situations occur in parliamentary systems, the majority party almost always forms a *majority single-party cabinet* by itself.

Far more often, no party wins a majority of votes. In most multiparty countries, the typical election result is that no party has a parliamentary majority by itself—a minority situation. Most commonly under such circumstances, several parties (two, three, or as many as six or seven) join forces and form a *coalition cabinet* in which they are all represented. Sometimes, parties anticipate this need to form coalitions before the election. They may then make a formal agreement

with one another and inform the voters that they intend to govern together if they collectively get enough votes. The allied parties may thus encourage their voters to support the coalition partners' candidates where their own party's candidates seem weak and often take advantage of special provisions of voting laws. Many German and French governments have come to power in this fashion. In such cases, the voters can have a direct voice in the choice of the future Cabinet, much as they do in two-party systems. Voters are thus given a major role in choosing the direction of government policy.

But parties often do not make such preelection commitments. Even when they do, they often fail to get the support they would need to control a parliamentary majority. If no party or preelection coalition wins control of the legislature through the election, then parties may bargain after the election, or between elections, to form a new Cabinet.

Whether bargaining takes place before or after the elections, the parties in parliamentary systems typically have a lot of options concerning the composition of the Cabinet. In minority situations, the result can be either a minority government or a majority coalition of several parties. In some cases, a single party decides that it can form a minority cabinet alone, often because the other parties disagree too much among themselves to offer any alternative. Figure 6.2 illustrates these various possibilities. In the minority case, the parties in the Cabinet must continually bargain with other parties to get policies

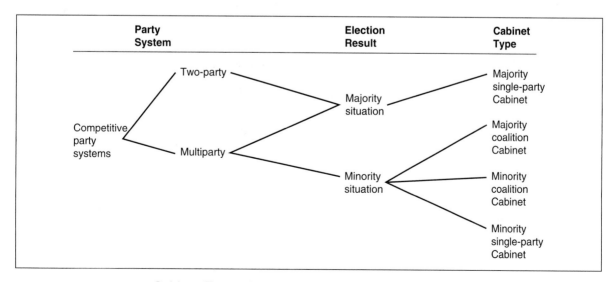

F I G U R E   6 . 2   Cabinet Formation in Parliamentary Democracies

adopted and even to remain in office. In majority coalitions, bargaining will take place primarily among coalition partners represented in the Cabinet. In both of these circumstances the power of the prime minister may depend on the bargains he can strike with leaders of other parties.

These complications illustrate two of the problems of combining parliamentary government with electoral systems of proportional representation. Such systems tend to produce minority situations. One problem with this is that the voters are often not given a very clear choice about who will control the executive branch. Instead, the parties may determine this behind closed doors after the election. Sometimes, the results are paradoxical, as when parties that have just lost votes in the elections are able to negotiate their way into a governing coalition. The second problem is that under minority situations, cabinets are sometimes unstable. Italy, for example, has on average had more than one change of government per year since World War II. Yet, such problems need not always emerge. In Germany, for example, cabinets have been quite stable and the voters have generally been given fairly clear options ahead of elections.

Functions of the Chief Executive

Typically, the chief executive is the most important structure in policymaking. The executive normally initiates new policies and, depending on the division of powers between the executive and the legislature, has a substantial part in their adoption. In presidential systems, the president very often has veto powers. Thus the chief executive not only has the first word in policymaking, he or she also typically has the last word. In parliamentary systems, on the other hand, the executive is less likely to be able to exercise a veto. The political executive also oversees policy implementation and can hold subordinate officials accountable for their performance. The central decisions in a foreign policy crisis are generally made by the chief executive: the president (George W. Bush in the Iraq War) or the prime minister (Margaret Thatcher in the Falklands crisis). Political initiatives and new programs tend to originate in the executive. A bureaucracy without an effective executive tends to implement past policies, rather than to initiate new ones. Without politically motivated ministers, bureaucracies tend toward inertia.

The decision of a president, prime minister, cabinet, or central party committee to pursue a new foreign or domestic policy will usually be accompanied by structural adaptations—the appointment of a vigorous minister, an increase in staff, the establishment of a special cabinet committee, and the like. Where the political executive is weak and divided, as in Fourth Republic France or contemporary Italy, (at least until recently,) this dynamic force is missing. Initiative then passes to the bureaucracy, legislative committees, and powerful interest groups, and general needs, interests, and problems may be neglected. In a separation-of-powers system when the presidency and the congress are controlled by different parties, even a strong president may be hampered in carrying out an effective policy. And if the president is hamstrung, the assembly is rarely able to fill the gap.

Chief executives also perform important system functions. Studies of childhood socialization show that the first political role perceived by children tends to be the chief political executive—the president, prime minister, and king or queen. In early childhood the tendency is to identify the top political executive as a parent figure. As the child matures, he or she begins to differentiate political from other roles, as well as to differentiate among various political roles (see Chapter 3). The conduct of the chief executive affects the trust and confidence that young people feel in the whole political system and that they carry with them into adulthood. The role of the chief executive in recruitment is obviously important. Presidents, prime ministers, and first secretaries have large and important powers to appoint not only cabinet and politburo members and government ministers but often judges, senior civil servants, ambassadors, and military officers as well. Typically, political executives can bestow honors and distinctions on members of the government and private citizens. The political executive also plays a central role in communication, in explaining and building support for new policies, or in improving performance in various sectors of the society and economy.

THE BUREAUCRACY

Modern societies are dominated by large organizations, and the largest contemporary organizations are government **bureaucracies,** or their systems of public administration. These agencies, by which we mean all the members of the executive branch below the top executive (president/monarch, prime minister, and cabinet) are generally in charge of implementing government policy. The size of government bureaucracies has increased over the course of the twentieth century. This is partly due to government efforts to improve the health, productivity, welfare, and security of their populations. In part, it may also be part of the tendency for government agencies, once they have been established, to seek growth for its own sake. In reaction to this tendency, and as part of the concern about government inefficiencies, there has in recent decades been a movement to reduce government budgets and to downsize the bureaucracy.

Structure of the Bureaucracy

The most important officials in bureaucracies are the experienced and expert personnel of the top **civil service.** The British "government," which we can think of as its top executive positions, consists of approximately 100 "frontbench" members of Parliament, some 20 of whom serve in the Cabinet, with the remainder named as ministers, junior ministers, and parliamentary secretaries. This relatively small group of political policymakers oversees some 3,000 permanent members of the **higher civil service,** largely recruited directly from the universities. They spend their lives as an elite corps, moving about from ministry to ministry, watching governments come and go, and becoming increasingly important as policymakers as they rise in rank. Below the higher civil service are a huge body of more than half a million permanent public employees, ordinary civil servants, organized into about 20 government departments and a number of other agencies. The total number of British civil servants rose from 100,000 in 1900 to more than 700,000 in 1979, but it then declined to under 500,000 under Conservative governments of the 1980s and 1990s.

The importance of the permanent higher civil service is not unique to Britain, though perhaps it has been most fully institutionalized there. In France, too, the higher civil service is filled with powerful generalists who can bring long tenure, experience, and technical knowledge to their particular tasks. In the United States, many top positions go to presidential appointees rather than to permanent civil servants. Despite this difference and a greater emphasis on technical specialization, there are permanent civil servants in the key positions just below the top appointees in such agencies as the Internal Revenue Service, the Federal Bureau of Investigation, the Central Intelligence Agency, the National Institutes of Health, and all the cabinet departments. These people tend to be specialists, such as military officers, diplomats, doctors, scientists, economists, and engineers, who exert great influence on policy formulation and execution in their specialties. Below these specialists and administrators are the vast numbers of ordinary government employees, postal workers, teachers, welfare case agents, and so forth, who see that governmental policies are put into practice. In 2004, the United States had 22 million public employees of all kinds, federal, state and local, or about 17 percent of the total labor force. In many European countries, that proportion is even higher, approaching a third of the labor force in Norway, Denmark, and Sweden.

The Functions of the Bureaucracy

Bureaucracies have acquired great significance in most contemporary societies. One reason is that the bureaucracy is almost alone in implementing and enforcing laws and regulations. In so doing, they may have quite a bit of discretion. Most modern legislation is general and can be effectively enforced only if administrative officials work out its detail and implementation. Policy implementation and enforcement usually depend on bureaucrats' interpretations and on the spirit and effectiveness with which they put it into practice. But the power of bureaucracies is not restricted to their implementation and enforcement of rules made by others. In Chapters 4 and Chapter 5 we discussed how bureaucratic agencies may articulate and aggregate interests. Departments like those for agriculture, labor, defense, welfare, and education may be among the most important voices of interest groups. Moreover, administrative agencies in modern political systems do a lot of adjudication. Tax authorities, for example, routinely determine whether citizens have faithfully reported their income and paid their taxes, and these authorities assess penalties accordingly. While citizens may in principle be able to appeal such rulings to the courts, relatively few actually do.

Finally, bureaucracies are involved in communication. Political elites, whether executives or legislators, base many of their decisions on the information they obtain from the public administration. Similarly, interest groups, political parties, the business elites, and the public depend on such information. Most major agencies in modern governments have spokespersons whose job it is to inform and influence the media. With the increasing media power in modern societies, top government executives are eager to present their versions of events. Leaks of secret or confidential information and intelligence have become a veritable flood. Increasingly, however, large parts of the journalistic professions refuse to recognize any limits on the publication of private as well as political information. Thus political executives and bureaucracies can no longer control information in the ways that they formerly did. In dealing with the media, top administrators now must have more complex strategies and professional assistance. The art of "spin control" has replaced their reliance on classification and "executive privilege."

Bureaucracy and Performance

We commonly use the term "bureaucracy" to refer to all systems of public administration. Strictly speaking, however, bureaucracy refers to a particular way of organizing such agencies, a practice that gained favor in the latter part of the nineteenth century and the beginning of the twentieth century. According to the classical German sociologist Max Weber, bureaucracies have the following features: (1) decision making is based on fixed and official jurisdictions, rules, and regulations; (2) there are formal and specialized educational or training requirements for each position; (3) there is a hierarchical command structure: a firmly ordered system of super- and subordination, in which information flows upward and decisions downward; (4) decisions are made on the basis of standard operating procedures, which include extensive written records; and (5) officials hold career positions, are appointed and promoted on the basis of merit, and have protection against political interference, notably in the form of permanent job tenure. No organization is perfectly bureaucratic in this sense, but professional armies come reasonably close, as do tax revenue departments.

These features of bureaucracies have a number of salutary effects. They promote competence, consistency, fair treatment, and freedom from political manipulation. Keep in mind what life could be like without bureaucracies. Before the advent of modern bureaucracy, public officials were often a sorry lot. Some of them inherited their jobs; others got them through family or political connections. Yet others bought their posts and used them either to enrich themselves or gain social status (or both). Many saw them strictly as a sideline and devoted little time to their duties. No wonder, then, that public officials were often incompetent, uninterested in their jobs, corrupt, or all of the above. They often used their powers arbitrarily, to favor friends and neighbors, and to the disadvantage of others. Given the lack of rules and records, aggrieved citizens typically had few recourses.

But the negative connotations that the word "bureaucracy" has taken on suggest that such organizations have liabilities as well. Bureaucratic organizations have a tendency to become stodgy, rule-bound, inflexible, and insensitive to the needs of their clients. In many cases, bureaucrats also have few incentives to be innovative and efficient, or even to work very hard. Although bureaucracies are supposed to be politically and ideologically neutral, in fact they tend to be influenced by the dominant ideologies of the time, to have conservative propensities, and to pursue institutional interests of their own.[19] Bureaucracies may present special problems in periods of major social change. When the Bolsheviks (Communists) took power in Russia in 1917, they had to depend on military officers and officials of the Czarist regime until they could train their own. In post-Communist societies in the 1990s, the resistance and inertia of the old governmental and economic bureaucracies have hampered government reforms and transitions toward democracy and economic freedom. Many citizens are exasperated with bureaucracy and its propensities for inefficiency and lack of responsiveness. This frustration is reflected in popular cynicism as well as in periodic attempts to reform government.

Mark Nadel and Francis Rourke suggest a variety of ways that government and societal agencies may influence and control bureaucracies, externally or internally.[20] The major external government control is the political executive. Although presidents, prime ministers, and ministers formally command subordinate officials and may have the power to remove them for nonperformance of duty, executives and bureaucracies actually mutually depend on one another. Top executives typically try to persuade; rarely do they go to the extreme of dismissing or transferring civil servants. Centralized budgeting and administrative reorganization are other means of executive control. The threat to take away resources or authority may bring bureaucratic implementation into greater conformity with the aims of the political executive.

Modern authoritarian systems discovered that they could achieve more efficient and effective control by simultaneously manipulating political socialization, political recruitment, and political communication. Socialization efforts are made to instill loyalty and to limit and regulate information. But if recruitment is made a part of a larger pattern of control, it is hardly neglected. Leadership selection in the former Soviet Union was accomplished through a device called *nomenklatura*. Under this procedure important positions were kept under the direct supervision of a party agency whose officials had the final word on recruitment. Moreover, the party offered a complicated set of inducements to control the behavior of the chosen officials. These inducements made it difficult for any but the topmost officials to have much freedom of action. Soviet leaders used normative incentives, such as appeal to party, ideology, and national idealism; financial incentives, such as better salaries, access to finer food and clothing, better housing, and freedom to travel; and coercive control, such as reporting by police, party, and bureaucrats. They used demotion or imprisonment, even execution, as penalties. To avoid a coup by police or military forces, the varied layers of command and inducement structures were interwoven, so that no layer could act independently.

In democracies assemblies and courts also help control the bureaucracy. Legislative committee hearings or judicial investigations may bring bureaucratic performance into line with political desires. Sweden invented the institution of the **ombudsman** to prevent bureaucrats from doing injury or injustice to individuals.[21] This invention has been copied by a number of other states. In the Scandinavian countries, Britain, Germany, and elsewhere ombudsmen now investigate citizen claims that they have suffered injury or damage as a result of government action. Ombudsmen typically have no power of their own, but report to the legislature for remedial action. Their cases rarely lead to criminal conviction, but often government officials change their policies as a result of embarrassing publicity. Thus, ombudsmen offer a more expeditious and less costly procedure than court action. Among the extragovernmental forces that constrain bureaucracies are public opinion and the mass media, as well as interest groups of various kinds.

Not all controls on bureaucrats are external. Internal controls, such as advisory committees, are appointed to oversee the impartiality of their performance. Another way of controlling bureaucracy is to decentralize it, thereby bringing agencies closer to their clients. Finally, the attitudes of the bureaucrats themselves affect their responsiveness and responsibility. The norms and values that bureaucrats bring with them into public service, and the standards and obligations they are taught to respect, have an important bearing on bureaucratic performance.

All such controls on civil servants tend to be less effective outside the advanced industrial democracies. Authoritarian systems lack many of these controls, particularly external ones, such as elected political executives and legislators, independent courts, free mass media, and interest groups. Therefore, authoritarian regimes are particularly prone to bureaucratic inefficiency and inertia. Moreover, in many nonindustrial countries, mass media are neither independent nor influential, few citizens participate in politics, and lower-level government employees are poorly trained and paid—all conditions that encourage bribery, extortion, and bureaucratic mismanagement.[22]

Successful democracy requires that public policies made by national assemblies and chief executives be implemented fairly and effectively; democracy depends on the rule of law. When ruling parties demand kickbacks of public money from construction firms seeking public works contracts, the democratic process is subverted by rent-seeking politicians. (See Chapter 1 and Box 1.4.) Similarly, when tax officials and border authorities are open to cash payments to overlook tax deficiencies and customs violations, democratic law making is undermined. Citizens who must bribe teachers to get education for their children or health officials to get immunizations are deprived of benefits of democratic public policies. Such practices are all too common in the poorer nations of the world.

T A B L E   6 . 4   Perceived Corruption and Economic Development Level*

Country	Perceived Corruption Index (0 = Corrupt) (10 = Clean)	Economic Development Level (PPP)
Britain	8.7	24,468
United States	7.7	34,870
Germany	7.3	25,530
Japan	7.1	27,430
France	6.3	25,280
Brazil	4.0	7450
Mexico	3.6	8770
China	3.5	4260
Egypt	3.4	3790
India	2.7	2450
Russia	2.7	8660
Nigeria	1.6	830

*Economic development level from World Bank, downloaded from www.worldbank.org/data on Sept. 24, 2002; Perceived Corruption Index from Transparency International, downloaded from www.transparency.org/cpi/index on April 24, 2003.

Failure of the rule of law is difficult to study systematically, but some comparative insight into corruption in public bureaucracies is provided by the surveys of perceptions of corruption on the part of business people, academics, and analysts in different countries. These have been combined into a Corruptions Perception Index, which rates about one hundred countries each year on a scale from 0 ("highly corrupt") to 10 ("highly clean"). Table 6.4 shows the ratings for 2002 (based on a three year moving average) of our usual twelve countries. As we see, all of our countries experience some levels of corruption, with even Britain's 8.7 less than ideal. (The top country rated in 2002 was Finland at 9.7.) But Britain, the United States, Germany and Japan (despite individually notorious cases in each), rate in the top half of the scale and countries. Brazil, Mexico, China and Egypt are far more corrupt, with scores in the range of 4.0 to 3.4, while Russia, plagued by many problems of its dual economic and political transitions, scores even worse, as does India. Nigeria, despite its recent efforts at democratic transition, is perceived as one of the world's most corrupt countries, with a score of 1.6. Comparisons of the perceived corruption scores with the Purchasing Power Parity measure of economic wealth and productivity in column two show that corruption and the failure of the rule of law are very strongly associated with poverty and underdevelopment, as well as with direct indicators of popular misery (also see Table 7.3).[23]

The ills of bureaucracy, including inefficiency and inertia, are pandemic. This is truly a dilemma because we are unlikely to invent any schemes for carrying out large-scale social tasks without the organization, division of labor, and professionalism that bureaucracy provides. Its pathologies can only be mitigated. The art of modern political leadership consists not only of defining and communicating appropriate goals and policies, but also of getting them implemented by a massive and complex bureaucracy—how and when to press and coerce it, reorganize it, reward it, teach it, or be taught by it.

KEY TERMS

assemblies
authoritarian regimes
bicameralism
bureaucracy
Cabinet
chief executives

civil service
confidence relationship
constitutional regimes
decision rules
democracy

democratic presidential regime
federal systems
higher civil service
impeachment
independent central banks

judicial review
ombudsman
parliamentary regimes
policymaking
semi-presidential regime
separation of powers

SUGGESTED READINGS

Aberbach, Joel, Robert D. Putnam, and Bert A. Rockman. *Bureaucrats and Politicians in Western Democracies.* Cambridge, MA: Harvard University Press, 1981.

Döring, Herbert, ed. *Parliaments and Majority Rule in Western Europe.* New York: St. Martin's Press, 1995.

Huber, John D. *Rationalizing Parliament.* Cambridge, England: Cambridge University Press, 1996.

Katzenstein, Peter. *Small States in World Markets.* Ithaca, NY: Cornell University Press, 1985.

Lijphart, Arend. *Democracy in Plural Societies.* New Haven, CT: Yale University Press, 1977.

———. *Patterns of Democracy: Government Forms and Performance in Thirty-Six Countries.* New Haven, CT: Yale University Press, 1999.

Linz, Juan and Arturo Valenzuela, eds. *The Failure of Presidential Democracy: Comparative Perspectives.* Baltimore, MD: Johns Hopkins University Press, 1994.

Mainwaring, Scott and Matthew Shugart, eds. *Presidentialism and Democracy in Latin America.* New York: Cambridge University Press, 1997.

March, James G. and Johan P. Olsen. *Rediscovering Institutions: The Organizational Basis of Politics.* New York: Free Press, 1989.

North, Douglass. *Institutions, Institutional Change, and Economic Performance.* Cambridge, England: Cambridge University Press, 1990.

O'Donnell, Guillermo and Philippe Schmitter. *Transitions from Authoritarian Rule.* Baltimore, MD: Johns Hopkins University Press, 1986.

Powell, G. Bingham. *Contemporary Democracies.* Cambridge, MA: Harvard University Press, 1982.

Riker, William H. *Federalism: Origin, Operation, and Significance.* Boston, MA: Little, Brown, 1964.

Sartori, Giovanni. *Comparative Constitutional Engineering.* New York: New York University Press, 1997.

Secondat, Charles de, Baron de Montesquieu. *The Spirit of the Laws.* London: Hafner, 1960.

Shugart, Matthew, and John Carey. *Presidents and Assemblies: Constitutional Design and Electoral Dynamics.* Cambridge, England: Cambridge University Press, 1992.

Stone-Sweet, Alec. *Governing with Judges: Constitutional Politics in Europe.* Oxford: Oxford University Press, 2002.

Strøm, Kaare. *Minority Government and Majority Rule.* Cambridge, England: Cambridge University Press, 1990.

Tsebelis, George and Jeannette Money. *Bicameralism.* Cambridge, England: Cambridge University Press, 1997.

Weaver, Kent and Bert Rockman, eds. *Do Institutions Matter? Government Capabilities in the United States and Abroad.* Washington: Brookings Institution, 1993.

Weber, Max. "Bureaucracy." In H. H. Gerth and C. Wright Mills, eds. *From Max Weber.* New York: Oxford University Press, 1976, pp. 196–244.

Weingast, Barry R. "Political Foundations of Democracy and the Rule of Law." *American Political Science Review* 91, no. 2 (June 1997): 245–63.

ENDNOTES

1. For a skeptical view of constitutional design, see James G. March and Johan P. Olsen, *Rediscovering Institutions: The Organizational Basis of Politics* (New York: Free Press, 1989), pp. 171–172. For a more sanguine argument, see Giovanni Sartori, *Comparative Constitutional Engineering* (New York: New York University Press, 1995).

2. Samuel Huntington, *The Third Wave: Democratization in the Late Twentieth Century* (Norman, OK: University of Oklahoma Press, 1991).

3. Adam Przeworski, Michael E. Alvarez, Jose Antonio Cheibub and Fernando Limongi, *Democracy and Development* (NY: Cambridge University Press, 2000).

4. John Locke, *Two Treatises of Government,* ed. Peter Laslett (Cambridge, England: Cambridge University Press, 1960); Charles de Secondat, Baron de Montesquieu, *The Spirit of the Laws* (London: Hafner, 1960).

5. *The Federalist: A Commentary on the Constitution of the United States* (Washington: National Home Library Foundation, 1937).

6. On presidential decree powers see John M. Carey and Matthew S. Shugart, *Executive Decree Authority* (New York: Cambridge University Press, 1998); for more general discussions of presidential powers see Matthew S. Shugart and John M. Carey, *Presidents and Assemblies: Constitutional Design and Electoral Dynamics* (Cambridge, England: Cambridge University Press, 1992); and Scott Mainwaring and Matthew S. Shugart, eds., *Presidentialism and Democracy in Latin America* (New York: Cambridge University Press, 1997.)

7. It is important to avoid confusion between the formal titles of government officials and the source of their selection and bases of their powers—which determine the type of political system. For example, Germany is a parliamentary system, whose executive is headed by a prime minister, although his official title is Chancellor; and as in many parliamentary systems the German head of state is a ceremonial president, chosen by the legislature, with little policymaking power. See also Table 6.2

8. Arend Lijphart, *Democracy in Plural Societies* (New Haven: Yale University Press, 1977); G. Bingham Powell, *Contemporary Demcracies* (Cambridge: Harvard University Press, 1982); Arend Lijphart, *Patterns of Democracy: Government Forms and Performance in Thirty-Six Countries* (New Haven: Yale University Press, 1999.)

9. Juan Linz and Arturo Valenzuela, eds., *The Failure of Presidential Democracy: Comparative Perspectives* (Baltimore, MD: Johns Hopkins University Press, 1994). Also see Przeworski, et. al., *Democracy and Development,* 2000, pp. 128–136.

10. Donald Horowitz, "Comparing Democratic Systems," in Larry Diamond and Mark F. Plattner, eds., *The Global Resurgence of Democracy* (Baltimore: Johns Hopkins University Press, 1993), pp. 127 ff.

11. Philippe Schmitter and Gerhard Lehmbruch, *Trends Toward Corporatist Intermediation* (Beverly Hills, CA: Sage, 1979).

12. See the discussion and references in Arend Lijphart, *Patterns of Democracy*, 1999, Ch. 13.

13. Arend Lijphart, *Patterns of Democracy*, 1999, p. 226.

14. George H. Gadbois, Jr., "The Institutionalization of the Supreme Court of India," in John R. Schmidhauser, ed., *Comparative Judicial Systems* (London: Butterworth Enterprises, 1987), pp. 111–142.

15. Donald S. Lutz reports that the U.S. Constitution, amended 26 times in 202 years (at the time of his writing in 1991) had been formally changed far less often than the cross-country average of about 2.5 amendments per year. "Toward a Theory of Constitutional Amendment," *American Political Science Review* 88 (1994), pp. 355–370. However, the Japanese constitution, of about average rigidity, had never been amended. Also see Ivo Duchachek, *Power Maps: Comparative Politics of Constitutions* (Santa Barbara, CA: ABC Clio Press, 1973), pp. 210 ff.

16. For a survey of parliamentary committees in Europe, see Ingvar Mattson and Kaare Strøm, "Parliamentary Committees," in Herbert Doring, ed., *Parliaments and Majority Rule in Western Europe* (New York: St. Martin's, 1995), pp. 249–307.

17. See Pippa Norris, "Legislative Recruitment," in Lawrence LeDuc, Richard G. Niemi, and Pippa Norris, eds., *Comparing Democracies* (London: Sage, 1996), pp. 184–215; and Richard E. Matland, "Women's Representation in National Legislatures: Developed and Developing Countries," *Legislative Studies Quarterly* 23, No. 1 (February 1998): 109–125.

18. See the different chapters in Michael Laver and Kenneth A. Shepsle, *Cabinet Ministers and Parliamentary Government* (New York: Cambridge University Press, 1994.)

19. See Joel Aberbach, Robert D. Putnam, and Bert A. Rockman, *Bureaucrats and Politicians in Western Democracies* (Cambridge, MA: Harvard University Press, 1981).

20. Mark V. Nadel and Francis E. Rourke, "Bureaucracies," in Fred Greenstein and Nelson Polsby, eds., *Handbook of Political Science,* vol. 5 (Reading, MA: Addison-Wesley, 1975), pp. 373–440.

21. See Frank Stacey, *The British Ombudsman* (Oxford, England: Clarendon Press, 1971); Roy Gregory and Peter Hutchesson, *The Parliamentary Ombudsman: A Study in the Control of Administrative Action* (London: Allen and Unwin, 1975).

22. On the difficulties involved in reducing administrative corruption in developing countries, see Robert Klitgard, *Controlling Corruption* (Berkeley, CA: University of California Press, 1989).

23. For statistical analysis explaining scores on the Corruption Perception Index, see Daniel Triesman, "The Causes of Corruption: A Cross-National Study," *Journal of Public Economics* 76 (June 2000): 399–457, who suggests lower levels of economic development, shorter exposure to democracy, and federalism among factors encouraging more perceived corruption.

7

Public Policy

In this chapter, we shift our focus to **public policies,** to all those authoritative public decisions that governments make. We shall refer to them as the **outputs** of the political system. Policies or outputs are normally chosen for a purpose; they are meant to promote end results that we shall refer to as political **outcomes.** Different policy instruments may be more or less efficient ways to reach the outcomes that policymakers ultimately want. We therefore want to know the relationships between political outputs and outcomes. Whether a certain outcome is good or bad ultimately depends on normative criteria that we call **political goods and values.** And whatever values and goals policymakers and citizens have will surely affect their evaluation of the political outcomes they actually reach. Since politicians and citizens often disagree over political goods and values, it is important to keep these goals in mind when we study public policy. In this chapter, we shall discuss these aspects of public policy in order, but we begin by considering what governments do.

GOVERNMENT AND WHAT IT DOES

Governments do many things. Some of them are timeless, similar in kind to what happened in the ancient world. In the days of the Roman Empire, for example, defense against external and internal enemies was a major government responsibility. It continues to be so in most societies today. In other ways, governments today do things that were unthinkable in the past. For example, contemporary governments regulate telecommunications and air traffic, policy areas that were unknown until the twentieth century.

Governments as Producers

What governments do can be summarized under several labels. First, governments produce many goods and services, though exactly which varies a great deal. While in most societies, governments provide law enforcement and postal services, in many countries they go far beyond such service provision. In the former Soviet Union and other communist states, governments owned and operated most major industries and produced everything from military equipment to consumer goods such as clothing and shoes. In a capitalist society such as the United States, the government produces far fewer goods, particularly consumer products. In other advanced industrial societies, such as much of Western Europe, the government is a larger producer than in the United States, but a far smaller one than in the former Soviet Union. Governments control a number of industries in many states, but the range is very different. In recent decades, one study shows, governments in the United States employed only 1 percent of the persons engaged in mining and manufacturing and 28 percent of those working for public utilities supplying gas, water, and electrical power; whereas in France, the corresponding figures were 8 percent and 71 percent. Capitalist, free-market societies tend to have governments that are less active as producers than have socialist societies. Yet, there is no society in which the government produces no goods and services, and similarly no state in which all industries are run by the government. Even in the former Soviet Union, part of the agricultural sector was private, as were many simple consumer services such as baby-sitting. Other ostensibly communist societies, such as Poland in the 1980s or China today, feature a lot of private enterprise, particularly in the consumer goods sector.

Public Policies

The importance of governments goes far beyond their role as producers of goods and services. Indeed, this may not even be their most important role in most contemporary states. Governments also engage in various forms of public policy, which is the focus of this chapter. Public policies may be summarized and compared according to outputs—that is, according to the actions governments take to accomplish their purposes. We classify these actions or outputs under four headings:

1. the **extraction** of resources—money, goods, persons, and services—from the domestic and international environments;
2. the **distribution**—of money, goods, and services;
3. the **regulation** of human behavior—the use of compulsion and inducement to enforce extractive and distributive compliance or otherwise bring about desired behavior; and
4. the **symbolic policies**—political speeches, holidays, rites, public monuments and statues, and the like—used by governments to exhort citizens to desired forms of behavior, often to build a sense of community or to celebrate exemplary conduct (see Chapter 1).

Night Watchman State, Police State, Welfare State, Regulatory State

Political systems have different policy profiles. Some governments produce a lot of goods and services but regulate little. Elsewhere, the government may be heavily engaged in extraction and distribution, but relies on the private sector to produce most goods and services. We can classify states broadly according to their mix of policies and activities. For example, it is customary to contrast the **night watchman state** of the nineteenth century with the more expansive forms of government that have emerged in the twentieth century. The night watchman state is a Lockean state (see Chapter 1), primarily concerned with regulation aimed at preserving law, order, and commerce, and the protection of its citizens.

The twentieth century saw the creation of the **police state,** the **welfare state,** and the **regulatory state.** The police state regulates much more intrusively and extracts resources more severely. The most oppressive forms of the police state have been associated with the totalitarian ideologies (Nazism, fascism, and communism) that have also left their mark on the past century. Fascist and communist governments typically call on their citizens to devote a lot of time to military or other community service.

The welfare state, which is found particularly in more prosperous and democratic societies, engages itself extensively in distributive activities to provide for the health, education, employment, housing, and income support of its citizens. For this purpose, it also has to extract (tax its citizens) more heavily. The welfare state originated in Germany in the late nineteenth century but has spread to most developed societies. Finally, the regulatory state has evolved in all advanced modern societies in response to the growing complexity of modern life.

In the first chapter of this book, we discussed three important challenges facing many contemporary states: building community, fostering development, and securing democracy and human rights. Many public policies are wholly or in part directed at these challenges. Public policies are designed to strengthen national identity and community by reinforcing the status of a common language or culture, or by promoting allegiance to a shared political heritage. A host of economic policies aims to promote economic and social development and to distribute its benefits more or less broadly. Finally, other policies seek to establish or enhance mechanisms (democratic institutions) that enable citizens to control political decisions. In the past century most Western nations have been transformed from authoritarian, or oligarchic, regimes to democracies. Government policy has increasingly been used to meet popular needs and demands. Yet we cannot infer that everything democratic governments do is in the best interest of their citizens.

EXTRACTION

Let us now turn to the four types of public policy we have identified above, beginning with extraction. All political systems extract resources from their environments and specifically from their members. When simple societies go to war, for example, individuals of specific age groups (most commonly young men) may

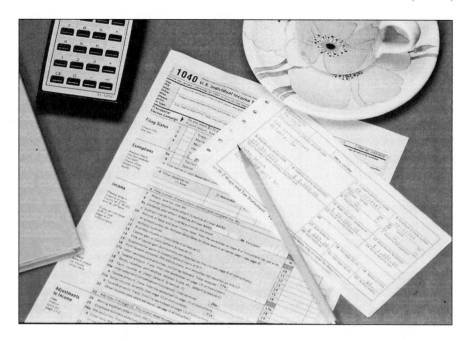

America's annual April 15th anguish is exemplified by the Form 1040 on some taxpayer's table along with the cup of coffee to keep him awake.

Bard Wrisley/Liaison International

be called on to fight. Anthropologists have estimated that in some hunter-gatherer societies, such obligations have been so onerous that about half of all males have died in warfare (Thomas Hobbes would not have been surprised). Such direct extraction of services is still found in modern states, in the form of compulsory military service, jury duty, or compulsory labor imposed on those convicted of crime.

The most common contemporary forms of resource extraction, however, are taxation and borrowing. **Taxation** is the extraction for governmental purposes of money or goods from members of a political system, for which they receive no immediate or direct benefit. Tax policies are designed to meet a lot of different objectives, which sometimes conflict. On the one hand, governments often want to collect as much tax revenue as possible from their citizens in order to finance various services. On the other hand, they do not want to kill the goose that lays the golden egg. The more governments tax their citizens, the less these people are inclined to work, and if the tax burden becomes too onerous, they may leave the country altogether. Another common trade-off in tax policies is between efficiency and equity. *Efficiency* means extracting the most tax revenue possible at the lowest cost to economic production. *Equity* means taxing in such a way that, as much as possible, no one is unfairly burdened, and particularly so that those who have the least are spared. In most soci-

eties, the tax system is designed to redistribute wealth in favor of the less well-off. Therefore, income taxes are generally progressive, which means that citizens with greater incomes are taxed at higher rates than those who earn less. Yet, there is a limit to how progressive income taxes can be. Highly progressive income taxes can reduce people's incentive to work and hurt capital formation. Therefore, they are often inefficient.

Personal and corporate income taxes and taxes on capital gains and wealth are called **direct taxes,** since they are directly levied on persons and corporations. Such taxes, as well as property taxes, tend to be progressive. But although corporate income taxes are meant to be progressive, corporations often avoid them through creative accounting or by moving their operations to countries where taxes are lower. If personal income taxes become too high, similar things can happen. **Indirect taxes** include sales and value-added taxes, excise taxes, and customs duties. Their distributive effects depend on who purchases the relevant commodities and services. Since the poor spend more of their income on food and clothing than do those who are better off, sales (or value-added) taxes on such necessities are regressive (which means that the poor pay relatively more than the rich). But indirect taxes on luxury goods may be progressive, since the poor rarely purchase yachts, fine jewelry, or private planes. Payroll

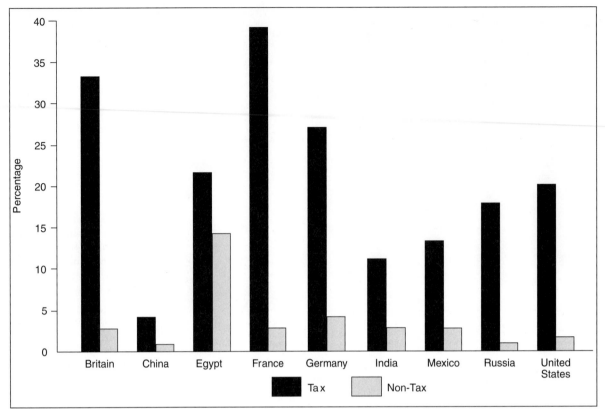

FIGURE 7 . 1   Central Government Revenue as a Percentage of GDP
and by Source of Revenue for Selected Countries, 1997

Source: World Bank, *World Development Report, 1999–2000* (New York: Oxford University Press, 2000), Table 14, pp. 256–57.

taxes, which are often used to finance pensions (e.g., social security in the United States), tend to hit the middle class, since the wealthy often receive a larger share of their income in the form of interest or capital gains. Such taxes on wages also penalize people in the labor force relative to retirees and homemakers and can therefore hurt employment or drive businesses into the "underground economy" in which they do not report their incomes.

Political systems that rely heavily on sales and payroll taxes are less likely to attain a progressive tax structure overall. On the other hand, such taxes are less "visible" than income taxes and seem to generate less resentment and tax avoidance. In many countries, particularly where the government does not have good financial records, indirect taxes are easier to collect. Finally, the more mobile a tax object is, the more difficult it is to tax. Financial investments tend to be highly mobile, which makes them difficult to tax. Land and buildings, on the other

hand, are not very mobile at all, and many states tax them substantially.

Besides redistribution and efficiency, tax policies are often designed to promote certain social values, such as charity, energy conservation, or home ownership. For example, many countries stimulate home ownership by making mortgage interest payments tax deductible. The rationale is that home ownership promotes stable families who take an active interest in their neighborhoods. On the other hand, if such tax incentives are too generous, they can cause economic distortions and reduce output. Families may overinvest in housing, so that businesses are starved of capital. Moreover, mortgage deductions are primarily a middle-class benefit of little use to the truly poor, since they rarely own their own homes.

Figure 7.1 shows the central government revenues as a percentage of **gross domestic product (GDP),** the total value of goods and services produced by a country's residents in a year. For the average country in Figure 7.1, about a fifth of the GDP is extracted by the central government's taxes, but in some countries the proportion is much higher. Regional and local taxes add to the tax burden. In federal systems, such as Brazil, Germany, India, Russia, and the United States, these can increase the total tax burden by a third or more.[1]

Governments also derive revenues from non-tax sources (the lighter columns in Figure 7.1), such as administrative fees and income from business enterprises that they run. The total size of government revenue from all these sources in some advanced capitalist countries is not radically smaller than that of Eastern European countries when they were under Communist control.

Growing tax burdens have led to taxpayer revolts and some scaling back of government extraction. But Sweden still extracts more than 50 percent of its GNP in taxes and France comes close to the 50-percent mark. Britain and Germany (after taking account of their subnational governments) are among a number of advanced industrial societies that collect revenue at around the 40-percent level of GDP, while the United States and Russia extract about a third. Outside the European–North American area, central government revenue rarely exceeds 20 percent of GDP. Egypt, with its substantial public sector, is an exception. Much of its revenue comes from public enterprises and foreign aid. The central government revenue of India is under 15 percent, or about a third more if we add state and local governments.

The tax profiles of different states depend on the kinds of taxes imposed, the distribution of income and wealth, the consumption patterns of different population groups, and the mobility of capital and labor. In Germany and Britain most of the revenue comes from social security and income taxes, but Germany relies far more heavily on social security payments and Britain more on income taxes. India and Mexico receive most of their revenue from indirect taxes. Heidenheimer, Heclo, and Adams classify the tax systems of the advanced free-market economies of the **Organization for Economic Cooperation and Development (OECD)** countries into three categories: (1) heavy social security tax systems (including Germany, Austria, the Netherlands, France, and Italy), which receive one-third to one-half of their revenue from social security, which is imposed more or less equally on both employers and employees; (2) the United States and Japan, which

fall the farthest below average in total tax burden and rely heavily on direct taxes rather than on sales and consumption taxes; and finally (3) countries such as Sweden and Norway, which impose the highest tax burdens of all the OECD countries and rely on all three types of taxation—direct, indirect, and social security payments but impose particularly burdensome social security payments on employers.[2]

Although overall tax burdens continue to grow, income tax rates have decreased in Western countries since the early 1980s, as there has been a shift from direct income taxes to less visible indirect consumption taxes. From 1975 to 1990 British top marginal income tax rates declined by 43 percentage points, U.S. federal rates by 42 points (though they then rose by about 13 points by the end of the Clinton administration, but have come down by about 4.5 points under President George W. Bush), Swedish rates by 35 points, and Japanese rates by 25 points. The average decline in top tax rates for all OECD countries was 18 percent.[3] Tax rates have come down because of the spread of economic views that stress the importance of entrepreneurial incentives for productivity. Lower marginal income tax rates stimulate economic activity and lessen incentives for tax evasion, but they may cause growing income inequalities.

DISTRIBUTION

Government not only takes—it also gives away, and that is what we call distribution. Distributive policies include the allocation by governmental agencies of various kinds of money, goods, services, honors, and opportunities to individuals and groups in the society. They can be measured and compared according to the quantity of whatever is distributed, the areas of human life touched by these benefits, the sections of the population receiving these benefits, and the effectiveness of the distributive program.

Figure 7.2 reports central governmental expenditures on health, education, and defense as a percentage of GDP. Clearly, central government expenditures depend a great deal on economic development. Developed countries generally allocate from one-half to two-thirds of their central government expenditures to education, health, and welfare. France, Germany, and Britain spend more than two-thirds of their budgets here, as compared with just under one-half in the United States, where a larger share of health care is in the private sector. Developing

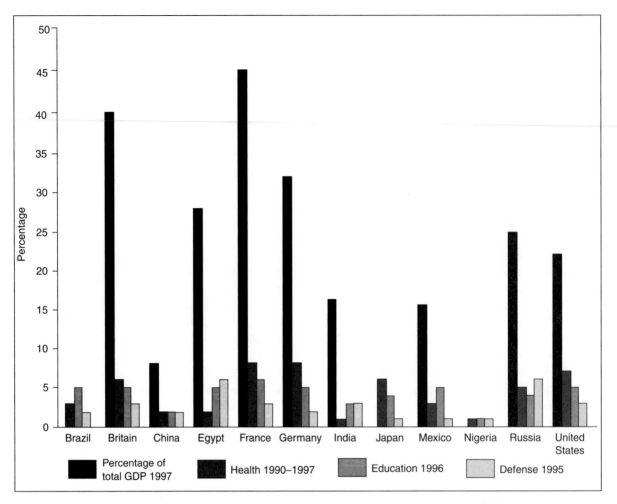

F I G U R E   7 . 2   Central Government Expenditures as a Percentage of GDP and by Object of Expenditure, 1990–1997

Source: World Bank, *World Development Report: 1999–2000* (New York: Oxford University Press, 2000), Table 14, pp. 256–257; Table 7, pp. 242–243; Table 6, pp. 240–241; Table 17, pp. 262–263.

countries such as India and Nigeria spend very little on health, but typically a little more on education. Low-income countries face a tragic quandary: While they urgently need to upgrade the skills of their workforces, their commitments in education and health are insufficient to make rapid headway. The government in a country such as Nigeria seems hardly to touch its people. India's efforts are only slightly greater. Sadly, the countries that "need" it the most have the least to spend on education and health.

National security spending shows a different pattern. Particularly among less-developed countries, spending varies as much with the international envi-

ronment as with overall economic means. Some states that are locked in tense international confrontations, such as in the Middle East, or that are trying to exert international influence, make extraordinary defense efforts. Because of its worldwide security commitments, the United States is by far the heaviest military spender, though between the end of the Cold War and September 11, 2001, U.S. defense spending decreased. Relative to the size of the national economy, however, Egypt spent more on defense in 1995 than did the United States. Japan, which spends as much as most Western countries on health and education, was very low in defense efforts. Prior to the water-

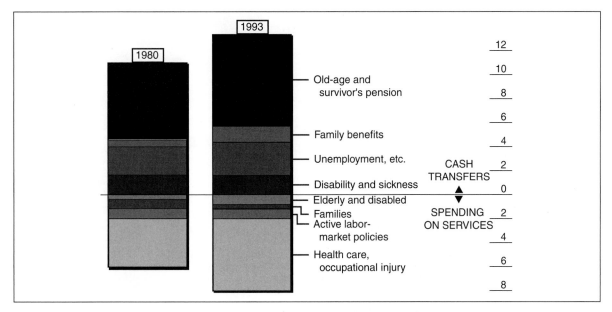

F I G U R E   7 . 3   The Welfare State in OECD Countries
(OECD Average Transfers and Spending as Percent of GDP)

Source: "Privatising Peace of Mind," *The Economist* (October 24, 1998): p. 4.

shed year of 1989, the Soviet Union and the Communist countries of Eastern Europe spent less on education, health, and welfare than the democracies of Western Europe. As the new democracies of the former Communist bloc have introduced market economies, their government revenue and expenditure patterns have become more similar to the West.

Poor nations, with limited budgets and many pressing demands, cannot easily spare the resources for health and education. Also, in both absolute and relative terms, social security expenditure in poor nations tends to be limited. But in these societies the aged and the infirm typically receive some care through the extended family. Just as our GNP measures fail to include the subsistence economy and therefore underreport the wealth of the poorest countries (see Chapter 1), our measures of educational and health expenditures may similarly underreport the efforts of the poorest states. Many developing societies still have a preindustrial welfare safety net for many citizens.

The Welfare State

The twentieth century has witnessed a vast increase in the scope of distributive policies in industrial societies. This has largely been associated with the growth of the welfare state. The welfare state generally refers to a set of government, and sometimes private, policies in the areas of old age pensions (known in the United States as social security), health, sickness, and accident insurance, unemployment benefits, and the like. Over time, welfare state policies have come to include such benefits as housing subsidies, child and childcare benefits, and other distributive policies. The first modern welfare state programs were introduced in Germany in the 1880s. In response to Germany's rapid industrialization and urbanization, the government began offering social insurance programs that protected workers against unemployment, accidents, sickness, and old age poverty. During the twentieth century, most industrialized states have adopted and greatly expanded welfare state policies, particularly in the period from the Great Depression of the 1930s until the 1970s.

Figure 7.3 shows that the welfare state in advanced capitalist (OECD) countries has continued to grow during the 1980s and 1990s, albeit at a somewhat slower rate. As the figure shows, welfare state spending consists of two major categories: cash transfers to individuals and families, and direct

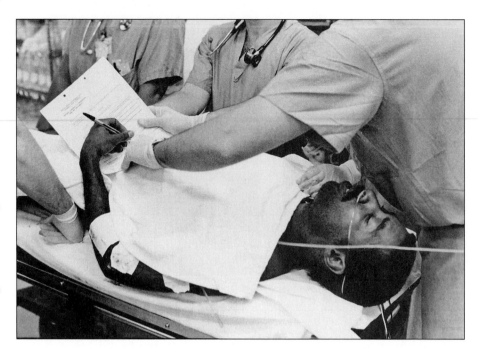

A seriously injured man is wheeled on a gurney into the emergency room of a Detroit, Michigan, hospital. He must sign the Medicaid form in order to activate his health benefits.

Leonard Freed/Magnum Photos, Inc.

government spending on services. Though both categories have grown, the transfer programs remain the largest. Among the individual programs that make up the welfare state, old-age pensions (social security) and health care loom particularly large. In many European countries with jobless rates of up to 10 or 15 percent, unemployment benefits are another major government outlay.

Not all welfare states are alike. Even among the advanced industrial countries, some welfare states are more extensive than others, and different political systems emphasize different programs and benefits. All the wealthier nations make efforts to assist the aged, the disabled, and the unemployed; however, differences in expenditures reflect policy and historical experience. The U.S. model stresses equality of opportunity through public education. In contrast, on the European continent, social security and health programs have traditionally taken precedence over education. The United States made a much greater effort, and much earlier, in mass education than did most European nations. On the other hand, Americans began spending on social insurance and public services much later, and still do less in this area. Americans have historically put much more emphasis on equality of opportunity and less on welfare obliga-

tions than Europeans. This may reflect the U.S. heritage as a nation of immigrants, many of whom have arrived poor and been expected to prosper by their own efforts.

Also, it is important to keep in mind that many welfare services in the United States are provided by private foundations, churches and other religious organizations, and individuals. In 1997 Americans made private donations of $143 billion to nonprofit organizations. More than three-fourths of these gifts came from living individuals, many of them persons of very limited means. The nonprofit sector of the U.S. economy accounts for 8 percent of the gross domestic product, more than twice as much as in 1960. It employs close to 10 percent of the American workforce, more than the federal and state governments combined.[4] The nonprofit sector exists in other developed states as well, but generally on a much smaller scale.

Since World War II especially, governments have greatly expanded their spending on a wide range of benefits. Education is one of the most important of these. Developing societies have made large efforts to provide at least primary education for all their citizens, while most of the more developed societies have also experienced a huge increase in secondary and university enrollments. A few decades ago, fewer than 5 percent of young adults in most European countries were able to pursue a university or college education. Today, those numbers have risen to 40 percent or more (see Table 7.5). In most of these countries, the majority of colleges and universities are public. Consequently, government spending on secondary and higher education has risen very substantially.

As government expenditures have grown to between one-third and one-half of the national product in most industrial democracies, they have caused serious concern about the costs of welfare state programs and the ability of future generations to pay for them. One of the most serious problems is that at the same time that senior citizens are qualifying for greater pension benefits and health care costs are rising rapidly, the ranks of the elderly are swelling relative to those in the workforce. This is reflected in the dependency ratio, which is the proportion of those outside the workforce (because they are too young or too old) to those in the working-age population. Figure 7.4 shows that over the next decades, dependency ratios will increase in all advanced industrial societies, and particularly in such countries as Japan. That means that fewer and fewer working people will have to pay higher and higher taxes just to support existing health and welfare programs. In the United States, Medicare and Social Security may incur large deficits in the future. In other countries, social welfare programs are already costing more than their designated taxes are bringing in.

Another problem with some welfare state policies is that they give citizens few incentives to behave responsibly. For example, generous unemployment or sick leave policies may give people little incentive to work. Norway and Sweden are among the leading countries in the world in life expectancy and public health statistics. Yet, workers in these countries are on sick leave about twice as often as those elsewhere in Europe, as the average Swedish worker misses about five or six weeks of work per year. And in Norway, more than 10 percent of the working-age population is on disability pensions. The reason, at least in part, is that unusually generous sick leave benefits let workers keep virtually their entire pay from the first day that they miss work, and that it is relatively easy to qualify for disability benefits. But these policies are costly. In Sweden, sick pay and disability benefits account for more than 10 percent of the government's total spending.

These widely perceived problems with the welfare state have stirred efforts to prevent further increases in spending obligations (entitlements) and to contain the costs of those already in effect. Conservative parties in particular have stressed setting limits on public expenditures and labor costs.[5] Thus the gradual expansion of welfare benefits that characterized most of the twentieth century can no longer be taken for granted.

REGULATION

Regulation is the exercise of political control over the behavior of individuals and groups in the society. Governments regulate the lives of their citizens in many ways. Although we usually associate regulation with legal coercion or its threat, there are other ways to regulate as well. Governments may control behavior by offering material or financial inducements or by persuasion or moral exhortation. For example, many governments try to reduce tobacco use by a combination of methods: (1) bans on smoking, sales, or advertising, (2) sales ("sin") taxes, and (3) information campaigns to convince citizens of the hazards of tobacco use.

Regulation occurs for a number of reasons, as we have discussed in Chapter 1. As social contract theorists such as Hobbes and Locke realized, government regulation can facilitate many beneficial activities. Economic production and commerce, for example, rely on government regulation to establish and protect property rights and to enforce contractual obligations. At the same time, citizens and consumers often demand regulations that protect them against fraud, manipulation, and obnoxious externalities such as toxic waste and environmental degradation. Increasingly, governments and international organizations, such as the European Union, have been involved in setting product standards, particularly for such products as pharmaceuticals and food. Governments also regulate to protect their citizens, and often particularly children and women, against physical and other abuse, and some protections are extended to animals and the natural environment as well.

Government regulation has proliferated enormously over the last century or so, due to new objective needs as well as citizen demands. Industrialization

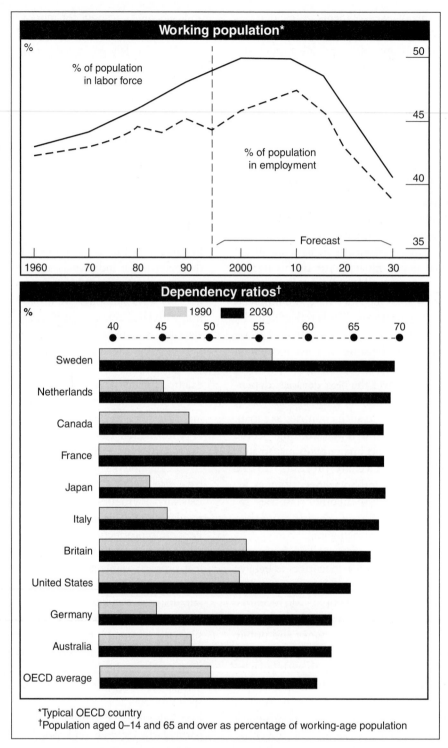

FIGURE 7.4   The Shrinking Working Population

Source: "Privatising Peace of Mind," *The Economist* (October 24, 1998): p. 9.

and urban concentration have caused problems in traffic, health, and public order. Industrial growth has created problems of industrial safety, labor exploitation, and pollution. Moreover, the growth of science and the belief that humanity can harness and control nature have led to increased demands for governmental action. Finally, changes in citizen values can lead to demands for new kinds of regulation. Thus, in recent decades regulation in the United States has extended to include gun control, protection of voting rights, prohibition of discrimination in employment, pollution, and the like. At the same time, however, in most modern nations regulation of birth control, abortion, divorce, blasphemy, obscenity, and sexual conduct has lessened.

But even though there are many similarities in regulative policies across the world, states often differ substantially in their policy profiles. Patterns of regulation vary not only with industrialization and urbanization, for example, but also with cultural values. In the study of public policy, we describe and explain such differences between political systems by asking the following questions:

1. What aspects of human behavior and interaction are regulated and to what degree? Does the government regulate such domains as family relations, economic activity, religious activity, political activity, geographic mobility, professional and occupational qualifications, and protection of person and property? These questions have to do with the *domain* of government regulation.

2. What social groups are regulated, with what procedural limitations on enforcement and what rights? Are these sanctions applied uniformly, or do they affect different individuals or groups differently? Are there rights of appeal? Such questions help us identify the *subjects* of regulation.

3. What sanctions are used to compel or induce citizens to comply? Does the government use exhortation and moral persuasion, financial rewards and penalties, licensing of some types of action, physical confinement or punishment, or other forms of coercion? These questions help us map the *instruments* or *mechanisms*, of regulation.

TABLE 7.1   Political Rights and Liberties Ratings for Selected Countries 2003–2004

Country	Political Rights	Civil Liberties
Brazil	2	3
Britain	1	1
China	7	6
Egypt	6	5
France	1	1
Germany	1	1
India*	2	3
Japan	1	2
Mexico	2	2
Nigeria	4	4
Russia	6	5
United States	1	1

*Rating for India explicitly excludes Kashmir, which was rated 5, 5.

Source: Expert ratings of political rights and civil liberties for each country on 1 (highest) to 7 (lowest) scale, provided by Freedom House from their website, www.freedomhouse.org. Downloaded January 14, 2005.

Although all modern states use sanctions, they vary in their goals and strategies. Yet, one aspect of regulation is particularly important politically: government control over political participation and communication. Recall from earlier chapters that democracy requires political competition. Governments in authoritarian systems often suppress political competition by prohibiting party organization, voluntary associations, and political communication. Government regulation in this area therefore has a crucial effect on democracy. Yet, focusing on the suppression of rights should not give us the idea that governmental regulation is always negative. Our civilization and amenities depend on regulation. Government regulation commonly promotes such values as the safety of persons and property, sanitation, prevention of environmental pollution, safe disposal of toxic wastes, maintenance of occupational safety, and equal access to housing and education.

Table 7.1 shows the political rights and civil liberties ratings for the countries included in this book, based on expert judgments. Political rights refer to citizen opportunities to participate in the choice of political leaders—voting rights, the right to run for office, and the like. Civil liberties refer to protections in such areas as freedom of speech, press, assembly, and religion, as well as to procedural rights, such as trial by a jury of peers and bans on arbitrary or cruel treatment. The rich democratic countries all have ratings of 1 or 2 for both political and civil rights. India, Brazil, and Mexico, which have improved significantly in recent years, follow next. At the other extreme, China, Egypt, and most recently Russia substantially suppress both political rights and civil liberties. China in particular has tried to control the media comprehensively and sets few limits on government regulation vis-à-vis the individual. Nigeria is rated in the middle. These rankings, of course, vary over time. Nigeria's military governments of the 1990s were repressive and frequently brutal, earning scores of 7 and 6 before power was turned over to an elected civilian president in 1999. Rights and liberties in the United States have improved since the civil rights movement of the 1960s.

There is a strong correlation between political and civil rights. No country that scores high on participatory rights is very low on civil liberties, and no country low on participatory rights is high on civil liberties. This suggests a strong relationship between popular participation and the rule of law and equitable procedure. In a cross-national study of governmental repression in 153 countries during the 1980s, Steven C. Poe and C. Neal Tate concluded that democratic political institutions and conditions of peace and social order best explained positive civil and political rights records. Authoritarian states and those involved in internal or international war were the most frequent civil rights violators. A high level of economic development also helped explain a strong rights record.[6]

COMMUNITY-BUILDING AND SYMBOLIC POLICIES

A fourth type of output is symbolic policies. Much communication by political leaders takes the form of appeals to the courage, wisdom, and magnanimity embodied in the nation's past; or appeals to values and ideologies, such as equality, liberty, community, democracy, communism, liberalism, or religious tradition; or promises of future accomplishment and rewards. Political leaders appeal to such values for different reasons—

for example, to win elections or get their own pet projects enacted. But at the same time many symbolic appeals and policies have the purpose of building community—for example, by boosting people's national identity, civic pride, or trust in government.

Symbolic outputs are also intended to enhance other aspects of performance: to make people pay their taxes more readily and honestly, comply with the law more faithfully, or accept sacrifice, danger, and hardship. Such appeals may be especially important in times of crisis. Some of the most magnificent examples are the speeches of Pericles in the Athenian Assembly during the Peloponnesian War, or those of Franklin D. Roosevelt in the depths of the Great Depression, or of Winston Churchill in World War II, when Britain stood alone after the fall of France. But symbolic policies are important even in less extreme circumstances. Public buildings, plazas, monuments, holiday parades, and civic and patriotic indoctrination in schools all attempt to contribute to the population's sense of governmental legitimacy and its willingness to comply with public policy.

OUTCOMES: DOMESTIC WELFARE

While we can describe different government policies, it is not always clear what their consequences will be. How do extractive, distributive, regulative, and symbolic policies affect the lives of citizens? Unexpected economic, international, or social events may frustrate the purpose of political leaders. Thus a tax rebate to increase consumption and stimulate the economy may be nullified by a rise in the price of oil. Increases in health expenditures may have no effect because of unexpected epidemics or rising health costs, or health services may not reach those most in need. Sometimes policies have unintended consequences that may be undesirable, as when the introduction of benefits for troubled social groups lead others to simulate the same troubles. Consequently, to estimate the effectiveness of public policy, we have to examine actual welfare outcomes as well as governmental policies and their implementation.

Table 7.2 compares a number of welfare indicators. The first two columns report measures of economic well-being or its lack: growth in private consumption and the share of the population living on less than $2 per day. The severe problems of Nigeria

T A B L E   7 . 2   Welfare Outcomes for Selected States, 1990–1998

Country	Growth in Private Consumption per Capita % Annual 1980–1997[*]	Population Below $2 per Day %, ca. 2000	Access to Safe Water (%) Mid–1990s	Access to Sanitation (%), Mid–1990s
Brazil	0.2	25.4	72	67
Britain	1.8	ND	100	100
China	4.5	53.7	90	21
Egypt	1.3	52.7	64	11
France	1.1	ND	100	96
Germany	ND	ND	ND	ND
India	1.9	86.2	81	16
Japan	ND	ND	96	100
Mexico	0.0	42.5	83	66
Nigeria	–2.6	90.8	39	36
Russia	ND	25.1	ND	ND
United States	1.1	ND	ND	ND

[*]Corrected for distribution.

Source: World Bank, *Entering the 21st Century: World Development Report 1999–2000* (New York, Oxford University Press, 2000), pp. 232–233; *World Development Indicators 2000*, Tables 2.4, 2.15. Retrieved May 12, 2000 from http://www.worldbank.org/data/wdi2000/pdfs/tab2_4.pdf,2_15.pdf; World Bank, *Building Institutions for Markets: World Development Report 2002* (New York, Oxford University Press, 2002), pp. 234–235; Table 2.

are particularly notable: not only does the vast majority of the population live on less than $2 a day, which is also true in India, but private consumption spending actually declined in the 1990s. The latter columns report the availability of critical public facilities: safe water and sanitation. Table 7.3 reports on health outcomes, including life expectancy, infant mortality, the health of children, and fertility. Table 7.4 tells us about access to communication and information, such as telephones, newspapers, television, and personal computers. Table 7.5 compares educational efforts and the extent to which countries at various levels of economic development succeed in increasing literacy. All of these data show how governmental and private efforts, in societies at different levels of economic development and of differing social structures and cultures, affect human life chances. Although natural resources and socioeconomic structure constrain these outcomes, government and private efforts can make a big difference.

In Chapter 1, we saw how income distribution tends to be most unequal in medium-income developing societies, such as Brazil, and more equal in advanced market societies as well as in low-income developing societies, such as India (Table 1.4). In his studies of European economic history, Simon Kuznets showed that in the early stages of industrial-

ization income distribution became more unequal, whereas in later stages of industrialization income distribution again came closer to equality.[7] This "Kuznets curve" is explained by the fact that in the early stages of modernization, the large sector of traditional farmers tends to be left behind as industry and commercial agriculture begin to grow. At higher levels of economic attainment, however, the number of poor farmers is reduced compared with the industrial and service sectors. In addition, when trade unions and political parties develop in democratic countries, they tend to bring about public policies that make income distribution more equal through taxation, wage policy, and welfare state policies.

Economic development affects economic prosperity, public health provisions such as sanitation and availability of potable water, and access to the outside world through telephone and television, roads, and other infrastructure. During the 1990s, the average public health expenditure per capita for the economically developed countries was $2505, compared with $182 for the developing countries. The average number of physicians per 1000 persons in the developed world was 2.8, as compared with 1.3 in the developing world. While most of the people of the developed world had access to safe water, this was true for only about half of the population of the less-advantaged

T A B L E   7 . 3   Health Outcomes for Selected Countries, 1990–1998

Country	Public Health Expenditure as % of GDP	Physicians per 1000 Citizens	Life Expectancy at Birth, 1999	Infant Mortality per 1,000 Live Births	Infant Health: % Malnutrition Under Age 5	Fertility Rate
Brazil	3.4	1.3	67	33	6	2.3
Britain	5.9	1.6	77	6	ND	1.7
China	2.0	2.0	70	31	16	1.9
Egypt	1.8	2.1	67	49	15	3.2
France	7.1	2.9	79	5	ND	1.8
Germany	8.3	3.4	77	5	ND	1.4
India	0.6	.4	63	70	53	3.2
Japan	5.9	1.8	81	4	ND	1.4
Mexico	2.8	1.2	72	30	14	2.8
Nigeria	0.2	.2	47	76	39	5.3
Russia	4.5	4.6	66	17	3	1.2
United States	6.5	2.6	77	7	ND	2.0

Source: World Bank, *Entering the 21st Century: World Development Report 1999–2000* (New York, Oxford University Press, 2000), pp. 232–33; World Bank, *World Development Indicators 2000*, Tables 2.14, 2.16, 2.18. Retrieved May 12, 2000 from http://www.worldbank.org/data/wdi2000/pdfs/tab2_14. pdf,2_16.pdf,2_18.pdf; World Bank, *Building Institutions for Markets:World Development Report 2002* (New York, Oxford University Press, 2002), pp. 232–33; Table 1.

T A B L E   7 . 4   Communication and Information, 1995–1998

Country	Newspapers	Televisions	Telephones, Main Lines	Personal Computers
Brazil	40	316	121	30.0
Britain	329	645	557	263.0
China	ND	272	70	8.9
Egypt	40	122	60	9.1
France	218	601	570	207.8
Germany	311	580	567	304.7
India	ND	69	22	2.7
Japan	518	707	503	237.2
Mexico	97	261	104	47.0
Nigeria	24	66	4	5.7
Russia	105	420	197	40.6
United States	215	847	661	458.6

Note: Per 1,000 people unless otherwise indicated.

Source: World Bank, *World Development Indicators 2000*, Tables 5.10, 5.11, 5.12. Retrieved May 12, 2000 from http://www.worldbank.org/data/wdi2000/ pdfs/tab5_10.pdf,5_10.pdf,5_12.pdf.

areas. In Nigeria, for example, only 39 percent of the population has access to safe water. The country has a high birth rate, but almost one out of ten infants fails to survive the first year of life; and more than one-third of Nigerian children under the age of five suffer from malnutrition. On the average, Nigeria has only a single physician per 20,000 inhabitants, and its citizens have a life expectancy at birth of just 47 years (compared with 75–80 years in advanced industrial countries).

Nigeria demonstrates the ills of poverty, but some poor countries cope more successfully with their challenges than others. The importance of culture for pub-

T A B L E   7 . 5   Education and Literacy, 1997–1998

Country	Public Education Expenditure As Percent of GDP, 1997	Percentage of Relevant Age Group Enrolled, Secondary, 1997	Percentage of Relevant Age Group Enrolled, Tertiary, 1997	Percentage 15 Years and Above Illiterate, All, 1998	Percentage 15 Years and Above Illiterate Female, 1998	Female Share of Labor Force, 1998
Brazil	5.1	66	15	16	16	35
Britain	5.3	92	52	ND	ND	44
China	2.3	70	6	17	25	45
Egypt	4.8	75	23	46	58	30
France	6.0	99	51	ND	ND	45
Germany	4.8	95	47	ND	ND	42
India	3.2	60	7	44	57	32
Japan	3.6	100	43	ND	ND	41
Mexico	4.9	66	16	9	11	33
Nigeria	0.7	33*	4	39	48	36
Russia	3.5	88	41	1	1	49
United States	5.4	96	81	ND	ND	46

*"Gross," rather than "net," enrollment.

Source: World Bank, *World Development Indicators 2000*, Tables 2.9, 2.10, 2.12, 2.13. Retrieved May 12, 2000 from http://www.worldbank.org/data/ wdi2000/pdfs/tab2_9.pdf,2_10.pdf,2_12.pdf,2_3,pdf; total literacy from http://www.worldbank.org/data/databytopic/ILIT.pdf.

lic policy is suggested by the comparison between China and India. With a similarly low GNP per capita, Chinese average life expectancy is 70 years and infant mortality is 31 per 1,000 live births, while those of India are 63 years and 70 per 1,000, respectively. China has five times as many physicians as India relative to its population. Half of India's children under five are undernourished, as compared to a fifth of those in China.

While the incidence of infant mortality and malnutrition is much lower in advanced economies, these problems are still serious among the poor in advanced industrial countries such as the United States. Although Table 7.3 does not show this (because it shows only government, not private, health spending), the United States spends the largest proportion of its GNP on health care of any state (approximately 15 percent). At the same time, however, the United States has a somewhat higher infant death rate than Japan and Western Europe, due to more widespread poverty, drug abuse, and unequal access to health care. As Table 7.3 shows, Japan has an exceptional record in health outcomes. It has the longest life expectancy and the lowest infant mortality rate among all our countries. But its fertility rate

of 1.4 means a declining population. (With no net migration, a fertility rate of approximately 2.1 results in a steady-state population.)

Table 7.4 provides a brief picture of the communications infrastructure. In the developed countries on the average there is a telephone for every two persons; in Nigeria there are as few as four to a thousand. Television has become widely available even in countries at middling development levels (e.g., Brazil and Mexico). Personal computers, however, are much more rare outside the advanced industrial economies. Whereas the relative incidence of television sets is less than three times higher in the United States than it is in Brazil, the relative frequency of personal computers is 15 times higher.

Table 7.5 provides us with a picture of educational attainment. The first column, showing public education expenditure as a percentage of GDP, gives a rough measure of the "priority" given to education. Remember, however, that private schools, which in some countries are very common, are not counted here. Countries such as Egypt devote similar percentages of their GNP to education as do the advanced industrial societies. Hence we may say that they are making proportionally similar efforts to ed-ucate their populations. But the differences in dollar expenditures per student are very large. China and India spend less generously on education, even rela-tive to the size of their economies. Nigeria spends the least of all and requires only children from ages 6 to 12 to attend school. The outcomes are largely what we might predict from these differences in output. Nigeria has only a third of the appropriate age co-hort in secondary education, by far the poorest record of these countries. India's figures are double that. The figures for Egypt are even better—75 per-cent in secondary schools, and 23 percent in col-leges, universities, and other postsecondary educa-tional and training institutions. At the high end in educational outcomes, France, Germany, Japan, and Britain have virtually all of their primary and sec-ondary school-age children in schools, and about half of the college-age population is in some form of advanced education. In the United States, college education is even more common.

The payoffs of development and investment in education are clearly reflected in literacy rates. Nearly half of all Egyptians, Indians, and Nigerians are unable to read or write. Yet China, with a simi-larly low GNP and small investment in education, has only 17 percent illiteracy. But because they are often based on the number of school years com-pleted, not on actual reading ability, literacy figures are a crude measure of skill and competence and must be treated with caution. The high official liter-acy figures in the United States, for example, conflict with studies showing substantial functional illiteracy among American adults.

Women in developing countries are especially likely to lag behind in literacy. For example, fewer than half of all adult females in Egypt and India are re-ported to be literate. The discrepancy between male and female literacy rates tells us something of the sta-tus of women. Where women make up a smaller pro-portion of the labor force (as shown in the last column in Table 7.5), female illiteracy also tends to be most common. Faced with poverty, disease, and the absence of a social safety net, parents in poor countries tradi-tionally want to have many children, to ensure that some survive and can support them in old age. But large families tend to mean that women have few op-portunities to educate themselves or hold jobs outside the home. The self-interest of parents in having large

families often also conflicts with population control and economic development. Modernizing the status of women generally makes them better informed and more capable of making choices that lead to a more stable and healthy population. As women are educated and/or enter the labor force, they recognize the advan-tages of smaller families and become more aware of the importance of education and adequate health care.

Table 7.5 also reveals the sobering difficulties of trying to change societies, even in an area such as lit-eracy, where modern methods and technology are available. It is hard for a poor country to spend a high percentage of its GNP on education, because it must then make sacrifices elsewhere. And the effects are limited if much of the country's productive effort has to go into feeding a rapidly growing population. No matter how large the educational effort may be, it does not translate into much per child, because the resource base is small and the population is growing rapidly. Moreover, since most older people are illiter-ate, the net effect on literacy is slow.

DOMESTIC SECURITY OUTCOMES

As Thomas Hobbes would have reminded us, main-taining domestic law and order and protecting per-sons and property are among the most basic govern-ment responsibilities. Without them the conduct of personal, economic, and civic life are impossible. It is therefore worrisome that until recently crime rates have been on the increase in many advanced indus-trial countries, as well as in the developing world. Thus in the United States the crime rate increased by almost 15 percent between 1982 and 1991. In France the 1990 incidence of crimes against persons and property was almost twice that of 1975. In Russia the crime rate doubled between 1985 and 1993, as that country experienced the collapse and remaking of a moral and legal order. The country now has a mur-der rate three to four times as high as the United States. Brazil and Mexico also have considerably higher murder rates than the United States, while those of such European countries as England, France, and Germany are a small fraction of the American numbers. China has similarly low murder rates, whereas Japan and Egypt are even lower.

High crime rates are primarily a problem of the larger urban areas where much of the population of modern countries resides. In modern and modernizing societies, despite increasing expenditures on law enforcement, the physical safety of our persons and possessions has over the past several decades been declining. Wealth and income may increase rapidly, but the liabilities of modernization include the anxiety over personal safety that is so common in urban life. The causes of this development are complex. Rapidly increasing migration into the major cities, either from the domestic countryside, or from poorer foreign countries, has increased diversity and conflict. Such urbanization is found in virtually all advanced industrial countries, but its pace is even more explosive in many developing countries such as Brazil and Nigeria, and the problems of poverty and infrastructure are far more severe. The newly arrived city-dwellers often find themselves uprooted from their cultures, unwelcome, without a job, and living in squalor. The weakening and even the breakdown of the nuclear family have impaired the capacity of modern cultures to transmit effective standards of conduct to the young. Also, inequality of income and wealth, unemployment, and the hopelessness of life prospects in the big city lie behind this general decline in public order and safety. In the former Communist countries the situation is compounded by the fact that traditional standards of law and morality have collapsed.

Yet, crime rates have recently come down significantly in the United States and some other countries. The number of murders per 100,000 inhabitants in the United States peaked at 9.4 in 1994, and declined to 6.8 in 1997 (see Figure 7.5). There are several reasons that crime rates have recently come down in the United States and elsewhere. One is a strong economy, in which more young people have been able to find jobs. A second reason is stricter law enforcement.

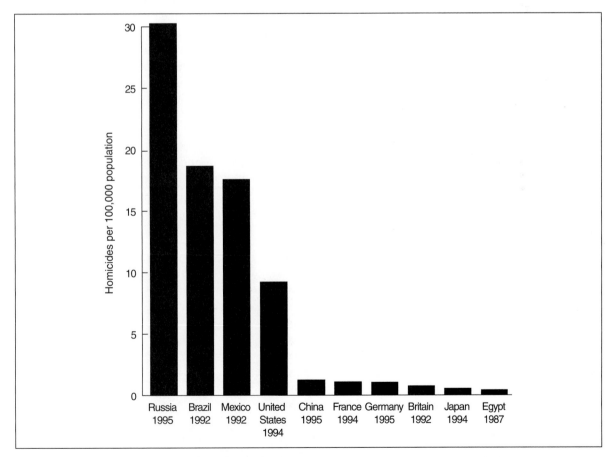

FIGURE 7.5   Homicides per 100,000 Population in Selected Countries, 1987–1995

Source: United Nations Demographic Yearbook, 1996 (New York: United Nations, 1996).

This is reflected in part in the number of police officers relative to total population, which ranges from one police officer for every 350 persons in the United States, to 820 in India, and 1,140 in Nigeria. In the United States, both federal and state governments have also sought to reduce crime by increasing the length of imprisonment. By removing the criminally prone from the streets, these authorities have succeeded in cutting the crime rate, but at the cost of an exploding prison population. According to a recent study, the United States now imprisons more people than any other country—perhaps half a million more than communist China. The total prison population in the United States is around 1.8 million, including more than 1 million in custody primarily in state prisons, and 600,000 in local jails, awaiting sentencing or serving short sentences. This population has been increasing at a rate of more than 50,000 per year. Similarly, the French prison population almost doubled between 1983 and 1990.[8] A third cause of lower crime rates has been a decrease in the number of youth at the age at which most crimes are committed. Yet, as the 15–25-year-old male population in the United States is now on the rise, we can expect violent crime to increase once again.

INTERNATIONAL OUTPUTS AND OUTCOMES

Most states engage in a great variety of international activities. Such economic, diplomatic, military, and informational activities may result in prosperity or depression, war or peace, secularization or the spread of particular beliefs.[9] The most costly outcome of the interaction among nations is warfare. Table 7.6 reports the numbers of deaths from international and internal collective violence for our twelve selected countries for almost the entire twentieth century (1900–1995). The figures are mostly civilian and military deaths from interstate warfare but also include the slaughter of civilians in the efforts to implement communism in the Soviet Union, the holocaust of European Jews under the German Nazis (the National Socialist Party) during World War II, many "ethnic cleansing" episodes in Europe and Africa, and civil wars in all parts of the world.

Table 7.6 shows the people of USSR-Russia, by a margin of more than two-to-one, to be the greatest victims of the tormented history of the twentieth century. The enormous Russian casualties during World War I destroyed the legitimacy of the Czarist regime. Its collapse was followed by the 1917 Bolshevik Revolution,

T A B L E   7 . 6   Deaths from Collective Civilian-Military Violence for Selected Countries, 1900–1995

Country	Civilian Deaths	Military Deaths	Unspecified Deaths	Total Deaths
Brazil	—	1,000	2,000	3,000
Britain	131,000	1,350,000	—	1,481,000
China	4,047,000	2,671,000	818,000	7,536,000
Egypt	51,000	28,000	—	79,000
France	490,000	1,830,000	—	2,320,000
Germany	2,232,000	7,150,000	—	9,382,000
India	889,000	71,000	37,000	997,000
Japan	510,000	1,502,000	—	2,012,000
Mexico	125,000	125,000	10,000	260,000
Nigeria	1,005,000	1,000,000	6,000	2,011,000
Russia/USSR	12,028,000	11,901,000	96,000	24,025,000
United States	—	524,000		524,000
TOTALS	21,508,000	28,153,000	969,000	50,630,000

Source: Adapted from Ruth Leger Sivard, "Wars and War Related Deaths, 1900–1995," *World Military and Social Expenditures 1996* (Washington: World Priorities, 1996), pp. 18–19. U.S. deaths add Korean and Vietnam war totals, from U.S. Department of State figures, to Sivard report of World War I and II deaths.

the Civil War (1918–1921), and Stalin's Great Terror (particularly in the 1930s), each of which cost the lives of millions. Soviet suffering climaxed in World War II with a total of seventeen million civilian and military dead. All told, the Soviet Union/Russia suffered more than 24 million civilian and military deaths in the wars and political horrors of the twentieth century.

Germany suffered the second-largest number of deaths from twentieth-century collective violence. More than three million, mostly military, occurred in the First World War. In World War II Germany suffered almost five million military deaths and another one and three-quarter million violent civilian deaths for a total of almost nine and one-half million. Other countries with huge losses include China, with a vast number of civilian casualties, and Japan, whose more than two million deaths occurred mainly among military personnel during World War II but include half a million civilians, notably many residents of Hiroshima and Nagasaki. French and British sufferings were of roughly similar magnitude, with the French losses somewhat higher than those of Britain. Both countries took horrendous military casualties in the trench warfare of World War I. Since the Civil War the United States has largely avoided the horrors of large-scale fighting on its own soil but still suffered over 120,000 deaths in World War I and close to half a million in World War II. While in the Korean and Vietnam wars, America suffered only moderate losses by these terrible standards, Korean and Vietnamese military and civilian dead were in the millions.

After World War II, the most devastating conflicts have occurred in the Third World. Many African countries, newly independent from about 1960, but with borders arbitrarily drawn by colonial powers, have serious problems of national cohesion and have suffered from chronic civil war. Large-scale civil war in Nigeria 1967–1970 cost perhaps more than a million lives, and more sporadic conflict has continued to the present time. In 2002, for example, when the country hosted an international beauty contest, it led to violent clashes between Muslims and Christians and hundreds of deaths. The partition of formerly British India into India, Pakistan, and Bangladesh has been associated with numerous deadly conflicts within and between the three countries. Some two million lives, mostly civilian, have been lost, half of them in India. The aftermath of the Cold War has witnessed a wave of instability and conflict in Eastern Europe and Central Asia. The breakup of the Soviet Union and Yugoslavia has resulted in bloody border wars and secessional conflicts (e.g., in Croatia, Bosnia, and Kosovo in the former Yugoslavia, and Chechnya in Russia). These conflicts have brought another wave of ethnic slaughter, religious clashes, and struggles for power between different warlords.

The Uppsala Conflict Data Project reports 103 armed conflicts (defined as involving at least 25 deaths) in the world from 1988 through 1997. Only six of these, including the continuing clashes between India and Pakistan, were interstate conflicts; most were civil wars occurring within current state boundaries. In 1997, a fairly typical year, there were 33 conflicts in progress, of which seven involved more than 1000 deaths.[10] The deadly costs of international warfare have gradually escalated. One authority estimates that more than 90 percent of the war deaths since 1700 have occurred in the twentieth century. Civilian deaths caused by war have increased even more rapidly than military ones. In the last decades of the century, more than three-quarters of the war deaths have been civilian.[11]

The United Nations in the post–Cold War world has intervened in some of these conflicts by providing peace-keeping missions when the parties to conflicts are ready to accept these mediations; more rarely as peace-makers when the conscience of the world cannot blink at cruel televised events. A case in point was the UN intervention in Bosnia and later in neighboring Kosovo; or in the transformation of the peace-keeping mission in the civil war in the West African state of Sierra Leone into a peacemaking effort. The UN's effectiveness in controlling both domestic and international collective violence depends on the maintenance of consensus among the great powers. How tenuous this consensus can become is illustrated in the troubled efforts of the UN to disarm Iraq after the Gulf War of 1990–1991 and later to prevent Saddam Hussein's government there from producing weapons of mass destruction.

The economic costs of national security are also high. Most major countries face a massive national debt that often includes large deferred costs of borrowing for earlier wars and the maintenance of national defense. Current defense expenditures, plus the interest costs of past conflicts, might have been

United Nations weapons inspectors arrive at the Al-Rasheed missile propellant compound in Iraq in January 2003.

AP/Wide World Photos

spent on more constructive public objects or left for private consumption or investment. Yet, states feel that they need to spend significantly on national defense because they are still governed by the "security dilemma"—they have to "take out insurance" against the possibility that their neighbors might be aggressive. While military expenditures in the world have declined since the collapse of the Soviet Union, the horrors of September 11, 2001, have led to a new costly mobilization of resources against international terrorism.

POLITICAL GOODS AND VALUES

If we are to compare and evaluate public policy in different political systems, we need to consider the political goods that motivate different policies. That leads us back to the issues we discussed in Chapters 1 and 2, to the functions and purposes that governments serve. This book is organized around the concepts of system, process, and policy. We can think about values as "political goods" related to each of those levels of analysis.

At the system level, there is a long tradition in political analysis that emphasizes order, predictability, and stability. Citizens are most free and most able to act purposefully when their environment is stable, transparent, and predictable. We call these conditions **system goods** since they reflect the functioning and effectiveness of the whole political system. While people generally want some measure of

change and new opportunities, most prefer stability to abrupt and unforeseeable change. Political instability—constitutional breakdowns, frequent leadership changes, riots, demonstrations, and the like—upsets most people's plans and can cost lives and material destruction. System goods have to do with the regularity and predictability with which political systems work, but also with their ability to adapt to environmental challenges.

Regularity and adaptability are typically somewhat in conflict. There are times when order and stability are at the top of the agenda. In the United States, the administration of Warren Harding after World War I was such a period, called "a return to normalcy." There was a similar withdrawal from mobilization after World War II and the Korean War. On the other hand, the 1930s and the 1960s were periods of change and adaptation, in which the reach of governmental powers was extended. But the stress on change and adaptation can also be a call for reductions in the scope in government, as in the Thatcher administration in Britain or the Republican "Contract with America" of 1994–1995.

Another school of thought emphasizes goods associated with the political process—citizen participation and free political competition. Democracy is good and authoritarianism bad, according to this school of thought, because of the way citizens are treated in the process, and not because democracy, for example, produces better economic results. Democratic procedures and various rights of due process, then, are **process goods.** Process goods include participation, compliance, and procedural justice. We value participation not merely as a means to responsive government, but for its own sake, as it enhances citizen competence and dignity. Compliance with authority can also be a good, as individuals respond to the impulse to serve others, which can be one of humanity's most gratifying experiences. President John F. Kennedy in his inaugural address called on such impulses to serve and sacrifice when he said, "Ask not what your country can do for you; ask what you can do for your country." Procedural justice (trial by jury, habeas corpus, no cruel and unusual punishment) is another crucial process value, without which citizens would have much greater reasons to fear their governments.

Procedural goods also include *effectiveness* and *efficiency.* A preference for effectiveness means that we prefer policies that actually lead to their desired purpose to those that do not. Efficiency means that government policies should attain their objectives at the lowest possible cost. If two alternative policies would lead to the same result but at very different costs, we would prefer the policy with the lower cost. In designing government agencies, most of us would prefer institutions that are lean and inexpensive to bloated agencies that produce no better results.

A third and final focus is on **policy goods,** such as economic welfare, quality of life, freedom, and personal security. We value a political system that improves welfare, decreases inequalities, enhances public safety, enables people to live lives they want for themselves, and cleans up its environment, whatever the political process that produces these results. Well-meaning people do not always agree which of these policy goods are most important. Yet, there are at least two important criteria that most of us would agree that government policy should meet. The first is *fairness.* If government undertakes some public policy, we would like that policy to be fair. The problem is that people often disagree over what is fair. In some situations, and according to some people, fairness requires that all people are treated equally (as when family members attempt to divide a tempting pie). In other situations, fairness demands that individuals be treated as they deserve or by performance (as when grades are given in a

college course). And in yet other situations, fairness means that people are treated according to their needs (for example, in cases of medical treatment). Thus fairness can imply *equal treatment* in some cases, *just desserts* (reward in proportion to merit or contribution) in others, and *treatment according to need* in yet others. Many distributive policies—for example, pension systems such as social security in the United States—rely on some combination of these criteria.

The debate over these various conceptions of fairness is never settled. In most cases, however, fairness would rule out practices that are *arbitrary* or *partial.* Few of us would find it fair if government officials threw dice to determine who would be imprisoned or given pensions, or if they made such decisions solely on the basis of their personal prejudices or connections. We can think of fairness in this sense as reflected in the process good of *procedural justice.*

The second consideration is the promotion and preservation of *freedom.* As anarchists, libertarians, and other government skeptics would remind us, public policies should promote and protect freedom and basic human and political rights. If two policies are equally efficient and fair, then we would prefer the one that respects the rights and liberties of the citizens to the greater extent. But even in a democratic society, freedom is not always chosen over other political goods. The right to bear arms, protected in the Second Amendment to the U.S. Constitution, has recently become a hotly contested issue, as many Americans would like to prevent those most likely to cause harm from carrying lethal weapons. Similarly, freedom of speech is a Constitutional guarantee, but many citizens favor restrictions on speech that is insulting or offensive.

Liberty is sometimes viewed only as freedom from governmental regulation and harassment. Freedom is more than inhibition of government action, however, because private individuals and organizations may also commit infractions of liberty and privacy. In such cases, liberty may be fostered by government intervention. Much legislation against racial segregation and discrimination generally has been impelled by this purpose. Liberty to act, organize, obtain information, and protest is an indispensable part of effective political participation. Nor is it irrelevant to social, political, and economic equality. Prior to the

T A B L E   7 . 7   Political Goods

Levels of Political Goods	Classes of Goods	Content and Examples
System level	System maintenance	The political system is characterized by regular, stable, and predictable processes domestically and internationally.
	System adaptation	The political system adapts to environmental change and challenges.
Process level	Participation in political inputs	The political system is open to and responds to a variety of forms of political action and speech, which may directly produce a sense of citizen dignity and efficacy.
	Compliance and support	Citizens fulfill their obligations (e.g., patriotic service) to the system and comply with public law and policy.
	Procedural justice	Equitable procedure (due process) and equality before the law.
	Effectiveness and efficiency	Processes have intended effects and are no more cumbersome, expensive, or intrusive than necessary.
Policy level	Welfare	Growth per capita; quantity and quality of health and material goods; distributive equity.
	Security	Safety of person and property; public order and national security.
	Fairness	Non-discrimination in government policy; mutual recognition of individuals from different ethnic, linguistic, or other groups; protection of vulnerable or disadvantaged citizens.
	Liberty	Freedom from regulation, protection of privacy, and respect for autonomy of other individuals, groups, and nations.

breakdown of communism in Eastern Europe and the Soviet Union, it was a common view that the communist countries were trading liberty for equality, by contrast with capitalism, which was said to trade off equality for liberty. One important thing that has come to light after the collapse of communism is the extent of corruption and privilege, as well as economic stagnation, in communist societies. While they had surely traded off liberty for a basic security of employment, it was not clear that the communist bloc had otherwise gained much in the way of equality.

Table 7.7 draws on our three-level analysis of political systems to present a checklist of political goods or values. There is no simple way to say which value should prevail when they conflict. But it is different preferences between such values as freedom, fairness, and efficiency that set different cultures, parties, and political philosophies apart. One society or group of citizens may value fairness over liberty; another may make the opposite choice, as in

Patrick Henry's famous exclamation, "Give me liberty or give me death!"

STRATEGIES FOR PRODUCING POLITICAL GOODS

All political systems embody strategies for producing political goods, but different political regimes are designed to produce different combinations of political goods. The framers of the U.S. Constitution believed that separation of powers would protect liberty; Karl Marx believed that the "dictatorship of the proletariat" would lead to a just and harmonious society; Mussolini believed that a strong leader would increase national power and glory; and the Ayatollah Khomeini believed that a society modeled after the Koran, and administered by the clergy, would promote justice on earth and eternal salvation.

Since the collapse of the Soviet Union in 1991, democracy has seemed to be "the only game in town." Earlier in the twentieth century there have been several political ideologies in competition with political democracy—communism, fascism, corporatist authoritarianism, and the like. Fascism went down in flames in World War II. Communism all but collapsed in the late 1980s, drained of credibility by its policy failure and its corruption. Most of its successor regimes have democratized and established market economies. The dictatorships of Latin America, discredited by their cruelties and economic failures, have turned to the market and democracy. The postcolonial regimes of Sub-Saharan Africa, after a brief interlude of populist democracy in the 1960s, turned to authoritarian regimes of one kind or another. Then in recent years some of them have begun to experiment once again with democracy. But although democracy and the market economy have been the wave of the immediate past, other strategies may very well become credible once again. Below we spell out the major political-economic alternatives in the world today, beginning with the industrialized countries and moving on to the developing, or industrializing, ones.

Industrialized Nations

The industrialized democratic nations must reconcile pressures to maintain or increase government services with the need to accumulate resources for investment in economic growth. Many contemporary democratic industrial nations have relatively high unemployment and/or relatively slow rates of growth. The rise of the service economy and the emergence of environmental challenges have complicated the class structure and reduced the power of trade unions. Industrial pollution of land, air, and water divides nations differently, with a substantial part of the middle classes opposing growth that implies environmental degradation, and a substantial part of the working classes making the opposite choice. These dilemmas—both the old capital versus labor issues, and the newer service economy and environmental issues facing all advanced democracies—may be dealt with in a market-oriented fashion as in the Britain of Margaret Thatcher, and the United States of the Reagan era, or in a social democratic fashion as in Norway and Sweden.

But though there are policy differences between the market-oriented and social democracies, both types of democratic regimes have in the last decades reconsidered taxes, welfare, and regulation. The size, cost, and inefficiencies of government have become major political issues. In the United States both major political parties have embarked on efforts to limit and restructure government—the Republicans leading a campaign to contain spending and return powers to the state governments; and the Democrats with their efficiency program of "reinventing government." The environmental issue divides both right and left. In some European countries "Green," ecologically oriented, parties have emerged. By the late 1990s such parties had participated in coalition governments in Belgium, Finland, France, Germany, and Italy.

Industrial authoritarian nations come in leftist and rightist varieties. Franco Spain (1938–1975), Greece under the military dictatorship (1967–1974), the Chile of Pinochet (1973–1988), and the Brazil of "the generals" (1964–1985) are examples of right-wing authoritarianism. The military authoritarian regimes of Southern Europe and Latin America of the 1960s and 1970s suppressed popular political organization but granted considerable freedom to private enterprise. They sought to foster economic growth, though at the expense of increasing inequality of wealth and income. But their repressive policies eventually became unpopular. Where authoritarian right-wing regimes had produced good economic results, as in Spain and Chile, they were able to negotiate a peaceful transition to democracy. Elsewhere, as in Portugal and Argentina, they were toppled through popular unrest and revolutions.

Prior to the collapse of communism in Eastern Europe, the Soviet Union, Poland, and Hungary were industrialized authoritarian regimes of the left. Though many of these countries have now moved toward market economies and democracy, anti-Western groups in Russia and in states such as Belarus and Ukraine have seriously resisted such moves. In general, and across different regime types, the credibility of socialism and of high welfare expenditures has declined in the last decades, while that of the market economy has risen. It is still to be seen whether this is a pendular move, or whether the power of the state reached a historic high point in the 1980s. In most former communist states, the governments have now moved away somewhat from the market enthusiasm of the early days of reform. Democratic stability in Latin America and Eastern Europe may still hinge on their economic success. Thus, while there are currently few industrialized authoritarian regimes (whether radical or conservative), it would be a mistake to think that the category is no longer relevant.

Preindustrial Nations

The preindustrial nations face common challenges of modernization. There are some seven strategies of political development followed by preindustrial countries—one democratic and the six authoritarian regimes that follow.

Neotraditional Political Systems. Neotraditional political systems, the best exemplars of which are Saudi Arabia and the sheikdoms of the Persian Gulf, emphasize stability, the maintenance of an established order. Since these regimes are oil rich, they have so far been able to modernize selectively (for example, the military) and buy off opposition and discontent. But as they develop economically through their oil royalties, and as they provide health, educational, and other amenities to a substantial part of their populations, some political modernization may follow. This may in turn fuel the development of a political opposition and demands for reform.

Personal Rule. Most Sub-Saharan African states are not neotraditional, though they may contain traditional structures such as kingdoms or chiefdoms. The colonial boundaries inherited by most Sub-Saharan countries were artificial constructs that often included many different languages, ethnicities, and religions. The formally democratic regimes that were established after independence soon gave way to various versions of "personal rule."[12] The "personal ruler" is not simply a chief executive in the limited political sense; he has a "proprietary" relation to the regime, its institutions and agencies, and often exploits it for his personal purposes. Rent seeking is thus a serious problem in such countries, as in the case of President Mobutu of Zaire (see Chapter 1). Where these systems stabilize, the rulers maintain control through police suppression, patronage, spoils, and privileges distributed through clientelistic networks. Many of the personal rule regimes in

Sub-Saharan Africa are characterized by low (or even negative) growth, low life expectancy, low literacy, and low health standards. Since these regimes are economically unproductive, they have little legitimacy and are susceptible to military coups.

Clerico-Mobilizational Regimes. In the last decades, and principally in Islamic countries, a clerico-authoritarian mobilizational ideology has emerged. Clerico-mobilizational regimes are built on a religious authority for which they try to mobilize active support. They are antisecular in social matters (for example, regarding the status of women and family policies) and they restrict civil society through media censorship and suppression. They are authoritarian, but neither traditional nor technocratic. They want to control the modern media, use it for their own purposes, and clean up moral corruption. They are ambivalent in economic policy, urging market intervention from Koranic precepts, but in practice do not seriously interfere with banks and other economic institutions. They are nationalist and anti-Western.

This "fundamentalist" religious movement is represented in both branches of Islam—Shia and Sunni. The Shia version is exemplified in Iran, which is dominated by clerics and Islamic legislators and judges. Sunni Islam has similar radical theocratic movements, not only in the Middle East but in Afghanistan, Pakistan, and in the Islamic areas of Central Asia. Movements of this kind are also strong in the more secular states of Algeria, Egypt, and even Turkey. The fate of these new movements is still unclear. They may not be very effective in mounting an international coalition, and nationalism and the split between Shia and Sunni Muslims may impede collaboration.

Technocratic-Repressive. Governments adopting this approach promoted economic growth previously in Indonesia and in parts of South America, where a coalition of military and civilian technocrats and business interests suppressed participation and pursued a growth-oriented investment policy at the cost of growing economic inequality. Such Middle Eastern countries as Syria and Egypt still pursue this strategy. In other countries that have gone democratic, economic or democratic failures may lead to reversions to technocratic-repressive strategies.

Technocratic-Distributive. There also is a distributive, and more egalitarian, version of the modernizing authoritarian regime. One example is South Korea prior to its democratization. South Korea suppressed participation but encouraged some income redistribution along with growth. Early land reforms, rapid development of education, labor-intensive, export-oriented industrialization, and substantial American advice, support, and pressure marked the Korean experiment. Its economic success seems to have led to effective democratization.

Technocratic-Mobilizational. The last category, the authoritarian technocratic-mobilizational strategy, has been exemplified primarily by preindustrial Communist countries, and in a milder form by Taiwan. In these states, there is a single political party mobilizing and involving citizens in the political process. Thus, Mexico was dominated by the Partido Revolucionario Institucional (PRI), which incorporates the major interest groups of labor, business, and agriculture into its party organization, for more than a half-century. Competitive participation is suppressed or limited. Though there are few such states today, we cannot rule out the possibility that they may return. China, Vietnam, North Korea, and Cuba are the last remaining Communist societies, dominated by single mobilizing political parties. China, Vietnam, and even Cuba have opened their socialist economies to market forces. China has seen enormous growth (see Chapter 13), but the question is how long it can avoid some political pluralism. The non-Communist mobilizational systems vary substantially in success and in their policy emphases. Taiwan has combined growth and distributive equity, and in recent years politics has become increasingly competitive.

Democratization in Developing Countries

Just as democracy has become the "only political game in town," democratization and its consolidation have become the main preoccupations of many contemporary political scientists. Current understandings of transitions to democracy emphasize the importance of leadership, choice, and bargaining, whereas they tend to play down the importance of economic and social factors. Many scholars argue that democratization can occur wherever the lead-

ers, pressured or influenced by democratization elsewhere, begin moving in the democratic direction. The recent literature very persuasively emphasizes the uncertainty and unpredictability of democratic transitions.[13] While democratization is therefore uncertain, tentative, and reversible, "democratic consolidation" is a condition in which the main elites have accepted democracy and in which participatory behavior has been widely adopted among the general population.

Stable democracy seems to depend on the presence of a "civil society" based on free media and a lively associational life. These conditions in turn are associated with widespread literacy and rising economic standards. From this perspective a great many contemporary Third World democracies are not consolidated institutionally or culturally.[14] Yet, the democratization of Taiwan and South Korea suggests that industrialization, urbanization, education, and communication can indeed foster consolidation.[15] On the other hand, India, a democracy almost continuously since independence in 1947, demonstrates that even a relatively underdeveloped country can sustain democracy.

TRADE-OFFS AND OPPORTUNITY COSTS

One of the hard facts about political goods is that though each may be desirable, they cannot all be had simultaneously. A political system often has to trade off one value to obtain another. Spending funds on education is giving up the opportunity to spend them on welfare, or to leave them in the hands of consumers for their own use. These **trade-offs** and **opportunity costs** are also found in complicated decisions about investment for the future as opposed to present consumption, as when politicians have to decide how to fund future retirement benefits. Even more difficult are the trade-offs between security and liberty, or stability and adaptation, where the very concepts imply giving up some of the one for some of the other. Extreme liberty, as Hobbes would tell us, would make a highly insecure world where the strong might bully the weak and where collective action would be difficult. Yet, without liberty, security is of little value, as the prisoner is too well aware. Moreover, the trade-offs are not the same under all circumstances. Under some conditions increasing liberty somewhat will also increase security—for example, because riots against censorship will end. Under some conditions investment in education will be paid back many times in health and welfare, because trained citizens can better care for themselves and work more productively. Although in politics you cannot always "have your cake and eat it, too," one of the important tasks of social science is to discover the conditions under which positive and negative trade-offs occur.

Regrettably, political science has no way of converting units of liberty into units of safety or welfare. And because politics may involve violence on a large scale, we must acknowledge that we can never calculate the value of a political outcome gained at the cost of human life. People act as though they know how to make such conversions, but as political scientists we can only point to value judgments that people have been willing to make. The weight given to various goods differs across cultures and contexts. The advantage of a clear-cut ideology is that it provides a logical scheme that tells us how much one value should be traded against another, and thus offers orderly bases for choice. Such schemes may be invaluable for those pressed into action in the terrible circumstances of war, revolution, and famine. However, there is no ideology, just as there is no political science, that can solve all these problems objectively.

KEY TERMS

direct taxes

distribution

extraction

gross domestic product (GDP)

indirect taxes

neotraditional political system

night watchman state

opportunity cost

Organization for Economic Cooperation and Development (OECD)

outcomes

outputs

police state

policy goods

political goods and values

process goods

public policies

regulation

regulatory state

symbolic policies

system goods

taxation

technocratic

trade-offs

welfare state

SUGGESTED READINGS

Bratton, Michael and Nicholas Vandewall. *Democratic Experiments in Africa: Regime Transitions in Comparative Perspective*. New York: Cambridge University Press, 1997.

Castles, Francis G., ed. *The Comparative History of Public Policy*. Cambridge, England: Polity Press, 1989.

Dahl, Robert. *Democracy and Its Critics*. New Haven, CT: Yale University Press, 1989.

Diamond, Larry, ed. *Democracy in Developing Countries*. Boulder, CO: Lynne Rienner, 1992.

Flora, Peter and Arnold Heidenheimer. *The Development of Welfare States in Europe and America*. New Brunswick, NJ: Transaction Books, 1981.

Gourevitch, Peter. *Politics in Hard Times*. Ithaca, NY: Cornell University Press, 1986.

Heidenheimer, Arnold, Hugh Heclo, and Carolyn Teich Adams. *Comparative Public Policy*, 3rd ed. New York: St. Martin's Press, 1990.

Huntington, Samuel. *The Third Wave: Democratization in the Late Twentieth Century*. Norman, OK: Oklahoma University Press, 1991.

Jackson, Robert, and Carl Rosberg. *Personal Rule in Black Africa*. Berkeley, CA: University of California Press, 1982.

Katzenstein, Peter. *Small States in World Markets*. Ithaca, NY: Cornell University Press, 1985.

Lijphart, Arend. *Patterns of Democracy*. New Haven, CT: Yale University Press, 1999.

Lindblom, Charles E. *Politics and Markets*. New Haven, CT: Yale University Press, 1978.

Mainwaring, Scott, Guillermo O'Donnell, and Arturo Valenzuela. *Issues in Democratic Consolidation*. Notre Dame, IN: University of Notre Dame Press, 1992.

Marks, Gary and Larry Diamond, eds. *Reexamining Democracy*. Newbury Park, CA: Sage, 1992.

Olson, Mancur. *The Rise and Decline of Nations*. New Haven, CT: Yale University Press, 1982.

Olson, Mancur. *Power and Prosperity*. New York: Basic Books, 2000.

Putnam, Robert D. *Making Democracy Work*. Princeton, NJ: Princeton University Press, 1993.

Tsebelis, George. *Veto Players: An Introduction to Institutional Analysis*. Princeton, NJ: Princeton University Press, 2002.

Wilensky, Harold, *Rich Democracies: Political Economy, Public Policy, and Performance*. Berkeley, CA: University of California Press, 2002.

Wilson, James G. *The Politics of Regulation in the United States*. New York: Basic Books, 1980.

ENDNOTES

1. See World Bank, *Entering the 21st Century: World Development Report 1999–2000* (New York: Oxford University Press, 2000), Table A.1, pp. 216–217.

2. Peter Flora and Arnold Heidenheimer, *The Development of Welfare States in Europe and America* (New Brunswick, NJ: Transaction Books, 1981); Arnold Heidenheimer, Hugh Heclo, and Carolyn Teich Adams, *Comparative Public Policy*, 3rd ed. (New York: St. Martin's Press, 1990).

3. Heidenheimer, Heclo and Adams. *Comparative Public Policy*, pp. 211–219.

4. *The Economist* (May 30, 1998): 19.

5. See, for example, Samuel Brittan, *The Economic Consequences of Democracy* (London: Temple Smith, 1977); Michael Boskin, *The Crisis in Social Security* (San Francisco: Institute for Contemporary Studies, 1978); Mancur Olson, *The Rise and Decline of Nations* (New Haven, CT: Yale University Press, 1982).

6. Steven C. Poe and C. Neal Tate, "Repression of Human Rights to Personal Integrity in the 1980s: A Global Analysis," *American Political Science Review* 88, no. 4 (December 1994): 853–872.

7. Simon Kuznets, "Economic Growth and Income Equality," *American Economic Review* 45 (1955): 1–28.

8. World Bank, *World Development Report: Infrastructure for Development* (New York: Oxford University Press, 1994), Overview, pp. 1, ff.

9. Peter Gourevitch in his book *Politics in Hard Times* (Cornell University Press, 1986) analyzes the policy responses of five Western industrial nations—Britain, France, Germany, Sweden, and the United States—to the three world depressions of 1870–1890, 1930–1940, and 1975–1985. Gourevitch shows how these crises affected business, labor, and agriculture differently in each country; consequences for political structure and policy varied greatly. Thus the world depression of the 1930s resulted in a conservative reaction in Britain (the formation of a "National" government), a moderate left reaction in the United States (the "New Deal"), a polarization and paralysis of public policy in France ("Immobilisme"), a moderate social democratic reaction in Sweden, and a radical right and left polarization in Germany, leading to a breakdown of democracy and the emergence of National Socialism. While the causes of World War II were complex, the pacifism of Britain, the demoralization and defeatism in France, the isolationism of the United States, and the nihilism and aggression of Germany were all fed by the devastating worldwide economic depression of the 1930s.

10. Summarized in "States in Armed Conflict," produced by the Department of Peace and Conflict Research, Uppsala University, Sweden, at their website, www.peace.uu.se, consulted May 15, 2000. For a more complete account see Peter Wallensteen and Margareta Sollenberg, "Armed Conflict and Regional Conflict Complexes, 1989–97", *Journal of Peace Research*, 35, no. 5, (1998).

11. Ruth Leger Sivard, *World Military and Social Indicators* (Washington: World Priorities, 1993), p. 20.

12. Robert Jackson and Carl Rosberg, *Personal Rule in Black Africa* (Berkeley, CA: University of California Press, 1982).

13. See, among others, Guillermo O'Donnell and Philippe C. Schmitter, *Transitions from Authoritarian Rule: Tentative Conclusions About Uncertain Democracies* (Baltimore, MD: Johns Hopkins University Press, 1986); Samuel Huntington, *The Third Wave: Democratization in the Late Twentieth Century* (Norman, OK: University of Oklahoma Press, 1991); Terry Karl, "Dilemmas of Democratization in Latin America," in *Comparative Politics* (October 1990): 1–22; Nancy Bermeo, "Rethinking Regime Change," *Comparative Politics* 22, no. 3: 359–377; Giuseppe Di Palma, *To Craft Democracies* (Berkeley, CA: University of California Press, 1990); Gary Marks and Larry Diamond, eds., *Reexamining Democracy* (Newbury Park, CA: Sage, 1992).

14. Larry Diamond, "Toward Democratic Consolidation," *Journal of Democracy* 5, no. 3 (July 1994): 4–17; Lawrence Whitehead, "The Consolidation of Fragile Democracies," in Robert A. Pastor, ed., *Democracy in the Americas* (New York: Holmes and Meier, 1989); Samuel J. Valenzuela, "Democratic Consolidation in Post Transitional Settings," in Scott Mainwaring, Guillermo O'Donnell, and Arturo Valenzuela, *Issues in Democratic Consolidation* (Notre Dame, IN: University of Notre Dame Press, 1992); Scott Mainwaring, "Transition to Democracy and Democratic Consolidation: Theoretical and Comparative Issues," in Mainwaring, et al., *Issues*. Terry Karl and Philippe Schmitter, "Modes of Transition in Latin America," *International Social Science Journal* 138 (May 1991): 269–284. Larry Diamond, *Political Culture and Democracy in Developing Countries* (Boulder, CO: Lynne Rienner, 1994), ch. 1; Robert D. Putnam, *Making Democracy Work* (Princeton, NJ: Princeton University Press, 1993).

15. Daniel Lerner, *The Passing of Traditional Society* (Glencoe, IL: Free Press, 1958); Seymour M. Lipset, "Some Social Requisites of Democracy," *American Political Science Review* (September 1959): 69–105; Karl Deutsch, "Social Mobilization and Political Development," *American Political Science Review* (September 1961): 493–514.

Politics in England

Richard Rose

COUNTRY BIO—UNITED KINGDOM

Population:	59.2 million	**Language(s):**	English, Welsh (about 600,000), Scottish form of Gaelic (about 60,000)
Territory:	94,525 sq. mi		
Year of Independence:	from twelfth century	**Religion:**	Anglican 26.1 million, Roman Catholic 5.7 million, Presbyterian 2.6 million, Methodist 1.3 million, Other Christian 2.6 million, Muslim 1.5 million, Hindu 500,000, Sikh 330,000, Jewish 260,000, Other 300,000, no religion 7,700. The remainder refused to report a religion in the 2001 census.
Year of Current Constitution:	unwritten; partly statutes, partly common law and practice		
Head of State:	Queen Elizabeth II		
Head of Government:	Prime Minister Tony Blair		

In a world of new democracies, England is different, because it is an old democracy. Unlike new democracies in Eastern Europe, Latin America, and Asia, England did not become a democracy overnight due to the collapse of a dictatorship. It became a democracy by evolution rather than revolution. Democratization was a slow process that occurred over the centuries. The rule of law was established in the seventeenth century; the accountability of the executive to parliament was established by the eighteenth century; political parties organized in the nineteenth century; and, even though competitive elections had been held for more than a century, the right of every adult man and woman to vote was not recognized until the twentieth century.

The evolution of democracy in England also stands in contrast to the dominant European practice of countries switching between democratic and undemocratic regimes. Whereas the oldest English person has lived under the same constitution all his or her life, the oldest Germans have lived under four or five constitutions, two democratic and two or three undemocratic.[1]

The gradual evolution of political institutions means that at no point in history did representatives of the English people meet together to decide what kind of government they would like to have, as happened in the American constitutional convention of the 1780s, and in dozens of new democracies in the past two decades. Politicians have been socialized to accept institutions as a legacy from their predecessors; these are the rules of the game by which they compete for office. Ordinary citizens have been socialized to accept established institutions too.

The influence of British government can be found in places as far-flung as Australia, Canada, India, and the United States. Just as Alexis de Tocqueville travelled to America in 1831 to seek the secrets of democracy, so might we journey to England to seek the secrets of stable representative government. Yet its limitations as a model are shown by the failure of many of the attempts to transplant its institutions to countries gaining independence from the British Empire, and even more by the failure of its institutions to bring political stability in Northern Ireland.

CURRENT POLICY CHALLENGES

When Tony Blair became prime minister in 1997, he declared a desire to create a New Britain, a "cool Britannia" having more in common with the world of pop stars and Princess Diana than the world of Winston Churchill. Yet rebranding a country is not as easy as rebranding pop groups or designer fashions.

To win office Blair created what he called a "New" Labour party with a vague Third Way philosophy, offered as an alternative to socialism as well as to unfettered capitalism, and modelled on the strategy of President Bill Clinton. In setting out Labour's manifesto, Blair proclaimed, "We are proud now to be the party of modern, dynamic business, proud now to be the party of law and order, proud now to be the party of the family, and proud now to be the party pledged not to increase income tax."[2] He pledged a pragmatic government that would do "what works," and appealed to the voters to "trust me."

By his lifestyle and rhetoric, Blair has shown that he believes in opportunity for all, and especially for aspiring Britons whose votes are critical for winning reelection. However, winning elections has challenged Blair to deliver campaign promises (Box 8.1). Blair now recognises: "In opposition announcement is the reality. For the first period of time in government, there was a tendency to believe the same situation applied. It doesn't. The announcement is only the intention."[3]

Blair's government has benefited from an abnormally lengthy economic boom, providing additional public revenue without raising taxes. This is important, as an aging population requires more health care, an educated population demands better education for their children, and a more prosperous society wants a better environment to match improved housing. The Labour government has sought to achieve greater efficiency by imposing more centralized controls and performance targets on public sector agencies.

From the right, the **Conservative Party** attacks the government for not being radical enough in promoting private initiatives and for overriding constitutional conventions. The **Liberal Democrats** criticize the government for not raising taxes a little in order to have more money to spend in raising health and education standards and for undermining legal protections of human rights. Tony Blair is

---

B O X   8 . 1   **Accomplishments and Frustrations of Tony Blair**

Tony Blair became leader of the Labour Party in opposition with the goal of winning elections. To make the party electable, he abandoned traditional commitments to the trade unions and to socialist values and centralized power in the prime minister's office. The strategy of refashioning the Labour Party has produced three successive election victories.

The Labour government has maintained Margaret Thatcher's principle of avoiding any increase in income tax. Much of the credit for managing the economy went to his Treasury minister, Gordon Brown. The government also implemented Labour's long-standing programme of constitutional reforms, including the devolution of powers to elected assemblies in Scotland and Wales, and enacting human rights legislation.

In foreign policy Blair's chief initiative has been cooperation in military action with the United States. After the 9/11 terrorist attack, he has allied Britain with policies of President George W. Bush, notwithstanding

major opposition in Parliament. Although claiming to want Britain to be at the heart of Europe, Blair has not sought to adopt the euro in place of the pound and has refrained from campaigning for measures to increase British support for the European Union.

Labour won the 2005 election even though it took only 35 percent of the vote. Distrust in Blair was blamed for this fall in vote and it encouraged speculation about when he would resign during his third term in office. Concurrently, Blair has pledged education, health, and pension reforms that can only show their consequences years after he has left office. Blair has explicitly rejected the liberalism of the 1960s and endorsed measures reducing legal and judicial restraints on government action.*

*Cf. Tony Blair, *New Britain: My Vision of a Young Country* (London: Fourth Estate, 1996); Anthony Seldon, *Blair* (New York: Free Press, 2004).

content to be attacked from both sides, believing that centrist policies will best maintain the support of most voters.

While the Blair administration has promoted decentralization to Scotland and Wales, critics charge that his "control freak" mentality is centralizing too much power in the hands of prime ministerial advisers who concentrate on promoting favorable headlines in the media and pushing civil servants to produce what makes for good headlines. Moreover, in the wake of terrorist attacks the government's adoption of wide-ranging powers to control the population have been criticized by civil liberties groups as anti-liberal, a charge the prime minister accepts as proof of his toughness.

In a changing world, the big question is: Where does England belong? Geographically, it is an offshore island of Europe. **Insularity** is one of its most striking cultural characteristics. Although the **United Kingdom** is a member of the European Union, the government's commitment to the European Union remains limited. Blair has pledged to put British interests "first, second, and last" in negotiations about the European Union. However, any attempt by Blair to cooperate with the other 24 member states of the European Union will inevitably result in compromises that British critics of the European Union will denounce as "giving away" Britain's sovereignty.

Historically, the country's ties are with English-speaking countries on other continents, including the United States. By deciding to ally himself with President George W. Bush in the war in Iraq, Blair has shown that today, as in Winston Churchill's time, a special relationship with the United States is valued more than ties to Europe.

THE CONSTRAINTS OF HISTORY

The Making of Modern England

The legacy of the past limits current choices, and England has a very long past. For much of its history, England was governed by the rule of law but the government was not democratic. However, the establishment of lawful procedures to check the arbitrary authority of the King made possible the gradual evolution of a democratic political system.

Compared with its European neighbors, England has been fortunate in solving many of the funda-

mental problems of governance early. The Crown was established as the central political authority in medieval times. The supremacy of the state's power over the church was settled in the sixteenth century when Henry VIII broke with the Roman Catholic Church to establish the Church of England. The power struggle between Crown and Parliament was resolved by a civil war in the seventeenth century in which Parliament triumphed and a weakened monarch was then restored. Parliament became able to hold the Crown accountable by the eighteenth century, but Parliament represented only a small portion of the population.

There is no agreement among political scientists about when England developed a modern system of government.[4] A constitutional historian might date the change at 1485, the start of the centralizing Tudor monarchy; an economic historian from the beginning of the Industrial Revolution about 1760, and a frustrated reformer might proclaim that it hasn't happened yet. The most reasonable judgment is that modern government developed during the very long reign of Queen Victoria from 1837 to 1901, when government institutions were created to cope with the problems of a society that was increasingly urban, literate, industrial, and critical of unreformed institutions.

The 1832 Reform Act started a gradual process of enfranchising the masses. A majority of English males got the right to vote by 1885. Concurrently, Conservative and Liberal party organizations began to contest elections nationwide. The right to vote was extended to all adult men and women in 1918. The **Labour Party**, founded in 1900 to secure the representation of manual workers in Parliament, first briefly formed a minority government in 1924.

The Industrial Revolution created a demand for government to make cities safe and healthy. In the mid-nineteenth century aristocratic institutions of governance were transformed into a system that could enact and implement laws on public health and education and collect the taxes needed to pay for new public services. The 1906 Liberal government introduced old-age pensions and unemployment insurance; slowly these programs were expanded. The gross national product (GNP) increased greatly, and the share claimed by government increased even more. In 1890 public spending was equal to 8 percent of GNP; in 1910 the share had risen to 12 percent and by 1920 to 26 percent.

A tunnel underneath the English Channel between England and France, opened in 1994, provides a physical link between Britain and the Continent. In political geography, however, England remains an "offshore" member of the European Union, seeking weak rather than strong ties with its continental neighbors.

Reuters Bettmann/Corbis

For the past half century, public spending has fluctuated around two-fifths of the gross national product. The creation of a modern system of government does not make the problems of governing disappear. England emerged on the winning side in two world wars, but its political influence was reduced. Political developments since can be divided into five stages.

First, during World War II an all-party coalition government led by Winston Churchill laid the foundations for a **mixed economy Keynesian welfare state**. The government created full employment to fight the war and rationed food to ensure "fair shares for all." From this coalition emerged the Beveridge Report on social welfare, John Maynard Keynes's Full Employment White Paper of 1944, and the Butler Education Act of 1944. These three measures—the first two named after Liberals and the third after a Conservative—were landmarks in the development of the British welfare state. The fair shares policy was continued by the Labour government of Clement Attlee elected in 1945 and the National Health Service was established. Coal mines, gas and electricity, railways, and the steel industries were nationalized (that is, taken into government ownership). By 1951 the Labour government had exhausted its catalog of agreed changes.

In the second stage, the Conservatives, in office from 1951 to 1964, maintained a consensus on social policy. Administrations under Winston Churchill, Anthony Eden, and Harold Macmillan were anxious to assure the electorate that they could be trusted to conserve a widely popular welfare state. Keynesian techniques for promoting economic growth, full employment, and low inflation showed evidence of success. Rationing was ended and living standards rose.

The third stage commenced in the early 1960s with a flood of books on the theme "What's wrong with Britain?" Continuities with the past were attacked as the dead hand of tradition. Politicians promoted managerial activism. Labour, Liberal, and Conservative politicians denounced "stagnation" and competed in prescribing activist measures, ushering in what Michael Mora has described as an age of "hyper-innovation."

The Labour Party won the 1964 election under Harold Wilson campaigning with the vague activist slogan, "Let's go with Labour." New titles were given government department offices, symbolizing a desire to change for its own sake. Behind the entrance of these restyled offices, the same people went through the same routines as before. The economy did not grow as predicted, and in 1967 the Wilson government was forced to devalue the pound and

BOX 8.2 The Meaning of Thatcherism

Among British prime ministers, Margaret Thatcher was unique in giving her name to a political ideology, **Thatcherism**. She believed in strong government—as long as it was in her hands. In foreign policy she was a formidable proponent of what she saw as Britain's national interest in dealings with the European Union and in alliance with President Ronald Reagan. The 1982 Argentine invasion of the Falkland Islands, a remote British colony in the South Atlantic, led to a brief and victorious war against Argentina. Thatcher was also quick to assert her personal authority against colleagues in the Cabinet and against civil servants.* The autonomy of local government was curbed by central government, and a property tax on houses replaced by a poll tax on each adult.

Thatcher's central conviction was that the market offered a cure for the country's economic difficulties. As Milton Friedman, the Nobel Prize-winning monetary economist, noted: "Mrs. Thatcher represents a different tradition. She represents a tradition of the nineteenth-century Liberal, of Manchester Liberalism, of free market free trade."[†] In economic policy the Thatcher administration experienced both successes and frustrations. Her anti-inflation policies succeeded but unemployment doubled. Industrial relations acts gave members the right to elect their union's leaders and vote on whether to hold a strike. She introduced what were described as "businesslike" methods for managing everything from hospitals and universities to museums, hoping to reduce public spending and taxation.

*Cf. Dennis Kavanagh, *Thatcherism and British Politics* (Oxford, England: Oxford University Press, 1990); and Margaret Thatcher, *The Downing Street Years* (New York: HarperCollins, 1993).

[†]"Thatcher Praised by Her Guru," *The Guardian* (London), March 12, 1983.

---

seek a loan from the International Monetary Fund. Labour lost the 1970 election.

The major achievement of the 1970–1974 Conservative government under Edward Heath was to make Britain a member of what was then the European Community and is now the European Union. Doing so divided his own party and the opposition. In trying to limit unprecedented inflation by controlling wages, Heath risked his authority in a confrontation with the National Union of Mineworkers. The result was a stalemate, and industry working a three-day week because of a shortage of coal. The prime minister called an election. The "Who Governs?" election of February 1974 showed many voters rejecting both major parties. The Conservative share of the vote dropped to 38 percent and Labour's to 37 percent, while the Liberal vote more than doubled to 19 percent. Due to anomalies in the electoral system, Labour won the most seats in the House of Commons, but no party had an absolute majority there. Labour formed a minority government, with Harold Wilson again prime minister. A second election in October 1974 gave Labour a bare majority. Inflation, rising unemployment, and a contraction in the economy caused this policy to collapse. James Callaghan succeeded Wilson as prime minister in 1976. Keynesian policies were abandoned in 1977

when Labour again relied on a loan from the International Monetary Fund to stabilize the pound.

The 1979 general election was won by the Conservatives under Margaret Thatcher, the first woman to serve as prime minister of a major European country. She ushered in the fourth stage, making a radical break with the past. She regarded the economic failures of previous governments as arising from too much compromise and too little conviction. "The Old Testament prophets did not say 'Brothers, I want a consensus.' They said: 'This is my faith. This is what I passionately believe. If you believe it too, then come with me.'"[5] Above all, she believed that the market rather than government should make the most important decisions in society (Box 8.2).

Divisions among opponents enabled Thatcher to lead her party to three successive election victories although never winning more than 43 percent of the total vote. Militant left-wing activists seized control of the Labour Party. Under Michael Foot its 1983 election manifesto was described by a Labour MP as the longest suicide note in history. In protest, four former Labour Cabinet ministers formed a centrist Social Democratic Party (SDP) in 1981 and made an alliance with the Liberal Party. After Thatcher's third successive election victory in 1987, the SDP leadership merged with the Liberals to form the Liberal Democrats.

While preaching against big government, Thatcher did not court electoral defeat by imposing radical cuts on the biggest spending and most popular programs of the government. In consequence, public spending continued to grow in the Thatcher era. It was 40 percent of the gross domestic product in her last full year in office. While the Conservative majority in Parliament endorsed Thatcher's policies, it did not win the hearts and minds of the electorate. When voters were asked on the tenth anniversary of Thatcher's period in office whether or not they approved of "the Thatcher revolution," less than one-third responded yes.[6]

Within the Conservative Party, Thatcher's increasingly autocratic treatment of Cabinet colleagues created resentment, and during her third term of office this was reinforced by unpopularity in opinion polls. In autumn 1990, disgruntled Conservative members of Parliament (MPs) forced a ballot for the party leadership. In the first round, the prime minister won just over half the votes of Conservative MPs. But under the party's complicated rules for electing a leader, this was not enough to confirm Thatcher in office; she resigned. In the subsequent ballot, Conservative MPs elected a relatively unknown John Major as party leader.

In his first electoral test in 1992, John Major won an unexpected and unprecedented fourth consecutive term for the Conservative government. Shortly after the 1992 election his economic policy of a strong British pound crashed under pressure from foreign speculators. Major was criticized by Thatcherites in the Conservative Party for agreeing to the Maastricht Treaty on expanding the powers of the European Union. Although personally above suspicion, Major's administration was plagued by the exposure of Conservative MPs' **sleazy** behavior, involving sex, money, or both. By 1993 Major reached the lowest popularity rating in the history of the Gallup Poll. The Major government held onto office and Thatcherite economic policies such as the privatization of the coal mines and railways were pursued.

A fifth stage in postwar British politics opened after Tony Blair became Labour leader in 1994. Blair was elected leader because he did not talk or look like an ordinary Labour Party member. Instead of being from a poor background, he was educated at boarding school and studied law at Oxford. Instead of having grown up in the Labour movement, his parents were Conservatives, and he joined the Labour Party due to the encouragement of a girlfriend, Cherie Booth (now his wife and a very successful lawyer). His qualities appealed to middle-class voters whose support Labour needed to move from opposition to government. Labour won a landslide majority in the House of Commons in the 1997 election, even though it received a smaller share of the popular vote than Margaret Thatcher in 1979, because the Conservative vote fell to its lowest share since 1832. In June 2001, Blair led Labour to another landslide victory over a demoralized opposition. But the longer he has been in office the more he has expressed frustration with the obstacles that British government creates to his hopes for changing Britain overnight.

Blair's decision to commit Britain to go to war in Iraq in 2003 alongside the United States caused a bitter division within his party. Official inquiries into the "spin" that Blair gave for going to war showed that he had exaggerated or misread intelligence briefings, and opinion polls showed that a majority of Britons no longer trusted Blair. Under pressure from Labour critics, Blair has had to interrupt foreign policy forays to show that he is concerned about improving social conditions in Britain.

The continuity of England's political institutions through the centuries is remarkable. Prince Charles, the heir to an ancient Crown, pilots jet airplanes, and a medieval-named Chancellor of the Exchequer pilots the British pound through the deep waters of the international economy. Yet symbols of continuity often mask great changes in English life. Parliament was once a supporter of royal authority. Today Parliament is primarily an electoral college deciding which party leader is in charge of government.

THE ENVIRONMENT OF POLITICS

One Crown but Five Nations

The Queen of England is the best known monarch in the world, yet there is no such entity as an English state. In international law, the state is the United Kingdom of Great Britain and Northern Ireland. The United Kingdom was created in 1801 as the climax of a process of expansion begun in the twelfth century. Great Britain, the principal part of the

T A B L E   8 . 1   National Identity

	England	Scotland	Wales	N. Ireland Prot.	N. Ireland Catholic
THINKS OF SELF AS:					
British	38	35	33	67	15
English	57	2	8	—	—
Scottish	2	52	—	—	—
Welsh	1	—	57	—	—
Ulster	—	—	—	20	6
Irish	1	11	—	8	69
Other, don't know	1	10	2	5	10
Total	100	100	100	100	100

Source: Richard Rose, *The Territorial Dimension in Government: Understanding the United Kingdom* (Chatham, N.J.: Chatham House, 1982), p. 14.

United Kingdom, is divided into three parts: England, Scotland, and Wales. **Scotland** was once an independent kingdom; since the 1707 Act of Union, there has been a common Parliament for the whole of Great Britain. However, the Scots have retained separate legal, religious, and educational institutions. **Wales** was joined with England in the sixteenth century and administered thereafter as if it were a part of England. Its most distinctive feature is the ancient Welsh language. The fourth part of the United Kingdom, **Northern Ireland**, consists of six counties of Ulster. The remainder of Ireland broke away to form a separate state in 1921 as the culmination of a rebellion against the Crown launched in Dublin in 1916.

In national identity, the United Kingdom is a multinational state as its citizens differ in how they describe themselves (see Table 8.1). In England people often are confused about the difference between being English or British and use the terms interchangeably. When asked to give their national identity, a majority describe themselves as English. In Scotland, more than half see themselves as Scots. In Wales, where three-quarters of the population does not speak Welsh, more than half say they are Welsh. In England, Scotland, and Wales, at least one-third see themselves as primarily British. Just as people in Texas can see themselves as both Texans and Americans, many see themselves as having a secondary British identity as well as well being English, Scots, or Welsh. In Northern Ireland, people divide into two nations. Most Catholics see

themselves as Irish while the great majority of Protestants see themselves as British.

The parties competing for seats differ in each nation of the United Kingdom. Northern Ireland is extreme, for British parties do not contest seats there. In Scotland, four parties compete. In the 2005 general election the Labour Party won more than two-thirds of the seats with two-fifths of the vote in competition with the Liberal Party, the pro-independence Scottish National Party and the fourth-place Conservative Party. In Wales, the nationalist party, Plaid Cymru, came fourth in votes. The most distinctive feature of Welsh politics is the high Labour vote.

Historically, Scotland and Wales have been governed by British Cabinet ministers accountable to the Westminster Parliament. Under pressure from nationalist parties campaigning for independence, the Labour Party adopted a policy of creating elected Assemblies in Scotland and in Wales. Referendums on devolution were held in September 1997. In Scotland, 74 percent voted in favor of a Scottish Parliament in Edinburgh while Welsh voters endorsed an Assembly in Cardiff by 50.3 percent.

A Parliament in Scotland with powers to legislate, tax, and spend was first elected in May 1999 under a system of proportional representation. In the second election to the 129-seat Parliament held in May 2003, the Labour Party won 32 percent of the proportional representation vote and 50 seats and the pro-independence Scottish National Party gained 27 seats with 21 percent of the vote. The

A Parliament has met in London by the River Thames for more than 700 years, and the clock tower of Big Ben is famous as a symbol of democracy in Canada and Australia as well as in Europe.

Steve Vidher/Leo de Wys, Inc.

Conservative Party won 13 percent of the vote and 18 seats, and the Liberal Democrats 10 percent of the vote and 17 seats. The Green Party, Scottish Socialists, and other parties together won 17 seats and almost one-quarter of the vote. As the party with the most seats, Labour provides the First Minister, but to achieve a majority in the Scottish Parliament, it has needed to form a coalition government with the Liberal Democrats.

After the May 1999 Welsh Assembly election, Labour formed a minority government. In the May 2003 election, Labour's share of the vote went up to 37 percent and it won half of the 60 seats in the Assembly. In second place was the Welsh Nationalist Party (Plaid Cymru), with 12 seats and 20 percent of the vote. The Conservatives gained 11 seats with 19 percent of the vote and Liberal Democrats won 6 seats with 13 percent of the vote. Powers over Welsh legislation and total public expenditure remain in the hands of a British Cabinet minister.

Northern Ireland is the most un-English part of the United Kingdom. Formally, it is a secular polity, but differences between Protestants and Catholics about national identity dominate its politics. Protestants, comprising about three-fifths of the population, want to remain part of the United Kingdom. Until 1972 the Protestant majority governed through a

home-rule Parliament at Stormont, a suburb of Belfast. Many of the Catholic minority did not support this regime; they wanted to leave the United Kingdom and join the Republic of Ireland, which in its constitution claimed the territory of Northern Ireland.

Since the start of demonstrations by Catholics against discrimination in Northern Ireland in 1968, it has been in turmoil. Demonstrations turned to street violence in August 1969, and the British Army intervened. The illegal **Irish Republican Army (IRA)** was revived and in 1971 began a military campaign to remove Northern Ireland from the United Kingdom. In retaliation, Protestants organized illegal armed forces too. Since August 1969, more than 3,200 people have been killed in political violence. After adjusting for population differences, the deaths from political violence are equivalent to more than 110,000 political deaths in Britain or more than 500,000 deaths in America.

British policy in Northern Ireland has been erratic. In 1969 the British Army went into action to protect Catholics. In 1971 it helped intern hundreds of Catholics without trial in an unsuccessful attempt to break the IRA. In 1972 the British government abolished the Stormont Parliament, placing government in the hands of a Northern Ireland Office under a British Cabinet minister. In 1985 the British government took the unprecedented step of inviting the Dublin-based government of the Republic of Ireland to participate in institutions affecting the governance of part of the United Kingdom.

A stable agreement about Northern Ireland requires the acceptance by paramilitary organizations on each side of the religious divide as well as of parties solely committed to parliamentary politics. In 1994 the IRA announced a cessation of its military activity, and Sinn Fein, the party political wing of the Irish Republican Movement, agreed to talks. Protestant paramilitary forces also ceased activities. On Good Friday, 1998, an agreement was reached for an elected power-sharing executive and cross-border institutions involving both Dublin and Belfast. The basic principle of the agreement, power-sharing, is the opposite of British government. Whereas in Westminster the majority party in the Commons can form a government on its own, in Northern Ireland government must be a coalition of representatives of both Protestants and Catholics.

The election of a Northern Ireland Assembly in June 1998, led to a power-sharing executive including the Ulster Unionist Party, the nonviolent Social Democratic and Labour Party (SDLP), and Sinn Fein, a party linked politically with the IRA. The Democratic Unionist Party led by Dr. Ian Paisley did not join the administration. When the IRA failed to produce sufficient tangible evidence that it was decommissioning arms, the power-sharing executive collapsed Northern Ireland is once again under "temporary" direct rule from Westminster, and a 45 million dollar bank robber and a brutal murder by the IRA have questioned Sinn Fein's commitment to a non-violent resolution of the conflict. In the 2005 election, the Democratic Unionist Party won the most seats and Sinn Fein came second.

The United Kingdom is a union—that is, a political system having only one source of authority, the British Parliament. However, institutions governing the United Kingdom are not uniform. Distinctive administrative institutions exist in Scotland and Wales, and **devolution** increases their political legitimacy by creating popularly elected assemblies. Northern Ireland has always been the subject of exceptional legislation.

Even though there is no agreement about what being English means, there is no doubt about which nationality is the most numerous. Politics in England is the focus of this chapter because England dominates the United Kingdom. Its population constitutes five-sixths of the total of the United Kingdom, and the remainder is divided among three different nations. No United Kingdom government will ever overlook what is central to England, and politicians who wish to advance in British government must accept the norms of English society. During the 1997 election campaign, Blair reminded Scottish voters, "Sovereignty rests with me, as an English MP, and that's the way it will stay."[7]

A Multiracial England

Through the centuries England has received a relatively small but noteworthy number of immigrants from other parts of Europe. The Queen herself is descended from royalty who came from Hanover, Germany, to assume the English throne in 1714. Until the outbreak of anti-German sentiment in World War I, the surname of the royal family was Saxe-Coburg-Gotha. By royal proclamation George V changed the family name to Windsor in 1917. Most post–World War II immigrants have been attracted to England by jobs. Since the late 1950s job seekers have been arriving from the West Indies, Pakistan, India, and other parts of what was once the British Empire and is now a multiracial Commonwealth. In addition, there is a substantial inflow and outflow of people from Australia, Canada, the European Union, and the United States spending a few years in England for study or work.

The new Commonwealth immigrants have only one characteristic in common: they are not white. Beyond that, immigrants share neither culture nor religion. West Indians speak English as their native language and have a Christian tradition; immigrants from India and Pakistan are Hindus, Muslims, or Sikhs and most speak English as a second language. The smaller number of African immigrants are divided by nationality. Chinese from Hong Kong have a distinctive culture too. Altogether, more than half of New Commonwealth immigrants have come from the Indian subcontinent, a quarter are black people from the Caribbean or Africa, and about a tenth are Chinese or other Asians from outside the Indian subcontinent.

The 2001 census estimated the nonwhite population of the United Kingdom had risen from 74,000 in 1951 to 4.6 million, almost 8 percent of the population. Public opinion has opposed unlimited immigration of nonwhites, and both Conservative and Labour governments have passed laws limiting the number of nonwhite immigrants.

With the passage of time the nonwhite population is becoming increasingly British born and educated. This makes the important issue: What is the position of British-born offspring of immigrants? Whatever their country of origin, they differ in how they see themselves: 64 percent of Caribbean origin identify as British, as do more than three-fifths of Pakistanis, Indians, and Bangladeshis, and two-fifths of Chinese. Laws to encourage better race relations and antidiscrimination measures have been enacted. However, provisions for enforcement by the courts are very weak in comparison with American legislation. After the 9/11 terrorist attacks in America, the Labour government has shifted emphasis from promoting multiculturalism to stressing the integration of immigrant families into the British way of life.

Immigrants and their offspring are being integrated into electoral politics, as residential concentration makes local politicians aware of their impact as a voting bloc. There are now hundreds of elected nonwhite councillors in local government; a disproportionate number are Labour. The 15 nonwhite MPs in the Commons today come from diverse backgrounds: India, Pakistan, Aden, Ghana, and the West Indies.

Political disturbances around the world have added a fresh issue, an increasing number of immigrants who claim to be refugees from trouble areas in the Balkans, the Middle East, and Africa. Some have valid credentials as refugees whereas others have been smuggled to England and arrive with false papers. In response to popular concern, the Blair government has promised to be tougher in enforcing asylum laws.

Insularity and Involvement

For centuries the English Channel has represented a literal as well as a symbolic gulf between England and continental Europe. The opening in 1994 of the Channel Tunnel linking England and France has not closed the gap. More than half of Britons say they do not feel at all European, and only 23 percent say that they feel strongly or somewhat European. Depending on circumstances, politicians claim that England is close to the United States, or to the Commonwealth countries scattered around the globe, or to Europe.[8]

Insularity is not to be confused with isolation. Britain is a member of more than 125 different international bodies, including the United Nations, the European Union, and NATO. The British Empire has been replaced by a free association of 54 sovereign states—the Commonwealth—with members on every continent. The independent status of its chief members is shown by the absence of the word "British" from the name of the Commonwealth. Commonwealth countries from Antigua and Australia to Zambia and Zimbabwe differ greatly from each other in wealth, language, culture, and religion, and in their commitment to democracy.

Britain's foreign policy since the end of the Second World War has been a story of contracting commitments. Britain took a lead in establishing NATO to involve the United States in the protection of Western Europe from the Soviet Union. Militarily, it has been dependent on high-tech hardware bought from the United States while retaining an armed force with upwards of 300,000 persons in uniform, including a major military presence in Iraq since 2003. Blair sees Britain's role as a key link in the creation of "one polar power which encompasses a strategic partnership between Europe and America."[9]

However, there has been limited popular support for the country acting like a global policeman. When a Gallup Poll asked whether people would rather Britain were a leading world power or a small neutral country like Sweden or Switzerland, 49 percent chose being a small power as against 34 percent wanting the country to be a world power.[10] Whereas military force is rarely used, economic transactions are continuous. England depends on world trade, importing much food and many raw materials. To pay for imports, England exports a wide range of manufactured goods, as well as "invisible" services provided by financial institutions in the city of London.

Speeches by the prime minister and head of the Treasury do not determine the foreign exchange value of the pound. This is decided in international markets in which currency speculators play a significant role. The value of the British pound in exchange for the dollar has ranged from above $2.50 to less than $1.25. In spring, 2005 the pound's value fluctuated around $1.90.

As England's world position has declined and the importance of countries such as Germany and France has risen, the government has looked to Europe. In a jet age, the English Channel is no longer a barrier to travel to the European continent. Television and the Internet carry news, sports, and entertainment across national boundaries. Economic ties have grown. For example, the Ford Motor Company links its manufacturing plants in England with factories across Western Europe, just as it links Ford factories between American states. Public opinion and politicians have remained divided about what role Britain can or should play in Europe. When the European Community was established in 1957, Britain did not join, because the government considered the country distant from the problems of continental neighbors ravaged by war. It joined in 1973.

European politics has grown in significance, symbolized by the Community changing its name to the European Union. Powers to promote a Single European Market enable the EU to impose regulations affecting British business and limit the scope for London to give subsidies to industries and firms in trouble. British ministers spend an increasing amount of their time negotiating with their opposite numbers in other countries of the European Union on matters ranging from political fundamentals to whether British beer should be served in metric units or by the traditional measure of a British pint.

The British government cannot insulate the country from changes in the world. English people cannot choose to be a small, rich country like Switzerland or Sweden. The effective choice today is between England being a big, rich country or a big, relatively poor European country. Exchanging nominal sovereignty to participate in the European Union presents no problems to governments in small countries, which have always recognized the influence of bigger neighbors. However, it is a shock to many British politicians who pride themselves on Britain's traditional involvement in three different international settings, the Commonwealth, Europe, and a "special relationship" with the United States.

The diversity of political outlooks within the European Union is so great after its enlargement to 25 member states that government ministers can normally find allies for any British cause. But to do so the government must be fully committed to involvement in the European Union. Seven years after becoming prime minister, Tony Blair has yet to convince fellow EU members that Britain is no longer an island but an integral part of Europe. The indictment of the American diplomat, Dean Acheson, a generation ago continues to ring true: "Great Britain has lost an empire and has not yet found a role."[11]

THE STRUCTURE OF GOVERNMENT

We must understand what government is as precondition of evaluating what it does. Descriptions of a government often start with its constitution. However, England has no written constitution. At no time in the past was there a break with tradition that forced politicians to write down how the country should be governed.

The **unwritten constitution** of England is a jumble of acts of Parliament, judicial pronouncements, customs, and conventions about the rules of the political game. The vagueness of the constitution makes it flexible, a point that political leaders such as Margaret Thatcher and Tony Blair have been ready to exploit to increase their own power. Instead of giving written guarantees to citizens, as the American Bill of Rights does, the rights of English people are meant to be secured by trustworthy governors. In the words of a constitutional lawyer, J. A. G. Griffith, "The Constitution is what happens."[12]

Comparing the written American and the unwritten English constitution emphasizes how few are the constraints of an unwritten constitution (Table 8.2). The U.S. Constitution gives the Supreme Court the final power to decide what the government may or may not do. In England, by contrast, the final authority is Parliament, where the government of the day commands a majority of votes. The Law Lords and the Judicial Committee of the Privy Council can resolve disputes about the interpretation of Acts of Parliament but not declare an Act unconstitutional. The Bill of Rights in the U.S. Constitution allows anyone to seek redress in the courts for infringement of personal rights, whereas in England an individual who believes his or her personal rights are infringed by an act of Parliament had no redress through the courts until the Blair government, instead of preparing a British code of rights, simply incorporated the European Convention of Human Rights into the laws of Britain. Whereas amendments to the U.S.

T A B L E   8 . 2   Comparing an Unwritten and a Written Constitution

	England (unwritten)	United States (written)
Origins	Medieval customs	1787 Constitutional Convention
Form	Unwritten, indefinite	Written, precise
Final power	Majority in Parliament	Supreme Court
Bill of individual rights	No	Yes
Amendment	Ordinary vote in Parliament; unprecedented action by government	More than majority vote in Congress, states
Centrality in political debate	Low	High

Constitution must receive the endorsement of well over half the states and members of Congress, the unwritten constitution can be changed by a majority vote in Parliament, or by the government of the day choosing to act in an unprecedented manner.

English courts claim no power to declare an act of Parliament unconstitutional. Courts ask whether the executive acts within its statutory powers. Many statutes delegate broad discretion to a Cabinet minister or public authority; the courts hesitate to question how the executive exercises its delegated discretion. Even if the courts rule that the government has improperly exercised its authority, the effect of such a judgment can be annulled by a subsequent act of Parliament retroactively authorizing an action.

The **Crown** rather than a constitution symbolizes the authority of government. However, the monarch is only a ceremonial head of state. The public reaction to the accidental death of Princess Diana was a media event but it was not a political event like the assassination of President Kennedy. Queen Elizabeth II does not influence the actions of what is described as Her Majesty's Government. While the queen gives formal assent to laws passed by Parliament, she may not publicly state any opinion about legislation. The queen is expected to respect the will of Parliament, as communicated to her by the leader of the majority party in Parliament, the prime minister.

What constitutes the Crown? No simple answer can be given. The Crown is a symbol to which people are asked to give loyalty. It does not refer to a particular community of people. The idea of the Crown combines the dignified parts of the constitution, which sanctify authority by tradition and myth, with the efficient parts, which carry out the work of government.

In everyday political conversation, English people talk about government, not the constitution. The term **government** is used in many senses (Figure 8.1). People may speak of the Queen's government, to emphasize enduring and nonpartisan features, or they may refer to Tony Blair's government to stress its personal and transitory features, or to a Labour or Conservative government to emphasize partisanship. The term government officials usually refers to civil servants. Collectively, the executive agencies of government are often referred to as **Whitehall**, after the London street in which many major government offices are located. **Downing Street**, where the prime minister's residence is located, is a short and narrow street off Whitehall. **Parliament**—that is, the popularly elected House of Commons and the nonelected House of Lords—is at the bottom end of the street called Whitehall. Collectively, these institutions are often referred to as **Westminster**, after the district in London in which they are located.

What the Prime Minister Says and Does

Within the Cabinet, the **prime minister** occupies a unique position, sometimes referred to as primus inter pares (first among equals). But as Winston Churchill once wrote, "There can be no comparison between the positions of number one, and numbers two, three or four."[13] However, the preeminence of the prime minister is ambiguous. A politician at the apex of government is remote from what is happening on the ground. The more responsibilities attributed to the prime minister, the less time there is to devote to any one task. Like a president, a prime minister is the prisoner of the political law of first

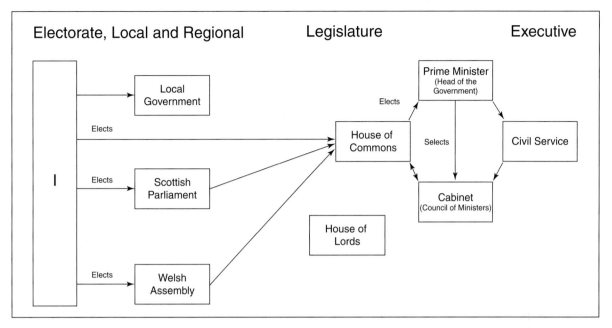

FIGURE 8.1   Structure of the British Government

things first. The imperatives of the prime minister are as follows.

1. *Winning elections.* A prime minister may be self-interested but he or she is not self-employed. To become prime minister, a politician must first be elected leader of his or her party. The only election that a prime minister must win is that as party leader. Six of the eleven prime ministers since 1945—Winston Churchill, Anthony Eden, Harold Macmillan, Alec Douglas-Home, James Callaghan, and John Major—initially entered Downing Street during the middle of a Parliament rather than after a national election. In the 17 elections since 1945, the prime minister of the day has ten times led the governing party to victory and seven times to defeat.

2. *Campaigning through the media.* A prime minister does not need to attract publicity; it is thrust upon him or her by the curiosity of television and newspaper reporters. Media eminence is a double-edged sword. When the news is bad, such as rising unemployment or popular concern about crime, the news puts the prime minister in an unfavorable light. While the personality of a prime minister remains relatively constant, during a term of office his or her popularity can fluc-

tuate by as much as 30 or 40 percentage points in public opinion polls.[14]

3. *Patronage.* To remain prime minister, a politician must retain the confidence of his party. He can silence potential critics by appointing a quarter of MPs in the governing party to jobs in the government as ministers or junior ministers; they sit on front bench seats in the House of Commons. MPs not appointed to a post are backbenchers; many ingratiate themselves with the party leader in hopes of becoming a government minister. In making ministerial appointments, a prime minister can use any of four different criteria: (a) personal loyalty (rewarding friends); (b) co-option (silencing critics by giving them an office so that they are committed to support the government); (c) representativeness (for example, appointing a woman or someone from Scotland or Wales); and (d) competence in giving direction to a government department.

4. *Parliamentary performance.* The prime minister appears in the House of Commons weekly for half an hour of questions from MPs, engaging in rapid-fire repartee with a highly partisan audience. Unprotected by a speechwriter's script, the prime minister must show that he or she is

a good advocate of their views or suffer loss of support. He or she occasionally makes statements to the House.

5. *Making and balancing policies.* Leading government is a political rather than a managerial task. When a prime minister asks an awkward question or gives advice, no Cabinet minister can ignore it. Foreign affairs are the overriding concern of a prime minister, because of the need to deal with heads of governments around the world. When there are conflicts between international and domestic policy priorities, the prime minister is the one person who can strike a balance between pressures from the world "out there" and pressures from the domestic electorate. The number of "intermestic" policies (that is, problems combining both an international and domestic element) is increasing.

While the formal powers of the office remain constant, individual prime ministers have differed in how they view their job, and in their political circumstances (see Figure 8.2). Clement Attlee, Labour prime minister from 1945 to 1951, was a nonassertive spokesperson for the lowest common denominator of views within a Cabinet consisting of very experienced Labour politicians. When an aging Winston Churchill succeeded in 1951, he concentrated on foreign affairs and took little interest in domestic policy; the same was true of his successor, Anthony Eden. Harold Macmillan intervened strategically on a limited number of domestic and international issues, while giving ministers great scope on everyday matters. Alec Douglas-Home was weak because he lacked knowledge of economic affairs, the chief problem during his administration.

Both Harold Wilson and Edward Heath were initially committed to an activist definition of the prime minister's job. However, Wilson's major initiatives in economic policy were unsuccessful. In 1974 the electorate rejected Heath's aggressive direction of the economy, and Wilson won office promising to replace confrontation between management and unions with political conciliation. James Callaghan, who succeeded Wilson in 1976, also emphasized consensus.

Margaret Thatcher had strong views about many major policies; associates gave her the nickname TINA because of her motto: There Is No Alternative. Thatcher was prepared to push her views

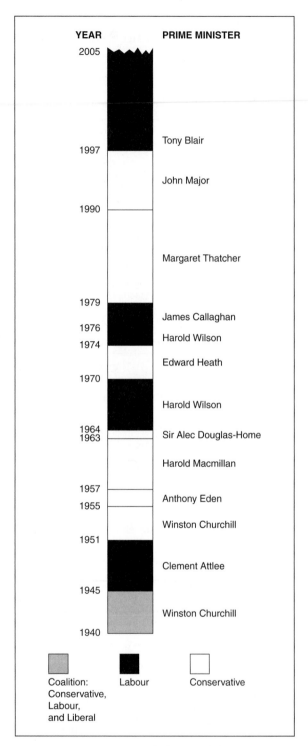

FIGURE 8.2   Prime Minister and Governments Since 1940

During the Iraq War, Tony Blair was the foreign leader closest to President Bush.

AP/Wide World Photos

against the wishes of Cabinet colleagues and civil service advisers by any means necessary. In the end, her "bossiness" caused a revolt of Cabinet colleagues that helped bring about her downfall, and made colleagues welcome John Major in place of a hectoring leader. However, his conciliatory manner was often interpreted as a sign of weakness, and sniping from ministers led Major to refer to his Cabinet colleagues as "bastards."

Tony Blair has carried into Downing Street the priority he gave to campaigning while in Opposition, and brought with him a media staff of "spin doctors" under the leadership of a pro-Labour tabloid journalist, Alastair Campbell. A former editor of *The Times* has charged that Campbell has "imposed the fixations of the press on a compliant government."[15] The media staff are unprecedented in their number, professional skills, and readiness to assert themselves. The emphasis is on "soft" media appearances, for example, on breakfast chat shows, rather than on tough confrontations with the Opposition in the House of Commons. In addition, Blair has brought a large policy staff into Downing Street, and given senior staff formal authority to give orders to civil servants and informal sanction to tell Cabinet ministers what the prime minister wants. This has led to charges of government by "Tony's cronies" and of the politicization of civil servants, who are expected to generate the headlines that

Number Ten wants. Producing the policies needed to back up headline-seeking statements is much more difficult, as the prime minister has learned.

Blair's innovations in campaigning and in Downing Street have led to criticisms that he has created a presidential system. However, by comparison with an American president, a British prime minister has less formal authority. The president is directly elected for a fixed four-year term. A prime minister is chosen by colleagues for an indefinite term—no longer than the life of a Parliament—and is thus less secure in office. The president is the undoubted leader of the federal executive and can dismiss Cabinet appointees with little fear of the consequences; by contrast, senior colleagues of a prime minister, such as Gordon Brown, are potential rivals for leadership and are kept in Cabinet to prevent them from challenging the incumbent from outside it. With the support of the Cabinet and the majority of the governing party's MPs, a prime minister can be far more confident than a president that major legislative proposals will be enacted into law. Although the president is the chief executive branch of the federal government, the White House is without authority over Congress, state and local government, and the judiciary. The prime minister is at the apex of a unitary government, with powers not limited by the courts or by a written constitution.

BOX 8.3   Departmental Organization and Reorganization

British government departments are multipurpose administrative units created as a result of the growth of government and brought together through a series of reorganizations justified by efficiency, policy, fashion, or political expediency.* For example, since 1964 responsibilities for trade, industry, and technology have been placed in departments labelled Trade and Technology, then Trade and Industry, separate departments for Trade and for Industry, and once again reunited as a single Trade and Industry department. Each time that the title on the front door of the department was changed, most officials and programs continued as before. The Cabinet of Tony Blair in January, 2005 had the following departments:

1. External affairs: foreign and commonwealth office; Europe; defence; international development
2. Economic affairs: treasury; trade and industry; transport
3. Law: Lord chancellor and law Officer's department; home office; constitutional affairs
4. Social services: health; social security; education and skills; work and pensions; culture, media, and sport
5. Territorial: environment, food and rural affairs; communities and local and regional government; housing and planning; some parts of constitutional affairs; the Northern Ireland Office
6. Managing government business: Office of Deputy Prime Minister, Leader of the House of Commons; Chief Whip in the House of Commons; Leader of the House of Lords; Chancellor of the Duchy of Lancaster

*See Richard Rose, *Ministers and Ministries: A Functional Analysis* (Oxford, England: Clarendon Press, 1987).

The Cabinet and Cabinet Ministers

The **Cabinet** consists of senior ministers, members of either the House of Commons or House of Lords and appointed by the prime minister. As ministers are leading figures in the majority party in Parliament, they contribute to what Walter Bagehot described as "the close union, the nearly complete fusion of the executive and legislative powers."[16]

The Cabinet has historically been the forum in which the prime minister brought together leading members of the governing party, many with competing departmental interests and personal ambitions, to ensure agreement about major government policies. This was possible because the convention of Cabinet responsibility requires that all Cabinet ministers and their deputies give public support (or at least, refrain from public criticism) of what the government is doing, even if they have opposed a policy in private. A minister who is unwilling to share responsibility has been expected to resign office, and it is rare for a minister to resign because of policy differences.

The Cabinet is no longer a place for collective deliberation in policy. A half century ago there were almost two Cabinet meetings a week with many taking several hours to arrive at a political consensus. By the time of John Major shorter meetings occurred less than once a week. Tony Blair has further reduced meetings and cut their average length to under an hour. Instead of being a forum for consultation, Cabinet meetings are now a forum in which Number Ten exhorts ministers to produce good news and bury bad news. Cabinet ministers remain important as department heads, for most decisions of government are taken within departments, and departments are responsible for overseeing all the services of government, which are usually delivered by public agencies distant from Whitehall and subordinate to it (Box 8.3).

The most important departments are the Treasury, which is responsible for taxing, spending, and managing the economy; the Home Office, responsible for police, immigration, and security; and the Foreign Office, although its head often acts as a subordinate to the prime minister. Other departments are prominent when their subject matter is in the news: for example, if there is a rail crash then the minister for Transport answers for what has happened.

Major Whitehall departments differ greatly from each other. For example, the Home Office has a staff approximately ten times larger than the Treasury. Because of the importance of the economy, however, the Treasury has more senior civil servants. The Home Office has more staff at lower levels because of the scale of its routine tasks involving supervision of police, fire, prison, drugs, cruelty to animals, control of obscene publications, race relations, and so on. The Treasury concentrates on one big task, the management of the economy. The varied tasks of the Home Secretary make him or her much more vulnerable to adverse publicity if, for example, a convicted murderer escapes from prison. But the job of the Chancellor of the Exchequer, the minister in charge of the Treasury, is more important politically, insofar as economic performance affects the governing party's electoral fate. Moreover, Gordon Brown, the current Chancellor, has a power base in the Labour Party independent of Tony Blair and is often described as his potential successor.

A minister has many roles; initiating policies, selecting among alternatives brought forward from within the department, or avoiding a difficult or unpopular decision. A minister is responsible for actions taken by thousands of civil servants nominally acting on the minister's behalf and must answer for agencies to which Whitehall is increasingly contracting out responsibility for delivering public services. In addition, a minister is a department's ambassador to the world outside, including Downing Street, Parliament, the mass media, and pressure groups. Not least, Cabinet ministers are individuals with ambitions to rise in politics.

The typical minister is not an expert in a subject but an expert in parliamentary politics, willing to deal with any department that offers opportunities to further his or her political career. A minister learns on the job. Usually, an MP is first given a junior post as an Under Secretary, with limited policy responsibilities. He or she may then be promoted to Minister of State, a position with broader and more important departmental duties, for example, looking after primary education in the Department of Education. The final step up the career ladder is to become head of a department and a full member of the Cabinet.

The political reputation of Cabinet ministers depends on their success in promoting the interests of their department in parliament, in the media and in battles within Whitehall. Cabinet ministers are willing to go along silently with their colleagues' proposals in exchange for endorsement of their own mea-

sures. However, ministers often have to compete for scarce resources, making conflict inevitable between departments. Regardless of party, the defence and education ministers will press for increased spending while treasury ministers oppose such moves. Cabinet ministers prefer to resolve their differences in Cabinet committees including all ministers whose departments are most affected by an issue or by lobbying Downing Street for the prime minister's support.

Tony Blair's concern with continuous campaigning by presenting good news through the media has led him to give his personal staff at Downing Street greater influence over what ministers say and do—insofar as it attracts media attention. However, Blair does not have any more time during the week to go into the details of policy, and because he has never been a departmental minister, his public remarks sometimes show naivete about how government actually works.[17]

The Civil Service

Although government could continue for months without new legislation, it would collapse overnight if hundreds of thousands of civil servants stopped administering laws and delivering public services. The largest number of civil servants are clerical staff with little discretion; they undertake the routine activities of a large bureaucracy. Only if these duties are executed satisfactorily can ministers have the time and opportunity to make new policies. The most important group of civil servants is the smallest: the few hundred higher civil servants who advise ministers and oversee work of the departments. Top British civil servants deny they are politicians because of the partisan connotations of the term. However, their work is political because they are concerned with formulating, revising, and advising on policies. A publication seeking to recruit bright graduates for the higher civil service declares: "You will be involved from the outset in matters of major policy or resource allocation and, under the guidance of experienced administrators, encouraged to put forward your own constructive ideas and to take responsible decisions."

Top civil servants are not apolitical; they are bipartisan, being ready to work for whichever party is the winner of an election. Their style is not that of the professional American athlete for whom winning is all-important. English civil servants have grown up playing cricket; its motto is that winning is less important than how one plays the game. The relationship between ministers and higher civil servants is critical. Ministers expect higher civil servants to be responsive to their political views and to give advice consistent with their outlook and that of the governing party and Downing Street. Civil servants like working for a political heavyweight who can carry the department's cause to victory in interdepartmental battles. A busy politician does not have time to go into details; he or she wants a brief that can catch a headline or squash criticism. Civil servants prefer to work for a minister who has clear views on policy, but they dislike it when the views proclaimed will get the department into trouble later because they are impractical.

In the traditional Whitehall model, both ministers and civil servants concentrated on political management rather than administrative concerns. Civil servants were expected to think like politicians, anticipating what their minister would want and objections that would be raised by Parliament, pressure groups, and the media. Ministers were also expected to think like civil servants, recognizing all the obstacles to achieving politically desirable goals, and scaling down their ambitions when ways could not be found to overcome these obstacles. The Thatcher government introduced a new phenomenon in Whitehall: a prime minister who believed civil servants were inferior to business people because they did not have to "earn" their living—that is, make a profit. Management was made the buzzword in Whitehall, and departments were supposed to be run in a businesslike fashion, achieving value for money so that the government could profit politically by cutting taxes. Parts of government departments were "hived off" to form separate public agencies, with their own accounts and performance target, However, when an agency's task is politically sensitive, such as the marking of national school examinations, the education minister cannot avoid blame if there are major errors in marking examinations.

The Blair government has continued Thatcherite attempts to make the civil service more businesslike, in hopes it can thereby provide more public services without raising taxes. In addition, it has made political advisers important in formulating policy, leading to criticisms from the independent official Committee on Standards in Public Life. Some civil servants fear that efforts to "modernize" the civil service are a mask for appointing officials who are pliable in the hands of ministers.

After years in office, Tony Blair has attacked the consequences of government by political advisers and spin doctors. In a leaked memo to Cabinet ministers he has criticized them for "too often" rushing out policies "in ignorance of the risks," thus making the government look bad.[18]

The Role of Parliament

The principal division in Parliament is between the party with a majority of seats in the House of Commons and the opposition party. The government gets its way because its members are the leading politicians in the party with a majority in the Commons. If a bill or a motion is identified as a vote of confidence in the government, the government will fall if it is defeated. MPs in the majority party almost invariably vote as the party leadership instructs, because only by voting as a bloc can their party maintain control of government. The instrument by which party discipline is imposed is known as a **whip**. This word actually has a double political meaning. It refers, on the one hand, to a member of parliament whose responsibility is to enforce party discipline. Each party will have a number of such offices, with the top officer known as the chief whip. On the other hand, the word "whip" also refers to a document issued by these party officials, on a weekly basis, which tells the party members how to vote on upcoming bills and how important each of these bills is. In nine out of ten votes in the Commons, voting is 100 percent along party lines. If a handful of MPs votes against the party whip or abstains, this is headlined as a rebellion. The government's state of mind is summed up in the words of a Labour Cabinet minister who declared, "It's carrying democracy too far if you don't know the result of the vote before the meeting."[19]

Whitehall departments draft bills presented to Parliament. Only a very small percentage of amendments to legislation are carried without government backing. Moreover, the government rather than Parliament sets the budget for government programmes. The weakness of the British House of Commons stands in marked contrast to the U.S. Congress, where each house controls its own proceedings independent of the White House and can be at loggerheads when different parties control each branch. An American president may ask Congress to enact a bill but cannot compel a favorable vote.

The first function of the Commons is to weigh political reputations. MPs continually assess their colleagues as ministers and potential ministers. A minister may win a formal vote of confidence but lose status if his or her arguments are demolished in debate.

Secondly, MPs in the governing party have private access to government ministers. The whip is expected to listen to the views of dissatisfied backbench MPs and to convey their concerns to ministers. In the corridors, dining rooms, and committees of the Commons, backbenchers can tell ministers what they think is wrong with government policy. However, MPs are unwilling to vote against their party if it threatens to bring down the government. The opposition cannot expect to alter major government decisions because it lacks a majority of votes in the Commons. The opposition accepts the frustrations going with its minority status for the life of a Parliament, because it hopes to win a majority at the next election.

Publicizing issues is a third function of Parliament. Debates in the House of Commons are losing importance; only one-sixth of backbenchers regularly listen to their colleagues' speeches in the House of Commons. An MP has much more access to the mass media than an ordinary citizen. Television has access to Parliament, but news programs usually show only sound bites.

Talking about legislation is a fourth function of the House of Commons. Backbench MPs can demand that the government do something about an issue. The procedures of the Commons force a minister to explain and defend a bill in detail. In theory a government bill can be substantially amended or even withdrawn as a consequence of criticism in Parliament—but such incidents are rare. Laws are described as acts of Parliament, but it would be more accurate if they were stamped "Made in Whitehall."

Fifth, MPs scrutinize how Whitehall departments administer public policies. An MP may write to a minister, questioning a departmental decision called to his or her attention by a constituent or pressure group. MPs can request the parliamentary commissioner for administration (also known as the ombudsman, after the Scandinavian prototype) to investigate complaints about maladministration. Committees scrutinize administration and policy, interviewing civil servants and ministers. However, as a committee moves from discussing details to questions of political principle, it raises the question of confidence in the government. Party loyalty usually guarantees that the government will not lose a committee vote.

A newly elected MP contemplating his or her role as one among 646 members of the House of Commons is faced with many alternatives. An MP may decide to be a party loyalist, voting as the leadership decides, without participating in deliberations about policy. The MP who wishes more attention can make a mark by brilliance in debate, by acting as an acknowledged representative of a pressure group, or in a nonpartisan way—for example, as a wit. An MP is expected to speak for constituency interests, but constituents accept that their MP will not vote against party policy if it is in conflict with local interests. The only role that an MP rarely undertakes is that of lawmaker.

Among modern Parliaments, the House of Lords is unique because none of its members (who are referred to as "peers") are elected. More than one-eighth of the members of this second chamber have inherited a peerage from an ancestor who may have received it several centuries ago. Others serve in the House of Lords because they are senior judges or bishops of the Church of England. But today a large majority of the members of the House of Lords are life peers who have been given a title later in life for achievement in one or another public sphere, including membership in the House of Commons. In 1999 the Labour government abolished the right of all but 92 hereditary peers to sit in the House of Lords. No party has a majority there. Among its 704 members, one-third are Conservative, one-third are Labour, 69 Liberal Democrats, and the remainder divide into a number of non-party categories.

The government often introduces relatively noncontroversial legislation in the Lords if it deals with technical matters, and it uses the Lords as a revising chamber to amend bills. In addition, the Lords can discuss public issues on matters of partisan controversy or on such cross-party topics as pornography or the future of hill farming. The Lords cannot veto legislation, but it can and does amend or delay the passage of some government bills. The limited influence of both houses of Parliament encourages proposals for reform. Backbench MPs perennially demand changes to make their jobs more interesting and to give them more influence. Labour MPs, especially women elected since 1997, have criticized procedures inherited from past centuries as inappropriate for the new millennium. However, the power to make changes rests with the government rather than the House of Commons. Whatever criticisms MPs made of Parliament while in opposition, once in Cabinet party leaders have an interest in existing arrangements that greatly limit the power of Parliament to influence or stop what ministers do.

While all parties accept the need for some kind of second chamber to revise legislation, there is no agreement about how it should be composed or what its powers should be. Many politicians argue for an elected upper house, but the last thing the government of the day wants is a reform that gives the upper chamber enough legitimacy to challenge a House of Commons that invariably endorses government legislation.

Government as a Network

The ship of state has only one tiller—but more than one pair of hands give it direction. In an era of big government, power does not rest in a single individual or office; it is manifest in a network of relations within and between a network of institutions. Policymaking involves the interaction between prime minister, ministers, and leading civil servants, all of whom share in what has been described as the "village life" of Whitehall—and this English village is far smaller and more intimate than the city full of politicians inside the Washington beltway.[20]

Within the Whitehall network, a core set of political figures are especially important in determining policies. The prime minister is the single most important person in government. Since there is no written constitution, a determined prime minister can challenge the status quo and seek to turn government to fresh ends. For example, Margaret Thatcher entered office with a large agenda of market-oriented policies that she wished to promote, and stamina and determination to push through policies against opposition from Cabinet colleagues as well as civil servants.

To say that the prime minister makes the most important decisions and departmental ministers the secondary decisions begs the question: What is an important decision? Decisions in which the prime minister is not involved affecting such issues as social security are more numerous, require more money, and affect more lives than most decisions taken in Downing Street. Scarcity of prime ministerial time is a major limitation on the influence of the prime minister. In the words of one Downing Street official, "It's like skating over an enormous globe of thin ice. You have to keep moving fast all the time."[21]

The head of the Treasury, the Chancellor of the Exchequer, takes many decisions with broad political ramifications too about measures to promote economic growth, taxation, and public expenditure. Chancellor Gordon Brown is extremely influential on domestic policy because he heads the department deciding how much spending ministers can spend and he has a base of support among Labour MPs independent of the prime minister. Within each department, the permanent secretary, its highest-ranking civil servant, usually has much more knowledge of a department's problems than does a transitory Cabinet minister.

In his first term, Tony Blair emphasized making Whitehall a campaigning organization, trebling the number of policy advisers attached to Downing Street and departments, and raising the priority given to managing news and staging media events. By "loaning" his authority to staff to use in discussions with civil servants and ministers, he has increased the collective influence of Downing Street within government. But the use of the prime minister's name by powerful advisers has also created adverse media publicity due to a "war of leaks" between political advisers.

In his second term, Blair gave priority to supporting antiterrorist actions of President George W. Bush. His argument for going to war in Afghanistan and Iraq invoked high moral principles; the methods that his spin doctors and political advisers used to make the case produced two public inquiries into the use and abuse of military intelligence. The second, chaired by a former head of the civil service, concluded of Blair's method of government: "We are concerned that the informality and circumscribed character of the government's procedures which we saw in the context of policy-making towards Iraq risks reducing the scope for informed collective political judgment."[22]

POLITICAL CULTURE AND LEGITIMACY

Politics is about the articulation of conflicting beliefs about who should govern and what government should do. There are three different political justifications of who should be involved when important political decisions are made.

The **trusteeship theory of government** assumes that leaders should take the initiative in deciding what is in the collective public interest. It is summed up in the epigram, "The government's job is to govern." Tony Blair can argue that as head of the majority party in parliament he has the legitimate right to decide what government does. The trusteeship doctrine is always popular with the party in office because it provides a justification for doing whatever the government wishes. The opposition party rejects this theory because it lacks the power of government.

The **interest group theory of government** sees government's role as balancing the demands of competing groups and classes in society. From this perspective, parties and pressure groups advocating group or class interests are more authoritative than individual voters.[23] Traditional Conservatives emphasized harmony between different classes in society, each with its own responsibilities and rewards. The socialist vision of group politics emphasized class divisions between trade unions and business, each seeking to use government to advance their interests, with the former having more votes and the latter more financial capital. With changes in British society, party leaders have distanced themselves from organized interests as they realize that votes are cast by individuals rather than business firms or trade unions.

The **individualist theory** of representation emphasizes that political parties should represent people rather than organized group interests. In the 1980s Margaret Thatcher was an outspoken advocate of economic individualism, regarding each person as responsible for his or her achievement of welfare through the marketplace. She even went so far as to declare, "There is no such thing as society." Liberal Democrats put more emphasis on individual freedom from collective constraints. Tony Blair has

similarly accepted offering individuals more choice in public services. However, individuals are rarely offered a referendum allowing them to vote directly on what government does—and holding a referendum and determining the question put is in the hands of the government of the day. The powers of British government are limited by cultural norms concerning what government should and should not do. In the words of one High Court judge: "In the constitution of this country, there are no guaranteed or absolute rights. The safeguard of British liberty is in the good sense of the people and in the system of representative and responsible government which has been evolved."[24]

However authority is justified, the great majority of English people find it inconceivable that there should be a fundamental change in the way the country is governed. Even Nationalist parties in Scotland and Wales do not reject parliamentary institutions; what they want is an independent Parliament for Scotland and for Wales.

The unresponsiveness of government to Parliament has encouraged popular protest—but the legitimacy of government means that protest is usually kept within lawful bounds. For example, the latest World Values Survey in Britain found that nearly everyone said they had or might sign a petition and half said they had or might participate in a lawful demonstration, but only one-sixth said they had or might consider an illegal occupation of a building or factor.

The legitimacy of government is evidenced by the readiness of the English people to comply with basic political laws. Law enforcement does not require large numbers of armed police. In proportion to its population, England's police force is smaller than that of America, Germany, or France. The crimes that occur in England are antisocial actions such as street violence, rather than political crimes against the state, such as assassinations. The one notable exception is Northern Ireland, where many major crimes, from murder to bank robbery, are carried out with the political objective of overturning an elected government.

The legitimacy accorded to the government is not the result of economic calculations about whether the British form of parliamentary democracy "pays" best, as rational choice theories propound. During the depression of the 1930s, British Communist and Fascist parties received only derisory votes, while their support was great in Germany and Italy. Likewise, inflation and unemployment in the 1970s and 1980s failed to stimulate extremist politics.

The symbols of a common past, such as the monarchy, are sometimes cited as major determinants of legitimacy. But surveys of public opinion show that the Queen has little political significance; her popularity derives from the fact that she is nonpolitical. The popularity of a monarch is a consequence, not a cause, of political legitimacy. In Northern Ireland, where the minority denies the legitimacy of British government, the Queen is a symbol of divisions between British Unionists and Irish Republicans who reject the Crown.

Habit and tradition appear to be the chief explanations for the persisting legitimacy of authority. A survey asking people why they support the government found that the most popular reason was "It's the best form of government we know." Authority is not perfect or even trouble free: It is valued on the basis of experience. Winston Churchill delivered a very English justification of the country's democracy when he told the House of Commons: "No one pretends that democracy is perfect or all wise. Indeed, it has been said that democracy is the worst form of government, except all those other forms that have been tried from time to time."[25]

Abuses of Power

The government of the day can only claim its authority is legitimate if it acts within the rule of law. In constitutional theory, Parliament can hold ministers accountable for abuses of power by the government. In practice, Parliament is an ineffective check on executive power, because the executive consists of the leaders of the majority party in Parliament. When a member of the government is under attack, the tendency of MPs in the governing party is to close ranks in defense of a colleague. The power of the government to get away with mistakes is supported by official secrecy. The Whitehall view is that information is a scarce commodity that should not be given out freely; publicity about policymaking is not in the "public (sic)" interest, for it can make government appear uncertain or divided about what should be done. Politicians often hide their deliberations behind the veil of collective Cabinet responsibility. The Whitehall view is restrictive: "The need to know still dominates the right to know."[26] Secrecy remains strong because it serves the interests of the most important people in government, Cabinet ministers and civil servants. The Public Information Act of 2005 reduced the executive's power to keep secret the exchange of views within the Whitehall network, but whitehall remains far behind the open government practices of Washington.

Both ministers and senior civil servants are prepared to mislead parliament and the public. William Waldegrave, the Conservative minister nominally responsible for open government, told a Commons select committee in 1994 that "in exceptional cases it is necessary to say something that is untrue in the House of Commons."

When accused in court of telling a lie about the British government's efforts to suppress an embar-

---

B O X   8 . 4   Conflicting Loyalties Among Civil Servants

The inability of Parliament to hold the government of the day accountable for palpable misdeeds disturbs senior civil servants who know what is going on and risk becoming accessories before the fact if they assist ministers in producing statements that mislead Parliament. Some even challenge the doctrine that a civil servant must support a minister, whatever the official's personal opinion. In one well-publicized case, a Ministry of Defence official, Clive Ponting, leaked to the House of Commons evidence that questioned the accuracy of government statements about the conduct of the Falklands War. He was indicted and tried for violating the Official Secrets Act. The judge asked the jury to think about the issue this way: "Can it then be in the interests of the state to go against the policy of the government of the day?" The jury concluded that it could be; Ponting was acquitted. However, most senior civil servants are unwilling to become whistle-blowers challenging actions of ministers, thereby jeopardizing their own careers.

*Graham Wilson and Anthony Barker, "Whitehall's Disobedient Servants? Senior Officials' Potential Resistance to Ministers in British Government Departments," *British Journal of Political Science* 27, No. 2 (1997): 223–46.

rassing memoir by an ex-intelligence officer, the then head of the civil service and secretary to the Cabinet, Robert Armstrong, described the government's statements as "a misleading impression, not a lie. It was being economical with the truth." Abuses of executive power have created tensions for civil servants who believe that their job is not only to serve the popularly elected government of the day but also to prevent abuse of the powers of governance. This has led civil servants at times to leak official documents with the intention of preventing government from carrying out a policy that the leaker believes to be unethical or inadvisable (Box 8.4).

Citizens have reacted to changing standards of political behaviour by distrusting their elected representatives. Only a third of Britons report that they have a great deal or quite a lot of confidence in Parliament. The press and trade unions, institutions that theories of civil society describe as important in holding government accountable, are trusted by even fewer people. The most trusted public institutions today are those that maintain authority, led by the armed forces and the police (Figure 8.3).

The decline of ministerial accountability to parliament has encouraged the courts to become more active in making rulings against the elected government of the day. Judges today are ready to find grounds to nullify the way that ministers exercise their powers when they regard actions as going beyond what is authorized in an Act of Parliament. Britain's membership in the European Union and adherence to the European Convention of Human Rights offers additional grounds for nullifying actions by ministers. Such decisions are embarrassing for the government of the day while not involving a frontal challenge to the authority of an Act of Parliament.

Terrorist activities challenge conventional norms of the uses and abuses of power, and successive British governments have faced such challenges since the civil rights demonstrations of 1968–1969 were superseded by violent and murderous actions by illegal Protestant and Catholic groups, including the Irish Republican Army, which regards its use of violence as a legitimate means of liberating Northern Ireland from British rule. Their violence has been

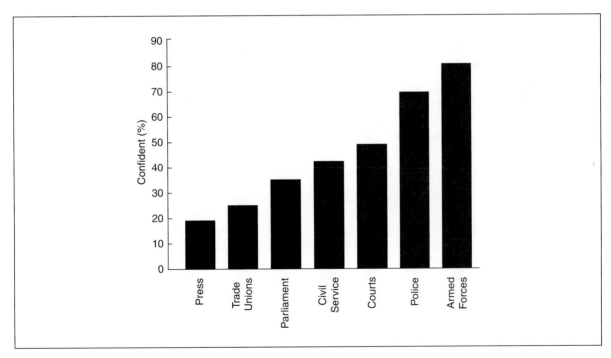

FIGURE 8.3   Trust in Political Institutions

Source: Ronald Inglehart, et al., World Values Survey and European Values Survey, 1999–2001. Ann Arbor: Interuniversity Consortium for Political and Social Research. Interviews conducted in Great Britain, October–November 1999 (N = 1000).

met by Crown forces "bending" the law. On Bloody Sunday, 1971, British soldiers shot and killed Irish protesters peacefully demonstrating in Londonderry. In England police have fabricated evidence or extracted confessions from some suspected of IRA terrorist violence, with the result that convictions have sometimes been voided subsequently by courts on appeal.

Culture as a Constraint on Policy

English people simultaneously value their form of government while making many specific criticisms about how it works. In the phrase of the English writer E. M. Forster, they give "two cheers for democracy." The values of the political culture impose limitations on the scope of public policy. Cultural norms about freedom of speech prevent political censorship. In the "swinging 1960s," laws against homosexual relations were repealed and abortion legalized, and AIDS has been treated as a disease rather than as a cause of shame or moralizing. Cultural expectations also influence what politicians must do. Regardless of party preference, the great majority of British people believe that government ought to provide education, health services, and social security. Today, the most significant limits on the scope of public policy are practical and political. Public expenditure on popular policies such as the health service is limited by the extent to which the economy grows and the reluctance of the Labour or Conservative governments to raise more money for health care by increasing taxes or by imposing limited charges of some sort for the use of health services.

POLITICAL SOCIALIZATION

Socialization influences the political division of labor. At an early age children learn about social differences relevant to politics; a small proportion become interested in politics, a larger proportion become apathetic, and the median person takes some but not that much interest in politics. The predispositions that a young person forms by the time she or he is old enough to vote are modified by adult experience. A middle-aged English person has voted in five or six general elections and is likely to evaluate subsequent political events in the light of what has already been learned.

Family and Gender

The family's influence comes first chronologically; political attitudes learned within the family become intertwined with primary family loyalties. A child may not know what the Labour or Conservative party stands for, but if it is the party of Mom and Dad this can be enough to create identification with a party.

The influence of family on voting is limited; 36 percent do not know how one or both of their parents usually voted, or their parents voted for opposing parties. Among those who report knowing which party both parents supported, just over half vote as their parents have done. In the electorate as a whole, only 35 percent say that they know how both parents voted and that they voted for the same party.[27] Children also acquire a religious identification from their parents but except in Northern Ireland, religion no longer has a substantial influence on voting, and there are no groups comparable to the American religious right.

Children learn different social roles according to gender, yet as adult citizens men and women have the same legal right to vote and participate in politics. Bipartisan interest in appealing to women is illustrated by the 1976 Sex Discrimination Act, prohibiting discrimination in employment. It was enacted by a Labour government following a report by a Conservative government.

Today all political parties seek the votes of women, since women are a majority of the electorate. However, parties do not want to offend men, for even though they are a minority, they constitute 48 percent of the electorate. Whether politicians are talking about economic, social, or international issues, they usually stress common concerns of both men and women. At each general election, women divide between parties in much the same way as men (Table 8.3).

Men and women tend to have similar political attitudes. On most political issues women divide into two contrasting groups, and the same is true of men. For example, more than half of women and half of men favor capital punishment and a substantial minority in each group oppose it. Even on the issue of

T A B L E   8 . 3   Social Differences and Voting (percentage of voters in 2005)

	Labour	Conservative	Liberal/Democratic	Other
Gender				
Women	37	33	23	7
Men	36	33	23	9
Difference	1	0	0	2
Age				
18–34	37	28	22	8
35–54	41	29	22	8
55+	32	41	20	8
Difference, young/old	5	13	7	1
Class				
Middle	33	36	24	7
Working	41	29	20	9
Difference, top/bottom	8	7	4	2

Source: YouGov post-election online panel survey of 3,749 electors, weighted to represent the British population, and published in the *Daily Telegraph*, London, 9 May 2005.

sex and nudity in the media, which registers a substantial difference of 20 percentage points, both women and men differ among themselves. Gender differences are less important than class, age, or education as an influence on party loyalties.

Gender differences do, however, lead to differences in political participation. Even though women constitute more than half the electorate, men are almost twice as likely as women to be local government councillors. Women constitute almost half the employees in the civil service, but they are heavily concentrated at lower-level clerical jobs; women hold about 10 percent of the top appointments in the civil service. A record number of women candidates stood for the Commons in 2001 but male candidates still outnumbered women by a margin of more than four to one. A total of 125 women were elected to the House of Commons, but it remains more than four-fifths male.[28]

Education

Even though individuals have different IQs, each vote counts equally in the ballot box. Yet education has traditionally assumed inequality. The majority of the population was once considered fit for only a minimum of education; in today's electorate the oldest voters left school at the age of 14 and the median voter by the age of 17. The highly educated are a small fraction of the population; they expect and are expected to play a leading role in politics.

Within the state system, the great majority of pupils attend comprehensive secondary schools, which recruit students of all levels of ability. Within the school, pupils are often divided into an academic stream being taught at a more advanced level than the average American high school education, and many who leave with only a basic education. Less than 6 percent of young persons attend "public" schools, that is, fee-paying schools which are private. Whereas half a century ago England had few universities, today almost one-half of young persons are in postsecondary institutions, many of which lack the facilities of established research universities.

The stratification of English education used to imply that the more education a person had, the more likely a person was to be Conservative. This is no longer the case. People with a university degree or its equivalent are currently less likely to vote Conservative than people with a minimum of education. The minority who are most educated now divide their vote between all three big parties, with the Liberal Democrats doing relatively well.

Education is strongly related to active participation in politics. The more education a person has, the greater the possibility of climbing the political ladder. People with a minimum of education constitute more than half the electorate but less than half of all local government councillors and less than 2 percent of all MPs. Whereas at one time graduates of Eton, Harrow, and other leading public schools predominated in Cabinet, today less than a third of all MPs have attended public schools.

The relatively small percentage of university graduates in the country constitutes 70 percent of all MPs. The expansion of universities has broken the dominance of Oxford and Cambridge; barely one-third of graduate MPs went to these two traditional institutions. The concentration of graduates from many different British universities in top jobs is a sign of a meritocracy, in which governors qualified by education replace an aristocracy based on birth and family. Yet leading posts can still go to those who have a common touch, as indicated by attendance at a state secondary school. John Major attended state secondary schools and did not go to university. Whereas the Labour prime minister Tony Blair went to Scotland's major fee-paying public school, the three Conservative leaders he defeated electorally all went to state schools.

Class

The concept of **class** can refer to occupational status or serve as a shorthand term for income, education, and prestige. Occupation is the most commonly used indicator of class in England. Manual workers are usually described as the working class and non-manual workers as the middle class.

Historically, party competition has been interpreted in class terms; the Conservative Party has been described as a middle-class party, and Labour as a working-class party. One reason why class appears relatively important in England is the absence of big divisions on race, religion, or language, as in the United States, Canada, or Northern Ireland. Today, the upper class no longer commands deference and celebrities owing their prominence to television and achievements in sports, rock music, or making money are better known than Dukes or Earls. Tony Blair is comfortable mixing with rock musicians and with the new rich from the entertainment industry.

Most Britons have a mixture of middle-class and working-class attributes. The mixed class group has been increasing, as changes in the economy have led to a reduction in manual jobs and an increase in middle-class jobs. Many occupations such as computer technicians and office workers now have an indeterminate status and voting behavior. The relationship between class and party has become limited.

No party now wins as much as half the vote of middle-class electors, and Labour wins just two-fifths the vote of manual workers (Table 8.3). Due to the cross-class appeal of parties, only two-fifths of voters were middle-class Conservatives or working-class Labour voters. The Liberal Democrats and other smaller parties draw a fifth or more of the vote in every class. Less than one in seven voters conforms to the stereotype of a middle-class person (nonmanual occupation, above-average education, homeowner, no trade union membership, and subjective identification with the middle class), or its counterpart working-class stereotype.

Socioeconomic experiences other than occupation also influence voting. At each level of the class structure, people who belong to trade unions are more likely to vote Labour than Conservative. Housing creates neighborhoods with political relevance. About one-sixth of voters live in local government-owned houses clustered together on a housing estate specifically identified as such. Labour wins more than half of the vote of local council tenants, while, regardless of class, Conservatives do relatively well among homeowners.

Mass Media

The mass media tends to reenforce differences arising from class and education. The British press is sharply divided into a few quality papers, such as *The Times, The Guardian, Daily Telegraph, The Independent* and *The Financial Times,* that carry news and comment at an intellectual level higher than American newspapers, and mass circulation tabloids that concentrate on trivia and trash such as *The Sun,* Britain's biggest selling newspaper. Most papers tend to lean toward one party but not uncritically so. When the Conservatives became unpopular with the electorate in the 1990s, some newspapers that were previously pro-Conservative sought to follow their voters in admiring Tony Blair. He actively courted the support of right-wing newspapers but following his fall in popular approval during the Iraq War former press allies became vocal critics.

Historically, radio and television were a monopoly of the British Broadcasting Corporation (BBC). Seeking to educate and to elevate, the BBC was also very respectful of all forms of authority, including government. The introduction of commercial television in the 1950s and commercial radio in the following decade has made all broadcasting channels populist in competing for audiences. There are now five channels plus cable TV and a great variety of radio stations. The law forbids selling advertising to politicians, parties, or political causes.

Current affairs programs often seek audiences by exposing alleged failings of government, and TV personalities make their names by the tough cross-examination of politicians of all parties. However, the government of the day controls the renewal of broadcasting licenses and, in the case of the BBC, the annual fee of about $200 that every viewer must pay for noncommercial BBC programs. Broadcasters try to avoid favoring one party, recognizing that over a period of years control of government and decisions about licenses and fees are likely to change hands between parties. Public opinion polls show that television is the primary source of political news and it is much more trusted than the press. Since political socialization is a lifetime learning process, the loyalties of voters are shaped by an accumulation of influences. In the course of a lifetime, an individual develops values expressing what government ought to do. These political values are independent of family and socioeconomic interests. Economic values concerned with trade unions, the welfare state, business, and privatization influence choices between parties. "New" noneconomic values such as protecting the environment and morality account for little variation in the vote, because parties usually lack a distinctive and well-established position.

How the government handles current issues affects the economy and public expenditure, but the judgments that people make about government performance reflect their preexisting values, and this is particularly true of popular evaluations of party and leader images. The influence of such current issues and ephemeral personalities is often overrated, for those who focus on today's events forget that voters have had a lifetime to learn which party they prefer.

POLITICAL PARTICIPATION AND RECRUITMENT

Participation

If political participation is defined as paying taxes and drawing benefits from public programs, then everyone is involved, for public policies provide benefits at every stage of life, from maternity allowance to mothers through education, employment and unemployment benefits, health care, and pensions in old age.

An election is the one opportunity people have to influence government directly. Every citizen aged 18 or over is eligible to vote. Local government officials register voters, and the list is revised annually, ensuring that nearly everyone eligible to vote is actually registered. Turnout at general elections has averaged 77 percent since 1950. However, in the 2001 election it fell to 59.4 percent. The Labour government responded by experimenting with voting by post, sending ballots to all persons whose names are on the electoral register. When this was tried in the 2004 European Parliament election, three-fifths of those sent a postal ballot did not send it back and there were well publicized cases of fraud. In 2005 turnout was 61.3 percent.

The wider the definition of political participation, the greater the number who can be said to be at least indirectly or intermittently involved in politics (Figure 8.4). Two-fifths have signed a petition on a public issue; a third say that they feel close to a political party. Political values can also be reflected in refusing to buy a product: one-quarter say that politics has affected their shopping by leading them to boycott a product. The most politically involved are a tenth or less of the electorate, those who say they are very interested in politics, took part in a demonstration, or are active in a party or pressure group. If holding or contesting public office is the measure of political participation, the proportion is less than 1 percent of the electorate.

Although political activists are a minority of the electorate, their actions are the focus of much political news. Because of the concentration of the media and politics, a London-based protest with a few thousand people can get press coverage,

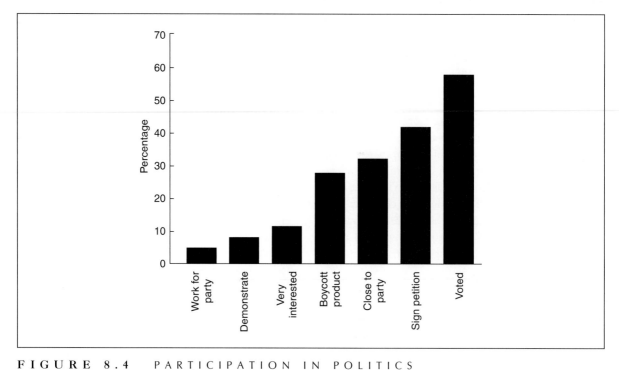

FIGURE 8.4   PARTICIPATION IN POLITICS

Source: Roger Jowell and the Central Coordinating Team, European Social Survey 2002/03. London: Centre for Comparative Social Surveys, City University. Interviews conducted in the United Kingdom, September 24, 2002 to February 4, 2003 (N = 1908).

even though those participating are only one–one-hundredth of 1 percent of the electorate.

Political Recruitment

The most important political roles in Britain are those of Cabinet minister, higher civil servant, and intermittent public person, analogous to informal advisers to an American president. Each group has its own recruitment pattern. To become a Cabinet minister, an individual must first be elected to Parliament and spend years attracting positive attention there. Individuals enter the civil service shortly after leaving university by passing a highly competitive entrance examination; promotion is based on achievement and approval by seniors. Intermittent public persons gain access to ministers and civil servants because of their expertise or position in organizations outside politics, or because they are personally trusted by leading politicians.

In all political roles, starting early on a political career is usually a precondition of success, because experience is positively valued. But aspiring Cabinet ministers are not expected to begin in local politics

and work their way gradually to the top at Westminster. Instead, at an early age an individual becomes a "cadet" recruit to a junior position such as a parliamentary assistant to an MP or a "gofer" for a Cabinet minister. This can lead to a central political role after gaining skill and seniority.

Geography is a second major influence on recruitment. Ministers, higher civil servants, and other public persons spend their working lives in London. A change at Downing Street does not bring in policymakers from a different part of the country, as can happen in the White House when a president from Texas succeeds a president from Arkansas. Since London is atypical of the cities and towns in which most British people live, there is a gap between the everyday lives of policymakers and the majority on whose behalf they act.

Cabinet Ministers

For a person ambitious to be a Cabinet minister, becoming an MP is the necessary first step. Nomination for a winnable or safe seat in the House of Commons is in the hands of local party selection committees. A candidate does not have to be resident in the constituency in which he or she is nominated. Hence, it is possible for a young person to go straight from university to a job in the House of Commons or party headquarters, and then look around the country for a nomination for a winnable seat, a process that takes years. Once selected for a constituency in which his or her party has a big majority, the MP can then expect to be reelected routinely for a decade or more.

After entering the House of Commons, an MP seeks to be noticed. Some ways of doing so—for example, grabbing headlines by questioning the wisdom of the party leadership—make it difficult to gain promotion to ministerial rank. Other approaches assist promotion, such as successfully attacking opposition leaders in debate or being well informed about a politically important topic. So too does showing loyalty to the party leader.

Only Members of Parliament can become Cabinet ministers. Yet experience in the Commons does not prepare an individual for the work of a minister. An MP's chief concerns are dealing with people and talking about what government ought to do. A minister must also be able to handle paperwork, relate political generalities to specific technical problems facing a ministry, and make hard decisions when no alternative is popular.

The restriction of ministerial appointments to experienced MPs prevents a nationwide canvass for appointees. A prime minister must distribute about 100 jobs among approximately 200 MPs in the governing party who have had experience in Parliament and not ruled themselves out of consideration for office on grounds of parliamentary inexperience, old age, political extremism, personal unreliability, or lack of interest in office. An MP has a better than even chance of a junior ministerial appointment if he or she serves three terms in Parliament. Exceptionally, Tony Blair has given peerages and ministerial posts to personal supporters who thus depend on loyalty to him rather than to their standing with their constituency electorate and Labour Party.

A minister learns on the job. Usually, an MP is first given a junior post as an Under Secretary and then promoted to Minister of State before becoming a full member of the Cabinet. In the process, an individual is usually shuffled from one department to another, having to learn new subject matter with each shift of departments. The average minister can expect to stay in a particular job for about two years, and never knows when the accidents of politics—a death or an unexpected resignation—will lead to a transfer to another department. The rate of ministerial turnover in Britain is one of the highest in Europe. The minister who gets a new job as the result of a reshuffle usually arrives at a department with no previous experience of its problems. It takes time to learn how to deal with the particular problems of a department. Anthony Crosland, an able Labour minister, reckoned: "It takes you six months to get your head properly above water, a year to get the general drift of most of the field, and two years really to master the whole of a department."[29] A minister's lack of substantial expertise in his or her department has produced criticism of the recruitment system.

Higher Civil Servants

Whereas MPs come and go from ministerial office with great frequency, civil servants have a job in Whitehall for the whole of their working lives. Higher civil servants are recruited without specific professional qualifications or training. They are meant to be the "best and the brightest"—a requirement that has traditionally meant getting a prestigious degree in history, literature, or languages. The Fulton Committee on the Civil Service recommended that recruits should have "relevant" specialist knowledge, but members could not decide what kind of knowledge was relevant to the work of government.[30] The Civil Service Commission tests candidates for ability to summarize lengthy prose papers, to resolve a problem by fitting specific facts to general regulations, to draw inferences from a simple table of social statistics, and to perform well in group discussions of problems of government.

Because bright civil service entrants lack specialized skills and need decades to reach the highest posts, role socialization into Whitehall by senior civil servants is especially important. The process makes for continuity, since the head of the civil service usually starts there as a young official under a head who had himself entered the civil service many decades before.

In the course of a career, civil servants become specialists in the difficult task of managing political ministers and government business. As the television series, *Yes, Minister* shows, they are adept at saying "yes" to a Cabinet minister when they mean "perhaps" and saying "up to a point" when they really mean "no." Increasingly, ministers have tended to discourage civil service advisers from pointing out obstacles to what the government wants to do; they are looking for "can do" advisers from outside the civil service as well as inside. The Blair government has greatly expanded the appointment of two types of political advisers. The largest number are aptly called political advisers, for their job is to mobilize political support for the government and for the Cabinet minister to whom they are assigned. Because their background is in party politics and the media, they bring skills that civil servants often lack. But because they have no prior experience of the civil service, they are often unaware of its conventions and legal obligations. The methods used by political appointees to put a desirable spin on what the government is doing can backfire and cause public controversy.

Another category of political advisers are experts with specialist knowledge about such problems as environmental pollution or experimental medical procedures such as cloning. While they may be inexperienced in the ways of Whitehall, they can contribute expertise that is often lacking in government departments, and they are often long-time supporters of the governing party too.

Most leaders of institutions such as the universities, banks, churches, and trade unions do not think of themselves as politicians and have not stood for public office. They are principally concerned with their own organization. But when government actions impinge on their work, they become involved in politics, offering ministers advice and sometimes criticism. They are thus intermittent public persons.

Selective Recruitment

Nothing could be more selective than a parliamentary election that results in one person becoming prime minister of a country. Yet nothing is more representative, because an election is the one occasion when every adult can participate in politics with equal effect. Traditionally, leaders in English society had high social status and wealth before gaining political office. Today, England has experienced the rise of the full-time professional politician. Aristocrats,

business people, or trade union leaders can no longer expect to translate their high standing in other fields into an important political position. As careers become more specialized, a professional politician gains increased expertise in his or her own sphere but becomes increasingly remote from other spheres.

The greater the scope of activities defined as political, the greater the number of people actively involved in government. Government influence has forced company directors, television executives, and university heads to become involved in politics and public policy. Leadership in organizations outside Whitehall gives such individuals freedom to act independently of government, but the interdependence of public and private institutions, whether profitmaking or nonprofit, is now so great that sooner or later they meet in discussions about what constitutes the public interest.

ORGANIZING GROUP INTERESTS

Civil society—that is, institutions independent of government—has flourished in Britain for centuries. So confident are leaders of civil society of their position that they readily discuss public affairs with government officials in expectation that they can exert pressure on behalf of interests they represent.

The Confederation of British Industries is the chief representative organization of British business. As its name implies, its membership is large and varied. The biggest firms or industries usually make direct representations to ministries for trade and industry. The Institute of Directors represents the highest-paid individuals at the top of large and small businesses. Banks and financial institutions in the City of London have their own channels of representation through the Bank of England, the central Bank, and directly to the Treasury. The comparable organization of labour is the Trades Union Congress (TUC); its members are trade unions that sometimes represent workers with conflicting interests, such as between those in low paid jobs and highly paid workers. Most member unions of the TUC are affiliated with the Labour Party, and some leading trade unionists have been Communists or Maoists. None has ever been a supporter of the Conservative Party. The membership of trade unions has shifted from industrial workers in coal and railways to white-collar workers in the public sector, such as teachers and health service employees. Changes in employment patterns have eroded union membership; less than one-third of the British labour force now belongs to unions.

Unlike political parties, interest groups do not seek influence by contesting elections; they want to influence policies regardless of which party wins. Nonetheless, there do remain ties between interest groups and political parties. Trade unions have been institutionally part of the Labour Party since its foundation in 1900. The connection between business associations and the Conservatives is not formal, but its private enterprise philosophy is congenial to business. Notwithstanding common interests, both trade unions and business groups demonstrate their autonomy by criticizing partisan allies acting against the group's interest.

Party politicians seek to distance themselves from pressure groups. Conservatives appreciate that they can only win an election by winning the votes of ordinary citizens, including some trade union members. Tony Blair's success in distancing himself from unions by attracting big donations from multimillionaires to finance his campaigning activities has led union leaders to attack his government as unsympathetic and threaten to withdraw cash contributions that are vital to meet the costs of the party's organizations. A few small unions have left the Labour Party.

To lobby successfully, interest groups must be able to identify those officials most important in making public policy. They concentrate attention on Whitehall. When pressure groups were asked to rank the most influential offices and institutions, they named the prime minister first by a long distance, Cabinet ministers second, the media third, and senior civil servants fourth (Figure 8.5). Less than 1 percent thought MPs outside the ministerial ranks were of primary importance. However, pressure groups do not expect to spend a lot of time in Downing Street. Most pressure group contacts are with divisions of government departments concerned with issues of little public concern but of immediate interest to the group. Groups that stir up confrontational media publicity make it difficult to gain a sympathetic private hearing from government departments.[31]

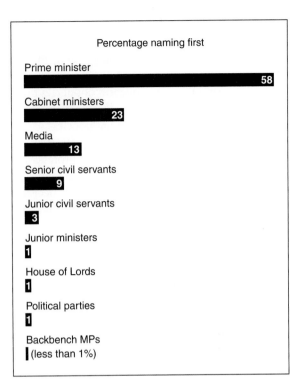

FIGURE 8.5   Pressure Group View of Who Holds Most Power

Source: Survey of officials of business, labor, and campaign groups, as reported in Rob Baggott. "The Measurement of Change in Pressure Group Politics." *Talking Politics* 5, No. 1 (1992): 19.

What Interest Groups Want

The scope of group demands varies enormously from the narrow concerns of an association for single parents to the encompassing economic policies of organizations such as the Confederation of British Industries and the Trades Union Congress. Groups also differ in the nature of their interests; some are concerned with material objectives, whereas others deal with single causes such as violence in the media or race relations. Most interest groups pursue four goals:

1. Information about government policies and changes in policies
2. Sympathetic administration of established policies
3. Influence on policymaking
4. Symbolic status, such as being given the prefix "Royal" in their title

Whitehall departments are happy to consult with interest groups insofar as they can provide government officials with reciprocal benefits:

1. Cooperation in the administration of existing policies
2. Information about what is happening in their field
3. Evaluation of the consequences of policies under consideration
4. Assistance in implementing new policies

As long as the needs of Whitehall and interest groups are complementary, they can bargain as professionals sharing common concerns. Both sides seek a negotiated agreement. This avoids contested decisions being made by politicians who know less and care less about details than interest groups and civil servants involved in departmental administration.

Organizing for Political Action in Civil Society

The more committed members are to a pressure group's goals, the more confidently leaders can speak for a united membership. Consumers are more difficult to organize because they are interested only in goods and services, not in their relations with other customers; they are a category rather than a social group. Changes in the economy, in class structure, and in the life styles of generations have resulted in a decline in the "dense" social capital networks of villages. Individuals are now free to choose among a variety of networks. As a trade union leader has explained, "Our members are consumers too."[32]

Whitehall civil servants find it administratively convenient to deal with united interest groups that can implement agreements. But decades of attempts to plan the British economy demonstrate that business and union leaders cannot guarantee that their nominal followers will carry out bargains that leaders make. Group members who care about an issue may also disagree about what their leaders ought to do. Individuals usually have a multiplicity of identities that are often in conflict—for example, as workers desiring higher wages and as consumers wanting lower prices. The spread of mass consumption and decline in trade union membership has altered the balance between these priorities.

Even if a pressure group is internally united, its demands may be counteracted by opposing demands from other groups. This is normally the case in economic policy, where interests are well defined, well organized, and competing. Ministers can play off producers against consumers or business against unions to increase their own scope for choice and present their policies as "something for everybody" compromises.

The more a group's values are consistent with the cultural norms of society as a whole, the easier it is to equate its interest with the public interest. But in an open society such as England the claims of one group to speak for the public interest can easily be challenged by competing groups.

The centralization of authority in British government means that interest groups must accept as given the political values and priorities of the governing party. Trade unions expect to see their influence increase when a Labour government is in office and business groups have similar expectations when the Conservatives are in power. However, a prime minister seeking to broaden the government's base of support can try to build bridges with nominal opponents too. Tony Blair's Labour government has conspicuously solicited support from business leaders.

Insider pressure groups usually have values in harmony with every party. These groups are often noncontroversial, such as the Royal National Institute for the Blind. The primary concern of permanent insiders is to negotiate on details of administration and finance, and to press for the expansion of programs benefiting the group. They advance their case in quiet negotiations with Whitehall departments. Demands tend to be restricted to what is politically possible in the short term, given the values and commitments of the government of the day.[33]

Outsider pressure groups are unable to negotiate because their demands are inconsistent with the party in power. If they are inconsistent with the views of the opposition as well, then outsider groups are completely marginalized. Excluded from influence in Whitehall, outsider groups often campaign through the media. To television viewers and readers of serious newspapers, their demonstrations appear as evidence of their importance; in fact, they are often signs of a lack of political influence.

Complete outsiders are excluded from Whitehall, whatever the government of the day, because their demands go against prevailing cultural norms. For example, the Ministry of Defence does not consult pacifist groups, for there is nothing to negotiate when principles are mutually exclusive. Green pressure groups face the dilemma of campaigning for fundamental change in hopes that eventually White-hall departments will turn their way, or working within the system in order to improve the environment to some extent but not as much as ecologists would like.

Keeping Pressure Groups at a Distance

For a generation after World War II ministers endorsed the corporatist philosophy of bringing together business, trade union, and political representatives in tripartite institutions to discuss such controversial issues as dealing with inflation and unemployment, and the restructuring of declining industries. Corporatist bargaining assumed a consensus on political priorities and goals and that each group's leaders could deliver the cooperation of those they claimed to represent. In practice, neither Labour nor Conservative governments were able to maintain a consensus. Nor were interest group leaders able to deliver their nominal followers. By 1979, unemployment and inflation were both out of control.

The Thatcher administration demonstrated that a government firmly committed to distinctive values can ignore group demands and lay down its own pattern of policy. It did so by dealing at arm's length with both trade unions and business groups. Instead of consulting and negotiating with interest groups, it practised state-distancing, keeping the government out of everyday marketplace activities such as wage bargaining and deciding prices and investment.

A state-distancing strategy concentrates on policies that government can carry out without the agreement of interest groups. It emphasizes the use of legislation to achieve goals, since no interest group can defy an act of Parliament. Laws have reduced the capacity of trade unions to frustrate government policies through industrial action. The sale of state-owned industries has removed government from immediate responsibility for the operation of major industries. The Labour government transferred to the Bank of England responsibility for monetary policy. At the same time it kept in the Treasury's hands the right to set policy goals for which the Bank is responsible.

State-distancing places less reliance on negotiations with interest groups and more on the independent authority of the Crown. Business and labor are free to carry on as they like—but only within the pattern imposed by the government's policy and legislation. Most unions and some business leaders do not like being "outside the loop" when government makes decisions. Education and health service pressure groups like it even less, because they depend upon government appropriations to fund their activities and cannot effectively turn to the market as an alternative source of revenue.

While in opposition, Tony Blair often spoke about the need to achieve "the reinvention of community,"[34] implying endorsement of corporatist institutions of cooperation between representatives of different groups in society. However, since becoming prime minister, Blair has made sure that meetings with groups are on terms laid down by Downing Street. When conflicts are apparent between groups, he avoids taking sides or getting involved in brokering agreements. He prefers to remain on the sidelines, lecturing conflicting groups to cooperate in a vaguely defined public interest.

PARTY SYSTEM AND ELECTORAL CHOICE

British government is party government, for parties nominate parliamentary candidates and elect a leader who is prime minister or in charge of the Opposition. An election gives voters the choice of deciding between parties competing for the right to govern.

A Multiplicity of Choices

A general election must occur at least once every five years; within that period, the prime minister is free to call an election at any time. Although every prime minister tries to pick a date when victory is likely, this desire is often denied. An election offers a voter a very simple choice between several candidates wanting to represent one of the 646 constituencies of the House of Commons. The party leader's name is not on the ballot. Within each constituency, the winner is the candidate who is first past the post—that is, the candidate with the largest number of votes even though his or her plurality falls short of half the vote.

If only two parties contest a constituency, the candidate with the most votes will have an absolute majority. But since three or more candidates now contest each constituency a candidate with the most votes may still have less than half the total vote thanks to multiple competitors dividing the majority of the vote. In a hard-fought contest between four parties in Inverness in 1992, the Liberal Democrats won the seat with only 26 percent of the vote. In hundreds of seats, no candidate gets as much as half the vote and there is no provision for a runoff election, as in France, to produce a winner with majority support.

The winner nationally is the party that gains the most constituency seats. In 1951 and in February 1974, the party winning the most votes did not win the most seats and thus did not form the government. Today, the Labour Party can win an absolute majority in the House of Commons with a smaller share of the vote than the Conservative Party, because its electoral strength is concentrated rather than spread evenly through the country. Between 1945 and 1970 Britain had a two-party system, because the Conservative and Labour parties together took an average of 91 percent of the popular vote and in 1951 as much as 97 percent (Figure 8.6). The Liberals had difficulty fielding candidates to contest most seats and even more difficulty in winning votes.

Support for the two largest parties was evenly balanced; Labour won four elections and the Conservatives won four.

In a two-party system the failure of one party tends to benefit its opponent. However, when both the largest parties are discredited, this gives other parties an opportunity to gain support. A **multiparty system** emerged in the elections of 1974. The Liberals won nearly one-fifth of the vote, and the Nationalists did well in Scotland, Wales, and Northern Ireland. Together, the Conservative and Labour parties took only 75 percent of the vote. The 1980s saw the Labour Party vote plummet as the Alliance of Liberals and Social Democrats won almost a quarter of the popular vote. Although the Alliance broke up after the 1987 election, the fragmentation of voters and parties has continued since.

1. In England, three parties—Labour, Conservatives, and Liberal Democrats—compete for votes and an anti-European Union United Kingdom Independence Party also fights a majority of seats. In Scotland and Wales there are normally four parties, for the Scottish National and Plaid Cymru

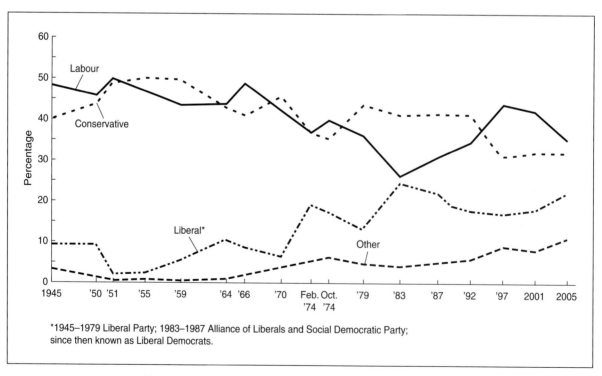

*1945–1979 Liberal Party; 1983–1987 Alliance of Liberals and Social Democratic Party; since then known as Liberal Democrats.

FIGURE 8.6   Votes Cast in General Elections Since 1945

(Welsh Nationalist) parties win seats too. In Northern Ireland, at least five parties normally contest seats.

2. The two largest parties do not monopolize the vote. Since 1974, the Conservative and Labour parties together have won an average of three-quarters of the vote and in the 2005 election gained just 67 percent of the vote.

3. The two largest parties nationally are often not the two front-running parties at the constituency level. In the 2005 election, the first and second parties in England were Labour and the Conservatives; in Scotland, Labour and the Liberal Democrats; in Wales, Labour and the Conservatives. The Conservatives won only one seat in Scotland and three in Wales. In Northern Ireland the Democratic Unionists and Sinn Fein, which is linked with the IRA, were the largest parties and all 18 seats were won by parties that did not contest seats in Great Britain.

4. More than half a dozen parties consistently win seats in the House of Commons. In 2005 "third" parties won 94 seats in the Commons.

5. Significant shifts in voting usually do not involve individuals moving between the Labour and Conservative parties but in and out of the ranks of abstainers or between the Liberal Democrats and the two largest parties.

To win a substantial number of seats in the House of Commons, a party must either gain at least one-third of the popular vote nationally or concentrate its votes in a limited number of constituencies. Nationalist parties in Scotland, Wales, and Northern Ireland win seats because they concentrate their candidates in one part of the United Kingdom. Although the Liberal Democrats win more than a fifth of the popular vote, because their support is spread relatively evenly across the country, their candidates are far more likely to finish second or third rather than first.

Britain has a system of disproportional representation that manufactures a House of Commons majority for one party with barely two-fifths of the popular vote. The Liberal Democrats are specially disadvantaged by the electoral system. In a totally proportional system of representation, the party's vote share in 2005 would have given it 142 seats; it gained less than half this number. Even more important, in a proportional representation system Labour's vote would have given it 227 seats, far short of a parliamentary majority. In a PR system, forming a government would require a coalition between at least two parties, since none would have a majority of parliamentary seats. In the Scottish Parliament, which is elected with proportional representation, coalition government is the norm.

Defenders of the British electoral system argue that proportionality is not a goal in itself. The **first-past-the-post system** is justified because it places responsibility for government in the hands of a single party. This justification is used in the United States, where the president can be described as representing all the people, even if he has won less than half the vote. By contrast, in countries such as Italy and Belgium proportional representation makes the choice of the parties forming a coalition government the outcome of intensive bargaining between parties that have received anything from one-third to 5 percent of the popular vote.

The strongest advocates of proportional representation are the Liberal Democrats, the party that would benefit most from a change in the electoral system. A change is also supported by those who believe that a coalition government is a better government because it encourages broader interparty consensus.

Successive British governments have altered the electoral system for contests that do not affect the composition of the Westminster Parliament. Northern Ireland elections have used proportional representation for more than three decades. The Scottish Parliament and Welsh Assembly are elected by systems involving proportional representation and so are British Members of the European Parliament. The Mayor of Greater London is elected by the alternative vote, ensuring that the winner is the first or second choice of more than half the voters.

Before winning a majority in 1997, Tony Blair encouraged talk about introducing proportional representation and proposals have been put forward by a government-appointed Commission. But this produced a countermobilization in defence of the current system from many MPs elected by first past the post and by trade unions who fear that a coalition government would be less sympathetic to its interests than a government consisting solely of Labour MPs. In Britain the decision about what kind of voting system to have is not determined by reasoning from abstract principles but by the interests of the party in power.

Control of Party Organization

Political parties are often referred to as machines, but this description is very misleading, for parties cannot manufacture votes. Nor can a political party be commanded as an army can be commanded. Parties are like universities; they are inherently decentralized, and people belong to them for a variety of motives.

Much of the work of party organizations is devoted to keeping together three disparate parts of the party: those who vote for it; the small minority who are active in its constituency associations; and the party in Parliament. If the party has a majority in Parliament, the prime minister must make sure that the other parts of the party support his or her actions even if many party activists and MPs do not like what their leader is doing. The London headquarters of each party provides more or less routine organizational and publicity services to constituency parties and to the party in Parliament. Each party has an annual conference to debate policy and to vote on some policy resolutions. Constituency parties are nationally significant because each selects its parliamentary candidate. The **decentralization** of the selection process has allowed the choice of parliamentary candidates with a wide variety of political outlooks and abilities. The Thatcher era encouraged an ideological litmus test on both the right and the left. Under Tony Blair the Labour Party has introduced more central direction in choosing candidates. Left-wing Labour activists argued that central direction has been used to purge socialists and put in Blair loyalists. Blairites justified centralization on the grounds it would promote the adoption of more women candidates in winnable seats; the number of Labour women MPs rose from 37 in 1992 to 98 by 2005.

The Labour Party leader is elected by an electoral college composed of Labour MPs, constituency party members, and trade unions. As part of a drive to prevent criticism of the leadership and public disunity, Tony Blair has created a new party organization that increases his control of the party and reduces the influence of party activists and trade unions.

The Conservative Party in Parliament has been separate from the campaigning arm of the party, Conservative Central Office, and local constituency associations. Until 1965, the party leader was not elected but "emerged" as the result of consultation among senior MPs and peers (members of the House of Lords). Since then, the Conservatives have elected their leader, initially by a ballot of Members of Parliament and today by this ballot identifying two candidates who are then voted on by the party membership at large. The failure of Ian Duncan Smith, chosen as leader by the party membership even though he did not have the support of a majority of Conservative MPs, led to his replacement in 2003 by Michael Howard without a vote, because both MPs and constituency activists saw him as a credible leader in the House of Commons, and in campaigning. He resigned after losing the 2005 election.

The Liberal Democrats have a small central organization, in keeping with their relatively few MPs. Liberal Democrats have sought to build up the party's strength by winning council seats at local government elections. At parliamentary elections, it targets seats where the party is strong locally. This strategy has paid off; it has almost trebled its MPs from 22 in 1987 to 62 in 2005 while its share of the vote fell by 0.6 percent.

The party leader is strongest when he or she is also prime minister. Constitutional principles and Cabinet patronage strengthen a prime minister's hand. Moreover, an open attack on a prime minister threatens electoral defeat as a result of conflict within the party. At the 1998 Labour Party conference Tony Blair told his Labour critics that their choice was not between a Socialist or a Labour government, but between the Labour government or a Conservative government.

Party Images and Appeals

Differences of ideology are often simplified in terms of a left-right scale, with the left representing socialist values and the right the values of Conservatives. While the terminology of left and right is part of the language of elite politicians, it is rejected by the great majority of British voters. When asked to place themselves on a left-right scale, the median voter chooses the central position, and only a tenth place themselves on the far left or far right. Consequently, parties that veer to one or another extreme risk losing votes.

When public opinion is examined across a variety of issues, such as inflation, protecting the environment, spending money on the health service, and trade union legislation, a majority of Conservative, Labour, and Liberal Democratic voters tend to agree for the most part. Tony Blair has proclaimed the goal of making Labour a party that is "the political arm of none other than the British people as a whole." In articulating this view, Blair is denying the existence of politics—that is, debate about what the government of the day ought to do.

Big divisions in contemporary British politics often cut across party lines, for example, attitudes toward the European Union divide both Labour and Conservative MPs and so has the Iraq War. Any attempt to impute a coherent ideology to a political party is doomed to failure, for institutions cannot think, and parties are not organized to debate philosophy but to fight elections. Instead of campaigning in ideological terms or by appealing to collectivist economic interests, increasingly parties stress consensual goals, such as promoting peace and prosperity. They compete in terms of which party or party leader can best be trusted to do what people want. The titles of election manifestos are virtually interchangeable between the Conservative and Labour parties—and so too is much of their content (Table 8.4).

In office, the governing party has the votes to enact any parliamentary legislation it wishes, regardless of protests by the opposition. However, most of the legislation introduced by the government is non-controversial or so popular that the opposition does not dare vote against the bill's principle. For every

government bill that the opposition votes against on principle in the House of Commons, three are adopted with interparty agreement.[35] Prior to the 1997 general election, the Labour Party even pledged that it would not immediately alter the spending limits in the budget of the Conservative government.

Most policies of the government are not set out in its party manifesto; they are inherited from predecessors of the same or a different party. When the Thatcher administration entered office in 1979, it inherited hundreds of programs enacted by preceding governments, including some on the statute books since 1760. The median law was more than half a century old.[36] In more than a decade, the Thatcher administration introduced dozens of new programs. It also repealed programs inherited from its predecessors, and some of its own programs that were quickly recognized as mistakes. When Margaret Thatcher left office, two-thirds of the programs for which the government was responsible, such as the national health service, were those inherited from previous administrations. When expenditure is analyzed, the influence of the "dead hand" of the past is greater still. Only 11 percent of public expenditure was devoted to programs that Thatcher started and almost three-quarters went to programs based on laws enacted before the end of World War II.

The freedom of action of the governing party is limited by constraints embedded in the obligations of office. Once in office, ministers find that all the

TABLE 8.4   Consensual Title of Party Election Manifestos

Year	Conservatives	Labour
1964	Prosperity with a Purpose	Let's Go with Labour
1966	Action, Not Words	Time for Decision
1970	A Better Tomorrow	Now Britain's Strong–Let's Make It Great to Live In
1974	Firm Action for a Fair Britain	Let Us Work Together
1974	Putting Britain First	Britain Will Win with Labour
1979	The Conservative Manifesto	The Labour Way Is the Better Way
1983	The Challenge of Our Times	The New Hope for Britain
1987	The Next Moves Forward	Britain Will Win
1992	The Best Future for Britain	Time to Get Britain Working Again
1997	You Can Only Be Sure with the Conservatives	Because Britain Deserves Better
2001	Time for Common Sense	Ambition for Britain
2005	It's Time For Action	Britain Forward not Back

laws enacted by their predecessors must be enforced, even if the government of the day would not have enacted them. A newly elected government also inherits many commitments to foreign countries and to the European Union. As a former Conservative minister said of his Labour successors, "They inherited our problems and our remedies."[37]

CENTRAL AUTHORITY AND DECENTRALIZED DELIVERY OF GOVERNMENT POLICIES

In a unitary state, political authority is centralized. Decisions made by central government are of fundamental importance, for they are binding on all public agencies through the Acts of Parliament and regulations prepared in Whitehall. In addition, Whitehall controls taxation and public expenditure to a degree unusual among other member states of the European Union, where coalition government and federalism encourage territorial and functional decentralization.

For ordinary individuals the actions of government are tangible only when services are delivered to them in local schools, a doctor's office, or to their home. However, Whitehall departments usually do not deliver policies themselves. Most public goods and services are delivered by public agencies outside the framework of Whitehall ministries and five-sixths of public employees work for non-Whitehall agencies.[38] Thus, making and delivering public policies involves intragovernmental politics.

There are many reasons why ministers do not want to be in charge of delivering services. Ministers may wish to avoid charges of political interference (for example, tax collection by the Board of Inland Revenue). They may want to allow flexibility in the market (the Bank of England), lend an aura of impartiality to quasi-judicial activities (the Monopolies Commission), show respect for the extragovernmental origins of an institution (Oxford and Cambridge universities), allow qualified professionals to regulate technical matters (the Royal College of Physicians and Surgeons), or remove controversial matters from Whitehall (the Family Planning Association). Leading ministers, and above all the prime minister, prefer to focus upon the glamorous "high" politics of European and foreign affairs and economic manage-

ment. However, since "low level" services remain important to most voters' lives, ministers are under pressure to do something when there is evidence of declining standards in schools, lengthening queues for hospital admission, and an increase of crime on the streets.

While politicians can make headlines by announcing a good intention, turning popular intentions into a programme that delivers services to citizens requires scarce resources of time and money. Running the Whitehall obstacle race is the first step in intragovernmental politics. Interdepartmental negotiations are required to get ministers to agree how credit and responsibility is to be divided up; how a new programme relates to existing commitments; what agency should administer the programme; and how much money is needed. Since most new policies must take into account the effects of existing policies in a crowded policy "space," negotiations are often time consuming. From the point of view of a prime minister who believes that popular election makes it desirable to do many things, the process of turning desires into practical programmes is often frustrating.

Because of Treasury control of public expenditure, before a bill can be put to Parliament the Treasury must authorize the additional expenditure required. Ministers in charge of spending departments dislike constant Treasury reminders that there are strict cash limits on what they can spend. The limits exist because increased spending implies increased taxation. Gordon Brown has used his position as Chancellor of the Exchequer, the minister in charge of the Treasury, to enforce his priorities on other ministers. Because Brown has a power base in the governing party, he can even enforce Treasury policies against the prime minister. Every Chancellor gains power because limits on public revenue mean that, in the words of a veteran Treasury official, "the Treasury stands for reality."[39]

A departmental minister must pilot a bill through Parliament. While the votes needed to secure passage are assured, if a matter is controversial a minister will face attacks from the Opposition and a host of amendments designed to test the minister's understanding of a policy. In addition to running the Whitehall obstacle race, a minister often must negotiate agreement with public agencies outside Whitehall, and with affected interest groups. The formally centralized authority of the Crown co-exists with a maze of institutions with varying and overlapping territorial and functional responsibilities.

Local government is subordinate to central government, for the latter has the power to write or rewrite the laws that determine what locally elected governments do and spend, or even abolish local authorities and create new units of government with different boundaries. Changes in boundaries have reflected a vain search to find a balance between efficiency (assumed to correlate with fewer councils delivering services to more people spread over a wider geographical area) and responsiveness (assumed to require more councils with a smaller territory and fewer people). Local authorities, however organized, have been the chief institution for delivering such public services as education, police protection, refuse collection, housing, and cemeteries (Box 8.5). Collectively, local government accounts for about a fifth of total public expenditure.

Local council elections are fought on party lines. In the days of the two-party system, many cities were solidly Labour for a generation or more, while leafy suburbs and agricultural counties were overwhelmingly Conservative. The Liberal Democrats now win many seats in local elections and when no party has a majority introduce coalition government into town halls. However, being a councillor is usually a part-time job.

The Blair government has assumed that elected mayors are a good way of holding government accountable and effective and, incidentally, breaking the local power base of Labour veterans skeptical of Blair's new Labour Party. Downing Street introduced the direct election of the mayor of Greater London citing New York and Chicago as positive examples. However, it has refused to give it the independence in taxing and spending that American local government enjoys.[40] Blair's political initiative collapsed when a left-wing Labour populist, Ken Livingstone, won election as London's first mayor running as an independent against an official Labour candidate.

Local government in England is usually divided into two tiers of county and district councils, each with responsibility for some local services. The proliferation of public–private initiatives and special-purpose agencies has reduced the services for which local government is exclusively or primarily responsible. The Blair government has proposed an additional tier of regional government in England—but many local Labour councillors oppose this on the

BOX 8.5   Delivering Public Services on the Doorstep

The growth of government has caused the primary activities of government to shift from debates in Westminster to the delivery locally of everyday public services such as health care, education, and environmental protection and rubbish collection. Government on the scale that we know it today could not exist if all its activities were concentrated in London, for five-sixths of the country's population lives elsewhere. As the demand for public services has increased, government has grown chiefly through pluralization— that is, the multiplication of familiar institutions delivering such as schools and hospitals. Devolution to Scotland and Wales has added to decentralization, for Westminster gives institutions in Edinburgh and Cardiff the responsibility for delivering many everyday services, while keeping overall financial control in London.

Education is an example of the combination of central authority and localized service delivery. It is authorized by an act of Parliament, financed principally by central government, and the minister in charge of education is a Member of Parliament and Cabinet.

However, the delivery of primary and secondary education has been the responsibility of local government and of the school head and its board of governors. Dissatisfaction with local government has led Whitehall to establish secondary schools independent of local government but dependent on Whitehall.

Control of day-to-day activities within the school is in the hands of the teaching profession. Increasingly, central government seeks to monitor the performance of schools in nationwide examinations. But since the Department of Education employs only 1 percent of the people working in education, success depends on actions taken by others.*

*See Richard Rose, "From Government at the Centre to Government Nationwide," in Y. Meny and V. Wright, eds., *Centre-Periphery Relations in Western Europe* (London: George Allen and Unwin, 1985), pp. 13–32; and Richard Rose, "The Growth of Government Organizations," in C. Campbell and B. G. Peters, eds., *Organizing Government, Governing Organizations* (Pittsburgh: University of Pittsburgh Press, 1988), pp. 99–128.

grounds that powers would be taken from local government, and a plan for a North-East regional government was rejected by voters in a referendum there. Today there is a jumble of more or less local institutions and uncertainties about surviving a future reorganization.

Acts of Parliament make councils responsible for delivering major services, and central government financial grants and subsidies are the largest source of local government revenue. There is no local income tax, since the central government does not want to give local authorities the degree of fiscal independence that American local government has. The Thatcher government replaced the local property tax with a poll tax on every adult living in a local authority. It believed this would make voters more aware of the costs of local government and keep spending down. In practice, the tax was difficult to implement, and produced a political backlash. The Major government replaced the poll tax with a community charge that once again related local taxation to the value of the house as well as to the number of people living there.[41] The continued squeeze on central government grants to local authorities under the Blair government has pushed up the community charge tax and maintained local government finance as a subject of rancorous intragovernmental politics.

Both Conservative and Labour parties are centralist. **Centralization** is justified in terms of **territorial justice**—that is, the same standards of public policy ought to apply everywhere in the country. For example, schools in inner cities and rural areas should have the same resources as schools in prosperous suburbs. This can be achieved only if tax revenues are collected by central government and then redistributed from well-to-do to poorer parts of England. In addition, ministers emphasize that they are accountable to a national electorate of tens of millions of people, whereas local councillors are only accountable to those who vote in their ward. Instead of small being beautiful, a big nationwide electorate is assumed to be better. The statement—"Local councillors are not necessarily political animals; we could manage without them"—was made by a left-wing law professor.[42]

Devolution has given a degree of autonomy to the delivery of public services in Scotland, Wales, and Northern Ireland. The new Scottish Parliament has the right to enact legislation affecting a large range of social and public services of direct concern to individuals and communities, such as education, health, and roads. It is also responsible for determining spending priorities within the limits set by its block grant of money from the British Treasury. The Welsh Assembly has administrative discretion, but no legislative or taxing powers. Northern Ireland is exceptional, in that the key service is police and security—and this is kept under the control of British ministers, with the Army and intelligence services in the background.

Executive agencies are functional institutions headed by nonelected officials responsible for delivering many major public services. The biggest, the National Health Service (NHS), is not one organization but a multiplicity of institutions. It allocates money to hospitals and to doctors and dentists who operate as self-employed professionals, although nearly all their income is derived from the NHS and they must work to its guidelines. Access to the national health service is provided without charge to every citizen. But health care is not costless; central government picks up the bill. Because of this, the Treasury perennially seeks to limit the increase in health expenditure. The Treasury seeks to drive down prices for supplies, which it can do because it is a monopoly purchaser of many health-related goods and services. It has also sought to restrict the supply of medical services by limiting the number of hospital beds and the number of doctors that it trains and must pay for.

Public demand for more and better health care rises with the ageing of the population, since older people need more health care, and with the development of new and more expensive forms of medical treatment. The government's rationing of supply has led to lengthening queues, involving months of waiting before a person can see a medical specialist and months of additional waiting before a hospital operation is conducted. In its second term of office the Blair government has sought to deal with this problem by management changes intended to increase efficiency and by limited increases in public expenditure. It has not adopted the common practice of most European Union countries, asking patients to pay a limited part of the cost of seeing a doctor or getting hospital treatment.

British government sponsors more than a thousand **Quasi-Autonomous Non-Governmental Orga-**

nizations (**quangos**). Some quangos simply advise on policy while others deliver public services. All are created by an Act of Parliament or by an executive decision; their heads are appointed by a Cabinet minister; public money can be appropriated to finance their activities; and, when things go wrong, Parliament has difficulty in assigning responsibility for decisions.

Advisory committees draw on the expertise of individuals and organizations involved in programmes for which Whitehall departments are nominally responsible. Ministry of Agriculture officials can turn to advisory committees for detailed information about farming practices; the Department of Trade and Industry can turn to business associations on matters of trade and to industrial associations for information about a particular industry. Because they have no executive powers, advisory committees usually cost very little to run. Representatives of interest groups are glad to serve because this gives them privileged access to Whitehall and an opportunity to influence government in matters in which they are directly interested.

Administrative tribunals are quasi-judicial bodies that make expert judgments in such fields as medical negligence or handle a large number of small claims, such as disputes about whether the rent set for a rent-controlled flat is fair. Ministers may use tribunals to avoid involvement in politically controversial issues, such as decisions about deporting immigrants. Tribunals normally work much more quickly and cheaply than the courts. However, the quasi-judicial role of tribunals has created a demand for independent auditing of their procedures, to ensure that they are fair to all sides. The task of supervising some 70 tribunals is in the hands of a quango, the Council on Tribunals.

Turning to the Market

The 1945–1951 Labour government turned away from the market because its Socialist leaders believed that government planning was better able than private enterprise to promote economic growth and full employment. It nationalized many basic industries, such as electricity, gas, coal, the railways, and airlines. State ownership meant that industries did not have to run at a profit; some consistently made money while others consistently lost

money and required big subsidies. Government ownership politicized wage negotiations and investment decisions.

The Thatcher government promoted privatization, selling shares of nationalized industries on the stock market. Profitmaking industries such as telephones, oil, and gas were sold without difficulty. Selling council houses to tenants at prices well below their market value was popular with tenants. Industries that were losing money, such as British Airways, British Steel, and the coal mines, had to be reorganized, and unprofitable activities were shed to make them attractive to buyers. Industries needing large public subsidies to maintain public services, such as the railways, have continued to receive subsidies after **privatization**.

Privatization has been justified on grounds of economic efficiency (the market is better than civil servants in determining investment, production, and prices); political ideology (the power of government is reduced); service (private enterprise is more consumer-oriented than are civil servants); and short-term financial gain (the sale of public assets can provide billions in revenue for government). Although the Labour Party initially opposed privatization, it quickly realized it would be electorally disastrous to take back privatized council houses and shares that people had bought at bargain prices.

Since many privatized industries affect the public interest, new regulatory agencies were established to regulate telephones, gas, electricity, broadcasting, and water. Where there is a substantial element of monopoly in an industry, the government regulatory agency seeks to promote competition and often has the power to fix price increases at a lower rate than inflation. Even though it no longer owns an industry, government cannot walk away from obligations accepted by its Victorian forebears, such as securing public safety and health. When several fatal accidents occurred on railways whose track was the responsibility of a privatized agency, the Blair government took it over.

From Trust to Contract

Historically, the British civil service has relied on trust in delivering policies. British civil servants are much more rulebound than their German counterparts and less worried about being dragged into court to justify their actions than are American officials. Intragovernmental relations between Whitehall departments and representatives of local authorities have been regarded as a discussion in which consensual understandings would be arrived at and upheld by all sides without the force of law, or debate and division in Parliament. However, the Thatcher government considered lengthy deliberations to be inefficient obstructions to its political goals.

The "next steps" inkitiative has made contracts with independent agencies to undertake the day-to-day delivery of such central government services as automobile licenses, patents, and social security benefits from policymaking agencies. In addition, the government has sought to save money on capital expenditure and reduce the size of the public deficit through the private finance initiative, inviting banks and profitmaking companies to loan money for some or all of the costs of investment in public services such as toll bridges that have a capacity to generate revenue. The theory is that government can obtain the greatest value for money by buying services from the private sector, ranging from cleaning the floors or operating staff canteens in government offices to prison services.

Government by contract faces political limits because the departmental minister must answer to Parliament when something goes wrong. The Prison Service is a textbook example. It was established as an executive agency separate from the Home Office in 1993 to bring in private management to reduce unit costs in the face of a rising "demand" for prison services due to changes in crime rates and sentencing policies. However, when prisoners escaped and other problems erupted, the Home Secretary blamed the business executive brought in to head the Prison Service. The Prison Service head replied by attacking the minister's refusal to live up to the terms of the contract agreed between them.

The proliferation of many agencies, each with a distinctive and narrow responsibility for a limited number of policies, tends to fragment government. For example, a single parent may have to deal with half a dozen different agencies to secure all the public services to which she or he is entitled. The Blair government has reacted by endorsing the idea of "joined up" government, linking the provision of related services so that they can more effectively and easily be received by citizens. In order to achieve this goal, Whitehall must centralize powers that it has previously contracted out. Moreover, it must also centralize powers within Whitehall, a measure consistent with Tony Blair's creation of a large staff in Downing Street but inconsistent with the responsibility of individual Cabinet ministers for running their own departments.

The Contingency of Influence

The theory of British government is centralist: All roads lead to Downing Street, where the the prime minister and the Chancellor of the Exchequer have their homes and offices, and the Treasury and the Foreign Office buildings are only a few steps away. In practice, policymaking is multidimensional, for those involved can be divided horizontally between ministries, executive agencies, and other forms of quangos, and vertically between central government and local authorities and other nondepartmental public bodies that deliver services locally and functionally.

Influence is contingent: it varies with the problem at hand. Decisions about war and peace are taken at the very center by the highest-ranking political and military officials. By contrast, decisions about whether a particular piece of land should be used for housing are normally made by local authorities. Most political decisions involve two or more government agencies, and therefore require discussion and bargaining before a decision can be implemented. The making of policy is constrained by disputes within government much more than by differences between the governing party and its opponents. Many tentacles of the octopus of government work against each other, as each public agency claims to represent conflicting definitions of the public interest.

While the center of central government has been pressing harder on other parts of British government, Whitehall itself has been losing influence because of its obligations in the European Union. The Single Europe Act promotes British exports, but it also increases the scope for European Union regulation of the British economy. Whitehall has adopted a variety of strategies in its European Union negotiations, including noncooperation and public dispute. Ironically, it is just these tactics that local government and British executive agencies use when they disagree with Whitehall.

Why Public Policy Matters

However a citizen votes, she or he does not need to look far to see the outputs of government: if there is a school-age child or a pensioner in the house, the benefits to the family are continuous and visible. If a person is ill, the care provided by doctors and hospitals are important outputs of public policy; so too are police protection and tight controls of land use that maintain greenery even in urban landscapes. Today the average household annually receives two significant welfare state benefits, such as education, health care, or a pension. To produce the benefits of public policy, government relies on three major resources: (1) laws, (2) money, and (3) personnel. Most policies involve a combination of these resources, but they do not do so equally. Policies regulating individual behavior, such as marriage and divorce, are law-intensive; measures such as social security, that pay benefits to millions of people, are money-intensive; and the delivery of services such as health care is labor-intensive.

Laws are the unique resource of government, for private enterprises cannot enact laws and the contracts only operate if the laws of the land are respected. The British executive centralizes within it the power to draft laws and regulations that can be approved without substantial amendment by Parliament. Moreover, many laws give ministers significant discretion in administration. For example, an employer may be required to provide "reasonable" toilet facilities rather than having all features of lavatories specified, down to the size and height of a toilet seat.

Public employees are needed to administer laws and deliver major services. Privatizing public services has reduced the number of people counted as civil servants or public employees, but it has not reduced to the same extent the number who depend on public spending for their job. In total, more than a fifth of the entire British labor force depends on government for their job.

To meet the costs of public policy, British government collects almost two-fifths of the gross national product in taxation. Income tax accounts for 28 percent of tax revenue; the top rate of taxation is 40 percent. Social security taxes are paid by deductions from wages and additional contributions of employers; these account for an additional 17 percent of revenue. Since there are no state or local income taxes, a well-to-do English person can be taxed at a lower total rate than a well-off person living in New York City.

Taxes on consumption are important too. There is a value-added tax of 17.5 percent on the sale of almost all goods and services, and gasoline, cigarettes, and alcohol are taxed heavily too. In total, taxes on consumption account for one-quarter of all tax revenue. Since profits fluctuate from year to year, the government prefers businesses to pay taxes on their gross revenues through value-added tax and on their total wages bill, through the employer's contribution to social security. Taxes on the profits of corporations claim an eighth of tax revenue. Additional revenue is generated by the National Lottery, launched in 1993; more people play the lottery than vote in a general election.

Social security is the most costly programme of British government. It accounts for 38 percent of public expenditure (Figure 8.7). It is also the most popular, for it transfers money from government to more than 10 million older people receiving pensions, plus millions of invalids, the unemployed, women on maternity leave, and poor people needing to supplement their limited resources. Spending on health and education are second and third in their claims on the public purse. Together, these three social welfare programmes account for two-thirds of total public expenditure. A classic commitment of government—defence and maintaining public order and safety through the police, fire service, courts, and prisons—are fourth in importance.

Since there is no item in the public budget labelled as "waste," any government wanting to reduce public spending must squeeze existing programmes—and big savings can be made only by squeezing popular programmes such as health and education or pensions. But doing so would go against public opinion. When Margaret Thatcher entered office in 1979, the public divided into three almost equal groups: those wanting to spend more and tax more; those wanting to cut taxes even if it means a reduction in public services; and a large middle group wanting to leave things as they are. Thatcher's campaign to cut taxes and

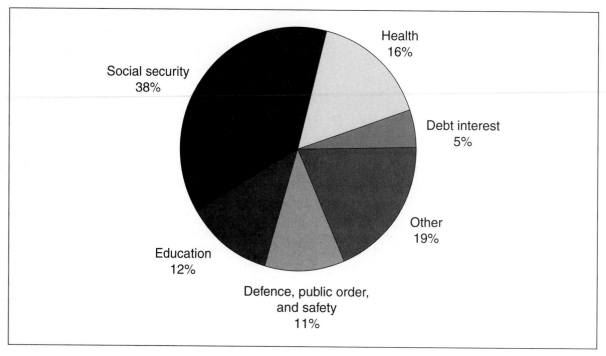

FIGURE 8.7   Public Expenditure by Program

Source: Office for National Statistics, 2004. *United Kingdom National Accounts: The Blue Book.* London: The Stationary Office, pages 276ff.

TABLE 8.5   Public Preference for More Taxing and Spending Rather than Less (in percentages)

	1983	1987	1991	1995	2001
Increase taxes and spending on health, education, and social benefits	32	50	65	61	59
Keep taxes and spending the same as now	54	42	29	31	34
Reduce taxes and spending	9	3	3	5	3
Don't know	5	5	3	3	4

Source: British Social Attitudes surveys, as reported in Alison Park, et al., eds., *British Social Attitudes: The 19th Report* (Thousand Oaks, CA: Sage Publications, 2002), p. 76.

public spending produced a reaction in favour of public expenditure. By the time she left office a majority favoured taxing and spending more on social programmes and this has remained the position since (Table 8.5). Tony Blair's government entered office with a pledge not to increase income tax. However, in order to finance increased expenditure on social programmes that are popular with the electorate, it has put up less visible "stealth taxes," such as the employer's contribution to social security, and taxes on insurance funds for pensioners. The effects of these tax increases are passed on to voters—but not in a form that they can easily see.

POLICY OUTCOMES AND CHANGES IN SOCIETY

Although living conditions reflect public policy, only a totalitarian regime claims responsibility for everything that happens in society. In an open society such as England, social conditions are a consequence of the interaction of public policies, the national and international economy, the not-for-profit institutions of civil society, and individual and household activities free of state control. The term welfare state is misleading. Total welfare in society is the sum of a "welfare mix," combining actions of government, the market, and the nonmonetized production of welfare in the household.[43]

Defence against threats to security at home and abroad is a unique responsibility of government. In an interdependent world, British government seeks to guarantee national security by participating in international alliances. Britain was a founder member of NATO, and has fought alongside American forces in the Gulf War in 1991, in Kosovo, and after September 11th, in Afghanistan and Iraq. Maintaining order at home requires the cooperation of others. This is clearest in Northern Ireland, as Whitehall negotiates with leaders of armed paramilitary organizations as well as with elected representatives. Crime prevention depends not only on policing but also on whether or not there are lots of unemployed youths ready to violate the laws in pursuit of money. Over the decades the crime rate has been rising, but it remains lower than in the United States.

Both Conservative and Labour governments accept responsibility for the economy. Most firms are profitmaking, consumers can spend money as they like, and wages and prices are principally decided in the market. Government influences the market through taxing and spending policies, interest rates, and policies for growth and unemployment. Increasingly, what happens to the British economy is also influenced by what happens in other countries of the European Union and on other continents too, and government cannot isolate the country from what happens elsewhere in the global economy.

In each decade since World War II, the British economy has grown, and compounding a small annual rate of growth over many decades cumulatively results in a big rise in living standards. Per capita national income has more than tripled since 1945. Many consumer goods that were once thought of as luxuries, such as owning a car or one's own home, are now mass consumption goods. Things unknown in 1945, such as air travel abroad or VCRs, are now commonplace. Between 1993 and 2003, the British economy grew at a rate of 2.9 percent annually, and over the decade it grew by 24 percent in total. This rate was much higher than France or Germany and almost as high as the United States.

Poverty can be found in Britain; the extent depends on the definition used. If poverty is defined in relative terms such as having less than half the average wage, this is consistent with a rising standard of living in absolute terms. If poverty is defined as being trapped at a low income level for many years, then less than 4 percent are longterm poor.

On all the major indicators of social well-being, the British people enjoy a higher standard of living today than a generation ago. Infant mortality has declined by more than four-fifths since 1951. Life expectancy for men and for women has risen by 12 years. A gender gap remains, as women on average live four years longer than men. The postwar expansion of schools has significantly raised the quantity of education available. Classes are smaller in size, and after leaving secondary school upwards of one-half of British youths go on to some form of further education, usually in institutions that did not exist in 1950. More than two-thirds of families now own their own home and nine-tenths report satisfaction with their housing.

The outputs of public policy play a significant part in the everyday life of all Britons. Everyone makes major use of health and education programs. Children at school or patients seeing a doctor do not think of themselves as participating in politics. Yet the services received are designed and paid for by government. Welfare state benefits—free education, health care, or the guarantee of an income in old age or unemployment—are so taken for granted today that most people see them as nonpolitical. They do not want a change in government after an election to cause radical changes in major social policies.

Popular Expectations

For a century commentators on English society have bemoaned the relative decline in the country's achievements compared with America and leading continental European countries. But ordinary people do not compare their lives with other countries; the most important comparison is with their own past. Evaluating change across time shows great improvements in the living conditions of most English people compared with their parents or grandparents. The longer the time span, the greater the improvements. Furthermore, in the production of such political "goods" as freedom from the state, confidence in the honesty of public officials, and administrative flexibility, British government remains an international leader. The great majority of people are proud of the achievements of Britain and would not want to be a citizen of any other country.

Frustration with government arises only if people expect it to be consistently very successful. But English people tend to have low expectations of government. In particular, decades of economic difficulties lowered expectations of what government can do to make the economy grow or prevent a rise in unemployment or inflation. Paradoxically, a government presiding over high unemployment and a slow growth economy would be living up to the pessimistic expectations of many. When there are low expectations, any time in which the economy does not get worse can be considered a reprieve from bad news. English people do not hold government responsible for what is most important in their lives; they evaluate their personal circumstances differently from public policy. When people are asked each year whether they think next year will be better or worse personally than the preceding year, on nine-tenths of the occasions a majority say they expect the coming year to be all right for themselves, even when many expect economic difficulties for the country as a whole. National prosperity is desirable but not a necessary condition for personal well-being. When people are asked to evaluate their lives, they are most satisfied with their family, friends, home, and job, and least satisfied with major political institutions of society.[44]

Satisfaction with the present goes along with acceptance of political change in principle. But there are disagreements about the direction of change—for example, whether Westminster should take more responsibility for public services or devolve more responsibilities locally, and whether Britain should align itself more closely with the United States or with the European Union. Even when goals are agreed, there are differences about the particular policy that can best achieve a given goal. Politics in England is thus an ongoing debate about the direction, the means, and the tempo of adapting old institutions and inherited policies to new circumstances in the twenty-first century.

KEY TERMS

Cabinet
centralization
class
Conservative Party
Crown
decentralization
devolution
Downing Street
first-past-the-post
    electoral system
government

individualist theory
insider and outsider
    pressure groups
insularity
Irish Republican Army
    (IRA)
Labour Party
Liberal Democrats
mixed economy
    Keynesian welfare
    state

multiparty system
Northern Ireland
Parliament
prime minister
privatization
Quasi-Autonomous Non-
    Governmental
    Organizations
    (quangos)
Scotland

sleazy
territorial justice
Thatcherism
trusteeship theory
    of government
United Kingdom
unwritten constitution
Wales
Westminster
Whitehall

INTERNET SOURCES

UK Government: www.direct.gov.uk

Parliament website: www.parliament.uk

Prime Minister's Office: www.pm.gov.uk

The BBC News Service: www.news.bbc.co.uk

The Political Studies Association in Britain: www.psa.ac.uk

SUGGESTED READINGS

Butler, D. E., and Geraint Butler. *Twentieth Century British Political Facts, 1900–2000,* 8th ed. London: Macmillan, 2000.

Butler, D. E., and Dennis Kavanagh. *The British General Election of 2001.* Basingstoke, England: Palgrave, 2001.

Flinders, Matthew. *The Politics of Accountability in the Modern State.* Aldershot: Ashgate, 2001.

George, Stephen. *An Awkward Partner: Britain in the European Community,* 3rd ed. Oxford, England: Oxford University Press, 1998.

Grant, Wyn. *Pressure Groups and British Politics.* New York: St. Martin's Press, 2000.

Hayward, Jack, Brian Barry, and A. Brown, eds. *The British Study of Politics in the Twentieth Century.* Oxford, England: Oxford University Press, 1999.

Independent Commission on Proportional Representation. *Changed Voting Changed Politics: Lessons of Britain's Experience of PR since 1997.* London: the Constitution Unit.

James, Simon. *British Cabinet Government,* 2nd ed., New York: Routledge, 1999.

Moran, Michael. *The British Regulatory State: High Modernism and Hyper-Innovation.* New York: Oxford University Press, 2003.

Norris, Pippa, ed. *Britain Votes 2001.* Oxford, England: Oxford University Press, 2001.

Norris, Pippa, and Joni Lovenduski. *Political Recruitment: Gender, Race, and Class in the British Parliament.* New York: Cambridge University Press, 1995.

Park, Alison, ed. *British Social Attitudes: The 20th Report.* Thousand Oaks, CA: Sage Publications, 2003.

Pattie, Charles, Patrick Seyd, and Paul Whitele. *Citizenship in Britain.* New York: Cambridge University Press, 2004.

Oliver, Dawn. *Constitutional Reform in the United Kingdom.* New York: Oxford University Press, 2003.

Rose, Richard. *Ordinary People in Public Policy.* Newbury Park, CA: Sage, 1989.

———. *The Prime Minister in a Shrinking World.* Boston: Polity Press, 2001.

Rose, Richard, and Phillip L. Davies. *Inheritance in Public Policy: Change Without Choice in Britain.* New Haven, CT: Yale University Press, 1994.

Saggar, Shamit, ed. *Race and British Electoral Politics.* London: UCL Press, 1998.

Seldon, Anthony. *Blair.* New York: Free Press, 2004.

Smith, Martin J. *The Core Executive in Britain.* London: Macmillan, 1999.

Social Trends. London: Stationery Office, annual.

Trench, Alan. *Has Devolution Made a Difference?* London: Imprint Academic, 2004.

Webb, Paul. *The Modern British Party System.* Thousand Oaks, CA: Sage Publications, 2003.

Whitaker's Almanack. London: J. Whitaker, annual.

Wilson, David, and Game, Chris. *Local Government in the United Kingdom,* 3rd ed. Basingstoke: Palgrave, 2002.

ENDNOTES

1. See Richard Rose, *What Is Europe? A Dynamic Perspective* (New York: Addison Wesley Longman, 1996), Ch. 3.

2. John Kampfner and David Wighton, "Blair Seals Labour's Switch to Low Tax Party," *Financial Times,* 27 March 1997.

3. Quoted in Krishna Guha, "Labour Escapes from Its Bloody Tower," *Financial Times,* 24 August 2002.

4. See Richard Rose, "England: A Traditionally Modern Political Culture," in Lucian W. Pye and Sidney Verba, eds., *Political Culture and Political Development* (Princeton, NJ: Princeton University Press, 1965), pp. 83–129.

5. Quoted in Richard Rose, *Do Parties Make a Difference?* 2nd ed. (Chatham, NJ: Chatham House, 1984).

6. Cf. Andrew Dilnot and Paul Johnson, eds., *Election Briefing 1997* (London: Institute for Fiscal Studies, Commentary 60, 1997), p. 2.

7. John Kampfner and David Wighton, "Reeling in Scotland to Bring England in Step," *Financial Times,* 5 April 1997.

8. *NOP Social and Political Research,* a nationwide survey of 1,921 respondents, March 17–23, 1995.

9. Philip Stephens and Cathy Newman, "We Need One Power, says Blair," *Financial Times,* 28 April 2003.

10. *Gallup Political and Economic Index,* London No. 390 (February 1993), p. 42.

11. "Britain's Independent Role About Played Out," *The Times* (London), 6 December 1962.

12. Quoted in Peter Hennessy, "Raw Politics Decide Procedure in Whitehall," *New Statesman* (London), 24 October 1986, p. 10.

13. Winston Churchill, *Their Finest Hour* (London: Cassell, 1949), p. 14.

14. See Richard Rose, "A Crisis of Confidence in the Party System or in Individual Leaders," *Contemporary Record* 9, No. 2 (1995): 273–93.

15. Simon Jenkins, "New Dogs, Old Tricks," *Sunday Times* (London), 21 March 2004.

16. Walter Bagehot, *The English Constitution* (London: World's Classics, 1955), p. 9.

17. See Richard Rose, *The Prime Minister in a Shrinking World* (Boston: Polity Press, 2001).

18. David Leppard and Robert Winnett, "Blair Blames Ministers for Policy Gaffes," *Sunday Times,* 18 April 2004.

19. Eric Varley, quoted in A. Michie and S. Hoggart, *The Pact* (London: Quartet Books, 1978), p. 13.

20. Hugh Heclo and Aaron Wildavsky, *The Private Government of Public Money* (London: Macmillan, 1974).

21. Bernard Ingham, press secretary to Margaret Thatcher, quoted in Rose, "British Government: The Job at the Top," in R. Rose and E. Suleiman, eds., *Presidents and Prime Ministers* (Washington, DC: American Enterprise Institute, 1980), p. 43.

22. Lord Butler, *Review of Intelligence on Weapons of Mass Destruction.* House of Commons Document 898. London: The Stationery Office, 2004, p. 160.

23. See Samuel H. Beer, *Modern British Politics,* 3rd ed. (London: Faber and Faber, 1982).

24. Lord Wright, in *Liversidge v. Sir John Anderson and Another,* 1941, quoted in G. Le May, *British Government, 1914–1953* (London: Methuen, 1955), p. 332.

25. House of Commons, *Hansard* (London: Her Majesty's Stationery Office), November 11, 1947, col. 206.

26. Cf. Colin Bennett, "From the Dark to the Light: The Open Government Debate in Britain," *Journal of Public Policy* 5, No. 2 (1985): 209; italics in the original.

27. See Richard Rose and Ian McAllister, *The Loyalties of Voters* (Newbury Park, CA: 1990), Ch. 3.

28. See Joni Lovenduski and Pippa Norris, eds., "Women in Politics," a special issue of *Parliamentary Affairs,* 49, No. 1 (1996).

29. Quoted in Maurice Kogan, *The Politics of Education* (Harmondsworth, England: Penguin, 1971), p. 135.

30. See the Fulton Committee, *Report,* vol. 1, pp. 27ff., and Appendix E, especially p. 162.

31. See Rob Baggott, "The Measurement of Change in Pressure Groups," *Talking Politics* 5, No. 1 (1992): 18–22.

32. Sir Ken Jackson, quoted by Krishna Guha, "Engineers and Electricians Turn Away from Moderate Traditions," *Financial Times,* 19 July 2002.

33. See W. A. Maloney, G. Jordan, and A. M. McLaughlin, "Interest Groups and Public Policy: The Insider/Outsider Model Revisited," *Journal of Public Policy* 14, No. 1 (1994): 17–38.

34. Tony Blair, *New Britain: My Vision of a Young Country* (London: Fourth Estate, 1996), p. 299.

35. For details, see Denis Van Mechelen and Richard Rose, *Patterns of Parliamentary Legislation* (Aldershot, England: Gower, 1986), table 5.2, and more generally, Rose, *Do Parties Make a Difference?*

36. Rose and Davies, *Inheritance in Public Policy,* p. 28.

37. Reginald Maudling, quoted in David Butler and Michael Pinto-Duschinsky, *The British General Election of 1970* (London: Macmillan, 1971), p. 62.

38. See *Better Government Services: Executive Agencies in the 21st Century.* (London: Office of Public Service Reforms and the Treasury, 2002).

39. Sir Leo Pliatzky, quoted in Peter Hennessy, "The Guilt of the Treasury 1000," *New Statesman,* 23 January 1987.

40. See Paul Peterson, "The American Mayor: Elections and Institutions," *Parliamentary Affairs* 53, No. 4 (2000): 667–79.

41. David Butler, Andrew Adonis, and Tony Travers, *Failure in British Government: The Politics of the Poll Tax* (Oxford, England: Oxford University Press, 1994).

42. J. A. G. Griffith, *Central Departments and Local Authorities* (London: George Allen and Unwin, 1966), p. 542. Cf. Simon Jenkins, *Accountable to None: The Tory Nationalization of Britain* (Harmondsworth, England: Penguin, 1996).

43. See Richard Rose, "The Dynamics of the Welfare Mix in Britain," in Richard Rose and Rei Shiratori, eds., *The Welfare State East and West* (New York: Oxford University Press, 1986), pp. 80–106.

44. Rose, *Ordinary People in Public Policy,* pp. 175ff.

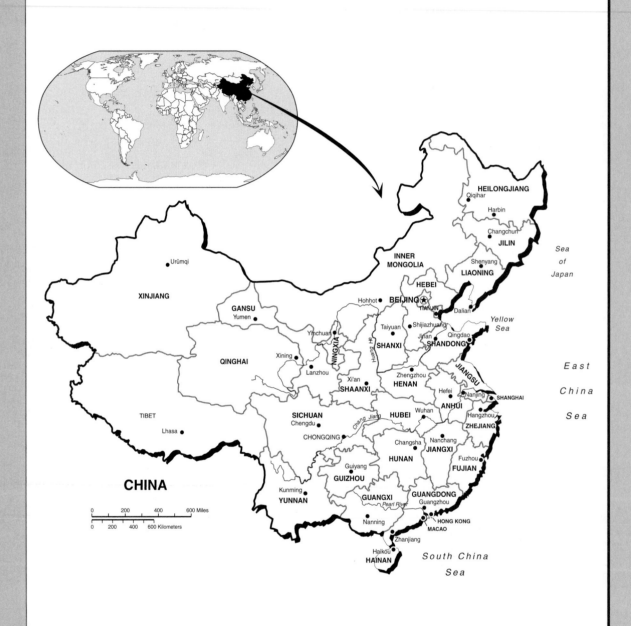

CHINA

0   200   400   600 Miles
0   200   400   600 Kilometers

CHAPTER

Politics in China

Melanie Manion

On October 1, 1949, Mao Zedong, the peasant revolutionary who had led the Chinese communists in war against the Japanese and in civil war, pronounced a basic communist victory, proclaimed a new regime, and promised a new era for China. From the centuries-old Gate of Heavenly Peace in Beijing, Mao formally inaugurated the People's Republic of China (PRC). For nearly three decades after, until his death in 1976, Mao was the chief architect and agitator for a comprehensive project of revolutionary transformation envisaged to lead a largely backward agrarian people to modernization, prosperity, and (ultimately) communist utopia. A few years after Mao's death, his successors officially and publicly rejected most of the premises, strategies, and outcomes of this revolutionary project, essentially declaring it a failure. They launched a new period of socialist reform, ongoing today. To be sure, reform in post-Mao China is not as radical or dramatic as the revolutions that toppled most of the world's communist regimes in 1989 and 1990. Nonetheless, the transformation is awesome.

Without publicly abandoning the ultimate goal of communism, Mao's successors have defined their current quest mainly in pragmatic economic terms, rather than utopian ideological terms. They have identified economic growth as the nation's highest priority and the Communist Party's main assignment. To achieve this objective, the communist party-state has largely retreated from 30 years of direct administration of the economy. Openly acknowledging the superiority of the capitalist experience, Chinese reformers are promoting a "socialist market economy," with a place for foreign investors, private entrepreneurs, family farms, and local community corporations. More than anything else, Chinese leaders have staked their legitimacy on the performance of this new economy.

While embracing economic markets, Chinese leaders have rejected political pluralism. The communist party-state was in clear evidence in Beijing on June 4, 1989, when the People's Liberation Army employed its tanks and machine guns to clear the streets and main public square of thousands of young protesters. The regime tolerates no open challenge to the Communist Party monopoly of political power. For most of the 1.3 billion ordinary Chinese, political reform is mainly reflected in a new official acceptance of a legitimate private sphere and a new official tolerance of political apathy. Compared with the Maoist years, when a hankering for a small private plot of land to farm or a taste for the music of Beethoven signified dangerous "bourgeois decadence," much less in daily life today is considered political. Moreover, under the new regime, ordinary citizens need not necessarily demonstrate active support for official policies and the political system—so long as they do not engage in active opposition. Chinese leaders have not charted a road toward liberal democracy, or at least not purposefully. Instead, the political system has become merely authoritarian in its limited reach, rather than pervasively totalitarian.

Yet, post-Mao reform is more than the retreat of the state from the economy and the imposition of fewer demands on citizens politically. A project of institutionalization is underway in China, to create an infrastructure promoting more transparency, stability, and responsiveness. In large part, this is to encourage investment and innovation, to support the goal of economic growth. At the same time, Mao's successors are also committed to political institutionalization for political reasons. They are attempting to build "sound organizational and working systems" that safeguard against arbitrary dictators and disruptive politics.[1] This has included better-crafted laws and a new legality, more assertive representative assemblies, and popularly elected grassroots leaders.

Much of China's recent transformation is only partly a direct result of the various policies that constitute reform. It is at least as much a byproduct of these policies. Reform has set in motion processes of economic, political, and social change that appear now largely beyond the control of leaders at the political center. Consider a few examples. Eased restrictions on population movement have created a "floating population" of perhaps 100 million internal migrants, most of them from the countryside and seeking work in towns and cities, many of them unregistered squatters, all of them representing a new tension between state control and market opportunity. Local governments, empowered by a new fiscal federalism, pursue and protect their negotiated economic claims from encroachment, at the expense of

a weakened central government with a steadily declining share of revenue. Growth in individual wealth and a telecommunications revolution beginning in the 1990s have permitted more than 22 million Chinese to link up with the outside world through their Internet connections, and this number is growing faster than anywhere else in the world.

CURRENT POLICY CHALLENGES

What key challenges confront Chinese policy makers as the new century begins? What major issues preoccupy ordinary citizens as they make their way in a rapidly changing China? The areas of concern are similar, the perspectives often different.

Chinese policy makers have largely abandoned the project of building community based on communist ideology. Instead, their popular appeals to a shared community mainly rest on the ideal of Chinese nationalism with strong historical roots. The 1997 transfer of sovereignty of Hong Kong from Britain to the PRC was a widely publicized historic milestone, offering a unique opportunity to build nationalist pride. Plans and promises of an eventual mainland unification with Taiwan (and threatening responses to intimations from Taiwan of a separate future) are usually framed in terms of a common Chinese history and culture that transcends current political frictions. Building community through Chinese nationalism also takes less overtly political forms, such as promoting Chinese achievements in international sports competitions. The prospect of hosting the 2008 Olympic Games has already become a unifying project, which will be cultivated for its potential to foster a sense of national unity and pride long after the medals have been counted. The nationalist approach to building community has other sides too. The angry crowds that threatened the American embassy in Beijing after the United States mistakenly bombed the Chinese embassy in Belgrade during the 1999 air war over Yugoslavia are one example. The cyber-war initiated by pro-China hackers into American government computers following the collision of an American spy plane and Chinese fighter jet in 2001 is another. In short, while Chinese policy makers are eager to promote Chinese nationalism in order to strengthen regime support, national sentiments among ordinary Chinese are not exclusively positive—and the tension between fostering and controlling nationalism is not always re- solved peaceably. Moreover, many in the non-Han minority nationalities such as Tibetans and Chinese Muslims do not view history so benignly.

Chinese policy makers have agreed to be judged mainly by their ability to foster economic develop- ment and deliver a better material life for Chinese citizens. On the one hand, China's development is beyond a doubt remarkable. Its economy grew at a rate of nearly 10 percent per year from 1980 to 2000, a record of sustained growth comparable only to Japan and Korea in the latter half of the twentieth century. China is now the world's seventh largest economy and second largest recipient of foreign di- rect investment. On the other hand, the "iron rice bowl" of permanent secure employment has been broken: a policy to merge, downsize, or close ineffi- cient state enterprises has furloughed millions of in- dustrial workers, often without compensation. In China's industrial cities, newly redundant workers gather together at enterprises or government offices to demand a basic livelihood. The social safety net is grossly inadequate to support the millions more re- dundant workers who would lose jobs if all or most loss-making enterprises went bankrupt. China's lead- ers have postponed the most politically difficult de- cisions of economic reform by continuing to extend bank credit to many large enterprises. The problem of livelihood for workers is a serious conundrum for Chinese policy makers. With good reason, they fear massive social unrest sparked by an urban working class advancing claims to economic rights denied them in the course of reform.

The effect of China's recent accession to the World Trade Organization (WTO) brings with it new opportunities for development, but also serious new challenges. Entry in the WTO will push reforms forward, but also exacerbate existing problems in the Chinese economy and tensions in Chinese soci- ety. Membership in the WTO brings with it signifi- cant short-term costs for China, in the form of in- creased unemployment and bankruptcies of domestic companies. Businesses that dominate the domestic market but are not efficient enough to compete successfully in international trade will suf- fer; these include many heavy industries and some agricultural sectors (such as wheat) in which China is not a competitive producer. Small-scale producers for local markets, which have enjoyed subsidies and

protection from local governments despite their inef- ficiency, will also bear the burden of costs due to WTO membership. In the short term, benefits will accrue mainly to China's exporting companies, mostly in light industries such as textiles and toys and mostly located in coastal regions. The growth of jobs in these industries will probably not counteract the loss of employment in the less competitive sec- tors, at least not very soon. Chinese policy makers face the prospect of an increase in labor protests and peasant riots in the near future.

While promoting a policy that "some get rich first," Chinese policy makers are acutely aware that the more needy Chinese deeply resent the newly conspicuous economic inequalities of the socialist market economy. Rural incomes are only about 40 percent of urban incomes, and coastal regions have been advantaged over the interior. As this cen- tury began, Chinese in modern Shanghai enjoyed an- nual incomes exceeding $3,700, while their counter- parts in backward Guizhou province made do with less then $300. While some Chinese struggle for a basic livelihood, there are also Chinese entrepre- neurs and venal officials who travel in luxury sedans, do business on cellular phones, and feast ostenta- tiously at expensive restaurants. Year after year, ordi- nary Chinese tell pollsters that corruption is the most serious problem in the country. Villagers rise up to protest abuses of power by "local emperors" impos- ing illegal fees and excessive taxes in the countryside. In the cities, Chinese grumble about the perceived ineffectiveness and insincerity of the official anticor- ruption effort: "not daring *not* to fight corruption, not daring to fight corruption seriously."

Unlike most other communist regimes, which toppled in the face of popular uprisings in the past two decades, China has experienced no second polit- ical revolution. Today, it is still a communist party- state. Chinese policy makers have promoted limited democratization, sometimes as an antidote to corrup- tion at the grassroots. While they have opened up po- litical processes to more diversified inputs, they have also firmly suppressed organized challenges to the communist party. A handful of leaders at the very top still monopolize the authority to choose what sorts of inputs from what sorts of groups are acceptable, and the decision rules are not always transparent.

Strikingly little remains of Mao's grand revolu- tionary schemes. Viewed from the perspective of the

1970s, the magnitude and pace of change in China in the 1980s and 1990s are practically unimaginable. Chinese politics today is "post-Mao" politics in the sense that there is a new regime, not simply a change of leaders—and, given its dynamics, there appears to be no turning back. Of course, without a grasp of China's rich political history, especially in the Maoist years, it is not only impossible to appreciate what has (and has not) changed, but also impossible to understand the crucial context of post-Mao reform: what has been rejected.

HISTORICAL SETTING

When ordinary Chinese today are asked about what it is they, as Chinese, are most proud, many respond: "our long history." Chinese civilization emerged more than six thousand years ago. As a polity, imperial China was the longest-lived major system of governance in world history, enduring as a centralized state ruled with little change in political philosophy or bureaucratic organization for more than two millennia until the fall of the Qing, the last dynasty, in 1911.[2] Traditional China was governed by an emperor and a unique bureaucracy of scholar-officials at the capital and in the localities, who gained their positions meritocratically through examinations that tested knowledge of the Confucian classics. Anyone was eligible to participate in the examinations, but successful performance required a classical education, usually through a private tutor, not available to most ordinary Chinese. **Confucianism** was basically a conservative philosophy. It conceived of society and the polity in terms of an ordered hierarchy of harmonious relationships. At the top of the hierarchy was the emperor, who maintained social order through his conduct as a moral exemplar. Confucianism blurred the distinction between state and society: it saw harmony (not conflict) as the natural social order; this harmony resulted because the virtuous emperor provided an example of correct conduct. Loyalty to the emperor was the highest principle in the hierarchy of relationships entailing mutual obligations throughout society.

From Imperial Order to the Struggle for a New China

This remarkable imperial order began to crumble in the mid-nineteenth century, when Qing rulers proved unable to uphold their political authority and maintain territorial integrity in the presence of large-scale domestic rebellion and foreign economic and military encroachment. The republic founded in 1912 did not restore order or sovereignty to China, but effectively collapsed within a few years, as dozens of Chinese regional warlords ruling with personal armies competed for control of territory.[3] Nearly four decades of political upheaval and continuous warfare ensued, as the Chinese sought solutions to the problems of governance that had brought down the Qing.

The dominant problems were the struggle for national sovereignty and the struggle for peasant livelihood. The former involved two sorts of claims: cession of Chinese territory in treaties imposed forcibly by Western powers beginning in the nineteenth century, and outright military invasion and occupation by the Japanese in the 1930s. As to the Chinese peasantry, poverty in the countryside due to socioeconomic conditions of exorbitant taxes, high rents, and usurious credit was aggravated by frequent floods and droughts, which usually brought ruin. An observer compared the condition of the Chinese peasant to a man standing up to his neck in water: one ripple would drown him.[4]

These two struggles were played out in the context of a competition to unify the country. By the 1920s, the **Nationalist Party** and army had emerged as the most prominent political and military force in the country. The Nationalists had their strongest social base in the urban areas; in the countryside, they were mainly dependent on the support of the landlord class. This largely explains Nationalist reluctance to implement land and social reforms to resolve the problems of Chinese peasants. Peasant poverty was exacerbated by absentee landlordism and the replacement of ties of mutual obligation with economic ties enforced by managing agents. Land distribution was not part of the Nationalist agenda; nor were tax controls or provision of cheap credit effectively implemented.

Between 1924 and 1927, the Nationalists allied with the communists in a battle to eliminate regional warlords and to unify China. By the late 1920s, the Nationalists had practically realized this aim. In 1927, they broke their alliance with the communists in a violent massacre that reduced the Communist Party from nearly 58,000 to 10,000 members. The break inaugurated a new civil war. In the end, the Nationalists were forced to retreat to the island of Taiwan in 1949. Only in 1991 did they formally acknowledge the civil war with the communists had ended.

By contrast with the Nationalists, the intellectual revolutionaries who founded the **Chinese Communist Party** in 1921 were unlikely contenders for power. The rise and eventual victory of the communists owe much to historic opportunities in the 1930s and 1940s. These opportunities were available for other forces to exploit too, but the communists exploited them best.[5] **Mao Zedong** emerged as leader of the communists in the mid-1930s, consolidating his leadership in the early 1940s.[6]

After the Nationalist attack in 1927, many communists retreated to the countryside. Mao had already reported on the spontaneous impulse for radical social change among the peasantry and had proposed a revolutionary strategy different from that suggested by communist theory or Russian experience. Mao rejected the idea that the Chinese communists could win power through a revolution of the small urban working class in China. Instead, he argued, a communist victory could only be achieved by providing leadership for a nascent rural revolution and building a guerrilla Red Army to surround the cities with the countryside. From a base in southeastern China, Mao and other communists implemented a program of political education and social change, including land redistribution. In 1934, a major Nationalist offensive forced them on a strategic retreat, the historic Long March, that ended at the caves of Yanan in China's northwest, where Mao and his communist forces, their numbers literally decimated, established their headquarters. From Yanan, they built on the strategy of rural revolution to further develop support in the countryside.[7]

The second indispensable component in communist victory was the 1937 Japanese invasion of central China, beyond territory in the northeast (Manchuria) that the Japanese had occupied since 1931.[8] Mao seized the strategic initiative to call for a truce in the civil war so that Chinese could unite to resist Japanese aggression. Nationalist leaders were initially wary. This combination of Nationalist reluctance and strong anti-Japanese sentiment in the cities and countryside earned the communists enormous popularity as the true nationalist resistance to foreign aggression. From 1937 to 1945, the communists

grew in force from 40,000 to more than a million. Japanese defeat in the world war ended the alliance between Nationalists and communists. A new civil war began.[9] In four years, the communists won victory, as peasant revolutionaries and Chinese nationalists. Once in power, they turned their energies to the construction of socialism.

POLITICAL HISTORY OF THE PRC

The history of the People's Republic of China (PRC) can be divided into three major periods. In the first, between 1949 and 1957, the Chinese adopted a "lean to one side" strategy, emulating the experience of the first and most powerful communist state, the Soviet Union. The second period began in 1958, when the Chinese introduced their own model of revolutionary development. Except for a few years at the beginning of the 1960s, this Maoist model prevailed until Mao's death in 1976. A short transitional period ensued, during which immediate problems of policy orientation and leadership succession were resolved with the arrest and trial of key radical leaders. In December 1978, the third period, a new era of socialist reform ongoing today, was inaugurated with a Central Committee declaration favoring learning from practical experience and rejecting the ideological constraints of Maoism—or any theory.[10] **Deng Xiaoping,** China's new "paramount leader," charted and presided over economic and political reforms. In the same sense that Chinese politics in the two decades ending in 1976 are appropriately characterized as the Maoist years, the last two decades of the twentieth century belong most to Deng—despite important differences in the power of these two leaders and how they wielded it.

The Chinese communists had won power largely by ignoring Soviet advice. Once in power, however, they looked to the Soviet Union for a plan to build socialism. They concluded a treaty of friendship and alliance in 1950. Soviet financial aid to China in the 1950s was not large. Mainly, aid was given in a massive technology transfer: over 12,000 Soviet engineers and technicians were sent to work in China; over 6,000 Chinese studied in Soviet universities, tens of thousands more in Soviet factories on short-term training courses. With this Soviet assistance, the Chinese developed heavy industry, establishing a centralized bureaucracy of planning agencies and in-dustrial ministries to manage the economy according to five-year plans. They nationalized private industry. In the early 1950s, they sent communists down to the grassroots to instigate and organize land reform, a violent "class struggle." Each peasant household was classified according to land holdings, and land seized from landlords was redistributed to poor peasants, the majority of the peasantry.[11] Agricul-tural collectivization followed. This process was also essentially coercive, especially in its later stages, but not as violent as land reform.

The "lean to one side" period did feature some Maoist strategies, especially in political participation and socialization. The Chinese implemented many policies by mobilizing the masses in intensive cam-paigns, with essentially compulsory participation. For the Chinese communists, potential regime oppo-nents such as intellectuals and capitalists were capa-ble of being politically transformed through prac-tices such as "thought reform." Communist leaders were sufficiently confident about the results of polit-ical education and regime accomplishments to invite nonparty intellectuals to voice criticism in the Hun-dred Flowers Campaign in 1957. When criticism was harsh, revealing weak support for the communist system, the leaders quickly reversed themselves. They launched an Anti-Rightist Campaign, which discovered more "poisonous weeds" than "blooming flowers." About a half million people, many of them intellectuals, were persecuted as "rightists" in a cam-paign that effectively silenced political opposition for 20 years.[12] Mass campaigns, political education, and political labeling were all coercive measures that resulted in the persecution of millions. To some ex-tent, this coercion had a characteristic Maoist (and Confucian) element: fundamentally, it rejected the Stalinist version of political purge as physical liqui-dation, because it viewed the individual as malleable and ultimately educable. Yet, "enemies of the peo-ple" were not usually spared: one to three million landlords and "counterrevolutionaries" were perse-cuted to death in the early 1950s alone.

In 1956, frictions in relations with the Soviet Union began to develop. Tensions increased throughout the 1950s, resulting in the withdrawal of aid and advisors and a Sino-Soviet split that shocked the world in 1960. Major irritants included Soviet reluctance to support efforts to "liberate" Taiwan,

Soviet unwillingness to aid China's nuclear develop-ment, and a relaxation of Soviet hostility toward the United States. At about the same time, Mao was re-considering his view of the Soviet model of develop-ment and developing his own radical model of building communism.

The first five-year plan had invested in heavy in-dustry, not agriculture. Following the Soviet model, central planners had not diverted resources from in-dustry to promote agricultural growth. In 1958, Mao proposed a strategy of simultaneous development of industry and agriculture, to be achieved in two ways: (1) the labor-intensive mass mobilization of peasants to increase agricultural output by building irrigation facilities and (2) the organization of primitive pro-duction processes to give inputs to agriculture (such as small chemical fertilizer plants and primitive steel furnaces to make tools) without taking resources from industry. A crucial element of Mao's solution was an increase in size of the collective farms. In or-der to build irrigation facilities, local communist of-ficials needed to control a labor force of large num-bers of peasants, larger than the current collectives that grouped together a few hundred households. By combining several collectives into one gigantic farm, Mao hoped to realize economies of scale. In 1958, with prodding from above, the people's communes were born, grouping together thousands of house-holds in one unit of economic and political organiza-tion managed by Communist Party officials.

The Maoist model was not simply an economic development strategy. It was fundamentally a political campaign, a point exemplified in the main slogan of the **Great Leap Forward:** "politics in command."[13] The Great Leap Forward abandoned most material rewards for moral incentives. By 1958, in Mao's view, Chinese peasants had demonstrated tremendous en-thusiasm and were ready to leap into communism, if properly mobilized by local leaders. In the politically charged climate, economic expertise was denigrated and caution criticized as lack of faith in the masses. Leaders in Beijing set output targets high, demanding that local leaders believe in the ability of the Chinese people to accomplish miracles. By implication, failure to achieve high targets could be due only to poor leadership. A dangerous vicious cycle was set in mo-tion: local leaders competed to demonstrate their po-litical correctness; when communes failed to meet targets set in Beijing, local leaders calculated output imaginatively to report targets had been met or exceeded; production results were increasingly exaggerated as reports went to higher and higher levels; the response from Beijing to the falsely reported leap in output was a further leap in targets.

In 1958, dislocation associated with forming the communes and peasant mobilization to help meet high steel output targets by making steel in primitive furnaces was so great that the autumn harvest was not all gathered. That year too, a false belief in excess production led to reduction in areas sown in grain. Even with reduced acreage, peasant contributions to agricultural labor were decreasing due to physical exhaustion, weak material rewards, and the abolition of private plots (and, in some cases, private property for complete communization). In 1959, when top Chinese leaders met to consider problems in the Leap, the Minister of National Defense criticized radicalism in policy implementation. In response, Mao accused the minister of factionalism, turned the meeting into a referendum on his leadership, and challenged others to dare to attack the Leap's radical principles. The meeting was a terrible turning point. With political correctness reasserted, radicalism in the Leap returned. Moreover, just as the 1957 Anti-Rightist Campaign had silenced opposition outside the party, Mao's 1959 accusations and threats effectively silenced opposition in the top echelons of party leadership.[14] That same year, large parts of China suffered from severe drought, others from severe flooding, in one of the worst natural disasters experienced in decades.

Over the next three years, the famine cost an estimated 27 million lives.[15] China retreated from Maoist radicalism. Mao retreated from day-to-day management of public affairs, but continued in his position as Communist Party chairman. In the early 1960s, the communes ceased to be relevant to agricultural production. Instead, peasant households contracted with the state for production, selling the surplus in newly established free markets. In industry, there was a renewed reliance on material incentives, technical expertise, and profitability as the standard to judge performance. The education system emphasized the creation of a knowledgeable and highly skilled corps of managers and leaders. Policy processes took into account advice by experts, rather than reliance on mass miracles.

By the mid-1960s, Mao had further developed his radical critique of the Soviet model and extended it to the Chinese experience. In China, Mao saw a "new class" of economic managers and political officials, privileged by elitist policies that increased social antagonisms. In 1966, Mao argued that many communist leaders (notably, China's head of state, Liu Shaoqi, but also others, including Deng Xiaoping) were corrupt "capitalist roaders" who opposed socialism and must be thrown out of power. He launched a Great Proletarian Cultural Revolution, yet another exercise in radical excess. The **Cultural Revolution** was simultaneously a power struggle, an ideological battle, and a mass campaign to transform culture. Compared to the Leap, its impact on the Chinese economy was minor. Its impact on society, especially in the cities, was devastating, however.

For Mao, the enemy of socialism was within the Communist Party. Unable to rely on the party to correct its mistakes, Mao instructed secondary school and university students to overturn "bourgeois culture" and "bombard the headquarters." The Communist Party became effectively powerless as an organization. For the first time since 1949, Chinese were free to organize politically. Unconstrained by the party, Chinese engaged in political action legitimated by their own interpretations of Mao Zedong Thought. Students formed radical Red Guard groups to criticize and persecute victims, often chosen quite arbitrarily or for reasons more personal than political. In schools, factories, and government agencies, those in power were criticized and persecuted. Persecution was frequently physical. It was not uncommon for victims to be held in makeshift prisons, forced to do harsh manual labor, and subjected to violent public "struggle sessions" to force them to confess their crimes. Many were "struggled" to death, and many others committed suicide. Factional fighting was inevitable, as rival Red Guard groups fought for power, each faction claiming true representation of Mao Zedong Thought.[16]

In 1967, the country was near anarchy. The schools had been shut down; most party and government offices no longer functioned; transportation and communications were severely disrupted; factional struggles were increasingly violent contests, some of them armed confrontations. Having unleashed social conflict, Mao had been able to manipulate it—but not to control it. Mao called on the army to restore order, a process that began in 1969.

The 1970s were years of more moderate conflict, mostly played out as a struggle at the apex of power rather than in society generally. Radical leaders (including Mao's wife) who had risen to power in the Cultural Revolution supported a continuation of radical policies. Other leaders, reinstated by Mao to balance the power of the radicals, supported policies of economic modernization. The conflict was ongoing at the time of Mao's death in 1976. Within two years, the economic modernizers had won. China embarked on a new course of socialist economic and political reform, different from anything in the experience of any communist system.

CHINESE SOCIETY

Chinese society has changed in various ways in the half-century since the communists came to power. These changes include social structural transformations engineered by the regime: the elimination of the landlord, capitalist, and small entrepreneurial classes in the 1950s, for example (although economic reforms of the 1980s and 1990s have promoted the resurgence of private entrepreneurs). This section focuses on basic features that make up the social environment for Chinese politics that have not undergone fundamental transformation but have changed only in degree, if at all.

First among these is China's huge population. When the communists came to power in 1949, China's population was 540 million. Today China remains the world's most populous country, with a population of 1.3 billion. As in the 1950s, most Chinese live in the countryside, although the proportion has been changing more rapidly in recent years. In the 1950s, about 85 percent of Chinese lived in the countryside; by 1980 that proportion had decreased only slightly, to 82 percent. More than two decades of economic reform produced significant transformation. De facto relaxation of rural to urban migration restrictions liberated the underemployed farming population to seek work in cities. Rural industrialization and the growth of towns also changed the situation. By the year 2000, only 64 percent of Chinese lived in the countryside. An increasing proportion of this rural population work at least part-time in industry. Before economic reforms in the 1980s, state-owned enterprises dominated industry in China. Today, rural collective industry, in the form of township and village enterprises under the

direction of local governments, is the most dynamic industrial sector.

The second basic feature involves geography: Although China is the second largest country in area (following Canada), the population is concentrated in the eastern third of the land. This is largely because only about a quarter of China's land is arable. Advances in agricultural mechanization and technology have not resolved China's serious land shortage. Population growth and reduction in cultivated area have exacerbated the problem. Despite strong efforts to preserve arable land for farming, China's leaders have been unable to reverse the reduction in cultivated area for a number of reasons. With decollectivization and the return of household farming, land is wasted on property borders. With the renewal of traditional practices in the more tolerant post-Mao environment, land is used as burial grounds, with graves replacing politically correct cremation. With increased prosperity in the countryside, villagers are building bigger houses. The basic problem of feeding China's large population can be expected to continue to loom large as more Chinese grow prosperous and change their diet: eating more, and eating more meat and less grain.

The third feature is that China is a multiethnic state. At least 92 percent of Chinese are ethnically Han, but there are 55 recognized **minority nationalities,** ranging in size from a few thousand to more than 15 million. Although minorities make up only a fairly small proportion of China's population, areas in which minorities live (usually called "autonomous" areas) comprise more than 60 percent of China's territory, and much of this is in strategically important border regions.[17] This includes Tibet (bordering India) and Xinjiang (bordering three new post-Soviet states), which have experienced fairly continuous minority unrest over the decades. The Chinese have maintained considerable armed forces in these areas to quell secessionist efforts.

Finally, Han Chinese share the same Chinese written language, a unifying force in China for more than two millennia, practically defining what it is to be Chinese. The same written language is spoken in many different dialects, however, often making communication difficult. Mandarin, based on the dialect of the Beijing locality, is the official language promoted by the communist regime through the education system and mass media.

A COMMUNIST PARTY-STATE

From top to bottom, Chinese politics has changed noticeably since the Maoist period. Yet, the essential form of the Chinese political system retains an organizational design borrowed decades ago from the Soviet Union and developed nearly a century ago in Russia by Lenin—the design of the communist **party-state.**

Lenin viewed political legitimacy in ways that justify a monopoly of power by a communist party elite that is not popularly elected. He believed that ordinary citizens do not understand their own real interests and that larger interests of society are not best advanced by aggregating interests that citizens articulate. According to Lenin, as ordinary citizens typically lack revolutionary consciousness and knowledge of communist theory, they are incapable of making the correct choices that will lead from capitalism to socialism and toward communism—a utopia characterized by a high level of economic prosperity, an absence of social conflict, and a minimal role for government. Lenin proposed a solution to this problem: a political party and political system built on the principles of guardianship and hierarchy.[18] To these two principles, Chinese leaders added the idea of the mass line, formulated by Mao in the 1940s. Guardianship and hierarchy define the communist party-state. The mass line adds another dimension, which moderates guardianship.

Guardianship describes the main relationship between the Communist Party and society. The party bases its claim to legitimate rule not on representation of the expressed preferences of a majority but on representation of the "historical best interests" of all the people. In theory, as most ordinary citizens do not know their best interests, society is best led by an elite vanguard party with a superior understanding of the historical laws of development. The Communist Party is therefore an exclusive organization—in China, membership is about 5 percent of the population—not a mass political party with membership open to all. The notion of Communist Party leadership is explicitly set forth in each of the four Chinese constitutions promulgated since 1949, as is

some version of the notion of dictatorship. Currently, the constitution describes the political system as a socialist state under the "people's democratic dictatorship." As the Communist Party is the only organization with the politically correct knowledge to lead society, it is the authoritative arbiter of the interests of the people. In effect, dictatorship in the name of the people is communist party dictatorship. Party leaders today are more informed of public opinion than in the past, but there is no place in the Chinese political system (or in Leninist theory) for organized opposition to Communist Party leadership.

Chinese Communist Party guardianship is, in theory, informed by the practice of the **mass line.** The party leads, but its leadership is not isolated from the opinions and preferences of the mass public. The degree to which mass preferences actually find expression in public policy depends on their fit with larger goals determined by party leaders. Party leaders at all levels (but especially at the grassroots) are supposed to maintain a close relationship with ordinary citizens so that the party organization can transform the "scattered and unsystematic ideas" of the masses into "correct ideas" and propagate them "until the masses embrace them as their own." In this way, policy is supposed to flow "from the masses to the masses."[19]

The internal organization of the Communist Party is organized around a hierarchy of party congresses and committees extending from the top of the system down to the grassroots. Lower party organizations are subordinate to higher party organizations, and individual party members are subordinate to the party as an organization. Inner-party rules for decision making are based on the Leninist principle of **democratic centralism.** Here, democracy refers mainly to consultation. It requires that party leaders provide opportunities for discussion, criticism, and proposals in party organizations (often including lower party organizations) as part of the normal process of deciding important issues or making policy. Centralism requires unified discipline throughout the party: top-level official party decisions are binding on party organizations and members. Centralism is never sacrificed to democracy. Party members are allowed to hold personal views contrary to party decisions and to voice them through proper party channels, but they are not free to act in ways that promote these views. According to the Communist Party constitution, the formation of "factions" or any sort of "small group activity" within the party is a punishable violation of organizational discipline. Communist Party hierarchy and the requirement that party members observe party discipline are designed as organizational guarantees that the party, in exercising leadership over society, acts as a unified force, responsive to the leadership of the highest level of party organization.

Ideology is today much less prominent (and less coherent) in Chinese politics than it was in the past. The principles of guardianship, hierarchy, and the mass line are not inconsequential abstractions, however. They have concrete practical implications, evident throughout the Chinese political system. Change in the system is evident too, of course, both as a product and byproduct of policies of reform in the past two decades. Yet, while the political reforms of the 1980s and 1990s are by no means trivial, they do not add up to fundamental systemic change. For now, as in the past, the design of the communist party-state is a fair model of the organization of political power in China.

POLITICAL STRUCTURES

The design of the communist party-state is perhaps most evident in the organization of power in two hierarchies of political structures, illustrated in Table 9.1. The focus here is politics at the national level, what the Chinese refer to as the political center of the system. Government executives, legislative assemblies, and bureaucracies are duplicated at each level of the political system by Communist Party executives, assemblies, and bureaucracies. In principle, there is a division of labor between party and government structures. In practice, the two often perform similar functions, with party structures and party officials exercising leadership over parallel government structures and government officials. This section on political structures distinguishes the party from the government, while elaborating the variety of mechanisms the party organization employs to exercise control over officials in party and government structures. The sections below on policymaking and policy implementation emphasize that, because of the interconnectedness of party and

T A B L E 9 . 1   Major Structures and Offices at the Political Center in 2005

Head of State: President of the PRC (Hu Jintao)			
Number of Members	Government Structures	Number of Members	Party Structures
	Executives		**Executives**
	Premier (Wen Jiabao)		General Secretary (Hu Jintao)
10	State Council Standing Committee	9	Politburo Standing Committee
35	State Council	24	Politburo
8	Central Military Commission Chairman (Jiang Zemin)	11	Central Military Commission Chairman (Ha Jintao)
	Administration		**Administration**
	State Council General Office		Secretariat
	Government ministries and commissions		Party departments
	Rule Adjudication		**Rule Adjudication**
	Supreme People's Court		Central Discipline Inspection Commission
	Supreme People's Procuratorate		
	Assemblies		**Assemblies**
159	National People's Congress Standing Committee	198	Central Committee
2,951	National People's Congress	2,120	National Party Congress

government, distinctions between party and government are of only limited use in understanding decision making in China. Both party and government structures have undergone changes since 1949. The description below focuses on the system that emerged in the 1980s and 1990s.

Government Structures

At the political center in Beijing, the key government structures are the **National People's Congress (NPC),** which is China's legislature, and the **State Council,** which exercises executive functions. Under the State Council are government ministries and commissions, which have ranged in number from 32 to 100 since 1949. Below the political center, government structures extend downward in a five-tiered hierarchy consisting of 31 provinces, 332 prefectures and large cities, 2,862 counties, 44,891 townships, and about 906,000 villages.[20] Local government structures (local people's congresses, local governments, and government departments) are found at the provincial, county, and township levels and in the large cities. The provincial level includes four huge cities (Beijing, Shanghai, Tianjin, and Chongqing) directly under the central government. Prefectures are formally "dispatched organs" of provinces, coordinating activity between governments at provincial and county levels. Villages are "autonomous mass organizations of self-government," which are not part of the formal state hierarchy.

According to the constitution, the highest organization of state authority is the NPC.[21] The NPC and its permanent body, the NPC Standing Committee, exercise legislative functions. NPC delegates are elected for five-year terms by delegates in provincial-level congresses and the armed forces. Normally, NPC delegates assemble once annually for a plenary session of about two weeks (although they did not meet at all in the years between 1965 and 1975). The number and composition of delegates is prescribed by law, but the NPC has always been huge. In 1986 the law set a ceiling of 3,000 delegates, which is about the number elected to each congress since 1983. By law, urban Chinese are overrepresented: a 1995 law set the ratio of rural to urban Chinese per NPC delegate at 4:1—already less unequal than in previous years, due to legal change as well as urbanization.

Formally, the NPC has extensive powers. This includes amendment of the constitution, passage and amendment of legislation, approval of economic plans and government work reports, and appointment of top state and government leaders. For most of the year, when the NPC is not in session, its Standing Committee of about 150 members, who reside in Beijing and meet regularly throughout the year, serves as the working legislative assembly. The 1982 constitution considerably strengthened the role of the NPC Standing Committee. It now exercises all but the most formal powers of the NPC and prepares the agenda for the annual NPC plenary sessions, when the full NPC typically ratifies its interim legislative actions.

Is the NPC (and its Standing Committee) a "rubber stamp" assembly? For the Maoist years, the answer is clearly "yes." In recent decades, however, the NPC has become more assertive, and its Standing Committee has assumed a greater role in law making. This is part of political reform undertaken in response to the extreme institutional nihilism of the Cultural Revolution. NPC assertiveness is evident in an increase in delegate motions (by an order of magnitude) and, more significantly, in dissenting votes. The practice of unanimous approval, once automatic, has ended, sometimes with embarrassing results. In 1998, 45 percent of NPC delegates demonstrated their disapproval of the government's failure to control corruption by abstaining or voting against the work report of the Chief Procurator. While this high level of dissent remains unusual for votes on work reports, economic plans, and official appointments, dissenting votes of 20 to 30 percent on draft laws are not uncommon. Actual failure to pass legislation submitted to the NPC has occurred on two occasions: a draft of the controversial Enterprise Bankruptcy Law was voted down in 1986, and a very restrictive draft of the Law on Public Demonstrations was voted down not long after the crushing of the 1989 mass protests. Both laws were sent back for substantial revision before securing the requisite majority approval in the NPC. A dramatic example of the new view of NPC authority occurred in 1989, when Hu Jiwei circulated a petition among fellow NPC Standing Committee members to call an emergency meeting of the NPC to exercise its constitutional power to repeal martial law.

The full NPC cannot be expected to function routinely as a credible legislature, because it is too large and meets too infrequently and briefly. More important is the lawmaking role of the less cumbersome NPC Standing Committee. In the early 1980s, many party and government elders retired from important positions in central and provincial administration to the NPC Standing Committee. Instead of retreating from political life, these elders used the Standing Committee as a channel for political influence. Their enhanced role was institutionalized with the establishment of a Legislative Affairs Committee (with significant staff) and permanent specialized legislative committees to consider draft legislation. With these changes, the NPC (and its Standing Committee) can no longer be dismissed as a rubber stamp. The legislature remains institutionally weak, however, for two main reasons, elaborated below: the practice of executive-led government (which does not distinguish the Chinese system from parliamentary systems in other countries) and the practice of Communist Party leadership (which is more fundamental).

In lawmaking, the State Council is the center of government activity, although this role too is newly enhanced.[22] The State Council is composed of the premier, who is head of government, and his cabinet of vice-premiers, state councillors, ministers, auditor general, and secretary general (currently at 35 members, all formally nominated by the premier and appointed by the NPC). In 2003, Wen Jiabao became premier, replacing Zhu Rongji, who had served since 1998. The State Council has its own Standing Committee that meets twice weekly, with members reporting on work in their assigned portfolios. As in parliamentary systems, the bulk of legislation is drafted by specialized ministries and commissions under the direction of the cabinet. Additionally, however, as most Chinese laws are drafted in general and imprecise language, they require detailed "implementing regulations" to produce any effect. These regulations are typically drafted by State Council ministries (under the direction of the newly reestablished State Council Legislation Bureau) and promulgated by the ministries or State Council without consideration by the NPC or its Standing Committee.

The Communist Party exercises direct leadership over government and legislative functions in a variety of ways. Before the NPC assembles, party leaders convene a meeting of all delegates who are members of the Communist Party (more than 80 percent of delegates elected to the Ninth NPC in 1998). At these meetings, leaders discuss the NPC agenda and offer "hopes" of the party leaders for the forthcoming session, including suggestions about the tone (how open or restrained NPC debate should be, for example). NPC powers of appointment are effectively nullified by party control over candidate nomination and the usual practice of an equal number of candidates and positions. For example, although the NPC formally appoints the president, vice president, premier, and cabinet members, there has never been more than one nominee for these positions and candidate nomination is decided at the party meeting convened before the NPC assembles. The only positions for which NPC elections have ever featured choice are the 1988 and 1998 elections to the NPC Standing Committee. Those elections featured no choice for positions of leadership, however, and only limited choice for regular NPC Standing Committee membership (about 6 percent more candidates than positions). As to lawmaking, Communist Party leaders have veto power over all legislation of consequence. The system of party review of legislation that emerged in the early 1990s rejects party micro-management of State Council or NPC Standing Committee work. Nonetheless, all important laws, constitutional amendments, and political laws submitted to the NPC or its Standing Committee must have prior approval by the party center. In short, the Chinese system is executive-led government, but with an important difference having to do with the role of the Communist Party.

The president of the PRC is head of state. This is a purely ceremonial office, held from 1993 to 2003 by Jiang Zemin, now held by **Hu Jintao.** Until the most recent party congress in 2002, Jiang was also head of the Communist Party organization, a position now held by Hu Jintao. Jiang continues to head the Central Military Commission, in which leadership of military forces is formally vested. The commission was established as a government structure only in 1982, but its Communist Party counterpart functioned long before then and remains in existence, headed by Hu Jintao since 2004, when Jiang relinquished the post to him.

Judicial authority rests with the Supreme People's Court at the center and with local people's courts below. Formally, the Supreme People's Court is responsible to the NPC. Courts at lower levels are responsible to the people's congresses at their respective levels and also take direction from courts above them. The Supreme People's Procuratorate, restored in 1978 after decades of neglect, is the central prosecutorial agency. It sits at the top of a hierarchy of procuratorates extending down to the county level, each formally responsible to a local people's congress and each also under the direction of the procuratorate above. The Supreme People's Procuratorate is responsible to the NPC. Procuratorates act as a bridge between public security agencies and the courts. They supervise criminal investigations, approve arrests, and prosecute cases. Beginning in the mid-1980s, the most important role of the procuratorates has been investigation and prosecution of corruption.

Party Structures

At the political center in Beijing, the key party structures are the National Party Congress and its Central Committee, the Politburo, and the Politburo Standing Committee. In addition, party departments are organized under a Secretariat. Below the center, down to the township level, are local party congresses and local party committees.

As in the government hierarchy, while the formal power of Communist Party structures is directly proportional to size of membership, actual impact on policy is inversely proportional to size. The Communist Party constitution vests supreme authority in the **National Party Congress,** but this structure is too big and meets too infrequently to play a significant role in political decision making. The Central Committee determines the number of congress delegates and procedures for their election. Since 1949, National Party Congresses have ranged in size from one to two thousand delegates, with recent congresses at about two thousand delegates, as shown in Table 9.2. In the past, the congresses met irregularly, but party constitutions since 1969 have stipulated that congresses are normally convened at five-year intervals. This has been more or less the practice since 1969 and has been strictly observed in the post-Mao years.

TABLE 9.2   Chinese Communist Party Congresses and Growth of Party Membership, 1921–2002

Congress	Year	Delegates	Party Members
1st	1921	12	More than 50
2nd	1922	12	123
3rd	1923	30	432
4th	1925	20	950
5th	1927	80	57,900[a]
6th	1928	84	40,000
7th	1945	544	1.2 million
Founding of the PRC, 1949			
8th	1956	1,026	11 million
9th	1969	1,512	22 million
10th	1973	1,249	28 million
11th	1977	1,510	35 million
12th	1982	1,575	40 million
13th	1987	1,936	46 million
14th	1992	1,939	51 million
15th	1997	2,108	58 million
16th	2002	2,120	66 million

[a]Communist party membership dropped from 57,900 to 10,000 after April 1927, when the Nationalists broke the "united front" with the communists with a massacre that decimated communist forces and ignited civil war.

Sources: Beijing Review 41, No. 8 (1998), 22; *People's Daily*, 2 September 2002.

Since the founding of the Communist Party in 1921, a total of 16 congresses have met, the most recent in November 2002.

National Party Congress sessions are short, about a week or two at most. A main function is to ratify important changes in broad policy orientation already decided by more important smaller party structures. Although party congresses yield no surprises, these changes receive their highest formal endorsement at the party congresses, and, therefore, the sessions have the public appearance of major historic events. A second function of the National Party Congress is to elect the **Central Committee,** which exercises the powers of the congress between sessions. Official candidates for Central Committee membership are determined by the Politburo before the congress meets. According to the 1982 party constitution, elections to the Central Committee are by secret ballot, and wide deliberation and discussion of candidates precedes them. Of course, centralism prevails: elections rarely offer choice (or much choice) among candidates.

The Central Committee is the Chinese political elite, broadly defined: it is a collection of the most powerful several hundred political leaders in the country. All Central Committee members hold some major substantive position of leadership, as ministers in the central state bureaucracy or provincial party leaders, for example. Membership on the Central Committee reflects this political power—it does not confer it. In this sense, the Central Committee is less important intrinsically as a political structure than extrinsically, for the different sorts of interests and constituencies represented by its members. Although the Central Committee does not initiate policy, changes in policy or leaders at the political center must be approved by it. This is done fairly routinely at plenary sessions now convened at least annually. Party leaders at the top rely on the bureaucratic and regional elites on the Central Committee to ensure that the "party line" is realized in practice. Central Committee membership brings these elites into the process as participants and, in effect, guarantors: in endorsing party policy, members also take on responsibility for its realization.

The Central Committee elects the **Politburo,** the Politburo Standing Committee, and the party general secretary—all of whom are also Central Committee members. These are the leaders at the very apex of the political system. The composition of these structures is determined by party leaders before the party congress, and elections are mainly ceremonial, featuring no candidate choice. The Politburo is the top political elite, usually no more than two dozen leaders, most of whom have responsibility for overseeing policymaking in some issue area. Its inner circle is the Politburo Standing Committee, typically no more than a half-dozen leaders, who meet about once weekly, in meetings convened and chaired by the party general secretary. Members of the Politburo and its Standing Committee are the core political decision makers in China, presiding over a process that concentrates great power at the top.

Since the abolition of the position of party chairman in 1982, the top party leader is the general secretary, a position held by Hu Jintao since 2002 (see Box 9.1). The change in terminology reflects the effort to promote collective leadership, a reaction against norms of past years when Mao presided as nearly all-powerful chairman of the party until his death in 1976. Yet, if general secretaries in the 1980s and 1990s have been less powerful than Chairman Mao, this has mainly to do with the unusual elite politics of the post-Mao transition period and especially the role of Deng Xiaoping.[23]

In communist systems, the death of the top leader creates a succession crisis: there is no formal or generally acknowledged position of second-in-command and no regularized mechanism to choose a new top leader. Mao's death ushered in a power struggle at the top, won by Deng and his fellow modernizers. Deng, already in his seventies at the time of Mao's death, chose to eschew top formal leadership of party or government in the interest of resolving the problem of succession. Under Deng, elite politics was organized as "leadership by lines." In the late 1970s, communist party elders who had formerly held important positions of power were reinstated after years of forced retirement during the Cultural Revolution. Within a few years, however, many of them retired (or semiretired) to the "second line," to serve as advisors and involve themselves only in major policy issues or broad strategy. At the very top, a half-dozen elders, all senior communist revolutionaries in their eighties or nineties, continued to play key roles in decision making and occupy formal positions of leadership, although not the top party or government positions. The best example, of course, was "paramount leader" Deng himself. Deng never held the top formal position of leadership in party or government, although he was on the Politburo

B O X   9 . 1   Hu Jintao and Political Succession

In November 2002, Jiang Zemin relinquished the key political position as Communist Party general secretary to Hu Jintao. This event marks the first time in PRC history that the transfer of party leadership has occurred as a regular matter at a party congress, rather than as a result of the death or political purge of the incumbent. Hu kept a low profile during his decade at the center of Chinese politics before 2002, but inklings of what his leadership may hold for China are nonetheless evident. Hu spent most of his adult life in some of the poorest regions of China, including Tibet. Yet, he does not appear to be an inward-focused politi-cal conservative. Typical of his generation of leaders, Hu is a technocrat: a graduate in hydraulic engineering of prestigious Qinghua University. He strongly sup-ported Jiang's call in 2000 to recruit the commercial, technical, and professional elite into the Communist Party. As president of the Central Party School, he su-pervised bold studies of political reform, including re-form of the party. More generally, Hu is a member of the "fourth generation" of Chinese leaders, the least dogmatic and most open-minded cohort to accede to top positions in Chinese politics. In March 2003, Hu succeeded Jiang Zemin as President of the PRC.

Standing Committee until 1987 and chaired the Cen-tral Military Commission until 1989. Just below this very small group at the top, elders retired to advisory positions on a Central Advisory Commission, set up in 1982. Other elders "retired" to formal positions on the NPC. Younger leaders were promoted to the top positions on the "first line," to allow them to de-velop their own bases of support and authority, with the support of their elder patrons.

Leadership by lines did not provide a smooth solution to the succession problem, however. In principle, elders on the second line used their pres-tige and informal power to support younger leaders in top executive positions. In practice, younger lead-ers on the first line, in the effort to establish their own authority, sometimes adopted positions at odds with the views of elder patrons. Friction with party elders resulted in two purges of top party executives in the 1980s: Hu Yaobang was dismissed as party general secretary in 1987, his successor Zhao Ziyang in 1989 (see Figure 9.1). The situation today is dif-ferent: by the mid-1990s, most of the elders at the very top, including Deng, had "gone to see Marx," and the Central Advisory Commission had been dis-mantled, having served its purpose of easing leaders into retirement. After a dozen years as party secre-tary and beneficiary of Deng's support until Deng's death in 1997, Jiang Zemin stepped down in 2002, lending his support to Hu Jintao.

The party has its own set of bureaucratic struc-tures, managed by the Secretariat. The Secretariat provides staff support for the Politburo, transforming Politburo decisions into instructions for subordinate party departments. Compared with their government counterparts, party departments are fewer in number and have more broadly defined areas of competence.

The Discipline Inspection Commission (DIC), a specialized rule adjudication organization subordi-nate to the Central Committee, was reinstated in 1978 to enforce standards of conduct for party members—including ideological, political, and organizational standards as well as party rules prohibiting various sorts of "inappropriate practices." An initial task for the DIC was to help restore political and organiza-tional order to the Communist Party, after serious damage to party discipline during and after the Cul-tural Revolution. Throughout the 1980s and 1990s, the DIC and local discipline inspection committees have investigated party members engaged in corrup-tion, and recommended disciplinary actions, ranging from a "warning" to expulsion from the party. In the 1980s and 1990s, discipline inspection committees meted out some form of punishment to more than 2.5 million party members, of which more than 500,000 were punished with expulsion from the party.

People's Liberation Army

The **People's Liberation Army (PLA),** which in-cludes the navy, air force, and army, has played a major role in Chinese politics. Party and army were practically inseparable until 1949. After 1949, the PLA participated in important nonmili-tary functions, such as economic construction. In the Cultural Revolution, the PLA was brought more directly into politics to resolve violent fac-tional struggles in society, at a time when party and government structures had been shattered. In

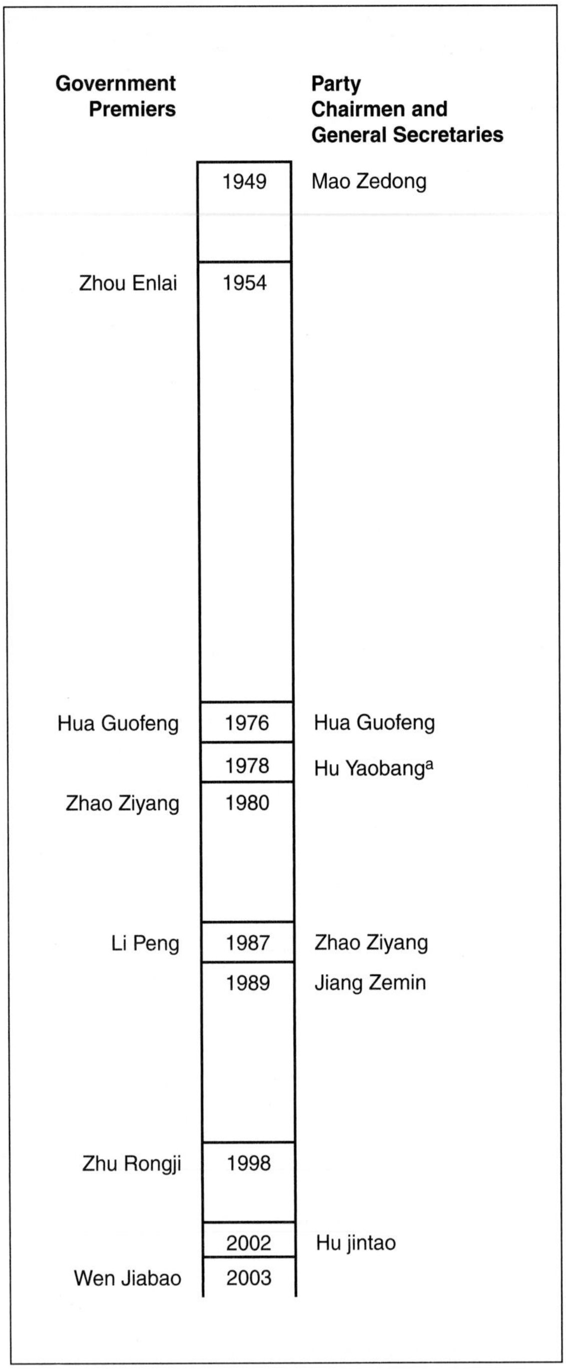

Government Premiers		Party Chairmen and General Secretaries
	1949	Mao Zedong
Zhou Enlai	1954	
Hua Guofeng	1976	Hua Guofeng
	1978	Hu Yaobang[a]
Zhao Ziyang	1980	
Li Peng	1987	Zhao Ziyang
	1989	Jiang Zemin
Zhu Rongji	1998	
	2002	Hu jintao
Wen Jiabao	2003	

FIGURE 9.1   Top Party and Government Executives, 1949–2003

[a]The office of party general secretary was revived in 1978. Hu Yaobang became general secretary while Hua Guofeng was chairman of the party. The office of chairman (and Hua's leadership role) was formally eliminated in 1982.

1989, the PLA was instrumental in crushing the mass protests.

The PLA does not dictate policy to party leaders, but it is the self-appointed guardian of Chinese sovereignty and nationalism, with a particular interest in preventing Taiwan's independence.[24] This is the issue with the greatest potential to spark military confrontation, and it is a matter the Chinese claim is completely internal.

Since the mid-1980s, the PLA has engaged in a program of military modernization and professionalization, increasing defense expenditures, procuring new weapons systems and technologies, and streamlining forces to realize a "smaller but stronger" force of 2.5 million. Despite this, the military gap between China and the West is not narrowing, but widening, as Western military technological advances continue at an increasingly rapid pace. The PLA is at least a decade behind in almost all weapons systems and remains predominantly a land force.

Party Leadership in Political Structures

Party and government structures from top to bottom are staffed by more than 40 million officials on state salaries. One important mechanism of party leadership, described above, is the structural arrangement: the duplication of political structures and the dominance of party structures and leaders over government structures and leaders. The Chinese Communist Party exercises leadership in political structures in other ways too. Among the most important are overlapping directorships, "party core groups," party membership penetration, and the *nomenklatura* system. Mechanisms of party leadership specific to policymaking are discussed in a later section.

The **nomenklatura system** is the most important mechanism by which the communist party exerts control over officials. In some sense, it is the linchpin of the political system. It refers to the management of all party and government officials (including state enterprise officials) in positions of importance by party committees exercising authority over all major personnel decisions such as appointment, promotion, transfer, and removal from office. Management authority is organized hierarchically and specified in lists of official positions. Any official at or above the rank of section chief is on such a list.[25] This amounted to about eight million officials in the late 1980s, and the number must be considerably higher now. At present, party committees, through their organization departments, directly manage all officials in positions one level down the administrative hierarchy. At the top of the system, the Politburo exercises direct management authority over all officials at the provincial level in the territorial hierarchy and at the ministerial level in the bureaucratic hierarchy—about 7,000 officials in all. This includes the entire NPC Standing Committee, for example.

While the reforms of the 1980s and 1990s significantly devolved economic authority, little effort has been made to diminish the *nomenklatura* system. The extension of management authority downward in a hierarchy of dyadic relationships that are known to officials has important implications. Party leaders have a means of ensuring that the real constituency of every important official is the superior party committee—and ultimately the Central Committee and its Politburo. In looking ahead to career advancement, then, even officials who owe their positions formally to elections must look upward to "selectorates" of party committees rather than only (if at all) downward to electorates of congress deputies and ordinary citizens. Otherwise, they can be penalized. For example, for his effort in 1989 to assert NPC authority to repeal martial law, Hu Jiwei was expelled from the NPC Standing Committee.

Another means by which the Communist Party exercises leadership over officials is in party membership penetration in political structures. The vast majority of officials in political structures (including government structures and positions filled by elections) are Communist Party members. At their places of work, officials are members of party committees, general branches, or branches located in a hierarchy of basic-level party organizations. They meet regularly to participate in party "organizational life," which is quite apart from their professional work. They are obliged to observe the inner-party discipline of democratic centralism. The routine activities of party branches in government offices are supervised by departments specially assigned to ensure that the Communist Party remains an active force in government structures. Because the party monopolizes opportunities to get along and ahead in the Chinese political system, the organizational hierarchy and party discipline designed to guarantee unified party leadership over society also promote party leadership in political structures.

Separate from the basic-level party organizations that bring party members in all workplaces under the communist party hierarchy are party core groups, formed in government structures only and composed of a handful of party members who hold the most senior positions.[26] The head of the party core group is normally also the head of the structure: for example, government ministers typically head party core groups of their respective ministries. Party core groups are appointed by the party committees one level up, and they answer to these party committees. While basic-level party organizations are mechanisms to promote unity and discipline under party leadership within political structures overall, party core groups are mechanisms to promote party leadership over leaders in their government host structures. Between 1987 and 1988, the system of party core groups was formally abolished (and many were actually dismantled) as part of a brief reform effort to separate party and government functions. Party core groups were quickly revived in 1989, however, after the purge of Zhao Ziyang, the leader most closely associated with the reform.

Finally, the structural distinctions illustrated in Table 9.1 mask significant overlap of directorates in party and government structures. The most obvious example is not illustrated in the table, however, as it changed with the most recent party congress. Until November 2002, Jiang Zemin was concurrently head of state, head of the party, and chairman of the Central Military Commission of both government and party. This particular concentration of high formal offices in one person is unprecedented in PRC history, but Hu Jintao may soon match it. The practice of "wearing two hats" (party and government) has always been common. Premier Wen Jiabao is also at the apex of party power, as a member of the Politburo Standing Committee. Wu Bangguo, who chairs the NPC Standing Committee, is also a member of the Politburo Standing Committee. Overlapping directorships were much more extensive in the past than they are now. Membership of local party committees and their parallel governments used to be indistinguishable. In the 1980s, overlapping directorships were retained at the political center but practically eliminated at lower levels.

ELITE RECRUITMENT

Some key features of elite recruitment emerge from the discussion above. First, membership in the Communist Party is a prerequisite for political elite status. Over the decades, the party has changed its focus of recruitment in society, reflecting larger changes in policy orientation. In the 1950s, for example, the party recruited most intensely among industrial workers, to build a more traditional communist party from a largely peasant base. In the Cultural Revolution of the 1960s and 1970s, radical leftist standards dominated—and recruitment was directed toward the less educated and less well-connected. In the 1980s and 1990s, the party focused its recruitment effort on intellectuals, professionals, and, since 2000, private entrepreneurs, all social groups identified as important for China's development as a prosperous nation. Second, the party controls not only accessibility to this fundamental prerequisite for elite status, but also possesses a powerful organizational mechanism to recruit and promote elites: the *nomenklatura* system. Both appointed and elected leaders are vetted for office, level by level, such that a party committee at some level is the real constituent for leaders below. Beijing has not relinquished this key power, despite significant economic decentralization in recent decades.

What determines who gets along and ahead in the Chinese political system? That is, what criteria have leaders at higher levels viewed as most important for promotion? While much is made of the role of informal politics in China, a systematic study of provincial leaders from 1949 to the present shows that economic performance is the most important determinant of elite promotion in the post-Mao era of reform.[27] Leaders in provinces with higher economic growth or revenue contributions to the center during their tenure are less likely to be demoted or retired from office. In short, to win the support of their real constituents in Beijng, provincial leaders have to "deliver the goods." This is not surprising, considering that leaders in Beijing have staked their claim to legitimacy on precisely this outcome.

RULE BY LAW

The principle of "rule of law" is traditionally associated with liberal democratic ideals. It implies a particular relationship between individuals and the state, the essence of which is protection of individual rights by limitations on arbitrary state power. Such limitations are enshrined in the law and in legal institutions. This notion makes no sense in traditional communist ideology, which does not view law (or the state) as neutral. From the communist viewpoint, law is part of politics. Law is viewed from the perspective of class struggle, as a weapon of the state to use in exercising dictatorship. Chinese communist leaders have never acknowledged rule of law as a legitimate view. In 1978, however, Chinese leaders began to revive and develop important ideas and institutions of legality that had flourished for a brief period in the 1950s. The new Chinese legality is a depoliticized view of law, which acknowledges **rule by law.**[28] Briefly, this means: there are laws, and all are equally subject to them. As the second principle is often violated, this may seem a trivial advance. It is not. The ongoing effort to establish rule by law in China has already changed the way Chinese act and think, in important ways.

The initial Chinese experiment with "socialist legality" began with the promulgation of the first constitution in 1954 and ended in 1957 with the Anti-Rightist Movement. Legalistic perspectives were rejected as examples of "bourgeois rightist" thinking. Legal scholars and legal professionals were criticized and labeled as "rightists." Work on development of criminal law stopped. Legal training and legal scholarship practically ceased. Defense lawyers disappeared from the legal process. Communist party committees took direct control of legal proceedings. The abandonment of law reached a peak during the Cultural Revolution, when violent "class struggle" and "mass justice" substituted for any regularized procedures to resolve social conflicts. This degree of radical lawlessness was not characteristic of the entire Maoist period, but a general official hostility to law prevailed from the late 1950s.

Legal reform began in 1978. The legal system, barely functioning at the time, required urgent action, for a number of reasons. First, there was an immediate need to establish legitimacy by righting past wrongs: investigating and reversing verdicts of dubious legality issued during the Cultural Revolution was a high priority. Second, Deng Xiaoping and other leaders wanted not only to restore public order and stability after years of chaos and uncertainty, but also to express their commitment to system building as a substitute for arbitrary political rule. Finally and not least of all, Chinese leaders hoped that the new legality would encourage economic investment and growth by promoting predictability—through transparent rules and impartial rule adjudication.

Rule by law requires laws. Nearly 30 years after the founding of the PRC, there was no criminal law. In 1978, Chinese leaders appointed committees of legal specialists to pick up work set aside for decades and to draft criminal codes for immediate promulgation. In 1979, the NPC passed the first criminal law and criminal procedure law. In the years that followed, as government agencies issued interim regulations that amended and clarified the hastily drafted laws, the NPC Legislative Affairs Committee worked on legal revisions. In 1996 and 1997, the NPC passed substantially amended and more precise versions of the laws. The 1997 amended criminal law takes into account changes in the Chinese economy that have created opportunities for economic crimes almost unimaginable in 1979 (such as insider securities trading, for example). It abolishes the vaguely defined crimes of "counterrevolution." The 1996 amended criminal procedure law grants the accused the right to seek counsel (a right rejected in the 1950s) at an early stage of legal proceedings.

Rule by law implies equality before the law. This idea stands in sharp contrast to both the politicized view of law in communist ideology and routine practices in the Maoist years. In 1978, the NPC restored the procuratorates, which had been abolished in the 1960s. A new important role of procuratorates in the 1980s and 1990s has been investigation and prosecution of official crimes, for which procuratorates have full independent responsibility, according to law. Chinese leaders have regularly and prominently voiced a commitment to equality before the law, stating that officials who abuse public office and violate laws must be punished. Equality before the law, labeled "bourgeois" in the 1950s, is featured in the 1982 constitution—which also, for the first time, subjects the Communist Party (not only party members) to the authority of the law. At the same time, as described in another section below, there has been an explosion of corruption in recent years. In practice, the Communist Party, through its political-legal committees and its system of discipline inspection committees, routinely protects officials from equality before the law in cases involving abuses of power.

At the end of the 1970s, most Chinese were ignorant of laws and mistrustful of legal channels, a reasonable position when politics routinely superceded law. In the 1980s, the authorities launched a number of campaigns to educate ordinary citizens about the content of important laws and about ideas such as equality before the law. Development of legal norms when legality has been actively denounced (not merely neglected) for decades has been difficult. Yet, ordinary Chinese do use law to pursue their interests. One indicator of the effect of the legal education effort is the growth in lawsuits against government agencies and officials under the administrative litigation law. The number of such lawsuits processed in the legal system has increased steadily since passage of the law in 1989, reaching nearly 80,000 cases tried in 1996. Even in cases not won outright in court, out of court settlements that favor plaintiffs have become sufficiently common to make lawsuits worthwhile.[29]

Legal reform has provoked criticism of Chinese law and legal practices outside China.[30] Three examples illustrate. First, Chinese criminal law stipulates the death penalty in "serious circumstances" of smuggling, rape, theft, bribery, trafficking in women and children, and corruption. In periodic intensive efforts to "strike hard" at crime, the authorities have resorted widely to capital punishment. Critics argue that capital punishment is excessively harsh for these crimes. Second, by design, criminal proceedings are inquisitorial (not adversarial), focused on determination of punishment (not guilt). As cases are prosecuted only after sufficient evidence has been collected to demonstrate guilt, most prosecutions result in guilty verdicts. The right to seek counsel at an early stage of proceedings is recognized in the law, but the requirement is only that a public defender be assigned no later than ten days before trial. By that time, the case has been prepared for prosecution, and usually a confession (for which the law promises leniency) has already been obtained. This practice of "verdict first, trial second" has been questioned and debated inside China and criticized outside China. Finally, despite abolition of specifically political crimes of counterrevolution, the Chinese authorities acknowledge "several thousand" political prisoners. While human rights groups estimate the number to be much larger, all critics view the situation as essentially inconsistent with the new law.

Nonetheless, the new legality has produced significant change. Today, the Chinese state is more

An unemployed writer and a street trader are about to be executed for arson in connection with demonstrations in Sichuan Province in June 1989. Demonstrations occurred in most cities in China at the time of the Tiananmen protests but usually without violence.

Pascal/Distribution Vu

constrained by laws and Chinese citizens freer by laws from political arbitrariness than ever before. Abuse of authority is acted on differently from before. The law is a weapon, because the regime has invested heavily in it. To the extent that, in practice, a double standard for citizens and officials persists, the law is a political weapon, which ordinary citizens can take up against perceived injustice. The official effort to build rule by law, by making law salient, has produced a basis for "rightful resistance" to hold the regime accountable to its own proclaimed standards.

POLITICAL SOCIALIZATION

Communist regimes tend to be not merely authoritarian but totalitarian in their reach. When communists gain power not through the ballot box but through victory in war, as did the Chinese, effective rule requires a major effort to build popular support for the regime and its goals. Further, embedded in the Leninist principle of Communist Party guardianship is the idea of tutelage: under socialism, the party rules as an enlightened vanguard, but the transition to communism requires that ordinary citizens acquire "revolutionary consciousness." This implies a huge project of social engineering, involving the de-

struction (or transformation) of tradition and inculcation of new socialist values.

The project to build "a new socialist man" was attempted with great thoroughness and zeal in Maoist China. How successful was the political socialization of the Maoist years? It is practically impossible to assess the degree to which revolutionary values were in fact internalized. Yet, a multitude of biographical and autobiographical accounts seems to indicate only a superficial victory of the regime—in transforming public discourse, from the traditional attachment to harmony and consensus to the communist principle of class struggle. During the Cultural Revolution, for example, ordinary Chinese proved adept at using stridently ideological language to pursue private goals, striking out at bosses and personal enemies with harmful political labels.[31] Political study also appears to have yielded little change in values. Over time, Chinese learned the rules of political conduct under the regime and acted out political study, criticism, and self-criticism as new political rituals.[32]

For ordinary Chinese, among the most important features distinguishing the Maoist from the post-Mao regime are the greatly reduced scope, less radical style, and substantially different message of the current political socialization effort. In defining economic growth as the main task of the regime, post-Mao reformers rejected a basic premise of political socialization in the Maoist years. According to Mao, ordinary Chinese, through political education, could undergo value change far in advance of the sorts of economic change that orthodox communist theory views as necessarily prior. For example, in the Great Leap Forward, Mao argued that Chinese peasants could be mobilized to "leap" into a communist way of thinking and acting, although the rural economy was far from producing the material abundance of a communist utopia. Mao also believed that intensive thought reform could transform the worldview of Chinese intellectuals and win them over to regime goals soon after the party had won power. The political socialization effort of Mao's successors has different and more modest aims. As discussed in the section on political participation below, Mao's successors no longer require active participation to support regime goals, much less internalization of regime values. Rather, it is generally sufficient that ordinary Chinese do not actively oppose the regime.

Post-Mao leaders have minimal political socialization aims for most Chinese. Basically, they demand passive support for the communist party as the only organization that can lead China to achieve its economic goals. Old appeals to ordinary Chinese to "serve the people" and "fight revisionism and self-interest" have been replaced by official encouragement to individuals and localities to enrich themselves (and, presumably, thereby enrich the country). For the most part, the inspirational revolutionary exemplars of Maoist years have been replaced by models of individual entrepreneurship. Indeed, in 2002 the communist party endorsed the remarkable principle that it represented not only ordinary working people, but also previously villified groups such as intellectuals and private entrepreneurs. Entrepreneurs were officially welcomed into the communist party.

The emphasis on individual prosperity and material incentives is a reversal in the content of norms promoted by the Communist Party. In terms of style too, socialization today has changed. It is far less intrusive than before. Radical efforts to transform the way ordinary Chinese think have been largely abandoned. Undoubtedly, this is partly because appeals to material self-interest are easier to promote than ideals of putting community and country first. Also, however, the retreat

from aggressive political socialization is a deliberate policy of political liberalization (to support economic goals) as well as a byproduct of economic liberalization.

Consider the issue of economic liberalization. One result of the economic policy of opening up to the outside is that Chinese leaders today cannot control information as in the Maoist years.[33] Ordinary Chinese are now routinely exposed to news and opinions about public affairs in their country through access to Hong Kong (which maintains relatively free and critical mass media) and the outside world in newspapers, books, radio and television broadcasts, and the Internet. In June 1998, Chinese citizens heard the president of the United States articulate an unambiguously critical American perspective on the status of human rights in China in a press conference that was televised live across the country. This sort of political liberalization is not only an inevitable byproduct of economic reform, however. It is also a policy choice. Post-Mao leaders have chosen to allow a variety of different messages to compete for the attention of ordinary Chinese. One result of this is the dilution in importance of the state-dominated mass media, with a virtual explosion of new publications in China today. In 1978, there were fewer than 900 periodicals and 200 newspapers with a provincial circulation in China; today, there are more than 8,000 periodicals and more than 1,000 provincial newspapers. To be sure, not all messages are acceptable. Yet, most of the new periodicals do not touch on politics, offering instead the latest perspectives on sports, fashion, music, and movie stars. New academic journals carry lively scholarly discussions about the economy, law, and politics—but Chinese leaders still reserve the right to shut down publications that in their view promote opposition to Communist Party rule.

The new content and style of political socialization is also clearly evident in the education system. Mao's successors inherited an educational system designed to build communist values—and fundamentally at odds with the priority of economic growth. During the Cultural Revolution, the "elitist" system of secondary and tertiary schooling was completely transformed. Secondary school graduates were sent to urban factories or rural communes to acquire at least a few years of work experience and learn from the masses. University entrance examinations were

Workers enjoy the ancient Chinese game of *weiqi* (Go), without fear of criticism for bourgeois decadence.

Lili Niu

replaced with recommendations by urban and rural grassroots leaders, based on demonstrated revolutionary political credentials. With the persecution of scholars and denigration of expert knowledge in the universities, the content of university education was redesigned to include more politics in every specialization and produce graduates who were more politically correct ("red") than technically skilled ("expert"). An entire decade was lost. The generation that missed out on a quality education during the Cultural Revolution, millions of them sent to the countryside to be educated by the peasantry, is known today as the "lost generation." In the late 1970s, acknowledging that economic modernization requires experts and a respect for expertise, Chinese leaders reinstated university entrance examinations and ordered university curriculum to be redesigned.

POLITICAL CULTURE

Older and middle-aged Chinese have experienced not only the radicalism of the Maoist years, but also more than two decades of "reform and opening" to the outside world. Young Chinese have only the personal experience of the relatively open post-Mao years, including the decade of the 1990s that saw the "third wave" of democratization, with the triumph

of democracy in nearly every communist country. When asked about the most memorable event in their lifetime, Chinese of all ages talk mainly about recent events such as the post-Mao reforms.[34] Surely recent changes, both inside and outside China, have left their imprint on the way Chinese view their government and their relationship to political authorities. Because Maoist-era leaders regarded social science with great suspicion, we have no good baseline of public opinion data by which to assess change over time in the beliefs of ordinary Chinese. We can say something about the Chinese political culture today, however, because of a recent explosion of survey research in China. This includes surveys organized and conducted by political scientists based in the United States. What is the orientation toward politics of ordinary Chinese? In particular, to what extent do the beliefs of Chinese seem conducive to political change in the direction of further democratization?

An important building block for democracy is a citizenry knowledgeable about politics and interested in public affairs, so as to be able to monitor the performance of representatives and leaders. Most ordinary Chinese follow public affairs at least weekly, mainly through radio or television programs and somewhat less through newspapers, but politics is not something that is a regular topic of discussion in China. A majority say they *never* talk about politics with others, a stark reflection of lack of active interest. Political knowledge and interest is not uniformly distributed in China, of course. A more active knowledge and interest is seen among men, the more highly educated, and Chinese with higher incomes, which is not so different from what we observe in other countries. Not surprisingly, Chinese in Beijing are much more interested in politics than Chinese overall, and in fact they discuss politics very frequently. Yet, even if we consider the situation of Chinese overall, which includes the relatively less knowledgeable and less interested rural population, political knowledge in China today is higher than in Italy in the early 1960s and political discourse higher than in Italy or Mexico in the early 1960s.[35]

How do the Chinese view their communist government? With the increased availability of information on other countries, including liberal democracies, do Chinese see their relationship with political authorities differently? Moreover, does the Chinese political culture reflect traditional values—the influence of Confucianism, which conceived of legitimacy to rule in moral terms? Perhaps the most interesting perspective on contemporary Chinese political culture is a comparative one that considers its fate across three different Chinese political systems. An extraordinary survey of a representative sample of Chinese in mainland China, Hong Kong, and Taiwan, conducted in 1993 and 1994, provides this perspective and helps to sort out different influences of traditional culture, political system, and socio-economic development.[36] Figure 9.2 compares

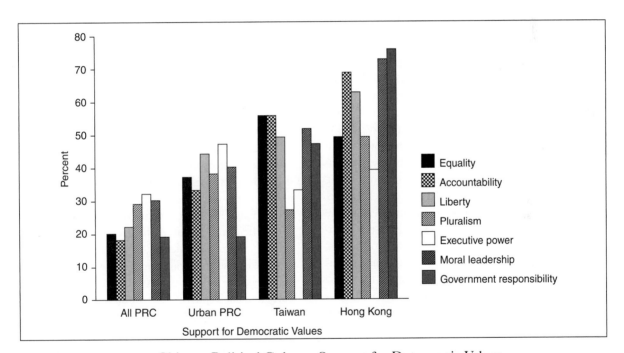

FIGURE 9.2   Chinese Political Culture: Support for Democratic Values in the PRC, Taiwan, and Hong Kong

Percent is percent expressing *disagreement* with statements below.
Equality: "Better educated people should have more say in politics."
Accountability: "Top government officials are like the heads of a big family. We should follow all their decisions on national issues."
Liberty: "The government should have the power to decide which opinions (perspectives) are to be circulated in a society and which are not."
Pluralism: "If there are several political groups, peace and harmony will be disrupted."
Executive power: "If a government is often constrained by an assembly, it will not be able to achieve great accomplishments."
Moral leadership: "We can leave everything to morally upright leaders."
Government responsibility: "The profusion of moral problems in society is the government's fault."

Source: Yun-han Chu and Yu-tzung Chang, "Culture Shift and Regime Legitimacy: Comparing Mainland China, Taiwan, and Hong Kong," in Shiping Hua, ed., *Chinese Political Culture, 1989–2000* (Armonk, N.Y.: M. E. Sharpe, 2001), pp. 332–333. Based on surveys conducted in 1993 and 1994.

responses of ordinary Chinese in the PRC, Hong Kong, and Taiwan to questions about political relationships. Five questions tap orientations to political equality, popular accountability, political liberty, political pluralism, and constraints on executive power. Two questions frame relationships in traditional Confucian terms of virtuous leaders and government responsibility for moral problems. Altogether, these questions probe Chinese support for values commonly associated with liberal democracy.

The array of responses in Figure 9.2 reveals a fairly consistent, easily interpretable, and striking pattern. First, there seems to be a strong impact of political system. A majority of Chinese in the PRC reject every democratic value, and support for democratic values is generally lowest in the PRC. This is not surprising. By the early 1990s, when this survey was conducted, Taiwan's process of democratization was well underway. Hong Kong, while still under British colonial rule, had enjoyed very significant civil liberties for decades and was taking initial steps to increase electoral competition. Second, the influence of non-Chinese political socialization is evident. The traditional Confucian orientation to the moral state is least evident in Hong Kong: nearly three-fourths of Hong Kong Chinese reject the views that everything should be left up to virtuous leaders and that the government is responsible for moral problems in society. By contrast, these views find overwhelming support in the PRC: they are rejected by only 30 and 19 percent, respectively. Chinese in Taiwan are somewhere in the middle, perhaps reflecting rule by a Chinese government but a society long open to outside influences. Third, and perhaps most interesting of all for speculation about support for democratization in the PRC, the responses show an impact of socio-economic development. This is most evident in a comparison of responses in the PRC overall with those in urban China only. With the exception of the last question, urban Chinese are much more supportive of democratic values than mainland Chinese generally. In fact, urban mainland Chinese have a stronger democratic orientation than their Taiwanese counterparts on some items. This contrast should not be exaggerated, however. Urban mainland Chinese are by no means overwhelmingly democratic: there is not a single democratic value on which we find majority support among them.

In sum, traditional Chinese values of hierarchical relationships and moral authority appear to prevail in the PRC. The mass political culture, especially in urban China, does not uniformly reject democratic values. Yet, overall, only about 20 to 30 percent of the population have orientations favorable to democratization.[37] The responses suggest that, barring the introduction of very major political change by the leaders themselves, popular disgruntlement about the performance of the government is unlikely to transform itself into collective action for regime change. Overall, the mainland Chinese are "elitist and authority-oriented," and this contributes to the stability of the communist regime.[38] Of course, most of these surveys were conducted about a decade ago—and China has continued to change, at an increasing pace.

POLITICAL PARTICIPATION

In the communist party-state, political participation, interest articulation, and interest aggregation are processes that are different from those normally found in liberal democratic systems. The source of difference is, of course, different conceptions of the relationship between leaders and citizens: the notion of guardianship is fundamentally incompatible with liberal democratic notions of representation. The Communist Party organization claims to represent the interests of all society, but it rejects, as unnecessary and unacceptable, organized interest groups independent of the Communist Party and political parties other than the communists. While there has been change in political processes in recent decades, the "officially acceptable" forms of political participation, interest articulation, and interest aggregation in the Chinese political system nonetheless continue to reflect the relationship of guardianship between party and society. Although moderated somewhat by the mass line, which emphasizes consultation, this relationship essentially structures political participation as a hierarchical top-down process, restricts interest articulation to individual contacting of officials, and leaves little place for interest aggregation outside the Communist Party. This section discusses political participation; the next section explores interest articulation and aggregation.

Officially Acceptable Political Participation

An important aspect of political reform undertaken after Mao's death in 1976 has been the redefinition of what constitutes "officially acceptable" political participation in the Chinese system. This is part of the process of political liberalization within a framework of Communist Party dominance. Guidelines for the new political participation are evident in three categories of rule changes that have routinized participation and reduced its burden for ordinary Chinese. The changes reflect an official reaction against the disruption that characterized mass participation in the Maoist years (especially during the Cultural Revolution), an official assumption that economic growth is predicated on order and stability, and an official recognition that changes in economic relationships require adjustments in political relationships.

The first category of rule changes involves political participation, which has become essentially optional for ordinary Chinese since the early 1980s. In the first 30 years of communist rule, for a broad range of political activities, failure to participate was considered tantamount to opposition to the communist regime. Today, politics intrudes far less in the lives of ordinary Chinese. The scope and demands of politics have shrunk. The single most important measure signifying this change is the official removal, in 1979, of all class and political labels. After 30 years, Chinese are no longer formally identified by class background or past "political mistakes." Not only does politics no longer dominate daily life, but in the diminished sphere of political activities, political apathy is no longer risky for ordinary Chinese. Certainly, local leaders continue to mobilize people for some activities (voting, for example), but political participation is no longer widely enforced in an atmosphere of coercion.

The second category has been the assiduous avoidance by the regime to rouse the mass public to realize policy objectives. In the Maoist years, by contrast, the quintessential form of political participation was the **mass mobilization campaign**—intensive, large-scale, disruptive group action, implemented by grassroots leaders. The Great Leap Forward launched in 1958 and the Cultural Revolution launched in 1966 were essentially mass campaigns, on a gargantuan scale (with some unique features, of course). Typically in mass campaigns, grassroots party leaders, responding to signals from the political center, roused ordinary Chinese to achieve regime goals of various sorts, often aimed at identified categories of enemies—such as "counter-revolutionaries" in 1950–1951, the "landlord class"

in 1950–1952, "rightists" in 1957, and "unclean cadres" in 1962–1963. Mass campaign methods were adopted for nonpolitical objectives too, such as the ill-conceived and ecologically harmful effort to eradicate "four pests" (sparrows, rats, flies, and mosquitoes) in 1956. Participation in campaigns was virtually compulsory. In the highly politicized environment that characterized all campaigns, lack of active enthusiasm was equated with lack of support for regime goals. Although undoubtedly a burden for the vast majority, the campaigns presented opportunities for the politically ambitious. For leaders at the grassroots, campaigns were opportunities to demonstrate to their superiors an ability to mobilize the masses to achieve extraordinary results. For some ordinary citizens, campaigns were opportunities to demonstrate activism and other political qualifications that might gain them membership in the Communist Party. For a great many others, however, campaigns were opportunities to settle personal scores by playing them out as political struggles. Not surprisingly, many political campaigns were accompanied by violence, justified in lofty political terms. Only three years after Mao's death, Chinese leaders issued an official rejection of mass campaigns as a mode of political participation. Many leaders who emerged at the top echelons of power in the late 1970s had themselves been victims of persecution in the Cultural Revolution. The social disorder of campaigns was rejected as antithetical to the new priority of economic growth.

The third category was the rejection of mass mobilization as the dominant mode of political participation. Chinese leaders have instead encouraged ordinary citizens to express their opinions and participate in politics through a variety of regular official channels, some new, others newly revived: offices of letters and visits, centers and telephone hotlines to report abuses of power, and letters to newspaper editors, for example.[39] Not least of all, the authorities have introduced important reforms in elections. As a consequence, political participation in China is varied and extensive in scope. In addition to the "officially acceptable" political activities noted above, Chinese regularly engage in personal contacting of officials to voice their concerns and (less regularly) a number of "officially unacceptable" activities. Table 9.3 shows findings from a survey conducted in Beijing in the late 1980s. The extent of

T A B L E   9 . 3   Political Participation in Beijing, 1983–1988 (Percent reporting having participated in political act)

Political Act	Percent
Voting for deputies to local people's congress, 1988	72.3
Voting for deputies to local people's congress, 1984	62.4
Contacting leaders of workplace	50.9
Complaining through bureaucratic hierarchy	42.8
Voting for leaders in workplace	34.7
Using connections (*guanxi*)	19.2
Complaining through trade unions	18.8
Working with others to solve social problems	16.1
Complaining through political organizations	14.9
Slowing down on the job	12.5
Writing letters to government officials	12.4
Giving gifts in exchange for help	8.2
Persuading others to attend campaign meetings for deputies	8.9
Complaining through people's congress deputies	8.6
Persuading others to attend campaign meetings or briefing meetings at workplace	7.7
Organizing others to fight against leaders	7.5
Writing letters to newspaper editors	6.7
Persuading others to vote for certain leaders in workplace elections	6.1
Persuading others to vote for certain deputies in local people's congress elections	5.2
Whipping up public opinion against workplace leaders	5.0
Persuading others to boycott unfair workplace elections	4.6
Reporting to complaint bureaus	4.0
Requesting audience with higher authorities	3.8
Persuading others to boycott unfair local people's congress elections	3.7
Bringing cases to court	1.7
Writing "big-character posters"	1.1
Participating in strikes	0.9
Participating in demonstrations	0.5

Source: Tianjian Shi, *Political Participation in Beijing* (Cambridge, MA: Harvard University Press, 1977), p. 94. Based on survey conducted in 1988–1989.

citizen participation in a wide range of activities—about a decade after Mao's death—is quite remarkable, not at all the picture of Maoist mobilization.

Elections and an electoral connection between citizens and leaders are integral to liberal democratic conceptions of representation. For this reason, governments and nongovernmental organizations in liberal democracies have paid close attention to electoral reforms in China. Indeed, many have provided support of various sorts (to train a new corps of election workers, for example), and the Chinese authorities have accepted this support. How do the electoral reforms fit into the framework of Communist Party guardianship?

Elections to local people's congresses in the Maoist years were political rituals, featuring no candidate choice and no secret ballot. Voters directly elected deputies to township-level congresses only; at higher levels, deputies were elected by congresses at the level immediately below. Such elections served as vehicles of regime legitimation, popular education, and political socialization—but they did not really allow ordinary citizens to choose representatives. In 1979, a new election law introduced direct election of deputies to county-level congresses, mandated secret ballots rather than public displays of support, and required the number of candidates to be one and a half times the number of deputies to be elected. Although local Communist Party organizations continue to play a key leadership role in election committees, essentially vetting candidates, not all candidates can win under current rules. Some officially nominated candidates lose elections. Indeed, some candidates officially designated for government office (which requires initial election to congresses) lose elections. A growing number of candidates who are not communist party members have competed and won in elections. A smaller number of government executives nominated by deputies are not official candidates and win without official endorsement.[40] An electoral victory signifies some degree of popular support, while losing signifies a problematic relationship with the mass public. At a minimum, the new rules are a means for the Communist Party organization to gauge popular views about local officials, diversify the pool from which leaders are recruited, and monitor local leaders. To be sure, the new rules have not produced radical change. Nor can such an outcome be expected without further change in rules: no platform of opposition to the Communist Party is permissible, and competition in elections to people's congresses is restricted to the township and county levels.

In 1997 and 1998, Jiang Zemin and the NPC proclaimed their support for more popular participation and more competition in elections to township people's congresses. The idea was neither new nor borrowed from the liberal democratic tradition. It emerged from a decade of practical experience with one of the more controversial political reforms of the post-Mao years: grassroots democratization in the Chinese countryside, formally approved in November 1987 when the NPC, after over a year of debate, passed a provisional version of the Organic Law on Village Committees. A final revised version was passed in November 1998. The law defines **village committees** as "autonomous mass organizations of self-government," popularly elected, in elections featuring choice among candidates, for three-year terms and accountable to a village council comprised of all adult villagers.

The introduction of popularly elected village committees in 1987 had not been a commitment to process but a gamble on outcomes by leaders at the political center. It was designed to strengthen state capacity to govern in the aftermath of agricultural decollectivization. In the early 1980s, the people's communes had been dismantled and replaced with township governments. Land and other production inputs were divided among peasant households to manage on their own, free markets were opened, most obligatory sales to the state were abolished, and private entrepreneurship was promoted.[41] The results of these reforms were successful by most economic standards, but disastrous in their consequences for rural leadership. As villagers gained greater economic initiative and autonomy, the power of the Chinese party-state to exact compliance was enormously weakened. By the mid-1980s, village leadership had seriously atrophied. Leaders were enriching themselves at the expense of the community, and villagers were resisting their efforts to implement unpopular policies. Violent conflicts between villagers and village leaders had become common. The revitalization of village committees in 1987 was designed to make the countryside more governable by increasing accountability. Presumably, villagers would be more responsive to leaders elected from below rather than those imposed from above as before.

With an average size of about 1,200 people, villages are small communities, where most adults have lived and worked together for decades—and could, therefore, be expected to know and elect capable and trustworthy leaders to manage village affairs. Presumably too, newly elected village leaders could serve as loyal agents of the Chinese party-state, guaranteeing policy implementation, acting as the "legs" of the township governments above them. Success required village management by leaders elected in processes featuring broad participation by ordinary villagers, electoral choice, and transparent procedures.

In 1997 and 1998, when top leaders affirmed the experience of village elections, most villages had undergone at least three rounds of elections, with enormous local variation in implementation. In many (perhaps most) villages, the village Communist Party branch controlled candidate nomination, there was no candidate choice for the key position of village committee director, and voting irregularities were common. Even in villages that made serious progress—with genuinely competitive elections, widespread popular participation in candidate nomination, and scrupulous attention to voting procedure—real managerial authority often resided not with the popularly elected village committee but with the village Communist Party branch. Fifteen years after passage of the draft law, too little is known to generalize about overall progress in village elections, its determinants, or its consequences.[42] Certainly, to the degree that the practices of grassroots democracy acquire the force of routine and expectations accumulate, however slowly, among nearly 900 million Chinese in more than 900,000 villages, political participation in the countryside will change profoundly. The 1998 version of the law cautioned against a liberal democratic understanding of where this process is meant to lead, however. A newly added article asserts the role of the Communist Party (not noted in the 1987 draft) in guaranteeing that village committees exercise their democratic functions.

Officially Unacceptable Political Participation

More dramatic than the reforms that have redefined officially acceptable political participation has been the political action of ordinary Chinese in city streets and squares beginning in the late 1970s. With strikes, marches, posters, petitions, and occupation of public spaces, ordinary citizens have acted as if political reform comprehended or condoned mass political action and public disorder. The official record suggests the contrary, however. In 1980, the right to post "big-character posters" (usually criticisms of leaders, written by individuals or groups and posted on walls), introduced during the Cultural Revolution, was removed from the Chinese constitution, and in 1982 the constitutional right to strike was rescinded. As for mass protests, the official view was made clear in 1979 with the introduction of the "four fundamental principles" that political participation must uphold: (1) the socialist road, (2) Marxism-Leninism-Mao Zedong Thought, (3) the people's democratic dictatorship, and (4) the leadership of the Communist Party. Of these principles, only the last is necessary to restrict political participation effectively, as the content of the first three has become what party leaders make of it. Participants (especially organizers) face real risks of physical harm and criminal punishment. Why then did ordinary citizens engage in mass protests with increasing frequency in the 1970s and 1980s? Why has urban worker and peasant unrest increased in the 1980s and 1990s?

Different sorts of "officially unacceptable" political participation have different explanations, but none can be explained without reference to the post-Mao reforms. On the one hand, economic reforms have produced some socially unacceptable outcomes: more (and more visible) inflation, unemployment, crime, and corruption, for example. Rural unrest has typically been triggered by local corruption and exaction of excessive (often illegal) taxes and fees. Peasant unrest sparked by these sorts of problems is by no means uncommon. Urban unrest—strikes, slowdowns, and demonstrations—has increased too, as state enterprises struggle to survive in the socialist market economy. Many enterprises have engaged in massive layoffs; others have been unable to pay bonuses and pensions. For the first time since 1949, many urban Chinese have been living on fixed incomes, no incomes, or unpredictable incomes as the cost of living increases. Since the beginning of industrial reform in the mid-1980s, the threat of urban unrest due to inflation and unemployment has consistently constrained plans of China's leaders to shut down large loss-making state enterprises.

In 1989, a different sort of urban unrest captured the attention of the world news media and, consequently, of the world. The demonstration that brought a million people to Tiananmen Square was the third major political protest movement since Mao's death. The first was in 1978–1979, the second in 1986–1987. All three differed fundamentally from the mass campaigns of the Maoist years, all were officially unacceptable, all were linked in some important way to official reforms and reformers, and all ended in failure for

In 1989, ordinary Chinese participated in the largest spontaneous protest movement the communists had ever faced. A lone protester shows defiance of regime violence in his intransigent confrontation with a Chinese tank.

AP/Wide World Photos

mass protesters (and resulted in setbacks to official reforms too).[43]

Despite links between protesters and official reformers, the post-Mao movements were not mass mobilization campaigns. As they were not explicitly initiated by the regime, once underway they could not be easily stopped with an official pronouncement from the political center. Instead, the authorities turned to coercive force wielded by the police, the armed police, and ultimately the army to terminate the protests with violence. The protests were officially unacceptable. This had less to do the substance of their demands than with their form of expression. The official consensus since December 1978 has been that the most important priority for China is economic growth, with social order and stability as prerequisites for growth. Mass protests are distinctly disorderly. Further, as a form of political participation, mass protests are a symptom of regime failure in two senses. First, by turning to the streets to articulate their demands, protesters demonstrate that official channels for expressing critical views are not working and that they do not believe the Communist Party claim that it can correct its own mistakes. Second, protesters are clearly not alienated from politics: while they reject official channels of participation, they are not politically apathetic; indeed, they articulate explicitly political demands despite serious risks and the difficulty associated with organizing outside the system. In short, political protests signify that mass political partici-pation can neither be contained within official channels nor deterred with liberalization and a better material life.

For the most part, despite some radical elements, the protests have not been blatantly antisystem in their demands. This does not appear to be merely strategic. Rather, the protests are something of a rowdy mass counterpart to the official socialist reform movement, exerting more pressure for more reform, and (while officially unacceptable) often linked with elite reformers. In the **Democracy Movement** of 1978–1979, Deng Xiaoping publicly approved many of the demands posted on Democracy Wall and published in unofficial journals, which called for a "reversal of verdicts" on individuals and political events. The demands were an integral part of the pressure for reform that surrounded the meetings of top leaders in late 1978, allowing elite reformers to argue for major changes in policy and political orientation. The poster campaign and unofficial journals were tolerated. To be sure, when a bold dissident named Wei Jingsheng demanded a "fifth modernization," by which he meant democracy of a sort never envisaged by the communists, the Chinese authorities promptly sentenced him to a 15-year prison term (ostensibly for revealing state secrets) and introduced the "four fundamental principles" to establish the parameters of acceptable debate (see Box 9.2).[44]

When the Communist Party congress convened in late 1987, party leader Zhao Ziyang acknowledged

---

B O X   9 . 2   Wei Jingsheng and the "Fifth Modernization"

In late 1978, in an atmosphere of great change that included official reversals of political verdicts of the Cultural Revolution, many Chinese began to gather regularly at a large wall close to Beijing's Tiananmen Square to post, read, and discuss political posters. One of the boldest posters to appear on Democracy Wall was an essay by Wei Jingsheng. It argued that the ambitious official program to modernize agriculture, industry, national defense, and science and technology could not succeed without a "fifth modernization"—democracy. In terms unacceptable to Chinese leaders, Wei asked: "The hated old political system has not changed. Are not the people justified in seizing power from the overlords?" Wei published more critical essays in his unofficial journal *Explorations*, one of more than 50 such journals circulating at the time. In March 1979, he posted an attack on Deng Xiaoping, asking: "Do we want democracy or new dictatorship?" Wei was tried and convicted of counterrevolutionary crimes and leaking state secrets to foreigners. After nearly 15 years, Wei was released from prison, only to be rearrested for dissident activities. In 1997, after years of pressure from human rights groups and governments outside China, China's most famous political dissident was released and exiled to the United States where he continues to act as critic of the Chinese communist regime.

conflicts of interest in society at the current time. The years 1988 and 1989 were high points for political liberalization. The political criticism expressed in Tiananmen Square in 1989 largely echoed public views of elite reformers in the party and government. From the perspective of communist authorities, the real danger in 1989 was not the content of mass demands but the organizational challenge: students and workers organized their own unions, independent of the party, to represent their interests. The challenge was exacerbated by an open break in elite ranks, when Zhao Ziyang voiced his support for the protesters and declared his opposition to martial law. Other party and government leaders and retired elders, including Deng Xiaoping, many of whom had been victims of power seizures by youths in the Cultural Revolution, viewed the problem as a basic struggle for the survival of the system and their own positions. The movement was violently and decisively crushed with tanks and machine guns in the **Tiananmen massacre** of June 4, 1989.[45]

All three protests ended in defeat for the participants: prison for the main protest organizers in 1979, expulsion from the Communist Party for intellectual leaders in 1987, and prison or violent death for hundreds in 1989. The defeats extended beyond the mass protest movement to encompass setbacks to the official reform movement too. When demands for reform moved to the city streets, more conservative leaders attributed the social disorder to an excessively rapid pace of reform. The result was a slower pace or postponement of reforms. Twice, the highest party leader was dismissed from office as a result of the mass protests (Hu Yaobang in 1987 and Zhao Ziyang in 1989), and the official reform movement lost its strongest proponent.

INTEREST ARTICULATION AND AGGREGATION

Most ordinary citizens engage in interest articulation without interest aggregation. This takes the form of personal contacting to articulate individual concerns about the effects of policies on their lives. Much of this interest articulation takes place at the workplace and might not be considered political in other systems. In the Chinese context, however, where the workplace is often an appendage of the state and controls resources and opportunities allocated by the market in capitalist systems, personal contacting

of grassroots bosses about individual concerns is part of politics. As shown in Table 9.1 above, more than 50 percent of those surveyed in Beijing in the late 1980s had engaged in precisely this sort of low-level politics. And more than 19 percent of those surveyed had made use of personal connections to open "back doors" to produce results more favorable than those expected through regular channels of bureaucratic allocation. For the most part, the function of interest aggregation is monopolized by the Communist Party, although the methods employed have evolved over the years.

Under the formal leadership of the Communist Party are eight "satellite parties," a legacy of the communist pre-1949 strategy of provisional cooperation with noncommunist democratic parties.[46] These parties have no real role in policymaking, but they are represented (with prominent nonparty individuals) in the Chinese People's Political Consultative Conference. In 1989 the Central Committee proposed greater cooperation with the noncommunist parties by regular consultation with their leaders on major policies—or at least a stronger effort to inform the parties of Communist Party policies. As recently as 1997, Jiang Zemin renewed the call for "multiparty cooperation." Of course, this call referred only to the eight officially tolerated parties. In 1998, the authorities arrested, tried, and imprisoned a veteran of the 1978–1979 Democracy Movement who attempted to register a fledgling China Democracy Party.

The other older formal organizations that aggregate like interests in the Chinese political system are the "mass organizations," extensions of the Communist Party into society, nationwide in scope and organized hierarchically. The All-China Federation of Trade Unions and the Women's Federation remain active and important mass organizations today. Mass organizations are led by Communist Party officials, who are specially assigned to these positions and who take direction from party committees. The main function of these organizations is not to aggregate and represent group interests for consideration in the policymaking process, but to facilitate propagation of party policy to the relevant groups. Essentially, mass organizations represent the interests of the Communist Party to the organized "interest groups" it dominates, not vice versa. The classic description of this relationship refers to mass organizations as "transmission belts" for the Communist Party.

A different set of associations, now numbering in the thousands, emerged in the 1980s. Officially, these are "nongovernmental associations," and the Chinese authorities view them as "bridges" between state and society. Generally, only one association is recognized as the bridge to a given sectoral constituency, which has prompted some Western scholars to see the associations as a corporatist arrangement, albeit in an authoritarian framework.[47] Among the most important and interesting associations are those organizing small, medium, and large Chinese businesses: the Self-Employed Laborers Association, the Private Enterprises Association, and the Federation of Industry and Commerce, respectively. Each was organized (and its members registered) under government auspices. In principle, the associations allow the government to control new sectoral interests, while providing a formal channel through which the interests can be articulated. In practice, there is great variation in the independence and influence of the associations. Generally, the associations are more influential at the grassroots, influencing local policy implementation. Some have attained significant national influence, however. Most notably, the Federation of Industry and Commerce has independent resources, which have permitted it to create a separate organizational network (chambers of commerce), a national newspaper, and a financial institution to provide credit to members. The autonomy from the state of nongovernmental associations is certainly not part of any political reform blueprint, but these associations may be the beginnings of a true civil society in China.

There are also known instances of organized articulation of interests by ordinary citizens to influence political decisions. An excellent example is the independent publication of *Yangtze! Yangtze!*, a collection of papers by scientists and environmentalists critical of the world's biggest and most controversial hydroelectric project, the Three Gorges Dam. The collection was released in early 1989 with the aim of influencing the widely publicized NPC vote to approve dam construction. Nearly a third of NPC delegates voted against the project or abstained. The government responded to this unprecedented display of opposition by postponing dam construction until the mid-1990s (see Box 9.3).

For the most part, however, articulation of interests by ordinary citizens is aimed not at influencing policymaking but at rectifying problems (usually official abuses) in policy implementation. A new resource for this sort of interest articulation is the new legality. Increasingly, groups with like interests but without formal organization (ordinary peasants, for example) have engaged in "rightful resistance," assembling to petition officials at higher levels to investigate and punish local leaders who violate laws and policies.[48] In these actions, citizens have used the law against officials to seek a reversal of perceived injustices. Rightful resistance is not individual articulation of grievances, but it instead takes the form of collective action through official channels. Although such organization is largely informal and ad hoc, it does constitute interest aggregation outside the Communist Party. Yet, as it uses official channels for the purpose of upholding the law,

---

BOX 9 . 3   The Three Gorges Dam

The Three Gorges Dam, currently under construction, is the biggest, most costly, and most controversial hydropower station ever built. It was conceived to regulate the flow of the Yangtze, the third most powerful river in the world. Three times in the past century, the river has flooded, killing hundreds of thousands. The dam will raise the water level about 330 feet higher than the current normal level. Building it will displace more than a million people. When completed, the dam will supply 10 percent of China's electric power, needed for industrial production and to achieve "basic electrification" of the countryside. Environmentalist opponents of the dam are concerned about damage to the ecosystem and endangerment of some species of fish and birds. Other critics are concerned because more than 100 significant archeological sites will be flooded. Serious opposition also focuses on safety issues: problems of sedimentation may cause floods upstream and weaken foundations of cities built on silt downstream. Most opponents suggest building several smaller dams, rather than one megadam. Concerns about safety reveal doubts that the government has appropriately considered expert advice in designing the project, which has been a Chinese dream for most of this century and has taken on significance as a political accomplishment.

leaders at the political center cannot view such actions as unacceptable.

POLICYMAKING AND IMPLEMENTATION

Today, it is practically inconceivable that a scheme such as the Great Leap Forward could be launched and implemented as it was in the 1950s. Controversial policies are no longer adopted at the whim of a single leader; experts play a significant role in policy formulation; experimentation in selected localities precedes widespread implementation; local authorities no longer slavishly sacrifice local development goals to meet unrealistic campaign targets dictated by the center.

The single most important difference distinguishing policy processes of the 1950s from those of the 1990s, however, is the recent greater reliance on negotiations and consensus building among a wider range of bureaucratic units and local authorities. This change is partly due to economic reforms that provide increased opportunities and incentives for departments and localities to devote resources to projects outside the state plan rather than to state-mandated projects. In discussing policy processes, the Chinese often refer to the following expression: "The top has its policies; the bottom has its countermeasures." Having renounced campaigns and purges, policy makers at the top have instead worked to forge agreements with a variety of players at the political center and in the localities so that policies adopted are implemented, not ignored or radically reshaped in the course of implementation. At the apex of the system, consensus building has become even more important after 1997, because no top party or government leader possesses the experience and personal prestige of a Mao Zedong or Deng Xiaoping.

The political structures described at the beginning of this chapter are essential points of reference for the description of policymaking and policy implementation here. In the Chinese communist party-state, however, key features of policy processes are not well illustrated by consideration of these formal structures alone. As elaborated below, the formal distinction between party and government structures is less relevant than it appears; at least one key structure does not appear on formal organizational charts; and authority is more fragmented and less well-bounded than formal structure suggests.

Policymaking

The main players in policymaking in the 1980s and 1990s have been found at three tiers of the political system, as shown in Figure 9.3 At the very top tier are the handful of political executives at the apex of the Communist Party: one preeminent party leader and other members of the Politburo Standing Committee (and sometimes the larger Politburo). Until about the mid-1990s, this top tier also included a small number of party elders. The executive generalists at the top are each typically responsible for at least one broad policy area. As a group, they decide and coordinate all major policy decisions. Below this top tier are the crucially important **leading small groups,** defined by broad functional sector, with sweeping mandates to preside over policy research, formulation of policy proposals, sponsorship of policy experiments, and drafting of policy documents.[49] Leading small groups are headed by leaders in the top tier of the policymaking process, although deputy heads are likely to be outside the top tier. There appears to be a norm that those who head leading small groups have some experience and expertise relevant to their portfolios. Leading small groups may also be established on a temporary basis to deal with crises or to exercise overall leadership over big projects.

Formally, the Politburo has the ultimate authority to determine major policies, but it probably meets in plenary session only about once monthly for a morning. These meetings appear to ratify policies already approved by the Politburo Standing Committee, although individual members of the Politburo play a more important role as deputy heads (or heads) of leading small groups. Standing Committee decisions are greatly influenced by the information and recommendations of the leader who heads the relevant leading small group. The most thorough consideration of policy options and shaping of policy decisions, then, probably occurs at the second tier, within leading small groups.

Leading small groups bring together all the senior officials with responsibility for different aspects of a functional area. These areas are defined in very comprehensive terms. For example, the responsibili-

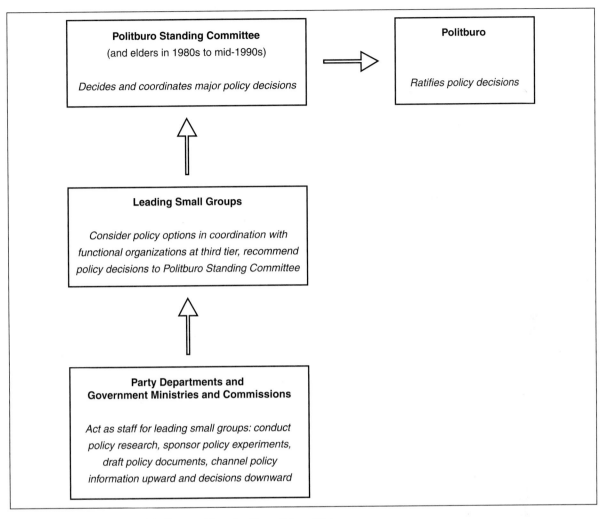

F I G U R E   9 . 3   Policymaking in Post-Mao China

ties of some of the most important leading small groups are defined in the following broad terms: party affairs, national security and military affairs, political and legal affairs, organization and personnel, finance and economics, and foreign affairs. Below leading small groups, at the third tier, are all the relevant administrative offices and departments (such as party departments and government commissions and ministries) that channel policy information upward and policy decisions downward. Units at the third tier are usually headed by members of the Secretariat or State Council Standing Committee (who might also be Politburo members).

Normally, a leading small group is composed of the group head, a deputy or two, members who

are on the group because of formally assigned functional duties in the bureaucracy, and discretionary members (such as advisors). Leading small groups have little staff of their own. The research centers and staff attached to offices and departments at the third tier do the actual work of gathering information and drafting policy documents. This means that the staff work for policymaking is done in departments of the party, government, or military—depending on the formal office of the leading small group head. Policy documents are issued not by leading small groups, which have no formal authority of their own, but by formal political structures (such as the Politburo, State Council, or Secretariat).

Fragmented Authoritarianism

Leading small groups are a coordinating mechanism in the Chinese political system, linking top political executives to bureaucracies and bridging bureaucratic systems. Coordinating mechanisms are particularly important to policymaking in the Chinese system because authority is formally structured so as to require the cooperation of many bureaucratic units, nested in separate chains of authority. Planning for the Three Gorges Dam megaproject, for example, required the active involvement of the State Planning Commission, State Science and Technology Commission, Ministry of Finance, Ministry of Water Resources and Electric Power, Ministry of Communications, six provinces, and the municipalities of Shanghai and Chongqing—in addition to political generalists at the top of the system. The fragmentation of formal authority and its resolution by formal and informal coordinating mechanisms at the top of the system have led some scholars to characterize the Chinese system as one of **fragmented authoritarianism.**[50]

In what ways is formal authority fragmented? The best example is the system of dual subordination. On the one hand, authority is organized in systems of functionally differentiated vertical bureaucracies in hierarchies that extend from ministries at the center to lower-level departments in the localities. Each ministry under the State Council is at the top of a hierarchy of subordinate departments that exist at the provincial, county, and township levels of government. On the other hand, the central ministry and subordinate departments are all government departments and, as such, subordinate to their respective governments too. The Chinese refer to the two structural arrangements as "lines" and "pieces." Authoritative communications are channeled from top to bottom (vertically, in lines) and also from governments to their departments (horizontally, in pieces). The two sorts of authority come together only at the level of the State Council. Simply put, then, all local government departments have two bosses in their formal authority relationships—not to mention their relationships with party departments in the same functional area and party committees with *nomenklatura* authority. In Chinese terminology, there are "too many mothers-in-law." The structure of formal authority routinely creates blockages in policy processes. Many policy issues cannot be resolved at lower levels but must be pushed up to a sufficiently high level that spans many authority structures and can overcome bureaucratic impasses below. In this context, it is not surprising that leaders at lower levels commonly exploit informal networks of interpersonal relationships, built up over the years, to articulate organizational interests and pursue organizational goals.

Obviously, the fragmentation of formal authority has implications for policy implementation too. For example, within the system of dual subordination, the Chinese formally distinguish "leadership relationships" (in which instructions from superiors are binding orders) from "professional relationships" (in which guidelines and opinions from superiors are nonbinding). How and how much guidelines from State Council ministries are implemented depends largely on the priority local governments attach to them. Without active local government support (which requires active local party committee support), the policies formulated in a ministry at the political center may be ignored, distorted, or implemented in a pro forma manner, without serious cost, by formally subordinate departments in the ministry's hierarchy.

Policy Implementation

Although the state has partially retreated from direct control over many aspects of the economy, politics, and society in recent decades, the proportion of decisions affecting all three spheres that is made at the political center in China is higher than that in liberal democracies. Considering this scope, the fragmented structure of authority, and the size and regional diversity of the country, policy makers are seriously constrained in their efforts to elicit effective policy implementation, despite the recent trend toward greater consultation and consensus building to bring relevant departments and localities into the policy process at an earlier stage. This section discusses problems of policy implementation in China. It is worth pointing out here, however, that despite problems and their consequences for unsuccessful policy implementation, the Chinese authorities have achieved policy success in two areas designated as vitally important for the country's development: promoting economic growth and controlling population growth. These accomplishments and the means of their attainment are examined at considerable length as part of the discussion of policy performance, later in this chapter. Here, the focus is on general issues in policy implementation.

The major issue of policy implementation is the monitoring problem, especially serious in China because of the constraints noted above.[51] How do China's policy makers ensure that central-level decisions are translated into actions at lower levels? Central authorities have a very limited capacity to monitor the many aspects of the economy, politics, and society affected by their policies. To cope, they adopt fairly simplistic performance indicators. Not only are these problematic as accurate measures of compliance, but also they can produce unanticipated results. Additionally, policy makers rely mainly on departments and localities, which have their own particular interests to pursue, for much of the information on which to base evaluations of performance. Leaders at the political center have attempted in recent years to develop channels of information independent of ministries and local governments. The State Statistical Bureau has been given more resources and responsibilities to gather and compile information relevant to policymaking and assessment of policy performance. Research institutes and public opinion polls have also played a greater role in channeling different sorts of information to leaders at the political center. The State Auditing Administration and the Ministry of Supervision, both newly established in recent years, are designed to improve central capacity to measure and monitor implementation. Nonetheless, central authorities are unable to verify most reports independently. As a result, information is routinely distorted to make policy implementors appear compliant. Policy makers appear to take this bias into consideration when assessing implementation.

As policy makers routinely communicate multiple (and conflicting) policy objectives downward through several channels, local authorities must arrive at a reasonable ordering of policy priorities. In deciding priorities, local objectives as well as the apparent priorities of the political center are considered. Local governments and parallel party committees are multitask agencies. Policy priorities communicated in documents channeled down the government functionally specialized line hierarchies may not be treated as policy priorities by local governments. Policies appear more likely to be implemented in conformity with central directives when signals from the center indicate that top leaders have reached a consensus among themselves and are paying attention. This sort of signal is generally communicated through documents issued by executive organizations (not simply central ministries) of the Communist Party (not simply the government). Party executives may also signal their attention to implementation of policy issues by speaking at work conferences convened to assess progress in particular areas or establishing an ad hoc leading small group to manage a particular policy problem.

Chinese politics presents no electoral incentives for top leaders to line up public policy with the expressed preferences of special interest groups or ordinary voters. To be sure, policy makers consult those players they view as relevant to policy outcomes. Yet, with restrictions on investigation or criticism by the mass media and the prohibition on organized opposition groups, policy makers face relatively little routine outside pressure in formulating policies. Despite increased consultation of players below the top tiers, the policymaking process is relatively closed, compared to liberal democracies. In a structural context that limits widespread input and provides no electoral connection to policy makers at the top, reshaping policy in the course of policy implementation is often the most effective way for officials to influence policy outcomes. Leaders at the political center accept a certain amount of "adaptation of central policy to local conditions"—indeed, this is a stock phrase of Chinese politics.

CORRUPTION

Economic reform has produced unprecedented growth and prosperity, but also the conditions for new forms of **corruption.** Since the early 1980s, the economy, no longer centrally planned but not fully marketized, has provided opportunities for officials to gain privately from abuse of their control over resources, contracts, and permissions. On the one hand, the new opportunities for corruption may have eased resistance to economic reform by officials with the most to lose from reform. On the other, abuse of public office to pursue private gain has grown in scope, scale, volume, and severity to become one of the gravest challenges facing the regime, even threatening the Chinese armed forces.[52] In public opinion polls conducted over the years, Chinese citizens consistently view corruption as a serious

BOX 9.4   Why Did the Rainbow Bridge Collapse?

Corruption is widely recognized as one of China's most serious problems. Bribery is pervasive in the Chinese construction industry. On January 4, 1999, the 102-meter long Rainbow Bridge in Chongqing municipality collapsed, killing 40 Chinese. Authorities soon discovered the bridge structure was seriously substandard, although constructed less than three years earlier. The bridge collapse led to the investigation and arrest of the chief contractor and the local deputy Communist Party secretary. While in charge of the Rainbow Bridge project, Secretary Lin Shiyuan had accepted more than $10,000 in bribes from the contractor, a former classmate, who was not qualified to undertake the construction project. Chongqing authorities ordered an immediate investigation of the quality of all local structures built in recent years. Problems and hidden dangers were discovered in many other structures, including another bridge built by the same contractor.

social problem, often the most serious problem. The huge 1989 mass protests, as much about corruption as about democracy, reflected and aired this view.

In the 1980s and early 1990s, illegal profiteering was a common form of corruption: taking advantage of a transitional reform policy that set two prices for the same production input, officials with control over resources obtained inputs at the lower official price and sold them at higher market prices. Asset stripping in state enterprises is another common form of corruption. Bribery is also common. Bribes are paid to officials to obtain government jobs, construction contracts, business licenses, and various permissions (see Box 9.4). Bribes are also paid to avoid taxes and circumvent regulations. In recent anticorruption campaigns, Chinese authorities have also targeted corruption in law enforcement and the criminal justice system itself—in the police forces, courts, and procuratorates. In 1997, authorities revealed that the country's top anticorruption chief himself had illicitly invested more than $7 million of funds seized in a major corruption case.

Chinese leaders are alarmed about rampant corruption, recognizing the threat to regime legitimacy and political stability. Since 1982, they have waged a nearly continuous corruption control effort. While corrupt officials have been prosecuted and punished, the battle against corruption suffers from a basic contradiction between Communist Party leadership and rule by law in China. In principle, as described above, equality before the law is a core component of the new legality. In practice, the Chinese legal system has not been used to full effect to control corruption. An important obstacle is a structural one, reflecting a more basic political obstacle. In 1978, party leaders reinstated discipline inspection committees, specialized departments subordinate to party committees at each level of the party hierarchy. Discipline inspection committees investigate misconduct and enforce ethical and political standards for party members. As the preponderance of officials are party members, discipline inspection committees investigate corruption. Regulations require the transfer of apparent criminal cases to procuratorates, but party investigations and party punishments generally precede criminal investigations. Procuratorates routinely encounter obstacles in their efforts to prosecute such cases, not only because officials call up networks of cronies for support but also because successful prosecution is botched when officials have sufficient time to destroy evidence. In principle, the system holds Communist Party members to a higher standard of conduct than ordinary citizens. In practice, exemption from prosecution and substitution of disciplinary action for criminal punishment are very common for officials (but not for ordinary citizens). Public cynicism about corruption control is understandable. In the instances that high-ranking officials are removed from office and sentenced through the legal system, many interpret it as the outcome of a political power struggle.

The problem of corruption and corruption control reflects a basic contradiction between the principles of Communist Party leadership and rule by law. If law is supreme, then the party is subordinate to law and under supervision by procuratorates and courts, not vice versa. So long as party leaders cannot commit to supervision by an impartial legal system, the building of a legal infrastructure will not amount to rule by law. Yet, to commit to such supervision calls into question party leadership and the foundations of the communist party-state.

POLICY PERFORMANCE

In late 1978, China's leaders defined economic growth as the most important policy priority for decades to come. Despite disagreement about the appropriate pace and scope of economic reform, there has been consensus on a broad strategy of retreat from direct state intervention. This means retreat from regular intervention through central government ministries and irregular intervention through disruptive political campaigns. The Chinese state has been achieving more by directly controlling less. This strategy has applied not only to economic goals but to most other policy goals in the 1980s and 1990s as well. The important exception has been population control, which Chinese leaders identified as a major policy priority in the late 1970s. The one-child family policy introduced in 1978 features the Chinese state in a more directly interventionist role in population control than ever before. This section examines the policies of economic reform and compulsory family planning, focusing on the role of the state in achieving policy goals.

Economic Reform

Although the Chinese have moved only slowly on political reforms, they have been much bolder in economic reforms. Since 1978, Chinese leaders have staked their political legitimacy on economic growth, more than anything else. For the most part, the gamble has succeeded. With the end of the Maoist era, Chinese economic growth, illustrated in Table 9.4, has been remarkable. Growth in China has been the highest in the world, averaging just under 10 percent per year between 1979 and 2000.[53] Some observers have speculated that China will replace Japan as the second largest economy in the world by the year 2010. Real per capita income has grown rapidly, to more than $800 by the end of the 1990s or nearly $4000 in purchasing power parity. Although China is obviously still very much a developing country, economic reform has been mainly a success story. How has it been achieved? Can it be expected to continue?

Mao's successors inherited a centrally planned economy, organized according to a Stalinist model bor-

TABLE 9.4   Economic Performance, 1980–2000 (in current yuan)

	GDP (billion yuan)	GDP per capita (yuan)
1980	451.8	460
1985	896.4	855
1990	1854.8	1634
1995	5847.8	4854
	8940.4	6972
2000	$1080 billion	$840 ($3,920 PPP)

Sources: China International Publishing Group and State Council Information Office, China Internet Information Center at http://www.china.org.cn; World Bank, *World Development Indicators 2002* (Washington, DC: World Bank, 2002): 18, 208.

rowed from the Soviet Union in the 1950s. Central government bureaucratic decisions, rather than market mechanisms, determined allocation through a "scientific" planning process. Nearly all industrial production was under "the plan" and took place in enterprises owned and directly managed by the state. Government economic ministries assembled and processed massive amounts of information about economic capacity (much of it greatly distorted by lower levels) and passed instructions about production down to individual enterprises in the form of planned inputs and outputs. Enterprise performance was evaluated according to fulfillment of the plan, and enterprises had little control over supply of inputs or choice of outputs. Prices were bureaucratically set at the center. Economic penalties for enterprise, managerial, or worker inefficiency were rare. Moreover, without scarcity prices, the concept of enterprise "profits" was not meaningful.

The strategy of economic reform pursued in China has been aptly described as a gradual growing out of the plan.[54] The Chinese did not initially set out with a stated goal or program to create their **socialist market economy.** Rather, economic reform has been an incremental process, often described with the Chinese phrase, "crossing the river by groping for stones." Initially, some top party leaders envisaged only a small secondary role for the market economy, as a "bird in a cage" of the planned economy. By the mid-1990s, however, the Chinese economy had basically grown out of the plan.[55]

Beginning with agricultural decollectivization in the early 1980s, Chinese leaders began to introduce

Economic reform has opened up opportunities for private entrepreneurship and increased the availability of goods and services for ordinary consumers.

Sean Sprague/Panos Pictures

market elements into the rural economy—and not only for agricultural production. Rural enterprises were allowed to expand into practically any product line, rather than being restricted to "serving agriculture," as before. Most of these industries were organized as "collective enterprises," with ownership by the local community at the township or village level and with strong direct involvement of local government in management. A two-track pricing system was introduced for industry. For state enterprises, most commodities had both a bureaucratically set price and a higher price determined by the market. State enterprises continued to produce according to the plan, but were also given expanded autonomy to produce above the plan and sell the additional commodities at market prices. New leasing and profit retention schemes were established, which for the first time provided incentives for state enterprises to organize production to earn profits rather than fulfill plan targets. State enterprises were also encouraged to transact with nonstate enterprises. For collective enterprises, which have never produced under the plan, production and sale of output was at market prices. In the mid-1980s, the absolute size of the planned sector was deliberately frozen, while growth of the market sector continued to be promoted. Consequently, the planned sector became less and less important in the economy overall.

The transformation is illustrated in Figure 9.4. In 1980, state enterprises accounted for nearly 80 percent of industrial production in China. By 2000, this proportion had been reduced to about 25 percent. While the rise of private industry (from practically nothing) has not been trivial in importance, it would be grossly inaccurate to describe the transformation as a shift from public to private industrial enterprise. Much of the change is accounted for by the explosive growth of township and village enterprises—that is, rural collective industry in which local government plays a very prominent role. These enterprises account for about 80 percent of industrial production in the collective sector.

The two-track pricing system allowed state enterprises to accommodate to market mechanisms gradually. Over the years, the number of commodities with bureaucratic prices was steadily decreased. By the mid-1990s, two-track prices were basically a thing of the past. Liberalization of prices has given the collective sector more than the state sector an advantage, because collective enterprises are typically smaller and have adapted production more flexibly to the changing market environment.

State enterprises have performed less well. Although they account for about 25 percent of industrial output, they employ nearly half of the urban workforce. Reforms of the 1990s were intended to resolve the problem of insolvent state enterprises, through mergers, sales, bankruptcies, and conver-

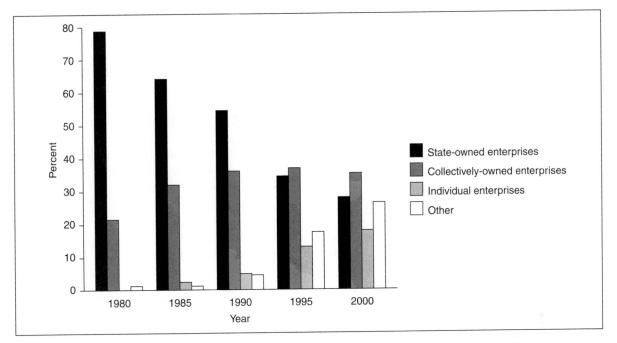

FIGURE 9.4   Growing Out of the Plan: Percentage Contributed to Total Value of Industrial Output, by Structure of Ownership and Management, 1980–2000

Note: "Individual" enterprises are privately owned enterprises with fewer than eight employees; "other" enterprises includes private enterprises with eight or more employees, joint ventures, and foreign-owned enterprises. Figures for 2000 are for 1999 year-end.

Sources: State Statistical Bureau, *A Statistical Survey of China 1997* (Beijing: State Statistical Publishing House, 1997), p. 7; *China Statistical Yearbook 2000* (Beijing: State Statistical Publishing House, 2000), p. 407.

sion to limited liability joint stock corporations. These reforms have proceeded very slowly. It is reasonable to say that the "iron rice bowl" has been broken, but there are probably 15 million redundant workers in state enterprises, and estimates of the number of furloughed workers come nowhere near this. For the most part, the state has continued to subsidize loss-making state enterprises through bank loans because Chinese leaders have viewed the prospect of massive urban unemployment that must accompany serious restructuring as politically unacceptable. In this sense, some of the most difficult problems of economic reform have been postponed by the adoption of a gradualist strategy.

As suggested above, one big task facing Chinese economic reformers in the new century is transformation of the banking sector. China's financial sector is almost wholly owned and dominated by government. A big problem is state enterprise indebtedness due to extension of state bank credit for essentially

political reasons. Another major task is creation of a legal and regulatory environment to support the socialist market economy. There has been progress in passage of legislation and training of legal specialists, including a new contingent of lawyers, but enforcement remains weak. The slow pace of legal institutionalization and the continued involvement of the government in economic decisions do much to explain the rise of corruption.

Compulsory Family Planning

While reducing state intervention to promote economic growth, policy makers have increased their intervention involving a new policy priority: population control. In 1953, the PRC's first census disclosed a population of 583 million, up 43 million since 1949. It continued to increase with widened access to health care, improved nutrition, and peace after decades of war. For most of the Maoist years, population planning was not actively promoted. Indeed, the economist Ma Yinchu was condemned as a rightist in 1957 for his advocacy of population control. In 1978, with the population close to a billion and amid rising concern about meeting economic goals and ensuring basic livelihood, employment opportunities, and social security support at the current rate of population growth, China's leaders declared population control a major policy priority. State-sponsored family planning was added to the constitution, and an ideal family size of one child was endorsed as national policy. According to this policy, most couples are required to stop childbearing after one or two births. Married couples in urban areas, with few exceptions, are restricted to one child. In rural areas, married couples are subject to rules that differ across provinces. In some provinces, two children are normally permitted; in others, only one child is permitted; in most provinces, a second child is permitted only if the first is a girl.

The **one-child family policy** is inherently difficult to implement in China, particularly in the countryside, where about 70 percent of Chinese live.[56] There, the population is relatively poorly educated and with poor access to public health facilities— circumstances that do not facilitate an effective family planning program. Traditional views about the family prevail: as in most agrarian societies, big families and many sons are viewed as ideal. Moreover, in China, a married daughter joins the household of her husband, while a married son remains in the household to support aging parents. Decollectivization and the return to household farming in the early 1980s enhanced the value of sons compared to daughters, for their labor power. The dismantling of the commune system has also left the state less able to monitor compliance, just as the new economic independence of peasants has left the state less able to enforce compliance. Finally, population control involves the state as the dominant decision maker in choices that are traditionally viewed, in China as elsewhere, as private family matters.

Despite the inherent difficulties, the Chinese have succeeded in curbing population growth dramatically, as is illustrated in Figure 9.5. A population structure normally resembles a pyramid: with relatively unchanged rates of births and deaths, the proportion of population from top to bottom is progressively bigger. The population pyramid in Figure 9.5 has two striking gaps. The first, located at about the middle of the pyramid, reflects fewer births as well as differentially more deaths among the young in the disasters following the Great Leap Forward (reflected here in 1957–1961 births). The second reflects the impact of family planning policies introduced in the 1970s, in particular, the one-child family policy adopted in 1978. Variation in policy emphasis by leaders at the political center is reflected in variation in number of births, beginning in the mid-1970s. Implementation of the one-child family policy began in 1979. In 1983, responding to concerns at the political center, implementation became more coercive. From 1984 through the late 1980s, policy was relaxed and implementation in the countryside faltered due to difficulties associated with decollectivization. Births rose immediately. From 1989 to the present, policy implementation has been stringent. Since the late 1980s, fertility has dropped to 1.9 births per woman, compared with a rate of 5.8 births in 1970. In the 1990s, the population has been growing at the rate of 1 percent per year, compared with a rate of 2.7 percent in 1970. Urban-rural differences are very significant, however. Urban births have shown a very strong effect of population control policies beginning in the mid-1970s, with no rebound. In the cities, the one-child family appears to be the accepted norm. In the countryside, however, any relaxation of policy has been reflected in immediate big increases in births.[57]

These results are largely the result of policy, not of the normal economic trend whereby populations move from high birth rates and high death rates to low birth rates and low death rates as the economy develops. This has happened in China, but the fluctuation in births is highly sensitive to fluctuations in policy and its implementation.

Policy implementation has taken a number of forms: a legal requirement of late marriage, a requirement of insertion of an intrauterine device after a first birth, and a requirement of sterilization of one partner after a second birth. There are incentives to sign a one-child family certificate after the first birth, including priority in entrance to schools and funding for health fees for the child. Fines are imposed on the family for policy violations. Birth planning workers at the grassroots are given birth quotas from higher levels, which they allocate on the basis of family circumstances. Implementation is easier in the cities than in the countryside: both partners typically work outside the home, facilitating monitoring and imposition of

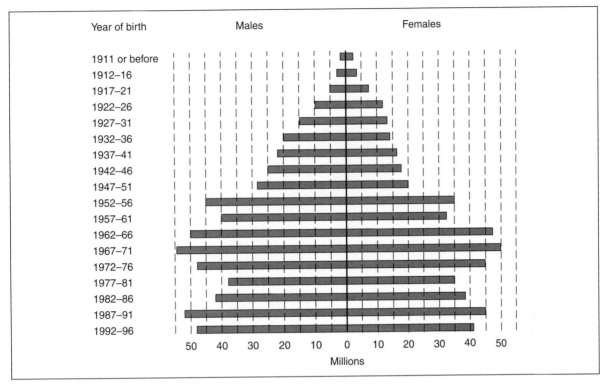

FIGURE 9.5   Estimated Midyear Population Structure, 1996

Source: Projections by the U.S. Bureau of the Census, based on birth rates from the Chinese State Statistical Bureau and preliminary results from the 1995 1 percent sample census. From Judith Banister, "China: Population Dynamics and Economic Implications," edited by the Joint Economic Committee, U.S. Congress in *China's Economic Future: Challenges to U.S. Policy* (Armonk, NY: M. E. Sharpe, 1997), p. 347.

penalities; workers have retirement pensions; and living conditions are cramped. In the countryside, since the late 1980s, implementation is mainly the responsibility of a woman serving on the village committee. From the perspective of leaders at the political center, abortion is basically a sign of failure, not success, in policy implementation. At the grassroots, from the perspective of birth planning workers, however, the obvious fact is that abortions do not add above-plan births. Undeniably, birth planning workers have incentives to encourage abortions and face few disincentives for doing so.

In recent years, policy makers have expressed concern about a perverse result of compulsory family planning: the shortage of young girls, compared with boys. In the 1990 census, "missing girls" show up as girls who should be alive and counted, based on the number of boys counted in each cohort, but who for whatever reason are not counted in the census. The problem of missing girls is increasingly se-

vere by cohort: of children born between 1979 and 1982, 3 percent of girls are missing; of children born between 1988 and 1990, 6 percent of girls are missing, for example. The most recent census reveal growth in birth disparities from a national average of 111 newborn boys to 100 newborn girls in 1990 to 117 boys for every 100 girls in 2000. Much larger disparities were found in rural southeastern and central China. These figures compare with an international average of about 106 boys to 100 girls.

The shortage of girls reflects the traditional Chinese preference for male children in the context of compulsory family planning. Traditional practices of female infanticide as well as abandonment and severe neglect of girls beyond infancy have led to excess female infant mortality. Not least of all, missing girls are increasingly the result of sex-selective abortion, made possible with the widespread use of ultrasound technology in the early 1980s.

China's success in reducing population growth has strong supporters and detractors outside the country. On the one hand, the United Nations Commission on Population and Development sees China as a spectacular success story. On the other, compulsory family planning and particularly the practice of abortion has provoked strong criticism from human rights advocates and governments in liberal democracies, including the United States. The official Chinese response has focused on "economic rights" that the government argues would be denied all Chinese in the decades to come if population growth is not brought under control.

HONG KONG

In 1842 and 1860, the island of **Hong Kong** and adjacent territory on the Chinese mainland was ceded by treaty to Britain in perpetuity. In 1898, more adjacent territory was ceded in a 99-year lease. These cessions were largely the outcome of British victory in wars fought to impose trade on China. For nearly a century, Hong Kong (including the adjacent territories) was a British colony, ruled by a governor appointed in London. Hong Kong flourished economically, with a disciplined labor force of Chinese immigrants, a free-market economy, and a government commitment to rule of law and civil liberties but not elected government. In 1984, the Chinese communist authorities elaborated the principle of **"one country, two systems,"** applicable to Hong Kong after 1997. China and Britain signed a Joint Declaration: Hong Kong would revert to Chinese sovereignty in 1997, but would continue to enjoy "a high degree of autonomy." The Chinese agreed that Hong Kong would enjoy economic, financial, and monetary autonomy, maintaining its capitalist system, legal system, and way of life for 50 years. At midnight on June 30, 1997, Hong Kong became a special administrative region of communist-ruled China.

The British had made little effort to democratize politics in Hong Kong through the 1980s. The governor had consulted business elites and other key constituencies on policy affairs, but there had been no elected legislature or government. Nor had political parties really developed in such an environment. All this changed in 1989. The Tiananmen massacre galvanized Hong Kong Chinese and British expatriates into efforts to accelerate the pace of political democratiza-

tion before 1997. In 1991, in the first direct elections to the Legislative Council, only a third of the legislative deputies were directly elected. In 1995, a controversial electoral reform bill introduced by Governor Christopher Patten guided elections: for the first time, ordinary Hong Kong citizens elected all deputies in the Legislative Council. Hong Kong's most liberal democratic parties, whose leaders included the outspoken critic Martin Lee, branded a "subversive" by Chinese communist authorities, won overwhelmingly in geographic voting districts. Openly pro-Beijing forces did poorly. Communist authorities rejected the elections and the legislature as violations of the Basic Law, Hong Kong's miniconstitution passed in China's National People's Congress in 1990. They supervised selection of a chief executive and provisional legislature in 1996. At the moment of the historic handover, this chief executive and provisional legislature officially replaced the governor and the legislature elected in 1995.

China's reaction to democratization in the mid-1990s increased apprehensions about prospects for autonomy in Hong Kong as a special administrative region. Yet, since the handover, Beijing authorities have been less heavy-handed than feared. Hong Kong today enjoys mostly the same civil liberties as under British rule. Human rights organizations and pro-democracy organizations that monitor and support progress in the PRC have bases in Hong Kong. Hong Kong newspapers provide information about politics in the PRC and are critical in ways not permitted on the mainland. In view of the weak legitimacy of the provisional legislature, the Hong Kong government proclaimed as its key aim for the 1998 elections, "A credible legislature will be elected." Democrats ultimately prevailed, as in 1995. Chinese communist authorities hope that success in implementing one country, two systems in Hong Kong will woo Taiwan back to the PRC too. Indeed, the principle was originally designed with Taiwan in mind.

TAIWAN

Taiwan, governed by the Nationalists as the **Republic of China** since 1945, lies a mere 100 miles off the east coast of the Chinese mainland. Communist "liberation" of Taiwan became moot when the United States sent its Seventh Fleet to the Taiwan Strait, declaring an American interest in the security of Taiwan after the outbreak of the Korean War in the 1950s. For the next three decades, the Chinese routinely bombarded offshore islands of Taiwan and continued to threaten liberation by military force. For the most part, however, it was a cold war—and until the 1970s, Taiwan was the clear winner, enjoying international recognition as the sole legitimate representative of China. In the 1970s, two major events affected Taiwan's status. In 1971, Taiwan lost its membership in the United Nations and its seat on the Security Council to China; in 1979 the United States recognized China diplomatically, downgrading the relationship with Taiwan to one of unofficial liaison. Today, fewer than 30 countries recognize Taiwan. These events have put China in a position of relative strength.

In 1979 China launched a peaceful offensive, calling on "Taiwanese compatriots" to support immediate steps to establish direct links, direct exchanges, and a process leading ultimately to peaceful reunification. The response of Taiwan's government to one country, two systems has been an assertion of the status quo of two separate political entities and a vague commitment to eventual unification on the basis of a "democratic, free, and equitably prosperous China." The two sides have engaged in negotiations on and off over the years. Since democratization in the late 1980s, Taiwan's leaders are more constrained than ever to represent majority public opinion, which does not support unification with the mainland. The election of a pro-independence party candidate to the presidency in 2000 has exacerbated friction across the Taiwan Strait.

CHINA'S POLITICAL FUTURE

Two main themes have run through this study of Chinese politics today. First, despite very significant economic liberalization and a nascent political institutionalization, Chinese politics takes place within the boundaries of what is still essentially a communist party-state. Second, the dramatic changes sweeping the Chinese economy, polity, and society, many of which now seem beyond the control of political leaders, are as much a byproduct of reform as a direct product of reform policies. The first theme cautions against liberal democratic optimism when considering China's political future. The second reminds us that the script of the political future will not be written by Chinese communist leaders alone.

In this new century, China must confront a number of key issues that will significantly determine its development. Can "organizational and working systems" that bolster and foster economic growth and safeguard against political arbitrariness actually be created within the confines of the communist party-state? Chinese leaders view with approval East Asian models that combine political authoritarianism with economic liberalism, but it is quite doubtful that lessons from tiny Singapore, for example, are applicable in China's huge political economy. Moreover, these models have not proved resistant to the democratization that Chinese leaders categorically reject.

Around the world, political change has created in the late twentieth century an age of democratization—the result, in many countries, of revolutions that toppled communist regimes older than the Chinese regime. What are the prospects for democracy in China? Will the "third wave" of world democratization reach China early in the twenty-first century?

Certainly, liberal democratic ideals and practices are quite alien to Chinese culture. Chinese history provides no examples of democratic rule, and the Chinese cultural tradition expresses no concerns to protect individuals by checking state power. Past experience and cultural tradition, then, offer little encouragement to those looking for the seeds of democratization in China. Yet, authoritarianism has not survived intact with economic modernization in many East Asian countries with a similar lack of historical and cultural foundations for democracy. To be sure, even with continued economic growth, China will differ from these countries for many years to come. It will be bifurcated in its development: middle-class prosperity will slowly emerge in the big cities and coastal regions, but Chinese in the countryside will remain relatively poor for some time.

With reform, for most ordinary Chinese, the party has demanded less and delivered more in recent decades. Unlike communist parties that gained (and held) power with the aid of Soviet troops and tanks, the Chinese Communist Party has indigenous and nationalist roots. It is less likely to collapse in the face of the sort of mass discontent that toppled communist regimes in Eastern Europe. More likely, the party will continue to transform China in the years to come and to transform itself in order to continue to rule. Whether that transformation ultimately amounts to a top-down revolution that incrementally overturns Leninist foundations remains to be seen.

KEY TERMS

Central Committee

Chinese Communist Party

Confucianism

corruption

Cultural Revolution

Democracy Movement

democratic centralism

Deng Xiaoping

fragmented
   authoritarianism

Great Leap Forward

guardianship

Hong Kong

Hu Jintao

leading small groups

Mao Zedong

mass line

mass mobilization
   campaign

minority nationalities

National Party Congress

National People's
   Congress (NPC)

Nationalist Party

nomenklatura system

one-child family policy

one country, two systems

party-state

People's Liberation Army
   (PLA)

Politburo

rule by law

socialist market economy

State Council

Taiwan (Republic of
   China)

Tiananmen massacre

village committees

INTERNET SOURCES

http://www.china.org.cn/. China Internet Information Center, State Council Information Office. Authorized website of Chinese government, link to National People's Congress. Access to government White Papers, news, statistical data.

http://www.chinadaily.com.cn. *China Daily.* News from China directed toward external readership.

http://english.peopledaily.com.cn/home.shtml. *People's Daily.* Official newspaper of Communist Party of China.

http://www.scmp.com. *South China Morning Post.* News about Hong Kong and mainland China, from Hong Kong.

http://www.wws.princeton.edu/~lynn/Chinabib.pdf. Contemporary China Bibliography, Professor Lynn White, Princeton University.

http://www.uschina.org/. United States–China Business Council. Analysis and advocacy of policy issues of interest to US corporations engaged in business relations with China.

SUGGESTED READINGS

Baum, Richard. *Burying Mao: Chinese Politics in the Age of Deng Xiaoping.* Princeton, NJ: Princeton University Press, 1994.

Bernstein, Thomas B. and Xiaobo Lu. *Taxation without Representation in Contemporary Rural China.* New York: Cambridge University Press, 2003.

Bianco, Lucien. *Origins of the Chinese Revolution, 1915–1949.* Stanford, CA: Stanford University Press, 1971.

Chang, Jung. *Wild Swans: Three Daughters of China.* New York: Anchor, 1991.

Dickson, Bruce J. *Red Capitalists in China: The Party, Private Entrepreneurs, and Prospects for Political Change.* New York: Cambridge University Press, 2003.

Gilley, Bruce. *Model Rebels: The Rise and Fall of China's Richest Village.* Berkeley: University of California Press, 2001.

Goldman, Merle and Roderick MacFarquhar, eds. *The Paradox of China's Post-Mao Reforms.* Cambridge, MA: Harvard University Press, 1999.

Lardy, Nicholas R. *Integrating China into the Global Economy.* Washington, DC: Brookings Institution, 2002.

Li, Cheng. *China's Leaders: The New Generation.* Lanham, MD: Rowman and Littlefield, 2001.

MacFarquhar, Roderick, ed. *The Politics of China: The Eras of Mao and Deng,* 2nd ed. Cambridge, England: Cambridge University Press, 1997.

Oi, Jean C. *Rural China Takes Off: Institutional Foundations of Economic Reform.* Berkeley: University of California Press, 1999.

Saich, Tony. *Governance and Politics of China.* New York: Palgrave, 2001.

Spence, Jonathan D. *The Search for Modern China.* New York: Norton, 1990.

Weston, Timothy B. and Lionel Jensen, eds. *China Beyond the Headlines.* Lanham, MD: Rowman and Littlefield, 2000.

Wong, Jan. *Red China Blues.* Sydney, Australia: Doubleday, 1996.

Yabuki, Susumu and Stephen M. Harner. *China's New Political Economy,* rev. ed. Boulder, CO: Westview Press, 1999.

ENDNOTES

1. The earliest and best expression of this commitment is in Deng Xiaoping, "On the Reform of the System of Party and State Leadership," August 18, 1980, in *Selected Works of Deng Xiaoping, 1975–1982* (Beijing: Foreign Languages Press, 1984): 302–25.

2. For a good, very readable discussion of Chinese history beginning with the late Ming (seventeenth century) and extending into the 1980s, see Jonathan D. Spence, *The Search for Modern China* (New York: Norton, 1990). Other good historical overviews include Charles O. Hucker, *China's Im-*

perial Past: An Introduction to Chinese History and Culture (Stanford, CA: Stanford University Press, 1975) and Immanuel C. Y. Hsu, *The Rise of Modern China*, 5th ed. (New York: Oxford University Press, 1995).

3. See Hsi-sheng Chi, *Warlord Politics in China, 1916–1928* (Stanford, CA: Stanford University Press, 1976); Edward A. McCord, *The Power of the Gun: The Emergence of Modern Chinese Warlordism* (Berkeley: University of California Press, 1993).

4. R. H. Tawney, *Land and Labour in China* (London: Allen and Unwin, 1932).

5. See especially Lucien Bianco, *Origins of the Chinese Revolution, 1915–1949* (Stanford, CA: Stanford University Press, 1971). See also Benjamin Schwartz, *Chinese Communism and the Rise of Mao* (Cambridge, MA: Harvard University Press, 1951).

6. The classic political biography of Mao is Edgar Snow, *Red Star over China* (New York: Grove Press, 1968). Of the many excellent studies by Stuart R. Schram, see especially *The Political Thought of Mao Tse-tung*, rev. ed. (New York: Praeger, 1969), *The Thought of Mao Tse-tung* (Cambridge, England: Cambridge University Press, 1989), and his biography of Mao, *Mao Tse-tung*, rev. ed. (Harmondsworth, England: Penguin, 1967). After Mao's death, scholars appraised Mao and his legacy from a variety of perspectives in Dick Wilson, ed., *Mao Tse-tung in the Scales of History: A Preliminary Assessment* (Cambridge, England: Cambridge University Press, 1977).

7. An optimistic perspective on this period of formation for the party is found in Mark Selden, *The Yenan Way in Revolutionary China* (Cambridge, MA: Harvard University Press, 1971). See also Selden's *China in Revolution: The Yenan Way Revisited* (Armonk, NY: M. E. Sharpe, 1995).

8. See Chalmers A. Johnson, *Peasant Nationalism and Communist Power: The Emergence of Revolutionary China* (Stanford, CA: Stanford University Press, 1962).

9. See Suzanne Pepper, *Civil War in China: The Political Struggle, 1945–1949* (Berkeley: University of California Press, 1978).

10. For a good selection of essays offering a comprehensive overview of PRC history, see Roderick MacFarquhar, ed., *The Politics of China: The Eras of Mao and Deng*, 2nd ed. (Cambridge, England: Cambridge University Press, 1997). Other good discussions of post-Mao history are found in Richard Baum, *Burying Mao: Chinese Politics in the Age of Deng Xiaoping* (Princeton, NJ: Princeton University Press, 1994) and Harry Harding, *China's Second Revolution: Reform after Mao* (Washington: Brookings Institution, 1987). Good discussions of particular topics of reform are found in Merle Goldman and Roderick MacFarquhar, eds., *The Paradox of China's Post-Mao Reforms* (Cambridge, MA: Harvard University Press, 1999).

11. The classic account is by William Hinton, who observed land reform before 1949 in *Fanshen: A Documentary of Revolution in a Chinese Village* (New York: Viking, 1966).

12. Roderick MacFarquhar, ed., *The Hundred Flowers Campaign and the Chinese Intellectuals* (New York: Praeger, 1960); Fu-sheng Mu, *The Wilting of the Hundred Flowers Movement: Free Thought in China Today* (London: Heinemann, 1962).

13. See Dali L. Yang, *Calamity and Reform in China: State, Rural Society, and Institutional Change since the Great Leap Famine* (Stanford, CA: Stanford University Press, 1996).

14. See Frederick C. Teiwes, *Politics and Purges in China: Rectification and the Decline of Party Norms, 1950–1965* (Armonk, NY: M. E. Sharpe, 1979) and *Leadership, Legitimacy, and Conflict in China: From a Charismatic Mao to the Politics of Succession* (Armonk, NY: M. E. Sharpe, 1984).

15. See Jasper Becker, *Hungry Ghosts: Mao's Secret Famine* (New York: Free Press, 1996).

16. Some of the best accounts of the Cultural Revolution are biographical or autobiographical. See, for example, Gordon A. Bennett and Ronald N. Montaperto, *Red Guard: The Political Biography of Dai Hsiao-ai* (Garden City, NY: Doubleday, 1971); Jung Chang, *Wild Swans: Three Daughters of China* (New York: Anchor, 1991); Yuan Gao, *Born Red: Chronicle of the Cultural Revolution* (Stanford, CA: Stanford University Press, 1987); Liang Heng and Judith Shapiro, *Son of the Revolution* (New York: Knopf, 1983); Anne F. Thurston, *Enemies of the People: The Ordeal of the Intellectuals in China's Great Cultural Revolution* (Cambridge, MA: Harvard University Press, 1988); Daiyun Yue and Carolyn Wakeman, *To the Storm: The Odyssey of a Revolutionary Chinese Woman* (Berkeley: University of California Press, 1985); and Nien Cheng, *Life and Death in Shanghai* (New York: Grove Press, 1986);

17. See Dru C. Gladney, *Muslim Chinese: Ethnic Nationalism in the People's Republic* (Cambridge, MA: Council on East Asian Studies, Harvard University, 1991); Stevan Harrell, ed., *Cultural Encounters on China's Ethnic Frontiers* (Seattle: University of Washington Press, 1995).

18. An excellent discussion of guardianship is found in Robert A. Dahl, *Democracy and Its Critics* (New Haven, CT: Yale University Press, 1989), ch. 4. On Leninism in general, see especially Alfred G. Meyer, *Leninism* (Cambridge, MA: Harvard University Press, 1957).

19. Mao Zedong, "Some Questions Concerning Methods of Leadership," in *Selected Works of Mao Tse-tung*, vol. 3 (Peking: Foreign Languages Press, 1965), pp. 117–122.

20. I thank Mi Youlu, Managing Editor of *Township and Town Tribune* for these figures, which are for 1997.

21. On the changing role of the NPC, see Murray Scot Tanner, *The Politics of Lawmaking in Post-Mao China: Institutions, Processes, and Democratic Prospects* (New York: Oxford University Press, 1999) and "Breaking the Vicious Cycles: The Emergence of China's National People's Congress," *Problems of Post-Communism* 45, No. 3 (1998): 29–47. For an historical perspective, see Kevin J. O'Brien, *Reform without Liberalization: China's National People's Congress and the Politics of Institutional Change* (Cambridge, MA: Cambridge University Press, 1990).

22. See Murray Scot Tanner, "How a Bill Becomes a Law in China: Stages and Processes of Lawmaking," *China Quarterly*, No. 141: 39–64.

23. See the selection of essays in David Shambaugh, ed., *Deng Xiaoping: Portrait of a Chinese Statesman* (New York: Oxford University Press, 1995).

24. Tai Ming Cheung, "The Influence of the Gun: China's Central Military Commission and Its Relationship with the Military, Party, and State Decision-Making Systems," in David M. Lampton, ed., *The Making of Chinese Foreign and Security Policy in the Era of Reform* (Stanford, CA: Stanford University Press, 2001), pp. 61–90; Michael D. Swaine, "Chinese Decision-Making Regarding Taiwan, 1979–2000," in *The Making of Chinese Foreign and Security Policy in the Era of Reform*, pp. 289–336. On military modernization, see David Shambaugh

and Richard H. Yang, eds., *China's Military in Transition* (Oxford: Clarendon Press, 1997); David Shambaugh, "The People's Liberation Army and the People's Republic at 50: Reform at Last," *China Quarterly*, No. 159 (1999): 660–72.

25. See Melanie Manion, "The Cadre Management System, Post-Mao: The Appointment, Promotion, Transfer and Removal of Party and State Leaders," *China Quarterly*, No. 102 (1985): 203–33; John P. Burns, *The Chinese Communist Party's Nomenklatura System* (Armonk, NY: M. E. Sharpe, 1989) and "Strengthening Central CCP Control of Leadership Selection: The 1990 *Nomenklatura*," *China Quarterly*, No. 138 (1994): 458–91.

26. See Hsiao Pen, "Separating the Party from the Government," in Carol Lee Hamrin and Suisheng Zhao, eds., *Decision-Making in Deng's China: Perspectives from Insiders* (Armonk, NY: M. E. Sharpe, 1995), pp. 153–68.

27. See Zhiyue Bo, *Chinese Provincial Leaders: Economic Performance and Political Mobility since 1949* (Armonk, NY: M. E. Sharpe, 2002). For an earlier discussion of elite recruitment and mobility, based on case studies, see David M. Lampton, *Paths to Power: Elite Mobility in Contemporary China* (Ann Arbor, MI: Center for Chinese Studies, University of Michigan, 1986).

28. For an overview of the change, see Richard Baum, "Modernization and Legal Reform in Post-Mao China: The Rebirth of Socialist Legality," *Studies in Comparative Communism* 19, No. 2 (1986): 69–103. For notions underlying the change, see Carlos W. H. Lo, "Deng Xiaoping's Ideas on Law: China on the Threshold of a Legal Order," *Asian Survey* 32, No. 7 (1992): 649–65. For a description of the law in practice in post-Mao China, see James V. Feinerman, "Economic and Legal Reform in China, 1978–91," *Problems of Communism* 40, No. 5 (1991): 62–75; Pitman B. Potter, ed., *Domestic Law Reforms in Post-Mao China* (Armonk, NY: M. E. Sharpe, 1994) and "The Chinese Legal System: Continuing Commitment to the Primacy of State Power," *China Quarterly*, No. 159 (1999): 673–83; Stanley B. Lubman, *Bird in a Cage: Legal Reform in China After Mao* (Stanford, CA: Stanford University Press, 1999).

29. See Minxin Pei, "Citizens v. Mandarins: Administrative Litigation in China," *China Quarterly*, No. 152 (December 1997): 832–62.

30. See, for example, Donald C. Clarke and James V. Feinerman, "Antagonistic Contradictions: Criminal Law and Human Rights in China," *China Quarterly*, No. 141 (1995): 135–54.

31. See especially the biographical and autobiographical accounts noted above in note 16.

32. See Martin King Whyte, *Small Groups and Political Rituals in China* (Berkeley: University of California Press, 1974).

33. See the account of "thought work" in Daniel Lynch, *After the Propaganda State: Media, Politics, and "Thought Work" in Reformed China* (Stanford, CA: Stanford University Press, 1999).

34. M. Kent Jennings and Ning Zhang, "Collective Memories in the Chinese Countryside" (Paper presented at the Annual Meeting of the International Society of Political Psychology, July 2002, Berlin). Chinese who were adolescents during the Cultural Revolution also recall that event as memorable, more so than do Chinese in other age groups.

35. See Tianjian Shi, "Cultural Values and Democracy in the People's Republic of China," *China Quarterly*, No. 162 (2000): 540–59; Yang Zhong, Jie Chen, and John Scheb,

"Mass Political Culture in Beijing: Findings from Two Public Opinion Surveys," *Asian Survey* 38, No. 8 (1998): 763–83. For a comparative perspective, see Gabriel A. Almond and Sidney Verba, *Civic Culture: Political Attitudes and Democracy in Five Nations* (Princeton, NJ: Princeton University Press, 1963).

36. Yun-han Chu and Yu-tzung Chang, "Culture Shift and Regime Legitimacy: Comparing Mainland China, Taiwan, and Hong Kong," in Shiping Hua, ed., *Chinese Political Culture, 1989–2000* (Armonk, N.Y.: M. E. Sharpe, 2001), pp. 320–47. See also Tianjian Shi, "Cultural Values and Political Trust: A Comparison of the People's Republic of China and Taiwan," *Comparative Politics* 33, No. 4 (2001): 401–19.

37. This is the conclusion of Tianjian Shi, based on analysis of the same survey data. See "Cultural Values and Democracy in the People's Republic of China." See also Andrew J. Nathan and Tianjian Shi, "Cultural Requisites for Democracy in China: Findings from a Survey," *Daedalus* 122, No. 2 (1993): 95–123.

38. Two independent sets of surveys, including surveys of the more politically knowledgeable and interested Beijing population, conclude this in almost exactly the same words. See Shi, "Cultural Values and Democracy in the People's Republic of China," and Zhong, Chen, and Scheb, "Mass Political Culture in Beijing."

39. See the excellent discussion of forms of political participation in Tianjian Shi, *Political Participation in Beijing* (Cambridge, MA: Harvard University Press, 1997), ch. 2.

40. On the Maoist period, see James R. Townsend, *Political Participation in Communist China* (Berkeley: University of California Press, 1967). On post-Mao elections, see Andrew Nathan, *Chinese Democracy* (Berkeley: University of California Press, 1985); Robert E. Bedeski, "China's 1979 Election Law and Its Implementation," *Electoral Studies* 5, No. 2 (1986): 153–65; Barrett L. McCormick, *Political Reform in Post-Mao China* (Berkeley: University of California Press, 1990); J. Bruce Jacobs, "Elections in China," *Australian Journal of Chinese Affairs*, No. 25 (1991): 171–200; Melanie Manion, "Chinese Democratization in Perspective: Electorates and Selectorates at the Township Level. Report from the Field," *China Quarterly*, No. 163 (2000): 133–51.

41. On rural decollectivization, see especially Daniel Kelliher, *Peasant Power in China: The Era of Rural Reform, 1979–1989* (New Haven, CT: Yale University Press, 1992); Kate Xiao Zhou, *How the Farmers Changed China: Power of the People* (Boulder, CO: Westview Press, 1996).

42. See Melanie Manion, "The Electoral Connection in the Chinese Countryside," *American Political Science Review* 90, No. 4 (1996): 736–48; Tianjian Shi, "Economic Development and Village Elections in Rural China," *Journal of Contemporary China* 8, No. 22 (1999): 433–35; Anne F. Thurston, *Muddling Toward Democracy: Political Change in Grassroots China* (Washington, DC: United States Institute of Peace, 1999); Lianjiang Li, "Elections and Popular Resistance in Rural China," *China Information* 16, No. 1 (2002): 89–107.

43. On protest movements in the 1970s and 1980s, see especially Andrew J. Nathan, *Chinese Democracy* (Berkeley: University of California Press, 1985); Jeffrey N. Wasserstrom and Elizabeth J. Perry, eds., *Popular Protest and Political Culture in Modern China: Learning from 1989* (Boulder, CO: Westview, 1992); Gregor Benton and Alan Hunter, *Wild Lily, Prairie Fire: China's Road to Democracy, 1942–1989* (Princeton, NJ: Princeton University Press, 1995).

44. James D. Seymour, ed., *The Fifth Modernization* (Stanfordville, NY: Human Rights Publishing Group, 1980).

45. On the 1989 protests, see Michel Oksenberg, Lawrence R. Sullivan, and Marc Lambert, eds., *Beijing Spring, 1989: Confrontation and Conflict, The Basic Documents,* (Armonk, NY: M. E. Sharpe, 1990); Han Minzhu and Hua Sheng, eds., *Cries for Democracy: Writings and Speeches from the 1989 Chinese Democracy Movement* (Princeton, NJ: Princeton University Press, 1990); Tony Saich, ed., *The Chinese People's Movement: Perspectives on Spring 1989* (Armonk, NY: M. E. Sharpe, 1990); Jonathan Unger, ed., *The Pro-Democracy Protest in China: Reports from the Provinces* (Sydney: Allen and Unwin, 1991); Craig Calhoun, *Neither Gods Nor Emperors: Students and the Struggle for Democracy in China* (Berkeley: University of California Press, 1995).

46. See James D. Seymour, *China's Satellite Parties* (Armonk, NY: M. E. Sharpe, 1987).

47. See especially Jonathan Unger, "'Bridges': Private Business, the Chinese Government and the Rise of New Associations," *China Quarterly*, No. 147 (1996): 795–819; Jonathan Unger and Anita Chan, "Corporatism in China: A Developmental State in an East Asian Context," in *China After Socialism: In the Footsteps of Eastern Europe or East Asia?*, edited by Barrett L. McCormick and Jonathan Unger (Armonk, NY: M. E. Sharpe, 1996) pp. 95–129.

48. See the discussions in Li Lianjiang and Kevin J. O'Brien, "Villagers and Popular Resistance in Contemporary China," *Modern China* 22, No. 1 (1996): 28–61; Kevin J. O'Brien, "Rightful Resistance," *World Politics* 49, No. 1 (1996): 31–55; Kevin J. O'Brien and Li Lianjiang, "The Politics of Lodging Complaints in Rural China," *China Quarterly*, No. 143 (September 1995): 756–83.

49. The most thorough description and thoughtful analysis of leading small groups is by Carol Lee Hamrin, "The Party Leadership System," in Kenneth G. Lieberthal and David M. Lampton, eds., *Bureaucracy, Politics, and Decision Making in Post-Mao China* (Berkeley: University of California Press, 1992), pp. 95–124. See also David M. Lampton, ed., *The Making of Chinese Foreign and Security Policy in the Era of Reform* (Stanford, CA: Stanford University Press, 2001), especially the contribution by Lu Ning, "The Central Leadership, Supraministry Coordinating Bodies, State Council Ministries, and Party Departments," pp. 39–60.

50. See Kenneth Lieberthal and Michel Oksenberg, *Policy Making in China: Leaders, Structures, and Processes* (Princeton, NJ: Princeton University Press, 1988).

51. See David M. Lampton, ed., *Policy Implementation in Post-Mao China* (Berkeley: University of California Press, 1987); Yasheng Huang, "Administrative Monitoring in China," *China Quarterly*, No. 143 (1995): 828–43.

52. See especially Ting Gong, "Forms and Characteristics of China's Corruption in the 1990s: Change with Continuity," *Communist and Post-Communist Studies* 30, No. 3 (1997): 277–88; Xiaobo Lu, "Booty Socialism, Bureau-preneurs, and the State in Transition," *Comparative Politics* 32, No. 3 (2000): 273–94; Yan Sun, "Reform, State, and Corruption: Is Corruption Less Destructive in China Than in Russia?" *Comparative Politics* 32, No. 1 (1999): 1–20; James Mulvenon, *Soldiers of Fortune: The Rise and Fall of the Chinese Military-Business Complex, 1978–1998* (Armonk, NY: M. E. Sharpe, 2001).

53. This is based on official Chinese statistics, which probably overstate real growth rates. One estimate suggests average annual rate of GDP growth in the 1980s and 1990s may be as low as 7.9 percent rather than the official figure of 9.9 percent. Of course, this would still make China one of the five most rapidly growing economies in the world. See Nicholas R. Lardy, *China's Unfinished Economic Revolution* (Washington, DC: Brookings Institution, 1998). More recently, Thomas G. Rawski has ignited controversy with his significantly lower estimates of growth for 1998–2001 (i.e., annual growth rates ranging from −2.5 to 4.0 percent), based on low energy consumption. See "How Fast Is China's Economy Really Growing?" *China Business Review* 29, No. 2 (2002): 40–43.

54. See Barry Naughton, *Growing Out of the Plan: Chinese Economic Reform, 1978–1993* (Cambridge, England: Cambridge University Press, 1996).

55. A good summary of policy and achievements in Chinese economic reform is Susumu Yabuki and Stephen M. Harner, *China's New Political Economy*, rev. ed. (Boulder, CO: Westview Press, 1999).

56. See Susan Greenhalgh, Zhu Chuzhu, and Li Nan, "Restraining Population Growth in Three Chinese Villages, 1988–93," *Population and Development Review* 20, No. 2 (1994): 365–95.

57. See the excellent study by Judith Banister, "China: Population Dynamics and Economic Implications," in Joint Economic Committee, U.S. Congress, *China's Economic Future: Challenges to U.S. Policy* (Armonk, NY: M. E. Sharpe, 1997), pp. 339–60. On coercion in implementation, see John Aird, *Slaughter of the Innocents: Coercive Birth Control in China* (Washington, DC: AEI Press, 1990).

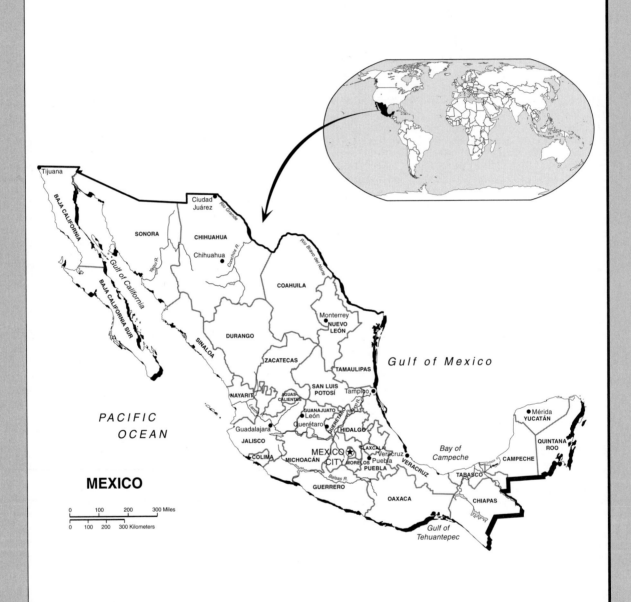

Tijuana

BAJA CALIFORNIA

Ciudad
Juárez

Rio Grande

SONORA

CHIHUAHUA

Conchos R.

Chihuahua

BAJA CALIFORNIA SUR

Gulf of California

Yaqui R.

COAHUILA

Rio Bravo del Norte

SINALOA

DURANGO

Monterrey
NUEVO
LEÓN

PACIFIC
OCEAN

ZACATECAS

TAMAULIPAS

Gulf of Mexico

NAYARIT

AGUAS
CALIENTES

SAN LUIS
POTOSÍ

Tampico

Lerma

GUANAJUATO
León
Querétaro

Pánuco R.

Mérida
YUCATÁN

Guadalajara

QUERÉTARO

HIDALGO

JALISCO

TLAXCALA

Veracruz

Bay of
Campeche

QUINTANA
ROO

MEXICO
CITY

MORELOS
Puebla

Puebla

VERACRUZ

CAMPECHE

COLIMA

MICHOACÁN

PUEBLA

MEXICO

Balsas R.

GUERRERO

TABASCO

CHIAPAS

OAXACA

Gulf of
Tehuantepec

| 0 | 100 | 200 | 300 Miles |
| 0 | 100 | 200 | 300 Kilometers |

Politics in Mexico

Wayne A. Cornelius and Jeffrey A. Weldon

COUNTRY BIO–MEXICO			
Population	100.2 million	**Head of Government**	President Vicente Fox Quesada
Territory	761,602 sq. mi		
Year of Independence	1810	**Language(s)**	Spanish, various Mayan, Nahuatl, and other regional indigenous languages
Year of Current Constitution	1917	**Religion**	nominally Roman Catholic 89%, Protestant 6%
Head of State	President Vicente Fox Quesada		

It is 8:00 on election night in 2000. Friends and family gather around televisions to watch the state-by-state returns and see how the next Congress will shape up. Exit poll results from the hottest races are announced. Computer-generated graphics showing vote trends flash on and off the screen. Returns are posted on the Internet as central election officials receive them. A few hours after the polls close, candidates begin appearing on television to concede defeat or claim victory. The outgoing president, whose party failed to elect its candidate, also goes on television to congratulate the winner and promise a smooth transition. Viewers heave a sigh of relief that the endless barrage of campaign commercials has ended and debate why things turned out as they did. The credibility of the results is not questioned.

What is striking about this picture is that it occurred not in the United States or some other "First World" country, but in Mexico, a country where the rigging of elections had been practiced systematically by the ruling *Partido Revolucionario Institucional* (PRI) for more than six decades. After the hotly contested but fraud-ridden presidential election of 1988, it took six days for the government to release even

preliminary results. Since then, Mexico has experienced a remarkable passage from a political system in which vote fraud and abuse of government resources by the ruling party were condoned by senior political leaders and cynically accepted by the general public to one in which government respect for voters' preferences is expected—indeed, demanded. This and other key elements of modern democratic politics are swiftly becoming routinized in Mexico.

Recurrent economic crises (1976–1977, 1982–1989, 1994–1996) were the most powerful catalyst for this revolution in citizen expectations. The vast majority of Mexicans suffered severe economic pain during these two decades, directly attributable to government mismanagement of the national economy. Millions of jobs were lost, real wages were stagnant or declining in all but a few years of the period, savings and businesses were decimated by inflation and currency devaluations, and government benefits for the middle and lower classes were slashed in the austerity budgets necessitated by the economic crises.

The 1988 presidential election brought a tidal wave of antigovernment protest voting, with the PRI's candidate eking out a bare majority victory.[1]

Zapatista leader Subco-
mandante Marcos arrives
in Mexico City in May 2001
to lobby the Congress to approve sweeping indigenous
rights legislation. The bill
was watered down before
passage and the Zapatistas
rejected it. The stalemate in
Chiapas continues.

AFP/Corbis; © Reuters NewMedia
Inc./Corbis

The government could contain the discontent and keep the PRI in power because it completely dominated the machinery of elections as well as the mass media. In the 1994 election, the PRI rode the coattails of the still highly popular President Carlos Salinas, and took advantage of public anxieties created by the Zapatista rebellion in Chiapas and a spate of high-profile political assassinations. PRI propaganda frightened voters with images of destabilizing violence and massive capital flight, in the event of an opposition party victory at the national level.

In the 2000 election, however, the *"voto de miedo"* (the fear vote) was overwhelmed by the *"voto de castigo"* (the punishment vote). Voters were furious at having been deceived twice by their government, first during the oil boom era of 1977–1981 and then during the Salinas presidency (1988–1994), periods when the government created an illusion of prosperity and boundless future economic gains. They were equally angry about rising street crime and mounting evidence of large-scale corruption in government under Salinas, who was almost universally blamed for the economic crisis that engulfed Mexico within weeks after he left office. For the first time in 71 years, the voters soundly rejected the presidential candidate of the PRI, turning to Vicente Fox, a maverick former Coca Cola executive-turned-politician who ran under the banner of the Alliance

for Change, a center-right coalition consisting of the **Partido Acción Nacional (PAN)** and the Partido Verde Ecologista de México (PVEM) (see Box 10.1).

Public confidence that a vote for some alternative to the PRI would actually be respected by the authorities had been boosted significantly by several rounds of reforms in the federal electoral law in the 1990s—changes that the government proposed and the PRI endorsed, under strong pressure from citizens and the opposition parties. These procedures added so many procedural safeguards into the conduct of elections that the worst, old-style forms of vote fraud (stuffing ballot boxes or stealing them, falsifying vote tallies, etc.) became virtually impossible without provoking a public uproar. Most importantly, the law created a new federal elections agency independent of government and PRI authority and made it responsible for organizing all phases of the electoral process, giving all parties access to the media, allocating public funds for campaigns, recruiting and training citizens to run the polling places, counting votes, and certifying the results.

The results of the 1997 elections for Congress had been a stunning setback for the PRI, which lost 112 races (out of 300 in which candidates were directly elected by majority vote rather than awarded their seats through a proportional representation formula). For the first time since 1929, the PRI had

BOX 10.1   The Watershed Election of 2000

The PRI's 71-year monopoly over presidential power in Mexico came to an end with the July 2, 2000 election. At that time it was the world's longest continually ruling party at the national level. In the run-up to the election, the PRI had tried desperately to shed its image as a corrupt, authoritarian party by holding a vigorously contested, open primary election to choose its presidential candidate, for the first time in its history not deferring to the preferences of the outgoing PRI president. The chosen candidate, Francisco Labastida, was a former state governor and middle-ranked technocrat under several PRI presidents. He tried but failed to distance himself sufficiently from the record of previous PRI governments. He was badly beaten in two nationally televised debates by the dynamic and plain-speaking candidate of the National Action Party, Vicente Fox. Labastida failed to excite even the PRI's own electoral base, despite spending more money on paid campaign advertising than any other candidate in Mexican history.

Fox appealed to the electorate seeking fundamental change in the Mexican political system. His campaign slogan was simple and potent: *"Ya!"*—"Change, now!" or "Enough, already!" He promised an economic policy "with a human face," and an end to corruption and rule by PRI narco-politicians. Distrusted as an outsider by his own political party, Fox created a nationwide network of private donors and campaign workers intensely loyal to him. Cuauhtémoc Cárdenas, running for president for the third time as the candidate of the Party of the Democratic Revolution (PRD), threatened to divide the anti-PRI vote, but his ineffectiveness as the first elected Mayor of Mexico City (1997–1999) undermined his popularity and helped Fox to convince Mexicans that they should vote strategically for him, as the opposition candidate most able to oust the PRI. The final results were: Fox, 42.5 percent; Labastida, 36.1 percent; Cárdenas, 16.7 percent; other candidates, 4.7 percent.

---

to surrender control of the Chamber of Deputies (the lower house of Congress) to a coalition of four opposition parties. The PRI also lost its two-thirds majority in the Senate, which is needed to approve constitutional amendments. In the 2000 elections, the PRI continued to lose ground in Congress. Currently there is no majority party in either house, although the PRI still controls a plurality of seats in both the Senate and the Chamber of Deputies (see Table 10.1 below). The PRI can be outvoted by a coalition of PAN, PRD, and smaller party members, but President Fox must assemble such coalitions on an issue-by-issue basis.

Beyond the division of power that has prevailed at the federal level since 1997, divided governments at the state level have become commonplace. During the 1989–1997 period, for example, seven states had legislatures controlled by a party different from that of the state's governor. Mexicans elected non-PRI candidates as governors in ten (out of 32) states during this period; prior to 1989 no opposition party victory at the state level had been recognized by the government. All this symbolizes Mexico's newly accelerated shift toward a much more competitive, pluralistic political system.

CURRENT POLICY CHALLENGES

Mexico entered the twenty-first century with huge social and economic problems: an economy that produces far too few jobs to accommodate the young people entering the labor market each year; an educational system sorely in need of modernization; a highly unequal distribution of income; a growing poverty population, with at least half of all Mexicans living below the official poverty line; acute environmental problems that damage the health of both rural and urban dwellers; and a criminal justice system that barely functions, routinely violates the human rights of citizens, and is heavily corrupted by drug trafficking. The PRI lost its grip on the Mexican political system in large part because it had failed to deal effectively with these problems. It remains to be seen whether the democratic "opposition," now in power, can manage them with conspicuously greater success.

Several emerging policy challenges will be no less daunting. As a developing country, Mexico has to play catch-up with its international trade partners and competitors. It must modernize its agricultural sector to allow it to survive competition from the

T A B L E   1 0 . 1   Composition of the Mexican Congress, 2000–2003

	Seats Won by Plurality Vote	Seats Won by P. R. System	Total	Percentage
Chamber of Deputies				
Partido Acción Nacional (PAN)[1]	80	71	151	30.2
Partido Revolucionario Institucional (PRI)	161	63	224	44.8
Partido de la Revolución Democrática (PRD)[2]	41	56	97	19.4
Partido Verde Ecologista de México (PVEM)[1]	3	14	17	3.4
Partido del Trabajo (PT)[2]	—	6	6	1.2
Convergencia	—	5	5	1.0
Total	**300**	**200**	**500**	**100**
Senate				
Partido Acción Nacional (PAN)[1]	37 (10)*	9	46	35.9
Partido Revolucionario Institucional (PRI)	47 (15)*	13	60	46.9
Partido de la Revolución Democrática (PRD)[2]	11 (7)*	4	15	11.7
Partido del Trabajo (PT)[2]	—	1	1	0.8
Partido Verde Ecologista de México (PVEM)[1]	1	4	5	3.9
Convergencia por la Democracia (CD)[2]	—	1	1	0.8
Total	**96**	**32**	**128**	**100**

[1]Alianza por el Cambio

[2]Alianza por México

*Numbers in parentheses are seats awarded by the "first minority" principle (first-ranked Senate candidate of the second-place party in every state).

United States and Canada, where subsidies and more efficient methods make agricultural goods cheaper. Mexico needs to replace its antiquated and inefficient labor law with new statutes that both protect workers and encourage job creation. It must renovate the energy sector—oil, electricity, and natural gas—either through increased government spending or by allowing greater private or foreign investment, which would require controversial constitutional amendments. An unfamiliar demographic problem is beginning to emerge—an aging population—and the Mexican people must soon bolster the funding of private and government-sponsored pension plans. Finally, the government must expand the tax base to provide the resources that will be needed to address all of the above-mentioned challenges.

On the political front, additional changes in electoral rules are needed to close loopholes concerning the financing of campaigns, to make it more difficult for elected officials to use government resources to promote their party's candidates, and to allow the im-

mediate reelection of legislators, which would make them more responsive and accountable to their constituents. But in terms of advancing Mexico's transition to a fully democratic system, these refinements may be less important than the rapidly spreading belief that alternation in power among Mexico's three main parties, at all levels of governance, is both desirable and achievable. In short, most Mexicans seem to have concluded that it is time to get on with the business of modern democracy.

HISTORICAL PERSPECTIVES

Colonialism and Church-State Relations

Long before Hernán Cortés landed in 1519 and began the Spanish conquest of Mexico, its territory was inhabited by numerous Indian civilizations. Of these, the Maya in the Yucatán peninsula and the Toltec on the central plateau had developed the most complex political and economic organization. Both of these civilizations had disintegrated, however, be-

B O X 1 0 . 2   Key Political Events in Mexico, 1810–2006

1810–1821	War of Independence against Spain.
1846–1848	War between Mexico and the United States.
1910–1920	Mexican Revolution.
1917	New Constitution is issued, incorporating Revolutionary goals and ideals.
1924–1928	Presidency of Plutarco Elías Calles.
1927–1929	Cristero Rebellion (Catholic Church vs. State).
1928	Alvaro Obregón is elected to the presidency; assassinated a few months later.
1928–1934	"Jefe Máximo" Plutarco Elías Calles rules from behind the scenes, under several provisional Presidents (the "Maximato" period).
1929	Plutarco Elías Calles establishes the Partido Nacional Revolucionario (PNR).
1934–1940	Presidency of Lázaro Cárdenas.
1938	President Cárdenas reorganizes the PNR, which becomes the Partido de la Revolución Mexicana (PRM); Cárdenas nationalizes the oil industry.
1939	Partido Acción Nacional (PAN) is founded.
1940–1946	Presidency of Manuel Avila Camacho.
1946–1952	Presidency of Miguel Alemán.
1946	PRM is restructured, renamed as the Partido Revolucionario Institucional (PRI).
1952–1958	Presidency of Adolfo Ruiz Cortines.
1958–1964	Presidency of Adolfo López Mateos.
1964–1970	Presidency of Gustavo Díaz Ordaz.
1968	Student protest movement challenges the government and is violently repressed (the "Tlatelolco massacre").
1970–1976	Presidency of Luis Echeverría.
1976–1982	Presidency of José López Portillo; period of the oil export boom.
1981–1982	Drop in world oil prices and rising interest rates cause economic collapse; Mexico is unable to service its external debt.
1982–1988	Presidency of Miguel de la Madrid.
1988–1994	Presidency of Carlos Salinas de Gortari.
1994	North American Free Trade Agreement (NAFTA) goes into effect; peasant rebellion erupts in the state of Chiapas; PRI presidential candidate Luis Donaldo Colosio is assassinated and replaced by Ernesto Zedillo; the peso is sharply devalued, provoking a deep economic crisis.
1994–2000	Presidency of Ernesto Zedillo.
1997–2000	The PRI lost the majority of seats in the Chamber of Deputies.
2000	PRI loses the presidency for the first time in 71 years.
2000–2006	Presidency of Vicente Fox.

fore the Spaniards arrived. Smaller Indian societies were decimated by diseases introduced by the invaders or were vanquished by the sword. Subsequent grants of land and Indian labor by the Spanish Crown to the colonists further isolated the rural Indian population and deepened their exploitation.

The combined effects of attrition, intermarriage, and cultural penetration of Indian regions have drastically reduced the proportion of Mexico's population culturally identified as Indian. By the 1990 census figures, 7.9 percent of the nation's population spoke an Indian language.[2] The Indian minority has been persistently marginal to the national economy and political system. Today, the indigenous population is heavily concentrated in rural communities that the government classifies as the country's most economically depressed and service-deprived, lo-

cated primarily in the southeast and the center of the country. They engage in rainfall-dependent subsistence agriculture using traditional methods of cultivation, are seasonally employed as migrant laborers in commercial agriculture, or produce crafts for sale in regional and national markets. The Indian population is an especially troubling reminder of the millions of people who have been left behind by uneven development in twentieth-century Mexico.

The importance of Spain's colonies in the New World lay in their ability to provide the Crown with vital resources to fuel the Spanish economy. Mexico's mines provided gold and silver in abundance until the wars of independence began in 1810. After independence, Mexico continued to export these ores, supplemented in subsequent eras by hemp, cotton, textiles, oil, and winter vegetables.

Since the Spanish conquest, the Roman Catholic Church has been an institution of enduring power in Mexico. Priests joined the Spanish invaders in an evangelical mission to promote conversion of the Indians to Catholicism, and individual priests have continued to play important roles in national history. Father Miguel Hidalgo y Costilla helped launch Mexico's war of independence in 1810, and Father José María Morelos y Pavón replaced Hidalgo as spiritual and military leader of the independence movement when the Crown executed Hidalgo in 1811.

During Mexico's post-independence period, institutional antagonisms between church and central government have occasionally flared into open confrontations on such issues as church wealth, educational policy, the content of public school textbooks, and political activism by the church. The constitutions of 1857 and 1917 formally established the separation of church and state and defined their respective domains. Constitutional provisions dramatically reduced the church's power and wealth by nationalizing its property, including large agricultural landholdings. The 1917 constitution also made church-affiliated schools subject to the authority of the federal government, denied priests the right to vote or speak publicly on political issues, and gave the government the right to limit the number of priests who can serve in Mexico. Government efforts during the 1920s to enforce these constitutional provisions led to a civil insurrection that caused 100,000 combatant deaths, uncounted civilian casualties, and economic devastation in a large part of central Mexico. The settlement of this "Cristero rebellion" established, once and for all, the church's subordination to the state, in return for which the government relaxed its restrictions on church activities in nonpolitical arenas.

This accord inaugurated a long period of relative tranquility in church-state relations, during which the government and the church ignored many of the anticlerical provisions of the 1917 constitution (such as the prohibition on church involvement in education). The central church hierarchy—among the most conservative in Latin America—cooperated with the government on a variety of issues, and the church posed no threat to the ruling party's hegemony.

Revolution and Its Aftermath

The nationwide civil conflict that erupted in Mexico in 1910 is often referred to as the first of the great "social revolutions" that shook the world early in the twentieth century. However, Mexico's upheaval originated within the country's ruling class. The revolution did not begin as a spontaneous uprising of the common people against an entrenched dictator, Porfirio Díaz, and against the local bosses and landowners who exploited them. Even though hundreds of thousands of workers and peasants ultimately participated in the civil strife, most of the revolutionary leadership came from the younger generation of middle- and upper-class Mexicans who had become disenchanted with three and a half decades of increasingly heavy-handed rule by the aging dictator and his clique. These disgruntled members of the elite saw their future opportunities for economic and political mobility blocked by the closed group surrounding Díaz. Their battle cry was "effective suffrage, no reelection"—the end of self-perpetuating dictatorship made possible by sham elections.

Led by Francisco I. Madero, whose family had close ties with the ruling group, these liberal bourgeois reformers were committed to opening up the political system and creating new opportunities for themselves within a capitalist economy whose basic features they did not challenge. They sought not to destroy the established order but rather to make it work more in their own interest than that of the foreign capitalists who dominated key sectors of Mexico's economy during the Porfirian dictatorship, a period called "the Porfiriato."

Of course, some serious grievances had accumulated among workers and peasants. Once the rebellion against Díaz got underway, leaders who appealed to the disadvantaged masses pressed their claims against the central government. Emiliano Zapata led a movement of peasants in the state of Morelos who were bent on regaining the land they had lost to the rural aristocracy by subterfuge during the Porfiriato. In the north, Pancho Villa led an army consisting of jobless workers, small landowners, and cattle hands, whose main interest was steady employment. As the various revolutionary leaders contended for control of the central government, the political order that had been created and enforced by Díaz disintegrated into

Peasants demonstrate against construction of a new international airport for Mexico City on their land. Their protests were successful in blocking the project, which would have been the largest public work built by President Vicente Fox's government.

AP/Wide World Photos

warlordism—powerful regional gangs led by revolutionary *caudillos* (political-military strongmen) who aspired more to increasing their personal wealth and social status than to leading a genuine social revolution.

The first decade of the revolution produced a new, remarkably progressive constitution, replacing the constitution of 1857. The young, middle-class elite that dominated the constitutional convention of 1916–1917 "had little if any direct interest in labor unions or land distribution. But it was an elite that recognized the need for social change. . . . By 1916, popular demands for land and labor reform were too great to ignore."[3] The constitution of 1917 established the principle of state control over all natural resources, subordination of the church to the state, the government's right to redistribute land, and rights for labor that had not yet been secured even by the labor movement in the United States. Nearly two decades passed, however, before most of these constitutional provisions began to be implemented.

Many historians today stress the continuities between prerevolutionary and postrevolutionary Mexico. The processes of economic modernization, capital accumulation, state building, and political centralization that gained considerable momentum during the Porfiriato were interrupted by civil strife from 1910 to 1920, but they resumed once a semblance of order had been restored. During the 1920s, the central government set out to eliminate or under-

mine the most powerful and independent-minded regional *caudillos* by co-opting the local power brokers, known as **caciques**. These local political bosses became, in effect, appendages of the central government, supporting its policies and maintaining control over the population in their communities. By the end of this period, leaders with genuine popular followings like Zapata and Villa had been assassinated, and control had been seized by a new postrevolutionary elite bent on demobilizing the masses and establishing the hegemony of the central government.

The rural aristocracy of the Porfiriato had been weakened but not eliminated; its heirs still controlled large concentrations of property and other forms of wealth in many parts of the country. Most of the large urban firms that operated during the Porfiriato also survived, further demonstrating that the revolution was not an attack on private capital per se. Except during the years of most intense violence (1914–1917), the Revolution had surprisingly minor effects on private investment and economic growth.

The Cárdenas Upheaval

Elite control was maintained during the 1930s, but this was nevertheless an era of massive social and political upheaval in Mexico. During the presidency of Lázaro Cárdenas (1934–1940), peasants and urban workers succeeded for the first time in pressing their claims for land and higher wages; in fact, Cárdenas actively encouraged them to do so. The result was an unprecedented wave of strikes, protest demonstrations, and petitions for breaking up large rural estates.

Most disputes between labor and management during this period were settled, under government pressure, in favor of the workers. The Cárdenas administration also redistributed more than twice as much land as that expropriated by all of Cárdenas's predecessors since 1915, when Mexico's land reform program was formally initiated. By 1940 the country's land tenure system had been fundamentally altered, breaking the traditional domination of the large haciendas and creating a large sector of small peasant farmers called *ejidatarios*—more than 1.5 million of them—who had received plots of land under the agrarian reform program. The Cárdenas government actively encouraged the formation of new organizations of peasants and urban workers, grouped the new organizations into nationwide confederations, and provided arms to rural militias formed by the *ejidatarios.* Even Mexico's foreign relations were disrupted in 1938 when the Cárdenas government nationalized oil companies that had been operating in Mexico under U.S. and British ownership.

The Cárdenas era proved to be an aberration in the development of postrevolutionary Mexico. Never before, nor since, had the fundamental "who benefits?" question been addressed with such energy and commitment by a Mexican government. Mexican intellectuals frequently refer to 1938 as the highwater mark of the Mexican revolution as measured by social progress, and they characterize the period since then as a retrogression. Certainly, the distributive and especially the redistributive performance of the Mexican government declined sharply in the decades that followed, and the worker and peasant organizations formed during the Cárdenas era atrophied and became less and less likely to contest either the will of the government or the interests of Mexico's private economic elites. De facto reconcentration of landholdings and other forms of wealth occurred as the state provided increasingly generous support to the country's new commercial, industrial, and financial elites during a period of rapid industrialization.

Critics of the Cárdenas administration have laid much of the blame for this outcome on the kind of mass political organizing that occurred under Cárdenas. The resulting labor and peasant organizations were captives of the regime—tied so closely to it that they had no capacity for autonomous action. Under

the control of a new group of national political leaders whose values and priorities were unfavorable to the working classes, these same organizations, after Cárdenas, functioned only to enforce political stability and limit lower-class demands for government benefits. "The institutional shell of Cardenismo remained," writes historian Alan Knight, "but its internal dynamic was lost. In other words, new drivers hijacked the jalopy; they retuned the engine, took on new passengers, and then drove it in a quite different direction."[4] In the long term, the principal beneficiaries of Cárdenas's economic project were the middle classes and unionized industrial workers—not peasants and the unorganized urban poor.

The Cárdenas era fundamentally reshaped Mexico's political institutions: The presidency became the primary institution of the political system, with sweeping powers exercised during a constitutionally limited six-year term with no possibility of reelection; the military was removed from overt political competition and transformed into one of several institutional pillars of the regime; and an elaborate network of government-sponsored peasant and labor organizations provided a mass base for the official political party and performed a variety of political and economic control functions, utilizing a multilayered system of patronage and clientelism.

By 1940 a much larger proportion of the Mexican population was nominally included in the national political system, mostly by their membership in peasant and labor organizations created by Cárdenas. No real democratization of the system resulted from this vast expansion of "political participation," however. Although working-class groups did have more control over their representatives in the government-sponsored organizations than over their former masters on the haciendas and in the factories, their influence over public policy and government priorities after Cárdenas was minimal and highly indirect. Policy recommendations, official actions, and nominations for elective and appointive positions at all levels still emanated from the central government and official party headquarters in Mexico City, filtering down the hierarchy to the rank and file for ratification and legitimation.

The Era of Hegemonic Party Rule

The political system shaped by Lázaro Cárdenas proved remarkably durable. From 1940 until the late 1980s, Mexico's official party-government apparatus was the most stable regime in Latin America. It had a well-earned reputation for resilience, adaptability to new circumstances, a high level of agreement within the ruling elite on basic rules of political competition, and a seemingly unlimited capacity to co-opt dissidents, both within and outside of the ruling party. As late as 1990, the celebrated Peruvian novelist Mario Vargas Llosa could plausibly describe Mexico's regime as "the perfect dictatorship," combining stability, legitimacy, and durability in a way that even the former Soviet Union and Castro's Cuba had never achieved.[5]

With the fall of the Communist Party of the Soviet Union in 1991, the PRI became the world's longest continuously ruling political party. Since 1929, when the "official" party was founded, both political assassination and armed rebellion had been rejected as routes to the presidency by all contenders for power. A handful of disappointed aspirants to the ruling party's presidential nomination mounted candidacies outside the party (in the elections of 1929, 1940, 1946, 1952, and 1988), but even the most broadly supported of these breakaway movements were successfully contained through government-engineered vote fraud and intimidation.

In the early 1970s concerns had been raised about the stability of the system, after the bloody repression of a student protest movement in Mexico City by President Gustavo Díaz Ordaz on the eve of the 1968 Olympic Games. Many analysts at that time suggested that Mexico was entering a period of institutional crisis, requiring fundamental reforms in both political arrangements and strategy of economic development. But the discovery of massive oil and natural gas resources during the latter 1970s gave the incumbent regime a new lease on life. The continued support of masses and elites was purchased with an apparently limitless supply of petro-pesos, even without major structural reforms. The government's room for maneuver was abruptly erased by the collapse of the oil boom in August 1982, owing to a combination of adverse international economic circumstances (falling oil prices, rising interest rates, recession in the United States) and fiscally irresponsible domestic policies. Real wages and living standards for the vast majority of Mexicans plummeted, and the government committed itself to a socially painful restructuring of the economy, including a drastic shrinkage of the sector owned and managed by the government itself.

The economic crisis of the 1980s placed enormous stress on Mexico's political system. In the July 6, 1988, national elections, the PRI suffered unprecedented reverses in both the presidential and congressional races. The vote share officially attributed to Carlos Salinas was more than 20 percentage points below that of PRI presidential candidate Miguel de la Madrid in the 1982 election. Ex-PRIista Cuauhtémoc Cárdenas, son of the much-revered former President Lázaro Cárdenas, heading a hastily assembled coalition of minor leftist and nationalist parties, was officially credited with 31.1 percent of the presidential vote—far more than any previous opposition candidate but probably much less than he actually received if the vote count had been honest.[6] A diminished PRI delegation still controlled the Congress, but the president's party had lost the two-thirds majority needed to approve constitutional amendments.

Carlos Salinas breathed new life into the creaking PRI apparatus. His brand of strong presidential leadership and his accomplishments—especially the toppling of corrupt labor union bosses, a sharp reduction in inflation, and the National Solidarity Program, a new-style antipoverty and public works program that increased government responsiveness to lower-class needs—sufficed to rebuild electoral support for the PRI and to paper over the cracks within the ruling political elite. Salinas opened the Mexican economy to foreign trade and investment, and privatized hundreds of inefficient state-owned companies. Mexico at last seemed poised to make a giant leap from Third World to First World status. While political liberalization had proceeded slowly and unevenly under Salinas, far behind the pace of his sweeping free-market economic reforms, Mexico appeared to be coasting inexorably toward a transfer of power to yet another PRI national government in 1994.

The illusion of proximate economic modernity and political inevitability was shattered on New Year's Day 1994, by a "post-modern" peasant revolt in Chiapas, Mexico's most underdeveloped and politically backward state. An estimated 2,000 primitively armed but well-disciplined Indian rebels seized control of four isolated municipalities and declared war on the central government—something that had not happened since 1938. Their demands for social justice and democracy resonated throughout Mexico, long after the initial skirmishes with the Mexican army had claimed at least 145 lives and a cease-fire had been negotiated. Suddenly, middle- and upper-class Mexicans, as well as foreign governments and investors, were reminded of the persistence of political repression, human rights violations, extreme poverty, and inequality in Mexico. The impoverished Indians who took up arms against the state in Chiapas symbolized the many millions of Mexicans who had been left behind in the drive for economic modernity and internationalism.

The unfinished business of Mexico's free-market economic revolution and the serious social dislocations that it had caused were, indeed, formidable; but they were still considered manageable, within the confines of the one-party-dominant system that had been institutionalized in the 1950s and 1960s. The rebels in Chiapas could be negotiated with and bought off, through a combination of carefully circumscribed political reforms, some land redistribution, and a massive infusion of government funds for social programs and infrastructure. The country could go on to hold national elections, installing another PRI president whose policy preferences differed little from those of his two predecessors, thereby locking in Mexico's new, market-driven, internationally "open" economic model.

Those comfortable assumptions were soon shattered as well. Less than three months after the Chiapas rebellion erupted, President Salinas's hand-picked successor, Luis Donaldo Colosio, was assassinated while campaigning in Tijuana, perhaps by conservative members of his own party. Colosio had launched his bid for the presidency with bold promises to accelerate the pace of political reform. Apart from raising the specter of uncontrolled political violence and an economy deflated by massive capital flight, Colosio's assassination—the first killing of a national-level political leader in Mexico since 1929—totally disrupted the traditional presidential succession process and reopened divisions within the national political elite that, as recently as 1988, had threatened to split the ruling party.

As in 1988, the fire was put out—but only temporarily. With a last great exertion of presidential will, Carlos Salinas imposed upon the PRI another hand-picked successor, economist-technocrat Ernesto Zedillo, to replace the slain Colosio. Rapid, skillful responses by Salinas's economic cabinet, strongly backed by the U.S. government, proved sufficient to calm the financial markets. In August 1994, in a high-turnout election that was judged by most independent observers at the time to be the cleanest in Mexico's postrevolutionary history, the opposition parties were soundly defeated. Not only did the PRI retain control of the presidency (albeit with just a plurality of 48.8 percent of the total votes cast), it also maintained an ample majority in the federal Congress.[7]

The appearance of restored stability created by the ruling party's impressive performance in the August 1994 elections was short-lived, however. In December 1994, a militarily insignificant renewal of the Zapatista rebels' activities in Chiapas, followed immediately by a sustained speculative attack on the overvalued peso by short-term foreign and domestic investors, opened a Pandora's box of economic and political troubles. What began as a currency and financial liquidity crisis quickly evolved into a massive capital flight and a deep recession. After publicly criticizing Zedillo and his cabinet ministers for provoking the economic crisis by mishandling the devaluation of the peso, ex-President Salinas went into de facto exile in Ireland.

By the late 1990s, the PRI once again appeared to be in a state of accelerated decomposition. Divisions within the party were deeper than at any time since the mid-1930s, when newly inaugurated, reform-minded President Lázaro Cárdenas forced a confrontation with long-time strongman and former president Plutarco Elías Calles and his conservative allies. With the defeat of its presidential candidate in 2000, the PRI lost control of the vast patronage resources of the central government, which were crucial to keeping it in power for more than seven decades.

International Environment

Since independence, Mexico's politics and public policies have always been influenced by proximity to the United States. Porfirio Díaz is widely reputed to have exclaimed, "Poor Mexico! So far from God and so close to the United States." Indeed, this proximity has made the United States a powerful presence in Mexico. A wide array of factors—the 2,000-mile land border between the two countries, Mexico's rich supplies of minerals, labor, and other resources needed by U.S. industry, and Mexico's attractiveness as a site for U.S. private investment—has made such influence inevitable.

Midway through the nineteenth century, Mexico's sovereignty as a nation was directly threatened when the U.S. push for territorial and economic expansion met little resistance in northern Mexico. Emerging from a war for independence from Spain and plagued by chronic political instability, Mexico was highly vulnerable to aggression from the north. By annexing Texas in 1845 and instigating the Mexican-American War of 1846 to 1848 (Ulysses S. Grant later called it "America's great unjust war"), the United States seized half of Mexico's national territory: disputed land in Texas, all the land that is now California, Nevada, and Utah, most of New Mexico and Arizona, and part of Colorado and Wyoming. This massive seizure of territory, along with several later military interventions and meddling in the politics of "revolutionary" Mexico that extended through the 1920s, left scars that have not healed. Even today, the average Mexican suspects that the United States has designs on Mexico's remaining territory, its oil, even its human resources.

The lost territory includes the U.S. regions that have been the principal recipients of Mexican immigrant workers in this century. This labor migration, too, was instigated mainly by the United States. Beginning in the 1880s, U.S. farmers, railroads, and mining companies, with U.S. government encouragement, obtained many of the workers needed to expand the economy and transport systems of the Southwest and Midwest by sending labor recruiters into northern and central Mexico.

By the end of the 1920s, the economies of Mexico and the United States were sufficiently intertwined that the effects of the Great Depression were swiftly transmitted to Mexico, causing unemployment to rise and export earnings and GNP to plummet. In response to these economic shocks, Mexico tried during the 1930s to reduce its dependence on the United States as a market for silver and other exports. The effort failed, and by 1940 Mexico was more dependent than before on the flow of goods, capital, and labor to and from the United States.

After 1940, Mexico relied even more heavily on U.S. private capital to help finance its drive for industrialization. The United States also experienced severe shortages of labor in World War II, and Mexico's dependence on the United States as a market for its surplus labor became institutionalized through the so-called *bracero* program of importing contract labor. Operating from 1942 to 1964, this program brought more than 4 million Mexicans to the United States to work in seasonal agriculture. After the demise of the *bracero* program, migration to the United States continued, with most new arrivals entering illegally. In recent decades the flow of migrant workers (and more recently, their dependents)

has been so heavy that by 2002 more than 9.7 million persons born in Mexico were living in the United States—equivalent to nearly 10 percent of Mexico's total population.[8]

The U.S. stake in Mexico's continued political stability and economic development has increased dramatically since World War II. In recent years Mexico has been the third largest trading partner of the United States (behind Canada and Japan). Employment for hundreds of thousands of people in both Mexico and the United States depends on this trade. In 1982, when U.S. trade with Mexico fell by 32 percent because of Mexico's economic crisis, an estimated 250,000 U.S. jobs were lost. Largely because of the late 1994 peso devaluation, which made Mexico's exports cheaper in the United States and U.S. products unaffordable to most Mexican consumers, the overall U.S. trade deficit soared to record levels in the first quarter of 1995.

Despite the sharp fluctuations in Mexico's economy since the early 1980s, that country is one of the preferred sites for investments by U.S.-based multinational corporations, especially for investments in modern industries like petrochemicals, pharmaceuticals, food processing, machinery, transportation, and athletic footware. Subsidiaries of U.S. companies produce half the manufactured goods exported by Mexico. Firms in Mexico's own private sector have actively sought foreign capital to finance new joint ventures and expand plant facilities. By the mid-1990s, total U.S. investment in Mexico was more than $115 billion.

Mexico's external economic dependence is often cited by both critics and defenders of the Mexican system as an all-encompassing explanation for the country's problems. In fact, economic ties between Mexico and the United States usually explain only part of the picture. And these linkages do not necessarily predetermine the choices of policy and development priorities that are set by Mexico's rulers. But Mexico's increasingly tight linkage to the U.S. economy limits the range of choices that can be made by Mexican officials; and economic fluctuations in the United States are a large source of uncertainty in Mexico's planning and policymaking.

The international environment of Mexico's political system was transformed fundamentally by the signing of the North American Free Trade Agreement (NAFTA) in 1993. NAFTA made Mexico a much more attractive investment site for U.S. firms seeking low-cost labor and for Asian and European firms seeking privileged access to the U.S. market. While Carlos Salinas opposed such an agreement during his 1988 presidential campaign, because "there is such a different economic level between the U.S. and Mexico," he soon found himself with no alternative to pursuing greater economic integration with the United States. With 1 million new job seekers entering its labor force each year, Mexico desperately needed to increase its rate of economic growth. The only way to do that while containing inflation was to stimulate a massive new infusion of investment capital from abroad. By 1998, thanks to NAFTA, Mexico had surpassed Japan to become the United States' second most important trading partner, after Canada.

Less than a year after NAFTA was implemented, the implications of the much closer linkage between the U.S. and Mexican economies became painfully clear, when a new financial crisis erupted in Mexico. While there was virtually no political constituency within the United States for a U.S. government "bailout" of Mexico, and no enthusiasm among Mexicans for taking on more foreign loans and using the country's oil revenues to collateralize them (just one of the stringent conditions imposed by the United States), neither government had any realistic alternative to such a rescue. A Mexican default on repayment of nearly $30 billion in *tesobonos* (short-term bonds issued by the Mexican treasury) held mostly by U.S. pension funds, mutual funds, and other institutional investors would have threatened the assets of many millions of American households whose money had been invested in the high-yielding Mexican government bonds. Moreover, a meltdown of the Mexican economy could have caused a dramatic surge in illegal immigration to the United States, in addition to those Mexicans who would be coming because of the 1994–1995 peso devaluation, which made the U.S. minimum wage more than 12 times higher than Mexico's. Consequently, a nearly $50 billion multilateral package of loan guarantees and credit line swaps—including $20 billion from a U.S. government currency stabilization fund—was made available to Mexico in January 1995.

The net macroeconomic impact of NAFTA has been positive for Mexico, as well as for the United States and Canada. However, North American economic integration has not lifted real wages in Mex-

ico, at least to the level that would deter emigration to the United States. And the benefits of NAFTA have been distributed quite unevenly within Mexico, with the roughly one-quarter of the economically active population still in agriculture being the most conspicuous losers.

POLITICAL CULTURE AND SOCIALIZATION

Most of what we know empirically about Mexican political culture is based on research completed during the period of sustained economic growth and virtually unchallenged one-party rule in Mexico, from 1940 to the mid-1970s. There is a growing body of survey-based research on attitudes toward political parties and other elements of mass political culture in the 1980s and 1990s, but not yet enough to confidently document the changes in core values, attitudes, and behaviors that most observers assume have occurred during the last two decades of economic and political crises.

The portrait of Mexican political culture that emerges from pre-1976 studies can be summarized as follows: Mexicans are highly supportive of the political institutions that evolved from the Mexican Revolution, and they endorse the democratic principles embodied in the Constitution of 1917. However, they are critical of government performance, especially in creating jobs, reducing social and economic inequality, and delivering basic public services. Most government bureaucrats and politicians are viewed as distant, elitist, and self-serving, if not corrupt. Mexicans traditionally have been pessimistic about their ability to affect election outcomes, anticipating fraud and regarding attendance at campaign rallies and voting as ritualistic activities.

On the surface, this combination of attitudes and beliefs seems to be internally contradictory. How could Mexicans support a political system that they see as unresponsive or capricious at best, in which they are mere "subjects" rather than true participants? Historically, popular support for the Mexican political system has derived from three sources: the revolutionary origins of the regime, the government's role in promoting economic growth, and its performance in distributing concrete, material benefits to a substantial proportion of the Mexican population since the Cárdenas era. Each of these traditional sources of support has been undermined to some extent in the last decade.

The official interpretation of the 1910 revolution stresses symbols (or myths) such as social justice, democracy, the need for national unity, and the popular origins of the current regime. The government's identification with these symbols was constantly reinforced by the mass media, public schools, and the mass organizations affiliated with the official party. Over the years, the party's electoral appeals were explicitly designed to link its candidates with agrarian reform and other revered ideals of the revolution, with national heroes like Emiliano Zapata and Lázaro Cárdenas, and with the national flag. (The PRI emblem conveniently has the same colors, in the same arrangement.) However, President Salinas broke decisively with so many tenets of "revolutionary ideology" (strict church-state separation, land reform, economic nationalism, etc.) that the PRI's claim to the revolutionary mantle became tenuous. Indeed, since the late 1980s, that mantle has been claimed by the neo-Cardenista opposition.

Relatively few Mexicans base their support for the system primarily on its revolutionary origins or symbolic outputs, however. For most sectors of the population, symbols were supplemented with particularistic material rewards: plots of land or titles to land that had been occupied illegally, schools, low-cost medical care, agricultural crop price supports, government-subsidized food and other consumer goods, and public sector jobs. For more than 40 years, the personal receipt of some material "favor" from the official party-government apparatus, or the hope that such benefits might be received in the future, ensured fairly high levels of mass support for the system. Even now, Mexicans' concept of democracy emphasizes economic and social outputs rather than procedural liberties.[9]

Despite their keen dissatisfaction with the government's recent management of the economy, corruption in government and the police, environmental pollution, and many other irritations, a plurality of Mexicans have remained "system loyalists." Indeed, Mexicans' pride in their country still seems rooted largely in their nation's political institutions. Survey data collected during the 1980s and 1990s consistently revealed the Mexican people's fundamental aversion to notions of radical transformation, especially if violence might result.[10] Nevertheless, most Mexicans today do not hesitate to criticize the

way in which their government functions, and many more of them feel free to demonstrate their dissatisfaction by voting to throw the rascals out. In 2000, Mexicans were much less risk-averse than in previous elections when they sized up the presidential candidates. Seventy-six percent of the respondents in a national pre-election survey who wanted Vicente Fox to be the next president agreed with the risk-taking statement, "He who risks nothing, gains nothing" while rejecting the status quo statement, "Better the Devil you know than the one you don't know." Among those who preferred PRI candidate Francisco Labastida, only 46% opted for the risk-taking statement.[11] Even though Labastida—a highly experienced technocrat-politician—was the "safe choice," his candidacy was doomed by his party's uneven performance since 1994.

Historically, most Mexicans tolerated corruption in government as a price to be paid in order to extract benefits from the system or to deal with police harassment. But the unbridled corruption of the López Portillo and Salinas administrations drastically reduced such tolerance, and an upsurge in drug-related corruption in the 1990s—reaching into the highest levels of the government bureaucracy and the national security apparatus—angered many Mexicans. They feared that their government had been taken over by "*narco-políticos*"—public officials in league with corrupt police and drug lords.

Mass Political Socialization

How do Mexicans form their attitudes toward the political system? In addition to the family, the schools and the Catholic Church are important sources of preadult political learning. All schools, including Church-affiliated and lay private schools, must follow a government-approved curriculum and use the same set of free textbooks, written by the federal Ministry of Education. Although the private schools' compliance with the official curriculum is often nominal, control over the content of textbooks gives the government an instrument for socializing children to a formal set of political values. This learning supports national political institutions and stresses the social and economic progress accomplished under postrevolutionary governments. Its impact is reflected in the beliefs of Mexican schoolchildren that their country has experienced a true social revolution; that, although this revolution is still incomplete, the government is working diligently to realize its goals; and that the president is an omnipotent authority figure, whose principal function is to maintain order in the country. Thus, despite the many egregious failures of presidential leadership that Mexicans have witnessed since the late 1960s, many of them continue to express a preference for strong, presidentialist government. However, education has increased criticism of the partisan politics and reduced tolerance for human rights violations by the military and police. Higher levels of education are also associated with stronger support for the right to dissent and other democratic liberties.

The Catholic Church has been another key source of values affecting political behavior in Mexico. Church-run private schools have proliferated in recent years, and along with secular private schools, they provide education for a large portion of children from middle- and upper-class families. Religious schools and priests have preached against socialism, criticized anticlerical laws and policies, and promoted individual initiative (as opposed to governmental action). They have also stressed the need for moral Christian behavior, which is seen as absent in the corrupt, self-serving, materialistic world of politics.

As adults, Mexicans learn about politics from their personal encounters with government functionaries and, increasingly, by participating in local community-based organizations and popular movements that seek collective benefits or redress of grievances of various sorts from the government. There has been an impressive proliferation of popular movements in Mexico since 1968, when the student protest movement was violently repressed. The catalysts for this new wave of popular movements include gangsterism in government-affiliated labor unions, increasingly blatant PRI vote fraud in state and local elections during the 1980s, the nationalization of Mexico's banks by President José López Portillo in 1982, the fumbling government response to the Mexico City earthquakes of 1985, and the implementation of neoliberal economic policies that adversely affected low- and middle-class segments of the society. While most of these popular movements are quite localized in scope and concerns, a few have grown to embrace thousands of Mexicans in many different states. Examples include a dissident teach-

ers' union movement that began in the late 1970s; the Civic Alliance, a coalition of hundreds of nongovernmental organizations, independent labor unions, and popular movements that has mobilized tens of thousands of Mexican citizens and hundreds of foreign observers to scrutinize the conduct of each national election since 1994; and a peasant movement that permanently blocked construction of a new international airport for Mexico City on their land in 2002.

The PRI-government apparatus systematically used the mass media as an agent of political socialization. Although the government did not frequently censor the media directly, there were significant economic penalties for engaging in criticism or investigative reporting that seriously embarrassed the president. For example, government advertising—a major source of revenue for most newspapers and magazines—could be withheld from offending publications. The Salinas administration ended the long-standing practices of bribing reporters to get favorable treatment and threatening to cut off newsprint to troublesome periodicals. Nevertheless, by the late 1990s only a handful of Mexico City newspapers and dissident news magazines were vigorously, dependably, critical of the government.

Since the PRI lost control of the presidency in 2000, the mass media are much more openly critical of government performance. Many newspapers and news magazines retain their PRI partisan bias and energetically criticize the PANista president. The independent media have kept up their intense scrutiny of the executive branch and are also highly critical of what they see as incompetence and inefficiency in Congress. Whatever they say about a president or his administration, however, the print media reach only a tiny fraction of the Mexican population (even the largest Mexico City newspapers have circulations under 100,000).

Until recently, television was virtually monopolized by a huge private firm, Televisa, that had a notoriously close working relationship with the PRI-government apparatus and invariably defended the incumbent president's performance. One of the consequences of the Salinas administration's privatization program was the break-up of Televisa's virtual monopoly. A formerly government-owned television channel in Mexico City has grown quickly into a rival network, TV Azteca, and Televisa itself has adjusted to the competition by giving much more coverage to opposition voices. Moreover, electoral system reforms enacted in 1996 require the Federal Electoral Institute to systematically monitor campaign coverage by the national and local electronic media, to determine whether they favor one party over another. These efforts have forced the media to act in a more balanced fashion. Consequently, exposure to the mass media no longer socializes the Mexican public to a particular set of political orientations sanctioned by incumbent authorities.

Political Participation

Traditionally, most political participation in Mexico has been of two broad types: (1) ritualistic, regime-supportive activities (for example, voting, attending campaign rallies), and (2) petitioning or contacting of public officials, to influence the allocation of some public good or service. People participated in PRI campaign rallies mostly because attending might have a specific material payoff (a free meal, a raffle ticket, a T-shirt), or because failure to do so could have personal economic costs. For example, union members who failed to attend such rallies could expect to lose a day's pay. As they went to the polls, Mexicans knew that they were not selecting those who would govern but merely ratifying the choice of candidates made earlier by the PRI-government hierarchy. Some voted because they regarded it as their civic duty, others because they wished to avoid difficulty in future dealings with government agencies. (By law, voting is obligatory in Mexico, and evidence of having voted in the most recent election has sometimes been required to receive public services.) Some voted in response to pressures from local *caciques* and PRI sector representatives. And some, especially in rural areas, freely sold their votes in return for handouts from local officials.

As elections have become moments of genuine political confrontation in many parts of Mexico, the ritualistic quality of voting and participation in campaign activities has diminished. Since 1994 Mexico has experienced an explosion in political participation, evidenced not only by the virtually nonstop protests of citizens' movements of all types but by a sharp rise in turnout in federal elections. The turnout of registered voters rose from 49 percent in the 1988 presidential election, to 61 percent in the midterm 1991 elections, to 78 percent in the 1994 presidential

election—a 28 percentage-point increase, in six years (see Figure 10.1). Turnout dipped to 64 percent in the 2000 presidential elections, mainly because so many former PRI voters stayed home.

Unfortunately, valid comparisons with electoral participation rates in the pre-1988 period are impossible, since the 1988 presidential election was the first for which reasonably accurate turnout figures were made public. In all previous national elections, the government inflated turnout statistics in an effort to convince Mexicans and the outside world that it had succeeded in relegitimating itself in impressive fashion. Inflated turnout figures were also the inevitable consequence of the ruling party's most commonly used method of committing vote fraud—simply adding votes to the PRI column. Even in the 1994 election, such "overvoting" was not entirely absent; the PAN found 936 precincts (about 1 percent of the total) in which reported voter turnout exceeded 100 percent of the registered voters. But taking the 1988 turnout figure as a fairly credible benchmark, we can have confidence that what has occurred since then represents a real increase in electoral participation.

How can we explain this participation explosion? Results from various preelection and exit polls in 1994 suggest that two key factors were responsible. First and foremost was the new, fraud-resistant electoral system installed between 1993 and 1994. Citizens were drawn to the polls by the novelty of an election in which, for the first time, they perceived a better-than-even chance that their vote could actually matter—that it would be respected by the government. Prospective voters trusted the process created by professionals in the newly reconstituted federal elections commission sufficiently to overcome their usual expectations of fraud. Second, voters perceived that the ruling party was actually vulnerable to defeat, a perception powerfully reinforced by the dismal performance of the PRI's Ernesto Zedillo in the first-ever, face-to-face, nationally televised debate among presidential contenders. The ruling party's perceived vulnerability motivated both PRI and opposition party sympathizers to go to the polls. As long as electoral politics remain as competitive, and potential voters continue to believe in the security of the electoral system, we can expect further, gradual movement toward a genuinely participant political culture in Mexico.

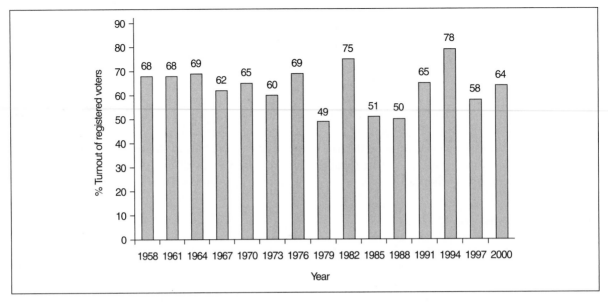

F I G U R E   1 0 . 1   Turnout of Registered Voters in National Elections, 1958–2000*

*The eligible electorate for 1952 includes all males aged 21 or over. Women received the franchise in 1958. Beginning in 1970, the legal voting age was lowered to 18.

Source: Data from Comisión Federal Electoral for 1958–1991; from Instituto Federal Electoral for 1994–2000.

POLITICAL STRUCTURE AND INSTITUTIONS

Mexico's political system has undergone dramatic transformations in practice and style, if not in form, during the last decade. It has moved steadily and smoothly from an authoritarian regime with democratic trappings to a democratic state, without a fundamental change in the line-up of political actors.

Mexican politics has long defied easy classification. In the 1950s and 1960s some U.S. political scientists depicted the regime as a one-party democracy that was evolving toward "true" (North Atlantic-style) democracy. They recognized certain imperfections, but in the view of these analysts, political development in Mexico was simply incomplete. After the government's massacre of student protesters in 1968 and 1971, most analysts described the system as authoritarian, but even this characterization was subject to qualification. By the 1990s, Mexico seemed to belong to a rapidly expanding category of hybrid, part-free, part-authoritarian systems that did not conform to classical typologies. Such labels as selective democracy, hard-line democracy, *demo-*

cradura (a Spanish contraction of "democracy" and "dictatorship"), and modernizing authoritarian regime were applied to such systems. These are characterized by partly competitive (though not necessarily fair and honest) elections that install governments more committed to maintaining political stability and labor discipline than to expanding democratic freedoms, protecting human rights, or mediating class conflict. Some regimes of this type are more likely to tolerate undemocratic practices (for example, electoral fraud and selective repression of dissidents) than others.

For most of the period since 1940, Mexico had a pragmatic and moderate authoritarian regime, not the zealously repressive kind that emerged in the southern cone of Latin America in the 1960s and 1970s. It was an institutional system, not a personalistic instrument, which dealt successfully with one of the most difficult problems for nondemocratic systems: leadership renewal and executive succession. The Mexican system was inclusionary, favoring cooptation and incorporation over exclusion or elimination of troublesome political forces. (However, the more repressive forms were never abandoned completely. The disappearances of hundreds of leftist militants in the 1970s and early 1980s, and President Salinas's attempt to completely marginalize the Cardenista left during his term are important exceptions to this historical pattern.) The government strove to incorporate the broadest possible range of social, economic, and political interests within the official party, its affiliated "mass" organizations, and opposition groups whose activities were sanctioned by the regime. As potentially dissident groups appeared, their leaders usually were co-opted into government-controlled organizations, or new organizations were established under government auspices as vehicles for emerging interests. Sometimes, emerging opponents of the regime were encouraged to create their own small but tame political parties. However, when confronted with opposition groups or movements that could not be co-opted (for example, students in 1968; the Cardenista left from 1987 to 1994; the Zapatista rebels in Chiapas since January 1, 1994), the regime responded punitively.

On paper, the Mexican government is structured much like the U.S. government: a presidential system, three autonomous branches of government (legislative, executive, and judicial) with checks and balances, and federalism with considerable autonomy at the local (municipal) level (see Figure 10.2). Until the late 1990s, however, Mexico's system of government was in practice far removed from the U.S. model. Decision making was highly centralized. The president, operating with relatively few restraints on his authority, completely dominated the legislative and judicial branches. Supreme Court justices were presidentially appointed and confirmed by a simple majority of the PRI-dominated Senate. Each incoming president replaced most justices, which made the judges agents of the executive branch. Until 1997, the ruling PRI continuously controlled both houses of the federal legislature. Opposition party members could criticize the government and its policies vociferously; but their objections to proposals initiated by the president and backed by his party in Congress rarely affected the final shape of legislation. Courts and legislatures at the state level normally mirrored the preferences of the state governors, many of whom themselves were hand-picked by the incumbent president.

Until recently, the overwhelming majority of those elected to public office in Mexico were, in effect, political appointees—named to their positions by higher-ups within the PRI-government apparatus. Selection as candidate of the PRI was tantamount to election, except in a handful of municipalities and congressional districts where opposition parties were so strong that they could not be ignored. Since re-election to office is prohibited at all levels of government, those elected on the PRI ticket were accountable and responsible not primarily to the people who elected them but to their political patrons within the regime. Most citizens who bothered to vote did so with little or no expectation that their votes would influence the outcome of the election, nor the subsequent behavior of the winner. Nominating conventions—if held at all—were attended only by party activists, whose role was to ratify the choices made in private by officials at higher levels.

These and other features of the Mexican system as it operated until 1997 are common to authoritarian regimes elsewhere: limited (not responsible) pluralism; low popular mobilization, with most citizen participation in the electoral process mobilized by the government itself; competition for public office and government benefits restricted mainly to those who support the system; centralized, often arbitrary decision making by one leader or a small group; and extensive government manipulation of the mass media. Now, however, a government that resembles the U.S. political system on paper is beginning to do so in practice, as well.

In 1988 the ruling party's control of the Congress was weakened significantly, setting the stage for a new era in executive-legislative relations. In that year's national elections, 66 PRI district-level candidates for seats in the lower house of Congress were defeated—nearly as many as the total of ruling party candidates defeated in all elections between 1946 and 1985. Between 1988 and 1991, the PRI was reduced to a bare working majority in the Chamber of Deputies (260 out of 500 seats), and for the first time since the ruling party was founded in 1929, opposition party candidates were elected to the Senate (4 out of 64 seats). Because the PRI no longer commanded a two-thirds majority in the lower house, President Salinas had to negotiate with the opposition party delegations (he chose to deal mostly with the PAN) to secure passage of key legislation amending

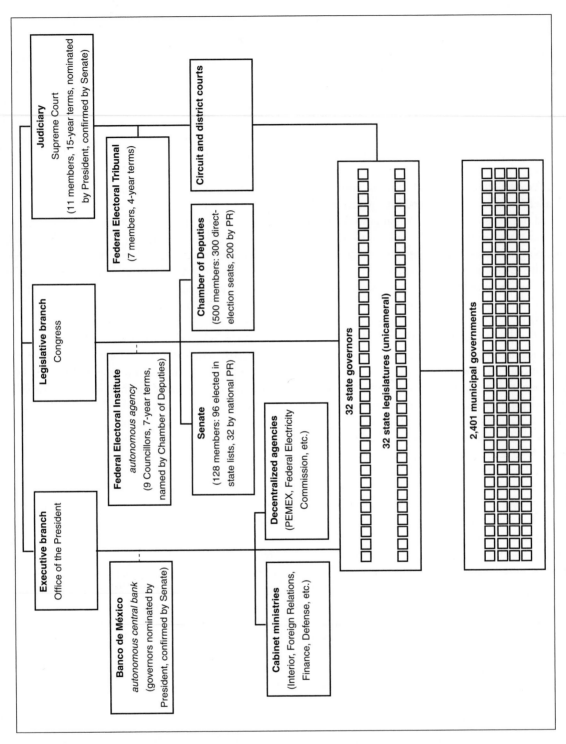

FIGURE 10.2   Structure of Mexico's Federal Government

the constitution.[12] Moreover, the Congress had ceased to function as a reliable instrument for internal distribution of power and its perks with the ruling party. With the recognition of so many opposition victories for congressional seats in 1988, aspiring PRIistas had to face the reality that nomination by their party was no longer equivalent to election. The tradition of the *carro completo* (clean sweep) by PRI candidates had ended.

The electoral law reform of 1993 further transformed the Congress by greatly increasing the representation of opposition parties in the Senate. The Senate was doubled in size (the current rules call for three senators per state, plus 32 senators elected by proportional representation in a closed national list). The reforms guaranteed that the opposition parties, combined, would control at least one-third of the Senate seats, as compared to less than 5 percent during the 1988–1993 period. The 1993 reforms also expanded the opposition parties' presence in the Chamber of Deputies, guaranteeing that no party could have more than 300 out of 500 seats under most circumstances.

As part of an overall strategy to broaden the base of support for his administration, President Zedillo offered to share power with the Congress in several key areas. Shortly after taking office, Zedillo announced his "commitment to forge a new balance of powers," and challenged the deputies to assert their constitutionally prescribed authority as never before. He proposed congressional approval of all major judicial appointments as well as oversight of all federal spending by a new auditing agency under congressional control.

The Congress, including the PRI's delegation, responded to Zedillo's challenge. In March 1995, after some 50 PRI deputies threatened to vote against a key element of the government's postdevaluation austerity plan—an increase in the value-added tax, which is levied on virtually all goods and services, from 10 percent to 15 percent—Zedillo found it necessary to aggressively lobby the congressional leaders of his own party to secure approval of the much-despised tax increase. Only Zedillo's arm twisting, combined with PRIistas' fears that the president would begin working directly with the opposition party members if his own party split on this crucial vote, prevented a wholesale breakdown of party discipline.

Since 1997, the government has lacked a majority in either or both chambers of Congress. Vicente Fox and future presidents will have to lobby and negotiate with Congress on a routine basis. The era when Congress's sole functions were to serve as a debating arena for the opposition parties (and for factions within the ruling party until the whips were applied) and as a rubber stamp for decisions already taken by the president has clearly ended.

Federalism

Despite the federalist structure of government that is enshrined in the 1917 constitution and legal codes, with their emphasis on the *municipio libre* (the concept of the free municipality, able to control its own affairs), in practice the Mexican political system has usually functioned in a manner classified as **political centralism.** From the 1920s through the Salinas presidency, the concentration of decision-making power at the federal level in most policy areas was continuous. Control over the preparation, conduct, and validation of elections—placed entirely at the municipal and state levels by the initial postrevolutionary electoral code, enacted in 1918—also passed to agencies that were part of the federal government apparatus or state-level entities controlled by federal authorities. A high degree of political centralism has been considered one of the main factors underlying Mexico's long-term political stability, although recent research at the state and local levels has demonstrated that political control by the center has been far less complete than is commonly assumed.[13]

Mexico is divided into 31 states and the Federal District, each one divided into **municipios**—politico-administrative units roughly equivalent in size and governmental functions to county governments in the United States. The *municipio* is governed by an *ayuntamiento,* or council, headed by a *presidente municipal* (mayor). Municipal officials are elected every three years.[14] Each successive layer of government in Mexico is significantly weaker, less autonomous, and more impoverished than the levels above it. In 1994, for example, the *municipios'* share of total public spending was 4 percent, the states' share was 16 percent, and the federal government made 80 percent of public expenditures. In the same year, the federal government took in 98 percent of all public revenues obtained through taxation, while the states collected 1.5 percent and the *municipios,* 0.5 percent. Municipal governments controlled by the PAN have had much greater success in increasing self-generated revenues than those controlled by the PRI, which typically deferred to the federal government.[15]

All of Mexico's seven most recent presidents entered office pledging to renew the "struggle against centralism," but serious efforts to decentralize have been made only since 1984. Under de la Madrid and Salinas, a limited form of revenue sharing was implemented and the federal constitution was amended to enhance the capacity of local governments to raise their own revenues. Partially successful efforts were also made to shift decision-making authority over public education and health care from the federal government to the states.[16] At the same time, the Salinas administration's **National Solidarity Program (PRONASOL)**—its principal social program, reaching into more than 95 percent of the country's 2,378 municipalities—was structured and administered to reinforce highly centralized presidential rule.[17]

More assertively than any of his predecessors, President Zedillo vowed to reduce centralism. He went so far as to sign an agreement with the country's state governors and mayors calling for constitutional amendments that would provide the legal framework for "a new Mexican federalism." Zedillo promised a more equitable distribution of federal funds to the states, and devolution of some functions that had been usurped by the federal government. But some federal ministries, especially the Treasury Department, have resisted further revenue sharing with municipal governments, on the grounds that they lack the administrative capacity to make effective use of additional resources.

The state governors represent another potential obstacle to the "new federalism." The governors retain control over all resources transferred from the federal government, and effective administrative decentralization down to the municipio level would require them to relinquish a major portion of their political power—something that they have successfully resisted. It is clear that, even under a president strongly committed to redistributing resources and sharing power with subnational units of government, movement toward U.S.-style federalism in Mexico will meet with opposition from many different quarters, including the federal government and the states themselves.

The Legislative Branch

Mexico's political system has been commonly described as presidentialist or presidentially centered. Nonetheless, these characterizations were based on observed practices in a dominant-party regime, in which the institutional rules of the party had overwhelmed the formal constitutional rules. A careful examination of the Mexican Constitution reveals a president who is among the more constitutionally constrained in Latin America and a Congress with strong, sometimes dominant powers over the other branches of government. The difference between the informal and formal institutions is the history of the PRI government.

The federal Congress has two houses: a 128-member upper chamber, the Senate; and a 500-member lower house, the Chamber of Deputies (see Figure 10.2). Both chambers employ a so-called mixed-member system in which some of the members are elected by plurality vote in single-member districts, while others are elected by a system of compensatory proportional representation on closed party lists.[18] The current electoral rules for the Senate, dating to 1996, call for plurality elections in each of the 32 states whereby each party nominates a slate of two Senate candidates. The party that wins a plurality elects both candidates from the slate to the Senate. The party that places second sends the first candidate on the list to the upper chamber. Furthermore, 32 senators are elected by proportional representation on closed national lists, so that each party that wins at least 2 percent of the national vote elects its proportional share of the 32 list senators. The rules prevent any party from winning more than two-thirds of the seats in the Senate except under extraordinary circumstances (a party would have to place first in every state and win more than two-thirds of the national vote).

For the Chamber of Deputies, 300 members are elected by plurality in single-member districts, and an additional 200 deputies are elected by proportional representation in five regional closed lists. In general, each party that wins at least 2 percent of the national vote is entitled to its proportional share of the list deputies with a few restrictions. First, no party can ever have more than 300 total seats, which restricts the largest party to less than the two-thirds majority required for constitutional reforms. Second, no party's share of the total number of seats can exceed by more than 8 percent its share of the national vote. This means that in order to win a majority in the lower chamber, a party must win more than 42 percent of the vote and a sufficient margin of victory over the second place party (usually around four percentage points) to win enough districts.

The mixed-member system directly affects the party system. Usually, plurality systems lead to two-party systems, as the voters find that it is better to coordinate their votes toward one of the two leading parties rather than waste them on third-party candidates. Proportional representation systems tend to create multiparty systems, because votes for the larger minority parties are not wasted. In Mexico, the mixed-member system has yielded a three-party system, in which most regions now have two-party systems (respecting the tendencies of the plurality system) but nationally the vote is split into three main blocs. The three parties with significant representation in the Mexican Congress are the PRI (with 42 percent of the seats in 2000 and 45 percent in 2003), the PAN (with 41 percent in 2000 and 30 percent in 2003), and the PRD (with just over 10 percent in 2000 and 19 percent in 2003).[19] The low threshold allows small parties to attain representation in the Chamber of Deputies, as well: for the 2003–2006 term, the Green Party, the Workers' Party, and Convergencia (a party with regional strength in the Gulf and in the Southeast states) won seats.

The mixed-member system complicates creating majorities in either chamber. Since the 8-percent rule on maximum overrepresentation was established in the lower house, no party has been able to achieve a majority. The Senate rules went into effect fully for the first time in the 2000 elections. Now, when the race is close between the first- and second-place parties, it is also unlikely that a majority party will emerge in the Senate. This means that the party of the president will rarely have a majority in Congress, thus creating a situation of divided government.

Like the U.S. Constitution, the 1917 Mexican Constitution lists the legislative branch first. The Congress is primarily responsible for enacting nearly all public policy, with only a few exceptions. The president has constitutionally delegated decree powers only over questions of land reform (expropriation decrees) and tariffs and quotas in international trade (in which he can unilaterally adjust tariffs and quotas if the circumstances call for modifications). All regular legislation must be approved by both chambers in the same form, and then submitted to the president for publication. The president must publish the bill within ten days or return the bill to the chamber of origin. The presidential veto can take two forms: one is a regular veto, in which the president expresses his rejection of a bill; the second is a corrective veto, in which the president requests that Congress amend the bill. In either case, Congress can insist on the original text of the bill by a two-thirds vote, after which the president must publish the legislation. In case of corrective vetoes, Congress often modifies the bill as requested (usually because of technical errors in the text) and sends it back to the president for promulgation.

Each of the two chambers has exclusive powers and areas of specialization. The Chamber of Deputies specializes in fiscal legislation. All revenue bills must originate in the lower chamber, and the Chamber of Deputies has exclusive powers over appropriations and budget oversight. The president submits the budget to the lower chamber on November 15, including the annual revenue law, adjustments in tax rates, and the spending bill. The fiscal year begins on January 1 of the following year, but the congressional term is supposed to end on December 15, giving the Congress only one month to review the president's budget. The Chamber of Deputies first approves the revenue and tax legislation, sending it to the upper chamber for Senate approval. However, only the Chamber of Deputies approves the appropriations legislation. This bill is sent directly to the president after floor approval, and prevailing constitutional doctrine establishes that the president does not have the power to veto this bill. This gives the Chamber of Deputies extraordinary influence over the federal public administration. Likewise, the lower chamber has exclusive powers over budgetary oversight and approves the public accounts.

The Senate has exclusive power to oversee foreign affairs. The Mexican president conducts foreign relations under constitutionally specified doctrines (such as self-determination, non-intervention, and the peaceful solution of conflict), and the upper chamber has the power to monitor foreign affairs. It approves treaties submitted by the president by a majority vote. Jointly with the Chamber of Deputies, the Senate must approve all foreign travel by the president. If the Congress does not approve of the executive's foreign policy, the president would be unable to conduct foreign affairs outside of Mexico's borders.

The Senate also has the power to remove state governors and depose state legislatures. The Constitution allows the Senate to topple state governments when it recognizes that the state can no longer provide for domestic security. This requires a vote of the upper chamber; afterwards, the president proposes a list of three candidates from which the Senate elects the interim governor by a two-thirds vote. Prompted by PRI presidents, the Senate deposed many governors during the twentieth century, though usually for political reasons rather than for security motives.

Federal deputies and senators have shown extraordinary levels of party discipline in recent years. For example, during the last two years of the 57th Legislature (1997–2000), on average 99.6 percent of the PRIista deputies voted together on party bills. Party cohesion for the PANista deputies in the 57th Legislature was about 92 percent, and for PRDista deputies, 93 percent. During the 58th Legislature (2000–2003), cohesion among PAN deputies increased to 94 percent, and hit 98 percent during the first two years of the 59th (2003–2004). Meanwhile, PRI discipline declined to 90 and 87 percent in the first two terms that it did not hold the presidency.

High party discipline in Mexico has two main sources.[20] First, consecutive reelection for deputies and senators is prohibited. This nearly eliminates accountability of the representatives to their constituents. Voters can neither reward their legislators for good performance nor punish them for bad representation. Since federal legislators are not required to seek cues from their electorate, they look elsewhere for guidance, and the party leadership is more than willing to provide it. Second, nomination procedures in each of the parties are relatively closed. The leadership traditionally has selected candidates directly in the PRI and the PRD, while PANista candidates are nominated in closed (but competitive) conventions of party activists. This further focuses the legislators on party leadership, because without the support of the party elite their political futures would be dismal.

Because each party generally votes as a bloc in Congress, this creates incentives for the leaders of each of the parties to negotiate bills among themselves rather than allow the rank and file members to work out compromises in committee. Other rules of Congress grant extensive authority to the coordinators of the parties (such as the power to assign members to committees and dole out office space and expense accounts to the deputies). Together, these institutions create a highly centralized legislative branch. When the president was recognized as the natural leader of the majority party in the Congress, the centralized tendencies in that branch allowed him to rule as a near dictator without changing any constitutional norms.

The Executive Branch

Despite the constitutionally limited powers of the executive branch, no one would dispute that the

TABLE 10.2   Party Cohesion in the Chamber of Deputies: Party Votes, 1998–2004 (percentages)

		PRI	PAN	PRD	PVEM	PT
57th Legislature	Mean	99.6	92.2	92.8	97.5	88.9
(1998–2000)	s.d.	1.3	12.6	13.9	8.0	16.4
58th Legislature	Mean	90.0	94.3	91.5	95.8	97.3
(2000–2003)	s.d.	13.3	12.6	15.5	9.3	9.7
59th Legislature	Mean	87.3	98.0	95.0	96.3	96.8
(2003–2004)	s.d.	13.6	7.8	10.1	10.3	9.2

Note: Data for the 59th Legislature through December 31, 2004. Party votes are roll calls in which at least one party dissented from the rest. Party cohesion is the percentage of the party voting with the majority of that party. "s.d." is the standard deviation.

Source: For the 57th Legislature, "Institutional and Political Factors in Party Discipline in the Chamber of Deputies, 1998–2002," presented at the First Latin American Political Science Congress, Salamanca, Spain, July 2002. Data for the last two legislatures calculated by Weldon.

president had been the dominant political actor for the greater part of the last century in Mexico. In addition to his rather modest constitutional powers, the Mexican president possessed a broad range of unwritten but generally recognized "metaconstitutional" powers that traditionally ensured his dominance over all of the country's other political institutions.[21] Mexicans use the term ***presidencialismo*** to connote this extraordinary concentration of powers, formal and informal, in the hands of the president, and the implication that incumbents frequently abuse these powers in pursuit of personal and political ends.

On any issue of national political significance, the federal judiciary would take its cue from the incumbent president. Until very recently, the Supreme Court never found presidential decisions or legislation enacted at the behest of the president to be unconstitutional, and Congress never challenged presidential appointments to or dismissals from the federal judiciary. The president had the informal power to seat and unseat state governors, mayors, and members of Congress. For example, during President Salinas's term, 17 state governors resigned, most under pressure from Los Pinos (the residence of the Mexican president). From 1929 through 1994, the president also functioned as the "supreme head" of the official party, choosing its leaders, dictating his legislative proposals to the PRI delegation in Congress, shaping the party's internal governance, imposing his personal choices for the PRI's gubernatorial and congressional candidates, and—most importantly—controlling the selection of the party's next presidential nominee.

The absence of a rigid, fully elaborated political ideology made it possible for a Mexican president to have a pragmatic, flexible program and style of governance. The so-called ideology of the Mexican Revolution was never more than a loosely connected set of goals or symbols. Today, there are only a few tenets of "revolutionary" ideology that must be scrupulously observed, such as the constitutionally mandated no-reelection principle for the presidency: the president is limited to a single six-year term.[22]

By the late 1980s, conventional wisdom held that traditional Mexican *presidencialismo*—especially if defined as the ability of the president to take unilateral actions that may be damaging to the interests of political and economic elites—was dead, the victim of the excesses and leadership failures of the last three presidents. Upon taking office in De-

cember 1988, Carlos Salinas challenged that notion through a succession of bold strokes against the fiefdoms that had increasingly faced up to presidential prerogatives during the preceding four administrations (for instance, the oil workers' union), and by embracing new policies that entailed large political risks (a free trade agreement with the United States and Canada). These actions proved that the essential powers of Mexican *presidencialismo* were still intact, at least for the time being, and could be used to effect sweeping political and economic change. These powers were grounded most importantly in the official party and the president's role as party leader.

During the PRI's seven decades of rule at the national level, three factors were required to create strong presidentialism.[23] First, the president's party had to have a majority in both chambers of Congress. Under **divided government,** the opposition majorities in Congress are unlikely to follow the dictates of the president. Second, there must be high levels of discipline in the majority party of Congress. This was achieved by the mechanisms described above. If there is insufficient discipline, the Mexican president would look more like most U.S. presidents, because the members of Congress act as free agents. Third, the president must be considered the leader of his party. In the 1930s, the first two factors were in place, but the leader of the party, Plutarco Elías Calles, received all of the benefits of the disciplined party, not the president. After Cárdenas reorganized the official party along lines of authority that led directly to himself, strong *presidencialismo* was finally achieved.

All three key ingredients of strong presidentialism were generally in place from 1946 to 1994. Even a bare 52-percent PRI majority in the 54th Legislature (1988–1991) was sufficient to maintain a strong presidency for Salinas. His successor, Ernesto Zedillo, adhered to a very different model of presidential leadership. Most importantly, Zedillo refused to assume the president's traditional role as leader of the PRI. He publicly pledged to refrain from interfering in internal party matters, including candidate selection. He committed himself to working with the opposition party delegations in the Congress, not just with the PRI, which held a majority in the first half of his term. He also assured that, unlike his predecessors, he would not involve himself in adjudicating disputed elections, thereby serving notice to the

PRI that the president could no longer be relied upon to be the ultimate guarantor of the party's electoral victories. Finally, Zedillo approved the arrest and jailing of Raúl Salinas, eldest brother of the ex-president, on charges of having masterminded the assassination of the PRI's second-ranking official in September 1994. In 1999, Raúl Salinas was convicted of homicide and sentenced to 50 years in prison (since reduced). Thus did Zedillo break the "rule of impunity" that had always protected former presidents, their close relatives, and principal aides from prosecution for corruption or politically motivated crimes committed during their terms.

The most important test of Zedillo's resolve to recast the institution of the presidency came as his term was ending. Tradition dictated that, at that point, he would exercise his metaconstitutional power as incumbent president to select his own successor, with minimal input from other key actors in the ruling coalition. In September 1990 Luis Echeverría became the first former president to publicly acknowledge this crucially important, unwritten rule of the Mexican political system. Also by tradition, those who aspire to the PRI's presidential nomination could not openly campaign for it, or even admit that they were seeking the presidency. Instead, supporters of the major contenders worked diligently behind the scenes to advance their man's prospects and to discredit the other contenders.

In 1987, in response to widespread criticism of the traditional, secretive selection process, Miguel de la Madrid, acting through the nominal head of the PRI, publicly identified six "distinguished party members" as precandidates for the PRI's 1988 presidential nomination, and arranged for them to present their ideas to PRI notables at semipublic breakfast meetings. These appearances represented only a cosmetic change in the presidential succession process, however, because they provoked neither real debate nor public campaigning by the hopefuls,

President Vicente Fox on his inauguration day, flashing his trademark "YA!" ("NOW!") sign

AFP/Corbis

and the outgoing president remained firmly in control of the nomination process.

Confident in his metaconstitutional prerogatives, Carlos Salinas dispensed with such cosmetic measures in 1993 and 1994 when he chose two of his cabinet members—initially Luis Donaldo Colosio and, following his assassination during the campaign, Ernesto Zedillo—to succeed him. The process through which the PRI's presidential candidates were selected was as closed and secretive as ever, even though Salinas's imposition of Zedillo to replace the slain Colosio was briefly and openly resisted by the PRI hierarchy. But public scrutiny of Salinas's second-choice candidate was expanded enormously by Zedillo's participation in the first-ever, face-to-face, nationally televised debate among the principal presidential candidates. The mere fact that a PRI presidential candidate had agreed to debate directly with his opponents on national television was a major irreversible step toward a more democratic presidential succession.

In the presidential succession of 2000, Zedillo took the considerably more radical step of keeping his hands off the PRI's nominating process. PRI leaders—with President Zedillo's blessing—opted to hold a nationwide primary election in November 1999 to determine the party's 2000 presidential candidate. Four veteran PRI politicians entered the race, campaigned actively for the nomination, and debated each other on national television. The winning candidate, Francisco Labastida, was widely considered to be Zedillo's favorite, if for no other reason than that he had been the Interior Minister (the top post in the cabinet) under Zedillo. Nonetheless, if he had a favorite candidate, Zedillo kept it to himself. The primary was considered a great success by the media and the party, and after some counseling from the president, the losers accepted defeat. However, seven months after the first open PRI primary for the presidency, the PRI candidate himself had to accept defeat in the general election.

Executive-Legislative Relations

The dynamics of executive-legislative relations in Mexico used to be determined by the metaconstitutional powers of the president. The operation of the three key factors outlined above—unified government, high party discipline in the ruling party, and the recognition of the president as the de facto head of the party—explained a compliant Congress. Today, now that the first and third factors no longer hold (thus making the second factor less relevant), executive-legislative relations follow constitutional rather than partisan norms, and Mexico either enjoys or suffers from the everyday republican conflicts of separation of powers.

Comparing the levels of productivity of the last five legislatures allows us to evaluate the executive's influence over the legislative branch under varying conditions of the metaconstitutional conditions listed above, as well as the relative strength of the president's party in the lower chamber (see Table 10.3). During the 54th Legislature (1988–1991), the first half of the Salinas presidency, the PRI held a small majority of 52 percent of the lower chamber. Despite the marginal majority, 98.6 percent of the executive's public bills were approved. Of the 110 bills approved during the 54th Legislature, nearly two-thirds had originated in the executive branch. The 55th Legislature (1991–1994) gave the PRI and Salinas a large majority in the Chamber of Deputies, around 63 percent. Again, 98.5 percent of the president's public bills were approved. More than three out of every five bills that were eventually approved in the lower chamber had been introduced by the executive. During both Legislatures, the three conditions for metaconstitutional power were strongly in place.

During the 56th Legislature (1994–1997), the first half of President Zedillo's term, the president was no longer functioning as de facto leader of his party: Zedillo had promised to keep a healthy distance between himself and the PRI. Nevertheless, Table 10.3 indicates that the lower chamber approved 98.9 percent of his bills, thanks to the three-fifths majority held by the ruling party. Nearly three-quarters of all of the bills approved by the chamber had originated in the executive branch. Although the president had claimed that he was no longer interested in being the head of the PRI, it appears that the party was not yet listening.

In the 57th Legislature (1997–2000), divided government prevailed for the first time since 1928. The PRI held just under 48 percent of the seats in the lower chamber, while the PAN and the PRD each had about a quarter of the seats. Thus, the first of the conditions for metaconstitutional power—unified government—was eliminated. Under divided government 90 percent of the president's bills

TABLE 10.3   Sponsorship and Approval of Public Bills in the Chamber of Deputies, 1988–2004

Legislature	% of Deputies from President's Party	Sponsor*	% of Total New Bills Introduced	% of Total Bills Approved	% of Sponsor's Bills Approved
54th (1988–1991)	52	Executive	22.8	65.1	98.6
		Deputies	77.2	34.9	15.6
		Other	0.0	0.0	—
		Total	**100.0**	**100.0**	**34.5**
55th (1991–1994)	63	Executive	42.4	62.6	98.5
		Deputies	56.3	36.5	38.5
		Other	1.3	0.9	50.0
		Total	**100.0**	**100.0**	**50.0**
56th (1994–1997)	60	Executive	33.8	74.2	98.9
		Deputies	61.7	24.2	16.2
		Other	4.5	1.7	16.7
		Total	**100.0**	**100.0**	**42.7**
57th (1997–2000)	48	Executive	10.1	31.0	90.0
		Deputies	81.9	59.6	20.8
		Other	7.9	9.4	32.2
		Total	**100.0**	**100.0**	**28.6**
58th (1997–2003)	41	Executive	6.8	23.7	89.9
		Deputies	77.3	57.7	18.4
		Other	15.8	18.6	30.0
		Total	**100.0**	**100.0**	**24.9**
59th (2003–2006)	30	Executive	3.9	12.1	72.3
		Deputies	79.8	61.8	17.4
		Other	16.4	26.1	35.4
		Total	**100.0**	**100.0**	**22.4**

*"Other" includes bills introduced by state legislatures, revenue bills presented in the lower chamber by senators, and bills that originated in the Senate that had been introduced there by senators. Executive bills that originated in the Senate are classified under the "Executive" category.

Source: *Diario de los Debates* and the *Gaceta Parlamentaria* of the Chamber of Deputies. Data compiled by María del Carmen Nava Polina, Jorge Yáñez López, and Claudia Y. Carmona M., under the direction of Jeffrey Weldon. Data for the 58th Legislature are through August 31, 2002. Data for the 59th Legislature are through December 31, 2004.

were approved—a decline of nine percentage points from the previous legislature. In fact, two executive-introduced bills were defeated: the revenue law for 1998 (a substitute bill was subsequently approved) and a bank bailout bill. Since 1928, a majority of the bills that the Chamber of Deputies approved had originated in the executive branch. In the 57th Legislature, this trend was abruptly reversed: only 31 percent of the bills approved in the term had been introduced by the executive, while nearly 60 percent had been sponsored by deputies.

By the time that the 58th Legislature had convened in 2000, metaconstitutional presidentialism

had ended. The first condition—unified government—remained unfulfilled. The PAN held only 41 percent of the seats in the lower chamber. In fact, the PAN delegation occasionally voted against the preferences of the president, as they did in 2001 when they opposed allowing representatives of the Zapatista rebels to speak from the podium of the Chamber of Deputies. Nearly 90 percent of Fox's bills were approved during the 2000–2003 term, an achievement no different from Zedillo's under divided government. However, nearly every bill that Fox had sent to Congress had been extensively amended in at least one of the chambers. Never before has a higher percentage of executive bills been amended, either in committee or on the floor.

In the 2003 election, the Green Party took their 5 to 6 percent share of the votes to the PRI in a partial alliance that eventually covered 99 districts. The shift of these votes from the PAN to the PRI led to a significant shift of seats in the second half of the term (if the Green vote shares are removed from both the 2000 and 2003 elections, then both the PAN and the PRI lost total shares of the vote in 2003—the 2003 election was more a realignment in electoral coalitions than a victory for the PRI). The PRI ended up with nearly 45 percent of the seats, while the PAN won only 30 percent. The PRD also increased its size in the lower chamber, winning nearly one-fifth of the seats, mostly due to district victories in the Federal District. Through the end of December 2004, only 72 percent of the president's bills have been approved. Only 12 percent of the bills approved by the Chamber of Deputies have originated in the executive branch.

Mexico's first "opposition" president has had difficult relations with a Congress in which the opposition parties—when united—have majority control. In March 2001, Fox introduced a major tax reform that would have placed a 15-percent value-added tax on food, medicines, books, and private school tuition. Opposition legislators in the Chamber of Deputies, led by the PRI and the PRD, strongly opposed this provision, and the PAN was reluctant to join what appeared to be a lost cause in support of their president. After several months of intense debate, the value-added tax proposal was killed and replaced by a 5-percent excise tax on certain "luxury" goods, which failed to raise much revenue and was later abandoned. In April 2002, with the PRI and PRD members again leading the pack, the Senate denied Fox permission to make a trip to several U.S. and Canadian cities, to demonstrate its opposition to various elements of his foreign policy. The trip was cancelled.

Executive-legislative relations have worsened during the second half of Fox's term. The proposal to raise the value-added tax was reintroduced in the fall of 2003, but the Chamber of Deputies defeated the bill on the floor. Later, the lower chamber rejected Fox's request to receive a medal from the UN Food and Agriculture Organization, demonstrating opposition to his agricultural policies. This was the

first time that a permission for an international or foreign medal had been denied to the president.

In the fall 2004 term, the opposition coalition in the Chamber of Deputies amended Fox's revenue bill, increasing dependence on oil sources as a part of expected federal revenue and raising the deficit target. The opposition also modified considerably the federal appropriations bill, decreasing or eliminating a number of federal programs and increasing pork-barrel expenditures for PRI and PRD states. Fox vetoed the appropriations bill; this was the first budget veto cast by a president since 1933. The Chamber of Deputies disputed the veto by filing a suit in the Supreme Court, claiming that the president did not have the constitutional power to veto the budget (despite the fact that there had been 45 vetoes of the budget between 1917 and 1933, none of which had been challenged on constitutional grounds by Congress). The Supreme Court suspended the expenditures to which the president had objected, and the constitutionality of the veto over the budget will be decided during 2005. Such tests of will between the executive and legislative branches are increasingly common in Mexico's era of divided government, with the judicial branch assuming an increasingly important role as arbiter between the two branches.

RECRUITING THE POLITICAL ELITE

What kinds of people gain entry into Mexico's national political elite, and who makes it to the top? At least since the days of the Porfiriato, the Mexican political elite has been recruited predominantly from the middle class. The 1910 revolution did not open up the political elite to large numbers of people from peasant or urban laborer backgrounds. That opening occurred only in the 1930s, during the Cárdenas administration, and then mainly at the local and state levels rather than the national level elite. By 1989, only 8.3 percent of all state governors, senators, cabinet, and subcabinet members had peasant or working-class origins; in a sample of 1,113 federal government bureaucrats, only 0.7 percent said that their fathers were peasants while 0.9 percent described them as workers.[24]

In recent *sexenios,* the national political elite has become more homogeneous in several important

---

BOX 10.3 The Career of Vicente Fox

1942: Born in Mexico City. Raised on a ranch in Guanajuato state. Father was a medium-sized landowner, producing vegetables and raising cattle. Mother was born in Spain, which made Fox ineligible for the presidency until an amendment to Article 82 of the constitution went into effect for the 2000 election.

1960: Began undergraduate study at Universidad Iberoamericana, Mexico City, majoring in business administration, but did not complete requirements for the B.A. degree until 1999.

1964–1979: Employed by Coca-Cola de México, starting as a route salesman and rising to general manager of national operations.

1979: Returned to Guanajuato to run family businesses.

1987: Entered party politics, encouraged by fellow-businessman and 1988 PAN presidential candidate Manuel Clouthier. Nominated as PAN candidate for federal Congressman in 1988.

1988–1991: Member of Congress (Chamber of Deputies), representing a district in León, Guanajuato.

1991: Ran for Governor of Guanajuato, as PAN candidate. Fox claimed victory in an election marred by PRI fraud, but the PRI candidate was declared the winner with 53 percent of the votes. After sustained protests by Fox's supporters, President Salinas imposed an interim PANista governor. Fox vowed to leave politics until Salinas's term ended (*"una huelga política"*). Fox's marriage ended in divorce.

1995–1999: Governor of Guanajuato, elected with 58 percent of the votes.

1999: Nominated as presidential candidate of the PAN.

2000–2006: President of Mexico.

---

ways. Its members have been drawn increasingly from the ranks of *capitalinos*—people born or raised in Mexico City. By the 1980s more than half of the presidential cabinet had been born in Mexico City and an even higher percentage had been raised there.[25] Postgraduate education, especially at elite foreign universities and in disciplines like economics and public administration, has become much more important as a ticket of entry into the national political elite. Over half of the cabinet members appointed by Presidents de la Madrid, Salinas, and Zedillo had studied economics or public administration, and over half of those who received training in these subjects at the graduate level did so in the United States. The economic cabinets of these three presidents were filled with recipients of Ph.D.s from universities such as Harvard, MIT, Stanford, Yale, and the University of Chicago. Typically, the PRIista **técnicos** spent their entire career within the government bureaucracy, especially the financial and planning agencies, never engaging in partisan politics. Ernesto Zedillo was the fifth man in a row to become president of Mexico without having held any previous elective office.

The economic policy debacles presided over by technocrat presidents and cabinet ministers in the 1990s discredited this breed of Mexican officials in the eyes of the public as well as the party leaderships. Significantly, a national PRI assembly in 1996 removed most technocrats from the line of presidential succession by requiring the party's future presidential nominees to have previously held elective office. Relatively few card-carrying technocrats found their way into the cabinet of Vicente Fox, who favored persons with non-governmental experience, a bachelor's or master's degree in business administration, educated in Mexico—like himself (see Box 10.3).

Since the 1970s, kinship ties have become more important as a common denominator of those who attain top positions of political power. Increasingly, such people are born into politically prominent families that have already produced state governors, cabinet ministers, federal legislators, and even presidents. And these political families are increasingly interconnected: At least one-third of the government officials and politicians interviewed by one researcher for several books on the Mexican political elite were related to other officials, not counting those related through marriage and the traditional rite of *compadrazgo* (becoming a godparent to a friend's child).[26] Family connections can give an aspiring political leader a powerful advantage over rivals.

The growing importance of kinship ties and other indicators of increasing homogeneity in personal backgrounds causes some observers to worry that Mexico's political elite is becoming more closed and inbred. While its social base may indeed be narrowing, the modern Mexican political elite still shows considerable fluidity; the massive turnover of officeholders every six years is proof of that. In the years of PRI dominance, 80 percent of the top 200 officeholders were replaced every 12 years, and 90 percent every 18 years. At the end of each administration, nearly one-third of the top-level players actually drop out of political life.[27] This helps to explain why in Mexico, unlike other postrevolutionary countries such as China and (until recently) the Soviet Union, the regime did not become a gerontocracy. In fact, the median age of cabinet members and presidential aspirants in Mexico has been dropping; in recent *sexenios,* most have been in their late 30s or early 40s.

INTEREST REPRESENTATION AND POLITICAL CONTROL

In Mexico's presidentialist system, important public policies used to be initiated and shaped by the inner circle of presidential advisers before they were even presented for public discussion. Thus, most effective interest representation took place within the upper levels of the federal bureaucracy. The structures that aggregate and articulate interests in Western democracies (the ruling political party, labor unions, and so on) actually served other purposes in the Mexican system: limiting the scope of citizens' demands on the government, mobilizing electoral support for the regime, helping to legitimate it in the eyes of other countries, distributing jobs and other material rewards to select individuals and groups. For example, the PRI typically had no independent influence on public policymaking; nor did the opposition parties, except where they controlled state or local governments.

From the late 1930s to the PRI's defeat in 2000, Mexico had a **corporatist** system of interest representation in which each citizen and societal segment was expected to relate to the state through a single structure "licensed" by the state to organize and represent that sector of society (peasants, urban unionized workers, businesspeople, teachers, and so on). The official party itself was divided into three **sectors:** (1) the Labor Sector, (2) the Peasant Sector, and (3) the Popular Sector, a catch-all category representing various segments of the middle class (government employees, other white-collar workers, small merchants, private landowners) and residents of low-income urban neighborhoods. Each sector in the PRI is dominated by one mass organization; other organizations are affiliated with each party sector, but their influence is dwarfed by that of the "peak" organization. Thus, the ***Confederación de Trabajadores de México* (CTM)** has dominated the Labor Sector; the *Confederación Nacional Campesina* (CNC) the Peasant Sector; and the *Confederación Nacional de Organizaciones Populares* (CNOP) the Popular Sector.

A number of powerful organized interest groups—foreign and domestic entrepreneurs, the military, the Catholic Church—were not formally represented in the PRI. These groups often dealt directly with the government elite, often at the presidential or cabinet level. They did not need the PRI to make their preferences known. They also had well-placed representatives within the executive branch who could be counted on to articulate their interests. In addition, the business community was organized into several government-chartered confederations. Since the Cárdenas administration, all but a small minority of the country's industrialists were required by law to join one of these employers' organizations, which channeled business interests into a few, well-controlled outlets. These confederations still exist, but the Supreme Court ruled in 1999 that compulsory membership was an unconstitutional restriction on the freedom of association.

Because the ruling party and the national legislature did not effectively aggregate interests in the Mexican system, individuals and groups seeking something from the government often circumvented their nominal representatives in the PRI sectoral organizations and the Congress, and sought satisfaction of their needs through personal contacts within the government bureaucracy. These **patron-client relationships** compartmentalized the society into discrete, noninteracting, vertical segments that served as pillars of the regime. Within the lower class, for example, unionized urban workers were separated from nonunion urban workers; *ejidatarios* from small private landholders and landless agricultural workers.

The middle class was compartmentalized into government bureaucrats, educators, health care professionals, lawyers, economists, and so forth. Thus competition between social classes was replaced by highly fragmented competition within classes.

The articulation of interests through patron-client networks assisted the PRI regime by fragmenting popular demands into small-scale, highly individualized or localized requests that could be granted or denied case by case. Officials were rarely confronted with collective demands from broad social groupings. Rather than having to act on a request from a whole category of people (slum dwellers, *ejidatarios,* teachers), they had easier, less costly choices to make (as between competing petitions from several neighborhoods for a paved street or a piped water system). The clientelistic structure thus provided a mechanism for distributing public services and other benefits in a highly selective, discretionary if not always arbitrary manner. This system put the onus on potential beneficiaries to identify and cultivate the "right" patrons within the government bureaucracy. The prohibition on consecutive reelection prevented local elected officials from taking on the role of patron. As they could be neither punished nor rewarded for their performance, elected politicians abdicated this responsibility, and it was only natural that the bureaucracy would replace them in the role of patron.

In the last twenty years, the appearance of independent citizens' organizations not tied into the PRI regime's clientelistic networks introduced new complexity and uncertainty into the political system. These movements developed partly in response to the economic crises of the 1980s and 1990s, partly because of the lack of policy progress in resolving public security problems, partly because of the declining responsiveness of existing state-chartered "mass" organizations, and partly as a result of general societal modernization (greater competition in mass communications, higher education levels, urbanization, changes in occupational structure, and the like). The attractiveness of independent popular movements also reflected the disdain with which the entrenched, state-affiliated organizations were regarded by the Mexican public. The PRI's sectoral organizations were viewed by most Mexicans as corrupt, manipulative, self-serving extensions of the state bureaucracy that provided no effective representation of their interests.

After the dismal performance of the sectoral organizations in delivering votes to Carlos Salinas in the 1988 presidential election, the dysfunctional nature of the corporatist system of interest representation became a matter of urgent concern for the government elite. Salinas and PRI leaders chose to deemphasize, if not eliminate, the role of the discredited sectors in interest articulation and aggregation. They decided that ossified corporatist structures should be supplemented with territorially based "movements" and committees, led by new cadres who could distance themselves (and, implicitly, the PRI itself) from the detested bosses who ran the sectoral organizations and foster a more direct relationship between the PRI and individual citizens.

Through the National Solidarity Program, the Salinas administration created what amounted to a parallel structure of interest representation that was very much territorially based and not at all dependent on the PRI's sectors. More than 150,000 Solidarity Committees were established in less than five years in low-income urban neighborhoods and rural communities throughout the country, partly as a mechanism for rebuilding electoral support for the PRI by demonstrating that the system could respond more rapidly to citizen demands for services and urban infrastructure. The Solidarity program contributed significantly to the PRI's impressive recovery in the 1991 midterm elections. After his break with Carlos Salinas, President Zedillo cancelled the Solidarity program, which was regarded as an instrument of *Salinismo.* Parts of the program were spun off into regional development projects administered by state governments; other parts were attached to the Finance Ministry through a new plan (PROGRESA) that provides direct cash assistance to the poorest Mexican families. In both cases, clientelistic ties to the presidency were eliminated. The partisan benefits of Solidarity's remnants still accrue to state governors, but today nearly half of the states are not controlled by the PRI.

Unquestionably, the Mexican regime's vaunted political control capabilities were weakened by the economic and political crises of recent sexenios. Nevertheless, the traditional instruments of control—patron-client relationships, *caciquismo* (local-level boss rule), the captive labor movement, selective repression of dissidents by government security forces—are still effective in some PRI-controlled states.

POLITICAL PARTIES

The Partido Revolucionario Institucional

The Partido Revolucionario Institucional (PRI) was founded in 1929 by President Plutarco Elías Calles to serve as a mechanism for reducing violent conflict among contenders for public office and for consolidating the power of the central government, at the expense of the personalistic, local, and state-level political machines of the decade following the 1910–1920 revolution. Between 1920 and 1929, there had been four major rebellions against the national executive by these subnational political machines. As historian Lorenzo Meyer has observed, the PRI was a party born not to fight for power, nor to share it with the opposition, "but rather to administer it."[28]

For more than half a century, the ruling party served with impressive efficiency, as a mechanism for resolving conflicts, for co-opting newly emerging interest groups into the system, and for legitimating the regime through the electoral process. Potential defectors from the official party were deterred by the government's manipulation of electoral rules, which made it virtually impossible for any dissident faction to bolt the party and win the election. Dissident movements did emerge occasionally, but before the neo-Cardenista coalition contested the 1988 election, no breakaway presidential candidacy had been able to garner more than 16 percent of the vote (by official count).

In 1938 President Lázaro Cárdenas transformed the official party from a mechanism for elite conflict resolution and co-optation into a mass-based political party that could be used explicitly to build popular support for government policies and mobilize participation in elections. Cárdenas accomplished this by merging into the official party the local-, state-, and national-level organizations of peasants and urban workers that had been created during his presidency. This reorganization established the party's claim to be an inclusionary party—one that would absorb the diverse economic interests and political tendencies represented in Mexican society. By including lower-income sectors, it reinforced the revolutionary credentials of the party, as well. The official party and its affiliated mass organizations occupied so much political space that opposition parties found it difficult to recruit supporters.

From the beginning, the official party was an appendage of the government itself, especially of the presidency. It was never a truly independent arena of political competition. A handful of nationally powerful party leaders, such as Fidel Velázquez, the patriarch of the PRI-affiliated labor movement until his death in 1997, occasionally constrained government actions, but the official party itself never determined the basic directions of government economic and social policies. Indeed, one of the key factors underlying the erosion of party unity and discipline since the late 1980s and the PRI's overwhelming defeats in state-level elections beginning in 1995, leading to its loss of the presidency in 2000, was the party's inability to distance itself from the unpopular austerity policies made by the technocrats in the federal government.

The official party traditionally enjoyed virtually unlimited access to government funds to finance its campaigns. No one knew how much was actually being siphoned from government coffers to the PRI, because Mexico had no laws requiring the reporting of campaign income and expenditures. When a PANista government took power in the state of Baja California in 1989, it found bank and legal records showing that more than $10 million in government funds had been channeled to the PRI for its 1989 gubernatorial campaign in that state. Reforms to the electoral code between 1993 and 1994 established minimal public reporting requirements for campaign income and expenditures, as well as Mexico's first-ever limits on individual and corporate contributions to electoral campaigns.

In the 1993–1994 electoral code reforms, ceilings on private contributions were set very high—the equivalent of $650,000 for an individual contribution. With its privileged access to financing from big business, the PRI continued to outspend its opponents by a huge margin, even without cash from government sources. In 1994, the PRI legally spent $44 million on its presidential campaign. It had even more money to spend on its campaigns, at all levels, than ever before, despite the contribution limits included in the electoral code reforms. In the same year, Roberto Madrazo, the PRI candidate for governor in the state of Tabasco, spent in excess of $50 million on his campaign—many times the limit for a gubernatorial race. This abuse came to light only after the defeated PRD candidate produced massive, incontrovertible evidence.

Yet another round of electoral reforms, passed by Congress in 1996, limited total private contributions to any party to 10 percent the total amount of regular public financing to all parties, and no individual can contribute more than 0.05 percent of the total regular public financing. Also, the reforms greatly increased public funding for all parties. The law also added a new prohibition on "the use of public resources and programs to benefit any political party or electoral campaign." The abuses did not disappear, however. After the 2000 presidential election, won by the PAN, the federal internal auditor discovered that the government-owned oil company, PEMEX, had made a $140 million loan to the oilworkers' union, one of the two most important PRI-affiliated labor unions. These funds were subsequently donated to the campaign of PRI candidate Francisco Labastida. By late 2002, the Attorney General's office was preparing to prosecute the directors of PEMEX, the leaders of the union, and the financial officers of Labastida's campaign.

As the party in power, the PRI profited from a vast network of government patronage through which small-scale material benefits could be delivered to large segments of the population. The president himself controlled a large slush fund ("*la partida secreta*"), authorized each year by Congress as part of the federal government budget, that could aid PRI officials and finance the party's campaigns as needed. During the Salinas *sexenio*, the National Solidarity Program delivered some $15 billion in benefits, ranging from refurbished schoolrooms and scholarships to keep low-income children in school, to health clinics, paved streets, potable water and sewage systems, housing, and support for small-business development. These small-scale investments were especially visible in the vote-rich urban slums, where the Cardenista coalition had won most of its support in 1988. In the 1991 congressional elections, persons who had personally benefited from the Solidarity program were strongly disposed to vote for PRI candidates. In 1994, just in time for national elections, the government launched PROCAMPO, a program offering direct cash payments to millions of subsistence farmers. Some 2.8 million PROCAMPO checks were delivered to beneficiaries within the two months preceding the August 1994 elections. By the late 1990s, in the context of an increasingly competitive electoral system, such "incumbency advantages" were being intensely criticized by the opposition parties and the media. Responding to this pressure,

Ernesto Zedillo virtually eliminated the presidential "secret budget" (see Figure 10.3).

Historically, the official party's most potent advantage over the competition was its ability to commit electoral fraud with relative impunity. A wide variety of techniques were used: stuffing the ballot boxes; disqualifying opposition party poll watchers; relocating polling places at the last minute to sites known only to PRI supporters; manipulating voter registration lists, padding them with nonexistent or nonresident PRIistas, and/or *rasurando* ("shaving off") those who are expected to vote for opposition parties; issuing multiple voting credentials to PRI supporters; buying, "renting," or confiscating opposition voters' credentials, often in return for material benefits; organizing *carruseles* ("flying brigades") of PRI supporters transported by truck or van to vote at several different polling places; and so forth. Moreover, in the past, the PRI held majority representation in all of the state and federal government entities that controlled vote counting and certification. The PRI could count on these bodies to manipulate the tallies to favor its candidates or, in cases where the opposition vote got out of control, nullify the unfavorable election outcomes. Adding votes to the PRI column, rather than taking them away from opposition parties, was the most common form of electoral fraud. In some predominantly rural districts, this practice led to election results in which the number of votes credited to the PRI candidate exceeded the total number of registered voters, or even the total number of adults estimated from the most recent population census.

In a successful effort to build up domestic and international credibility for the 1994 national elections, the Salinas government introduced a number of important safeguards against fraud. New, high-tech, photo-identification voter credentials were issued to virtually the entire 42.5 million-person electorate. The Federal Electoral Institute (IFE) was greatly strengthened and given greater autonomy. The PRI and its government representatives were denied a majority on the IFE's decision-making board. A new system of independent electoral tribunals was established to adjudicate election disputes, and a special prosecutor's office was established to investigate alleged violations of the electoral laws. The law defined a broad range of electoral offenses—not previously subject to prosecution—as electoral crimes (though the special prosecutor was appointed by the president and reported

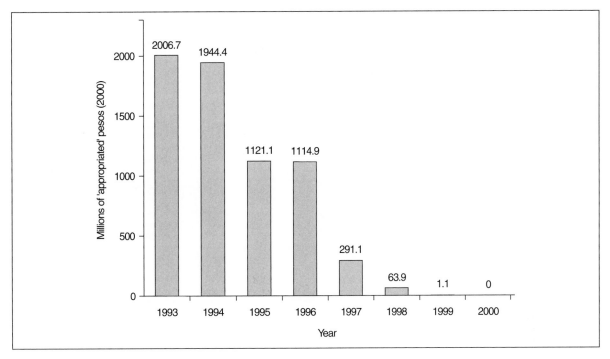

F I G U R E   1 0 . 3   *La Partida Secreta* (The President's Secret Budget)

Source: Santiago Levy, "El Presupuesto de Egresos de la Federación," *Este País* (Mexico), October 2000, p. 3.

to the federal attorney general, who was unlikely to bring charges against important PRI leaders or government officials). The role of independent, Mexican citizen observers in monitoring the casting and tallying of votes was formally recognized, and the presence of foreign electoral observers (euphemistically termed "international visitors") was legalized. Exit polls of voters and "quick counts" of the actual vote in sample precincts by the IFE as well as private organizations were authorized and publicly announced on election night.

Taken together, these innovations, which cost the Mexican taxpayers more than $1 billion, represented a major advance toward improving the security, professionalism, and fairness of the Mexican electoral system. However, various types of irregularities—especially violations of ballot secrecy and efforts by local bosses to induce voters to support the PRI—were still widespread in the more isolated, rural areas. Subsequent state and local elections in various parts of the country have demonstrated that subnational PRI leaders continue to use direct threats and other forms of intimidation, particularly against peasant voters.

The 1996 electoral reform greatly increased the institutional autonomy of the IFE. The Interior Minister was removed as president of the Institute and replaced by a nonpartisan president and eight nonpartisan commissioners. These nine electoral commissioners were elected for a seven-year term by a two-thirds vote of the Chamber of Deputies. Since no party can control more than 60 percent of the seats in the lower chamber, the IFE commissioners are elected by consensus of all of the parties. In the 1997 and 2000 national elections there was very little evidence of fraud. Since the IFE controls most of the process in a nonpartisan manner, the remaining sources of electoral fraud are vote-buying (still common in some states, especially in the Southeast), and the buying or renting of voter credentials. Both practices are illegal, but neither is easy for federal electoral authorities to police.

The share of the vote claimed by the PRI has been declining for three decades, but until recently, the erosion was gradual and did not threaten the party's grasp on the presidency and state governorships (see Figure 10.4). In the 1980s and 1990s, however, Mexican

Members of Mexico's newly independent Federal Electoral Institute (IFE) vote on a motion in 1997.

Instituto Federal Electoral, Mexico

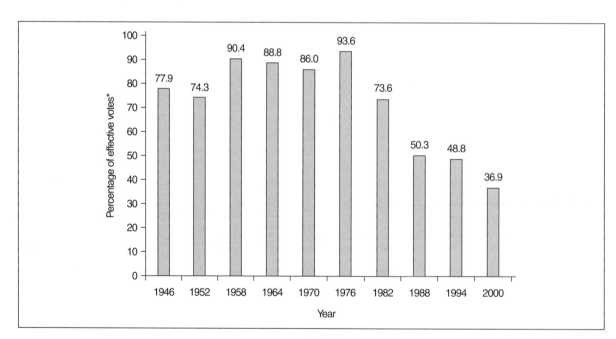

FIGURE 10.4 Support for PRI's Presidential Candidate, 1946–2000

*Percentage base includes votes cast only for registered and nonregistered candidates.

Note: The 1976 PRI candidate, José López Portillo, ran virtually unopposed because the PAN failed to nominate a candidate. The only other significant candidate was Valentín Campa, representing the Communist Party, which was not legally registered to participate in the 1976 election. More than 5% of the votes were annulled.

Source: Data from Comisión Federal Electoral, 1946–1988; from Instituto Federal Electoral, 1994–2000.

T A B L E   1 0 . 4   Electoral Competition in National Elections, 1964–2000 (percentage of 300 federal electoral districts)

Election Year	PRI Monopoly[a]	Strong PRI Hegemony[b]	Weak PRI Hegemony[c]	Two-party Competition[d]	Multiparty Competition[e]	Opposition Victory[f]
			Type of Competition			
1964	28.1%	52.2%	4.5%	14.0%	—	1.1%
1967	24.2	61.2	3.6	9.7	—	1.2
1970	27.0	53.9	1.7	17.4	—	—
1973	18.7	51.3	4.1	21.8	1.0%	3.1
1976	35.8	44.6	6.7	11.9	0.5	0.5
1979	9.4	48.0	12.3	6.3	22.7	1.3
1982	1.3	51.7	6.3	26.1	14.0	0.3
1985	3.3	41.7	9.0	21.0	21.3	3.7
1988[g]	1.0	19.0	15.0	8.3	34.0	22.7
1991	—	21.7	16.0	18.0	41.0	3.3
1994	—	2.3	8.3	26.0	55.4	8.0
1997	—	—	2.7	12.0	40.3	45.0
2000	—	—	1.0	8.3	34.7	56.0

[a]PRI monopoly = PRI vote > 95 percent.

[b]Strong PRI hegemony = PRI vote < 95 percent but > 70.

[c]Weak PRI hegemony = PRI vote < 70 percent, but the difference between PRI and second party in district is > 40 percentage points.

[d]Two-party competition = PRI vote < 70 percent, difference between PRI and second party is < 40 percentage points, second party vote > 25 percent, and third party vote < 10 percent.

[e]Multiparty competition = PRI vote < 70, difference between PRI and second party is < 40 percentage points, and second party vote < 25 percent or third party vote > 10 percent.

[f]Opposition victory = any party's vote > PRI vote.

[g]For 1988, opposition victories include those won by the Cardenista coalition of parties.

Source: Leopoldo Gómez and John Bailey, "La transición política y los dilemas del PRI", *Foro Internacional*, 31:1 (July–September 1990), p. 69. Calculations for 1991 and 1994 from Joseph L. Klesner, "The 1994 Mexican Elections: Manifestation of a Divided Society?" *Mexican Studies*, 11:1 (winter 1995), p. 141; for 2000 from Joseph Klesner, "Electoral Competition and the New Party System in Mexico," paper presented at the Annual Meeting of the American Political Science Association, August 30–September 2, 2001, p. 49.

elections became much more competitive. The proportion of electoral districts dominated to varying degrees by the PRI dropped dramatically, from 70 percent in 1979 to 1 percent in 2000. In the 2000 elections, the PRI faced significant competition from one or more opposition parties in 99 percent of the 300 electoral districts (see Table 10.4). The "Soviet-style" precincts that regularly delivered 98 to 100 percent of their votes to PRI candidates have disappeared.

In the last four elections, the PRI has done best among older voters, the less educated, and low-income people (see Table 10.5). It has also held the loyalty of a plurality of union members. However, the corporatist vote in general is no longer a dependable source of support for the PRI, and the low mobilization of these voters was one of the major reasons for its defeat in the 2000 elections.

Another key factor accounting for the long-term decline in the PRI's effectiveness as a vote-getting machine is the massive shift of population from rural to urban areas that has occurred in Mexico since 1950. In that year, 57 percent of the population lived in isolated rural communities of fewer than 2,500 inhabitants. By 1990 less than 29 percent lived in such localities. This massive rural-to-urban migration is reflected in occupational statistics: During the last four decades, the proportion of Mexico's economically active population employed in agriculture dropped from 58.3 to 26.8 percent. In urban Mexico, authoritarian control mechanisms are less efficacious. Education and income levels are higher,

TABLE 10.5   Party Choice in 2000 Presidential Election, by Type of Locality, Region, Gender, Age, and Education (in percentages)

	PAN	PRI	PRD	Others
Total	44	37	16	3
Type of Locality				
Urban	49	32	16	3
Rural	30	50	19	1
Mixed	35	45	19	1
Region				
North	48	39	12	1
Center-West	46	39	12	3
Center	42	35	20	3
South	42	26	20	2
Gender				
Male	46	33	19	2
Female	42	41	14	3
Age				
18–24	48	34	17	1
25–29	46	35	16	3
30–34	48	34	16	2
35–39	47	28	12	3
40–44	40	37	20	3
45–49	42	38	19	1
50–54	44	41	13	2
55–59	28	47	24	1
60 +	33	42	24	1
Education				
None	28	48	22	2
Primary	32	48	19	1
Secondary	46	36	15	3
College Preparatory	50	30	17	3
University +	58	24	15	3

Source: Nationwide exit poll conducted by *Reforma* newspaper, July 5, 2000.

and the middle classes—which provide a considerable share of the opposition vote—are larger. A smaller proportion of the population is subject to pressures from local-level PRI bosses.

The PRI is significantly weaker in cities with 100,000 or more inhabitants, where more than half of the Mexican population now lives. Mexico City has been a particular disaster area for the PRI in recent elections. The PRI lost the mayoral races in Mexico City by large margins in 1997 and 2000. If senate, city council, and federal deputy losses are included, the PRI has gone 0 for 159 in the last two elections in Mexico City. Even in rural areas, however, the PRI's formerly safe vote continues to erode. While the PRI

still gets a higher share of the vote in rural areas than any other party, the average vote for PRI candidates in rural precincts fell to 40 percent in 2000, continuing a trend that began with the 1982 national elections.

The PRI has had to adjust from being an official party—a political machine based on incumbency advantages—to being a party out of power. PRI legislators for the first time have had to figure out how to vote without presidential leadership. The whole party has had to define its ideology as a political party, not as an instrument of power. In an effort to clarify party ideology and redefine the lines of power in the party, the PRI held a national, open election to select the party president in 2002. The two candi-

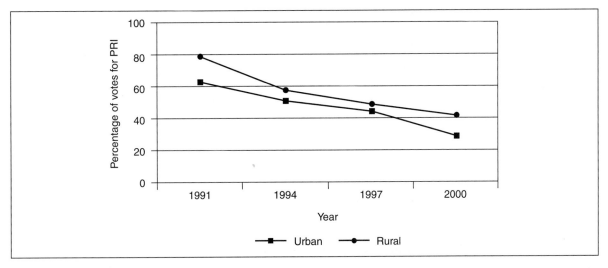

F I G U R E   1 0 . 5   PRI's Vote Share, by Type of Locality

Sources: For 1991–1997, Jorge Buedía, "El elector mexicano de los noventa: un nuevo tipo de votante?" *Política y Gobierno*, Vol. 7, No. 2 (2nd semester, 2000); for 2000; unpublished data from Análisis de Resultados de Comunicación y Opinión Pública, S.A. de C.V. (Mexico City).

dates were Roberto Madrazo, who had lost the presidential primary in 1999 and was considered to be the more populist and modern leader, and Beatriz Paredes, the leader of the PRI faction in Congress, who was more closely identified with defeated presidential candidate Francisco Labastida and the party bureaucrats. This time Madrazo won, due mostly to his close alliance with the teachers' union, one of the few corporatist organizations that has retained a capacity to mobilize voters.

Madrazo has not yet defined a strategy to recover support for the PRI, in part because the PRI must both cooperate enough with the PAN and the president to avoid being labeled as intransigent, and distance itself enough from the president and his party to establish the PRI's brand label. The main issues that distinguish the PRI from the Fox government so far are taxes (the PRI wants less), spending (the PRI wants more), and reform of the government-owned electrical energy industry (the Fox administration wants increased private investment in this sector and advocates changing the constitution to attract it; the PRI is torn between allowing more private investment without constitutional changes and maintaining a state monopoly in the utility).

The Partido Acción Nacional (PAN). The PAN's regional strongholds include several northern states (Baja California, Chihuahua, San Luis Potosí,

and Nuevo León), the center-west states of Jalisco, Guanajuato, and Aguascalientes, the central core region (the Estado de México, Querétaro, Morelos, and the Federal District), and Yucatán and Veracruz. Between 1989 and 2000, the PAN won gubernatorial elections in nine states (Baja California, Chihuahua, Guanajuato, Jalisco, Nuevo León, Querétaro, Aguascalientes, Morelos, and Yucatán), and it managed to create a de facto two-party system in these states. In 1995, the PAN retained control of the governorship of Baja California, thereby accomplishing something that no opposition party had previously done: to transfer power from one elected opposition governor to another. The PAN failed to retain the governorship of Chihuahua in 1998 and Nuevo León in 2003, losing to the PRI. However, PAN candidates won their third consecutive races for governor in Guanajuato (2000) and Baja California (2001), and also maintained control of Jalisco (2001). The PAN picked up the governorships of San Luis Potosí in 2003, and took Tlaxcala from the PRD in 2004. Between 2003 and 2004, the party also lost very close races to the PRI in Campeche, Sinaloa, Veracruz, and Oaxaca, all previously PRI strongholds. Over the last decade, the PAN has governed nearly all of the 20 largest cities in Mexico, with the conspicuous exception of Mexico City, and has also governed most of the capital cities of the country.

The PAN was established in 1939, largely in reaction to the leftward drift of public policy under President Lázaro Cárdenas, particularly his policies in support of socialist public education. Its founders included prominent Catholic intellectuals who espoused an early Christian Democratic ideology, and the party has traditionally opposed government restrictions on Church activities. The party attacked political centralism and advocated expanded states' rights long before it was fashionable to do so. The PAN's principal constituency has always been the urban middle class, but is has also attracted votes among the socially conservative peasants and the urban working class.

Between 1964, when a primitive form of proportional representation increased opposition presence in the Chamber of Deputies, and the mid-1990s, when the PAN was governing many municipal and state governments, the focus of PANista representation was in the federal Congress, especially the lower chamber (the first PANista was elected to the Senate only in 1991). In these years, PAN deputies would typically begin their congressional terms fighting electoral fraud from the previous election, in an attempt to increase the number of PANista deputies. Then they would settle in and begin to propose legislation. Until the Salinas years, these bills would almost always be ignored in the chamber at the time of introduction; but eventually most of the PAN's legislative proposals were adopted by the federal executive and reintroduced and approved by Congress. Among the PANista ideas later embraced by PRI governments were increased proportional representation in both chambers of Congress, autonomous electoral courts and electoral agencies, the permanent voting credential, increased municipal autonomy, increased autonomy and authority for the Supreme Court, increased self-governance for the Federal District (Mexico City), federal revenue-sharing with the states, liberalization of the social security systems, a national consumer protection agency, and profit-sharing with employees.

The ideological position of the PAN has been relatively constant over the last six decades. It could be classified as the center-right, with strong elements of Christian socialism (which covers a wide range of policies, from center-left on labor issues to right-of-center on abortion), combined with traditional liberal attitudes on trade, municipal decentralization, and general democratization. The PAN's relative position on the political spectrum has depended mostly on the positioning of the PRI, whose pendulum has shifted to positions clearly to the left of the PAN (as in the 1970s) or to the right of the PAN (as was the case from 1988 to 2000).

Statistical analysis of roll-call votes in the 57th Legislature (1997–2000) places the PAN at the center of the political spectrum, to the left of the PRI. Although roll calls are not available for earlier years, congressional debates suggest that the PAN held a similar position for most of the Salinas and Zedillo years. Despite the nationalist and populist background of their party, PRI deputies found themselves voting to the right of the PAN because they had to support the neoliberal economic policies and austerity measures of PRI presidents. However, during the 58th Legislature, under a PANista president, PAN members generally voted to the right of the PRI. Now it is the PAN deputies who must support the austerity programs of their president, while PRI deputies are liberated to vote their conscience and constituencies rather than take cues from the president.

The PAN has worked long and hard to develop a strong network of grass-roots militants. While clearly the leader today among Mexico's parties in terms of organizational strength, the PAN is a party with several major weaknesses. Since the mid-1970s it has been divided into moderate-progressive and militant-conservative ("neo-PANista") factions, which have jockeyed for control of the party machinery and carried out purges of opposing faction members when they were in power. The more pragmatic, moderate-progressive faction has been in control of the party since 1989. Vicente Fox's ideology is closer to the moderate-progressives than to the neo-PANistas.

The challenge to the PAN now is to make the adjustment from a party of opposition to a party of government. The transition has been difficult for some PANistas, who still act as if they were in the opposition, challenging the president because he is the president. The PAN must find a way to continue embracing Fox's main campaign message of change while at the same time being the party of the government. The PAN and the government have at times struggled over the definition of change, and it has been particularly difficult to bring about fundamental economic reforms without majorities in the federal chambers. Furthermore, change has been impeded by the reces-

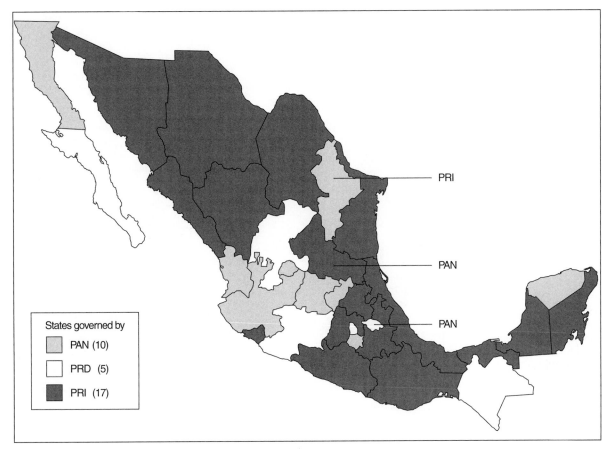

States governed by
PAN (10)
PRD (5)
PRI (17)

FIGURE 10.6   States Governed by Three Main Parties, December 2004

PAN-governed states include Aguascalientes, Baja California, Guanajuato, Jalisco, Morelos, Nayarit, Querétaro, San Luis Potosí, Tlaxcala, and Yucatán.
PRD-governed states include Baja California Sur, Chiapas, Distrito Federal, Michoacán, and Zacatecas.
PRI-governed states include Campeche, Chihuahua, Coahuila, Colima, Durango, Guerrero, Hidalgo, México, Nuevo León, Oaxaca, Puebla, Quintana Roo, Sinaloa, Sonora, Tabasco, Tamaulipas, and Veracruz.

sion that hit at the beginning of Fox's presidency, which has reduced the government's latitude by restricting the size of the federal budget.

At the beginning of the Fox administration, some PANistas complained that the president had not named enough members of the party to positions in the federal government. In fact, few members of Fox's cabinet have a long history in the party, and the dearth of PANistas is even more conspicuous at the subcabinet level. Some ministries are nearly devoid of PANistas. In contrast, the Fox administration has complained at times of lack of support from PANista legislators for key parts of the president's agenda, such as making peace with the Zapatista rebels in Chiapas by granting sweeping new rights to the indigenous population.

The Partido de la Revolución Democrática (PRD).
Before 1988, the Mexican left had spawned political parties like the Partido Popular Socialista (PPS), which for decades served as a home for moderate socialists and other left-of-center politicians willing to collaborate with the government and even to endorse the PRI's presidential candidates, in exchange for a seat in Congress. The more independent left—that is, those who did not cooperate openly with the ruling party—was traditionally represented by the *Partido Comunista Mexicano* (PCM). The Communists were allowed to compete legally in elections during the presidency of Lázaro Cárdenas, but their party was subsequently outlawed and did not regain its legal representation until 1979, when its congressional candidates won 5 percent of the vote.

Cuauhtémoc Cárdenas, candidate of the PRD, casts his ballot in the 1997 election that made him the first popularly elected mayor of Mexico City.

Instituto Federal Electoral, Mexico

During most of the 1980s, even in the face of Mexico's gravest economic crisis since the 1910 Revolution, and despite a series of party mergers intended to reduce the fractionalization of the leftist vote, the parties on the left lost ground electorally. They were hampered by constant internal squabbling (motivated mostly by personalistic rivalries, and to a lesser extent to ideological cleavages), and inability to do effective grassroots organizing, and an identification with discredited, statist economic policies.

The key to the left's rejuvenation in 1988 was a split within the PRI leadership—the most serious since the early 1950s. In August 1986 a number of nationally prominent PRI figures, all members of the party's center-left wing, formed a dissident movement within the PRI known as the Corriente Democrática (CD). They were led by Porfirio Muñoz Ledo (former head of the PRI, runner-up candidate for the party's presidential nomination in 1976, former secretary of labor and secretary of education), and Cuauhtémoc Cárdenas, who was just finishing his term as governor of the state of Michoacán. The CD criticized the de la Madrid administration's economic restructuring program and sought a renewed

commitment by the PRI to traditional principles of economic nationalism and social justice. Most urgently, CD adherents called for a top-to-bottom democratization of the PRI, beginning with the elimination of the *dedazo* (the unilateral selection by the outgoing president) as the mechanism for determining the party's presidential candidate. The CD's proposals were widely interpreted as a last-ditch attempt by the PRI's traditional politicos to recover leadership of the party by influencing the outcome of the 1987–1988 presidential succession. The CD's demands for reform were resoundingly rejected by the PRI hierarchy, and its leaders formally split from the party in October 1987.

Confronted with the defeat within the PRI, Cárdenas accepted the presidential nomination of the Partido Auténtico de la Revolución Mexicana (PARM), a conservative, nationalist party established by another group of dissident PRIistas in 1954. Later, four other parties—all on the left and including the remnants of the old Mexican Communist Party—joined the PARM to form a coalition, the Frente Democrático Nacional (FDN), to contest the 1988 presidential election, with Cárdenas as their candidate. Before joining the Cárdenas coalition, the leftist parties had been attracting only insignificant support in public opinion polls, and some were in danger of losing their legal registration. As members of a center-left coalition led by a political figure with broad popular appeal, they stood to gain a great deal. Soon after the 1988 elections, however, the left's long-standing ideological and personalistic cleavages reasserted themselves, and by 1991, when midterm elections were held, most of Cárdenas's 1988 coalition partners had gone their separate ways, leaving the newly constituted PRD as the principal standard-bearer of the left. Even within the PRD, serious disagreements emerged over such issues as the degree of democracy in internal party governance and strategies for dealing with the government (dialogue and collaboration on certain issues versus permanent confrontation).

The left's problems in the early 1990s were not all self-inflicted. Under Salinas, the government showed no inclination to negotiate seriously with the Cardenista left. Salinas's own contemptuous attitude toward the PRD was summed up by his public comment in response to protests by PRD legislators that disrupted his final state-of-the-nation address in November 1994: "I neither see them nor hear them." Under Salinas, the government showed much greater willingness to recognize electoral victories of the PAN than those claimed by the PRD, except for local offices in Cárdenas's home state of Michoacán. Conflicts between PRD militants and PRI *caciques* have been bitter, with hundreds of PRD activists murdered since the party was created in 1989. The behavior of the PRI-government apparatus in several key elections held during the Salinas *sexenio* signaled that it would never allow a PRD government to come to power at the state level, anywhere in the country. When the PRD's victories at the municipal level were recognized, the city governments under its control were punished and starved for resources by PRI state governors.

President Zedillo opened a new chapter in PRD-government relations, recognizing Cuauhtémoc Cárdenas's overwhelming victory in the 1997 mayoral race in Mexico City. In 1998–1999 the PRD won gubernatorial elections in the states of Zacatecas, Tlaxcala, and Baja California Sur. In 2000, it picked up the state of Chiapas, and again won the Mexico City mayoralty. In 2001, the PRD finally won

Cárdenas's home state of Michoacán, after choosing his son, Lázaro, for governor. In all of these elections except for Mexico City and Michoacán, the victorious candidates were defectors from the PRI who had been passed over for the party's gubernatorial nomination. These outcomes illustrate a key advantage for the PRD in Mexico's current three-party competition: In places where the PRI organization is fractured by internal rivalries, where the local factions are unable to reach consensus on a candidate, the PRD is usually the main beneficiary. For PRIistas whose political aspirations are thwarted by their own party, the PRD—the party run by ex-PRIistas—is a natural new home.

Until 2000, the PRD continued to take policy positions to the left of the ruling party on some issues (for example, arguing against the use of any taxpayer money to bail out bankers who made bad loans during the Salinas *sexenio*). Its differences with most recent government policies were matters of degree, pacing, and how much was being done to ameliorate the social costs of these policies, rather than their basic direction. During the 57th Legislature (1997–2000), when for the first time the PRI lost a majority in the lower chamber, the PRD tended to vote with the PAN and against the PRI on issues of political reform and to enhance the oversight of the legislative branch over the federal executive. On most economic issues, the PAN and the PRI voted together, with the PRD often voting against.

In the 58th Legislature (2000–2003), the PRD took a more radical stance on policy issues and has been more intransigent in its relations with the other parties. In part this is due to the diminished presence of the party in the Congress—about 60 percent smaller than the PRD delegation in the 1997–2000 period. It now introduces bills that call for a major restructuring of the Mexican political system, including the emasculation of the federal executive. Some of the bills have proposed the introduction of a parliamentary system with an elected president, something like the presidential-premier system in France. The PRD has called for increased proportional representation and the abolition of the single-member districts (where the PRD does relatively less well).

In its early years, the PRD did a poor job of mobilizing previously uncommitted voters. It had retained many of the urban working-class voters who traditionally supported the parties of the independent left, but it was not very successful in establishing ties with the popular movements that had developed outside of the PRI-affiliated corporatist structures. However, its ties to the rural areas were underdeveloped, and the PRD had been dominated by Mexico City-based politicians and intellectuals for whom the provinces hardly existed. Central party leaders often shortchanged local organizers in their allocation of party funds.

The future of the PRD is to be found in the Federal District, Michoacán, Guerrero, Baja California Sur, and perhaps in Tabasco and Oaxaca. The front-runner for the PRD presidential nomination for 2006 is Mexico City major Andrés Manuel López Obrador, who has very high approval ratings in the city. However, he is facing impeachment charges in the lower chamber. If he is impeached and eliminated from contention, the PRD can always return to Cuauhtémoc Cárdenas, who has already announced that he is running in his fourth consecutive presidential contest.

The divisions in the PRD are much worse than those that have affected the PAN. For example, the rivalry between Cárdenas and Muñoz Ledo, which began soon after the PRD was formed, came to a head in the 57th Legislature. Muñoz Ledo had been selected as the floor leader of the party in the Chamber of Deputies, but he eventually left the party to run for the presidency under the banner of the PARM (just as Cárdenas had done in 1988). Then he abandoned his campaign and endorsed Fox in the late spring of 2000, and was later designated as ambassador to Belgium and the European Union and has played an important role in the state reform process. The PRD has attempted to resolve the personalistic differences in the party by holding open national elections (basically a primary) to select the party president. However, the losers in these elections have often charged the winning side with electoral fraud—a surprising charge for a party that spent most of the 1990s complaining of fraud by the PRI.

GOVERNMENT PERFORMANCE

Promoting Economic Growth and Reducing Poverty

There is little debate about the importance of the state's contribution to the economic development of Mexico since 1940. Massive public investments in infrastructure (roads, dams, telecommunications,

electrification) and generous, cheap credit provided to the private sector by Nacional Financiera and other government development banks made possible a higher rate of capital accumulation, stimulated higher levels of investment by domestic entrepreneurs and foreign corporations, and enabled Mexico to develop a diversified production capacity second only within Latin America to that of Brazil.

From 1940 until well into the 1970s, a strong elite consensus prevailed on the state's role in the economy. The state facilitated private capital accumulation and protected the capitalist system by limiting popular demands for consumption and redistribution of wealth; it established the rules for development; and it participated in the development process as the nation's largest single entrepreneur, employer, and source of investment capital. The state served as the "rector" (guiding force) of this mixed economy, setting broad priorities and channeling investment (both public and private) into strategic sectors. Acting through joint ventures between private firms and state-owned enterprises, the government provided resources for development projects so large that they would have been difficult or impossible to finance from internal (within-the-firm) sources or through borrowing from private banks.

The result, from the mid-1950s to the mid-1970s, was the much-touted "Mexican miracle" of sustained economic growth at annual rates of 6 to 7 percent, coupled with low inflation (5 percent per annum between 1955 and 1972). By 1980 the gross national product had reached $2,130 per capita, placing Mexico toward the upper end of the World Bank's list of semi-industrialized or "middle-developed" countries. As sole proprietor of PEMEX, the state oil monopoly, the government was responsible for developing the crucial oil and natural gas sector of the economy. By the end of the oil boom (1978–1981), oil was generating more than $15 billion a year in export revenues and fueling economic growth of more than 8 percent per year—one of the world's highest growth rates.

It is the distributive consequences of this impressive performance in economic development and the manner in which it was financed by the government since the 1970s that have been criticized in retrospect. From Miguel Alemán (1946–1952) to the present, all but one or two of Mexico's presidents and their administrations reflected the private sector's contention that Mexico must first create wealth and then worry about redistributing it—the belief being that the state would quickly be overwhelmed by popular demands that it could not satisfy. By the early 1970s, however, there was convincing evidence that an excessively large portion of Mexico's population was being left behind in the drive to become a modern, industrialized nation.

This is not to say that some benefits of the development process did not trickle down to the poor. From 1950 to 1980, poverty in absolute terms declined. The middle class expanded to an estimated 29 percent of the population by 1970. From 1960 to 1980 illiteracy dropped from 35 to 15 percent of the population, infant mortality was reduced from 78 to 70 per 1,000 live births, and average life expectancy rose from 55 to 64 years. Clearly, the quality of life for many Mexicans—even in isolated rural areas— did improve during this period, although several other Latin American countries (Chile, Colombia, Costa Rica, Cuba, Ecuador, El Salvador, and Venezuela) achieved higher rates of improvement on indicators of social well-being than did Mexico during the same period.

There was, however, a dark side to Mexico's "economic miracle." From 1950 to the mid-1970s, ownership of land and capital (stocks, bonds, time deposits) became increasingly concentrated. Personal income inequality also increased, at a time when, given Mexico's middle level of development, the national income distribution should have been shifting toward greater equality, according to classical economic development theory. Indeed, Mexico apparently had a higher overall concentration of income in the mid-1970s than in 1910, before the outbreak of the revolution. By 1977 the poorest 70 percent of Mexican families received only 24 percent of all disposable income, while the richest 30 percent of families received 76 percent of income. Survey data collected by INEGI, the government's statistical research agency, suggest that the country's income distribution became slightly more equal between 1977 and 1984, but this may have been due to the extraordinarily large number of new jobs created during the oil boom years of 1978 through 1981, most of which were eliminated during the severe economic contraction of 1982 through 1988. In any case, the long-term trend toward a higher degree of income inequality soon reasserted itself. Inequality increased by 10 per-

cent between 1984 and 1989, before leveling off during the 1989–1992 period.

Other social indicators mirror the pattern of personal income distribution. By 1989 more than one-quarter of Mexican children under five years of age in rural areas were malnourished; the incidence of severe malnutrition among such children had risen by 100 percent during the preceding ten years. While 78 percent of Mexico's elementary school-age children were enrolled in 1990, only 54 percent of those starting primary school finished it. Among the dwellings included in the 1990 census, 57 percent had no sewerage connections, 50 percent had no piped water inside the dwelling, and 13 percent had no electricity.

On every indicator of economic opportunity and social well-being, there are vast disparities among Mexico's regions and between rural and urban areas. Unemployment and underemployment are concentrated overwhelmingly in the rural sector, which contains at least 70 percent of the population classified by the government as living in extreme poverty. The rate of infant mortality in rural areas is nearly 50 percent higher than the national average. Interregional disparities in social well-being are equally extreme. In 1990 the percentage of persons with incomes lower than two minimum salaries (a bare subsistence level) ranged from 40 percent in Baja California to 80 percent in Chiapas. A composite index of social well-being in 2000 shows the Federal District (Mexico City) and the northern border states as being the most privileged, and the southern states (especially Chiapas, Oaxaca, and Guerrero) as the most marginalized (see Figure 10.7). Gross domestic product per capita in the same year was 8 times higher in the Federal District than in Oaxaca, for example. This pattern of extreme spatial inequalities has remained essentially unchanged for several decades.

The policies and investment preferences of Mexico's postrevolutionary governments contributed much to the country's highly inegalitarian development. At minimum, the public policies pursued since 1940 failed to counteract the wealth-concentrating effects of private market forces. Evidence is strong that some government investments and policies actually reinforced these effects. For example, during most of the post-1940 period, government tax and credit policies worked primarily to

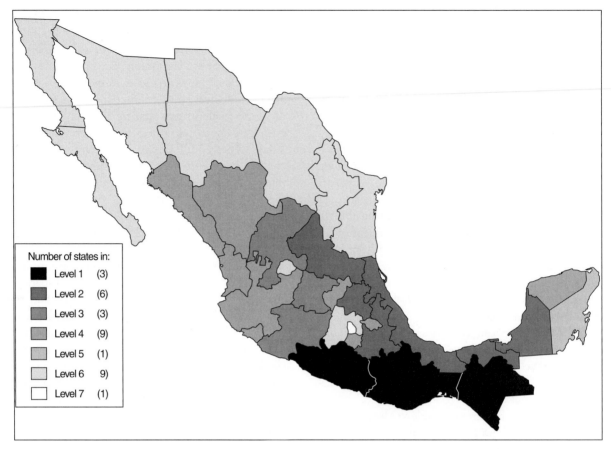

FIGURE 10.7   Levels of Social Well-Being by State, in 2000

Level 1: Chiapas, Guerrero, Oaxaca.
Level 2: Campeche, Hidalgo, Puebla, San Luis Potosí, Tabasco, Veracruz.
Level 3: Guanajuato, Michoacán, Zacatecas.
Level 4: Colima, Durango, Jalisco, Morelos, Nayarit, Querétaro, Sinaloa, Tlaxcala, Yucatán.
Level 5: Quintana Roo.
Level 6: Aguascalientes, Baja California, Baja California Sur, Coahuila, Chihuahua, México, Nuevo León, Sonora, Tamaulipas.
Level 7: Distrito Federal.

Note: Level of social well-being is measured by characteristics of dwellings (have electricity, refrigerator, television, concrete vs. dirt floors, sewerage connection, private bathroom; number of rooms; use something other than firewood or coal for cooking) and population characteristics (percentage economically active; literate; 6–19-year-olds who attend school; receive health care; live in urban area; average number of children born to women over 12 years of age).

Source: Instituto Nacional de Estadística, Geografía e Informática, www.inegi.gob.mx

the advantage of the country's wealthiest agribusiness and industrial entrepreneurs. Government expenditures for social security, public health, and education remained relatively low by international standards. By the late 1970s, Mexico was still allocating a smaller share of its central government budget to social services than countries like Bolivia, Brazil, Chile, and Panama. The slowness with which basic social services were extended to the bulk of the population in Mexico was a direct consequence of the government's policy of keeping inflation low by concentrating public expenditures on subsidies and infrastructure for private industry, rather than on social programs and subsidies to consumers.

Even during the period between 1970 and 1982, when populist policies were allegedly in vogue and government revenues were expanding rapidly because of the oil export boom, public spending for programs like health and social security remained roughly constant, in real per capita terms. The economic crisis that erupted in 1982, after an unprecedented run-up in Mexico's domestic and externally held debt, made it impossible to maintain even that level of government commitment to social well-being. By 1986 debt service was consuming over half of the total federal government budget, necessitating deep cuts in spending for health, education, consumer subsidies, and job-creating public investments. Social welfare expenditures per capita fell to 1974 levels. Mexico's macroeconomic adjustment program was considerably more severe than those in other major Latin American countries that also experienced debt crises during the 1980s. The severity of the adjustment is reflected particularly in minimum real wages, which fell by two-thirds between 1980 and 1989. Despite a modest resurgence of economic growth in the early 1990s, by the end of the Salinas *sexenio* real wages for most Mexicans had still not recovered their levels of 1981. The economic crisis of the mid-1990s caused most Mexicans to lose whatever ground they had gained during the Salinas years.

Under Mexico's four most recent presidents, the government has implemented a **neoliberal economic development model** stressing the need to give much freer rein to market forces. The primary objective of this "technocratic free-market revolution" has been to attract more private investment (especially foreign capital) and thereby push up Mexico's rate of economic growth. While drastically shrinking the public sector of the economy through a sweeping privatization program and opening up nearly all sectors of the economy to private investment (including those formerly reserved to the state), the technocrats were unwilling to completely surrender the government's traditional "rectorship" role in the economy. "The new [government] elite did not believe that the market, left to its own devices, would resolve all problems through invisible hands."[29]

This concern is reflected in the considerable spending by the last two technocratic administrations on social welfare initiatives like Salinas's National Solidarity Program and Zedillo's PROGRESA program—both explicit efforts to constuct a minimal safety net for the millions of low-income Mexicans who were the short-term "losers" from neoliberal economic policies and trade liberalization under NAFTA. But these carefully targeted social programs were not sufficient to offset the structural impoverishment caused by

falling real wages, the elimination of millions of jobs, and the slashing of most consumer subsidies.

A controversial national survey conducted jointly by a United Nations agency and the Mexican government in 1992 found 37.2 million Mexicans (43.8 percent of the total population) living at or below the official poverty line. An independent, academic study using official and private sector statistics found that from 1963 to 1981, before the shift to neoliberal economic policies, the proportion of Mexico's population living below the poverty line had dropped from 77.5 to 48.5 percent; however, from 1982 to 1992, the trend was reversed, with the poverty population rising to 66 percent.[30]

Whatever statistical base is used, it is clear that the new, market-oriented development model thus far has exacerbated—not alleviated—Mexico's poverty and inequality problems, even when the model was apparently working well in macroeconomic terms (that is, from 1989 through 1992).[31] Moreover, Mexico's experience with rapid economic growth during the "miracle" years of the 1950s and 1960s and the oil boom of the late 1970s and early 1980s suggests that without strong, sustained government action to correct for market failures and improve human capital endowments through education and job training, income concentration and related social problems will continue unabated.

Net job creation in Mexico under neoliberal economic policies since the late 1980s has been anemic, despite a huge influx of foreign capital. This dismal performance can be explained in part by the fact that well over half of the foreign funds received by Mexico during this period were invested in stocks, short-term government-issued bonds, and other financial instruments, rather than in job-creating, direct investment projects. Equally important, the government's strategy of promoting export-led development has induced many private firms to become more competitive in the global marketplace by shedding labor and becoming more capital-intensive.

Thus it has yet to be proved that economic liberalization and free trade can yield significantly higher rates of economic growth and job creation, especially in Mexico's small- and medium-sized businesses (only about one in ten of these businesses export anything).[32] The character of economic development being generated in Mexico by the neoliberal model seems incompatible with the country's overwhelming social requirements. There is a growing consensus that the government will have to do much more to upgrade workers' skills through vocational education and subsidized, on-the-job training if Mexico is to realize a greater return from its painful shift to an open, market-oriented development strategy. A fundamental reform of the country's public education system will be necessary to achieve a better distribution of the gains from NAFTA.

Financing Development and Controlling Inflation

From 1940 to 1970, Mexico's public sector acquired an international reputation for sound, conservative monetary and fiscal policies. This conservative style of economic management, coupled with Mexico's long record of political stability, gave the country an attractive investment climate. By 1982 this image had been shattered; the public sector (and much of the private sector) was suffering from a deep liquidity crisis, and inflation had reached levels unheard of since the first decade of the Mexican Revolution, when paper currencies lost most of their value. What happened?

The basic difficulty was that the government had attempted to spend its way out of the social and economic problems that had accumulated since 1940, without paying the political cost that sweeping redistributive policies would have entailed. Instead, it attempted to expand the entire economic pie by enlarging the state's role as banker, entrepreneur, and employer. Throughout the period since 1940, and especially after 1970, Mexico's public sector expanded steadily while its revenue-raising capability lagged. The result was ever-larger government deficits, financed increasingly by borrowing abroad.

For most of the post–World War II period, Mexico's tax effort—its rate of taxation and its actual performance in collecting taxes—was among the lowest in the world. Officials feared that any major alteration in the tax structure would drive domestic and foreign capital out of the country. Two modest attempts at tax reform, in 1964 and 1972, failed because of determined opposition from the business community. When the private sector refused to accede to higher taxes, the Echeverría administration opted for large-scale deficit financing, external indebtedness, and a huge increase in the money supply. The public sector itself was vastly enlarged, increasing the number of state-owned enterprises from 84 in 1970 to 845 in 1976. Fiscal restraint was finally forced on the government by depletion of its currency reserves in 1976.

Echeverría's successor, José López Portillo, at first attempted to reverse the trend toward larger government deficits, but the effort was abandoned when the treasury began to swell with oil export revenues. Again, the temptation was to address basic structural problems by further expanding the state sector, and López Portillo found it impossible to resist. Oil revenues seemed to be a guaranteed, limitless source of income for the government. Mexico borrowed heavily abroad, anticipating a steady rise in oil prices. When world oil prices declined in 1981 and 1982, the government was forced to suspend repayment of the foreign debt and negotiate a long-term reduction in interest rates—the first of several debt "restructurings," the most recent of which was completed in 1990.

Deficit financing, especially in the context of the overheated economy of the oil boom years, also touched off a burst of inflation. The average annual inflation rate rose from 15 percent during Echeverría's presidency (nearly triple the average rate between 1940 and 1970), to 36 percent under López Portillo and 91 percent during the de la Madrid *sexenio* (159 percent in 1987). Both the de la Madrid and Salinas administrations made reducing the inflation rate their top economic priority, but Salinas was much more effective in bringing inflation under control than his predecessor. His principal instrument was price and wage controls, enforced by a formal, government-business–organized labor "pact" that was renewed six times, with some adjustments, at 12- to 18-month intervals. This form of shock therapy brought the inflation rate down to single digits by 1994.

The other key to Salinas's success in fighting inflation was deep cuts in spending to reduce and eventually eliminate the public deficit, coupled with unprecedented steps to boost federal government revenues. These measures included the sale or closure of hundreds of state-owned enterprises, vigorous enforcement of the tax laws (only two individual tax evaders had been caught and imprisoned between 1921 and 1988), and the introduction of a 2 percent annual tax on total business assets, intended to reduce manipulations that had previously enabled 70 percent of Mexico's businesses to evade paying any taxes.

Even after the Salinas administration's "successful" tax reform, however, the federal government still obtained most of its revenues (over 60 percent) from socially regressive indirect taxes, primarily the value-added tax levied on about 70 percent of all goods and services. Personal income tax rates for the wealthiest Mexicans were actually reduced from 50 percent in 1988 to 35 percent in 1990, and a proposed tax on capital gains by individual investors in the stock market was shelved. "As on previous occasions, the government decided it was too risky to tax the savings of the richest Mexicans. The threat of capital flight . . . remained a powerful constraint on the government's taxing powers."[33]

The deep financial crisis that erupted in the first month of Ernesto Zedillo's presidency raised serious questions about the wisdom of the Salinas administration's obsessive pursuit of one-digit inflation, as well as its decision to "live with" a seriously overvalued peso until after the August 1994 national elections—indeed, until after President Salinas had left office. An earlier, staged devaluation would have boosted inflation and interest rates at a politically inopportune moment, but it could have prevented the financial panic and massive capital flight that followed the sudden, mega-devaluation of December 20, 1994. More than $10 billion in investment capital fled Mexico within a week; the peso had to be sharply devalued, eventually losing more than half of its value against the U.S. dollar; and the government came within a few days of insolvency as its foreign currency reserves were depleted.

Salinas and his financial ministers were also justly criticized for creating illusions of prosperity by financing a huge current accounts deficit (resulting mostly from a flood of consumer imports) with short-term, highly speculative capital. That "hot money"—mostly from large, U.S. institutional investors—flowed into *tesobonos,* the high-yielding, U.S. dollar-denominated bonds with maturities ranging from 28 to 180 days that were issued by the Mexican Treasury in prodigious quantities beginning in 1989. By the end of 1994, Mexico's debt in *tesobonos* had grown to almost $30 billion, and with the central bank's reserves virtually depleted by its efforts to fend off six speculative attacks on the peso during 1994, there was no way to pay off these bonds as they matured. Only massive financial assistance from the United States prevented a default and a general collapse of the Mexican economy.

How could a technocratic government that had earned worldwide respect for its skillful management of the economy, even in the midst of the political shocks of 1994, have erred so grievously? Most likely, a combination of political and personal factors led to the debacle: the government's need to paper over the financial cracks that were developing in order to achieve a decisive PRI victory in the 1994 elections; Carlos Salinas's desire to protect his image in the midst of a difficult and ultimately unsuccessful campaign to become head of the World Trade Organization after he left the presidency; the ineptitude and inexperience of newly inaugurated President Zedillo's economic team in dealing with skittish private investors. In any case, the Mexican government suffered a severe loss in credibility abroad, and the average Mexican has paid—and will continue to pay—a high price for the politically motivated manipulation of macroeconomic policy.

Establishing the Rule of Law

The one area of performance in which the Mexican government has been failing most conspicuously, especially since the mid-1990s, is the administration of justice. From the poorest urban workers to middle-class professionals to the richest business tycoons, Mexicans are appalled and incensed that the government seems totally incapable of dealing effectively with the epidemic of violent street crime—armed robberies, muggings, kidnappings, rapes, and homicides. Surveys show that virtually every resident of Mexico City in the late 1990s had either been a crime victim or had a close relative or friend who had suffered the same fate in recent years. Increasingly, middle- and upper-class Mexicans are protecting their children by sending them abroad to be educated, and there has been a sharp increase in emigration to the United States by Mexican businessmen who are no longer willing to risk being targeted by criminals.

The crisis of public security in Mexico is real, not just perceived. During the 1990s there was a significant increase in violent crimes. Nationally, homicide rates rose by nearly 20 percent from 1990 to 1995, and by far more in many of the states (for example, 230 percent in Guerrero; 211 percent in Chihuahua). Statistics on street crime (robberies, assaults, muggings) showed an even steeper increase in the mid-1990s. In Mexico City, the total number of crimes reported to police doubled from 1993 to

1997. And official crime statistics have understated the magnitude of the problem because of widespread underreporting. For example, it is estimated that only 15 percent of crimes actually committed in Mexico City are reported to police, due to citizens' low expectation that the perpetrators will be caught and punished, and to fears of reprisals by either criminals or the police.

This is the type of government performance failure for which Mexicans have the least tolerance, according to innumerable public opinion polls as well as election results. Cuauhtémoc Cárdenas's job performance rating as mayor of Mexico City fell throughout 1998 and 1999, mainly because his PRD government was making so little evident progress in reducing street crime. And voters are punishing political parties for their failures in this area. In 1998, for example, the PAN lost control of the governorship of Chihuahua, partly because of the previous PANista governor's lackluster record in crime-fighting.

The swelling public clamor to establish the rule of law in Mexico encompasses a broad range of demands: make the system of justice work more efficiently (i.e., actually solve crimes, try and jail the perpetrators); reduce police corruption and brutality; ensure that people accused of crimes are treated fairly, respecting their constitutionally guaranteed rights and liberties, regardless of social class or political connections; make the system of justice equally accessible to citizens seeking redress of grievances; make elected officials accountable, legally, for their actions ("end impunity"); and increase the independence of the judiciary, especially vis-à-vis the executive branch.

President Zedillo began tackling the rule of law problem by addressing the last of these demands. In his first significant official act upon taking office in December 1994, he replaced all but two of the incumbent Supreme Court justices and reduced the size of the Supreme Court from 24 to 11 justices. He changed the terms of the justices from six-year periods, coinciding with the six-year presidential term, to fixed, 15-year terms. He also changed the requirement for confirmation of Supreme Court justices by the Senate, from a simple majority to two-thirds of the Senate. This means that the president's nominees must attract at least some votes from the opposition parties; they cannot be rubber-stamped by a PRI majority. Finally, Zedillo expanded the judicial review powers of the Supreme Court by explicitly granting the Court the ability to declare acts of Congress and other federal government actions unconstitutional. This power was implicit in the 1917 Constitution but it had never been exercised. The 1994 judicial reforms, enacted by Congress at Zedillo's behest, made it more than an abstract concept. All this was an attempt by Zedillo to restore some measure of public confidence in the country's judicial institutions, after a year in which several high-profile political assassinations had gone unsolved and unpunished, and distrust of the entire justice system had risen to unprecedented levels.

The 1994 reforms made it possible for the opposition parties to bring various laws and government actions forward to the Supreme Court for constitutional review. For example, the cases brought in 1995 and 1996 included challenges to an increase in the federal sales tax that the Congress (then under PRI control) had approved in 1995. Demands for investigations of human rights violations, such as a massacre of unarmed peasant political activists by state police in Guerrero, also came before the court. Another case, brought by the PRI governor of Tabasco, challenged the authority of the federal Attorney General to investigate his alleged campaign-spending law violations. And yet another case challenged the president's use of the military to deal with the Zapatista rebellion in Chiapas, without first declaring an official state of emergency. Several of these cases were dismissed on legal technicalities. In other cases, a 6-to-5 majority of the justices ruled against the federal government's position, but under the 1994 judicial reforms it would have taken a *supermajority* of 8 out of 11 justices to strike down a law or official action as unconstitutional, so the Court's decision had no practical impact in these cases.

These outcomes illustrate a major limitation of Zedillo's 1994 judicial reforms: The requirement that laws can be declared unconstitutional only with a supermajority ruling of Supreme Court justices is a very high threshold, one that can stymie the Court in dealing with the most sensitive political issues rulings.[34] In short, while Zedillo was willing to expand the Supreme Court's powers of judicial review and thereby reduce its subordination to the executive, he wanted to keep the Court on a fairly short leash.

Another major limitation of the 1994 reforms is that they apply only to the top level of the federal judiciary: state-level courts continue to function as before, and the federal Supreme Court must still rely on state-level officials to implement its rulings. In the campaign spending and human rights violation cases mentioned above, PRI-dominated state legislatures simply ignored or overturned the Supreme Court's rulings. Until court decisions based on abstract principles of law cannot be undermined by political actors whose interests could be damaged by those rulings, the goal of a "government of laws, not men" will remain elusive in Mexico.

To the average citizen, what matters most is being liberated from the constant preoccupation with matters of personal security: how to avoid becoming a victim of violent crime. The causes of rising crime rates in Mexico are not difficult to identify. In the 1990s, Mexico became an increasingly important conduit for illegal drugs destined for the U.S. market. In states where drug trafficking is concentrated (Baja California, Chihuahua, Sinaloa, Jalisco), a high percentage of violent crime is related to the operations of drug cartels. Drug trafficking has also contributed mightily to the corruption of police, prosecutors, judges, and military personnel.

The police forces—federal, state, and local—themselves are a major source of Mexico's crime problem. Not only are they corruptible, because of low pay and low professionalization, they actually commit a sizable portion of crimes, especially in large cities. In recent years, most of the kidnappings of urban residents, carried out to extort money from them and their relatives, have involved former or active-duty police officers. A remarkably large number of Mexican police officers are actually wanted for crimes, but the warrants for their arrest never get served because the offenders are protected by corrupt superior officers. Simply firing criminal elements in the police forces is not the solution, since they only return to the street as civilians, committing crimes with impunity.

Ironically, the transition to a more democratic political system—and more specifically, the breakdown of centralized political controls that is a key element of that transition—has probably contributed to the increase in crime committed by law-enforcement personnel. For decades, agents of the PRI tightly controlled the country's security apparatus, extending all the way up to the president. As the PRI-dominated political system crumbled, the security forces had no masters; they now worked for themselves, pursuing their own interests. As in today's Russia, the breakdown of central controls gives police greater discretion to pursue criminal activity of various kinds, without fear of detection and punishment.

Social and economic factors have also contributed powerfully to the recent epidemic of crime in Mexico. As shown in Figure 10.8, crime increased steeply in Mexico City beginning in 1995, the first full year of the deep economic crisis touched off by the megadevaluation of the peso in December 1994. Nationally, the rise in violent crime in the 1990s coincided with a sharp increase in the number of people living in poverty, the number of unemployed and severely underemployed people, and greater inequality in the distribution of personal income. These negative changes in social welfare were direct consequences of the implementation of the government's neoliberal economic policies since the mid-1980s—policies that, at least in the short term, produced a relatively small number of "winners" and many more "losers."

In a quantitative analysis of homicide rates in a national sample of 1,750 *municipios* in Mexico, a general index of poverty was, by far, the single most important predictor of homicide rates at the local level in 1990. Other indicators of economic distress—the unemployment rate and the degree of income inequality in a *municipio*—were also significant predictors. So were certain demographic variables, like the percentage of single mothers.[35] The frequency of female-headed households is an indicator of the breakdown of the Mexican family structure, which is strongly related to adverse economic conditions and the necessity for household heads to migrate to the United States for long periods to supplement the family's income.

Finally, the inefficiency or malfunctioning of the criminal justice system is a major contributor to crime in Mexico. The actual probability of being caught, convicted, and serving substantial prison time is far too low to serve as a significant deterrent to crime. For example, out of every 100 crimes reported in Mexico City during 1997, only four cases resulted in the apprehension of the perpetrators and their imprisonment for more than a few days; 75 percent of the cases were simply filed away—dropped for lack of evidence. The investigations of these crimes were never carried out, or failed to turn up any evidence

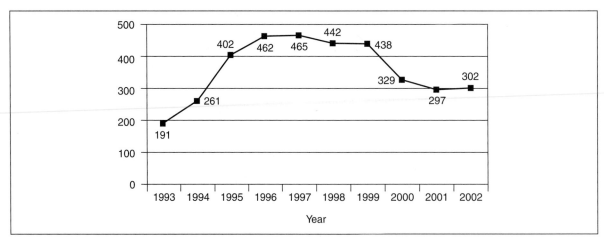

FIGURE 10.8   Crimes Reported in Mexico's Federal District (Mexico City), 1993–2002 (daily average)

Note: Reported crimes include robberies of passerby, on public transport, of vehicle, of house, of business, violent homicide, aggravated assault and rape. Information is updated until May 1, 2002.

Source: Procuraduría de Justicia del Distrito Federal's website: www.pgjdf.gob.mx

that would hold up in court, or were truncated because of police corruption. A similar analysis at the national level reveals that only 3.7 cases out of every 100 crimes reported during 1996 went to trial and resulted in putting criminals in jail.[36]

Potential remedies for Mexico's dysfunctional criminal justice system include tighter screening, testing, and monitoring of law enforcement personnel; higher pay and better training for police; replacing state and local police with military officers and enlisted men; further democratization, leading to alternation in power by political parties at a national level, which would make federal police forces more accountable to elected officials; and sustained and more egalitarian economic growth, to reduce the necessity to commit crimes of property. None of these possible remedies is a panacea, and several have already been tried, to no avail (for example, militarization of state and local police forces, as was done in Mexico City and the state of Baja California in the late 1990s). The deficient administration of justice is likely to remain Mexico's most intractable public problem for many years to come.

MEXICO'S POLITICAL FUTURE

In the months following Vicente Fox's victory in the presidential elections there was a major debate among

Mexican intellectuals and the political elite over whether the country had successfully completed its transition to democracy, with the alternation of power in the presidency, or whether further and deeper structural reforms would be necessary before Mexico should be classified as a democratic republic.

It is certain that elections in Mexico at the federal level are now as democratic as nearly any other country in the Americas. Electoral law reforms have ended many forms of fraud that were typical in the past. The Federal Electoral Institute has a strong reputation as a guardian of democracy. The current IFE commissioners will leave office after the 2003 midterm elections, but no one doubts that the next batch of commissioners will have similar values. Considering that the PRI-government apparatus functioned as a political machine, in which maintaining power in the executive branch was absolutely necessary to maintain the incentive structure for the rest of the political elite, the end of PRI domination of the presidency arguably has concluded the authoritarian era of Mexican politics. Without the presidency, the PRI cannot be the same. If the PRI recovers the presidency in 2006, it would have spent six years restructuring the internal incentives, six years searching for an ideology. Therefore, the PRI would be a different party, and by then the democratic transition could have been consolidated. Of course, if the PRI fractures in the meantime and fails to win back the presidency in 2006, most analysts would clearly classify the Mexican transition as concluded.

At the same time, many argue that a mere alternation in power is insufficient to consolidate a democratic transition. They claim that structural reforms, especially a comprehensive state reform, is required before the transition to democracy can be completed. The basic argument follows the patterns of democratic transition in Spain, where the transition was prolonged and required the commitment of all of the major political actors to act together in moderation to protect the new democracy. In the first months after Mexico's 2000 election, there was a major movement to replace the 1917 Constitution, creating a system with a weaker president and stronger Congress, courts, and state governments. There has been talk of changing the electoral formulas once again (though, of course, each party proposed formulas that were either more or less proportional, according to their relative electoral strengths).

The political strategies that follow from these two concepts of Mexico's transition are very different. The notion that the political transition was completed with the alternation in power in 2000 leads to political actors facing up to the problem of divided government, accepting that the electorate gave mixed signals on election day, and allowing each branch of government to make the best of the situation considering the constitutional powers that it holds. Therefore, the Congress should not consider executive bills to be untouchable (and considering the frequency with which they are amended in the chambers, this certainly seems to be the case). The president should use his constitutional decree powers and his veto as he sees fit, and not worry that their use be considered an affront to the legislative branch. The Supreme Court should arbitrate. Both the president and the parties in Congress should use publicity in the press to get their message out and pressure the other branch to give in.

Those who believe that Mexico should follow the lead of the Spanish transition call for national political accords and consensus on all basic matters of governance. They believe that the constitutional boundaries between the branches must be redefined, again by consensus. (Proponents of this plan in the executive branch want to create a strong, flexible presidency, while those in the opposition parties want congressional dominance or even parliamentary government.) They believe that a politician—especially a president—who goes public to appeal for support is playing outside of the bounds of proper behavior during a period of transition (they call it *Chavismo,* after Hugo Chávez, the current populist president of Venezuela).

Of course, Mexico in the first years of the twenty-first century is not Spain in the last half of the 1970s. The PRI-government apparatus was a political machine, not a fascist military government. Zedillo was certainly not a Franco; nor was Salinas, nor even Díaz Ordaz. A transition toward a different form of government is possible if the three main parties agree (which is unlikely), but a lack of change in form of government does not mean that Mexico is less democratic. On the other hand, though it is highly unlikely that Fox will ever govern like a PRI president or that a "PAN-government apparatus" will emerge anytime soon, there is no guarantee that the PRI would not return to its old ways of governance if it recovers the presidency in 2006.

Thus, where is Mexico today? There is little doubt that Mexico should now be classified as a democracy in terms of electoral transparency and even personal freedoms. Despite all of the sound and fury between the executive and legislative branches under divided government, there is also little doubt that Mexico has now one of the most stable democratic political systems in Latin America—certainly closer to Chile and Costa Rica than to Brazil, Argentina, or Venezuela. There are still electoral shenanigans in some state elections, but at the national level, when the attention of all of the major parties is closely focused on the process, recent elections have been remarkably clean. The main question remaining is not whether Mexico needs a state reform to become democratic, but rather whether a democratic Mexico will opt for a state reform because a sufficient number of parties and political actors believe that such change is convenient.

KEY TERMS

cacique
Cardenismo
Confederación de Trabajadores de México (CTM)
corporatism/corporatist
divided government
municipio

National Solidarity Program (PRONASOL)
neoliberal economic development model
Partido Acción Nacional (PAN)

Partido de la Revolución Democrática (PRD)
Partido Revolucionario Institucional (PRI)
patron-client relationship
political centralism

presidencialismo
sectoral organizations
   sectors (of the PRI)
sectors
sexenio
técnico

INTERNET SOURCES

President's Office: **http://www.presidencia.gob.mx**

Chamber of Deputies: **http://www.diputados.gob.mx**

Senate: **http://www.senado.gob.mx/ingles**

Latin America Information Network for Mexico: **http://www.lanic.utexas.edu/la/mexico**

SUGGESTED READINGS

Bailey, John and Jorge Chabat, eds. *Transnational Crime and Public Security: Challenges to Mexico and the United States.* La Jolla, CA: Center for U.S.-Mexican Studies, University of California-San Diego, 2002.

Bruhn, Kathleen. *Taking on Goliath: Mexico's Party of the Democratic Revolution.* University Park, PA: Pennsylvania State University Press, 1997.

Camp, Roderic A. *Generals in the Palacio: The Military in Modern Mexico.* New York: Oxford University Press, 1992.

———. *Crossing Swords: Politics and Religion in Mexico.* New York: Oxford University Press, 1997.

———. *Mexico's Mandarins: Crafting a Power Elite for the Twenty-First Century.* Berkeley: University of California Press, 2002.

Centeno, Miguel Angel. *Democracy Within Reason: Technocratic Revolution in Mexico,* 2nd ed. University Park, PA: Pennsylvania State University Press, 1997.

Chambers, Edward J. and Peter H. Smith, eds. *NAFTA in the New Millennium.* La Jolla, CA and Edmonton, Canada: Center for U.S.-Mexican Studies, University of California-San Diego and University of Alberta Press, 2002.

Cook, Maria L. *Organizing Dissent: Unions, the State, and the Democratic Teachers' Movement in Mexico.* University Park, PA: Pennsylvania State University Press, 1996.

Cornelius, Wayne A., David Myhre, Todd Eisenstadt, and Jane Hindley, eds. *Subnational Politics and Democratization in Mexico.* La Jolla, CA: Center for U.S.-Mexican Studies, University of California-San Diego, 1999.

Domínguez, Jorge I. and James A. McCann. *Democratizing Mexico: Public Opinion and Elections.* Baltimore, MD: Johns Hopkins University Press, 1995.

Domínguez, Jorge I. and Chappell Lawson, eds. *Mexico's Pivotal Democratic Election.* Stanford, CA and La Jolla, CA: Stanford University Press and Center for U.S.-Mexican Studies, University of California-San Diego, 2003.

Domínguez, Jorge I., James A. McCann, and Alejandro Poiré, eds. *Toward Mexico's Democratization: Parties, Campaigns, Elections and Public Opinion.* New York: Routledge, 1999.

Foweraker, Joe and Ann L. Craig, eds. *Popular Movements and Political Change in Mexico.* Boulder, CO: Lynne Rienner, 1990.

Harvey, Neil. *The Chiapas Rebellion: The Struggle for Land and Democracy.* Durham, NC: Duke University Press, 1998.

Knight, Alan. *The Mexican Revolution,* 2 vols. Lincoln: University of Nebraska Press, 1990.

Krauze, Enrique. *Mexico—Biography of Power: A History of Modern Mexico, 1810–1996.* New York: HarperCollins, 1997.

Lawson, Chappell, *Building the Fourth Estate: Democratization and the Rise of a Free Press in Mexico.* Berkeley, CA: University of California Press, 2002.

Levy, Daniel C., Kathleen Bruhn, and Emilio Zebadúa, *Mexico: The Struggle for Democratic Development.* Berkeley, CA: University of California Press, 2001.

Middlebrook, Kevin J. *The Paradox of Revolution: Labor, the State, and Authoritarianism in Mexico.* Baltimore, MD: Johns Hopkins University Press, 1995.

Rodríguez, Victoria E., ed. *Women's Participation in Mexican Political Life.* Boulder, CO: Westview, 1998.

Rodríguez, Victoria E. and Peter M. Ward, eds. *Opposition Government in Mexico.* Albuquerque: University of New Mexico Press, 1995.

Roett, Riordan, ed. *The Challenge of Institutional Reform in Mexico.* Boulder, CO: Lynne Rienner, 1995.

———, ed. *Mexico's Private Sector: Recent History, Future Challenges.* Boulder, CO: Lynne Rienner, 1998.

Rubin, Jeffrey. *Decentering the Regime: Ethnicity, Radicalism, and Democracy in Juchitán, Mexico.* Durham, NC: Duke University Press, 1997.

Serrano, Mónica, ed. *Governing Mexico: Political Parties and Elections.* London: Institute of Latin American Studies, University of London, 1998.

Smith, Peter H. *Labyrinths of Power: Political Recruitment in Twentieth-Century Mexico.* Princeton, NJ: Princeton University Press, 1979.

Snyder, Richard. *Politics after Neoliberalism: Reregulation in Mexico.* Cambridge, UK: Cambridge University Press, 2001.

Ward, Peter M. *Mexico City,* 2nd ed. New York: Wiley, 1998.

Ward, Peter M. and Victoria E. Rodríguez. *Bringing the States Back In: New Federalism and State Government in Mexico.* Austin: Lyndon B. Johnson School of Public Affairs, University of Texas-Austin, 1999.

ENDNOTES

1. PRI candidate Carlos Salinas de Gortari was credited with 50.74 percent of the valid votes cast. However, if the 695,042 "spoiled" ballots and 14,333 votes cast for nonregistered presidential candidates are included in the calculation, Salinas won by only a plurality of 48.7 percent.

2. This represents an undercount, since the census identifies as Indians only persons over the age of five. Indians of all ages constitute an estimated 15 percent of the total population.

3. Peter H. Smith, "The Making of the Mexican Constitution," in William O. Aydelotte, ed., *The History of Parliamentary Behavior* (Princeton, NJ: Princeton University Press, 1977), p. 219.

4. Alan Knight, "Cardenismo: Juggernaut or Jalopy?" *Journal of Latin American Studies* 26:1 (1994): 107.

5. Quoted in Denise Dresser, "Five Scenarios for Mexico," *Journal of Democracy* 5, No. 3 (July 1994): 57.

6. The actual extent of irregularities in the 1988 presidential vote will never be determined. Within a few hours after the polls closed, with early returns showing Cárdenas ahead by a significant margin, top authorities ordered the computerized count to be suspended. When results for a majority of the country's polling places were announced six days later, Salinas had won. There is no corroborating evidence from exit surveys of voters, because the government denied permission for such surveys in 1988. The PRI-controlled Congress later ordered the ballots stored in its basement to be burned, thereby eliminating any possibility of challenging the election outcome. Study of the partial, publicly released results and preelection polling data has led most analysts to conclude that Salinas probably did win but that his margin of victory over Cárdenas was much smaller than the 19-point spread indicated by the official results.

7. According to statistics of the Federal Electoral Institute (IFE), Zedillo won 50.18 percent of the valid votes—that is, excluding "spoiled" ballots and write-in votes cast for unregistered candidates. However, if the calculation is based on total votes cast (including those annulled by electoral authorities), Zedillo's share of the vote declines to 48.77 percent.

8. *Binational Study on Migration Between Mexico and the United States* (Washington and Mexico City: U.S. Commission on Immigration Reform and Secretaría de Relaciones Exteriores, 1997), p. ii.

9. See Roderic A. Camp, *Citizen Views of Democracy in Latin America* (Pittsburgh, PA.: University of Pittsburgh Press, 2001).

10. For illustrative survey data from the early 1990s, see Jorge I. Domínguez and James A. McCann, *Democratizing Mexico: Public Opinion and Electoral Choices* (Baltimore, MD: Johns Hopkins University Press, 1996), pp. 29–47.

11. Mexico 2000 Election Panel Study, round 1 (data available at: http://web.mit.edu/polisci/faculty/C.Lawson.html).

12. Constitutional reforms are very common in Mexican law because regular statutory reforms or new policy programs frequently require constitutional sanction before they can be enacted. Therefore, constitutional reforms in Mexico are not only questions of basic structural or political reform but also matters of public policy.

13. See Alan Knight, "Historical Continuities in Social Movements," in Joe Foweraker and Ann L. Craig, eds., *Popular Movements and Political Change in Mexico* (Boulder, CO: Lynne Rienner, 1990), pp. 78–102; Jeffrey W. Rubin, *Decentering the Regime: Ethnicity, Radicalism, and Democracy in Juchitán, Mexico* (Durham, NC: Duke University Press, 1997); Heather Fowler-Salamini, "De-Centering the 1920s: *Socialismo a la Tamaulipeca,*" *Mexican Studies* 14, No. 2 (Summer 1998): 287–327; Wayne A. Cornelius, Todd Eisenstadt, and Jane Hindley, eds., *Subnational Politics and Democratization in Mexico* (La Jolla, CA: Center for U.S.-Mexican Studies, University of California-San Diego, 1999).

14. Until recently, each *presidente municipal* typically was hand-picked by higher-ups within the PRI-government apparatus, normally a federal congressman and the state governor.

15. Victoria Rodríguez and Peter Ward, *Political Change in Baja California: Democracy in the Making?* (La Jolla, CA: Center for U.S.-Mexican Studies, University of California-San Diego, 1995), pp. 112–14.

16. See Victoria E. Rodríguez, *Decentralization in Mexico: From Reforma Municipal to Solidaridad to Nuevo Federalismo* (Boulder, CO: Westview, 1997); and Peter M. Ward and Victoria E. Rodríguez, *Bringing the States Back In: New Federalism and State Government in Mexico* (Austin, TX: Lyndon Baines Johnson School of Public Affairs, University of Texas-Austin, 1999).

17. John Bailey, "Centralism and Political Change in Mexico: The Case of National Solidarity," in Wayne A. Cornelius, Ann L. Craig, and Jonathan Fox, eds., *Transforming State-Society Relations in Mexico: The National Solidarity Strategy* (La Jolla, CA: Center for U.S.-Mexican Studies, University of California-San Diego, 1994), pp. 97–119.

18. For a recent discussion of mixed-member electoral systems in general, and comparisons between Mexico's electoral regime with similar systems, see *Mixed-Member Electoral Systems: The Best of Both Worlds?,* ed. Matthew Soberg Shugart and Martin P. Wattenberg (Oxford: Oxford University Press, 2001).

19. The figures are means, as the size of the party delegations changed frequently as deputies switch parties or become independents.

20. See Jeffrey A. Weldon, "Political Sources of *Presidencialismo* in Mexico," in Scott Mainwaring and Matthew Soberg Shugart, eds., *Presidentialism and Democracy in Latin America* (New York: Cambridge University Press, 1997), pp. 225–58.

21. For a conventional interpretation of the powers of the Mexican president, see Luis Javier Garrido, "The Crisis of *Presidencialismo,*" in Wayne A. Cornelius, Judith Gentleman, and Peter H. Smith, eds., *Mexico's Alternative Political Futures* (La Jolla, CA: Center for U.S.-Mexican Studies, University of California, San Diego, 1989), pp. 417–34.

22. The purported rationale for this principle, applied to the president in the 1917 Constitution and extended to members of Congress in 1933, was to ensure freedom from self-perpetuating, dictatorial rule in the Porfirio Díaz style. However, the real reason for prohibiting the consecutive reelection of deputies and senators was probably to cut the ties between local political bosses and their federal legislators, at a time that the ruling party was seeking greater centralization of authority.

23. See Weldon, "The Political Sources of *Presidencialismo* in Mexico."

24. Centeno, *Democracy Within Reason,* p. 112.

25. Centeno, *Democracy Within Reason.*

26. Unpublished data from Roderic A. Camp. See also Roderic A. Camp, "Family Relationships in Mexican Politics," *Journal of Politics* 44 (August 1982): 848–62; Smith, *Labyrinths of Power,* pp. 307–10.

27. Smith, *Labyrinths of Power,* ch. 6.

28. Lorenzo Meyer, "La democracia política: esperando a Godot," *Nexos* 100 (April 1986): 42.

29. Centeno, *Democracy Within Reason,* p. 194.

30. United Nations/CEPAL and INEGI, "Informe sobre la magnitud y evolución de la pobreza en México, 1984–1992," unpublished report, Mexico City, October 24, 1993; Eduardo Hernández and Julio Boltvinik, "Informe sobre la pobreza en México," Universidad Nacional Autónoma de México and El Colegio de México, Mexico City, April 1995.

31. A wealth of statistical data demonstrating these trends can be found in Enrique Dussel Peters, *Polarizing Development: The Impact of Liberalization Strategy* (Boulder, CO: Lynne Rienner, 2000).

32. Calculated from survey data reported in Clemente Ruiz Durán and Carlos Zubirán Schadtler, *Cambios en la estructura industrial y el papel de las micro, pequeñas, y medianas empresas en México* (Mexico City: Nacional Financiera, 1992), p. 158.

33. Carlos Elizondo, "In Search of Revenue: Tax Reform in Mexico under the Administrations of Echeverría and Salinas," *Journal of Latin American Studies* 26(1), February 1994, pp. 159–90.

34. Sara Schatz, "A Neo-Weberian Approach to Constitutional Courts in the Transition from Authoritarian Rule: The Mexican Case, 1994–1997," *International Journal of the Sociology of Law* 26 (1998): 217–44.

35. Andrés Villarreal, "Structural Determinants of Homicide in Mexico" (paper presented at the annual meeting of the American Sociological Association, January 5, 1999).

36. Guillermo Zepeda Lecuona, "La inseguridad pública en México" (paper presented to the Research Seminar of the Center for U.S.-Mexican Studies, University of California-San Diego, October 28, 1998).

NIGERIA

0   50   100   150 Miles
0   50   100   150 Kilometers

Lake
Chad

Sokoto R.
Sokoto
Birnin
Kebbi   SOKOTO
Lamfara R.
Katsina
KATSINA
JIGAWA
Hadejia R.
Ditse
YOBE
Maiduguri
KEBBI
ZAMFARA
Gusau
Kano
KANO
Damaturu
BORNO
Komadugu Gana R.

KADUNA
Kaduna R.
Kaduna
BAUCHI
Bauchi
Gombe
NIGER
Kainji
Reservoir
Minna
Jos
GOMBE
ADAMAWA

Niger R.
ABUJA
ABUJA
FCT
Lafia
PLATEAU
Yola
Jalingo
KWARA
Ilorin
NASARAWA
Benue R.
Taraba R.

OYO
Lokoja
KOGI
Makurdi
TARABA
Osogbo
EKITI
Ado-Ekiti
Ibadan
OSUN
Akure
BENUE
Abeokuta
ONDO
EDO
Benin
City
ENUGU
OGUN
Enugu
EBONYI
Lagos
Asaba
Awka
Abakaliki
LAGOS
Bight of
Benin
DELTA
ANAMBRA
IMO
ABIA
CROSS
RIVER
Yenagoa
Owerri
Umuahia
Calabar
RIVERS
Uyo
BAYELSA
Port
Harcourt
Gulf of Guinea
AKWA
IBOM

Niger R.

11

Politics in Nigeria

Robert J. Mundt and Oladimeji Aborisade

COUNTRY BIO—NIGERIA			
Population	120 Million	Head of State	President Olusegun Obasanjo
Territory	356,668 sq. mi	Head of Government	President Olusegun Obasanjo
Year of Independence	1960	Language(s)	English (official), Hausa, Yoruba, Igbo (there are 250 other ethnic groups)
Year of Current Constitution	1979 constitution still partially in force; draft 1995 constitution was published in 1999, revised the same year and then called "the 1999 Constitution."	Religion	Muslim 50%, Christian 40%, indigenous beliefs 10%

In the African context Nigeria is a megastate. Even on a world scale, Nigeria is a major country. Larger than France or Britain, it claims over one-fifth of the people in Africa and has the world's largest black population. Its petroleum and its substantial standing military force guarantee its prominence in international relations; and with 45 universities, Nigeria contains a large proportion of Africa's centers of learning and research.

For these reasons alone, one should know about Nigeria. But learning about Nigeria is also an efficient approach to learning about Africa, because Nigeria embodies much of the variety of African political experience within its borders. Its traditions include the large-scale emirates of the north and the small kingdoms and village-level republics of the south. Although both were administered by Britain, the north and south of Nigeria experienced different versions of colonial rule. Its culture is divided by ethnicity and also by religion, especially between Christians and Muslims. Its history since independence in-

cludes coups, countercoups, and civil war; recently, along with many other Africans, Nigerians have been groping toward a renewal of democracy. The problems and prospects of many African ministates are found in Nigeria, but at a more daunting scale and level of complexity. To know Nigeria is not necessarily to know Africa, but to one who is well acquainted with the Nigerian experience there will be little that is surprising in politics elsewhere on the continent.

Nigeria's prominent place in the world is more potential than real, however, because in recent years Nigeria has been a *sick* giant. Its economy is in shambles and the provision of public services has broken down. This chapter examines the causes of this illness and the likelihood of recovery.

CURRENT POLICY CHALLENGES

Of all the countries considered in this book, Nigeria might be the only one whose continued existence is currently in doubt. The country's ethnic, regional, and religious divisions have intensified in recent years, and important political actors have recently suggested breaking up the country into a weak federation or even completely independent states if political power cannot be distributed in a manner all can accept. This situation is not all that unusual: Nigeria has existed for only 42 years. After roughly 70 years of existence, the United States and the Soviet Union each split apart over regional and policy issues (the Civil War and the breakup of the Soviet Union); and definitions of Canada and of the United Kingdom remain open to question in some quarters today. It may be easier to explain why Nigeria is likely to fall apart in the short term than it is to specify conditions for its long-term stability.

It is against this stark reality that politics and policy must be viewed in Nigeria today. In 1999 Nigeria returned to formal civilian rule, when Olusegun Obasanjo was elected president. A few weeks later a new democratic legislature was also elected. In 2003, President Obasanjo was reelected in a landslide, and his party also captured most other important political offices. Even though Nigeria has returned to constitutional rule, that constitution will continue to be tested by Nigerians' frustration over the failure of their potentially wealthy country to provide basic human needs, education, potable water, reliable transportation and communications, and politics free of rampant corruption. Income levels per capita are barely a tenth of income in the United States or Western Europe, and among the 178 nations ranked in the United Nations' Human Development Index, Nigeria ranked number 148—among the poorest quarter of nations. Similarly, the 2002 Corruption Perceptions Index developed by Transparency International ranked corruption levels in Nigeria as second worst among the 102 nations studied.

From the outset, the government has struggled to move Nigeria in a new direction. If a democratic regime cannot address these demands in reasonably short order, that regime will suffer the fate of those before it and chaos or renewed authoritarian rule will be the likely outcome. Yet, Nigerians always seem to draw on a wellspring of optimism, even as they maintain an attitude of skepticism. The following analysis will help the reader determine the degree to which that optimism is warranted.

THE EFFECTS OF HISTORY

More than 30 years ago, anthropologist Clifford Geertz titled an essay on the developing nations "Old Societies and New States."[1] This is an apt characterization of Nigeria, for although the concept of Nigeria dates only to 1914, and the independent state only to 1960, the cultures that compose it have ancient roots.

In one sense, then, there are "many" Nigerias. That is, there are distinct political cultures with precolonial origins, and there are the varied colonial experiences of north, east, and west. We will consider these causes of variety separately.

The Enduring Effects of Precolonial Events

Our images of precolonial Africa have been plagued by misunderstandings, sometimes in the form of simple ignorance, but often the result of prejudice. Many in the industrial world still view traditional Africa as "primitive," composed of a series of "tribes."[2]

A common response is that "Africa had its empires also." As we shall see, this is quite true. However, to insist that empires are a sign of advanced culture is to accept that the successful implementation of authoritarian rule over large numbers of people is "civilized." It can be argued that those peoples who at the village level developed complex systems of limitations on their rulers were at least as politically sophisticated as those who built empires. All these peoples interacted in trade, cultural diffusion, and war for many centuries before the creation of today's nation-states, and their belief systems were as complex and nuanced as any in the world.

To reiterate, there was no single Nigeria a century ago. Some of the peoples inhabiting the land that now constitutes Nigeria were organized only at the village or extended family level (for example, the **Igbo** in the southeast), while in other areas there were kingdoms and states. Where one group had subjugated the peoples around them, we can identify empires, such as that of Kanem-Bornu around Lake Chad between the eleventh and fourteenth centuries, the Oyo Empire in the western region of present-day Nigeria from the thirteenth to the eighteenth centuries, and the Fulani Empire of the nineteenth century.[3]

The **Hausa** people began forming city-states in northern Nigeria between 1000 and 1200 A.D., and came under the influence of Islam no later than the fifteenth century. By the next century, mosques and Koranic schools were flourishing and Hausa princes were international rivals of Morocco and the Ottoman Empire. The fortunes of these systems waxed and waned through the centuries, but they were decisively changed when non-Hausa court officials rose against them early in the nineteenth century. These officials were **Fulani,** a people with their origins in western Sudan who had entered into the Hausa lands as herders and, more importantly, as teachers, traders, and eventually court advisers. By their own accounts they were ardent Muslims who found the Hausa leaders lax in their faith and decadent. A Fulani scholar and preacher, Usman dan Fodio, inspired a religious and political revolt against the Hausa kings (he found responsive audiences to his denunciation of taxes, even among Hausa commoners). A Fulani-dominated caliphate was established in Sokoto, now northern Nigeria. This Fulani Empire controlled most of the north until the British defeated it in 1903. Sokoto retains its role as the Muslim religious capital of Nigeria to this day. The Hausa and Fulani cultures have become so intertwined, with extensive intermarriage and with Hausa the primary language of both, that the dominant culture of the north is usually referred to as **Hausa-Fulani.** The descendants of the rulers of the Hausa-Fulani kingdoms, identified by the Islamic title *emir*, continue to hold court in the major cities of northern Nigeria.

In the forest region the **Yoruba** and Bini peoples of the southwest began forming kingdoms between the twelfth and fifteenth centuries at Oyo, Ife, and Benin. In the seventeenth and eighteenth centuries the kingdom of Oyo subdued its rivals and extended its control over the entire southwest Nigeria. These political systems developed intricate methods of limiting the powers of their rulers. For example, the ruler of Oyo, the Alafin, was chosen by a council of chiefs, the Oyo Mesi. The Historian Michael Crowder recounts that "if they felt the Alafin had exceeded his powers [the Oyo Mesi] could divine that all was not well between the Alafin and his spiritual double and force him to commit suicide. . . . However, the Oyo Mesi were restrained from abuse of this power by the fact that one of their number had to die with the Alafin."[4] Clearly, limited government has other sources than the Magna Carta and comes in a variety of forms. The successors to the Yoruba

kings, or *obas*, continue to act out symbolic leadership roles in many cities in southwestern Nigeria.

Because Nigeria was defined through the colonial experience, we must ask how and why the eventual British domination occurred. The immediate cause for British interest in West Africa was trade, and the first such international trade of any importance was in slaves. Coastal groups began exchanging captives for goods with European trading ships as early as the sixteenth century. Wars among the various kingdoms ensured a plentiful supply of captives, particularly in southwestern Nigeria. For the next 300 years this trade was sustained: Benin, Lagos, Bonny, and Calabar thrived as slave trade centers exporting upward of 20,000 persons per year to the Americas. Nigeria lost some of its most able-bodied inhabitants during those "barren three centuries" of relations between Europe and Africa.

In 1807 the British parliament outlawed the slave trade. In a remarkable turnabout, the British navy replaced British slave ships and began patrolling the West African coast to cut off the trade, which was not, however, completely eliminated until about 1850. The established slave-trading patterns were gradually converted to other goods. British consuls established themselves on the coast and began to intervene in local politics, favoring those candidates for ruling positions who would give them commercial advantages over other European traders. The British succeeded in obtaining treaties of British protection and trade along the coast. These were treaties between unequals, increasingly favorable to the British as they first established commercial and then political control.

The Colonial Interlude (1900–1960)

With tongue in cheek, Nigerian journalist Peter Enahoro once described his nationality in this fashion: "Today, the conglomeration of tribes assembled compulsorily at the 1884 Berlin conference are assigned as Nigerians—for want of a substitute collective noun."[5] Indeed, the name "Nigeria" itself was coined by Flora Shaw, an Englishwoman who later married Sir Frederick Lugard, the architect of colonial Nigeria. Enahoro's characterization refers to the origins of Nigeria's boundaries and those of most countries of contemporary Africa. In order to avoid war resulting from the competition for colonies, the great European powers met as the Conference of Berlin in 1884–1885 and divided Africa into spheres of influence. In effect, the European powers decided to seize control of the continent rather than merely trade with its rulers and merchants. In a wave of negotiations, imperialist wars, and conquests, their efforts were successful, and by the beginning of World War I in 1914 maps of Africa showed clearly drawn lines with areas color-coded according to the European power claiming control. Thus in 1886 the Royal Niger Company was granted a royal charter to control Nigerian trade. That charter was replaced in 1900 by the creation of the Colony of Lagos and the Protectorates of Northern and Southern Nigeria.

There was an unfortunate interaction between the colonial penetration and West Africa's natural environment: Cultures tend to be affected by climate and ecology, as people adapt differently to life in the rainforest, grasslands, or desert. In West Africa, the prevailing climate and ecological zones run east and west (see Figure 11.1). However, the colonial thrust was from the coast of the Gulf of Guinea inland, and

colonial boundaries were established on the coast and then extended northward, intersecting the climate zones. This virtually guaranteed that the colonies thus established would be composed of peoples coming from vastly different cultures.

Nigeria first became an entity in 1914, when the Northern and Southern Protectorates and Lagos were brought under a single colonial administration. This unifying action was largely symbolic, however, as its two parts continued to be governed separately. The Northern and Southern Provinces replaced the Protectorates, each under a lieutenant governor. Northern Nigeria remained apart as such political structures as a legislative council evolved in the south. Northerners did not sit on the Nigerian Legislative Council until 1947. Indeed, the North proved to be the perfect setting for the "indirect rule" elaborated by Governor Lord Lugard: The British administration would not intervene directly into everyday life in its colonies, but would support the rule of traditional leaders such as the Fulani emirs. This, Lugard argued, was the most efficient

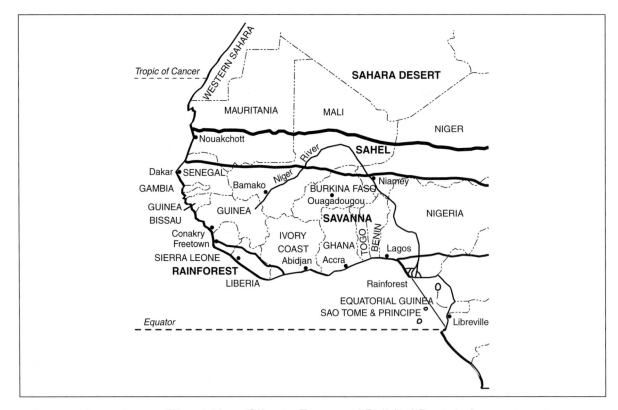

FIGURE 11.1   West African Climate Zones and Political Boundaries

means of controlling the colonies. In southern Nigeria, however, Western-educated elites challenged the authority of the traditional rulers where they existed (as among the Yoruba); in southeastern Nigeria, among the Igbo and other peoples, there really were no traditional kings or chiefs. Attempts to create village chiefs where the concept was unknown produced results that were sometimes comical and often tragic. Novelist Chinua Achebe has an English colonial officer describe such a situation:

> Chief Ikedi was still corrupt and high-handed but he had become even more clever than before. The latest thing he did was to get his people to make him an *obi* or king, so that he was now called his Highness Ikedi the First, Obi of Okperi. This among a people who never had kings before! This was what British administration was doing among the Ibos, making a dozen mushroom kings grow where there was none before.[6]

Thus the different applicability of indirect rule served to further distinguish the political experiences of the regions.

The British colonial administration also faced the problem of incompatible objectives. In order to make the colony self-sustaining, Britain needed an export economy. However, the conversion of peasant societies from subsistence to a market orientation eroded the foundations of traditional rule. Except in the north, chiefs and kings had no traditional right to collect taxes, yet this became a central duty in the colonial system. Also, the development of a modern system of transportation and communication, necessary to stimulate commerce, encouraged the movement of people from the countryside to cities and from one part of the country to another, all under the protection of the colonial authorities. Urbanized populations and immigrants from other cultures could scarcely be expected to show deference to traditional rulers, nor did they see any good reason for paying taxes.

Along with commerce and administration, the British brought missionaries and education. Missionaries of many denominations—Anglicans, Presbyterians, Catholics, Baptists, Adventists, and others—brought the gospel to Nigeria, although only to the south; the northern emirates had an understanding with the British that Christian proselytizing would not be permitted in their domains. Christianity spread especially rapidly in the south-

east, and somewhat less so in the southwest; with it went formal schooling. As Nigerian children learned the English language and customs, they acquired the tools with which to challenge colonial rule on the rulers' own terms. However, the Western-educated elite that emerged came largely from the south. Thus, the culture is divided north and south along religious lines, but the difference has to do with much more than religion.

Modern constitutional development began within a few years of the creation of Nigeria as a single colony, with elective office first provided in 1922. An early nationalist leader, Herbert Macaulay, established a political party soon thereafter. As a Nigerian-centered political life grew up among the formally educated, other organizations arose, and the British colonial administration was pressed with demands for participation. The spirit of the times was captured by Nigerian writer Wole Soyinka as he recalled that:

> Suddenly there was Oge-e-e-ed Ogendengbe (Herbert) Macaulay and there was Ze-e-e-ek (Nnamdi Azikiwe, nationalist leader). His oratory, we learnt, could move mountains. Some young, radical nationalists were being jailed for sedition, and sedition had become equivalent to demanding that the white man leave us to rule ourselves.[7]

From then on, constitutions promulgated by various governors (and named after them) were always somewhat behind the expectations of Nigerian political activists. What southern politicians judged conservative, however, was usually seen as radical by the conservative elites in the north. These differences of opinion among Nigerians resulted in 1954 in the creation of a federal system of three regions, Northern, Eastern, and Western. A single ethnic group dominated each region: The Hausa-Fulani in the north, the Yoruba in the west, and the Igbo in the east. Under pressure from their leaders, the Eastern and Western regions received self-government in 1957; the North became self-governing in 1959, a few months before national independence.

Nigerian Independence

As Nigeria approached independence, there was a general consensus that the nation should come to independence as a single country. Independent Nigeria was born on October 1, 1960.

Nigeria's independent governments at the federal and state levels experienced a very short "honeymoon." Within two years, conflict had torn apart the ruling coalition in the Western Region. The next year suspicions about the national census (see below) destroyed what little trust there was among the regions. Finally, in 1965 law and order broke down in the Western Region over election-related fraud and violence, and the military ended the First Republic in a January 1966 coup.

An awareness of these experiences is critical to an understanding of political conflict in independent Nigeria. Although the colonial experience was comparatively brief, it left a legacy of political ideas that were difficult to reconcile with precolonial values and structures. Many modern Nigerians remain profoundly Yoruba or Hausa; but is there a role for obas and emirs in modern Nigeria? This is not just a clash between the "traditional" and the "modern," because there are many, perhaps hundreds of "traditions." The blending of these various influences was all the less likely given the short time allowed for political evolution prior to independence. Nigerians and other Africans are today grappling with the resultant confusion, which has produced political instability, economic woes, and constant military interventions. And the difficulties on Nigeria's road to national unity are obviously related to the absence of any start in that direction prior to independence.

ENVIRONMENTAL POTENTIAL AND LIMITATIONS

Why has Nigeria's economic development been so dismal? Why are most of its people so poor? Are these conditions the result of physical environment, history, and socioeconomic context, or do they result from the Nigerian political process and the policy decisions that Nigerian governments have made?

Nigeria is counted among the world's less developed, or Third World, countries. Its gross national product in 1997 was $30.7 billion, or $260 per capita (see again Figure 11.4). This put it well below the United Nations criterion for "low-income countries," which was a per capita GNP of less than $750. Furthermore, from 1980 to 1991 GNP per capita actually declined by 1.7 percent annually. Its gross national product in 2000 was $32.8 billion, or $260 per capita. Controlling for purchasing power parity (PPP), per capita GPA was $790.

Conditions Affecting Agricultural Production and the Sale of Primary Commodities

Colonial policies not only retarded Nigeria's political development but also had profound, if mixed, effects on her economy. Since early in the colonial period, southern Nigerians have been producing cocoa, palm oil, timber, and rubber. The timber, sold mostly as tropical hardwoods for use in furniture and construction, came from the now-dwindling rainforests in the south. In the north the principal market products were cattle, hides and skins, cotton, and peanuts.

The growth of trade in these commodities was not entirely spontaneous. The British interest in Nigeria was primarily commercial, with its origins in the United Africa Company (UAC). When the UAC was granted a charter as the Royal Niger Company in 1886, it was given police and judicial power, and authorized to collect taxes and to oversee commerce. Not surprisingly, its policies aimed at developing the Nigerian economy to be compatible with British needs. Also, public sentiment in Britain never solidly favored creating a colonial empire, and powerful voices in Parliament favored keeping the costs of empire to a minimum. Colonial administrations were under heavy pressure to be self-sufficient—to develop local sources of revenue to cover their costs of administration. As a result, colonial administrators pressured peasant farmers away from subsistence agriculture and into commercial farming, particularly of export crops. Furthermore, cost-efficient marketing meant emphasis on just a few of the most needed products; in Nigeria (and elsewhere in West Africa), these turned out to be palm oil, cocoa, peanuts, and cotton. Thus British raw material priorities and the need to provide a self-sufficient colonial administration distorted African economies toward dependence on the sale of a small number of primarily agricultural commodities.

The combination of population growth and the commercialization of agriculture strained relationships between agricultural techniques and the ecology that had been in place for centuries. Colonial officials sometimes assumed that productivity could be greatly increased in tropical regions with the introduction of "modern" methods without recognizing the different ecological conditions of production

A street market bustles at an exit to the raised super-highway connecting Lagos Island to the mainland.

A. Hermann/UPI Bettmann/Corbis

in a tropical setting. Lush tropical rainforest could not simply be replaced by plantations. Rainfall, temperature, and soil conditions meant that farming techniques effective in England or North America would be unsuccessful or even disastrous. Only gradually, and much later, were the efforts of agronomists applied to maximizing agricultural production in the tropics, especially to food production for local consumption. There is still a large "research deficit" between the resources expended for agricultural research in temperate zones, as opposed to that in tropical zones.

Thus, Nigeria came to independence with an economy typical of Africa and other Third World areas. It was based on the production and export of agricultural commodities, principally palm oil (of which Nigeria was the world's leading exporter) and cocoa. Because Nigeria was larger and more ecologically diverse than most African colonies, its exports showed greater diversity than in the typical case. Still, production in each of its regions was focused on one or a few commodities, and the country as a whole depended on commodity markets in the industrial countries for its foreign exchange.

Like other newly independent countries, Nigeria broke with some colonial economic development policies, especially as concerned the need to diversify production. But the need for foreign exchange meant that agriculture continued to emphasize exportable commodities, even as investment capital was largely directed toward industrialization. Economists in both the industrial and Third World countries associated industry with prosperity, and agriculture was seen as the "cash cow" from which to extract savings for investment in other areas. Also, Nigerian government officials, trained in the need to balance budgets, balanced appropriations bills with overly optimistic estimations of "expected revenue."

When these fell short, the difference was made up from cash reserves accumulated by the Central Produce Marketing Board. However, "since those reserves were derived from the price differential between what was paid to the farmer and what the Board earned in export earnings . . . for close on a decade, Nigeria existed only through the exploitation of her farmers."[8]

In addition to keeping agricultural prices low to provide such reserves, Nigerian governments also tried to satisfy urban demands for cheap food by holding down the price paid to farmers in the domestic market. This contributed to the unattractiveness of agricultural work, and enhanced the lure of the cities.

Disease

Physical illness is a part of the human condition, and the higher disease rates of poorer nations are largely explained by the lack of resources to acquire medicines, medical facilities, and personnel. But environment contributes as well: Some of the most common human diseases, including malaria, can only survive in tropical climates. In tropical Africa, virtually every long-term resident carries the malaria virus, and large proportions of the population are affected by it. It is usually not fatal, but it is extremely debilitating, and it has a documented effect on labor productivity. Various river-borne diseases also account for long-term illness and fatalities, contributing especially to the high mortality rate among children. As with agricultural problems, research can attack these diseases; yet a vastly disproportionate share of the world's resources applied to health problems is focused on ailments more common to the industrialized world. In recent times, AIDS has topped the list of most dreadful diseases in Africa, affecting at least 33 percent of adults in Zimbabwe, 39 percent in Botswana, and over 4 million Nigerians. The AIDS epidemic is slowing down the agricultural economy in particular and national productivity in general.

Population Growth

Nothing is more striking to a visitor to Nigeria than the youth of the population; everywhere there are multitudes of children. About one-half the Nigerian population is less than 15 years of age.[9] Children are considered a valuable resource in labor-intensive agricultural societies, and in a country with high in-fant mortality rates and no social security system, parents would be imprudent not to have enough children so that some would grow up to provide for them in their old age. This behavior becomes dysfunctional at the societal level, of course, as increasing populations struggle to survive on a limited physical environment. Between 1975 and 2000, the population of Nigeria grew an average of 2.9 percent annually. With slow economic growth (only about 2.4 percent annually in the 1990s), this means when measured in per capita terms, GDP growth was actually negative. During this same period, the urban population grew from approximately 23 percent to 44 percent, a major leap. In this environment of rapid population growth and urbanization, children become economic liabilities. Thus, the "dependency ratio" (the proportion of the nonworking population to the working population) has steadily risen since the early 1960s, placing a great strain on the country's underdeveloped facilities for social welfare and education.[10]

Counting the population in Nigeria has always been controversial because of its implications for the distribution of resources and political districting. The government's official population count in 1991 was 88.5 million but there has not been a widely accepted census since 1963 (see pp. 734–735). Population totals for Nigeria therefore vary widely. In 2000, the United Nations estimated the population was 113.8 million, while the World Bank the year before put the figure at 123.9 million. If we accept the United Nations estimate and projected growth as accurate, Nigeria's population pressures will soon be staggering (see Figure 11.2), growing to 165.3 million in 2015 and over 200 million in 2025.

Urbanization

Nigeria shares a pattern of urbanization common in Africa: Although the country is still primarily rural, it is urbanizing rapidly. Nigeria's population is projected to be over 50 percent urban by the year 2010. In the process, the development of urban infrastructure is added to the long list of demands on government. For example, the government ministry in charge of Abuja, the federal capital, announced in 2002 that the population of the city had exceeded 4 million whereas city planners had estimated that the population would only be about 1.5 million at this stage of development.[11]

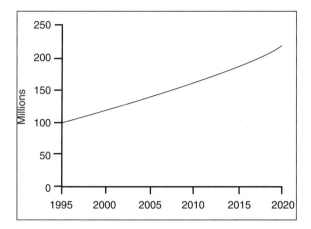

FIGURE 11.2 Nigeria's Projected Population Growth, 1995–2020

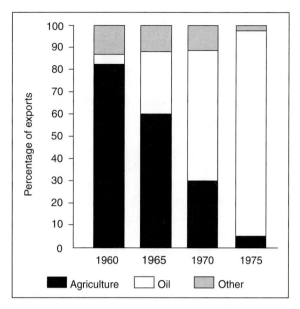

FIGURE 11.3 Composition of Nigerian Exports

Source: Peter O. Olayivola, *Petroleum and Structural Change in a Developing Country* (New York: Praeger, 1987).

The population shift means that a smaller proportion of the labor force is available for agricultural work. That is a normal pattern of modernization, of course, but unless the productivity of agricultural workers increases, it means a drop in food production per capita. That has been the Nigerian experience: Self-sufficient in food at independence, Nigeria is now heavily dependent on imports, paid for from oil revenues.

Petroleum

The magnitude of Nigeria's petroleum reserves became apparent in the 1950s with the first shipload of crude exported in 1958. Nigeria was engulfed in a bloody civil war from 1966 to 1970, which brought a halt to oil exports. At war's end, however, Nigerian petroleum production began to boom, and grew at a dramatic rate through the 1970s. Although such a valuable mineral resource is an asset to any country, its effects on Nigeria were not all beneficial. The country's economy became distorted by the great disparity of value between petroleum and the traditional agricultural products: Soon young workers were abandoning their farms and villages and flocking to the cities and the oil fields.

Oil revenues peaked in 1979. World demand for oil decreased each year from 1979 to 1983. At the same time, oil production in non-OPEC countries, especially Mexico, Norway, and the United Kingdom, grew substantially. Nigeria's planners were slow to realize the implications of rising supply

and stagnant demand. The glory days of seemingly limitless oil revenues ended abruptly in April 1982, when production of crude oil in Nigeria dropped from 2.1 million to .9 million barrels per day; oil export revenues fell correspondingly, from $1.35 billion to $.7 billion per month. In the preceding decade, Nigeria had become dependent on oil revenues for imports and large-scale development projects. As was commonly the case in the Third World, Nigeria fell behind in its debt payments, which forced the government to impose unpleasant austerity measures. A further fall in oil prices in 1986 pushed the country into a severe recession from which it has never recovered. Moreover, Nigerian fortunes became even more closely tied to oil revenues: Figure 11.3 shows that the source of Nigeria's hard currency shifted dramatically from agricultural products to petroleum in the early 1970s; since that time petroleum has accounted for over 90 percent of export earnings.

The Geographic Distribution of Natural Resources: Political Effects

Nigeria's oil fields are found in the Niger delta basin, an area of 70,000 square kilometers, or 8 percent of the country. As a natural resource that is both geographically concentrated and far more valuable than any other, Nigerian petroleum presents a classic problem for distributive justice. To Nigerian federal governments, it is a "national patrimony." Its potential value was an important motivation behind the Eastern Region's declaration of independence as **Biafra** in 1966, and oil certainly helps explain why the rest of the country was so obstinately determined to keep the region within Nigeria. But had Biafra maintained its independence, the question of oil field ownership would not have gone away, for the people who traditionally inhabited that area were minorities in the Igbo-dominated Biafra. And even though the federal government won the civil war, local peoples continue to protest the spread of oil wealth over the whole country while their land pays the price of environmental degradation from the oil operations, and southern Nigerians in general wonder why the riches should be shared with the distant north. The oil-producing region is the least developed in Nigeria and unrest will continue there until the Delta peoples believe they have been fairly treated. On top of this, in recent years bitter and violent combat has broken out among the youth of the various Delta peoples. Petroleum-related tragedy struck in October 1998 when a broken oil pipeline at the town of Jesse ignited into an inferno that resulted in over 700 deaths.

The International Environment

Nigeria, like most African countries, has been profoundly affected by its birth at the height of the Cold War, and by the sudden end of the bipolar war with the dissolution of the Soviet Union. During the Cold War, new nations were pressured to choose sides. The West and East granted foreign aid to developing nations as a reward for loyalty. Nigeria at independence was considered to be conservative and "prowestern," especially in contrast to such radical regimes as that of Kwame Nkrumah in Ghana. The prime minister at independence, Tafawa Balewa, announced the country's gratitude "to the British whom we have known first as masters, then as leaders, and finally as partners, but always as friends."[12]

Many Nigerian intellectuals equated the West's capitalism with colonialism, however, which they contended continued after independence through **neocolonial** economic ties. Political discourse through the first 30 years of Nigerian independence was often based on the ideological poles of capitalism and socialism, and relationships with the major powers involved staking a position between the two camps. In the civil war that resulted from the Eastern Region's declaration of independence as Biafra in 1967, the Soviet Union sided with the Nigerian federal government, while the U.S. government attempted to maintain a neutral position, even though the Biafran cause was widely supported by Americans. Economics finally dictated Nigeria's international position: The West was best equipped to prospect for Nigeria's oil fields, and only the West had the technology to extract and market this natural resource. Thus developed a close relationship between the Nigerian federal government and some of the world's major oil companies.

The end of the Cold War brought a new era to the relations of Nigeria and other poorer nations with the industrial world. The West's fear of the spread of communism had caused them to pay some attention to even the smallest and least-endowed countries. In the colonial period, Britain had provided virtually all foreign aid to Nigeria. In the Cold War environment at independence, Nigeria adopted a deliberate policy of diversification that diluted British influence and brought aid from the United States, Canada, the European Common Market (now the European Union), Japan, and Sweden. By the 1990s, however, those Third World countries without significant resources or with serious developmental problems were simply less interesting to the developed world; it is commonly perceived that Africa particularly has been "marginalized." In the Nigerian case, official loans and grants have not loomed large in recent years in any event, given access to oil revenues; foreign aid represented only about $2 per person in 1990.

Another problem in Nigeria's relationship (and that of Africa as a whole) with the industrial world has been much more serious: A massive and increasing international debt. Nigeria shared in a common Third World experience following the oil crisis of 1973. A sudden boom in oil prices resulted in huge new deposits in the world's banks. This surge in deposits without an increase in the demand for credit posed a serious problem to the lending agencies: They had to find borrowers. The increasing value of

As the oil boom drained the rural workforce, signs urged Nigerians to return to agriculture.

Bruno Barbey/Magnum Photos, Inc.

Nigeria's commodities made the nation appear extremely creditworthy. Although Nigeria's military government at the time was already busy spending the booming oil profits, there was a great demand for new infrastructure and for an expansion of public services. Banks had little difficulty convincing the Nigerian government to borrow additional sums. This borrowing seemed to make sense to all sides, given high inflation, rising prices for commodities, and the "excess liquidity" of bank deposits. Late in the 1970s commodity prices fell, however, and petroleum prices also did not remain as high as predicted. Third World debt mushroomed in the 1980s and several governments defaulted. Nigeria's indebtedness grew from $8.9 billion in 1980 to $34.5 billion in 1991; by 1995 it represented 274.5 percent of the annual value of the country's exports, and 140.5 percent of GNP. After the transition to democracy, President Obasanjo made debt reduction a high priority for his administration and in 2000 Nigeria rescheduled $20 billion of its debt. In 2001, total external debt still stood quite high at $32.1 billion. However, increasing world oil prices has decreased the share of exports that go towards debt servicing to roughly 4.3 percent, rather than 1990's unmanageable 22.6 percent.

A final aspect of Nigeria's international environment is its regional context, West Africa. As an accident of colonial rule, Nigeria is entirely surrounded by former French colonies—Benin (formerly Dahomey), Niger, and Cameroon. Because France and the French-speaking West African countries have been suspicious of Nigeria's intentions and have developed close economic ties among themselves, Nigeria has had difficulty in developing the leadership role in the region that its size and strength would suggest.

POLITICAL CULTURE AND SUBCULTURES

The political culture of Nigeria is extremely heterogeneous and complex. Analysis of it must take into account a Western value system overlaid on those of its various precolonial traditions; it must assess the impact of a variety of religious beliefs and of the continuing effects of Christian and Muslim proselytizing efforts. Since the colonial experience have come new divisions based on social class and on the different experiences of urban and rural dwellers. The whole range of modern political ideologies is found among the belief systems of the politically active population. Here we will give greatest attention to the political implications of ethnic identity, religious beliefs, social and economic status, contact with urban life, and civil society.

Ethnic Identity

Because of the geographic separation of ethnic groups, Nigerians can be easily identified based on language and cultural traits. These groups vary tremendously in size, and only three of them—the Hausa, Yoruba, and Igbos—are particularly numerous and influential in the country's politics. The influence of these three major groups is a cause of great concern to the remaining minority groups. Because there has been a high degree of geographical separation of ethnic groups in Nigeria (a result of the country's policies during and since the colonial period), Nigerians can easily identify the origins of their fellow citizens by observing their dialect (or accent in English), their manner of dress (if it is traditional), and in some cases by "tribal marks," patterned facial scars that formerly were created as part of rites of passage to indicate ethnic identity. There are also differences in wealth and political awareness.

In the absence of a widely accepted census, the size of Nigerian ethnic groups can only be approximated. Approximately one-half of the country's population is in the north, and about one-fourth each in the southeast and southwest. The Hausa represent about two-thirds of the north's total population, the Igbo about two-thirds in the east, and the Yoruba about two-thirds in the west. Thus, other groups represent about one-third in each region, and one-third overall. Here we will briefly consider the three largest groups.

Hausa-Fulani. The Hausa-Fulani people mostly live in the northern half of the country. As noted earlier, this hyphenated identity came from the imposition of Fulani rule over the Hausa population in the nineteenth century. The two cultures became intricately intertwined, although they have never become completely homogenized. Thus, the term "Hausa" is often used as a short form of "Hausa-Fulani." "Hausaland" actually straddles the border between Nigeria and Niger to the north, a former French colony, and the people in these two countries maintain many cultural and commercial ties. A greater proportion of Hausas engage in subsistence agriculture and live in rural villages than is true of southern Nigerians. There are sizable Hausa communities in cities all over Nigeria, where they carry on trade and commercial activities while maintaining kin and client relationships with their home region. The vast majority of Hausas (but not all) are Muslim. The Hausa heartland is itself still organized as a series of emirates: Each of the major cities in northern Nigeria is the seat of an emir, one of the kings through whom the British applied their indirect rule. There is no official role for the emirs in modern Nigeria, and their unofficial role is hotly disputed, even in the north. Yet they retain great influence in their localities and, through Hausa prominence in national politics, in the rest of the country as well.

Igbo. The **Igbo** (also spelled **Ibo**) occupy the southeastern part of the country, from the banks of the Niger River east. Most of the region is developed for market agriculture, with Igbo farmers growing palm products, rice, and yams. The Igbo people lived in politically independent, socially endogamous villages, usually no larger than 8,000 people and did not have a sense of common Igbo identity until the colonial period.

The Igbo are known for the enthusiasm with which they adopted Western culture. Although the encounter with British colonialism was a wrenching shock forcefully described in Chinua Achebe's novel *Things Fall Apart*, the Igbo responded enthusiastically to Western education and the missionaries who brought it, and aggressively sought advancement in modern commerce and civil service. Igbo people also emigrated widely throughout the country and seem less concerned than other groups with maintaining separate communities where they are "strangers." (In Nigeria, the term "stranger" refers specifically to a person living outside his or her "home" community.) They are employed on the basis of their education and modern skills in all parts of the country, including the north.

Igbo officers led the first military coup in 1966, and thousands of Igbos living in northern cities were attacked and killed in the reaction to that coup. The Igbos retreated to their home region and the next year followed the call of one of their own, Lieutenant Colonel Ojukwu, in the secession from Nigeria of Igbo-dominated Biafra. The three-year civil war that ended in the defeat of Biafra in 1970 caused great hardship, but within a few years Igbos were again active in commerce (they were by then generally barred from government work in other localities) across the land. Nevertheless, the Biafran experience and the civil war left long-term mistrust between the Igbos and other Nigerians.

Yoruba. The **Yoruba** mostly live in the southwestern part of Nigeria, including the metropolitan area of **Lagos,** the former federal capital and major urban center. Traditionally subsistence farmers, rural Yoruba people began growing cocoa and palm products for export in the colonial period. Although they share a common language, traditional religion, and myths of origin, the precolonial Yoruba were divided into a number of independent and warring kingdoms that give them separate identities today as Ijebu, Egba, Awori, Oyo, Ekiti, Igbomina, and others. The Yoruba have a long tradition of commerce, and both men and women are prominent in trade networks and markets throughout West Africa.

The Yoruba kingdoms were marked by complicated institutions that balanced power between an *oba* (king) and lineage chiefs, as in the relationship between the Alafin of Oyo and the Oyo Mesi described earlier. In their effort to impose indirect rule, the British upset these structures by supporting the obas against all challengers. In the process, the obas frequently became autocratic and lost much of their legitimacy with their own people; their influence in contemporary politics varies greatly, but is generally much less than that of the northern emirs.

Because the Yoruba had, on the one hand, a highly stratified society complete with kings and, on the other hand, were quite receptive to missionaries and their schools, they are often seen as in an intermediate position between the stratified and change-resistant Hausa and the egalitarian and innovative Igbo. In their sometimes strident assertion of their identity and interests, they also have provoked their share of mistrust among other Nigerians, as their candidates have generally been shut out of national leadership positions.

Given the ethnic-based strife so common in the world today, it should not come as a surprise that group identities are deeply rooted and emotionally charged in Nigeria as well. Ethnic rivalries often have their roots in precolonial warfare and are frequently refreshed by economic rivalries. While nationalism may serve as a cement where the feeling is shared by a country's entire population, the same feeling at a subnational level can destroy a political system. In Nigeria, these attachments are multilayered, and different levels of association can become charged at different times, as demonstrated in the Ibadan/Ijebu rivalry (see Box 11.1). Strong ethnic ties often are felt and expressed in kinship terms, and thus are often central to the definition of self. However, the Nigerian case demonstrates that ethnicity is often wrongly understood as primordial. While ethnic identity indeed has ancient roots, this does not mean that one's ethnic identity is identical with that of one's distant ancestors. In Africa, and in Nigeria in particular, we see extraordinary change, as in the bonding of two separate groups to form the Hausa-Fulani culture, in the emergence of a "Yoruba" identity over what were previously separate societies in conflict, and in the formation of an Igbo identity among villagers who previously were largely unaware of one another. Both in the colonial period and since, ethnic identities have been manipulated for political purposes.

In Nigeria some of the first associational groups were based on the perception of common ethnic

---

BOX 11.1   The Ibadan Ijebu Controversy

Ibadan is one of the two largest cities in Nigeria. An old Yoruba city, it is plagued by a historic rivalry between its two major groups, the Ibadan and the Ijebu—both claiming descent from Oduduwa (whose descendants seem as quarrelsome as Abraham's!) The Ijebu lived closest to the coast and thus were the first to enter into commerce with European traders. Their attempt to control trade with the interior—that is, with Ibadan—is said to have produced their long-standing animosity. At the same time, the animosity is not always felt at the individual level, for intermarriage between the two groups is common.

bonds in "nontraditional" settings. As a student in London, the early nationalist leader Obafemi Awolowo formed the *Egbe Omo Oduduwa* as a cultural organization grouping expatriate Yorubas. This group was to become the basis for the Action Group, the political party Awolowo later formed.

Because the major ethnic groups are regionally based, political issues affecting such groups are often defined geographically, and Nigeria has preserved a sense of permanent attachment between a people and its "traditional" homeland to the degree that it is more difficult to become a "citizen" of another state in Nigeria than it would be for a Nigerian to acquire citizenship in many foreign countries. The ethnic exclusiveness found in each state and local authority is euphemistically referred to as Nigeria's "federal character," and has strong effects on the nature of national policy. Thus, as Nigerians respond to educational or economic opportunities in other parts of the country, they find it necessary to organize into ethnic associations for protection and promotion of their interests. Hausas in the south usually live in a ghetto called the *Sabo*, where they speak their language and practice their Muslim faith. Nigerians at the lowest socioeconomic level often belong to a single association, that of their ethnic group; the more educated members of these "stranger" communities will often overlay the purely ethnic associations with others in which they interact across ethnic lines.

Multiple ethnic identities even at the local level have had a fragmenting effect on political structure. Particularly since 1976, there have been numerous disputes over the site of local government headquarters, with the "loser" often petitioning to the state and federal governments for a division of the local government area. The conflict between the Ife and Modakeke in Oranmiyan local government (see Box 11.2) is but one of many examples that could be cited. Local ethnic conflict affects policy outputs as well, where local governments build health centers or markets that are not used by some ethnic groups, thus throwing off planners' projections.

Religion

Each of the groups identified above had traditional religious institutions and beliefs in place long before the arrival of Christianity and Islam. In some cases these earlier beliefs have maintained their vigor, especially among many Yoruba.

B O X 1 1 . 2   The Conflict Between Modakeke and Ile-Ife

Early in the nineteenth century, Yorubas from Old Oyo were driven south by a Fulani invasion, and some settled in and around Ile-Ife. They were at first well received by Ile-Ife's traditional ruler, the Ooni, but soon got into a violent quarrel with the local population. The Oyo refugees were then reduced to servitude, and some were sold into slavery. Later, however, in an internal dispute, they sided with the ruler, who rewarded them with a settlement of their own, Modakeke. Strife continued between the two groups, and in an 1882 battle the Modakeke burned down the sacred city of Ife. Throughout the colonial period, the Ooni often used their conflict to play one group against the other. As independence neared, the Modakeke sought a local government independent of Ife. Also, the Ife leaders supported the Action Group (party), while Modakeke supported the National Council of Nigeria and the Cameroons (NCNC). After independence, Ife and Modakeke were in the same local government (Oranmiyan), but fought constantly until Oranmiyan was split in 1989. There was peace until August 1997, when the government moved one local government from an Ife to a Modakeke location and then to supposedly neutral ground. Violent conflict broke out among young men of each side. Whole villages were burned and hundreds of lives were lost. In January 1999, the Osun State Administrator invited the two communities to an open meeting, at which both groups agreed to a ceasefire. The Ooni stated that he had in fact requested General Abacha to create a new state, and that Abacha had declined but had given him the new local government as a consolation prize. The traditional leader's request and the government's response inadvertently rekindled historic animosities, with tragic results. In April 2002, the Federal Government mandated Osun State to create an Area Office for Modakeke as a peace process. The Area Office was created without delay and it is yielding some positive results within Modakeke community.

However, the missionaries brought their religion with formal education in the southern regions; most major Christian churches are well established in the south, and indigenous Christian sects have split off from them in a myriad of denominations. Not surprisingly, the Christian denominations themselves tend to be geographically and ethnically concentrated, with a higher proportion of Roman Catholics among the Igbo, a Baptist concentration among the Yoruba of Ogbomoso, the Evangelical Church of West Africa predominant in Igbomina and Kwara State, and so on. A significant proportion of Yoruba—perhaps half—are Muslim. Under the agreement between the colonial administration and the northern emirates, Christian proselytizing was barred from the north, and, except for the "strangers" living there, almost the entire population is at least nominally Muslim, and the Hausa bring their religion with them when they move south. This movement is offset by the establishment of churches in northern cities by immigrants mostly from the south.

Missionaries built and staffed the great majority of schools during the colonial period. Thus the north-south education gap, with its effect on political awareness, attitudes toward civil rights, and the like itself derives from the prohibition of missionaries in the north.

There is, then, an overlay of religion on ethnicity that intensifies the north-south cultural split, and the case can be made that the most sensitive issues now involve religion rather than ethnicity. This is more dangerous, because the sharp north-south divide is blurred by multiple ethnic identities but is focused by the Christian-Muslim dichotomy. Nigeria has a special problem in this regard in that the Christian–Muslim split is near 50–50, whereas in almost all other African states Muslims are either the large majority of the population or compose a clear minority. Samuel Huntington has divided the world into nine "civilizations." He foresees that "fault lines" among them will be the major loci of conflict in years to come, and notes specifically that "the overwhelming majority of fault line conflicts . . . have taken place along the boundary looping across Eurasia and Africa that separates Muslims from non-Muslims." The greatest potential for strife, he suggests, is where these lines split a single country.[13]

The brother of Usman dan Fodio, the leader of the nineteenth-century *jihad* (holy war) in northern Nigeria, wrote a four-volume work on the nature of legitimate Islamic government. It does not allow for the possibility of a conflict between secular concepts of justice and welfare and those in the *sharia* (Muslim religious law). These values are well-rooted in the region: A survey of 686 students at Bayero University in Kano in 1983 found that 92 percent of them "believed an Islamic state was inherently superior to a secular state."[14] In the 1980s the Maitatsine Islamic movement, composed largely of young men marginalized by the socioeconomic changes of the period, rioted against the Christian presence in northern Nigeria (as well as against police repression) with loss of life estimated in the thousands. On the other side, a failed coup against the Babangida regime in 1990 is widely thought to have been a "Christian coup against the northern Muslim leadership."[15] Because fundamentalist elements in both Christianity and Islam have frequently found it unacceptable to live in a pluralist society, those seeking a basis for political stability in Nigeria must be sensitive to finding a balance between the two major faith groups. For that reason there was great distress in the south when, in 1986, President **Babangida** proposed that Nigeria join the Organization of the Islamic Conference (OIC), a group of more than 50 predominantly Muslim countries formed in 1970. In 1991, Babangida asserted that the membership was "in abeyance," which is perhaps the only resolution of the issue that will not exacerbate religious tensions.

The Evolution of Nigerian Nationalism

All of our preoccupation with Nigerian subcultures should not obscure the fact that the British colonial administration was responding to Nigerian nationalist forces when they granted independence in 1960. There were three major sources of nationalist sentiment. The first was a small number of freed slaves from North America and others of African descent from the Caribbean who settled on the West African coast and developed a culture unrelated to any of those indigenous to the country. Second, nationalist fervor grew out of the experience of Nigerians who fought for the British in World War II and felt frustration at the lack of recognition of their service. A third category of nationalists consisted of those Nigerians who studied in England and especially in the United States, including one of the most prominent among them, **Nnamdi Azikiwe** (see Box 11.3).

BOX 11.3   The Story of Nnamdi Azikiwe

Although an Igbo, Nnamdi Azikiwe was born in Zungeru in northern Nigeria in 1904. He received his basic education in Nigeria, then went to the United States where he studied at Lincoln University in Pennsylvania, Stores College in West Virginia, and the University of Pennsylvania. He also worked in the United States as a coal miner, laborer, and dishwasher. Upon his return home he joined the Nigerian Youth Movement. His interest in self-rule led to his presence at the founding of the National Council of Nigeria and the Cameroons (NCNC) and to his founding of a pro-self-rule newspaper, the *West African Pilot*. He then moved to the Gold Coast (now Ghana), where he published an article, "Has the African a God," that resulted in a sedition charge. He won his case on appeal and went on to serve as the premier of the Eastern Region, and from 1963 to 1966 as president of Nigeria. He died in 1996 at the age of 92.

Although they came from a variety of ethnic backgrounds, in their quest for independence, these activists developed a sense of Nigerian nationalism and succeeded in forming cross-ethnic alliances.

Civil war also stimulated Nigerian nationalism. The two military coups before the Biafran war were clearly ethnic in their origins. However, the Biafran conflict brought together a military force that was cross-ethnic (excluding, of course, Igbos, who were at the heart of the Biafran succession). Although the officer corps is increasingly dominated by Muslims, it has continued to recruit nationally.

A study of Nigerian political culture must focus on orientations toward national (federal) political institutions. Nigerians oriented toward public political activities can be identified by (1) exposure to formal education and (2) involvement in the modern economy. As concerns interest in public policy, many Nigerians, particularly in rural areas and in the north, are *subjects,* not *participants.* Although such people may be unaware of, and uninterested in, issues of general political concern, they still have to deal with local government officials on issues affecting themselves and their families. In Nigeria, as elsewhere in Africa and the Third World, such concerns are likely to be handled through personal interest contacting. In a cross-national study conducted in the early 1990s, Nigerians were more likely than most to feel that the government should provide for individual needs (see Figure 3.3).[16] In most cases, such contacting is part of a *clientelist* arrangement: Citizens go to an individual who is politically influential for help and expect to "pay" for help through a long-term arrangement that may include payment in kind (as in bribes), or by turning out to vote when asked to do so, even while remaining uninterested in politics. Political activity is widespread and virtually all-embracing; interest in public affairs is strongly conditioned by education and employment.

Democratic Norms and Values

In order to assess Nigeria's chances for achieving political democracy, we must first consider the distribution of norms that might support democratic institutions. The legitimacy of opposition, manifested as tolerance for criticism, opposition, and competition for control, is an obvious prerequisite for stable democracy.[17] The performance of political activists in Nigeria from 1960 on suggests problems, even under democratic civilian regimes. As single parties gained control in each region, opponents were treated very roughly, often in the physical sense, with armed thugs hired to disrupt their meetings and attack their leaders.

Nevertheless, while an interest in the welfare of the nation over that of more particular groups may not characterize large numbers of Nigerians, even among the politically active, a truly Nigerian political culture has emerged across a large proportion of the politically aware population. Two values are widely held: freedom and public accountability.[18] A survey of university students found a nuanced view of democracy: Democracy was defined in terms of results such as good government and responsiveness, rather than by process; politicians were denigrated and there seemed to be little confidence in the wisdom of the electorate.[19] Yet, as a "bottom line," a large majority of the students still favored a full, election-based democracy.

BOX 11.4   The Igbo Women's War

" In November of 1929, thousands of Igbo women . . . converged on the native Administration centers. . . . The women chanted, danced, sang songs of ridicule, and demanded the caps of office (the official insignia) of the Warrant Chiefs. . . . At a few locations the women broke into prisons and released prisoners. Sixteen Native Courts were attacked, and most of these were broken up or burned. . . . On two occasions, British District Officers called in police and troops, who fired on the women and left a total of more than 50 dead and 50 wounded. No one on the other side was seriously injured." The women's actions were "an extension of their traditional method for settling grievances with men who had acted badly toward them."

Source: Judith Van Allen, "'Aba Riots' on 'Ibo Women's War'? Ideology, Stratification and the Invisibility of Women," in Nancy J. Hafkin and Edna G. Bay, eds. *Women in Africa: Studies in Social and Economic Change* (Stanford, CT: Stanford University Press, 1976), pp. 59–85.

The Political Role of Women

In Nigeria's ethnic diversity, the position of women varies considerably. In Igbo, Yoruba, and other southern Nigerian traditions, women had considerable control over their own affairs in what anthropologists label "dual-sex" systems. That is, there were parallel systems of political and social organization for men and women. P. C. Lloyd concluded that "the Yoruba wife's status is characterized by great overt submission to her husband together with considerable economic independence."[20] Scholars of colonial history contend that women lost most of their autonomy under colonialism, because British custom at the time gave women less control of their own affairs than did the African societies they controlled. A famous case in point is the Igbo "Women's War" (referred to by the colonial government as the "Aba riots"), in which Igbo women used traditional means of protest against taxation and were harshly repressed by the colonial government (see Box 11.4).

In the north, Islamic custom greatly restricts women's roles in society. Although Hausa women have considerably more freedom than their counterparts in the Middle East, including significant roles in local production and trade, they generally are not allowed an active political role at independence. Northern women voted for the first time in 1979.

The contemporary involvement of women in political leadership is similar to that of many countries: in most parts of the country, Nigerian women vote in equal numbers with men but are generally under-represented in politics. In the 1998/1999 elections, out of 109 Senate seats, men held 106 of Senate seats and women held 3; men held 348 seats in the House of Representatives and women 12; men held 767 positions as local government chairmen and only 7 were women; 7665 Councilors were men and 75 were women.

Political Corruption

A traveler on Nigerian roads meets frequent police checkpoints and barricades. Ostensibly in place to check for arms and smuggled goods, their actual function is to extort payments from travelers by uncovering various minor violations. Many Nigerians do not take offense at this behavior, noting that police officers' pay is low and often comes late. Travelers leaving the country through Murtala Muhammed International Airport in Lagos are routinely asked for "gifts" or subjected by police and customs officials to harassment designed to elicit bribes. This, of course, is petty activity compared with the huge sums high government officials have extracted from investors and contractors, sometimes as much as 25 percent of a contract. Pervasive corruption has been a problem ever since the late colonial era; it was the central theme of Chinua Achebe's novel *No Longer at Ease,* in which an idealistic young administrator is gradually pressured by personal problems and the prevalence of corruption into accepting bribes. Achebe is only one of many Nigerians to condemn corruption; each political regime comes to power promising to eliminate the practice and punish offenders, only to fall into the same pattern. The huge sums of money that passed through officials' hands as a result of the oil boom greatly aggravated the problem: Unprecedented forms of flagrant corruption appeared when oil revenues began to fill the federal treasury of General Yakubu Gowon in the early 1970s. His military governors spent large sums on openly lavish lifestyles, thus tarnishing the image of the military, which had supposedly come to power in reaction to the corruption of the First Republic. The coup against Gowon in 1975 was a direct result, as was the assassination of his successor General Murtala in 1976.[21] Succeeding regimes have all found it impossible to control the demands of those in public office to share in a "national cake," and Achebe asserts that corruption has grown more "bold and ravenous" under each new regime.[22] Although there is no firm evidence, it is widely believed that the deceased leader **Sani Abacha** and his family channeled enormous sums of money from petroleum revenue accounts into their private coffers at home and abroad. As part of its campaign to promote transparency in government and fight corruption, the Obasanjo administration has successfully recovered $2 billion from the Sani Abacha family. The Nigerian public is highly ambivalent about the corruption problem, frequently complaining about it and condemning it, but generally resigned to its pervasive presence.

POLITICAL SOCIALIZATION

Nigerians develop their political beliefs and attitudes through the influence of socialization "agents" such as the family, primary and secondary groups, formal education, the media, and government-sponsored activities.[23] A caveat is necessary, however, when comparing the political socialization process in Nigeria to the established liberal democracies. Political socialization in the developed world occurs through fairly stable institutions. We treat the fluidity of party alignments in France or events such as the Vietnam War in the United States as exceptional, whereas in Nigeria people have grown up under political arrangements that shift constantly, even to their very core. Add to this the upheaval of urbanization and of the sudden and dramatic impact of petroleum on the culture and the economy, and the need for a different perspective on socialization is apparent. Nevertheless, there is a universal quality to the importance of the agents of socialization identified above, even as the nature of those institutions and the objects of political attitudes and values they shape may differ greatly from those in Europe or North America.

The Family

The family, whether nuclear or extended, remains the core unit of political activity in Nigeria. In many Nigerian traditions, families are identified with a particular trade or role in society. Thus, among the Yoruba a family of warriors is called *Jagunjagun,* farmers are *Agbe,* and traders are *Onisowo.* To traditionally minded Nigerians such identification remains important to the determination of one's appropriate role in modern politics.

Many Nigerians have grown up in polygamous families.[24] There is no law preventing a man from taking more than one wife, although Muslims are theoretically limited to a maximum of four and Christians of mainstream denominations to one. All indigenous traditions in Nigeria accept polygamy, and little stigma is attached to the practice. Some Christian denominations in Nigeria enforce monogamy only on those men who hold office in the church. However, in the economic difficulties of the 1980s and 1990s few have had the resources to support more than one household and formal polygamy, especially in urban households, is rare.

The large family units that result from polygamous households and the broader definition of family give kinship special political importance. A politician may be able to count on the support of literally hundreds of actual kin, and even larger numbers if one considers clan affiliations based on a sense of kinship even where exact genealogical ties cannot be demonstrated. Kinship provides the most powerful sense of identity and loyalty to many in Nigeria and elsewhere in Africa, and it is the model (and often the real-world basis) for clientelist relationships.

Schools

In most contemporary nations, the schools play a central role in developing a sense of community. This is clearly an important mission in Nigerian schools, and balancing various loyalties is a delicate task for Nigerian educators. Also, formal education is one of the principal benefits Nigerians expect from government. The school certificate is highly regarded throughout the developing world as a means to economic and social advancement, and this is especially true in Nigeria: "It seems safe to say that by the 1930s and 1940s no people in the world placed a higher value on education or regarded its consequences more optimistically than did the inhabitants of this area."[25]

As Nigeria approached independence in the 1950s, the two southern regions invested massively in expansion of their educational systems, especially at the primary level. There is a broad consensus that primary education should be free and universal. Beyond that basic agreement, however, Nigeria has struggled with how to shape the curriculum and how to make it available.

The oil boom of the 1970s stimulated a massive wave of secondary school expansion and the university system, which grew from one in 1948 to five in 1962 to 45 by 2002. Just between 1999 and 2002, sixteen state universities and six private ones were created. In addition to universities, the higher education system includes 75 polytechnics and colleges of technology and of education.

Even in the prosperous 1970s, a lack of resources threatened this educational boom, and there was a lack of properly trained instructors at all levels. With the economic collapse of the 1980s, funds for education dried up, and education suffered at all levels. More than ever, equal access has become illusory, a problem that becomes more acute as one moves from the primary to the secondary and to the postsecondary level. The bias is on the one hand socioeconomic—children of the elite occupy a disproportionate share of the seats—and also reflects gender.

In 1990, there were 76 female pupils in primary school to every 100 males, and 74 to every 100 males at the secondary level. Seventy-two percent of the primary school-age population was in school (compared to 68 percent for sub-Saharan Africa as a whole); 62 percent of males and 40 percent of females are literate, which is about the continent-wide mean. As a result, the level of political awareness has risen substantially, although there is a widened gap in this respect between north and south. It is clear that the national-level data mask persistent regional disparities: Total attendance figures are higher in the south, and primary school enrollments were almost evenly split by gender as of 1983, whereas girls constituted only 34 percent of pupils in the north.[26]

There have been indirect political effects of the education gap across regions. As the number of secondary graduates increased in the south, many of them sought jobs in the north and were embittered at northern rejection. At the same time, northerners grew alarmed at the prospect of being inundated by educated southerners. Differences in educational achievement thus contributed to the resentments that exploded in violence in 1966. Today northern political dominance in the face of higher educational achievement in the south continues to aggravate interregional political conflict.

Language is an aspect of community building that is often taken for granted, but language usage in

The conference center in Abuja, the new capital.

Betty Press/Woodfin Camp & Associates

school can have a major impact on political attitudes. As noted previously, English is the official language of Nigeria and remains the vehicle of instruction in Nigeria from primary school through the university. Furthermore, English is the language of government and, for the most part, of the mass media. Because English is a second language in most Nigerian homes, school plays an especially critical role in enabling access to the political system.

As a nation-building effort the three major indigenous languages—Hausa, Igbo, and Yoruba—are also taught through secondary school and are topics in the Senior School Certificate Examinations. Proficiency in English is required for admission to a university, where the local languages are used only in programs where they might specifically be required. The connection between English usage and government activities gives added weight to the usual relationship between education and political efficacy.

Whatever the effect of intentional socialization in the schools, studies of political culture invariably affirm the effect of education on political participation. This is especially true in less developed countries, where the cultural gap between those with and without formal education is especially great. Data from the 1999 World Values Survey in Nigeria finds that only 25 percent of illiterate Nigerians are very interested in politics, compared to 46 percent among the most educated.

The Mass Media

The presence of a lively and politically independent press goes back at least to Azikiwe's *West African Pilot.* By the time of independence a considerable number of competing newspapers existed in Nigeria (virtually all published in Lagos, then distributed nationwide). Yet the current combined circulation of daily newspapers is only about 2.7 million, or about 24 per 1,000 people.

The political effect of the press is naturally limited in a country where half the adults are illiterate. A 2000 survey found that approximately 30 percent of Nigerians get their news from newspapers at least once a week. Interest in politics is high, however, even among people who cannot read. That same survey reported that 64 percent of

Nigerians are somewhat or very interested in politics, and 65 percent say they discuss politics and the government with people "sometimes" or "often."[27] Today, newspaper readership includes all politically active Nigerians, and the perspectives in the press undoubtedly have a wide word-of-mouth circulation.

Virtually all Nigerians get their news from radio and 60 percent of Nigerians list television as a source of news at least once a week. Radio and television have always been state-controlled and thus are faithful purveyors of the government's "spin" on political events. Shortwave broadcasts from BBC, the Voice of America, and other outside sources have been available as independent sources for decades, however. In recent years, indigenous television competes with satellite news services and since 1999 new independent media outlets have opened. In the year 2000 alone, Nigerians saw several new newspapers launched and six new privately operated radio stations. Although only a tiny proportion of the country's population have access to satellite telecasts or the Internet, such advanced communications technology permits outside views of Nigerian events to be introduced into the country, then spread by word of mouth or reflected in the print media.

The authoritarian regimes imposed a substantial number of restrictions on the media. According to the Center for Free Speech, a Nigerian watchdog organization, the military issued 21 decrees between 1966 and 1995 limiting press freedoms or even proscribing particular publications outright. There was a high level of tensions between military governments and the press, and the life of a journalist was not easy. Many journalists were arrested and in 1986 a prominent critic of the government was killed by a letter bomb.

The constitution promulgated in 1999 reversed many restrictions instituted under General Sani Abacha and previous military rulers. Article 39 states: "Every person shall be entitled to freedom of expression, including freedom to hold opinions and to receive and impart ideas and information without interference." Although this guarantees broad freedom for the media, journalists can still face criminal punishment for defamation of public officials and a 1999 decree requires them to be accredited by a government-run media council. The government was also widely criticized for a raid on a major daily newspaper in 2000 for alleged failure to pay an overseas hotel bill.

The State

The Nigerian government has at its disposal the modern means of mass communication that oil revenues have allowed it to develop. Periodically it launches propaganda campaigns on one issue or another, as in Operation Feed the Nation and Free Primary Education (in the 1970s), the War Against Indiscipline (in the 1980s), or the more recent Road Safety Operation, for which the government recruited author Wole Soyinka as director.

As part of its "transition program" to democracy (between 1986 and 1993), the regime of General Ibrahim Babangida inaugurated a "Directorate for Social Mobilisation," also known as MAMSER (Mass Mobilization for Self-Reliance, Economic Recovery and Social Justice). MAMSER's ostensible purpose was to shape a mass political culture that would be congenial to democracy. The government devoted considerable resources to this effort, although many questioned its effectiveness and some its sincerity. In 1995 the Abacha regime replaced it with a smaller organization intended to work through local governments. In 1990 the Babangida regime also established a Center for Democratic Studies (CDS) in Abuja, to conduct research on democratization and present seminars on that topic for government officials. In 1996, it too was closed by Abacha.

Nigerian political attitudes are far more likely to be affected by everyday contact with the state than by the state's direct, intentional efforts to shape attitudes. In Nigeria's federal system, direct contact comes largely through local officials. Rural residents without English-language proficiency find that, even at the local level, officials are much more educated than they, and generally expect and get deference. Government is remote and must be approached through some form of informal mediation. For those with formal education, contact with local government is relatively simple; furthermore, because Nigerian policy is to hire civil servants from their home areas, there is neither a social nor a cultural difference between the educated citizen and the public servant. Nigerians expect to pay for expeditious service, and while they are aware of

norms of honesty and ethics that are higher than the behavior they perceive, they are not scandalized by the difference. Perceptions of policymakers are not usually the result of direct contact. Nigerians generally express great cynicism about the motivations of policymakers at all levels, civilian or military, but for the most part this results from media accounts of venality and corruption. Whether through direct contact or media portrayal, they most often get what they expect from governmental officials, which of course becomes a self-fulfilling prophecy:

> The Complete Nigerian civil servant unlike his predecessor is not self-effacing behind an array of coded titles. You meet him here, you see him there, and you talk to him yonder. He is eager to make your acquaintance. He takes you into little corners to confide in you. For instance, he tells you how much it would cost you to have your file speeded up, which I think is very nice.[28]

One would expect that the unhappy experience with military rulers would leave Nigerians cynical and disillusioned. There certainly have been such effects, but there is a remarkably abiding faith in the importance of politics, especially among the educated. There is an impact here of the oil economy. Profits from the sale of petroleum have flowed through the central government, so that the stake in access to those in government, especially at the top, is high. For many intellectuals, however, the knowledge that important resources will be distributed through the government is offset by the uncertainty of the outcome of any attempt to become involved. They tend, thus, to leave the political field to a collection of seasoned politicians, those who have assembled a voter base every time a regime has offered the prospect of new elections.

Contact with Urban Life

Massive population movement from the countryside to the cities is a nearly universal characteristic of less developed countries. In the Nigerian case, the oil boom of the 1970s accelerated this movement, as the massive infusion of wealth stimulated employment opportunities in construction and other areas. From 1970 to 1995, Nigeria's urban population increased from 20 to 39 percent of the total. The subsequent economic downturn left many of the new urban residents in an economically marginal position that was all the more precarious because they were removed from the possibility of subsistence production, the usual option of peasants when profits from marketed goods are low. In such an environment, urban residents are "available" for political mobilization; they are physically close to political institutions that might be held responsible for their problems, and communication about political events can spread quickly. In Nigeria, political unrest is directly felt in Lagos, where most national political institutions are located. This political consideration has contributed to the regime's decision to move the federal government to a new capital in Abuja, much farther to the north.

Religion

Given the importance of religion in many Nigerians' lives, it is not surprising that religious institutions and religious leaders affect political orientations. According to the same 2000 survey cited above, nearly 80 percent of all Nigerians say they belong to religious associations, and half of those say they are active members. A dramatic example is the activity against political authorities in northern Nigeria inspired by religious leader Alhaji Mohammed Marwa Maitatsine. In the 1970s, the rapid urbanization of the country produced a marginalized stratum of youth in the towns and cities of northern Nigeria. Fundamentalist Muslim reformers were active at the time, with financial support from Saudi Arabia and other Arab countries. The fundamentalist message, especially as preached in the Izala movement—an acronym for the Society for the Removal of Heresy and Reinstatement of Tradition—proved appealing to the young urban migrants and directed them religiously and politically against the dominant leadership in the north. They were thus mobilized into the region's political factionalism:

> Religion is a powerful instrument of mobilization in Northern Nigeria . . . ambitious politicians and local notables supported the creation of the Izala movement . . . support for a religious movement by a politician offers political rewards. This is all the more so given the fact that religious leaders mediate between the politicians and the civil society. Moreover, with the pledge by the military to hand over power in 1979, and

with the heightened inter- and intra-party competition, one observed an intensification of contacts between politicians, local notables and religious leaders.[29]

With the return of democracy in 1999, Nigeria has experienced a new wave of religious tension, especially in the north where several states have declared their intention to implement Sharia, or Islamic law. Christian associations have opposed these changes and the conflicts have sometimes been dramatic: At least 10,000 people have been killed in religious conflicts between 1999 and 2003.

POLITICAL RECRUITMENT

All the chief executives of Nigeria since independence are identified in Table 11.1. Several conclusions are apparent. First, northerners have dominated the leadership of the country under both civilian and military rule, in the first case because the population of the north is about the same as in the east and west combined, and in the case of the military regimes, because of increasing dominance of the officer corps by northerners.

In the early years of independence, a military career lacked prestige, especially among educated southerners. In an effort to speed the replacement of remaining British officers, the Balewa government actively recruited university graduates into the officer ranks. One result was the introduction of large numbers of educated Igbos into officer ranks; another was the politicization of the army. Three of the first six university graduates to enter the army led the first coup.

Because the military controlled the country between 1983 and 1999, an officer's commission has come to be seen as the most regular path to political power. It seems that the ethos of the military has changed in this regard. The first coup leaders in 1966 professed great regret at the necessity to intervene and promised that their stay would be temporary. They were removed and killed in the second 1966 coup before their sincerity could be tested. The longevity of General Gowon's regime was made necessary by the need to prosecute the civil war, and then to lay a constitutional framework for civilian rule. When Gowon seemed inclined to settle in for the long term, he was removed, and General Obasanjo set and abided by his 1979 deadline. Thus, through the first period of military rule, although

T A B L E   1 1 . 1   Nigerian Chief Executives, 1960–1999

Dates	Name	Title	Ethnicity	Cause of Departure
1960–Jan. 1966	Tafawa Balewa	Prime Minister	Hausa-Fulani (North)	Coup (killed)
1963–Jan. 1966	Nnamdi Azikiwe	President [appointed]	Igbo (East)	Coup (removed)
Jan.–July 1966	Agusi Ironsi	Military Head of State	Igbo (East)	Coup (killed)
July 1966–1975	Yakubu Gowon	Military Head of State	Tiv ("Middle Belt")	Coup (removed)
1975–1976	Murtala Muhammed	Military Head of State	Hausa-Fulani (North)	Coup (killed)
1976–1979	Olusegun Obasanjo	Military Head of State	Yoruba (Southwest)	Handed power to civilian government
1979–1983	Shehu Shagari	President	Hausa-Fulani (North)	Coup (removed)
1983–1985	Muhammed Buhari	Military Head of State	Hausa-Fulani (North)	Coup (removed)
1985–1993	Ibrahim Babangida	Military Head of State	Gwari (North)	Forced out of office
Aug.–Nov. 1993	Ernest Shonekan	Interim Head of State [appointed]	Yoruba (Southwest)	Forced out of office
Nov. 1993–June 1998	Sani Abacha	Head, Provisional Ruling Council	Kanuri (North)	Died in office
May 1998–May 1999	Abdulsalami Abubakar	Head, Provisional Ruling Council	Gwari (North)	Handed power to civilian government
May 29, 1999–	Olusegun Obasanjo	President	Yoruba (Southwest)	

there was serious profit taking on the part of many military leaders, none of them expected to have long-term political careers.

The second round of military power (1983 to 1999) produced a gradual change in the perspectives of at least some military officers. Many observers have wondered about the military leadership's annulment of the 1993 presidential election results and the abolition of state and local elective offices already filled. Most feel that if the presumed winner, Moshood Abiola, had been allowed to assume power, he would have been unable to deal effectively with the country's problems, would quickly have lost an already dubious legitimacy, and would thus have prepared the way for a return of the military with acceptance by the population. As it was, the Abacha regime faced massive resistance and was able to rule only on the basis of force, at least in much of the south. Many assume that Abacha's actions, while certainly supported by elements in the north that could not stomach a Yoruba president, also reflected the strong desire of a new generation of military officers to enjoy the fruits of power that come from oil revenues and from the potential profits that flow from the corruption of public office. The country witnessed open jockeying for positions as state governors or "chairmen" of local governments, which were allocated according to military rank. National-level of-

fices were usually filled by generals, brigadiers, or colonels; state governors were mostly colonels; and local chairmen were lieutenant colonels and majors, often retired from active service. Politics in Nigeria is still largely a game of money; therefore, the retired military, the business group, and some retired civil servants dominate the elective positions while a few academics have political appointments like minister, commissioner and the foreign service.

Nigerian universities produce large numbers of trained public administrators, and they follow long-term careers in federal, state, or local administration that usually are not affected by changes at the top. An analysis of the educational backgrounds of the "administrative class" (assistant secretaries to permanent secretaries) just before the restoration of civilian rule in 1979 showed that all but 11 percent of them held university degrees.[30] An appropriate educational level had come to be expected in the civil service.

There has been some upheaval in the civil service following regime changes: An estimated 11,000 administrators were removed when Murtala Muhammed came to power in 1975 and took vigorous action against corruption. But to the degree that the administrative system continues to function through the many regime changes, it does so because of the permanence of the civil service.

Recruitment into political positions at the local and state levels generally exclude "strangers," even though they may be long-time residents of a community and, of course, Nigerian citizens. There are some exceptions: where "strangers" are sufficiently numerous, they can run and win. In most places, however, regulations have expressly limited candidacy to indigenous candidates. In addition to simple democratic fairness, the advantage of creating a multiethnic council is that it stimulates identity and participation in the community on the part of populations that are otherwise excluded. The overriding characteristic of recruitment into political or administrative office, however, is the effort faithfully to "reflect the federal character of Nigeria"—that is, to fill positions to have a government that is an ethnic microcosm of the locality or state it controls.

In the past, appointments of military personnel to government posts also reflected the country's "federal character": Northern officers were appointed in the northern states, Yorubas and others from the southwest to states in that region, and so on, although Abacha introduced a pattern of more random assignments, placing southern officers in the North and vice versa. However, the highest military positions have come from the combat arms, which recently are dominated by northerners; without the northern preponderance in these positions, Abacha's control of the country could not have been maintained. Even northerners have not always been reliable: Press reports claimed that a majority of junior officers had voted in 1993 for the southern civilian, **Moshood Abiola**. Abacha's support base was narrowed even further when, in March 1995, he arrested former head of state **Olusegun Obasanjo** and one of the most prominent senior northern military leaders, Shehu Musa Yar'Adua. Obasanjo was released by Abubakar after Abacha's death in 1998; Yar'Adua died in prison in December 1997. The same month, Abacha arrested the chief of the general staff, General Oladipo Diya on the charge of plotting a military coup, and thus removed the most senior Yoruba officer. Ethnic politics are still very much dominating the politics of Nigeria. However, President Olusegun Obasanjo has made use of the zoning structure, which breaks Nigeria into six divisions for the purpose of appointments and the distribution of infrastructures,

but the minority—especially in the Delta areas of the oil producing region—would want more functional roles in government. On many occasions, the oil producing regions have usurped the laws and frictions developed between them. The federal government had to break it up. It is to be noted that the oil producing regions have been neglected even by other administrations.

POLITICAL STRUCTURE

It is open to question whether we can realistically describe the "structure" of the decision-making process in a country that has experienced five successful coups, three civilian constitutions, and a particularly amorphous arrangement from General Babangida's annulment of the 1993 elections to the election of Obasanjo in February 1999. It is, however, useful to be familiar with the range of constitutional arrangements the country has known and the patterns in their evolution.

The first political institution in which Nigerians participated as Nigerians was the legislative council mandated by the Clifford Constitution of 1922, which provided for elected representatives from Lagos. Elections were introduced in this way and stimulated political activity. Through successive constitutional changes in the 1940s and 1950s, elective office was extended to local and regional governments and the first provisions for a federal structure were introduced.

The Development of the Constitution of 1999

As President Babangida in 1992 and 1994 postponed the return to civilian rule, his standing with the population, and even within the military, moved ever lower. When he delayed announcing the outcome of the June 12, 1993, presidential election, apprehensions grew, for it was popularly believed that Moshood Abiola had won. Two days after the election, initial results released by the **National Election Commission (NEC)** showed that Abiola had won in 11 of 14 states. Later, a private human rights coalition, the Campaign for Democracy, published election results indicating that Abiola had won in 19 of the 30 states. A few days later, the military government declared the election invalid. At the same time, Babangida promised new elections, and once again promised a return to civilian rule. He appointed a transition committee chaired by a Yoruba, Ernest Shonekan, and Babangida vacated the capital without fanfare—in a technical sense meeting his deadline for the restoration of civilian rule. However, Shonekan had virtually no support and was pushed aside by General Sani Abacha three months later in November 1993. General Abacha maintained the myth of a return to civilian government and created a Constitutional Conference to draft yet another governing document. The Constitutional Conference was inaugurated on June 27, 1994, but two weeks earlier, on the anniversary of the annulled election, Moshood Abiola had declared himself president. Abiola was arrested on June 23, 1994 and charged with three counts of treason. One count stated that he "solicited, incited, addressed, and endeavored to persuade people to take part in unconstitutionally overthrowing the head of state," an ironic indictment from a government whose leader seized control by force. Abacha seemed to manipulate the system to remain president, but his strategy was aborted by his death of a reported heart attack in May 1998. Meanwhile, Abiola had maintained his claim from prison, but he also died of a reported heart attack two months after Abacha, just as he was negotiating his release with Abacha's successors, Abdulsalami Abubakar. The succession of deaths, first of Shehu Yar'Adua in prison (November 1997), then Abacha (May 1998), and Abiola (July 1998), was seen by many Nigerians as an entirely improbable set of events. Even though the departed represented an extreme range of political positions, conspiracy theories have since then been widely floated.

In the period from 1983 to 1999, politics in Nigeria took the form of a succession of military regimes that constantly planned a return to democracy. Administrative and judicial proceedings continued as though a constitutional structure were in place. The 1995 constitution was widely discussed and even cited as the basis for election procedures in 1997 and 1998—yet the document was only officially promulgated by General Abubakar in May 1999 as he handed power over to a civilian regime. The overall structure of the current constitutional is outlined in Figure 11.4.

Federalism

In a country as vast and complex as Nigeria, many political decisions are not made at the national level. A federal system was established as Nigeria moved to independence in 1954. In a uniquely Nigerian scenario, two of the regions, the Eastern and the Western, gained self-governing status in 1957; the North followed in 1959. Thus a very decentralized federal system was already in effect at independence. The Constitution of 1960 was explicitly federal, dividing responsibilities between the federal government and the three regions. Federalism has been a constant in the three constitutions (1963, 1979, and 1989) since that time, and in the constitution developed but never promulgated under Abacha in 1995 which Abubakar used as the basis for his return of the country to civilian rule in 1999. Indeed, it is difficult to imagine a stable political structure that would not allow a considerable devolution of power to leaders of the three major ethnic groups at least. There have been two attempts to impose a unitary system: In the first coup in 1966, General Ironsi attempted to end the autonomy of the regions, and there seemed to be a similar thrust in the aborted coup of 1990. In each case, reactions to the suggestion of a unitary system were decidedly cool.

In the face of formal federalism, however, stands a fiscal condition that calls the federal concept into question: All levels of government derive the largest portion of their revenues from the national oil monopoly, distributed through the national government. Beyond this fiscal fact of life, there has been the control of Nigeria by military governments for 29 of 43 years of independence. It is difficult to define federalism under a military chain of command. Nonetheless, any permanent civilian constitution will undoubtedly be genuinely federal. As political activists in the South have become convinced that northerners are bent on dominating any central government in Nigeria, they have argued for greater state or regional autonomy. Some southerners even call for separate military forces for the major regions. We can be certain that defining state and local government boundaries will continue to be a central issue confronting any regime, civilian or military.

In our discussion of culture, we noted the effect of ethnic fragmentation on local government boundaries. When the Federal Military Government

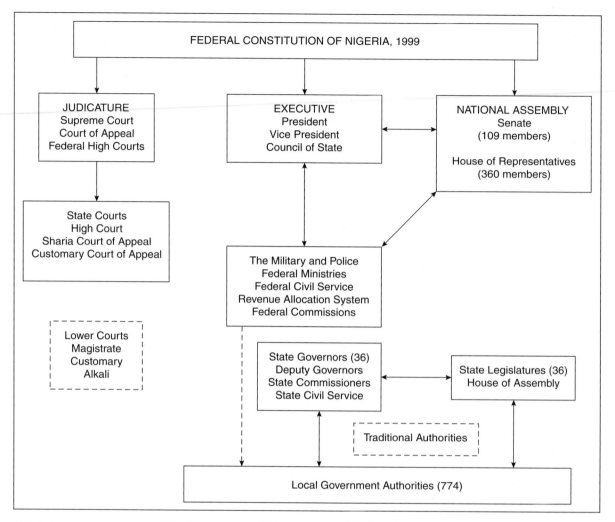

FEDERAL CONSTITUTION OF NIGERIA, 1999

JUDICATURE
Supreme Court
Court of Appeal
Federal High Courts

EXECUTIVE
President
Vice President
Council of State

NATIONAL ASSEMBLY
Senate
(109 members)

House of Representatives
(360 members)

State Courts
High Court
Sharia Court of Appeal
Customary Court of Appeal

The Military and Police
Federal Ministries
Federal Civil Service
Revenue Allocation System
Federal Commissions

Lower Courts
Magistrate
Customary
Alkali

State Governors (36)
Deputy Governors
State Commissioners
State Civil Service

State Legislatures (36)
House of Assembly

Traditional Authorities

Local Government Authorities (774)

FIGURE 11.4 The Structure of Government Under the 1999 Constitution

created 301 local government administrations (LGAs) in 1976, boundary lines were drawn in Lagos with minimal consultation locally, and communities were not allowed to change them. When the country returned to civilian rule in 1979, however, elected officials were much more receptive to demands for subdividing local government areas. Within a year there were 716 local governments, an increase of 238 percent. Naturally, such a large number of local administrations placed a heavy burden on a country with limited financial and human resources. Since the local governments themselves had little potential for generating revenue, they were unable to provide the services demanded by local populations. Interethnic competition to ensure respon-

sive government produced units that were unable to respond to those who had "won" their own local governments.

The next military government addressed this situation. After seizing power on December 31, 1983, they returned the country to 301 local governments, plus three in the new Federal Capital Territory. Even the military was susceptible to local demands, however: The number again began to grow, and now at the "grass roots" there are 774 LGAs, a new high.

State-level politics has often been dominated by local ethnic rivalries, as states are called upon to settle local government boundary disputes and to decide on the competence of various traditional institutions. Pressures analogous to those at the local level have led to an expansion of the number of states. The three colonial regions, which became the states of federal Nigeria, quickly became four. With the outbreak of civil war in 1967, the country was divided into 12 states, a number that was increased to 19 in 1976, to 30 in 1991, and to 36 in 1996 (plus the Federal Capital Territory; see Figure 11.5).

All these tensions finally converge at the national level, the source of most government resources. Recent federal governments have attempted to calm the ethnic struggle with a Nigerian version of affirmative action based on the country's "federal character." Various regions (and thus ethnic groups) are guaranteed a proportionate share of federal positions. This is an application of the consociational model, a common solution where countries are deeply divided by religion or ethnicity.[31] If appointments were made on competence alone, the educational advantage of the southernmost populations would result in their having a disproportionate share of civil service jobs. The major exception to apportioning positions according to federal character may be an indication of priorities. The Nigerian national football (soccer) team is not selected with attention to geographic representation!

Both the 1979 and 1989 constitutions describe a three-level federalism. In such other large federations as the United States, Canada, and Australia, the constitution focuses on the federal-state relationship, with local government principally in the domain of the state or province. The fact that Nigerian constitutions have specified a uniform structure and common functions for local government is rather unusual. While there are no doubt advantages to this uniformity of structure and function, it does not allow for local governments to reflect the diversity of local cultures present in the country, nor is experimentation possible of the sort that has produced the manager and commission systems at the local level in the United States. Since colonial times, however, local government has really been little more than local administration of federal policy, a situation unlikely to change until local governments acquire independent sources of revenue. Clearly, in an oil-centralized system the demand for local governments cannot be explained by the control of decisionmaking. Rather, ever more local government is

attractive because of the formula-driven allocation of funds that supports local activities. In 1981, the Second Republic's National Assembly decided to allocate 10 percent of federal revenues and 10 percent of state revenues to the localities. However, not only were state governments unwilling to abide by this mandate, but they frequently tapped for their own purposes the federal allocation that was transmitted to them for distribution at the local level. To remedy this situation, the 1989 Constitution provided direct payment of the federal allocation to local governments; in 1990 that allocation was increased to 15 percent, and a few years later to 20 percent of federal revenues, where it stands today.

The process of subdividing administrative and political units has fueled a growth of the public sector. Employment in the public service is an indicator of the growth of government. At independence, there were 71,693 employees of federal and regional government; by 1974 there were about 630,000, not counting the 250,000 in military service. A study of local governments in 1978 and 1979 found another 386,600 positions at that level, not counting general laborers or district or village heads. The drop in oil revenues in the mid-1980s brought an end to government growth. However, the Buhari administration imposed a 15 percent across-the-board personnel reduction that started a long period of stability in government employment.[32] Since 1999 competition among states for the distribution of federal revenues is acute in two arenas: First in disagreements between the president and the National Assembly over the amount of money that should be returned to the oil-producing areas, or what Nigerians refer to as the "derivation formula." Second, the controversy has played out between the states and the federal government in a series of major Supreme Court decisions in 2002 concerning states' entitlement to offshore oil revenues and the federal government's right to exempt certain expenses from funds distributed under the derivation formula.

Some suggest that a genuine federalism would help to cure Nigeria's political problems, which almost always involve the tremendously large stakes in the oil-rich nation's federal government. Perhaps a national government with limited resources would result in a federation that is not viewed as a high-stakes zero-sum game.

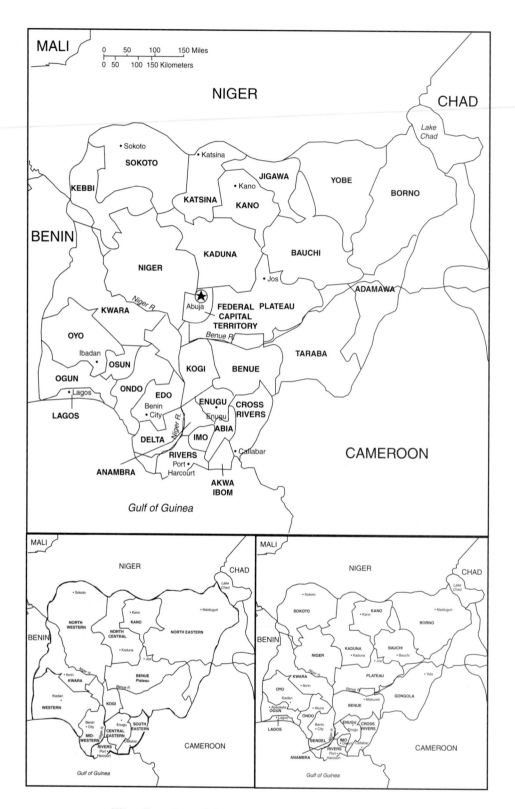

F I G U R E   1 1 . 5   The Creation of States, 1960–1997

Note: Lower left: Dark border shows original three regions, increased to four by the creation of the Midwestern Region, and to twelve in 1967. Lower right: Nineteen states, 1976–1991. Above: 30 states 1991–1997. (Current 36 states are shown at the beginning of the chapter.)

Parliamentary Versus Presidential Government

Without exception, British colonies came to independence with a parliamentary system based on the mother country's Westminster model. Initially Nigeria followed the Commonwealth pattern, with a ceremonial governor-general named by the British monarch. In 1963 the formal structure was redesignated a republic, with Nnamdi Azikiwe as president with mostly ceremonial powers; the parliamentary system was maintained, with a prime minister as head of government. Because Nigeria's first experience with civilian rule ended disastrously in 1966, it is not surprising that the previous system was called into question as a new constitution was being framed in the 1970s. The 1979 Constitution of the Second Republic was unabashedly modeled on the U.S. presidential model: An independently elected president was balanced against a two-house National Assembly at the federal level, with governors and legislatures following the same model at the state level. The disorder in the Second Republic might have brought presidentialism into disrepute as well, but the principal aspects of the presidential system were maintained in the 1989 and 1995 constitutions.

The 1999 constitution provides for an independently elected president and a dual chamber National Assembly at the federal level. Governors and single-house legislatures follow the same basic model at the state level. The Speaker of the House presides over the House of Representatives, while the President of the Senate, who is in the line of presidential succession after the vice president of the republic, presides over the upper chamber. Each of Nigeria's 36 states has three senators (plus one for the Federal Capital Territory of Abuja), while population determines the number of constituencies in each state for a total of 360 representatives. Senators and representatives serve four-year terms and are elected at the same time, rather than in staggered elections. One legacy of the long years of military rule is that many of these legislators—nearly 80 percent in both chambers—have no previous legislative experience. There are about 60 standing committees in each chamber with jurisdiction over different issues. Committees are still getting accustomed to their role in the legislative process, and many bills are not amended or debated until they reach the floor for debate. As permitted by the constitution, the Executive Branch introduced the federal budget and other major pieces of legislation, and how much the National Assembly can or should modify these bills has been a hotly contested issue since 1999. Differences of opinion between the two branches of government have been dramatic even though the president's party enjoys a majority in both chambers.

Nigeria's problems with achieving stable constitutional rule have made it an important case study in arguments over the relative advantages of the two systems in conditions of cultural pluralism. On the face of it, the fault may seem to lie with defects in the various constitutional frameworks, but the problem may actually be the intractable nature of Nigerian pluralism. A constitutional document cannot succeed at papering over a lack of trust among the country's subcultures. The lack of trust has led to suggestions of a "zoning" arrangement, which would require that the presidency and other top posts rotate automatically among the various geographical "zones" in the country, such that every major group could have a turn. The Constitutional Conference of 1995 gave a general endorsement to zoning at all levels of government—that is, for governorships of states and chairmanships of local governments as well as at the federal level. But would such a plan really inspire trust, or would it inspire officeholders to even more rapacious rent-seeking, knowing they would only be in a given office for one term?

The Judiciary

Nigeria came to independence with a well-established legal system that included a court system and a thriving legal profession in the British tradition. The federal and state courts are integrated into a single system of trial and appeal courts. Thus the 1999 Constitution provides a Supreme Court, a Court of Appeal, and state and federal High Courts with original and appellate jurisdictions. Traditional authorities maintain their greatest influence in their judicial powers, for states are explicitly allowed to constitute customary and Sharia (Muslim Koranic law) courts, both original and appellate. Ten northern states maintain *Sharia* courts, a point of contention between Muslim authorities and those who see such official recognition as divisive.

It has been one of the greater anomalies of Nigeria's often chaotic politics that the independent judiciary has survived, even through military regimes that rule by decree. The final blow to judicial independence may have come, however, under the Abacha regime, which showed no inclination to respect any semblance of legal system autonomy. It reacted to court orders by changing the rules—even constitutional provisions—that might be used against it. It also established special military tribunals for robbery and firearms violations, for the trial of Ken Saro-Wiwa and others in Ogoniland, and for those accused of supporting coups against Abacha in 1995 and 1997.

INTEREST ARTICULATION

There are at least two aspects of political influence in Nigeria. First is the effect of organized interest groups such as unions and trade associations and religious bodies. The second involves the more informal channels of participation through individual relationships often described by the term "clientelism."

Nigerian author Wole Soyinka describes how some of the first formal interest groups formed during the colonial period out of previously nonpolitical associations:

> Much later, we heard of the formation of the Nigerian Women's Union. The movement of the *onikaba*, begun over cups of tea and sandwiches to resolve the problem of newly-weds who lacked the necessary social graces, was becoming popular and nation-wide. And it became all tangled up in the move to put an end to the rule of white men in the country.[33]

The activities of formal associations and institutions often offer the most vigorous expression of societal independence from a government. Characteristically, voluntary associations were either brought under control or abolished in the authoritarian regimes that took hold in Africa soon after independence. This was not, however, the case in Nigeria, where even during military regimes organizations such as the Nigerian Women's Union have maintained an independent existence, even as their political influence was reduced.

Ethnic and Religious Associations

Many of the first formal associations in Nigeria had an ethnic base. The Igbo Federal Union (later the Igbo State Union) was "inaugurated by politically conscious representatives of the Igbo intelligentsia."[34] The *Egbe Omo Oduduwa* was organized among young, urban, Yoruba professionals. Minority groups especially found comfort in formal associations such as the Ibibio State Union, the Edo National Union, the Urhobo Renascent Convention, and others. These associations often formed the organizational base for parties, and contributed to the latter associations' ethnic orientations. In the north, where individual clientelist ties are relatively stronger, associations even of the ethnic type have played less of a role. An ethnic association of contemporary significance is the Movement for the Survival of the Ogoni People (MOSOP), founded by **Ken Saro-Wiwa.** MOSOP claims to speak for the 500,000 Ogoni people whose land is now occupied by Shell Oil drilling rigs. The Ogoni complain that they have borne the brunt of the inconvenience of Nigeria's oil industry and have received little in return. By the early 1990s they had begun to disrupt production, and Saro-Wiwa was arrested. He won his freedom and continued to campaign overseas against Shell Oil and the Nigerian government. When four Ogoni chiefs were murdered by young militants, Saro-Wiwa was again placed under arrest (along with 14 other Ogonis) and charged with murder for inciting the youths. In October 1995, he and eight codefendants were convicted by a military court and in November they were hanged, despite pleas of clemency from around the world. After five years in the grave, in July 2002, the federal government allowed their families to exhume bodies of Ken Saro-Wiwa and others for a proper burial.

As in many other countries, religious institutions and associations play an important part in Nigerian politics. These groups are especially durable and resilient, because when political activity is repressed they remain organized around denominational objectives, and where an ethnic association might have to play a less obvious role, neither Christian nor Muslim religious groups and leaders find it necessary to camouflage their identities. As in other countries, religious-based interest groups take several forms: The formal institutions (churches, Koranic schools), leadership roles such as bishops, pastors, and *mallams* (Muslim teachers and learned men), and voluntary denominational associations. The effectiveness of religious institutions in articulating concerns to government has been reduced by intergroup conflicts, most frequently between Christians and Muslims, that put the government in the role of mediator.

Not surprisingly, associational life is most active in the south; however, the north is home to an Islamic "mystic brotherhood," the *Tijaniyya,* which is particularly influential among lower-class Hausa Muslims and is looked on with suspicion by the representatives of orthodox Islam (another brotherhood, the *Khadiriyya,* is identified with the traditional elite of the north). The existence of such groups blurs the distinction between "modern" associations and "traditional" institutions.

Associational Groups

In the more urban and industrialized areas of the country, one encounters a range of associational interest groups common to the politics of any modern nation. Trade unions have played a role in Nigerian politics since the colonial period, sometimes collectively through the Nigerian Labour Congress (NLC) and its 17 affiliated unions. However, labor action is organized more frequently by sector. Groups representing the petroleum workers can have an immediate impact on the national economy and consequently have the potential for great political influence, as was demonstrated in 1994 strike actions by the **National Union of Petroleum and Gas Workers (NUPENG)** and the Petroleum and Natural Gas Senior Staff Association (PENGAS-SAN). Groups such as NULGE (the Nigerian Union of Local Government Employees) are especially influential because of their immediate impact on government.

Professional organizations such as the Nigerian Bar Association, the Nigerian Medical Association, and especially the Nigerian Union of Journalists, are politicized as issues concern them directly. Military governments periodically force the dissolution of such groups by arresting their leaders: After The NLC met in Kaduna in July 1994 and voted a general strike, the Abacha government arrested Frank Kokori, secretary of NUPENG, and most members of the petroleum industry unions eventually returned to work. (Kokori was one of the first political prisoners released by General Abubakar following the death of Abacha.)

The universities are another modern sector that has a tradition of political activism. Faculty (the term "staff" is used in Nigeria), as well as students, were some of the earliest critics of military rule, and military governments have tried to marginalize their role in the country. Strikes by staff and students are common, and the campuses were the most vocal opponents of Abacha's continuation of military rule. However, because recent military regimes have been content to let the universities deteriorate, campus political activities have not had the impact on policy as have parallel actions of, say, petroleum workers.

The National Democratic Coalition (NADECO) and the Campaign for Democracy (CD) are groupings of civil rights and democracy activists that are particularly influential in intellectual circles and among students. In 1994 they were at the front of much anti-Abacha activity. NADECO is seen as a predominantly Yoruba organization, and consequently is not strong outside the southwest. Another largely southwest-based opposition group the Joint Action Committee on Nigeria (JACON) formed in the last years of the Abacha regime. All these groups criticized General Abubakar's approach to a return to civilian rule.

During the long periods of military rule, politicians at all levels who were turned out by the military have constituted an interest group united around their desire to be allowed back into the circles of power. They were a force pushing for the return to civilian rule, even as many of them were content to be "co-opted" into administrative service under the military.

Nonassociational Groups

A clear Nigerian example of the nonassociational interest group, but shadowy in its definition, is the famous **"Kaduna Mafia."** Hardly any informal conversation on Nigerian politics fails to mention this network of powerful northern leaders who are said to maintain strong influence over the military and Nigerian politics. Richard Joseph offers this description:

> In a general sense [Kaduna Mafia] refers to members of the northern intelligentsia who assumed positions of political and social influence during the decade of military rule after the civil war. These individuals are, on the whole, better educated than their predecessors in the emirate North who held

similar positions in the first decade after independence. [They also] were less dependent on the patronage of the traditional rulers to advance in their careers.[35]

This group was highly influential in the Babangida years, but Sani Abacha distanced himself from them, and the arrest and death in prison of General Yar'Adua, a leading figure in the Kaduna Mafia, suggests that the organization has lost its influence, at least temporarily.

Given that most of Nigeria's labor force is involved in agriculture, one expects to find strong associational activity among farmers. However, the ethnic divisions in the country have prevented the formation of any national-level farm organizations. Those groups that do exist are usually engaged in local cooperative activities and are not active beyond the regional level. More commonly, the interest articulation activities of farmers are of the anomic protest variety (that is, spontaneous and unorganized), or take the form of clientelism (see below).

Finally, one institution is far more than an interest group: the military itself. We will address their political role later. The Nigerian military is not a cohesive interest, as was demonstrated in the transition from Abacha to Abubakar. The enlisted personnel and lower-ranking officers have not seen any direct benefit from military rule, and many supported efforts to return to civilian rule. Also, the country's ethnic divisions are reflected in the military as well, although they compete there with a well-ingrained military professionalism. The military rank-and-file were originally drawn mostly from northern non-Hausa minorities. Later recruitment drew from all over the country, but the minorities, especially from the "Middle Belt," remain disproportionately numerous. The early preponderance of Igbo officers ended with the second coup and the Biafran War, which resulted in the northern dominance in the officer corps that is present today. However, there is wide ethnic diversity among the officers, and ethnicity is only one factor in the complex disputes within the military. There is a constant possibility that new factions will emerge to challenge the current leadership, to forestall or delay the return to civilian control. The Abacha regime cited a conspiracy to that end when, in March, 1995, it ordered the arrest of "a group of over-ambitious and misguided officers and civilians." According to then second-in-command

General Oladipo Diya, the coup plotters included "a cross-section of the country, officers from all parts of the country." Ironically, Diya himself was arrested as part of an alleged coup plot two years later.

The role of a vital civil society as a balance to political authority was played by a range of interest groups in the wake of General Sani Abacha's seizure of power in November 1993. Trade unions and unions of the academic staff at secondary schools and the universities engaged in a series of strikes against the Abacha regime. These activities were designed to force Abacha to release Moshood Abiola from prison, to agree to political activity on Abiola's part, and to turn over power to a civilian regime. Their strike stimulated an increase in world prices of raw crude oil and in pressing shortages in refined petroleum products in Nigeria. Abacha responded by arresting the union leaders and replacing them with his handpicked successors. Many Nigerians thought that strike and demonstration action would force Abacha out, but he stubbornly clung to power until his death.

Abacha's regime was not without substantial support. An organization called the Association for a Better Nigeria, formed under Babangida, went to court to seek an injunction against certification of the 1993 election. This and other associations represented those in the country who profited from the existing arrangement and were not eager for a new constitutional regime, and so continued their vocal support of the Babangida and Abacha regimes both in Nigeria and abroad. These elements were largely discredited after Abacha's death, and a number of their leaders made public pleas for forgiveness.

Patron-Client Networks

An alternative structure for interest representation is found in the **patron-client network.** Powerful Nigerian political figures are able to mobilize support through personal "connections" with subordinates, who may themselves serve in a corresponding role of "patron" for a yet-lower set of "clients." **Clientelism** was an integral aspect of political life in the larger-scale precolonial systems of the Hausa, the Yoruba, and others. Those who are not represented by formal associations may be able to take advantage of their connections to achieve political ends, particularly at the local level, and where traditional rulers and their political systems maintain some influence.

Furthermore, the pattern of personal contacts is ingrained in the culture and thus remains important as an approach to powerful modern figures independent of any local traditional context.

Resting on these patron-client networks in Nigeria is a patronage system in which a ruler or official gives a public office to an individual client in return for his loyalty in delivering political support at some lower level. The prevalence of such a system in Nigeria is not dependent on particular regimes, civilian or military.[36] Their durability makes the "restructuring" of Nigerian administration difficult when regimes are under pressure to develop an "austerity" budget.

POLITICAL PARTICIPATION

The forms of action that Nigerians take in pursuit of political goals cover the whole spectrum of possibilities, from voting to participation in the terribly violent civil war of 1967–1970. Given the lack of either good census data or reliable voter registration figures, it is difficult to be precise about voter turnout figures, but estimates are in the range of 40 to 60 percent in some earlier elections, an impressive level for a majority poor and illiterate populace. Some of the explanation is found in the prevalence of patron-client systems, the "machine politics" that ties ordinary voters into the electoral process through personalistic ties with political activists.

Interest in elections, even in the mobilization of patron-client networks, declined during the long transition to civilian rule, but it rose again with the return to civilian rule. In the presidential election of February 1999, turnout was estimated at 52 percent.

Violence also is employed frequently, from the use of "thugs" by political parties in both republics to the confrontations with police in Lagos and the southwest during the last days of the Babangida regime and in the challenges to Abacha's seizure of power. Violence by the state, although less common than in many authoritarian regimes, has played a major role in Nigeria politics: Upward of 50 people were executed for participation in the failed coups of 1986 and 1990; death sentences against those accused in 1995 were not carried out, only because the PRC could not agree among themselves on whether to do so. The greatest example of political violence was, of course, the Biafran civil war in 1969 to 1996. Nigeria has experienced over 2 million deaths in wars from 1960 to 1992, the vast majority of them during the civil war.

Nigeria has been a highly politicized country ever since independence, although alienation and frustration with the failure to develop stable, honest, and responsive institutions are increasingly evident.

PARTIES AND ELECTIONS

After the Babangida government voided the national elections of 1993 and Abacha came to power, party activities were banned in Nigeria. The exception was the artificially created five-party system that contested local and state elections under Abacha; these parties were allowed to exist only if they refrained from any criticism of the regime, and they leaned so far in the other direction that all five named Abacha their presidential candidate! In 1998 the Abubakar regime allowed new parties to be formed and contested the 1998–1999 elections. The rebirth of party activity is evidence that the evolution of political parties and their effect on Nigerian politics is worthy of attention.[37]

The first modern party was formed by Herbert Macaulay in Lagos in 1923. Several such movements contended for power at the local level under the colonial regime, and a diverse nationalist movement emerged in 1944, under the leadership of Macaulay and Nnamdi Azikiwe, the National Council of Nigeria and the Cameroons (NCNC).[38] This organization advocated greater representation in the Nigerian colonial government. Chapters were established across Nigeria. However, when the British introduced a more democratic and decentralized constitution in 1951, the NCNC broke up along ethnic lines. The 1951 Constitution mandated indirect assembly elections in the three regions; Lagos was in the Western Region, where the Yoruba were in the majority. An opposition party, the Action Group (AG), emerged under the leadership of a young Yoruba lawyer, Obafemi Awolowo, with an initial organizational base in the *Egbe Omo Oduduwa,* a Yoruba cultural society. Although Azikiwe's NCNC won in multiethnic Lagos, the AG won the majority of seats in the Western Region. The NCNC won overall in the Eastern Region, where Azikiwe's own Igbo ethnic group was in the majority.

This is President Olusegun Obasanjo in a full Yoruba Agbada dress campaigning to the Yoruba people of the southwest—his own ethnic group—for his second term. In 1999, he did not get good support from the Yoruba. But in the election of 2003, the Yorubas gave him overwhelming support, because he had proved himself as a worthy leader.

AP/Wide World Photos

From the beginning there were forces within both the NCNC and the AG arguing for movement in a multicultural, issue-based, cross-regional direction. The Action Group was especially split along liberal (cross-regional, pushing for quick movement toward independence) and conservative (ethnic-based, evolutionary) lines. Elected offices were first established regionally, and only later (in 1957) at the national level, This favored the forces of regionalism. Azikiwe particularly was committed to action at the national level, but it became clear that a regional power base was essential, and Azikiwe also was constrained to center his party on its strength in the east. Thus the NCNC came to be identified with that region and the Igbo people (see Table 11.2).

In the north, Britain's successful application of indirect rule had resulted in an alliance between the colonial administration and the traditional emirs that impeded the formation of modern political movements. Whereas in the south such movements had arisen among a Western-educated elite outside the control of any traditional authority, in the north the only youth to receive a modern education came from the families of the traditional elites. Although reformist political organizations were formed, notably the Northern Elements' Progressive Union (NEPU) under Mallam Aminu Kano, they operated only at the margins and tension points of the emirates. A more conservative movement, the Northern Peoples' Congress (NPC), was taken over by the Sardauna (a

T A B L E 1 1 . 2   Ethnic Distribution of Party Leaders, 1958

Party*	Igbo	Yoruba	Hausa-Fulani
NCNC	49.3	26.7	2.8
AG	4.5	68.2	3.0
NPC	—	6.8	51.3

*NCNC: National Council of Nigeria and the Cameroons; AG: Action Group; NPC: Northern People's Congress.

Source: Richard Sklar and C. S. Whitaker, Jr., "Nigeria," in James S. Coleman and Carl Rosberg, eds., *Political Parties and National Integration in Tropical Africa* (Berkeley: University of California Press, 1964).

traditional title) of Sokoto and a Hausa commoner, Abubakar Tafawa Balewa. The NPC, the traditional emirates, and the preindependence administrative structure were intertwined such that young administrators could run successfully for public office, but only if they had the support of their administrative superiors and of the local traditional elite. This political structure grew up among a population that was not as educated (less than 15 percent were literate) as in the south, and that was much more loyal to their traditional authorities. In the 1959 Northern House of Assembly, 24 percent of NPC delegates were sons of incumbent or former emirs, and over a third were blood relatives of emirs. The elite origins of the party's officers and candidates were de-emphasized through both communal (ethnic) and religious (Islamic) appeals to the electorate. Not surprisingly, the NPC did not give high priority in its program to achieving national independence. The NPC was challenged in northern elections, but with only occasional success. Unlike the NCNC and AG, neither the NPC nor their northern rivals even tried to obtain political support outside their own region.

When General Ironsi assumed power following the breakdown of political order in the Western Region and the first coup, one of his first moves was to abolish all parties and a large number of political associations. The country remained without formal parties from 1966 until the preparations for a return to civilian rule in 1979. General Yakubu Gowon (head of state from 1966 to 1975) had considered the creation of a one-party state in Nigeria, with himself as leader of a "national movement." Nigeria's diversity and the plurality of its power bases made that concept impossible to achieve: To northern leaders, it suggested southern domination, while to the politicians waiting for the return of civilian rule, it meant the end of their ambitions. Gowon was unable to decide on a course of action and was deposed before any plan had been adopted.

After taking power, Murtala Muhammed set in motion a process to return to civilian rule. The military regime established a Constitution Drafting Committee, and in his address to its opening session, Murtala Muhammed laid down several principles relating to parties. He encouraged them to "discover some means by which Government can be formed without the involvement of political parties," but otherwise that they should draft a plan to guarantee "genuine and truly national political parties," while striving to work out "specific criteria by which their number would be limited."[39] The drafters responded with a constitution that was carefully crafted to promote national parties. It specified that to be elected president, a candidate would have to poll at least 25 percent of the votes cast in each of at least two-thirds of the states. Elections were to be controlled by a Federal Election Commission (FEDECO), with which all parties must register. Parties were to offer membership to any Nigerian, and party governing boards were to reflect the country's "federal character"—specifically, coming from at least two-thirds of the states. The Electoral Decree was published in 1978; in that same year political parties were again made legal, and they came in a flood—some 150 were formed.

The elections of 1979 and 1983 are difficult to analyze, because five parties competed for president, senate and house seats, and state assemblies with varying degrees of success. Looking at the Senate, House, and state assemblies overall, most states were controlled by a single party. Awolowo's United Party dominated five of the 19 states, all in the Yoruba west and the midwest (a "minority" area). Azikiwe's NPP carried three states, two of which were in the Igbo-dominated east. Aminu Kano's northern opposition party carried only its leader's own state, Kano, in the north. The GNPP won two states in the northeast, home region of its presidential candidate. However, the ethnic factor was complicated by the success of the NPN in building cross-regional alliances. The NPN controlled eight states; five of these were in the north, but three were in the southeast.

In order to participate in the elections of 1998 and 1999, parties were required to demonstrate a nationwide organization. On the basis of the cases they submitted, nine parties were qualified to compete in the local elections of December 1998. The three parties that received the highest number of votes in the 774 local governments were then allowed to compete in the state and national elections of 1999. The People's Democratic Party (PDP) won in 389 local governments, the All People's Party (APP) in 182, and the Alliance for Democracy (AD) in 100, with other parties winning in the remaining 103. As the presidential elections of February 1999 approached, the APP and AD negotiated to present a single candidate—in other words, the normal effect of a winner-take-all situation pushed toward the creation of a two-party system. There were ultimately just two candidates, Olusegun Obasanjo representing the PDP and Olu Falae leading the APP. Obasanjo won with 62.8 percent compared to Falae's 37.2 percent. The **Independent National Election Commission (INEC)** created by the Abubakar regime for this election declared Obasanjo the winner.

In 2003, Obasanjo ran for reelection. The APP, which had in the meantime renamed itself the **All Nigeria People's Party (ANPP),** selected Muhammed Buhari, another former military ruler, as its presidential candidate. Despite the internal tensions in the PDP, the party increased its majority in both houses of Congress and won 28 out of 36 governorships. Obasanjo was reelected by a landslide, winning almost twice as many votes as Buhari. He and the PDP particularly improved their position in the Southwest, where they captured five governorships from the AD. Table 11.3 shows the results of the 2003 elections. At every level, the PDP consistently demonstrated its dominance.

T A B L E   1 1 . 3   Results of 2003 National Elections

	PDP	ANPP	AD	Others
Presidential Vote	61.9%	32.2%	Did not contest	5.9%
National Assembly Vote (Seats)	54.5% (213)	27.4% (95)	9.3% (31)	8.8% (7)
Senate Vote (Seats)	53.7% (73)	27.9% (28)	9.7% (6)	8.7% (0)

Note: PDP: People's Democratic Party; ANPP: All Nigeria People's Party; AD: Alliance for Democracy.

Source: The Independent National Electoral Commission, preliminary results.

Ethnic Solidarity and Party Loyalty

Figure 11.6 shows the formation of Nigerian political parties, notably their reemergence with the same ethnic bases after suppression by military regimes. Governments, especially the military ones, have tried to force Nigerians to express their will through cross-ethnic parties. However, because ethnicity drives much of the political organizing in the country, political leaders have succeeded in subverting the goal of truly national parties through their calls to ethnic identity. A political career is started in a local community on an ethnic basis, and a cross-ethnic party is in that situation nothing more than a coalition of ethnic interests. The Hausas have been most successful in this situation; they captured the presidency each time this national office was filled by election until Obasanjo's victory in 1999. With envy and bitterness, many political activists in the south were convinced that the Hausas know they can assemble an electoral majority under their control and that they act accordingly. Many charged that Obasanjo, although not Hausa, could not have won without their support and was in effect the "northern" candidate.

The NPN won the ultimate prize, the presidency, in 1979, essentially on the basis of a combination of northern voters and minority voters in the southern regions. The most significant difference for parties between the First and Second Republics turned out to be the carving up of the original three regions into 19 states. Ethnic groups other than the "big three" were dominant in a number of these states and had thus broken free of regional ethnic dominance. Party strategists henceforth combined a strong base in one of the main ethnic group areas with a successful appeal for support among minorities and potentially among dissident groups in the home bases of the other two major groups.

The same five parties remained in existence through the four years of the Second Republic, and

contested again in 1983 for the presidency, seats in the Senate and House, and state-level positions. However, the smallest parties, the PRP and the GNPP, had been weakened by their lack of access to resources. And, as is normal in a presidential system where the ultimate prize, the presidency, is a winner-take-all election, there were pressures on the two major opposition parties to combine against the incumbent. Such cooperation proved impossible, however, when neither Azikiwe nor Awolowo would defer to the other as presidential candidate. In a campaign marked with violence and vote-rigging, the NPN won a solid victory, recording gains against the opposing parties in their home areas.

The NPN victory was short-lived. Three months into its second term it met an early demise at the hands of Nigeria's fourth military coup. Party financing in the 1983 elections was based on unprecedented political corruption, even as the country's financial situation had greatly deteriorated, and was among the reasons offered by the military for again abolishing the country's political parties. The public's acceptance of that action was rooted in the civilian government's failure to address in policy the issues raised during the campaign. For example, both the UPN and the NPP promised full employment and free education at all levels. These promises were beyond the regime's fiscal capacity and showed a serious lack of responsibility; it is not surprising that they contributed to voter cynicism.

The two-year reign of Muhammadu Buhari (1983–1985) presented no timetable for a return to electoral politics. However, Buhari's successor, Ibrahim Babangida, began outlining conditions for a return to civilian rule in 1986 that revealed his view of the country's problems. Babangida announced that 49 politicians convicted of corruption would be banned from politics for life. Between 1987 and 1989, a series of decrees created a National Election Commission (NEC) to replace the defunct FEDECO in

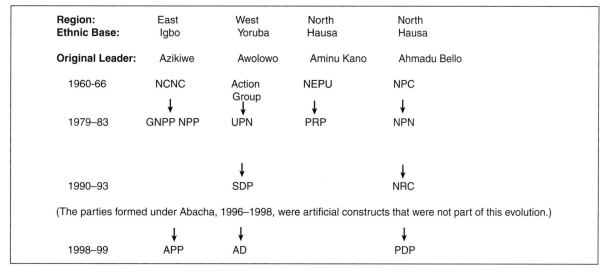

Region:	East	West	North	North
Ethnic Base:	Igbo	Yoruba	Hausa	Hausa
Original Leader:	Azikiwe	Awolowo	Aminu Kano	Ahmadu Bello
1960-66	NCNC	Action Group	NEPU	NPC
	↓	↓	↓	↓
1979–83	GNPP NPP	UPN	PRP	NPN
		↓		↓
1990–93		SDP		NRC

(The parties formed under Abacha, 1996–1998, were artificial constructs that were not part of this evolution.)

	↓	↓		↓
1998–99	APP	AD		PDP

F I G U R E   1 1 . 6   The Evolution of Political Parties in Nigeria

managing the electoral process. The NEC provided for nonpartisan local council elections in 1987, set a timetable for the creation of political parties and the sequential election of legislators and executives at the local, state, and national levels, and promulgated a constitution to come into effect in 1992.

The NEC was entrusted with the task of establishing guidelines for party formation that would result in the emergence of a de facto two-party system. In 1989 the ban on party activities was lifted and associations were invited to form, with the proviso that they have a national following and an internally democratic structure. Some 50 parties sprang up overnight.

The effect of forcing a two-party system on this political chaos was not clear. Some feared it would lead to a polarization along north-south, Christian-Muslim lines. Such a polarization would imply the papering over of serious splits among northerners and between powerful interests in the southeast and southwest; in this context, the emergence of two monolithic political movements would not automatically occur. Thirteen groups eventually petitioned the NEC for recognition. After careful scrutiny the NEC certified five parties to the Armed Forces Ruling Council (AFRC). The AFRC response was extremely innovative: All 13 associations, including those certified by the NEC, were dissolved, and two parties were established by the military government, perhaps the only time in history that an authoritarian leadership had imposed a two-party system!

Babangida charged the NEC to examine the various documents of the dissolved parties and synthesize them into two discrete philosophies, one for a party "a little to the left," the other to fit a party "a little to the right" on the political spectrum. However, they were to have identical constitutions, providing for the choice of candidates by primary election. Even the parties' names were assigned by the government: The party on the left would be the Social Democratic Party, that on the right the National Republican Council. The impact of the American model on Nigerian constitution making had never been more obvious.

The government built headquarters buildings for both parties at each local government and provided generous "take off grants" to sustain their organizing efforts. In a first round of elections, party officials at all levels were elected. However, powerful politicians had naturally formed parallel organizations and set about using their clientelist networks to capture one or the other party at various levels.

Nigerians reacted to these developments with a mixture of cynicism and hope. It was difficult for intellectuals to accept a "democracy" based on parties and elections mandated by an authoritarian government; yet it was the "only game in town" and promised to bring the country back to civilian rule, however constraining the new rules might be. Many participated in the 1990 elections of local government secretaries and councils under the two party labels. The next year saw the election of state governors and legislators and a

National Assembly. And the process was inevitably building to the election of a president, in 1992, at which time the military would hand over power.

The process was set back late in 1992 when the regime nullified the results of the parties' efforts to produce presidential candidates. The process had indeed been so poorly handled as to justify a postponement of the process. Yet Nigerians were ever more skeptical as to whether the military really intended to leave, or were just playing an elaborate game to buy time.

Babangida scheduled a new election for June 1993, ordered the parties to produce new candidates, and set August 27, 1993, as the date for turning over power to the civilian government. Under more careful control, the parties reconvened their national conventions and nominated new candidates. The National Republican Council selected a relatively unknown figure, Bashir Tofa (a Kanuri from the northeast), while the Social Democrats nominated a rich businessman from the southwest, Moshood Abiola. Abiola was inexperienced in politics but, like Tofa, had close ties to the military hierarchy. He seemed to have an ideal combination of identities for Nigeria's plural culture: Although a Yoruba, he, like his opponent, was also a Muslim. Significantly, both had been active supporters of the NPN in the Second Republic.

The election finally took place on June 12, 1993. Nigerian and international observers reported that it was a generally fair election, certainly the cleanest Nigeria had ever seen; the NRC had not announced any plans to contest the outcome. Perhaps equally as important as its relative fairness, the election produced a unifying outcome that was everything advocates of a two-party system could have desired. Abiola, from the south, appeared to have won a majority of the votes in nine northern states, including his opponent's home state of Kano. The results seemed to suggest that, under a two-party system, factionalism in each region and state could be exploited to prevent a strictly regional outcome.

The 1993 results were never officially announced, however, and two weeks later Babangida annulled the election. Party politics, even the contrived variety invented by the Babangida regime, had once again proved to be an exercise unacceptable to the military leadership and their allies. The Abacha regime announced guidelines for the creation of new

parties in June 1996, and political entrepreneurs immediately began forming alliances, even though NADECO and other opposition groups denounced the exercise as a sham. We have seen that the five parties certified for local elections in March 1997 all nominated Abacha for the presidency.

On July 20, 1998 Abubakar announced the dissolution of the five parties, the nullification of the local and state elections, and a new start toward democracy with freely formed parties and a promise to hand over power to an elected president on May 29, 1999. A new organ, the Independent National Electoral Commission, was created to supervise the electoral process. Of the nine parties originally certified in October 1998, the three that survived the local elections represented some degree of continuity with earlier party formations—each with a base among one of the three major ethnic groups. However, because of the requirement to have a national base and for other strategic considerations, the candidates of each party were not necessarily of the ethnic group presumably dominant in it. Most importantly, even though the PDP is said to have its base in the north, its leaders threw their support for the presidential nomination to General Obasanjo, who had only recently been released from Abacha's prison. As both a southerner (both he and his principal opponent Olu Falae were Yoruba) and a former military ruler, Obasanjo was seen by many both inside and outside the country as the individual most likely to provide effective leadership in the postmilitary state. However, some of those active in the various human rights and democracy movements were dubious that a former authoritarian leader was an appropriate president for a democratic state, and his northern backing raised doubts among many southerners. And the question still remained: Would the military be ready to return to the barracks? The answer came with the inauguration of Obasanjo as president on May 29, 1999.

In order for Nigeria's third attempt at democracy to succeed, President Obasanjo's administration will have to tackle significant problems including a depleted treasury, a bureaucracy in need of retraining, ethnic and religious conflict, economic stagnation, and widespread corruption. Even though the president's party holds a majority in the National Assembly, there have been significant tensions between the executive and legislative branches. Since 1999, corruption investigations have resulted in two changes of leadership in the Senate and one in the House. In 2002, PDP members in the Assembly responded with an impeachment campaign against President Obasanjo.

The elections of April 19, 2003, in Nigeria, were the first civilian conducted elections in 20 years. This represents a big step towards the establishment of an enduring democracy in Nigeria. Although there were some complaints of irregularities, the elections were said to be "free and fair." It was the first election in Nigeria where three retired army generals contested for the Presidency. President Olusegun Obasanjo won with 62% of the votes to Muhammed Buhari's 32%; other candidates had 6% including Odumegu Ojukwu, the former seccessionist leader of Biafra, 1967–1970. Olusegun Obasanjo's PDP has performed very creditably in all the elections—Senate, House of Representatives, and the Presidency. The Nigerian people showed good judgment by voting for his party, because he performed very well during his first term. Also, it was the first time in Nigeria when 30 political parties were registered, and 20 of them contested for the Presidency.

POLICY FORMATION AND IMPLEMENTATION

Many people have stopped bothering themselves with classifying African regimes as democratic or otherwise. They instead keep asking: How much do the regimes address themselves to the needs and aspirations of the people? I am one, I tell you, all these noises about democracy and democratic are mere luxuries to the sufferers.[40]

In comparing Nigeria's various civilian and military regimes, the ultimate question must always be their *performance*. This is certainly the "bottom line" for Nigerians, whose support of these various regimes is based on the quality of life they experience under them. This section thus focuses on the *decisions* governments have made, particularly in raising revenues, dispersing funds, and implementing programs; it will also discuss some background issues such as planning and conducting the federal census, the results of which underlie all policy; and finally it presents the constraints imposed on Nigerian decision making by the outside world, particularly in the World Bank-supported **Structural Adjustment Program.** Dealing with "SAP," as the

economic restructuring program is commonly called, leads us back to the discussion of environment with which we began. Policy relating to Nigeria's international economic situation has responded to initiatives from other African countries, world powers, international organizations, and multinational firms. Here we consider the critical constraints that the world economy puts on the choices available to a Third World country, even one as large and resource-rich as Nigeria.

Extractive Performance

The tax people brought this paper, they say that, because I have a large farm, I am to get a special assessment. They say that I am *Gbajumo* (well-to-do) because I have a large farm, but they say nothing about the thirteen children and four women who depend on the farm for gari [food], no. They say I am *gbajumo* with a large farm.[41]

Nigeria inherited a fiscal system in 1960 that depended mainly on taxes on international trade. Indirect taxes provided 64 percent of total revenues, direct taxes only 16.5 percent, and other revenues 19 percent. The colonial system had developed a revenue system that operated through agricultural marketing boards. Ostensibly created to provide price stability to farmers, marketing boards accumulated surplus funds in good years that tempted government officials with development projects in mind. Peasant farmers also paid direct taxes, of which they were much more aware: Widespread tax riots broke out in the Western Region in 1968 and 1969, a period during which tax collection was halted, eventually to be replaced by a lower, much simpler flat tax.

In the First Republic and under the Gowon administration, the state governments collected the personal income, sales, and poll taxes. Tax collections generally declined as new states were created, without fiscal institutions in place and with smaller tax bases than the old regions. At the same time, rising oil revenues strengthened the fiscal position of the federal government (and those states with oil fields).

Oil production began in earnest in 1958. At independence, the federal government was collecting modest royalties from private Western oil companies. In 1971, within a few years of the Biafran War, Nigeria joined the **Organization of Petroleum**

Exporting Countries (OPEC), and also formed the **Nigerian National Oil Corporation (NNOC)** to participate directly in oil production. NNOC acquired a one-third interest in the AGIP Company and Elf, both French-controlled firms. At the time, this was seen as retribution for French support of the Biafran separatist effort, but within a few years the government had acquired a majority interest in all oil production activities. The NNOC was merged with the Ministry of Petroleum Resources to form the Nigerian National Petroleum Corporation. Over this same period (the mid-1970s), petroleum prices had risen dramatically, from $3.30 per barrel in 1972 to $21.60 in 1979. Thus the sale of crude oil directly by the Nigerian federal government to multinational oil companies came to provide the greater part of federal government revenues and, through the federal system, of state and local revenues as well.

In a pattern typical of Third World oil exporting countries, Nigeria today depends almost entirely on the revenues from this single industry. Since there is no indication that the world's appetite for oil will diminish in the near future, it is a reliable revenue source that substitutes for the various forms of taxes on private income. Nigerians are fortunate that they have not been directly burdened with the cost of supporting government programs; they are perhaps unfortunate that governments, especially authoritarian military regimes, can tap this vast wealth without risking the wrath of taxpayers. The exceptions to this general rule are enterprises and property owners in Lagos state, which has a large share of the country's modern enterprises and generates over half its revenues, and the Ogonis and other peoples who inhabit the oil-producing region, who do not feel they benefit from the natural resources of their home area.

Given their control of vast petroleum reserves, Nigerian regimes have not actively sought large amounts of direct foreign aid. Whereas low-income countries received an average of $10.20 per capita ($24.50 excluding China and India) in 1991, Nigeria's per capita aid totaled only $2.60 that year—a mere 0.8 percent of GNP. At the same time, Nigeria used its oil reserves as the collateral for massive borrowing from foreign and international banks in the 1970s and 1980s. The funds supported massive capital expenditures, and gave Nigeria an enormous external debt, which rose from 10 percent of GNP to 140.5 percent between 1980 and 1995. Oil wealth did not bring the country financial independence; quite the contrary, the debt gives international lenders a predominant voice in Nigeria's allocation of public funding.

Distributive Performance

As a producer of high-grade petroleum, Nigeria has an unusually great potential to move out of the ranks of the less developed into the middle-income nations. In the 1970s, impressive projects such as road development and irrigation projects as well as the launching of Abuja as the nation's capital were signs that potential might become reality.

Unfortunately, political corruption grew apace, and probably began consuming a higher proportion of national wealth than in the pre-oil period. When oil revenues suddenly began their decline in 1980, "corruption and mismanagement prevented any kind of disciplined adjustment," and "the economy was plunged into depression and mounting international indebtedness. . . . Sucked dry of revenue by the corruption, mismanagement, and recession, state governments became unable to pay teachers and civil servants or to purchase drugs for hospitals, and many services (including schools) were shut down by strikes."[42]

In spite of the country's raw material advantage, Nigerians have not seen their lives improve in recent years. The United Nations Development Program publishes a Human Development Index based on three factors: life expectancy at birth, adult literacy, and per capita GDP. Table 11.4 shows some development rankings for Nigeria, its immediate neighbors (Benin, Niger, and Cameroon) and a sample of other countries. Nigeria has a rank of 148 out of 173 countries on the HDI, and a rank of 157 on per capita GDP alone. It is not surprising to find the less-developed countries low on these listings. However, GDP per capita is a good measure of distributive potential; thus the comparison of per capita GDP and the HDI ratings can be an indicator of how well a country has done for its people compared with other countries with similar capacity. Although the Nigerian data are comparable to those of its neighbors and to Africa as a whole, this suggests that the Nigerian advantage in oil revenue has had little noticeable impact on the overall quality of life (Table 11.4).

TABLE 11.4   Nigeria's Ranking on GNP per Capita
and Human Development Index (HDI)

Country	Life Expectancy at Birth, 2000	Adult Literacy Rate (%) 2000	Real GDP per Capita 2000*	Human HDI 2000	Rank in per Capita GDP, 2000	Rank by HDI	Per Capita GDP-HDI
United States	77.0	99.0	34,142	.939	2	6	–4
Japan	81.0	99.0	26,755	.933	11	9	2
Britain	77.0	99.0	23,509	.928	20	13	7
Mexico	72.6	91.4	9,023	.796	55	54	1
Botswana	40.3	77.2	7,184	.572	64	126	–62
Indonesia	66.2	86.9	3,043	.684	111	110	1
China	70.5	84.1	3,976	.726	96	96	0
Cameroon	50.0	75.8	1,703	.512	135	135	0
Nigeria	51.7	63.9	896	.462	157	148	9
Benin	53.8	37.4	990	.420	154	158	–4
Niger	45.2	15.9	746	.277	168	172	–4

Note: These figures are in U.S. dollars converted at Purchasing Power Parity (PPP) rates.

Source: UN Development Program, *Human Development Report 2002*

Budgetary priorities are important in analyzing distributive performance. In the case of a country ruled by the military for most of the last decade, one might expect that military expenditures would loom especially large. This is not the case in Nigeria, where published sources put the 2000 military budget at $234 million. At the peak of General Abacha's rule, the per capita expenditure on the military was only $2 per annum, for a rank of 154 out of 160 countries. However, there are believed to be significant additional military expenditures that are not publicly reported. Extremely modest in size at independence, Nigeria's armed forces grew to 250,000 at the height of the Biafran War. Then the Gowon regime began a program of gradual attrition that reduced the force to about 100,000 in the mid-1980s. Further shrinkage since then has resulted in a total force of 77,000 . This still leaves Nigeria a major military force, and despite its use as a springboard to political power, Nigeria's army remains one of the more professional on the continent. As discussed later, Nigerian leaders have used this military strength to maintain a high profile in West Africa.

Nigerians have a great enthusiasm for education, and parties and regimes have promised universal access to it. Some progress can be noted: In 1964 Nigeria ranked twenty-ninth among African nations in enrollments, with 5 percent of the school-age population in primary school; it was nineteenth in secondary enrollments, with 5 percent of the appropriate age group in school. Ten years later, 24 percent of the school-age population was in school, and Nigeria was fifteenth in Africa on this measure. In 1990, 60 percent of the school-age population was in primary school, an impressive accomplishment given population growth in that period; but it had fallen back to nineteenth in rank on the continent. Current information about primary and secondary enrollment is scarce, but youth literacy was 87 percent in 2000, up from 65 percent in 1985.

The Nigerian government's performance in the area of health has been mediocre. The 1990 expenditure of $906 million was only $9 per capita, compared with a continent-wide average of $24. Part of this poor performance is seen in the low foreign assistance component in Nigeria's effort: Only 6 percent of its health expenditure came from that source, the third lowest proportion in Africa. But here again there has been progress in outcomes: Nigeria's infant mortality rate has dropped from 185 in 1960, to 139 in 1970, 114 in 1980, and 83 in 1999. The under-five mortality rate was 151 in 1999, however, meaning roughly 15 percent of Nigerian children do not reach the age of five.

With petroleum firmly established as the major source of foreign exchange in Nigeria, and with that industry under government control, the distribution of wealth is heavily influenced by policy decisions.

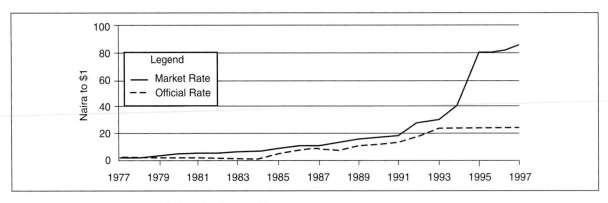

FIGURE 11.7   Naira Exchange Rate

Private consumption surged as oil revenues multiplied in the 1970s, about 8 percent per year. This average figure conceals tremendous increases in wealth at the top; the lower 40 percent of the population benefited very little. Government expenditure grew at an even greater rate than private consumption, both in absolute terms and as a proportion of GDP.[43] This aspect of expenditure, of course, includes sums lost in corrupt payments to individuals. Nigeria should have reaped another windfall during the Gulf War, as petroleum prices temporarily shot up, but increased revenues never showed up in national accounts. In 1994, economist Pius Okigbo examined the books of the Central Bank of Nigeria; he reported (as he left the country) that $12.6 billion were not accounted for. The skimming of oil profits had indeed reached astronomical proportions.

Income distribution is also affected by inflation, which followed from the rapid increase in the money supply during the 1970s oil boom and continued apace later on, as governments followed a time-honored approach to balancing budgets when revenues decline: They printed money. The result was continuous inflation, a problem that became especially serious in the 1990s, as shown in Figure 11.7. The case study (see Box 11.5) shows the effect of this inflation on individual income. Governments have attempted to deal with inflation by enforcing an official exchange rate for the **naira**—Nigeria's national currency. The result was a huge divergence in official and market exchange rates, causing chaos in the financial system. This dried up investments and stimulated corruption, since anyone with access to foreign exchange at the official rate can then sell the foreign currency "on the street" for a large profit. Since 1999, the govern-

ment has reduced its role in stabilizing the currency, along the value of the naira to be largely determined by forces of supply and demand.

As a policy issue, distribution in a large country such as Nigeria is also seen as a geographic question, not just one of policy priorities. Nigerians have a fondness for referring to the national budget as the "national cake," and they see state and local governments as the major recipients of slices. The federal government now spends between two-thirds and three-fourths of public monies, and also has great control over how the money distributed to state and local governments will be spent. On the contentious question of how to distribute resources as the number of states and local governments expanded, governments settled on relatively straightforward formulas, a combination of equality (across-the-board distributions to all states) and population. States other than Lagos now depend on the federal Revenue Allocation System (RAS) for 70 to 90 percent of their recurrent revenues. In order to fund local governments, the RAS was extended to cover them directly in 1981. Beginning in 1982, federal revenues were shared according to set percentages among the three levels of government. Given the set formulas in the RAS, it is not surprising that regions and localities strive for statehood and local autonomy, and that population counts loom large as a political issue.

Dealing with Debt and Structural Adjustment

During the 1970s oil boom, insufficient attention was paid to the productivity of the uses to which public funds were put. Much of the money was ap-

BOX 11.5   The Effects of Inflation: A Case Study

A young graduate with a new doctoral degree won a position as an instructor at a Nigerian university in 1977. His salary and benefits totaled 6,000 naira per year. At that time, one naira equaled $1.50, so his salary was the equivalent of $9,000—modest by industrial-world standards but very comfortable in Nigeria. Twenty years later, this same man achieved the rank of full professor, at a salary of 51,000 naira per year, with fringe benefits raising his total annual compensation to 90,000 naira. However, at the parallel market exchange rate of 80 naira to the dollar, his salary was the equivalent of $1,125 per year, a figure not taking into account the effect of inflation on

the purchasing power of the dollar since 1977. In 1998, a national review of faculty salaries increased the professor's salary to the equivalent of $5,000 per year. This discussion implies that salaries are regularly paid. However, in early 1999, the Abubakar government was in such financial straits that it failed to provide salary payments at all. In 2000 President Obasanjo improved the workers' pay generally and moved University teachers' pay to 130,000 Naira per month, the equivalent of $1000 dollars per month. He did this to discourage brain drain in Nigeria and to promote high level productivity in all sectors.

---

plied to an increase in welfare expenditures, to developing an unprofitable steel industry, and to building the new capital at **Abuja.** Late in the 1970s, commodity prices fell, while oil prices remained high; African governments borrowed at an even faster pace, and the continent's total indebtedness increased between 1978 and 1982 from $27 billion to $72 billion. As African governments became unable to make debt payments, international financial institutions, principally the International Monetary Fund (IMF) and the World Bank, were called in to monitor a restructuring and rescheduling of the debt. Nigeria's total indebtedness continued to increase in the 1980s, from $8.9 billion in 1980 to $34.5 billion in 1991; by 1991 it represented 257 percent of the annual value of the country's exports and 109 percent of GNP. The annual cost of servicing the debt consumed 25 percent of the value of exports (up from 4 percent in 1980); the weight of this burden almost ensured that the debt would continue to grow. Throughout the past decade, the question of how to deal with the external debt has been a principal focus of political discussion in Nigeria.

The debt problem that began under military rule became much more acute during the Second Republic (1979–1983). The Buhari regime approached the IMF for relief in the form of new loans and more favorable repayment terms but rejected the severe conditions the IMF attached to its help: The naira would have to be devalued, trade restrictions would have to be dropped, and subsidies for domestic gasoline consumption ended. These and similar measures have been the issues involved in

Nigeria's Structural Adjustment Program (SAP). It was clear to the military leadership that such measures would be extremely unpopular with the Nigerian public and would lead to outbursts of political violence. When Ibrahim Babangida seized power in 1985, he opened a "national debate" on the issue. He claimed to fashion a Nigerian version of structural adjustment (while at the same time negotiating with the IMF). As the program's austerity measures began to be felt, the SAP became extremely unpopular. In his parallel program of moving back toward civilian rule, Babangida forbade candidates to criticize the program, but at the same time he eased off on the necessary austerity measures. The net result was that, although Nigerians were suffering from the country's poor position in international finance, the SAP did not reduce the debt or reform the financial system. Rather than allow the naira to float as urged by the IMF, the Abacha regime maintained the official exchange rate of 22 naira to the dollar, a decision certainly supported by those who were able to take advantage of it. In 1995 the exchange rate was partially opened to market forces, but the N22 to $1 exchange rate was maintained for government transactions. This neither stabilized the economy nor satisfied the international sector. The total external debt reached almost $8 billion, and the Nigerian National Petroleum Corporation owed over $1 billion to its foreign partners. In responding to gasoline shortages, however, the government lowered the subsidy on petroleum products. Nigeria once had the lowest fuel prices in the world, but in 1994 gasoline prices were raised 400 percent—still at the lower end of the range of prices in the world. Holding the price down had deprived the country of gasoline, as stocks were spirited over the borders to fetch higher prices or sold along the roadside at "unofficial" prices. However, the sharp price rise seemed one more hardship to endure for those on low and fixed incomes, already suffering from rapid inflation. The discomfort increased when extreme fuel shortages reappeared in 1997. Long lines at official stations prompted a black market rate of up to 80 naira ($3.60) per liter, or about seven times the normal price; the shortage was attributed to deteriorating conditions in Nigeria's four refineries as well as to mismanagement and diversion of maintenance funds and to massive smuggling of petroleum out of the country for personal profit by high-placed government officials.

There could hardly be a more dramatic demonstration of policy failure: a country rich in petroleum incapable of providing its citizens with fuel. In 1998 the Abubakar government imposed a variety of measures to remedy the situation, from severe penalties for fuel diversion to emergency funds to repair refineries and pay for increased imports of refined petroleum. The government also raised the price at the pump from 11 to 25 naira per liter. At the same time, the government and its partner oil companies were bedeviled by increasing unrest and violence in the oil-producing areas and against the pumping operations themselves. By late 1998 these disruptions were having a serious impact on Nigerian oil production, a situation that complicated the inauguration of a stable civilian government. After President Obasanjo was inaugurated in May 1999, he tried to bring calm to the situation by voiding all contracts awarded in the six months prior to his administration. Since then, each attempt by the government in 2000, 2001, and 2002 to raise the price at the pump has been met with the return of lines at filling stations. Efforts to reduce government spending by eliminating the petroleum subsidy for domestic consumption remain highly controversial because it impacts not only the cost of public transportation but also food and other daily essentials.

Regulative Performance

At independence in 1960, the Nigeria Police Force was essentially regionalized. Because the police were frequently mobilized for political purposes during the rough and tumble politics of the 1960s, the military regime decided to consolidate the police function at the national level. It is this national police force that now enforces traffic laws and other government legislation. However, it is often still the case that "law and order" is maintained in individual communities—especially in rural areas—through traditional institutions and norms. Traditional leaders not only prevent deviant behavior but also take responsibility for the welfare of the "strangers" who, in accord with accepted procedures, have taken up residence in their communities.

Although Nigeria was under military rule from 1983 to 1999, the average citizen has not felt oppressed by an authoritarian state. That citizen is aware of the police presence at checkpoints along the country's highways, but fear of authority does not restrict the citizen's actions to any degree. As in most Third World countries, there simply are not the resources available to the Nigerian government to keep close tabs on its large population.

Nigeria's judicial system remains vigorous, and until the advent of Abacha's reign it had been surprisingly diligent at following a rule of law through the various informally constituted regimes. Still, military regimes intruded on that rule of law. The regime imposed the State Security (Detention of Persons) Decree in 1984, which allows detention without trial of those "suspected of posing a threat to national security." State officials seemed to intervene with increasing frequency into the judicial system where political questions are involved.

Freedom of expression was reduced even further as Sani Abacha held onto power. Repression touched members of the political and military elite and internationally famous figures who hitherto had appeared to be safe. In 1994, writer Wole Soyinka was prevented from leaving the country by air, and his passport was seized. (He later slipped across the border and criticized the regime from abroad until after Abacha's death.) Prominent political prisoners under Abacha included former head of state (and future president) Olusegun Obasanjo and Moshood Abiola and former presidential candidate Shehu Yar'Adua. Abacha showed himself to be unconcerned about international opinion in allowing the execution of Ken Saro-Wiwa in the face of an international outcry and in ignoring Pope John Paul II's plea for release of political prisoners during a 1998 visit.

The Census Issue.   One policy issue has overshadowed all the others since independence, because the outcome often determines how political goods will be distributed. A minor policy issue in some countries, in Nigeria population counts have been fraught with conflict. In a country where federal subsidies make up the lion's share of budgetary allocations at all levels, the distribution of population directly affects the distribution of resources. (Americans will recognize a similar issue that arose concerning undercounting of some ethnic groups and the homeless after the 1990 census in the United States, and in the debate over whether to use representative samples rather than the whole population in some aspects of the 2000 census.)

After a false start in 1962, a national census was conducted in 1963. It reported a total population of 55.6 million, making Nigeria the tenth largest country in the world. However, it found a majority of that population (30 million) to be in the north, a finding that was then and is always questioned by southern Nigerians, who maintain that a flyover or drive through the north and south will easily demonstrate that population densities are higher in the latter (although it is also true that the area of the north is much greater). Nevertheless, the 1963 census, or straight-line projections from it, remained the official source of population statistics for almost 20 years. At the same time, voices are continually raised in favor of a new "fair" count in the regions that perceive themselves undercounted.

> In 1973, General Gowon's Supreme Military Council attempted a census update, and ordered that enumerators be accompanied by unarmed soldiers. With the prestige and integrity of the armed forces behind the count, the resulting figures presumably could be trusted, and used for economic planning, electoral preparation, and military disengagement. Gowon's optimism was misplaced. The 1973 census figures, when finally released, appeared as politically manipulated and inflated as the discredited results of a decade earlier. . . . Apparent overcounting in certain areas, especially in the north, revived the latent fears of regional domination that periodically roil Nigerian politics.[44]

After almost two additional decades of continued reliance on the 1963 figures, the Babangida government commissioned a new census to be conducted by a National Population Commission. Following methodical pretesting and sampling, a census in November 1991 put the country's total population at 88.5 million, a substantial downward revision from estimates that had exceeded 100 million. According to this census, the highest population concentrations were in the states of Bauchi, Kaduna, Kano, Katsina, and Sokoto in the north, and Lagos, Oyo, and Rivers in the south. The census caused new consternation in the south, where feelings ran high that the figures had again been "cooked" to favor the north.

Conclusions on Performance

While our judgments on performance should be nuanced given the complexity of Nigeria's political environment and the problems it faces, an overall conclusion emerges unfailingly. In comparison to other countries with equivalent natural resources, skilled human resources, and size, Nigeria has not done well.

That outcome caused Chinua Achebe to write *The Problem with Nigeria,* in which he concluded that the "problem" was leadership. Until Nigerians can settle on a constitutional arrangement that provides responsive leadership from the national to the local level, the country will continue to fall far short of its potential. Although the Second Republic failed, it was a significant improvement over the first in reining in the politicization of ethnicity. There was reason to be optimistic that the constitution developed in the later years of the Babangida regime would introduce another increment of correction. Although Abubakar was able to move the country to civilian rule, his decision to base the transition on the poorly articulated constitution drafted under Abacha in 1995 did not inspire confidence in most Nigerians that the new regime would be based on the rule of law. Democracy cannot be "delivered" by a military regime; indeed, further progress in democratization will depend on the formation and maintenance of a coalition with the strength to force the country in that direction.

A fatal flaw in political culture may have developed in Nigeria since independence, and it is part of the "curse of oil": public policy is often seen in Nigeria as the "national cake," and the unfortunate analogy suggests that "they"—the government— bake a cake that is distributed in slices sized to match the political influence of various constituencies. At least at the mass level, constituencies are defined in ethnic terms, and politics becomes a competition among ethnic groups for larger slices of cake. The analogy could of course be used to describe the politics of many countries, but not to the extreme degree that it applies in Nigeria. There, communities look to the government to provide for them. A successful Nigerian constitution must not only provide responsive leaders; it must also shift responsibility so that extractive and distributive performance come from the same budget, and so that there is some relationship between the amounts one pays into and receives from the public sector. Public goals based on community effort were the norm in most Nigerian traditions; that norm must be rediscovered.

NIGERIA IN AFRICA AND IN THE WORLD

Nigeria (now along with South Africa) has the population and resource base to be a regional power, and it has stimulated hopes and fears among its neighbors concerning that potential. Under the First Republic (1960–1966), Nigeria generally focused inward and played a rather minor role in the continent's turbulent politics. But then came the civil war over Biafra in 1966; Nigeria's army grew from 10,000 to 250,000, the country's oil potential became known, and, as we have seen earlier, world powers took an interest in the war's outcome.

Some West African governments offered clear support to Biafra, a support Nigerians suspected grew from a desire to see their country divided up and thus reduced in influence. This was thought especially to be the case with Cote d'Ivoire (the Ivory Coast) under President Houphouet-Boigny, who favored Biafra with French support. When the war ended, relations among these countries were, as might be expected, strained.

Subsequently, Nigeria under General Gowon took a leading role in establishing, in 1975, the **Economic Community of West African States (ECOWAS),** hoping both to bring Nigeria closer to other West African countries while at the same time countering French influence in the region. The Ivoirian government had taken the lead in forming the Economic Community of West Africa, an exclusively French-speaking organization, and was wary of the predominant position that Nigeria might play in a

wider regional organization. But Nigeria was successful in first approaching Togo, Benin, and Niger, the French-speaking countries with which it already had close ties, offering attractive economic inducements that included special petroleum prices. With this group in hand, Nigerian diplomats cast their net wider, and the representatives of 16 West African governments signed the Treaty of Lagos. The ECOWAS treaty specified a two-year phase during which intracommunity tariffs would be frozen, followed by an eight-year period that would end with the removal of duties on trade among members. Finally, a common external tariff wall would be created.

Thus, West Africa under Nigerian leadership is partaking in the worldwide movement toward free-trade zones. As elsewhere, however, progress has been difficult. Ten years after its creation, ECOWAS reported that it had not made "tangible progress in practical terms," and by 1989 the member governments were $80 million in arrears in their contributions to the organization. The proportion of intracommunity trade in the member countries' total international trade has not changed since 1980. At the same time, ECOWAS has had better success as a regional political organization, especially in mediating disputes among member states, and in 1990 a Nigerian proposal was approved that created a Standing Mediation Committee.[45]

Nigeria has played a prominent role in the region through commitment of its substantial military capacity, notably in supplying the leadership and the majority of troops for ECOMOG, the ECOWAS-sponsored peacekeeping force in Liberia. That operation was viewed a success, with armed conflict halted and elections held. Nigerian troops have also been stationed in Sierra Leone to protect that country's borders from incursions of Liberian rebels, and have confronted a Sierra Leonean military junta that overthrew an elected civilian government, an action more than a bit ironic, given the origins of the Abacha regime. Nigeria has participated in wider-ranging United Nations operations in Lebanon, Rwanda, the former Yugoslavia, and Somalia. However, as in other countries, these overseas deployments are seriously questioned at home, given the country's financial difficulties.

Because of its prominence on the continent, Nigeria's international financial problems have been especially embarrassing. Forced along with other African nations to accept stringent structural adjustment planning from the World Bank and International Monetary Fund, Nigeria has reacted with frustration and anger and has led the region's governments in their critique of international lenders' policies, hosting the meeting that led to the Lagos Plan of Action as a response to international debt-structuring proposals.

Of all the world powers, France plays the most prominent role in West Africa. Although the French interest focuses on its own former colonies, in recent years the French believe that Nigeria's size and potential wealth should not be overlooked, and France actively promotes closer economic ties with Nigeria, a move that upsets Nigeria's French-speaking neighbors. The Western powers, especially Britain and the United States, were openly critical of Nigeria's military rulers and supported the country's return to civilian rule, especially during the Babangida regime and once again with Abdulsalami Abubakar. The United States and Britain condemned Babangida's 1993 election annulment, and they suspended aid as a result. However, this relationship was not important enough to Nigeria's rulers to modify their behavior. Presumably an embargo on purchases of Nigerian oil would have had that effect, but the industrial nations' governments did not have the will to take such a drastic step. Most observers saw the Abacha regime's treatment of dissenters as a calculation of how far they could silence opposition without provoking more severe international sanctions. In contrast, many Nigerians were critical of what they saw as the West's premature enthusiasm over actions that until then were only *promised* by Abubakar in 1998. Western support returned with enthusiasm upon Obasanjo's inauguration.

PROSPECTS FOR DEVELOPMENT

Nigeria's political and economic setbacks do not equal the tragedies of Rwanda or Somalia, but the frustrations are nonetheless deep and enduring. Billions of desperately needed naira have been wasted, a few have grown rich at the expense of the poor, and accountability in government has proved highly elusive. Poet Tanure Ojaide captured this frustration in "No Longer Our Own Country," written in 1986:

> We have lost it,
> the country we were born into.

> We can now sing dirges
> of that commonwealth of yesterday—
> we live in a country
> that is no longer our own.[46]

In much of the world, the attraction of democracy has been its association with prosperity. Like other people, Nigerians are more interested in the outcome of the political process than in the process itself. Calls for better leadership and the welcome initially extended to some military regimes suggest that Nigerians' highest priorities are economic security and the rule of law. If these could be provided by generals, the country would probably accept an authoritarian system. However, at least since Plato we have known that benevolent authoritarianism is an elusive concept. Western democracies have developed on the premise that democracy is a necessary, if not sufficient, condition for accountable leadership. And Nigerians have had enough opportunities to compare the results of military rule with their expectations so that a majority of them are ready for another try at elective civilian rule. Perhaps another constitutional correction will be enough to usher in the long-term political stability for which they have hoped.

We have focused the above discussion on those aspects of the Nigerian situation most amenable to correction. There remain several rather intractable problems that will only be overcome with truly revolutionary change. Larry Diamond has identified as a central problem for Nigeria the relationship between the economy and the state. In his words, "Stable democracy is associated with an autonomous, indigenous bourgeoisie, and inversely associated with extensive state control over the economy. In Nigeria, and throughout much of Africa, the swollen state has turned politics into a zero-sum game in which everything of value is at stake in an election, and hence candidates, communities, and parties feel compelled to win at any cost."[47] The answer appears to be the emergence of a vigorous private sector less dependent on government subsidies and freed from the kind of patronage costs that have drained the initiative and resources of the private sector. In West Africa and the world, Nigerians have a reputation for entrepreneurship. The challenge is to reduce the role of government to that of providing necessary infrastructure and public welfare safety nets so that Nigerian entrepreneurial initiative can thrive. Oil revenues remain critical. As the sense of public duty among some of the military elite declined from Gowon and Murtala to Babangida and Abacha, a subculture developed among officer ranks that can be identified as "when do I get my turn?" Such corruption of values is common, but the availability of oil revenues means that authoritarian leaders need not seek their rents directly from the populace. Rather, they have learned that all they must do is control the spigot and the narrow slice of the population that operates and protects it, and opponents will be helpless. The oil workers' unions and the people whose homelands are located where the drilling is done must be neutralized; the rest could safely be ignored.

Mancur Olson observed that "resolute autocrats can survive even when they impose heinous amounts of suffering upon their peoples. When they are replaced it is for other reasons (e.g., succession crises) and often by another stationary bandit." He then concluded that democracy appears under "historical conditions and dispersions of resources that make it impossible for any one leader or group to assume all power."[48] These conditions are not close at hand for Nigeria, with its economy overwhelmingly dependent on oil and the state's resources controlled directly by the regime. In this situation, interactions among the military become supremely important. Abubakar proved not to be "another stationary bandit," but instead represented a faction of military leaders with no taste for politics and a desire to re-professionalize the military services. Had he and his supporters not taken a longer-term view than Abacha, the continued existence of Nigeria as a single state would have been in doubt. After more than 15 years of continuous military rule and a great deal of oppression and misgovernment, there is hope that the Obasanjo administration may be able to achieve success in a diverse country like Nigeria, President Olusegun Obasanjo embarked on the privatization model. This model has achieved success in the areas of telephone and domestic transportation. Other areas in which very substantial progress has been made are: water, housing, and electricity. Nigeria is gradually becoming a service-oriented country, but it will take a while before the people will adjust.

KEY TERMS

Sani Abacha
Moshood Abiola
Abdulsalami Abubakar
Abuja
Nnamdi Azikiwe
Ibrahim Babangida
Biafra
clientelism, patron-client network
Economic Community of West African States (ECOWAS)
Hausa, Hausa-Fulani
Igbo (Ibo)
Independent National Election Commission (INEC)
Kaduna Mafia
Lagos
naira
National Election Commission (NEC)
National Union of Petroleum and Gas Workers (NUPENG)
neocolonial
Nigerian National Oil Corporation (NNOC)
Olusegun Obasanjo
Organization of Petroleum Exporting Countries (OPEC)
Saro-Wiwa, Ken
Structural Adjustment Program (SAP)
Yoruba

INTERNET SOURCES

National Orientation and Public Affairs Website: **http://www.nopa.net/**
Federal Government of Nigeria: **http://www.nigeria.gov.ng/**

Current information on Nigeria, including news from the major daily papers in Lagos, can be obtained through the Nigeria page of *Africa South of the Sahara: Selected Internet Resources*: **http://www-sul.stanford.edu/depts/ssrg/africa/guide.html**

SUGGESTED READINGS

Abernethy, David B. *The Political Dilemma of Popular Education: An African Case*. Stanford, CA: Stanford University Press, 1969.

Achebe, Chinhua. *A Man of the People*. New York: Doubleday-Anchor, 1967.

———. *The Trouble with Nigeria*. Enugu: Fourth Dimension Press, 1983.

Beckett, Paul, and Crawford Young, eds. *Dilemmas of Democracy in Nigeria*. Rochester, NY: University of Rochester University Press, 1997.

Coleman, James S. *Nigeria: Background to Nationalism*. Berkeley: University of California Press, 1958.

Crowder, Michael. *The Story of Nigeria,* 4th ed. London: Faber and Faber, 1978.

Diamond, Larry. *Class, Ethnicity, and Democracy in Nigeria: The Failure of the First Republic.* Syracuse, NY: Syracuse University Press, 1988.

———. "Nigeria: Pluralism, Statism and the Struggle for Democracy." In Larry Diamond et al., eds., *Democracy: Africa.* Boulder, CO: Lynne Rienner, 1988, pp. 33–91.

Diamond, Larry, Anthony Kirk-Greene, and O. Oyediran, eds. *Transition Without End: Nigerian Politics and Civil Society Under Babangida.* Boulder, CO: Lynne Rienner, 1997.

Dudley, Billy. *An Introduction to Nigerian Government and Politics.* Bloomington: University of Indiana Press, 1982.

Gordon, David F. "Debt, Conditionality, and Reform: The International Relations of Economic Restructuring in Sub-Saharan Africa." In Thomas M. Callaghy and John Ravenhill, eds., *Hemmed In: Responses to Africa's Economic Decline.* New York: Columbia University Press, 1993, pp. 90–129.

Graf, William D. *The Nigerian State: Political Economy, State Class and Political System in the Post-Colonial Era.* Portsmouth, NH: Heinemann Educational Books, 1988.

Guyer, Jane I. "The Spatial Dimensions of Civil Society in Africa: An Anthropologist Looks at Nigeria." In John W. Harbeson, Donald Rothchild, and Naomi Chazan, eds., *Civil Society and the State in Africa.* Boulder, CO: Lynne Rienner, 1994, pp. 215–29.

Joseph, Richard A. *Democracy and Prebendal Politics in Nigeria: The Rise and Fall of the Second Republic.* Cambridge, England: Cambridge University Press, 1987.

Kane, Ousmane. "The Rise of Muslim Reformism in Northern Nigeria: IZALA (The Society for the Removal of Heresy and Reinstatement of Tradition)," In Martin Marty and Scott Appleby, eds., *Accounting for Fundamentalisms.* Chicago: University of Chicago Press, 1994.

Koehn, Peter H. *Public Policy and Administration in Africa: Lessons from Nigeria.* Boulder, CO: Westview, 1990.

Lewis, Peter M., Pearl T. Robinson, and Barnett R. Rubin. *Stabilizing Nigeria: Sanctions, Incentives, and Support for Civil Society.* Washington: Brookings Institution Press, 1998.

Metz, Helen Chapin, Ed. *Nigeria: A Country Study,* (5th ed.) Washington: U.S. Government Printing Office, 1992.

Nafziger, E. Wayne. *The Economics of Political Instability: The Nigeria-Biafran War.* Boulder, CO: Westview, 1983.

Normandy, Elizabeth. "Nigeria." In Mark W. Delancey, ed., *Handbook of Political Science Research on Sub-Saharan Africa.* Westport, CT: Greenwood Press, 1992.

Ogbondah, Chris W. *Military Regimes and the Press in Nigeria, 1966–1993.* Lanham, MD: University Press of America, 1994.

Ohiorhenuan, John F. E. *Capital and the State in Nigeria.* New York: Greenwood Press, 1989.

Olagunju, Tunji, Adele Jinadu, and Sam Oyovbaire. *Transition to Democracy in Nigeria (1985–1993).* Ibadan, Nigeria: Safari Books, 1993.

Olayiwola, Peter O. *Petroleum and Structural Change in a Developing Country: The Case of Nigeria.* New York: Praeger, 1987.

Oyediran, O., ed. *Nigerian Government and Politics Under Military Rule 1968–79.* London: Macmillan, 1979.

Oyewole, Anthony. *Historical Dictionary of Nigeria.* Metuchen, NJ: Scarecrow Press, 1987.

Publius: The Journal of Federalism 21, No. 4 (Fall 1991) [special issue on Nigeria].

Soyinka, Wole. *AkÈ: The Years of Childhood.*

Suberu, Rotimi T. 1994. "The Travails of Federalism in Nigeria." In Larry Diamond and Marc F. Plattner, eds., *Nationalism, Ethnic Conflict, and Democracy.* Baltimore: Johns Hopkins University Press, 1994, pp. 56–70.

ENDNOTES

1. Clifford Geertz, *Old Societies and New States: The Quest for Modernity in Asia and Africa* (New York: Free Press of Glencoe, 1963).

2. Because Africans have frequently referred to their ethnic groups as "tribes" and to the conflicts among those groups as "tribalism" these terms seem appropriate to our discussion of ethnicity in Nigeria. The problem from an outside perspective is that the term tribe has been applied indiscriminately to small groups of villages or whole empires, and often in conjunction with the adjective "primitive." Thus "tribe" has lost any specific meaning and imparts prejudicial notions. One may ask whether, if the Yoruba or Igbo of Nigeria are tribes (of 30 or 40 million), are not the less numerous peoples known as Norwegians or Irish also tribes? What is the distinction? And if ethnic conflict in Africa is "tribalism," the same phenomenon in Yugoslavia, Britain, Germany, or the United States deserves the same label.

3. This discussion relies principally on A. Oyewole, *Historical Dictionary of Nigeria* (Metuchen, NJ: Scarecrow Press, 1987); Michael Crowder, *The Story of Nigeria,* 4th ed. (London: Faber and Faber, 1978); and James S. Coleman, *Nigeria: Background to Nationalism* (Berkeley: University of California Press, 1958).

4. Crowder, *The Story of Nigeria.*

5. Peter Enahoro, *How to be a Nigerian* (Ibadan, Nigeria: Caxton Press, 1966), p. 2.

6. Chinua Achebe, *Arrow of God* (Garden City, NY: Anchor Books, 1967) p. 65.

7. Wole Soyinka, *AkÉ: The Years of Childhood* (Ibadan, Nigeria: Spectrum Books, 1981) p. 200

8. Billy Dudley, *An Introduction to Nigerian Government and Politics* (Bloomington: University of Indiana Press, 1982), p. 230.

9. World Bank, *World Development Report 2001,* "World Development Indicators," (Washington: World Bank, 2000), p. 49.

10. Patrick Smith, "Economy" in *Africa South of the Sahara 1994* (London: Europa Publications, 1994), p. 660

11. "Abuja Faces Population Explosion Crisis," *This Day,* September 12, 2002.

12. E. Wayne Nafziger, *The Economics of Political Instability: The Nigeria-Biafra War* (Boulder, CO, Westview, 1983), p. 73.

13. Samuel P. Huntington, *The Clash of Civilizations and the Remaking of World Order* (Simon and Schuster, 1996), pp. 255–56. See also, Naomi Chazan and Victor T. Levin, "Africa and the Middle East: Patterns of Convergence and Divergence," in John W. Harbeson and Donald Rothchild, eds., *Africa in World Politics* (Boulder, CO: Westview Press, 1991), p. 208. The Census of 1963 found the population to be 47 percent Muslim, and 34 percent Christian, with 18.2 percent following African religions. However, the census figures are widely suspect, and the distinction between a Christian or Muslim and a traditional believer is quite arbitrary.

14. Barbara J. Callaway, *Muslim Hausa Women in Nigeria* (Syracuse, NY: Syracuse University Press, 1987), p. 93.

15. Chazan and Levine, "Africa and the Middle East," p. 207.

16. For earlier evidence of this same pattern see Sidney Verba, "The Parochial and the Polity," in Sidney Verba and Lucian Pye, eds., *The Citizen and Politics: A Comparative Perspective* (Stamford, CT: Greylock Publishers, 1978), pp. 3–28.

17. Robert A. Dahl, *After the Revolution* (New Haven, CT: Yale University Press, 1971); see also the discussion in Billy Dudley, *An Introduction to Nigerian Government and Politics* (Bloomington: Indiana University Press, 1982), pp. 80–83.

18. Larry Diamond, "Nigeria: Pluralism, Statism and the Struggle for Democracy," in Larry Diamond et al., eds., *Democracy in Africa* (Boulder, CO: Lynne Rienner, 1988), pp. 33–91.

19. Paul Beckett and James O'Connell, *Education and Power in Nigeria* (London: Hodder and Stoughton, 1977).

20. P. C. Lloyd, "The Yoruba of Nigeria," in James L. Gibbs, Jr., ed., *Peoples of Africa* (New York: Holt, Rinehart, and Winston, 1965), p. 565.

21. See the discussion in Billy Dudley, *An Introduction to Nigerian Government and Politics* (Bloomington: University of Indiana Press, 1982), pp. 80–83.

22. Chinua Achebe, *The Trouble with Nigeria* (Enugu, Nigeria, Fourth Dimension Press, 1983), p. 42.

23. The discussion that follows draws on Crawford Young's treatment of socialization in his chapter on "Politics in Africa" in earlier editions of this book.

24. In anthropological usage, polygamy is a general term for marriage to more than one spouse. Polygamy is preferred to describe the marriage of one man to more than one woman (and polyandry for the reverse). However, polygamy is the term in general use in Nigeria and elsewhere in English-speaking Africa.

25. David B. Abernethy, *The Political Dilemma of Popular Education* (Stanford, CA: Stanford University Press, 1969), p. 18. The description of education development that follows draws on this same source.

26. *Statistics of Education in Nigeria 1985–89* (Lagos, Nigeria: Federal Ministry of Education, 1990), p. 7

27. Afrobarometer Survey, "Attitudes Toward Democracy and Markets in Nigeria," 2000. United States Department of State, "Country Reports on Human Rights Practices: Nigeria," March 4, 2002. Committee to Protect Journalists, "Attacks on the Press 2001."

28. Peter Enahoro, *The Complete Nigerian,* (Lagos, Nigeria: Malthouse Press, 1992), p. 121.

29. Ousmane Kane, "The Rise of Muslim Reformism in Northern Nigeria," in Martin Marty and Scot Appleby, eds., *Accounting for Fundamentalism* (Chicago: University of Chicago Press, 1994).

30. Peter H. Koehn, *Public Policy and Administration in Africa* (Boulder, CO: Westview, 1990), p.16.

31. As noted in Chapter 5, the concept of consociational arrangement comes from Arend Lijphart, *Democracy in Plural Societies* (New Haven: Yale U.P., 1977).

32. Keohn, *Public Policy and Administration in Africa*, pp. 17–18, cites various sources for these totals.

33. Soyinka, Ake, pp. 199–200.

34. Richard Sklar and C. S. Whitaker, Jr., "Nigeria," in James S. Coleman and Carl G. Rosberg, Jr., eds. *Political Parties and National Integration in Tropical Africa* (Berkeley: University of California Press, 1964), p. 636.

35. Richard A. Joseph, Democracy and Prebendal Politics in Nigeria (Cambridge, England: Cambridge University Press, 1987), pp. 133–34.

36. Joseph, *Democracy and Prebendal Policy in Nigeria*. Joseph calls the Nigerian version of patronage prebendalism, "patterns of political behavior which rest on the justifying principle that such offices should be competed for and then utilized for the personal benefit of officeholders as well as for their reference or support group. The official public purpose of the office often becomes a secondary concern, however much that purpose may have been originally cited in its creation or during the periodic competition to fill it" (p. 8).

37. This account of party development through the first years of independence is taken from Sklar and Whitaker, "Nigeria."

38. "Cameroons" here refers to the English-speaking portion of the contemporary country of Cameroon (French Cameroun) on Nigeria's eastern border. The former German colony of that name was divided into League of Nations Trust Territories after World War I under British and French control. The NCNC was meant to include members from the British trust territory as well as from Nigeria, but in a pre-independence plebiscite, the English-speaking Cameroonians opted for incorporation into Cameroon. The NCNC then was renamed the National Convention of Nigerian Citizens.

39. Address of Brigadier Murtala Muhammed, reprinted as the preface to the *Report of the Constitution Drafting Committee* (Lagos, Nigeria: Ministry of Information, 1976), quoted in Dudley, *Introduction to Nigerian Government,* p. 127.

40. Letter to the editor, *Lagos,* 1983; quoted in Joseph, *Democracy and Prebendal Politics in Nigeria.*

41. Wole Soyinka, *AkÉ: The Years of Childhood,* p. 201

42. Larry Diamond, "Nigeria," p. 53.

43. I. William Zartman, with Sayre Schatz, "Introduction," in I. William Zartman, ed. The Political Economy of Nigeria (New York: Praeger, 1983), p. 13. The military figures cited above come from Ruth Sivard, "World Military and Social Expenditures 1996," (Leesburg, VA: WMSE Publications, 1996) and "The Military Balance 2001–2002" (London: Oxford University Press, 2001).

44. Claude E. Welch, *No Farewell to Arms?* (Boulder, CO: Westview, 1987), p. 10.

45. The preceding treatment of ECOWAS' formation is drawn from Carol Lancaster, "The Lagos Three: Economic Regionalism in Sub-Saharan Africa," in John W. Harbeson and Donald Rothchild, eds. *Africa in World Politics* (Boulder, CO, Westview Press, 1991), pp. 249–67.

46. Tanure Ojaide, *The Blood of Peace and Other Poems* (London: Heinemann, 1991), p. 9.

47. Diamond, "Nigeria", p. 69.

48. Mancur Olson, "Dictatorship, Democracy and Development," *American Political Science Review* 87 (September 3) : 573.

12

Politics in Russia

Thomas F. Remington

COUNTRY BIO—RUSSIA

Population:	145 Million	**Head of Government:**	Premier Mikhail Efimovich Fradkov
Territory:	17 million square kilometers	**Language(s):**	Russian, other
Year of Independence:	1991	**Religion:**	Russian Orthodox 70–80%, Muslim 8–9%, Buddhist 0.6%, Jewish 0.3%
Year of Current Constitution:	1993		
Chief of State:	President Vladimir Vladimirovich Putin		

REBUILDING RUSSIA

The year 2000 opened with a dramatic change of leadership in Russia. On December 31, 1999, President **Boris Yeltsin** appeared on Russian national television to announce that he was resigning as president of Russia as of midnight. Although Yeltsin's term was not due to expire until June 2000, he had decided to leave office early and turn the powers of the presidential office over to his prime minister, Vladimir Putin, who under the constitution was Yeltsin's successor. Just completed parliamentary elections had confirmed Putin's political strength. Yeltsin's departure gave Putin a strong advantage in the upcoming presidential election, which according to the constitution had to be held within three months of the president's leaving office. Putin's very first decree as acting president was to grant Yeltsin and his family lifetime immunity from all criminal prosecution. The manner in which the succession occurred was not illegal, but it reflected an unseemly bargain: Yeltsin was giving Putin the presidency in return for security for himself and his family.

Yeltsin's departure marked the end of a turbulent decade during which Russia struggled to shed its Communist past and create a new political and economic system. The change in regime from communism to democracy occurred largely without bloodshed, but produced an intense and protracted behind-the-scenes fight over power and property. Social inequality exploded: a handful of people grew fabulously wealthy from the privatization of state assets. At the same time, over 40 percent of the population sank into poverty as unemployment rose and high inflation destroyed incomes and savings. The social safety net wore thin. Crime and corruption proliferated. Discipline and accountability in the state bureaucracy—which had deteriorated in the late Communist period—broke down still further. The government attempted to carry out a far-reaching program of fiscal and monetary reform, but with only limited success. Entrenched bureaucratic interests fought at every turn to subvert the government's plans. Many people bitterly reflected that the expansion of democratic freedoms had brought more misery than progress.

Meantime Russians had to adjust to the fact that their country was no longer a great empire consisting of 15 ethnically diverse, nominally sovereign republics forming a single union. Now it was an independent state and its neighbors were likewise free and independent under international law. The political controls that the Communist Party had exercised over the economy, property, culture, and political decision making were gone. New institutions for coordinating the behavior of the citizens and territories of the country had not yet taken hold. The state was extremely weak, a problem made all the more serious because even after the dissolution of the Soviet Union, Russia was still by far the largest country in the world in physical expanse. Maintaining the unity of the country under those conditions was a severe challenge. President Putin's first priority, therefore, has been to restore order by recentralizing state power.

Russia's transition posed an especially serious challenge to governance because the breakdown of the Communist regime ended many of the political structures that had held the state together. The very identity of the state was in question because the Soviet Union itself dissolved in December 1991 and the 15 republics of the federal union became independent. Russians therefore had to redefine their political community around a smaller, national state, and to generate new bonds of loyalty to it. Creating a post-Communist state that was both governable and democratic was extremely difficult because the Soviet regime had left behind so few of the political prerequisites of legitimate democratic authority, such as developed political parties, an honest and professional bureaucracy, an independent judiciary, encompassing social interest groups, and a democratically oriented political culture. Finally, putting the country on a path of self-sustaining economic development after decades of stagnation and decline required the replacement of the old centralized planning system with an economy based on the market system and private property. In all three areas, Russia entered the new century having made halting, partial steps forward in some respects, but major steps backward in the quality of life and quality of government.

CURRENT POLICY CHALLENGES

Vladimir Putin, Yeltsin's successor as president, faces an agenda of enormous proportions. He seeks to rebuild the power of the central government after a decade in which power slipped away to powerful economic magnates and entrenched regional bosses. To do this he has worked hard to tighten administrative discipline in the state. He has had some success. After nearly 10 years of steady economic contraction, the economy began to grow again in 1999, and has registered steady growth since then. Putin has enjoyed high levels of popular confidence, giving him wide latitude in choosing his policies. Gradually his general policy course has become clearer. It has three main elements. In foreign policy, he seeks to integrate Russia more deeply into the international system economically and politically. In the economy, he is trying to put Russia on a course of high and self-sustaining economic growth through the discipline of the market and incentives for investment. In politics, he is quietly but steadily imposing a centralized system of rule that relies on police controls and allows little more than a symbolic role for political opposition. Observers call his ideal model of rule "managed democracy." He wants to preserve the formal trappings of constitutional democracy, but also to manipulate political processes to ensure the outcomes he wants. His strategy has been to remove or neutralize potential sources of opposition to his power while creating an environment conducive to business investment and economic growth. Like previous Russian rulers, he has consolidated his own power by replacing officials considered loyal to the previous leadership with new people tied to him personally. He made his career in the security police and he has filled a strikingly large proportion of senior state positions with officials from the police, secret services, and armed forces (see Box 12.1).

Putin has only been partially successful in realizing his goals. Much of the credit for the economic recovery goes to the high world market prices for oil and gas. Most of the ambitious fiscal and administrative reforms he has introduced have been blunted in implementation. Some of Putin's actions, such as the suppression of independent media and the campaign against the oil giant **Yukos**, have discouraged business investment and fueled capital flight, leading to slower economic growth. Putin's heavy reliance on the country's "power structures" (the interior ministry with its police and security troops, the regular armed forces, the law enforcement system, and the secret services) to remove or intimidate his rivals and to reinforce central control has chilled open public

BOX 12.1 Who Is Mister Putin?

Vladimir Putin's rise to power was so rapid that when he succeeded to the presidency, he was virtually unknown. A question often asked by Russians and foreigners alike was "Who is Mr. Putin?"

Vladimir Vladimirovich Putin was born on October 7, 1952, in Leningrad (called St. Petersburg since 1991), and grew up in an ordinary apartment. From early on, he took an interest in martial arts and became expert at judo. Inspired by heroic tales of the secret world of espionage, at the age of 16 he paid a visit to the local headquarters of the KGB, hoping to become an agent. There he was told, however, that he needed to go to university first. In 1970 he entered Leningrad State University and specialized in civil law. Upon graduation in 1975, Putin went to work for the KGB and was assigned to work first in counterintelligence, and then in its foreign intelligence division. Proficient in German, he was sent to East Germany in 1985. In 1990, after the Wall fell, Putin went back to Leningrad, working at the university but in the employ of the KGB. When a former law professor of his, Anatolii Sobchak, became mayor of Leningrad in 1991, he went to work for Sobchak. In the mayor's office he handled external relations, dealing extensively with foreign companies interested in investing in the city, and rose to become deputy mayor.

In 1996, Putin took a position in Yeltsin's presidential administration. He made a rapid career. In 1998, Yeltsin named Putin head of the FSB (the Federal Security Service—successor to the KGB), and in March 1999, secretary of the Security Council as well. In August 1999, President Yeltsin appointed him prime minister. Thanks to his decisive handling of the military operation in Chechnia, Putin's popularity ratings quickly rose. On December 31, 1999, Yeltsin resigned, making Putin acting president. Putin ran for the presidency and, on March 26, 2000, won with an outright majority of the votes.

As time passed, Putin's political persona became somewhat clearer. Uncomfortable with the give and take of public politics, he prefers the hierarchical style of organization used in the military and police. He is a pragmatist with no particular affection either for the Soviet or tsarist order. He recognizes that Russia must participate in the contemporary world economy rather than burden itself with new international conflicts. Skilled at projecting an affable, relaxed demeanor, he is also self-possessed and disciplined, and reveals little of himself in dealing with others. Like many previous Russian rulers, he has made the consolidation of his own political power his first priority.

---

discourse and judicial independence. This makes it harder for the center to monitor bureaucratic performance. Actual improvements in the quality of governance under Putin have been modest. Putin has been much more successful in undercutting democratic checks and balances on central power than in making the new authoritarian system work effectively. Putin appears to believe that by centralizing power and eliminating opposition he can make the bureaucracy a more effective instrument for achieving his goals. However, history suggests that administrative over-centralization usually ends up not strengthening but weakening state capacity.

HISTORICAL LEGACIES

The Tsarist Regime

The Russian state traces its origins to the princely state that arose around Kiev (today the capital of independent Ukraine) in the ninth century. For nearly a thousand years, the Russian state was autocratic.

That is, it was ruled by a hereditary monarch whose power was unlimited by any constitution. Only in the first decade of the twentieth century did the Russian tsar agree to grant a constitution calling for an elected legislature—and even then, the tsar soon dissolved the legislature and arbitrarily revised the constitution. In addition to autocracy, the historical legacy of Russian statehood includes absolutism, patrimonialism, and Orthodox Christianity. Absolutism meant that the tsar aspired to wield absolute power over the subjects of the realm. *Patrimonialism* refers to the idea that the ruler treated his realm as property that he owned rather than as a society with its own legitimate rights and interests.[1] This conception of power continues to exert an influence over state rulers today.

Finally, the tsarist state identified itself with the Russian Orthodox Church. In Russia, as in other countries where it is the dominant religious tradition, the Orthodox Church ties itself closely to the state, considering itself a national church. Traditionally it has exhorted its adherents to show loyalty and obedience to the state in worldly matters, in return for which the state treated it as the state church. This legacy is still manifested in the post-Communist rulers' efforts to associate themselves with the heritage of Russia's church, and in many Russians' impulse to identify their state with a higher spiritual mission.

Absolutism, patrimonialism, and Orthodoxy have been recurring elements of Russian political culture. But alternate motifs have been influential as well. At some points in Russian history, the country's rulers have sought to modernize its economy and society. Russia imported Western practices in technology, law, state organization, and education in order to make the state competitive with other great powers. Modernizing rulers such as Peter the Great (who ruled from 1682 to 1725) and Catherine the Great (1762–1796) had a powerful impact on Russian society, bringing it closer to West European models. The imperative of building Russia's military and economic potential was all the more pressing because of Russia's constant expansion through conquest and annexation of neighboring territories, and the ever-present need to defend its borders. The state's role in controlling and mobilizing society rose with the need to govern a vast territory. By the end of the seventeenth century, Russia was territorially the largest state in the world. But for most of its history, Russia's imperial reach exceeded its actual grasp.

By comparison with the other major powers of Europe, Russia's economic institutions remained backward well into the twentieth century. However, the trajectory of its development, especially in the nineteenth century, was toward that of a modern industrial society. By the time the tsarist order fell in 1917, Russia possessed a large industrial sector, although it was concentrated in a few cities. The country had a sizable middle class, although it was greatly outnumbered by the vast and impoverished peasantry and the radicalized industrial working class. As a result, the social basis for a peaceful democratic transition was too weak to prevent the Communists from seizing power in 1917.

The thousand-year tsarist era left a contradictory legacy. The tsars attempted to legitimate their absolute power by appealing to tradition, empire, and divine right. They treated law as an instrument of rule rather than a source of authority. The doctrines that rulers should be accountable to the ruled and that sovereignty resides in the will of the people were alien to Russian state tradition. Throughout Russian history, state and society have been more distant from each other than in Western societies. Rulers and populace regarded one another with mistrust and suspicion. This gap has been overcome at times of great national trials such as the war against Napoleon and later World War II. Russia celebrated victory in those wars as a triumphant demonstration of the unity of state and people. But Russia's political traditions also include a yearning for equality, solidarity, and community, as well as for moral purity and sympathy for the downtrodden. And throughout the Russian heritage runs a deep strain of national identification based on pride in the greatness of the country and the endurance of its people.

The Communist Revolution and the Soviet Order

The tsarist regime proved unable to meet the overwhelming demands of national mobilization in World War I. Tsar Nicholas II abdicated in February 1917 (March 1917, by the Western calendar). He was replaced by a short-lived provisional government which in turn fell when the Russian Communists—Bolsheviks, as they called themselves—took power in October 1917 (November, by our calendar). Their aim was to create a socialist society in Russia and, eventually, to spread revolutionary socialism throughout the world. Socialism, the Russian Communist Party believed, meant a society without private ownership of the means of production, where the state owned and controlled all important economic assets, and where political power was exercised in the name of the working people. **Vladimir Ilyich Lenin** was the leader of the Russian Communist Party and the first head of the Soviet Russian government. (Figure 12.1 lists the Soviet and post-Soviet leaders since 1917.)

Under Lenin's system of rule, the Communist Party controlled all levels of government. At each level of the territorial hierarchy of the country, full-time Communist Party officials supervised government. At the top, final power to decide policy rested in the CPSU (Communist Party of the Soviet Union) Politburo. Under **Joseph Stalin**, who took power after Lenin's death in 1924, power was even further

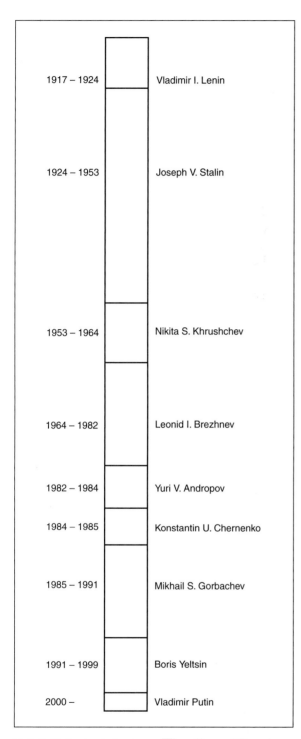

centralized. Stalin instituted a totalitarian regime intent upon building up Russia's industrial and military might. The state survived the terrible test of World War II, ultimately pushing back the German army all the way to Berlin. But, the combined cost of war and terror under Stalin was staggering. The institutions of rule that Stalin left behind when he died in 1953 eventually crippled the Soviet state. They included personalistic rule, insecurity for rulers and ruled alike, heavy reliance on the secret police, and a militarized economy. None of Stalin's successors could reform the system without undermining Communist rule itself.

As vast as the Soviet state's powers were, they were frustrated by bureaucratic immobilism. As in any organization, overcentralization undermined actual power, through distortions of information flow, tacit resistance to the center's orders by officials at lower levels, and the force of inertia. Bureaucratic officials were generally more devoted to protecting and advancing their own personal and career interests than in serving the public interest. By the time **Mikhail Gorbachev** was elected General Secretary of the CPSU in 1985, the political system of the USSR had grown top heavy, unresponsive, and corrupt. The regime had more than enough power to destroy any budding political opposition. However, it was unable to modernize the economy or improve living standards for the population. By the early 1980s, the economy had stopped growing and the country was unable to compete militarily or economically with the advanced countries of the West.

The youngest member of the Politburo at the time he was named party leader—he was only 54 when he took over—Gorbachev quickly grasped the levers of power that the system granted the General Secretary. He moved both to strengthen his own political base, and to carry out a program of reform.[2] Emphasizing the need for greater openness—**glasnost**—in society, Gorbachev stressed that the ultimate test of the party's effectiveness lay in improving the economic well-being of the country and its people. By highlighting such themes as the need for market relations, pragmatism in economic policy, and less secretiveness in government, he identified himself as a champion of reform. Gorbachev not only called for political democratization, but he pushed through a reform bringing about the first contested elections for local soviets in many decades. He

F I G U R E   1 2 . 1   Timeline of Russian Rulers Since 1917 and the Periods of Their Rule legalized private enterprise for individual and cooperative businesses and encouraged them to fill the many gaps in the economy left by the inefficiency of the state sector. He called for a "law-governed state" (*pravovoe gosudarstvo*) in which state power—including the power of the Communist Party—would be subordinate to law. He welcomed the explosion of informal social and political associations that formed. He made major concessions to the United States in the sphere of arms control. This resulted in a treaty which, for the first time in history, called for the destruction of entire classes of nuclear missiles.

Using to the full the General Secretary's authoritarian powers, Gorbachev quickly railroaded his proposals for democratization through the Supreme Soviet. In 1989 and 1990, Gorbachev's plan for free elections and a working parliament was realized as elections were held, deputies elected, and new soviets formed at the center and in every region and locality. When nearly half a million coal miners went out on strike in the summer of 1989, Gorbachev declared himself sympathetic to their demands.

Gorbachev's radicalism received its most dramatic confirmation through the astonishing developments of 1989 in Eastern Europe. All the regimes making up the Socialist bloc collapsed and gave way to multi-party parliamentary regimes in virtually bloodless popular revolutions. The Soviet Union stood by and supported the revolutions. The overnight dismantling of communism in Eastern Europe meant that the elaborate structure of party ties, police cooperation, economic trade, and military alliance that had developed with Eastern Europe after World War II vanished. Divided Germany was allowed to reunite.

In the Soviet Union itself, meantime, the Communist Party faced a critical loss of authority. The newly elected governments of the national republics making up the Soviet state one by one declared that they were sovereign. The three Baltic Republics declared their intention to secede from the union. Over 1989–1990, throughout the Soviet Union and Eastern Europe, Communist Party rule was breaking down.

Political Institutions of the Transition Period: Demise of the USSR

Gorbachev's reforms had consequences he did not intend. The 1990 elections of deputies to the Supreme Soviets in all 15 republics and for local soviets stimulated popular nationalist and democratic movements in most republics. In the core republic—Russia itself—Gorbachev's rival Boris Yeltsin won election as Chairman of the Russian Supreme Soviet in June 1990. As chief of state in the Russian Republic, Yeltsin was well positioned to challenge Gorbachev for preeminence.

Yeltsin's rise forced Gorbachev to alter his strategy. Beginning in March 1991, Gorbachev sought terms for a new federal or confederal union that would be acceptable to Yeltsin and the Russian leadership, as well as to the leaders of the other republics. In April 1991 he reached an agreement on the outlines of a new treaty of union with 9 of the 15 republics, including Russia. A weak central government would manage basic coordinating functions. But the republics would gain the power to control the economies of their territories.

Gorbachev had underestimated the strength of his opposition. On August 19, 1991, his own vice-president, prime minister, defense minister, KGB chairman, and other senior officials preempted the signing ceremony of the treaty by placing Gorbachev under house arrest and seizing state power. This was a fateful moment for Russia. In Moscow and St. Petersburg, thousands of citizens rallied to the cause of democracy and Russian sovereignty. The coup collapsed on the third day and Gorbachev returned to office again as president. But his power was now fatally weakened. Neither union nor Russian power structures heeded his commands. Through the fall of 1991, the Russian government took over the union government, ministry by ministry. In November 1991, President Yeltsin issued a decree formally outlawing the Communist Party of the Soviet Union. By December, Gorbachev was president without a country. On December 25, 1991, he resigned as president and turned the powers of his office over to Boris Yeltsin.[3]

Political Institutions of the Transition Period: Russia 1990–1993

The Russian Republic followed the example of the USSR and adopted its own constitutional amendments creating a Congress of People's Deputies and Supreme Soviet, and soon after, a state presidency. Boris Yeltsin was elected president of the Russian

BOX 12.2   Boris Yeltsin: Russia's First President

Boris Yeltsin, born in 1931, graduated from the Urals Polytechnical Institute in 1955 with a diploma in civil engineering, and worked for a long time in construction. From 1976 to 1985 he served as first secretary of the Sverdlovsk oblast (provincial) Communist Party organization.

Early in 1986 he became first secretary of the Moscow city party organization but was removed in November 1987 for speaking out against Gorbachev. Positioning himself as a victim of the party establishment, Yeltsin made a remarkable political comeback. In the 1989 elections to the Congress of People's Deputies, he won a Moscow at-large seat with almost 90 percent of the vote. The following year he was elected to the Russian republic's parliament with over 80 percent of the vote. He was then elected its chairman in June 1990. In 1991, he was elected president of Russia, receiving 57 percent of the vote. Thus, he had won three major races in three successive years. He was reelected as president in 1996 in a dramatic, come-from-behind race against the leader of the Communist Party.

Yeltsin's last years in office were notable for his lengthy spells of illness, and for the carousel of prime ministerial appointments he made. The entourage of family members and advisers around him, dubbed colloquially "the Family," seemed to exercise undue influence over him. Yet, infirm as he was, he judged that Russia's interests and his own would be safe in Vladimir Putin's hands. Instead of turning against Putin when Putin gained in power and popularity, Yeltsin chose to resign and turn the presidency over to Putin. His resignation speech was full of contrition for his failure to bring a better life to Russians. In retirement, Yeltsin entered a dignified private life, resurfacing with his old rival Mikhail Gorbachev for President Putin's inauguration on May 7, 2000.

Yeltsin's legacy is mixed. He was most effective when engaged in political battle, whether he was fighting for supremacy against Gorbachev, or fighting against the Communists. Impulsive and undisciplined, he was gifted with exceptionally keen political intuition. He regarded economic reform as an instrument in his political war with the Communist opposition, and used privatization to make it impossible for any future rulers to return to state socialism. Imperious and willful, he also regarded the adoption of the 1993 constitution as a major achievement and willingly accepted the limits on his presidential power that it imposed.

Federation in June 1991. Unlike Gorbachev, Yeltsin was elected in a direct, popular, competitive election, which gave him a considerable advantage in mobilizing public support against Gorbachev and the central USSR government (see Box 12.2).

Like Gorbachev before him, Yeltsin demanded extraordinary powers from parliament to cope with the country's economic problems. Following the August 1991 coup attempt, he sought from the Russian Congress of People's Deputies, and was given, the power to carry out a program of radical market-oriented reform by decree. Yeltsin named himself acting prime minister and formed a government led by a group of young, Western-oriented leaders determined to carry out a decisive economic transformation. The new government's economic reforms took effect on January 2, 1992. Their first results were felt immediately as prices skyrocketed. Quickly many politicians began to distance themselves from the program: even Yeltsin's vice-president denounced the program as "economic genocide." Through 1992, opposition to the reforms grew stronger and more in-transigent. Increasingly, the political confrontation between Yeltsin and the reformers on the one side, and the opposition to radical economic reform on the other, became centered in the two branches of government. President Yeltsin demanded broad powers to carry out the reform program, but parliament refused to adopt a new constitution that would give him the powers he demanded. In March 1993 a motion to remove the president through impeachment nearly passed in the parliament.

On September 21, 1993, Yeltsin declared the parliament dissolved, and called for elections to a new parliament. Yeltsin's enemies barricaded themselves inside the parliament building. After a 10-day standoff, the dissidents joined with some loosely organized paramilitary units outside the building and attacked the Moscow mayor's offices adjacent to the Russian White House. They even called on their followers to "seize the Kremlin." Finally, the army agreed to back Yeltsin and suppress the uprising by force.

The circumstances of the December 1993 parliamentary elections were hardly auspicious. Yeltsin's decree meant that national elections were to be held for a legislature that did not, constitutionally, exist, since the constitution establishing these institutions was to be voted upon in a referendum held in parallel with the parliamentary elections. Yet for all the violence surrounding its inception, the constitution approved in the December referendum has stayed in force since then.

THE CONTEMPORARY CONSTITUTIONAL ORDER

The Presidency

The 1993 constitution combined elements of presidentialism and parliamentarism. (See Figure 12.2 for a schematic overview of the Russian constitutional structure.) Although it provided for the separation of executive, legislative, and judicial branches and for a federal division of power between the central and regional levels of government, it gave the president wide power. The president is popularly

elected for a four-year term (under the constitution, he is limited to two terms). The president names the prime minister to head the government. Yet the government must have the confidence of parliament to remain in power. Although the constitution does not call the president the head of the executive branch, he is so in fact by virtue of his power to appoint the prime minister and the rest of the government, and his right to issue **presidential decrees** with the force of law. (The decree power is limited, however, because decrees may not violate existing law and can be superseded by legislation.)

Over the decade since the constitution was approved, some informal practices have come to govern the exercise of central power. For example, the president and government divide executive responsibility. The government, headed by the prime minister, is primarily responsible for economic and social policy. The president directly oversees the ministries and other bodies directly concerned with coercion, law enforcement, and state security—the

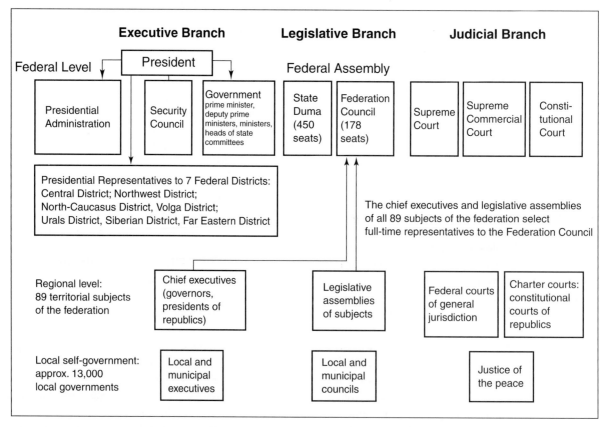

FIGURE 12.2   Russian Political System Under the 1993 Constitution

"power ministries." These include the Foreign Ministry, Defense Ministry, Ministry of Internal Affairs (which controls the regular police and security troops), Federal Security Service (FSB—formerly the KGB), and several other security and intelligence agencies. The president and his staff set overall policy in foreign and domestic domains, and the government develops the specific proposals and rules carrying it out. In practice, the government answers to the president, rather than to parliament. The government's base of support is the president rather than a particular coalition of political forces in parliament.

Despite the asymmetrical constitutional balance, the parliament does have some power. Its approval is required for any bill to become law. The State Duma (the lower house of parliament) must confirm the president's nominee for prime minister. If, upon three successive votes, the Duma refuses to confirm the nomination, the president must dissolve the Duma and call new elections. Likewise the Duma may vote to deny confidence in the government. If a motion of no confidence carries twice, the president must either dissolve parliament or dismiss the government. During Yeltsin's tenure as president, the Duma was able to block some of Yeltsin's legislative initiatives. Under Putin, however, it has largely been a rubber stamp. Conceivably, future presidents may have less of a free hand in their dealings with parliament than Putin does. The constitution allows for a wide range of types of relationship between president, government, and parliament, depending on the degree to which the president dominates the political system.

In addition to these powers, the president has a large array of other formal and informal powers in his constitutional capacity as "head of state," "guarantor of the constitution," and commander-in-chief of the armed forces. He oversees a large presidential administration which supervises the federal government and keeps tabs on regional governments. Informally, the administration also manages relations with the parliament, the courts, big business, the media, political parties, and major interest groups. A good indication of the degree to which Putin has revived Russia's traditional authoritarian style of rule is the informal rule that no significant political undertaking in Russia is possible without prior clearance from the presidential administration.

The president also oversees many official and quasi-official supervisory and advisory commissions. One of the most important is the **Security Council**, chaired by the president, which consists of a permanent secretary, the heads of the power ministries and other security-related agencies, the prime minister, and, more recently the finance minister and chairs of the two chambers of parliament. Its powers are broad but shadowy. Another prominent body advising the president is the **State Council**, which comprises the heads of regional governments. Both Yeltsin and Putin have regularly created and dissolved new institutions answering directly to the president. These improvised structures can be politically useful as counterweights to constitutionally mandated bodies such as parliament, as well as providing policy advice and feedback. They help ensure that the president is always the dominant institution in the political system, but they undermine the authority of formal institutions.

The Government

In contrast to most parliamentary systems, the makeup of the Russian government is not directly determined by the party composition of the parliament. Indeed, there is scarcely any relationship between the distribution of party forces in the Duma and the political balance of the government. Nearly all members of the government are career managers and administrators rather than party politicians. Overall, the government is not a party government, but reflects the president's calculations about how to balance considerations such as personal loyalty, professional competence, and the relative strength of major bureaucratic factions. When President Putin chose Mikhail Fradkov to be prime minister on March 1, 2004—two weeks *ahead* of presidential elections—the political establishment was taken by surprise. Fradkov was a relatively obscure figure who had headed the Federal Tax Police for two years. His very lack of independent political clout underscored the fact that Putin would be the main source of policy direction for the country.

Following a major restructuring in 2004, the Cabinet comprises 15 ministries and 3 state committees that in turn oversee dozens of other state committees and agencies responsible for managing the federal executive branch. The reform sought to replace the many ministries responsible for managing specific branches of the economy with a smaller number of ministries performing broad functions. Skeptics noted that although the aim was to streamline the structure of government, the total number of federal-level executive bodies rose from 57 to 72.[4]

The Parliament

The parliament—called the Federal Assembly—is bicameral. The lower house, the **State Duma**, combines single-member district representation and party-list proportional representation. The upper house, the **Federation Council**, represents each of Russia's 89 federal regions on an equal basis. Party factions dominate the proceedings of the State Duma, while the Federation Council avoids forming partisan groups.

Under President Yeltsin, the Federal Assembly was a modestly authoritative body. President Putin, however, has a degree of influence over both chambers that has turned them nearly into a rubber stamp for his legislative agenda. Whether this present state of affairs will last, however, is open to question. President Putin's domination of the political system may prove temporary, and popular demands for policy change and political representation may again make parliament a source of opposition influence. Russia's constitution can accommodate a variety of possible arrangements. In any case, the actual power of parliament will depend more on the evolution of the party system and other structures for aggregating popular demands than on formal constitutional rules.

The Duma has the right to originate legislation except for certain categories of policy which are under the jurisdiction of the Federation Council. As Figure 12.3 shows, upon passage in the State Duma, a bill goes to the Federation Council for consideration. The Federation Council can only pass it, reject it, or reject it and call for forming an agreement commission comprising members of both houses to iron out differences. If the Duma rejects the upper house's changes, it can override the Federation Council by a two-thirds vote and send the bill directly on to the president.

When the bill has cleared parliament, it goes to the president for signature. If the president refuses to sign the bill, it returns to the Duma. The Duma may pass it with the president's proposed amendments by a simple absolute majority, or override the president's veto, for which a two-thirds vote is required. The Federation Council must then also approve the bill, by a simple majority if the president's amendments are accepted, or a two-thirds vote if it chooses to override the president. On rare occasions, the Duma has overridden the president's veto and it has overridden Federation Council rejections more frequently. In other cases, the Duma has passed bills rejected by the president after accepting the president's amendments. Under President Yeltsin, political forces opposed to Yeltsin, particularly Communists and nationalists, held the majority in the Duma. But parliament and president generally worked to head off major confrontations.

The Duma's 450 members are elected in two ways. Half, or 225, are elected in **single-member districts** by a first-past-the-post, plurality rule. The other 225 are elected on party lists. A party receiving at least 5 percent of the vote on the party-list ballot is entitled to as many of the 225 party-list seats in the Duma as its share of the party-list vote. As in other proportional representation systems, votes cast for parties that fail to clear the 5 percent threshold go to winning parties. In the fall of 2004, however, President Putin proposed reforming the electoral system so as to eliminate all single-member district seats and elect all 450 deputies proportionally from party lists.

Nearly all Duma deputies either join party factions or form their own groups. Factions and groups enjoy desirable privileges in the Duma, including the right to committee chairmanships, office space, and recognition in floor debate. Faction leaders are represented on the governing body of the Duma, the Council of the Duma.

The December 2003 elections gave the forces aligned with President Putin an overwhelming majority in the Duma, which they have used to centralize power. The pro-Putin party is called **United Russia**, and it holds two-thirds of the seats in the Duma. Around 80 percent of all single-member district deputies joined the United Russia faction—a good indication of its drawing power. The new Duma that convened in January 2004 gave nearly all committee chairmanships to members of United Russia, and 8 out of the 11 members of the Council of the Duma are from United Russia. Since United Russia votes with a high degree of discipline, the Duma consis-

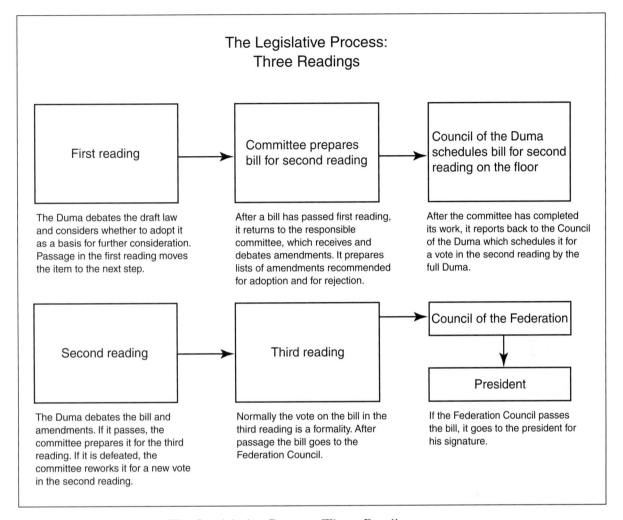

The Legislative Process:
Three Readings

F I G U R E   1 2 . 3   The Legislative Process: Three Readings

tently delivers the president legislative majorities. Other factions have very little opportunity to influence the agenda, let alone the outcomes of legislative deliberations.

Each deputy is a member of 1 of 29 standing committees with specific policy jurisdictions. As bills are submitted to the Duma, they are assigned to particular committees, which collect and review proposed amendments before reporting out the bills for votes by the full chamber with the committee's recommendations.

The Federation Council is designed as an instrument of federalism in that (as in the United States Senate) every constituent unit of the federation is represented by two representatives. Thus the popu-

lations of small ethnic-national territories are greatly overrepresented compared with more populous regions. The Federation Council has important powers. Besides acting on bills passed by the lower house, it also approves presidential nominees for high courts such as the Supreme Court and the Constitutional Court. It must approve presidential decrees declaring martial law or a state of emergency, or any acts altering the boundaries of territorial units. It must consider any legislation dealing with taxes, budget, financial policy, treaties, customs, and declarations of war.

Until a major reform pushed through by President Putin in the spring of 2000, its members were the heads of the executive and legislative branches of each constituent territory of the federation. Now, however, each governor and each regional legislature names a representative to the Federation Council to serve on a full-time basis. The governors appoint their representatives, who are then confirmed by the legislatures. The regional legislatures elect their representatives. They can recall their representatives at any time.

There is great deal of dissatisfaction over the current role of the Federation Council. Many believe that the composition of the chamber should be replaced with one providing that the members are popularly elected. This must be reconciled, however, with the constitutional requirement that the 2 members of the chamber from each of Russian 89 territorial subjects must represent the executive and legislative branches.

Executive-Legislative Relations

Relations between president and parliament during the Yeltsin period were often stormy. The first two Dumas, elected in 1993 and in 1995, were dominated by the Communist and other leftist factions hostile to President Yeltsin and the policies of his government. This was particularly true in areas of economic policy and privatization. On other issues, however, such as matters concerning federal relations, the Duma and president often reached agreement—sometimes against the resistance of the Federation Council, whose members fought to protect regional prerogatives.

The 1999 election produced a Duma with a pro-government majority. President Putin and his government built a reliable base of support in the Duma for their legislative initiatives comprising a coalition of four centrist political factions. The 2003 election produced a still wider margin of suppport for the president in the Duma and an overwhelming majority for the United Russia party. This means that the president does not need to expend much effort in bargaining with the Duma to win its support for his policies. Generally speaking, the pro-presidential deputies in the Duma need the Kremlin much more than the Kremlin needs them. As a result, the balance of power in the political system under Putin has shifted steadily away from the parliament and toward the president.

The Constitutional Court

The 1993 constitution provides for judicial review by the **Constitutional Court**. Its 19 members are nominated by the president but are subject to confirmation by the Council of the Federation. The Court is empowered to consider the constitutionality of actions of the president, the parliament, and lower-level governments. The court has carefully avoided issuing any decisions restricting presidential powers in any significant way. However, it has decided a number of thorny constitutional issues, including the relations between the two chambers of parliament and the delineation of powers between the central and regional governments. It has also consistently defended the rights of individual defendants in the criminal justice system. The court has also tended to uphold the sovereignty of federal law over the rights of the constituent territories of the federation. In 2000 the court ruled, for instance, that the national republics within Russia may not call themselves "sovereign" or claim ownership of the natural resources on their territories.

Central Government and the Regions

Following the breakup of the Soviet Union, many Russians feared that Russia would break up as well into a patchwork of independent fiefdoms. Certainly Russia's territorial integrity was subjected to serious strains. Under President Yeltsin, the central government granted wide autonomy to regional governments in return for political support. Under Putin the pendulum has swung back sharply toward centralization.

Demographic factors also affect Russia's territorial integrity. Eighty percent of Russia's population is ethnically Russian. None of its ethnic minorities accounts for more than 4 percent of the total (the Tatars form the largest of the ethnic minorities, constituting about 5.5 million of the 146 million total population). Rebuilding national community in post–Soviet Russia has been helped by Russia's thousand-year history of statehood. Yet until 1991, Russia was never constituted as a nation-state: under the tsars it was a multinational empire, and under Soviet rule it was nominally a federal union of socialist republics. State policy toward nationality has also varied over the centuries. In some periods, Russia recognized a variety of distinct ethnic-national communities and tolerated cultural differences among them. In other periods the state pressured non-Russian groups to assimilate to Russian culture.[5]

Russia was formally established as a federal republic under the Soviet regime. In contrast to the Soviet Union of which it was the largest component, only some of its constituent members were ethnic-national territories. The rest were pure administrative subdivisions, populated mainly by Russians. The non-Russian ethnic-national territories were classified by size and status into autonomous republics, autonomous provinces, and national districts. In many of them, the indigenous ethnic group comprised a minority of the population. Since 1991, the names and status of some of the constituent units have changed. As of 2004, Russia comprises 89 constituent territorial units. In Russian constitutional law, these are called the "subjects of the federation." They represent 6 different types of unit: 21 are republics, 6 are *krais* (territories), 10 are autonomous districts (all but one of them located within other units), 1 is an autonomous *oblast,* 2 are cities, and 49 are *oblasts.* Republics, autonomous districts, and the one autonomous oblast are units created specifically to give certain political rights to populations living in territories with significant ethnic minorities. Oblasts and krais are simply administrative subdivisions with no special constitutional status.

One of the centralizing measures President Putin has pursued is the merger of smaller ethnic regions into larger territorial units. The first such merger is between Perm' oblast and its neighbor, the Komi-Permyak autonomous district. Persuaded by a combination of pressures and material inducements from the central government, voters and officials in both regions approved the merger in December 2003. It will take effect in December 2005. Several similar mergers are now being negotiated, including the incorporation of Tiumen' oblast with two oil-rich autonomous districts that border it. Most observers believe that the Putin administration seeks to eliminate most or all of the smaller ethnic units by merging them into larger neighboring regions and reducing the patronage rights that come with their status as separate territorial units.[6]

The ethnic republics jealously guard their special status. From 1990 to 1992, all the republics adopted declarations of sovereignty and two made attempts to declare full or partial independence of Russia. In the mountainous region of the North Caucasus, between the Black and Caspian Seas, there lies a belt of ethnic republics that includes the Chechen Republic (**Chechnia**). Its leadership declared independence of Russia in 1991, an act Russia refused to recognize but did not initially overturn by force. The Tatar Republic also sought to separate itself from Russia. It is situated on the Volga, in an oil-rich and heavily industrialized region. Eventually Russia and Tatarstan worked out a treaty satisfactory to both sides, and the separatist movement in Tatarstan gradually subsided. In Chechnia, however, armed opposition failed to unseat the secession-minded leader. In December 1994 Russian forces attacked the republic directly, subjecting its capital city, Groznyi, to devastating bombardment. This forced tens of thousands of Chechen and Russian residents to flee the city and led to a protracted, destructive war. Fighting ceased in summer 1996 but resumed in 1999. Federal forces had established control over most parts of Chechnia by early 2000, but Chechen guerrillas continue to carry out ambushes and suicide attacks against federal units and have impeded the restoration of political order. Chechen terrorist groups have attacked civilian targets both in the North Caucasus region and in Moscow. One of the most shocking of these incidents was the seizure of a school in the town of Beslan, near Chechnia, in September 2004 (see Box 12.3). The brutal methods used by federal forces to suppress the uprising have fueled continuing hatred on the part of many Chechens against the federal government, which in turn facilitates recruitment by the terrorists. The 21 ethnic republics have the constitutional right to determine their own form of state power so long as their decisions do not contradict federal law. All 21 have established presidencies. In many cases, the republic presidents have constructed personal power bases around appeals to ethnic solidarity and the cultural autonomy of the indigenous nationality. In many cases they have used this power to establish personalistic dictatorships in their regions.

President Putin has made clear his intention to reassert the federal government's authority over the regions. The reform of the Federation Council was one step in this direction. In 2000 Putin pushed a law

BOX 12.3   Beslan

September 1 is the first day of school each year throughout Russia. Children, accompanied by their parents, often come to school bringing flowers to their teachers. A group organized by the Chechen warlord Shamil Basaev chose September 1, 2004, to carry out one of the most horrific incidents in the history of the Chechen wars. A group of heavily armed militants stormed a school in the town of Beslan, located in the republic of North Osetia, next door to Chechnia. Over 1,000 schoolchildren, parents, and teachers were taken hostage. The terrorists crowded the captives into the school gymnasium, which they filled with explosives to prevent any rescue attempt. Negotiations over the release of the hostages failed; the terrorists even refused to allow water and food to be brought into the school to relieve the hostages' suffering. Reports on the terrorists' demands varied. Some indicated that the terrorists demanded the release of some of their comrades who had been captured earlier that summer; other reports said that the terrorists called for the withdrawal of federal troops from Chechnia.

On the third day of the seige, something triggered the detonation of one of the bombs inside the school. In the chaos that followed, many of the children and adults rushed to escape. The terrorists fired at them. Federal forces stormed the school, trying to rescue the escaping hostages and to kill the terrorists. Many of the bombs planted by the terrorists exploded. Ultimately around 350 of the hostages died, along with all the terrorists, and an unknown number of security troops.

The media covered the events extensively. The Beslan tragedy had an impact on Russian national consciousness comparable to that of September 11 in the United States. While there had been a number of previous attacks tied to Chechen terrorists, none had cost so many innocent lives. Although many Russians blamed corruption and poor organization among the police for allowing the terrorists to take over the school initially and for failing to prevent the destruction at the end, they also recognized that the terrorists had made it impossible for the security forces to attempt a rescue for fear of provoking a massacre of the children.

Putin and other senior government officials claimed that the terrorists were part of an international terrorist movement aimed ultimately at the dismemberment of Russia itself. Putin studiously avoided linking the incident to Russian policy in Chechnia. In response to the crisis, Putin called for measures to reinforce national security, particularly in the North Caucasus, and to improve the effectiveness of federal police, security, and military agencies. He also called for several reforms of the political system, including an end to the institution of direct popular election of governors. Instead, he proposed that the president would nominate candidates for governor, and the regional legislatures would confirm them. This step, he said, would make governors more accountable for the safety and well-being of their regions. He also proposed eliminating single-member district seats in the Duma elections in favor of filling all Duma seats by party-list proportional representation. Most observers assumed that Putin wanted to make these changes anyway, and that the Beslan tragedy simply gave him a political opening to enact them. By the same token, however, Putin has placed his own political reputation on the line by tying his strategy of centralizing power to the goal of strengthening state security.

---

through parliament that gave him the ability to remove a governor if a court found that the governor had refused to act in line with the federal constitution and law. Needless to say, the governors strongly opposed these changes. But the Duma supported the proposal and, with some modifications, it was passed into law.

Putin's decree of May 13, 2000, also created seven new "federal districts." He appointed a special presidential representative to each district who monitors the actions of the regional governments within that district. This reform sought to strengthen central control over the activity of federal bodies in the regions. Often, in the past, local branches of federal agencies had fallen under the influence of powerful governors. Critics of Putin's reform complained that it was a step in the direction of creating a hyper-centralized, authoritarian system of rule. Defenders argued that many regions had effectively become personal dictatorships and that decisive steps were needed to bring them back under central control. Putin has moved carefully but steadily to limit the autonomy of governors. He has replaced most of the heads of regional police and security service administrations. But he has refrained from forcibly removing governors. The governors have generally avoided direct confrontations with Putin. Moreover, once

BOX 12.4   The 2004 Vladivostok Mayor's Race*

Even by the standards of Russian elections, the race for mayor of the city of Vladivostok in 2004 stood out for the scale of corruption. Vladivostok is the capital city of the Far East region. Governance in the region has been corrupt and incompetent, often resulting in disruptions in the supply of heat, electric power, and water. There has been a chronic power struggle between the governor of the region and the mayor of Vladivostok.

In February 2001 President Putin finally succeeded in dislodging the powerful governor of the region. Many thought that the destructive conflict between governor and mayor would finally end. However, the new governor, Sergei Darkin, continued to fight with the Vladivostok mayor. Darkin sponsored his own candidate for mayor in the 2004 election, Vladimir Nikolaev, who was a deputy in the local legislature and controlled a major fishing company. Nikolaev also had been convicted in 1999 of beating one local official and threatening to murder another (he began serving a three-and-a-half-year jail term, but was soon amnestied). Russian press reported that he heads a major organized crime group and bears the underworld nickname of "Winnie the Pooh."

The mayoral race was bitterly fought. During the campaign there were physical attacks on candidates, threats, abductions of newspaper distributors, and copious disinformation. No candidate won an outright majority in the first round, so a second round was scheduled. The two top finishers—Nikolaev, who received 26.8 percent and a former mayor, Viktor Cherepkov, who received 26.3 percent—entered the runoff. Nine days before the election, a bomb reportedly exploded at Cherepkov's headquarters. What finally forced Cherepkov off the ballot was not the bombing, however, but a court decision six days before the election that disqualified him from running for using illegal campaign methods.

Under normal procedures, Kopylov, who had received the next highest vote total in the first round, would have entered the runoff, but he refused. So did the person who received the fourth highest total. In the end, the man who came in fifth, with 3 percent, was Nikolaev's opponent. Nikolaev went on to win with 53 percent of the vote; 37 percent voted "against all."

Many observers wondered how to interpret the Kremlin's passivity in dealing with Vladivostok: Does it reflect Putin's indifference to local power struggles? Or is it a sign of Moscow's powerlessness in the face of entrenched corruption? Some cynics have even speculated that elections so scandalous are actually intended to discredit the very institution of elections in order to prepare the way for direct presidential rule.

*This account is based on a report by Vyacheslav Shirokov in *Russian Regional Report*, Vol. 9, No. 13, 20 July 2004; and Julie Corwin, "Vladivostok Sees Its Wildest Election Yet," RFE/RL Newsline, July 28, 2004.

Putin enacts the reform replacing direct election of governors with a system of appointed governors, they will be still more careful to appear politically loyal to the president.

Below the tier of regional government is a tier of units that are supposed to enjoy the right of self-government—municipalities and other local government units. There are some 13,000 of these local entities. Local governments have almost no independent sources of revenue. On average, they receive 90 percent of their budget funds from the regional and federal governments. Regional governments resist allowing local governments to exercise any significant powers of their own, and federal laws have been unable to alter this situation. In many cases, the mayors of the capital cities of regions are political rivals of the governors of the regions. Moscow and St. Petersburg are exceptional cases because they have the status of federal territorial subjects like republics and regions. Other cities lack the power and autonomy of Moscow and St. Petersburg, and must bargain with their superior regional governments for shares of power.

Before 2005, regional chief executives (generally called **governors**) were chosen by direct popular election. Since the enactment of Putin's recent reforms, however, the president appoints governors. Many citizens supported this change, believing that the institution of local elections had been discredited by corruption and fraud and that elections were more often determined by the influence of wealthy insiders than by public opinion (see Box 12.4). Putin clearly hopes that appointed governors will be more accountable and effective, but past experience suggests that centralizing power by itself is unlikely to improve state performance in the regions in the absence of other mechanisms for enforcing federal law.

Russia's post-Communist constitutional arrangements are still evolving. The political system allows considerable room for the arbitrary exercise of power and even, as under President Putin, the evisceration of democracy. Both Yeltsin and Putin have interpreted their presidential mandates broadly. President Yeltsin used his decree power to carry out a massive privatization program. He signed bilateral treaties with almost 50 individual regional governments. He also launched a brutal military campaign to suppress an independence movement in the Chechen Republic. He carried out all of these actions without seeking parliamentary approval. In one 18-month period between 1998 and 1999, he named and dismissed his prime minister four times.

President Putin has also used his powers expansively. In 2000 he issued a decree creating seven federal super-districts to facilitate central supervision of regional governments and he appointed representatives to oversee them. By decree he also created a new consultative structure of regional governors called the State Council. This was an effort to mollify the governors, whom he had deprived of seats in the Federation Council. Both institutional changes were not envisioned by the constitution, but also not specifically prohibited by it. The constitutional arrangements established under President Yeltsin had the potential to evolve toward democracy. A successful democratic transition, however, depends on more than a democratic constitution. The web of political institutions surrounding formal constitutional rules strongly shapes the way officeholders wield power. Informal rules can be far more important than formal rules. If rulers can circumvent formal limits on their power, constitutional structures may become irrelevant to the actual exercise of power.

Russia somewhat resembles the pattern that political scientist Guillermo O'Donnell has called "delegative democracy."[7] In such a system, common in Latin America, a president may win an election and then proceed to govern as if he were the sole source of authority in the country. The president exercises so much power over other political structures, thanks to his control of the police and military and his access to patronage, that he can negate the nominal separation of powers written into the constitution. In such a system, parliamentarians may use their positions not to represent constituents or craft legislation but to trade favors and enrich their friends and family. Judges may deem it safer to tailor their decisions to the wishes of powerful state officials. The editors of major newspapers bury stories unfavorable to the authorities. Interest groups curry favor with officials rather than mobilizing their supporters around particular policy positions. The leaders of opposition parties learn to accept their role on the sidelines.

Under Putin this pattern of "hollowed out democracy" has become evident. Without explicitly violating any constitutional limits on his power, and without abolishing elections or other democratic institutions, Putin has effectively negated the constitutional limits on his power built into the constitution. Using the president's extensive powers over the executive branch, he has neutralized and marginalized nearly all independent sources of political authority, while observing formal constitutional procedures. For example, he enacts his policy program by passing legislation through parliament rather than by relying on his decree power. But having used his control over electoral processes to secure overwhelming majority support in both chambers, parliamentary approval of his agenda is assured. As observers have pointed out, Putin appears to dislike the open give and take of democratic politics, preferring more familiar methods of behind-the-scenes bureaucratic maneuvering.[8] Putin's use of presidential power presents a sharp contrast to the Yeltsin period. Yeltsin used his presidential powers erratically and impulsively. But Yeltsin respected certain limits on his power: he did not suppress media criticism, and he tolerated political opposition. Faced with an opposition-led parliament, Yeltsin was willing to compromise with his opponents to enact legislation. However, Yeltsin grew dependent on a coterie of powerful financial-media-industrial **oligarchs** for support and let them acquire substantial influence. Likewise, Yeltsin allowed regional bosses to flout federal authority with impunity because he found it much less costly to accommodate them than to fight them.

The loss of state capacity under Yeltsin illustrates one danger of an overcentralized political system. When the the president does not effectively command the powers of the office, power drifts to other centers of power. Putin's presidency illustrates the opposite danger. When Putin took over, he was faced with the task of reversing the breakdown of political control and responsibility that had accelerated under Yeltsin. Although he has repeatedly called for a system based on respect for the rule of law, he has also steadily restored authoritarian rule. He captured the contradictory quality of this vision in his 2004 message to parliament, when he said that creating "a free society of free people is the very most important of our tasks" but at the same time warned that any attempts to effect a significant change in policy "could lead to irreversible consequences. And they must be absolutely excluded."[9]

RUSSIAN POLITICAL CULTURE IN THE POST-SOVIET PERIOD

Russian political culture is the product of centuries of autocratic rule, rapid but uneven progress of educational and living standards in the twentieth century, and rising exposure to Western standards of political life. The result is a contradictory bundle of values and beliefs: a sturdy core of commitment to democratic values is accompanied by pronounced disillusionment with the way democratization and market reforms have worked out in Russia. Russians rate the Soviet regime before perestroika positively as a time of relative security and prosperity, but reject the notion of bringing back communism. Forty-one percent of Russians say they would support a return to the Brezhnev era, but only 5 percent think that such an event is possible.[10] Over 70 percent of Russians regret the breakup of the Soviet Union, but 72 percent say that restoring it is neither possible nor necessary.[11]

Support for some features of a market economy is high but low for others. For example, surveys consistently find substantial support for the idea that the state should own all major industrial enterprises (about half the population expresses this opinion).[12] Only 21 percent of the population supports private ownership of land. On the other hand, the number of people who agree with the proposition that "it is immoral to be wealthy in a poor country" is declining with time, and more people now disagree with the idea (47 percent) than agree with it (39 percent).[13] Seventy percent of the population oppose ending the policy of allowing tenants to acquire their state apartments as private property at no charge.[14]

James Gibson sums up the findings of a number of studies by drawing three conclusions: there is rather extensive support in Russia for democratic institutions and processes so long as people see these as rights for themselves; there is much less support for extending rights to unpopular minorities; and the segments of the population who are the most exposed to the influences of modern civilization (younger people, more educated people, and residents of big cities) are also those most likely to support democratic values. This suggests that as Russia becomes more open to the outside world, support for democratic values will grow.[15]

Contemporary values and beliefs have been shaped by both long-term factors such as the rise in educational levels over the decades of Soviet rule, and by short-term factors such as the powerful impact of glasnost in raising popular aspirations for a standard of living close to that of the developed West. Public values were also shaped by the wrenching loss of familiar bearings as the old regime collapsed and with it, the very Soviet Union.

In his struggles with the Communist opposition, Yeltsin encouraged people to imagine that his leadership would usher in a new era of prosperity and freedom. Instead, poverty, unemployment, and inequality rose sharply, and privation led to the enrichment of a small class of ultra-rich tycoons who flaunted their quickly amassed fortunes. Organized crime flourished. The modest but universal social safety net of the Communist regime disintegrated. Little wonder that many Russians came to regard "democracy" as a bitter joke and the market economy as a mechanism for exploitation—just as Communist propaganda had taught. Democratization and economic liberalization became associated in Russians' minds with the breakdown of social and economic order since the late 1980s. Although Russians generally value the idea of democratic rights and freedoms, most people tend to consider them remote and unattainable in Russia.

Both nostalgia for the old order and aspirations for a better future set standards by which people judge the current regime harshly. Most Russians are highly critical of the performance of the current regime—apart from Putin. Russians think that the country's leaders are mainly concerned with their own power and wealth rather than with the country's well-being. A 2004 survey suggests the low esteem in which citizens hold their leaders (see Table 12.1). Although they have a low opinion of the authorities in general, Russians have varying levels of trust in different institutions. Table 12.2 indicates that the army

T A B L E   1 2 . 1   How Do You Regard the People Currently in Power? (in %)

They are people concerned only with their own material and career well-being.	53
They are honorable but weak people, unable to use power and ensure order and a consistent policy.	14
They are honorable but incompetent people who do not know how to lead the country out of its economic crisis.	9
They are a good team of politicians who are leading the country in the right direction.	13
Hard to answer.	11

February 2004, N=1600.

Source: Yuri Levada, "Svoboda ot vybora? Postelektoral'nye razmyshleniia," published on website Polit.ru, May 18, 2004.

and regional governors enjoy somewhat higher confidence than most other institutions; the table also confirms that Putin towers over all other structures. It is striking, however, that Russians ascribe the greatest power to some of the institutions in which they have the lowest confidence. This is particularly notable in the case of banks, industrial managers, and the State Duma.

Survey after survey shows that citizens have little faith in the current political system, although there is a good deal more confidence in Putin than in any other individual leaders or institutions. Since he has come into power, Putin's approval ratings have consistently remained between 70 and 80 percent, higher by far than any other leader or institution.[16] The number of Russians who approve of the activity of the prime minister (as of June 2004) is only 37 percent (44 percent disapprove) and only 38 percent give a favorable rating to the activity of the government as a whole, while 54 percent give it an unfavorable rating.[17] Russians give Putin credit above all for reversing the deterioration of living standards: 24 percent of the population cite this as his main achievement.[18] These figures show how successful Putin has been at taking credit for positive developments in the country and allowing the government to take the blame for continuing problems. Not surprisingly, Putin's popularity leads Russians to want to give him sweeping power over the political system. After the March 2004 presidential election, a nationwide survey found that 68 percent agreed with the statement that concentrating nearly all state power in Putin's hands "would be beneficial to Russia." Fifty-four percent believed that the best system would be one in which the government "is fully sub-

T A B L E   1 2 . 2   Trust in Institutions; Assessed Influence of Institutions

Institution	% Expressing Trust	% Ascribing Influence
Bankers, financiers	6	59
Governor of region	34	54
Television	29	43
Federal Security Service (FSB)	26	42
Army	34	38
Directors of industrial enterprises	8	36
Duma members	8	36
Newspapers	25	33
Parties	6	29
Constitutional Court	24	29
Police	15	28
SMD representative	11	23
President Putin	53	79

Source: New Russian Barometer X. Nationwide survey 17 June–3 July 2001. N=2000. Figures represent percentage of respondents giving each institution a rating of at least 5 on a 7-point scale. Cited in Richard Rose and Neil Munro, *Elections Without Order: Russia's Challenge to Vladimir Putin* (Cambridge: Cambridge University Press, 2002), p. 226.

Note: Question: To what extent do you trust each of these institutions to look after your interests?

Question: How much influence do you think each of the following groups has on Russian life today?

TABLE 12.3 Assessments of Current Political System

	Better (in %)	Same (in %)	Worse (in %)	Difference Between Better and Worse (%)
Everybody has freedom of choice in religious matters	79	16	5	74
One can join any organization one likes	75	18	7	68
Everybody has a right to say what they think	73	21	6	67
Everyone can decide individually whether or not to take an interest in politics	66	27	7	59

Source: New Russian Barometer VII. Nationwide survey, 6 March–13 April 1998. N=1904. Cited in Richard Rose and Neil Munro, *Elections Without Order: Russia's Challenge to Vladimir Putin* (Cambridge: Cambridge University Press, 2002), p. 67.

Note: Question: Compared to our system of government before perestroika, would you say that our current system is better, much the same, or not so good as the old system in the following respects.

ordinate to the president and his administration."[19] After the series of terrorist incidents in summer 2004, culminating with the Beslan school siege in September, the public supported Putin and his handling of the crisis while expressing sharp criticism of the police and security forces for allowing the terrorists to strike with impunity at civilian targets.

Russians' impatience with a separation of powers system, and their faith in Putin, does not mean that they do not also want democratic rights and freedoms for themselves. Indeed, paradoxically, many associate Putin with democracy. Over half of the population (55 percent) thought that following Putin's reelection as president in 2004 the country would develop as a democracy; the comparable figure in 2000 was only 35 percent.[20] Russians prize their right to criticize the authorities: 76 percent of respondents think it is permissible to criticize Putin, and 86 percent think criticism of the government is permissible.[21] And as skeptical as they are of elections, they nonetheless value the opportunity elections give them to choose representatives. Russians also value the freedoms that democratization has brought. Comparing the present system with the Soviet regime before Gorbachev, Russians recognize that they are much freer of state controls (see Table 12.3).

The political culture thus combines contradictory elements. Russians do value democratic rights, but experience has taught them that under the banner of democracy, politicians can abuse their power to the detriment of the integrity of the state and the well-being of society. They also feel powerless to af-

fect state policy. Little wonder that a leader such as Putin can command such widespread support despite the general mistrust Russians have for the post-Soviet political institutions. Russians see him as restoring order following a protracted period of social and political breakdown. Faced with a hypothetical choice between democratic freedoms and a guaranteed income, Russians are closely divided (see Table 12.4).

The survey results reported here illustrate the contradictory influences on Russian political culture. On the one hand, Russians associate democratization with loss and breakdown: the loss of the Soviet Union, the breakdown of familiar principles of political and economic organization, the deterioration of employment and social safety nets. On the other hand, Russians value democratic freedoms. There is considerable continuity with the past in support for the idea that the state should ensure society's

TABLE 12.4 Democratic Freedoms vs. Guaranteed Income

Agree	26%
More agree than disagree	17%
More disagree than agree	23%
Disagree	25%

Source: New Russian Barometer VII. Nationwide survey, 6 March–13 April 1998. N=1904. Cited in Richard Rose and Neil Munro, *Elections Without Order: Russia's Challenge to Vladimir Putin* (Cambridge: Cambridge University Press, 2002).

Note: Question: Are you agreed with the following opinion: If state guarantees to me a normal wage and decent pension, I am prepared to give up freedom of speech and the right to travel freely abroad.

prosperity and the citizens' material security.[22] More than in Western Europe or the United States, Russians believe that the state is responsible for providing a just moral and social order, with justice being understood as social equality more than as equality before the law.[23] This pattern reflects the lasting influence of traditional conceptions of state and society on Russian political culture. Still, few would support the reestablishment of Soviet rule or a reversion to a military dictatorship. Most people think that the tremendous upheavals they have experienced since the late 1980s will result in an improved life—not soon, but "eventually."[24]

Political culture is also shaped by slower-acting but more lasting influences, including the succession of generations, rising educational levels, and urbanization.[25]

The shift in values and beliefs has accelerated as new generations of young people are exposed to fundamentally different influences than those to which their parents were exposed. The older generation, for instance, views Stalin much more favorably than among the younger generations.[26] To a large extent, these differences are mutually reinforcing: the older generations tend to have lower levels of education and less exposure to the more cosmopolitan way of life of cities.

Political Socialization

The Soviet regime devoted enormous effort to political indoctrination and propaganda. The regime controlled the content of school curricula, mass media, popular culture, political education, and nearly every other channel by which values and attitudes were formed. The heart of Soviet doctrine was the Marxist belief that the way in which a society organizes its production—feudalism, capitalism, socialism, and so forth—determines the structure of values and beliefs prevalent in the society. The idea was that the ruling class in each society determines the basic ideology of the society. Therefore, Soviet propaganda and indoctrination emphasized that Soviet citizens were part of a worldwide working class movement to overthrow capitalism and replace it with socialism, in which there would be no private property. Needing to knit together a highly diverse multinational state, the Soviet regime downplayed national feeling and replaced it with a sense of patriotic loyalty to the Soviet state

and to the working class's interests in the worldwide class struggle.

Today the ideology of Russian education has changed significantly. In place of the idea of the class struggle and the international solidarity of the working class, textbooks stress love for the Russian national heritage. Historical figures who in the Communist era were honored as heroes of the struggle of ordinary people against feudal or capitalist masters are now held up as great representatives of Russia's national culture.[27] There is still a strong emphasis on loyalty to Russia as a state, but now it is wedded to Russian nationalism. This is logical, in view of Russia's effort to create a new sense of national community within the new post-Soviet state boundaries.

There is also a strong undercurrent of desire for some sort of restored union among at least some of the former Soviet republics. Russian television broadcasts pay considerable attention to activities in the "near abroad," as Russians term the other former Soviet republics. Russians continue to feel tied to the other republics by decades of shared social, economic, cultural, and political experience. Putin and other politicians actively play on this sentiment, calling for the reinforcement of ties between Russia and its neighbors in the Commonwealth of Independent States (CIS). Sergei Shoigu, the relatively popular minister for Emergency Situation, noted during the parliament election campaign in November 2003 that he hoped "to live to see the day when we have one big country within the borders of the [former] Soviet Union." A former KGB chairman went so far as to say that "if we do not reassemble the Soviet Union, we have no future at all."[28] Putin rarely goes so far as to call for rebuilding the Soviet Union, but he regularly declares that it is a strategic imperative for Russia to strengthen the CIS.[29] The neo-imperial currents running through Russian political culture undercut the effort to create a new post-Soviet national community based on democratic values.

The contradictory forces acting on political culture reflect both the dislocations of the transition from Soviet rule as well as aspirations awakened by the longer-term process of modernization. Support for democratic principles coexists with severe discontent with the way reform turned out in practice, nostalgia for the certainties of the Soviet order, and regret at the breakup of the Soviet Union. Russians value highly their right to vote, and they have exercised it actively in recent elections. Overwhelming majorities of the public rate the present regime preferable to the old Communist regime with respect to freedom of speech, freedom of religion, and freedom of association.[30] Russians are skeptical about their ability to influence the current political system but most regard Putin favorably, and if his efforts to raise economic growth rates and living standards are successful, confidence in the system as a whole will gradually rise. As Richard Rose argues, the reason Russians generally approve the current regime is not because they consider it to be ideal, but because it has improved economic well-being and they see little prospect for changing it.[31]

Political attitudes are relatively independent of citizens' evaluations of the performance of the current regime, but attitudes about the market economy have shifted markedly as the economic situation worsened in the 1990s. As time passes, support for democracy will therefore rest on two interacting forces: the turnover of generations, and the performance of the regime. The collapse of Communist rule and the promise of democratic equality awakened expectations that have been cruelly disappointed. Many Russians consider democracy an ideal that is unattainable for Russia at present, and are willing to settle for a regime that provides basic order and well-being.

POLITICAL PARTICIPATION

In a democracy, citizens take part in public life both through direct forms of political participation, such as voting, party work, organizing for a cause, demonstrating, lobbying, and more indirect forms of participation, such as membership in civic groups and voluntary associations. Both kinds of participation influence the quality of government. By means of collective action citizens signal to policymakers what they want government to do. Through these channels of participation activists rise to positions of leadership. But, despite the legal equality of citizens in democracies, levels of participation across groups in the population vary with differences in resources, opportunities, and motivations. The better-off and better-educated are disproportionately involved in political life everywhere, but in some societies the disproportion is much greater than in others.[32]

The Importance of Social Capital

A healthy fabric of voluntary associations has been recognized since de Tocqueville's time as an important component of democracy. As Robert Putnam has shown, participation in civic life builds social capital—reciprocal bonds of trust and obligation among citizens that facilitate collective action. Where social capital is greater, people treat one another as equals rather than as members of social hierarchies. They are more willing to cooperate in ways that benefit the society and improve the quality of government by sharing the burden of making government accountable and effective.[33] For example, where people feel less distance and mistrust toward government, governments are better able to float bonds to provide improvements to community infrastructure. People are more willing to pay their taxes, so that government has more revenue to spend on public goods—and less ability and less incentive to divert it into politicians' pockets. Both capitalism and democratic government rest on people's ability to cooperate for mutual benefit.

In Russia, however, social capital has historically been scarce compared with West European societies, and participation in civic activity has been extremely limited. Moreover, state and society have generally been separated by mutual mistrust and suspicion. State authorities have usually stood outside and above society, extracting what resources they needed from society but not cultivating ties of obligation to it. To a large extent, the gap between state and society still exists today in Russians' attitudes and behavior. Thus, although Russians turn out to vote in elections in relatively high numbers, participation in organized forms of political activity (that is, not simply talking about politics with others or engaging in protest) is low. Opinion polls show that most people believe that their involvement in political activity is futile, and have little confidence that government serves their interests.

Since the late 1980s, political participation, apart from voting, has seen a brief, intense surge followed by a protracted ebb. Membership in voluntary associations in contemporary Russia is extremely low. According to survey data, 91 percent of the population do not belong to any sports or recreational club, literary or other cultural group, political party, local housing association, or charitable organization. Four percent belong to sports or recreation groups, and 2 percent each say that they belong to a housing bloc, neighborhood association, or cultural group. Only half a percent report being a member of a political party. About 9 percent report attending church at least once a month, and about 20 percent say that they are members of trade unions. Attending religious services and trade union membership are very passive forms of participation in public life. Yet even when these and other types of participation are taken into account, almost 60 percent of the population still are outside any voluntary public associations.[34]

This is not to say that Russian citizens are *psychologically* disengaged from public life or that they are socially isolated. Half of the Russian adult population reports reading national newspapers "regularly" or "sometimes" and almost everyone watches national television "regularly" (81 percent). Sixty-nine percent read local newspapers regularly or sometimes. Sixty-six percent discuss the problems of the country with friends regularly or sometimes and 48 percent say that people ask them their opinions about what is happening in the country. A similar percentage of people discuss the problems of their city with friends.[35] Russians do vote in high proportions in national elections—higher, in fact, than their American counterparts.[36]

Moreover, Russians prize their right *not* to participate in politics.[37] Today's low levels of political participation are a reflection of the low level of confidence in political institutions and the widespread view that ordinary individuals have little influence over government. In one 2000 survey, 85 percent of the respondents expressed the opinion that they have no influence to affect the decisions of the authorities.[38] In another survey, 60 percent said that their vote would not change anything; only 14 percent of the respondents thought that Russia was a democracy while 54 percent said that "overall" it is not a democracy.[39]

The withdrawal from active political participation today results from the shattering of the expectations for change that rose to unrealistic levels in the late 1980s and early 1990s. Gorbachev's policy of relaxing controls on political expression and political participation stimulated a short-lived surge of involvement in many forms of public activity, including mass protests such as strikes and demonstrations, as well as the creation of thousands of new informal organizations. But this wave subsided in the early 1990s. The disengagement and skepticism reflected in public life today certainly reflects disillusionment with how conditions have turned out.

Elite Recruitment

Elite recruitment refers to the institutional processes in a society by which people gain access to positions of influence and responsibility. Elite recruitment is closely tied to political participation, because it is through participation in community activity that people take on leadership roles, learn civic skills such as organization and persuasion, develop networks of friends and supporters, and become interested in pursuing political careers.

In the Soviet regime, the link between participation and elite recruitment was highly formalized. The Communist Party recruited the population into a variety of officially sponsored organizations, such as the Communist Party, youth leagues, trade unions, and women's associations. Through such organizations, the regime identified potential leaders and gave them experience in organizing group activity. The party reserved the right to approve appointments to any position which carried high administrative responsibility or which was likely to affect the formation of public attitudes. The system for recruiting, training, and appointing individuals for positions of leadership and responsibility in the regime was called the **nomenklatura** system. Those individuals who were approved for the positions on nomenklatura lists were informally called "the nomenklatura." Many citizens regarded them as the ruling class in Soviet society.

The democratizing reforms of the late 1980s and early 1990s made two important changes to the process of elite recruitment. First, the old nomenklatura system crumbled along with other Communist Party controls over society. Second, although most members of the old ruling elites adapted themselves to the new circumstances and stayed on in various official capacities, the wave of new informal organizations and popular elections brought many new people into elite positions. Today the contemporary Russian political elite consists of a mixture of career types: some people have worked their way up through the state bureaucracy while others have entered politics through other channels, such as elective politics or business.

President Vladimir Putin offers a reassuring word to Russian citizens.

AFP/Corbis

As in other areas of political life, old Soviet institutional mechanisms for recruitment are being restored under Putin. In the Communist regime, the party maintained schools for training political leaders, where rising officials were given a combination of management education and political indoctrination. Today most of those schools serve a similar function as academies for training civil servants and are overseen by Putin's presidential administration. Moreover, elements of the old nomenklatura system are being restored with a view to ensuring that competent and politically reliable cadres are available for recruitment not only to state bureaucratic positions but even for management positions in major firms.[40]

There are two major differences between elite recruitment in the Communist regime and the present. The nomenklatura system of the Soviet regime ensured that in every walk of life, those who held positions of power and responsibility were approved by the party. They thus formed different sections of a single political elite and owed their positions to their political loyalty and usefulness. Today, however, there are multiple elites (political, business, scientific, cultural, etc.), reflecting the greater degree of pluralism in post-Soviet society.

Second, there are multiple channels for recruitment to today's *political* elite. Many of its members come from positions in the federal and regional executive agencies. Putin in particular has recruited officials for his administration heavily from among the police (the regular police and the security services) and from the military.[41] Other prominent political figures climbed the ladder by winning local or national elections, or after making successful business careers.

The formation of a business elite, in fact, is one of the most remarkable phenomena since the end of the Soviet regime. Many of today's successful businesspeople came out of the old Soviet nomenklatura, as old guard bureaucrats discovered ways to cash in on their political contacts and get rich quickly. Money from the Communist Party found its way into the establishment of many new business ventures, including several of the first commercial banks.[42] As early as 1987 and 1988, officials of the Communist Youth League (Komsomol) saw the possibilities of using the organizations' assets to set up lucrative business ventures, such as video salons, banks, discos, tour agencies, and publishing houses.[43] They took advantage of their insider contacts, obtaining business licenses, office space, and exclusive contracts with little difficulty. Some bought (at bargain basement prices) controlling interests in state firms that were undergoing privatization, and a few years later found themselves millionaires or billionaires.

Other members of the new business elite rose through channels outside the state. Many, in fact, entered business in the late 1980s, as new opportunities for legal and quasi-legal commercial activity opened up. A strikingly high proportion of the first generation of the new business elite comprised young scientists and mathematicians working in research institutes and universities. The new commercial sector sprang up very quickly. By the end of 1992 there were nearly 1 million private businesses registered, with some 16 million people working in them.[44]

The new business elite is closely tied to the state, sometimes in order to capture benefits, and sometimes because state officials keep business on a short leash. Financial-industrial conglomerates often cultivate strategic alliances with well-placed officials in the government. Both under Yeltsin and Putin, bureaucratic factions form around particular enterprises and industries. Businesses need licenses, permits, contracts, exemptions and other benefits from government. Political officials, in turn, need financial contributions to their campaigns, political support, favorable media coverage, and other benefits that business can provide. In the 1990s, the close and collusive relations between many businesses and government officials nurtured widespread corruption and the meteoric rise of a small group of business tycoons popularly known as oligarchs. The oligarchs took advantage of their links to President Yeltsin's administration to acquire control of some of Russia's most valuable companies. The prominence of the newly rich fed a strong public backlash that made it politically viable for President Putin to suppress some of them and destroy their business empires by police methods. The notion that businesspeople can make money honestly and benefit society by doing so strikes many people as a hopelessly naive proposition. Many therefore welcome a heavy-handed state to protect them from the power of the wealthy. But often when the state cracks down on a particular business empire, it is a maneuver by one bureaucratic faction to acquire control of a lucrative business asset from another, not a step toward the rule of law.

INTEREST ARTICULATION: BETWEEN STATISM AND PLURALISM

The political and economic changes of the last decade in Russia have had a powerful impact on the way social interests are organized. A far more diverse spectrum of interest associations has developed than existed under the Communist regime. There are tens of thousands of non-governmental organizations—a phenomenon that could not exist in the Communist society, when the Communist Party oversaw all organizations. The pattern of interest articulation, however, still reflects the powerful impact of state control over society as well as the sharp disparities in wealth and power that formed during the transition period. A few organizations have considerable influence in policymaking, while other groups have little. Patron-client networks between state officials and their patrons and their clients remain a persistent feature of political life. The old regime did not tolerate the open pursuit of any interests except those authorized by the state. Interest organizations such as trade unions, youth groups, professional societies and the like were closely supervised by the Communist Party. This statist model of interest articulation was upset by glasnost. Glasnost stimulated an explosion of political expression which in turn prompted groups to form and to make political demands and participate in elections. It is hard today to imagine how profound was the impact of glasnost on Soviet society. Suddenly it opened the floodgates to a growing stream of startling facts, ideas, disclosures, reappraisals, scandals, and sensations. Gorbachev was clearly surprised by the range and intensity of the new demands that erupted. In loosening the party's controls over communication sufficiently to encourage people to speak and write freely and openly, Gorbachev also relinquished the controls that would have enabled him to limit political expression when it went too far.

As people voiced their deep-felt demands and grievances, others recognized that they shared the same beliefs and values, and made common cause with them, sometimes forming new, unofficial organizations. Therefore, one result of glasnost was a wave of participation in "informal"—that is, unlicensed and uncontrolled—public associations. Daring publications in the media allowed people with common interests to identify one another and encouraged them to come together to form independent associations. When the authorities tried to limit or prohibit such groups, they generated still more frustration and protest. Associations of all sorts formed: groups dedicated to remembering the victims of Stalin's terror; ultra-nationalists who wanted to restore tsarism; nationalist movements in many republics. The devastating explosion of the nuclear reactor at Chernobyl in 1986 had a tremendous impact in stimulating the formation of environmental protest, linked closely to nationalist sentiment in Belarus and Ukraine.[45]

The elimination of the state's monopoly on productive property resulted in the formation of new interests, among them those with a stake in the market economy. No longer does the state demand that organized groups serve a state-defined political agenda, as was the case under the old regime. Now groups can form freely to represent a diversity of interests, compete for access to influence and resources, and define their own agenda. By 2001, there were over 300,000 non-governmental, non-commercial organizations registered with the government, of which around 70,000 were active.[46] Over 2 million people work in these organizations as activists and employees, and around 12–13 percent of the population receive assistance in some form from them.[47]

As new interest organizations have formed, they have entered into a variety of relationships with the state. Some organizations have survived into the new regime, clinging to their organizational assets and legacies and continuing to seek "insider" access to the state. Others that have sprung up from scratch also work closely with legislative and executive authorities, but others play "outsider" roles, trying to influence government by mobilizing public attention and support. The pattern of interest group activity is more pluralist than corporatist because the very rapidity with which new associations have formed has defeated efforts by both government and interest groups to form monopolistic, stable, comprehensive umbrella organizations that the state could treat as the official voice of a particular interest. In most cases, interest associations are too numerous, too weak internally, and too competitive for corporatism to succeed.

Let us consider three examples of associational groups: the **Russian Union of Industrialists and Entrepreneurs (RUIE)**, the **League of Committees of Soldiers' Mothers**, and the **Federation of Independent Trade Unions of Russia (FITUR)**. They illustrate different strategies for organization and influence.

The Russian Union of Industrialists and Entrepreneurs

Most formerly state-owned industrial firms are now wholly or partly privately owned. More and more industrial managers respond to the incentives of a market economy rather than those of a state socialist economy. Under the old regime, managers were told to fulfill the plan regardless of cost or quality. Profit was not a relevant consideration.[48] Now, more managers seek to maximize profits and increase the value of their firms. Although many still demand subsidies and protection from the state, more and more would prefer an environment where laws and contracts are enforced by the state, regulation is reasonable and honest, taxes are fair (and low), and barriers to foreign trade are minimized. These gradual changes are visible in the changing political interests of the association that represents the interests of big business in Russia, the Russian Union of Industrialists and Entrepreneurs, or RUIE. The RUIE is the single most powerful organized interest group in Russia. Its members comprise both the old state industrial firms (now mostly private or quasi-private) and the newer financial-industrial conglomerates headed by the oligarchs. Its long-time president is Arkadii Vol'skii, who had been a senior CPSU official. In the early 1990s the RUIE's lobbying efforts were aimed at winning continued state support of industrial firms and planning for a slow transition to a market economy. The RUIE also helped broker agreements between business and labor, and was a source of policy advice for government and parliament.

With time, the RUIE's political goals have shifted and its clout has grown. Policymakers in the Putin administration have institutionalized consultation with the RUIE in developing economic policy. The improvement in economic conditions at the end of the 1990s made the RUIE's members more interested in improving the business environment for Russia generally, rather than in capturing industry-specific privileges. The RUIE expanded its in-house capacity for working with the government and the parliament in drafting legislation. On a wide range of issues such as land reform; tax law; pension policy; bankruptcy legislation; reform of the natural gas, energy, and railroad monopolies; regulation of the securities market; and the terms of Russia's entry to the WTO, the RUIE has been active and influential in shaping policy. A measure of its stature is the fact that at its annual conference in June 2001, the prime minister, two deputy prime ministers, the minister of economic development, the head of the state pension fund, several governors, and officials from more than 50 regions attended.

Yet the limits of RUIE's power as the collective voice of big business are clear. When the Putin regime began its campaign to destroy the Yukos oil firm starting in July 2003 (see subsequent discussion), RUIE confined itself to mild expressions of concern. Its members, evidently fearful of crossing Putin, chose not to defend Yukos' head, Mikhail Khodorkovsky, or to protest the use of police methods to destroy one of Russia's largest oil companies. Instead, they promised to meet their tax obligations and to do more to help the country fight poverty. Putin pointedly avoided meeting with RUIE and other business association leaders from November 2003 to July 2004—and then agreed to meet with them only on the condition that the subject of Yukos not be discussed. Perhaps if big business had taken a strong and united stand, they could have influenced state policy. But the desire by each individual firm to maintain friendly relations with the government and fear of government reprisals undercut business's capacity for collective action.

The Yukos Affair One of the most widely publicized episodes of the Putin era concerns the state's drive to break up the powerful oil company Yukos, whose head, Mikhail Khodorkovsky, was one of the most prominent of Russia's new post-Communist magnates. Khodorkovsky began as one of a group of young Komsomol activists working in the Moscow city government in the late 1980s who used their Komsomol resources and connections to start a bank called Menatep. Financing from the Menatep bank enabled them to acquire—at a bargain basement price—80 percent of the shares of the Yukos oil company when the government privatized it in 1995. At first, Khodorkovsky sought to squeeze maximum profit from the firm. Soon, however, his business strategy changed, and he made Yukos the most dynamic of Russia's oil companies. Khodorkovsky discovered that by emulating Western business practices the company could increase its net worth and productive capacity. At its peak in 2002, the company's assets were worth about $20 billion, and Khodorkovsky owned nearly $8 billion. He was Russia's wealthiest citizen.

Meantime, Khodorkovsky created a foundation called Open Russia and launched several charitable initiatives. Khodorkovsky also was active in Russian politics, funding democratic parties, and sponsoring the election campaigns of several deputies to the State Duma. Detractors accused him of wanting to control parliament and even of wanting to change the constitution to turn it into a parliamentary system. There was talk that he intended to seek the presidency.

Without consulting with the Kremlin, he began talks with foreign oil companies on selling a significant share of Yukos stock. In April 2003, Yukos announced an agreement to merge with another Russian oil company, which would have created Russia's largest oil company. In June 2003 he signed an agreement with China for Yukos to build a major oil pipeline that would supply a quarter of China's oil imports. At a meeting at the Kremlin in February 2003, Khodorkovsky even crossed swords with President Putin over a deal by which a state-owned oil company had acquired a private firm, complaining openly to Putin that the deal was corrupt.

At some point in spring 2003, the Putin administration evidently decided that Khodorkovsky and Yukos had grown too independent and must be destroyed. In a series of actions beginning in July 2003, several top figures in Yukos and associated companies were arrested and charged with fraud, embezzlement, tax evasion, and even murder. One case involved a privatization deal going back to 1993. The police raided the offices of the company and a number of its affiliates. They even raided the office of an orphanage sponsored by Open Russia. In October 2003, Khodorkovsky was arrested and charged with fraud and tax evasion. The courts refused to release him on bail. At the end of December, the government opened another front against the company, charging it with failure to pay taxes in the years from 1998 to 2003. The tax ministry demanded that the company pay 100 billion rubles (about $3.4 billion) in unpaid taxes from 2000 and declared that more claims from 2001, 2002, and 2003 were pending. The government froze the company's bank accounts as collateral against the claims. In July 2004 the company defaulted on payments to foreign banks for loans and claimed that it could not meet the government's demands. It threatened that it would have to begin laying off workers. The government continued to step up its campaign against Yukos. In December 2004 it seized control of the company's largest production subsidiary (responsible for about 60 percent of Yukos' total oil output) and auctioned it off to an obscure company which the next day was bought by

Rosneft', a fully state-owned oil company headed by one of President Putin's top aides.

Analysts have suggested many reasons for the government's relentless campaign against Yukos, which has harmed Russia's economy. Yukos had been Russia's fastest-growing and most forward-looking energy company. It was responsible for the rapid growth of Russian oil exports, and was a model of the transformation of the "robber barons" of the 1990s into entrepreneurial capitalists. Indirectly, the government's campaign had a chilling effect on Russian and foreign investment. Some have suggested political motives, arguing that Khodorkovsky, through his refusal to kowtow to the authorities and his liberal spending in the political arena, was challenging Putin. Some have taken the authorities' explanations at face value, accepting the argument that Yukos had indeed engaged in shady tax-avoidance schemes and that it was getting no more than its just desserts. The problem with this explanation is the selective and coordinated nature of the campaign against Yukos. All major Russian companies had behaved as Yukos had, seeking to take advantage of legal loopholes in order to minimize taxes and maximize profits. But only Yukos was singled out for attention. The dismantling of Yukos and destruction of Khodorkovsky were very similar in this respect to the authorities' successful campaigns to break up the business empires of two other oligarchs in 2000, Boris Berezovsky and Vladimir Gusinsky, who had turned against Putin. In those cases as well, criminal and civil prosecutions were used as weapons to dismantle their companies and drive their leaders into exile overseas.

Another, more plausible, explanation for the Yukos affair is that it is part of a struggle among intra-bureaucratic factions over the distribution of control over profitable business assets. Whatever the motives for the authorities' actions, the Yukos affair shows that the regime will manipulate the legal system for political purposes, and that many of the most important political contests in Russia are fought out within the state bureaucracy rather than in the open arena of public politics.

The League of Committees of Soldiers' Mothers

The Soviet regime sponsored several official women's organizations, but these mainly served pro-

paganda purposes. During the glasnost period, a number of unofficial women's organizations sprang up. One such group was the Committee of Soldiers' Mothers. It formed in the spring of 1989 when some 300 women in Moscow rallied to protest the end of student deferments from military conscription. In response to their actions, Gorbachev agreed to restore the deferments. Since then the movement has grown, with local branches forming in hundreds of cities, joined together in the League of Committees of Soldiers' Mothers. Their focus has expanded somewhat but remains centered on the problems of military service. The league presses the military to eliminate the use of soldiers' labor in its construction battalions and to end the brutal hazing of recruits which results in the deaths (in many cases by suicide) of hundreds of soldiers each year. The league also helps young men avoid being conscripted.[49]

The onset of large-scale hostilities in Chechnia in 1994–1996 and 1999–2000 stimulated a new burst of activity by the league. It helped families locate soldiers who were missing in action or captured by the Chechen rebel forces. It sent missions to Chechnia to negotiate for the release of prisoners and to provide proper burial for the dead. It collected information about the actual scale of the war and of its casualties. It also continued to advise families on ways to avoid conscription and to lobby for decent treatment of recruits. Through the 1990s, it became one of the most sizable and respected civic groups in Russia. It can call upon a network of thousands of active volunteers for its work. They visit wounded soldiers in hospitals and help military authorities in identifying casualties. One of the movement's greatest assets is its moral authority as mothers defending the interests of their children. This stance makes it hard for their opponents to paint them as unpatriotic or power-hungry.

The league actively lobbies parliament (for example, it fought to liberalize the law on alternative civil service for conscientious objectors but with only modest success), but for the most part it concentrates on helping soldiers and their families deal with their problems. Thus it performs multiple functions, combining political goals with services to clients. Unlike many Russian associational groups, the league has chosen to remain independent of government, not seeking any special privileges or recognition.

Like many non-governmental organizations, the League of Committees of Soldiers' Mothers cultivates ties with peace and women's groups in Europe and North America, and has won widespread international recognition for its work. For some groups, such ties are a source of dependence, as organizations compensate for the lack of mass membership with aid and knowhow from counterpart organizations abroad. However, these dilemmas of organizational development have not been a serious problem for the soldiers' mothers movement, which has a vital and self-sustaining base of support for its activity despite the sometimes-hostile attitude of the authorities.[50]

The Federation of Independent Trade Unions of Russia

The Federation of Independent Trade Unions of Russia (FITUR) is the successor of the official trade union federation under the Soviet regime. Unlike RUIE, however, it has poorly adapted itself to the post-Communist environment even though it inherited substantial organizational resources from the old Soviet trade union organization. In the Soviet era, virtually every employed person belonged to a trade union. All branch and regional trade union organizations were part of a single labor federation, called the All-Union Central Council of Trade Unions. With the breakdown of the old regime, some of the member unions became independent, while other unions sprang up as independent bodies representing the interests of particular groups of workers. Nonetheless, the nucleus of the old official trade union organization survived, and is called the Federation of Independent Trade Unions of Russia. It remains by far the largest trade union federation in Russia. Around 95 percent of all organized workers belong to unions which at least formally are members of FITUR. The independent unions are much smaller. By comparison with big business, however, the labor movement is fragmented, weak, and unable to mobilize workers effectively for collective action.

FITUR inherited valuable real estate assets from its Soviet-era predecessor organization, including thousands of office buildings, hotels, rest homes, hospitals, and children's camps. It also inherited the right to collect workers' contributions for the state social insurance fund. Control of this fund enabled the official trade unions to acquire enormous income-producing property over the years. These assets and income streams give leaders of the official unions considerable advantages in competing for members. But the FITUR no longer has centralized control over its regional and branch members. In the 1993 and 1995 parliamentary elections, for instance, member unions formed their own political alliances with parties. Thus internal disunity is another major reason for the relative weakness of FITUR as an organization. Much of its effort is expended on fighting other independent unions to win a monopoly on representing workers in collective bargaining with employers rather than in joining with other unions to defend the interests of workers generally.[51]

The ineffectiveness of the FITUR is also illustrated by the tepid response of organized labor to the severe deterioration in labor and social conditions in the 1990s. There has been much less labor protest than might be expected. Unrest did increase through the 1990s, mainly because of wage arrears. Surveys find that in the 1990s, in any given year, three-quarters of all workers received their wages late at least once.[52] Teachers were particularly hard hit by the problem of unpaid wages and organized numerous local strikes. Waves of strikes by teachers shut down thousands of schools in the late 1990s. After 1999, teachers' protests subsided somewhat as wage arrears gradually were paid off thanks to the beginning of the economic recovery.[53]

We might wonder why there has not been more labor protest. One reason is workers' dependence on the enterprises where they work for a variety of social benefits which are administered through the enterprise, such as pension contributions, cheap housing, and access to medical clinics and day care facilities.[54] Another, however, is the close, clientelistic relationship between the leadership of the FITUR and government authorities. Like business, organized labor for the most part prefers to cultivate a clientelistic relationship with the political authorities rather than to stand independently of them.

New Sectors of Interest

In a time when people's interests themselves are changing rapidly, interest groups search for new roles. Some old groups decline, while new organizations form. In Russia, many new associations have formed around the interests of new categories of actors. Bankers, political consultants, realtors, mayors of small cities, mayors of large cities, judges, attorneys, auditors, television broadcasters, political consultants, and numerous other professional and occupational groups have all formed associations to seek favorable policies or regulate professional standards. Environmental groups, women's organizations, human rights activists, and many other cause-oriented groups have organized. Most of these operate in a particular locality, but a few have national scope.

The rules of the game for interest articulation are not well established. In the Yeltsin period, lobbying frequently took corrupt forms, including bribery of parliamentary deputies and government officials. By the end of the 1990s, more collective action by business and other sectors of interest was evident and there was more open bargaining over the details of policy.[55] Under Putin, however, policy-making is more centralized again, and interest groups are more dependent on the goodwill of the president for access. Still, organized interests still press their demands through the mass media, the parliament, and the government, and public pressure does have some impact on policymaking.

PARTIES AND THE AGGREGATION OF INTERESTS

Interest aggregation refers to the generalization of the demands of various groups of the population into programmatic options for government. Although other political institutions also aggregate interests, parties are the quintessential structure for this vital task. How well parties aggregate interests, define choices for voters, and hold politicians accountable is of critical importance to democracy.

In Russia, despite over a decade of post-Communist political development, the party system remains tenuous and fluid. There is considerable turnover in the parties that run in parliamentary elections from election to election. Politicians are constantly starting new parties, only to abandon them after the election. Voters have little sense of attachment to parties and more often associate them with particular politicians' personalities than with specific ideological stances. In the Duma, deputies do organize their political activity around party factions, but most of these parties have very weak roots

in society. Party activity in Russia is organized more around *patronage*—the delivery of particularistic benefits to favored client groups—than around mobilizing support for the achievement of *programmatic* goals.

The struggle between democratic reformers and their Communist opponents, which defined the politics of 1989–1991, helped shape the party system in the first half of the 1990s. Some parties allied themselves with the democratic movement, while others remain wedded to Marxist-Leninist ideology. Still others identify themselves with Russian nationalism. All three tendencies—democratic, communist, and nationalist—can still be found in the spectrum of Russia's political parties today.

Since the mid-1990s, however, ideological conflict has faded in importance. Instead there have been repeated efforts to create patronage parties with strong official sponsorship. Such a party is known as a **party of power**. It is a party that both state officials and voters recognize as enjoying the favor of power-holders. To the voters, such a party presents an image of continuity and stability. For officeholders, it is a vehicle for career advancement. At present United Russia embodies the model perfectly. However, in the 1990s there were several less successful predecessors that formed and faded away before United Russia came to dominate the political scene.

Each parliamentary election brings a new impetus to the formation of political parties. Presidential elections, however, have not had a similar effect. Because Russia's presidential system encourages the president to avoid making commitments to parties, presidential elections have tended to concentrate attention on the candidates' personalities rather than their policy programs, and therefore have undermined party development. Yet even in parliamentary elections, each new election presents voters with a substantially new set of party choices, making it hard for voters to develop any lasting attachments to parties or to make sensible judgments about parties' past or future performance.

Elections and Party Development

The 1989 and 1990 Elections   The development of parties began with the elections under Gorbachev to the reformed USSR and Russian Republic parliaments. Democratically oriented politicians coalesced

T A B L E   1 2 . 5   Party-List Vote in Duma Elections, 1993, 1995, 1999, and 2003

Party	1993	1995	1999	2003
Democratic Parties				
Russia's Choice	15.51	3.9	—	—
Union of Rightist Forces (SPS)	—	—	8.52	4.0
Yabloko	7.86	6.89	5.93	4.37
Party of Russian Unity and Concord (PRES)	6.76	—	—	—
Democratic Party of Russia (DPR)	5.52	—	—	.2
Centrist Parties				
Women of Russia	8.13	4.6	2.04	—
Civic Union[a]	1.93	1.6	—	—
Parties of Power				
Our Home Is Russia	—	10.1	1.2	—
Fatherland—All Russia (OVR)	—	—	13.33	—
Unity/United Russia[b]	—	—	23.32	38.2
Nationalist Parties				
Liberal Democratic Party of Russia (LDPR)[c]	22.92	11.2	5.98	11.6
Congress of Russian Communities (KRO)[d]	—	4.3	.62	—
Motherland (Rodina)	—	—	—	9.2
Leftist Parties				
Communist Party of the Russian Federation (CPRF)	12.4	22.3	24.29	12.8
Agrarian Party	7.99	3.8	—	3.69
Other parties failing to meet 5% threshold	10.98	26.81	12.55	11.1
Against all	4.36	2.8	3.34	4.8

Source: Compiled by author from reports of Central Electoral Commission.

[a]In 1995, the same alliance renamed itself the Bloc of Trade Unionists and Industrialists.

[b]In 2003, Unity ran under the name United Russia following a merger with the Fatherland party.

[c]In 1999, the LDPR party list was called the Zhirinovsky bloc.

[d]In 1999, this party was called "Congress of Russian Communities and Yuri Boldyrev Movement."

to form legislative caucus in the USSR Congress of People's Deputies in 1989, and in turn helped a broad coalition of democratic candidates run for the Russian Congress in 1990. In parliament, democratic factions competed for influence with communist, nationalist, agrarian, and other political groups. These parliamentary factions became the nuclei of political parties in the parliamentary election of December 1993.

Table 12.5 indicates the results of the party-list voting in the 1993, 1995, 1999, and 2003 elections, and Figure 12.4 shows the distribution of parliamentary parties' seats in the Duma following the 1999 and 2003 elections.

Parliamentary factions vary in their composition. A few have substantial numbers of both list and single-member district (SMD) deputies, but most are composed predominantly of one type of member or the other. Some factions are "start-up" groups made up of independents elected in SMD races who do not wish to affiliate themselves with the party factions, while for others, the core of their membership are deputies elected on the party list. In the case of United Russia in the current Duma, about 60 percent of the members are from single-member districts—which means that 80 percent of single-member district deputies elected in 2003 chose to join the United Russia faction. This is a good indication of the power of the United Russia bandwagon.

The 1993 and 1995 Elections   The 1993 election produced a shock—the pro-reform, pro-Yeltsin

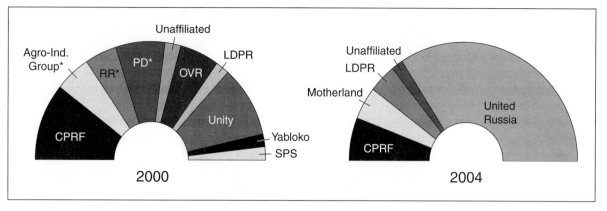

F I G U R E   1 2 . 4   Seat Shares of Parliamentary Parties in State Duma, 2000 and 2004

Source: Compiled by author from reports of State Duma.

Note: Figures taken as of January 2000 and May 2004. Percentages shift with time as members change factional affiliations. Note that United Russia was the result of a merger of the Fatherland party with Unity.

*These were groups made up of deputies elected in single-member districts who chose not to affiliate with any of the party-based factions, but were registered as official deputy groups on the basis of having at least 35 members. In the 2004 Duma, there were no such groups.

party, Russia's Choice, did unexpectedly poorly, while Vladimir Zhirinovsky's misleadingly named Liberal Democratic Party of Russia (LDPR) did unexpectedly well. The Communists (**Communist Party of the Russian Federation**, or CPRF) took about 10 percent of the seats. Altogether the democratic factions received about 38 percent of the seats in the Duma, the left about 20 percent, and centrist factions about 20 percent. No political camp had a majority, but Zhirinovsky's oppositional stance meant the anti-Yeltsin forces had a narrow majority.

In the 1995 elections a wide array of political groups competed—far more than could possibly be accommodated given that the same 5 percent threshold rule was kept. Some 43 organizations registered and won a spot on the ballot. In the end, only four parties crossed the 5 percent threshold: the Communists, Zhirinovsky's LDPR, the "Our Home Is Russia" bloc formed around Prime Minister Chernomyrdin, and the Yabloko party. Of these, the Communists were the most successful, winding up with nearly a third of the seats in the Duma. Altogether, half of the votes were cast for parties that failed to win any seats on the party-list ballot.

The 1996 Presidential Election   The 1995 parliamentary election was a test of strength for Russia's parties and leaders. The big unknown was how Yeltsin would perform in the 1996 presidential race.

At the beginning of 1996 his approval was in the single digits.[56] During the campaign, Yeltsin succeeded in persuading voters that the election was about a choice between him and a return to communism.

This strategy worked. Yeltsin's displays of vigor during the campaign, his lavish promises to voters, and his domination of media publicity, all contributed to a remarkable surge in popularity and a victory over Gennadii Ziuganov, his Communist rival (see Table 12.6).[57] The campaign took its toll on Yeltsin, however. Soon afterward he had major heart surgery and for much of his second term he was in poor health.

The 1999 Elections   The 1999 election was dominated by the question of who would succeed Yeltsin as president. Many federal and regional officeholders wanted to rally around a new "party of power" in order to protect their positions. A group of backroom Kremlin strategists formed a movement called Unity in late summer 1999. They wanted to create a political movement that state officials throughout the country could rally around in the parliamentary election. The party would serve as a political vehicle for Vladimir Putin, whom Yeltsin had just named prime minister and anointed as his successor. Conveniently, at the same time as Unity's formation and Putin's appointment, Chechen rebels launched raids into the neighboring region of Dagestan. Bombings of apartment buildings attributed to Chechen terrorists also

Gennadii Ziuganov rallies the Communist Party faithful under a portrait of Vladimir Lenin at a November 1998 anniversary celebration of the October Revolution.

Sergey Chirikov/Corbis/AFP

T A B L E   1 2 . 6   Presidential Election Results (in percent)

	First Round (June 16, 1996)	Second Round (July 3, 1996)
Boris Yeltsin	35.28	53.82
Gennadii Ziuganov	32.03	40.31
Aleksandr Lebed'	14.52	
Grigorii Yavlinskii	7.34	
Vladimir Zhirinovsky	5.70	
Svyatoslav Fedorov	0.92	
Mikhail Gorbachev	0.51	
Martin Shakkum	0.37	
Yurii Vlasov	0.20	
Vladimir Bryntsalov	0.16	
Aman Tuleev	0.00	
Against all candidates	1.54	4.83

occurred in Moscow and other cities. Putin's decisive handling of the military operations against the Chechen guerrillas gave him and the Unity movement a tremendous boost in popularity during the campaign. Unity, which had not even existed until late August, won 23 percent of the party-list vote.

Putin and the 2000 Presidential Race   The presidential election of 2000 occurred ahead of schedule due to President Yeltsin's early resignation. Under the constitution, the prime minister automatically succeeds the president upon the premature departure of the president, but new elections for the presidency must be held within three months. Accordingly, the presidential election was scheduled for March 26, 2000. The early election gave the front-runner and incumbent, Putin, an advantage because he could capitalize on his popular-

TABLE 12.7 Presidential Election Results, March 26, 2000 (in percent)

Vladimir Putin	52.94
Gennadii Ziuganov	29.21
Grigorii Yavlinskii	5.8
Aman Tuleev	2.95
Vladimir Zhirinovsky	2.70
Konstantin Titov	1.47
Ella Pamfilova	1.01
Stanislav Govorukhin	0.44
Yuri Skuratov	0.43
Alexei Podberezkin	0.13
Umar Dzhabrailov	0.10
Against all candidates	1.88

TABLE 12.8 Russian Presidential Election Results, 2004 (as % of valid vote)

Vladimir Putin	71.31
Nikolai Kharitonov	13.74
Sergei Glaz'ev	4.1
Irina Khakamada	3.84
Oleg Malyshkin	2.02
Sergei Mironov	.75
Against all	3.45
Turnout	64.4

Source: Central Electoral Commission.

ity and the country's desire for continuity. Putin ran the Russian equivalent of a "rose garden" campaign, preferring to be seen going about the normal daily business of a president rather than going out on the hustings and asking for people's votes. He counted on the support of officeholders at all levels, a media campaign that presented a "presidential" image to the voters, and the voters' fear that change would only make life worse. His rivals, moreover, were weak. Several prominent politicians prudently chose not to run against him. In the event, Putin won an outright majority on the first round. Table 12.7 shows the results.

The 2003 and 2004 Elections Under Putin the ideological divide between Communists and democrats that had marked the transition era disappeared. The political arena was dominated by the president and his supporters. The loyal pro-Putin party Unity was renamed United Russia after it merged with a rival party, Fatherland (headed by Moscow mayor Yuri Luzhkov). United Russia held almost a monopolistic position in the party spectrum, squeezing other parties to the margins. The magnetic attraction of a successful party of power was demonstrated vividly in the 2003 parliamentary election, when United Russia won 38 percent of the party-list vote and wound up with two-thirds of the seats in the Duma. The Communists suffered a severe blow, losing almost half their vote share, and the democrats did even worse. For the first time, none of the democratic parties won seats on the party-list

vote. The result underscored Putin's drive to eliminate any meaningful political opposition. Such an impressive showing for United Russia assured Putin's reelection as president. The March 2004 race was a landslide. Putin won easily with 71.31 percent of the vote (see Table 12.8). European observers commented that the elections were "well administered" but hardly constituted "a genuine democratic contest" in view of the president's overwhelming control of media coverage of the race and the absence of genuine competition.[58]

Party Strategies and the Social Bases of Party Support

Survey researchers have found differences in party support among various categories of the population. Factors such as household income, age, urban or rural residence, and education levels are related to differences in party preferences.[59]

Table 12.9 indicates how the parties differed in the social bases of their support in the 2003 Duma elections. Note that the table should be read downward. For example, it tells us that 64.5 percent of the Communist voters were 55 and over. The table shows that age, gender, education, and economic situation all influence party choice. For example, the Communists depended much more on older voters than do other parties, and on voters with lower levels of education and lower income levels. In contrast, United Russia drew its support from across the political spectrum. United Russia voters are distinctive because women predominate: 62 percent of their supporters were female. This fact is consistent with the observation that female voters in Russia tend to support parties promising stability and continuity in

TABLE 12.9   Social Bases of Support for Parties, Duma Parliamentary Election, December 2003 (in %)

Party Support by Age Group	Motherland	LDPR	United Russia	CPRF	Other Party	Against All	Did Not Vote	Total
18–24	3.8	19.2	13.9	1.8	9.6	10.3	17.3	13.7
25–39	14.1	31.3	22.8	9.1	23.9	33.8	36.1	28.5
40–54	37.2	38.4	29.3	24.5	31.4	33.8	25.5	28.7
55+	44.9	11.1	34.0	64.5	35.1	22.1	21.2	29.1
Total	100	100	100	100	100	100	100	100
By sex								
Male	43.6	60.6	38.0	49.5	44.1	43.3	46.6	45.3
Female	56.4	39.4	62.0	50.5	55.9	56.7	53.4	54.7
Total	100	100	100	100	100	100	100	100
By education								
Incomplete secondary	35.9	20.2	29.9	43.1	25.1	16.7	26.8	28.0
Secondary, specialist	47.4	65.7	55.6	45.9	49.2	65.2	58.4	56.0
Incomplete higher, higher	16.7	14.1	14.5	11.0	25.7	18.2	14.9	16.0
Total	100	100	100	100	100	100	100	100
By household economic situation								
Barely make ends meet	12.7	14.1	12.1	24.8	12.9	9.0	17.2	15.4
Enough for food	38.0	38.4	36.5	45.0	36.0	28.4	36.8	37.0
Enough for clothes	38.0	37.4	40.6	24.8	37.1	47.8	35.5	36.8
Enough for durables+	11.4	10.1	10.8	5.5	14.0	14.9	10.4	10.8
Total	100	100	100	100	100	100	100	100

Key: LDPR: Liberal Democratic Party of Russia (Zhirinovsky's party)
    CPRF: Communist Party of the Russian Federation

Source: New Russia Barometer XII, 12–22 December 2003, N=1601. From website: www.russiavotes.org accessed July 19, 2004.

Note: In each table, figures read downward. Each cell entry is the share of a given party's supporters represented by a given social category. Thus, of the supporters of the party Motherland, 3.8% were in the 18–24 age group; 29.1% of all voters were in the 55 years or older age group, but of Communist voters, 64.5% were in this age category.

policy. In other respects, however, United Russia's base of social support is strikingly broad, suggesting that the party is successful in positioning itself as a nonideological catch-all party.

Following their poor performance in the 2003 and 2004 elections, most parties have fundamentally rethought their strategies. Traditionally, the Communists have relied on their inherited organizational networks, their habits of party discipline, a clear-cut ideological profile, and their association with the socialist legacy of the old regime to attract voters. Some party strategists, however, believe that they

must change their message and their leadership in view of their dismal showing in 2003. Likewise, the democratic parties, such as the Union of Rightist Forces and Yabloko, are considering a merger. By competing against each other in 2003, they both fell below the 5 percent threshold. The nationalists found it difficult for them to identify any winning issues in the face of Putin's skillful manipulation of the idea of a strong state and continuity with Russia's past. Most politicians have recognized that career success today requires hitching their wagon to the dominant party of power—United Russia.

Toward Consolidation of the Party System?

Party development in Russia has been hampered by institutional factors, such as the powerful presidency. Strong presidentialism undermines the ability of parties to promise that electoral success will translate into policy influence, since the president can choose a government largely of his own liking. Moreover, both Yeltsin and Putin have avoided party affiliations, preferring to remain above the partisan fray. Under these circumstances, politicians have little incentive to invest their efforts in building up party organizations. As a result, parties are weak at performing the functions of aggregating the interests of citizens and formulating practical policy options. In turn, voters have little basis on which to form definite opinions and attachments about parties. There are also short-term reasons for the arrested development of political parties. Under Yeltsin, the power of regional political bosses and large business firms offered candidates and voters more useful resources for winning elections than parties could.[60] Moreover, under Putin, there was little room for any party other than United Russia.

The current situation is not likely to last indefinitely, however. The strongly presidential tilt to the constitution is not likely to change soon. But it is hard to predict what will happen once Putin no longer occupies the dominant political institution. If the system evolves in the direction of a European democracy, future presidents will need to consider the balance of political forces in the parliament in choosing a government. There will be a greater balance between president and parliament, and a greater role for parties and party competition. If, in contrast, Putin's authoritarian methods survive him, party competition will be nominal at best.

THE POLITICS OF ECONOMIC REFORM

The Dual Transition

Russia's transition was so wrenching because the country had to remake both its *political* and *economic* institutions following the end of communism. The move to a market economy created opportunities for some, and hardships for many more. Democratization opened the political system to the influence of groups that could organize to press for advantages for themselves. Many people who had modest but secure livelihoods under the Communist regime were ruined by inflation and unemployment when the planned economy broke down. A smaller number took advantage of opportunities for entrepreneurship or exploited their connections with government to amass sizable fortunes. The Russian case illustrates the danger that a transition to democracy and a market economy can get stuck partway, as power is captured by powerful entrenched interests that take advantage of the initial steps toward reform, only to block any further steps toward competition and an open economy.

Stabilization Russia pursued two major sets of economic reforms in the early 1990s, macroeconomic stabilization and privatization. Stabilization, also called structural adjustment (and sometimes **shock therapy**), is an austerity program for the economy. The government seeks to restore a macroeconomic balance between what society consumes and what it produces. It requires a painful dose of fiscal and monetary discipline. Stabilization gives the national currency real value, which requires eliminating chronic sources of inflation by cutting state spending, raising taxes, lifting price controls, and ending protectionism. Structural reform of this kind always lowers the standard of living for some groups of the population, at least in the short run.

Initially it was believed stabilization would be opposed by those whose living standards suffered as a result of the higher prices and lower incomes, such as workers in state enterprises, government employees, and pensioners. In practice, however, those who benefitted from the early steps to open the economy and privatize state assets then opposed any subsequent measures to carry economic reform through to its conclusion. This includes officials who acquired ownership rights to monopoly enterprises and then worked to shut out potential competitors from their markets. It also includes state officials who benefited from collecting "fees" to issue licenses to importers and exporters or permits for doing business, and entrepreneurs whose firms monopolize the market in their industry.[61] A fully competitive market system, with a level playing field for all players, would threaten their ability to profiteer from their privileged positions.

From Communism to Capitalism Communist systems differed from other authoritarian regimes in ways that made their economic transitions more difficult. This has been particularly true for the Soviet Union and its successor states. For one, the economic growth model followed by Stalin and his successors concentrated much production in large enterprises. This meant that many local governments are entirely dependent on the economic health of a single employer. The heavy commitment of resources to military production in the Soviet Union further complicates the task of reform in Russia, as does the country's vast size. Rebuilding the decaying infrastructure of a country as large as Russia is staggeringly expensive.

The economic stabilization program began on January 2, 1992, when the government abolished most controls on prices, raised taxes, and cut government spending sharply. Almost immediately, opposition to the new program began to form. Economists and politicians took sides. The "shock therapy" program was an easy target for criticism, even though there was no consensus among critics about what the alternative should be. It became commonplace to say that the program was all shock and no therapy.

By cutting government spending, letting prices rise, and raising taxes, the stabilization program sought to create incentives for producers to increase output and to look for new niches in the marketplace. In theory, increases in production should have driven down prices. But Russian producers did not respond by raising productivity. As a result, society suffered from a sharp, sudden loss in purchasing power. People went hungry, bank savings vanished, and the economy fell into a protracted slump. Firms that were politically connected were able to survive by winning cheap credits and production orders from government, which dampened any incentive for improving productivity. Desperate to raise operating revenues, the government borrowed heavily from the IMF and issued treasury bonds at ruinously high interest rates. IMF loans came with strings attached—the government pledged to cut spending further and step up tax collections as a condition of accepting IMF assistance, which fueled the depression further. Communists and nationalists got a rise out of audiences by depicting the government as the puppets of a malevolent, imperialist West.

Privatization Stabilization was followed shortly afterward by the mass **privatization** of state firms. In contrast to the shock therapy program, privatization enjoyed considerable public support, at least at first. Privatization transfers the legal title of state firms to private owners. Economic theory holds that under the right conditions, private ownership of productive assets is more efficient for society as a whole than is state ownership because in a competitive environment owners are motivated by an incentive to maximize their property's ability to produce a return. Under the privatization program, every Russian citizen received a voucher with a face value of 10,000 rubles (around $30 at the time). People were free to buy and sell vouchers, but they could only be used to acquire shares of stock in privatized enterprises or shares of mutual funds investing in privatized enterprises. The program sought to ensure that everyone became a property owner instantly. Politically, the program aimed to build support for the economic reforms by giving citizens a stake in the outcome of the market transition. Economically, the government hoped that privatization would eventually spur increases in productivity by creating meaningful property rights. Beginning in October 1992, the program distributed 148 million privatization vouchers to citizens. By June 30, 1994, when the program ended, 140 million vouchers had been exchanged for stock out of 148 million originally distributed.[62] Some 40 million citizens were, in theory, share owners. But these shares were often of no value, because they paid no dividends and shareholders could not exercise any voting rights in the companies.

The next phase of privatization auctioned off most remaining shares of state enterprises for cash. This phase was marked by a series of scandalous sweetheart deals in which banks owned by a small number of Russia's wealthiest tycoons—the so-called oligarchs—wound up with title to controlling packages of shares in some of Russia's most lucrative oil, gas, and metallurgy firms for bargain basement prices.[63]

A small group of such magnates devised a scheme in 1995 under which the government auctioned off packages of shares in several major state-owned companies in return for loans to the government. Under the plan, called **loans for shares**, if the government failed to repay the loans in a year's time, the shares would revert to the banks that made the loans. The government, not surprisingly, defaulted on the loans, letting a small number of oligarchs acquire controlling stakes in some of Russia's largest and most lucrative companies.

Consequences of Privatization   On paper, privatization was a huge success. By 1996, privatized firms produced around 90 percent of industrial output, and around two-thirds of all large and medium-sized enterprises had been privatized.[64] In fact, however, the actual transfer of ownership rights was far less impressive than it appeared. For one thing, the dominant pattern was for managers to acquire large shareholdings of the firms they ran. As a result, management of many firms did not change. Moreover, many nominally private firms continued to be closely tied to state life-support systems such as cheap state-subsidized loans and credits.[65]

The program allowed a great many unscrupulous wheeler-dealers to prey on the public through a variety of financial schemes. Some investment funds promised truly incredible rates of return. Most investors in Western companies would have regarded these claims as outrageous and fraudulent. Many people lost their savings by investing in funds that went bankrupt or turned out to be simple pyramid schemes. The Russian government lacked the capacity to protect the investors. Many people were disenchanted with the entire program as a result. Privatization was carried out before the institutional framework of a market economy was in place. Markets for stocks, bonds, and commodities were, and still are, small in scale and weakly regulated. The legislative foundation for a market economy has gradually emerged, but only after much of the economy was already privatized. Banks do a very poor job of mobilizing private savings into investment in Russian companies. For much of the 1990s, the lack of liquidity in the economy meant that enterprises failed

to pay their wages and taxes on time, and traded with one another using barter. By 1998, over half of enterprise output was being "sold" through barter trade.

The government fell into an unsustainable debt trap. Unable to meet its obligations, it grew increasingly dependent on loans. As lenders became increasingly certain that the government could not make good on its obligations, they demanded ever higher interest rates, deepening the trap. Ultimately the bubble burst. In August 1998, the government declared a moratorium on its debts and let the ruble's value collapse against the dollar. Overnight, the ruble lost two-thirds of its value and credit dried up.[66] The government bonds held by investors were almost worthless. The effects of the crash rippled through the economy. The sharp devaluation of the ruble made exports more competitive and gave an impetus to domestic producers, but also significantly lowered people's living standards.

As Table 12.10 shows, economic output in Russia fell for a decade before beginning to recover in 1999. The recovery is not due to a structural reform of the economy. There has not been a substantial overhaul of the banking system or the way industry is managed. The economy is still vulnerable to a downturn in the international economic situation, because Russia remains highly dependent on exports of natural resources: exports of oil and gas make up over half of Russian exports and a fifth of Russian GDP.[67] Still, a number of industries are showing real vigor. The oil industry has increased investment and output sharply and several oil companies have expanded their international distribution and marketing efforts. They have even invested in agriculture and food processing, which are also showing signs of recovery. Several domestic industries got a boost from the steep increase in the prices of imported goods. In an economy that was as deeply depressed as Russia's, even a small infusion of cash has a multiplier effect,

T A B L E   1 2 . 1 0   Russian Annual GDP Growth and Price Inflation Rates, 1991–2003 (in %)

	1991	1992	1993	1994	1995	1996	1997	1998	1999	2000	2001	2002	2003
GDP	−5.0	−14.5	−8.7	−12.6	−4.3	−6.0	0.4	−11.6	3.2	7.6	5.0	4.0	7.3
Inflation	138.0	2323.0	844.0	202.0	131.0	21.8	11.0	84.4	36.5	20.2	18.6	15.1	12.0

Note: GDP is measured in constant market prices. Inflation is measured as the percentage change in the consumer price index from December of one year to December of the next.

Source: Press reports of Russian State Statistical Service (www.gks.ru).

as enterprises are able to pay off arrears in back wages and taxes. In turn, these taxes allowed government to pay off its backlog of wages and pensions, in turn allowing consumer demand for industry's products to rise, and so on. These trends have raised living standards noticeably. Unemployment has fallen since the August 1998 crisis and the number of people living in poverty has declined by about one-third. President Putin has expressed satisfaction with the favorable trends in the economy, but has warned that they are not sufficient to achieve sustained and balanced development. He has called for doubling GDP in 10 years, which would require average annual economic growth of 7 percent per year for the next decade.[68] However, some of Putin's actions—such as the moves to drive the oil firm Yukos into bankruptcy and the jailing of its founder, Khodorkovsky—are having a chilling effect on business investment and make it that much harder for Russia to achieve high sustainable economic growth.

Social Conditions   Living standards fell deeply during the 1990s. A small minority became wealthy, and some households improved their lot modestly. Most people, however, suffered a net decline in living standards as a result of unemployment, lagging income, and nonpayment of wages and pensions.

A much larger share of the populace lives in poverty than during the Soviet era. As of 2004, about 30 million people, or about 20 percent of the population, live in poverty. High poverty rates are the result of unemployment and the lag of incomes behind prices. Unemployment, at about 8 percent, is much lower than its crisis level of 13 percent, but still is high for a country that was accustomed to nearly full employment in the Soviet period, and where the state-funded social safety net is weak.

As elsewhere in the former Communist countries, unemployment has affected women more severely than men. In Russia two-thirds of the unemployed are women and young people (and these are, of course, overlapping categories).[69] Also vulnerable to the economic trends of the past few years have been groups whose incomes are paid directly out of the state budget, such as those living on pensions and disability payments, as well as

teachers, scientists, and health care workers. Although they received periodic increases in pay, these usually were insufficient to keep up with increases in prices.

Inequality has also grown sharply since the end of the Soviet era. One commonly used measure of inequality is the Gini index, which is an aggregate measure of the total deviation from perfect equality in the distribution of wealth or income. In Russia, the Gini index nearly doubled during the early 1990s, rising from 26 in 1987–1990 to 48 in 1993–1994. Inequality in Russia was higher than any other post-Communist country except for Kyrgyzstan.[70] As the economy began to recover and poverty has declined, the gap between rich and poor has closed somewhat.

The erosion of public health is also tied to deteriorating economic performance. Mortality rates have risen, especially among males. In 2003, the president of the Russian Academy of Medical Sciences reported that mortality among men of working age had risen 80 percent in 10 years.[71] At present rates, he declared, of boys aged 16 in 2004, only half would survive to age 60. Life expectancy for males is only 58 while for females it is 72, a remarkable discrepancy, generally attributed to the higher rates of abuse of alcohol and tobacco among men. Other demographic indicators are equally grim. Every year Russia's population declines by a half a million people or more due to the excess of deaths over births. The rate of deaths per year is 70 percent higher than the rate of births.[72] Rates of incidence of HIV and other infectious disease, murders, suicides, drug addiction, and alcoholism are rising. Policy makers consider the demographic crisis to be one of the gravest threats to the country's national security.

Setting the country on a path of self-sustaining economic growth, where workers and investors are confident in their legal rights, requires a complete overhaul of the relationship of the state to the economy. The Soviet state used central planning to direct enterprises on what to produce and how to use resources. Much of the economy was geared to heavy industry and defense production, and government ministries directly administered each branch of the economy. The post-Communist state must have an entirely different relationship to the economy in order to stimulate growth. It must set clear rules for

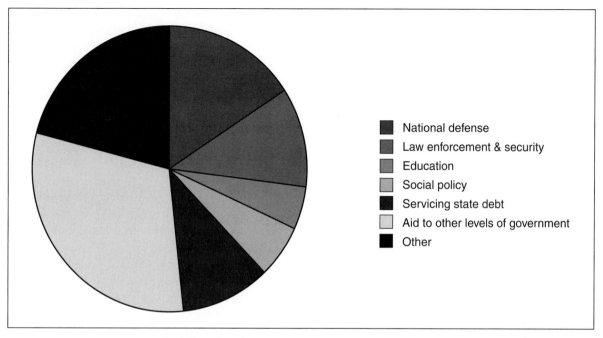

National defense
Law enforcement & security
Education
Social policy
Servicing state debt
Aid to other levels of government
Other

FIGURE 12.5   2004 Russian State Budget (in %)

economic activity, regulate markets, enforce the law, supply public goods and services, and promote competition. Shifting the structure of the state bureaucracy and the attitudes of state officials has been a herculean task.

We can get some idea of the legacy of the Communist system in the way the state was intertwined with the economy by looking at the structure of the state budget. Figure 12.5 shows the breakdown graphically. As a proportion of federal spending, defense (at 15.5 percent) is lower than in the United States (18.7 percent of federal spending in 2003). So is spending to service the federal debt (11 percent in Russia as opposed to 14.7 percent in the United States). The large spending for aid to regions and law enforcement makes it difficult for Russia to maintain an adequate social safety net or to maintain its education and health systems. Moreover, under Putin, defense and national security spending is rising, while education spending is falling.[73] The budget surpluses of the last four years made it possible for the government to meet its basic obligations, but spending was pared back so severely in the 1990s that many critical needs continue to go unmet. Only sustained economic growth will allow the government to rebuild the country's physical and social infrastructure.

RULE ADJUDICATION: TOWARD THE RULE OF LAW

The Law-Governed State

One of the most important goals of Gorbachev's reforms was to make the USSR a **law-governed state (pravovoe gosudarstvo)** rather than one in which state bodies and the Communist Party exercised power arbitrarily. Since 1991, the Russian leaders have asserted that the state must respect the primacy of law over politics—even when they took actions grossly violating the constitution. The difficulty in placing law above politics testifies to the lingering legacy of the old regime's abuse of the legal system. President Putin too has emphasized the rule of law (in a strange but memorable phrase, he once called for the "dictatorship of law") even while his actions have sometimes flagrantly infringed on the independence of the judiciary.

The struggle for the rule of law began well before Gorbachev.[74] After Stalin died, his successors ended mass terror and took significant steps to reduce the use of law for political repression. Still, throughout the late Soviet era, the Communist Party and the KGB often used legal procedures to give the mantle of legal legitimacy to acts of political repression. Although the prosecution of political dissidents has ended, the use of the legal system for political purposes by state authorities continues. Changes since 1991 represented some movement toward establishing an independent judicial branch, but under Putin political control over the legal system has started to grow again.

The major institutional actors in the legal system are the **procuracy**, the **judiciary**, and the **bar**. Each has undergone substantial change in the post-Communist period.

The Procuracy   Russia's legal system traditionally vested a great deal of power in the procuracy; the procuracy was considered to be the most prestigious branch of the legal system. The procuracy is comparable to the system of federal and state attorneys-general in the United States, but has more wide-ranging responsibilities and is organized as a centralized hierarchy headed by the Procurator-General. The procuracy is charged with fighting crime, corruption, and abuses of power in the bureaucracy. It investigates crimes and official malfeasance and seeks to ensure that all state officials and public organizations observe the law. Moreover, the procuracy oversees the entire system of justice. The procuracy has traditionally been the principal check on abuses of power by state officials. But it is inadequately equipped to meet the sweeping responsibilities that the law assigns to it, because of the difficulty of effectively supervising the vast state bureaucracy and overcoming the entrenched political machines of party and state officials.

The Judiciary   In contrast to the influence that the procuracy has traditionally wielded in Russia, the bench has been relatively weak. Trial judges are usually the least experienced and lowest paid of the members of the legal profession, and the most vulnerable to external political and administrative pressure. Successful judicial reform requires greater independence and discretion on the part of courts. Judges are being asked to raise their standards of professionalism at a time of rapid change in law, legal procedure, and social conditions. In a few instances, judges have been murdered when they attempted to take on organized crime. Many judges have left their positions to take higher paying jobs in other branches of the legal profession, but caseloads have risen substantially.

Policymakers pay lip service to the ideal of an independent judiciary but often violate it in practice. A number of reforms have the potential to increase judicial independence. Putin, for example, has backed a reform that will allow defendants in major criminal cases to request a trial by jury. Trial by jury has been tried out in several regions on an experimental basis and now will be implemented nationwide. It is opposed by the procuracy, because the prosecution has to work much harder to present a convincing case. It is also expensive, because court facilities must be expanded and jurors must be selected and paid. The goal of the jury system, however, is to make the judicial system more adversarial, so that the prosecution and the defense have equal status in the courtroom, and the judge becomes a neutral arbiter between them.

The Russian judiciary is a unitary hierarchy. All courts of general jurisdiction are federal courts, except for local justices of the peace. Most trials are held in district and city courts, which have original jurisdiction in most criminal proceedings. Higher-level courts, including regional and republic-level courts, hear appeals from lower courts and have original jurisdiction in certain cases. In turn, the Russian Supreme Court hears cases referred from lower courts and also issues instructions to lower courts on judicial matters. The Supreme Court does not have the power to challenge the constitutionality of laws and other official actions of legislative and executive bodies. The constitution assigns that power to the Constitutional Court. Under the constitution, the judges of the Supreme Court are nominated by the president and confirmed by the Federation Council.

There is a similar hierarchy of courts hearing cases arising from civil disputes between firms or between firms and the government called **commercial courts (arbitrazhnye sudy)**. Like the Supreme Court, the Supreme Commercial Court is both the highest appellate court for its system of courts as well as the source of instruction and direction to lower commercial courts. As with the Supreme Court, the judges of the Supreme Commercial Court are nominated by the president and confirmed by the Federation Council.

In recent years, the Supreme Commercial Court has handed down a number of major decisions that clarify the new rules of the economic game.

The Ministry of Justice oversees the court system and provides for its material and administrative needs. Its influence over the judiciary is limited, however, because it lacks any direct authority over the procuracy.

The Bar   Change of another sort has been occurring among those members of the legal profession who represent individual citizens and organizations in both criminal and civil matters: "advocates" (*advokaty*). They are comparable to defense attorneys in the United States. Their role has expanded considerably with the spread of the market economy. They have long enjoyed some autonomy through their self-governing associations, through which they elect officers and govern admission of new practitioners. In the past, their ability to effectively use their rights was limited, but in recent years their opportunities have risen markedly. Private law firms are proliferating. The profession is attractive for the opportunities it provides to earn high incomes.

Constitutional Adjudication   One of the most important reforms in post-Communist Russia's legal system is the establishment of a court for constitutional review of the official acts of government. The Constitutional Court has authority to interpret the constitution in a variety of areas. It has ruled on several ambiguous questions relating to parliamentary procedure. It has overturned some laws passed by national republics within Russia, and struck down several provisions of the Russian Criminal Code that limited individual rights. Generally, in disputes between individuals and state authorities, the court finds in favor of individuals, thus reaffirming the sphere of individual legal rights. It has consistently upheld the sovereignty of the federal constitution over regional governments.

However, the most important challenge for the court is the huge domain of presidential authority. The court has been reluctant to challenge the president. One of its first and most important decisions concerned a challenge brought by a group of Communist parliamentarians to President Yeltsin's decrees launching the war in Chech-

nia. The court ruled that the president had the authority to wage the war through the use of his constitutional power to issue decrees with the force of law. In other, less highly charged issues, the court established legal limits to the president's authority. For instance, the court ruled that Yeltsin could not refuse to sign a law after parliament had overridden his veto. However, in the more authoritarian climate under Putin, the court has not issued any rulings restricting the president's powers. Generally the court is sensitive to the political climate surrounding it, and takes care not to issue a ruling that would be ignored or opposed by the president.

Obstacles to the Rule of Law

Movement toward the rule of law continues to be hampered by the abuse of legal institutions by the political authorities and endemic corruption in state and society.

In the post-Soviet state the security police continue to operate autonomously. In the Soviet period, the agency with principal responsibility for maintaining domestic security was called the KGB (State Security Committee). The KGB exercised very wide powers, including responsibility for both domestic and foreign intelligence. Since 1991 its functions are split up among several agencies. The main domestic security agency is called the Federal Security Service (FSB). Although the structure and mission of the security agencies have changed, they have never undergone a thorough purge of personnel. No member or collaborator of the Soviet-era security services has been prosecuted for violating citizens' rights.

The security police are regarded as one of the more professionally competent and uncorrupted state agencies. However, despite being assigned new tasks such as fighting international narcotics trafficking and terrorism, they still demonstrate a Soviet-style preoccupation with controlling the flow of information about the country. For example, in 2001 the security police sent a directive to the Academy of Sciences demanding that scholars report all contacts with foreigners. Many similar Soviet-era police practices have been revived under Putin.

Another grounds for concern about the impartiality of the judicial system is a series of actions taken against independent media beginning in 2000.

These combined a variety of judicial tactics that included police harassment and criminal prosecution as well as civil actions such as bankruptcy proceedings. These actions forced the owners of two television companies to divest themselves of their media holdings and transfer ownership to companies loyal to the administration. As a result, Russia's two relatively autonomous national television companies, NTV and TV-6, lost their political independence; one respected liberal newspaper was shut down; and the entire media establishment was sent a strong signal that it would be wise to avoid crossing the current administration.

Corruption   Another serious obstacle to the rule of law is endemic corruption. Corruption increased substantially after the Soviet period. It is widespread both in everyday life and in dealings with the state. A recent large-scale survey by a Moscow research firm gives some indication of the nature and scale of corruption. At least half the population of Russia is involved in corruption in daily life.[75] For instance, the survey found that the probability that an individual will pay a bribe to get an automobile inspection permit was about 60 percent. The likelihood of paying a bribe to get one's child into a good school or college, or to get good grades, was about 50 percent. There was a 26 percent chance of paying a bribe to get a favorable ruling in a court case. The areas where the largest sums are spent are health care, education, courts, and automobile inspections; these alone make up over 60 percent of the money spent on bribes.[76]

Bribery in the dealings between business and the state is of a far larger magnitude. The survey's authors estimate that 82 percent of business firms engage in giving bribes to government officials, particularly those involved in licensing, taxation, and regulation. They calculated that the total annual cost of such corruption is $33.5 billion, a sum equivalent to about half of the federal budget.[77]

Corruption is hardly unique to Russia or to the former Communist world. However, it is especially widespread in Russia and the other former Soviet states. Corruption on this scale imposes a severe drag on economic development, both because it diverts resources away from public needs, and because it undermines people's willingness to invest in productive activity.[78] Moreover, much corruption is tied to organized crime, which bribes government officials for protection, and drives out legal businesses. For example, in a number of cases, criminal organizations have forced owners of legitimate businesses to sell out. The payment of protection money by businesses to organized crime groups is very widespread. The corruption of the police and courts ensures that such crimes go unpunished and forces legal businesses to compete in the corruption market with illegal ones.

A family in Chechnia surveys the damage to their home from the war.

Malcolm Linton/Getty Images

Corruption in Russia has deep roots and many Russians assume that it is ineradicable. Comparative studies of corruption demonstrate, however, that a culture of corruption can be changed by changing the expectations of the public and the government.[79] The key is for the political leadership to make a serious effort to combat corruption, and to back their commitment up with institutional reform and sustained attention to the problem. In Russia, corruption is so pervasive that it is a significant drag on the economy and the political system.

Reforms of the legal system have made some progress toward realizing the goal of the rule of law. Putin has taken a number of steps which, if fully implemented, would strengthen the judiciary's independence from both political pressure and corruption. At the same time, Putin's willingness to use the courts as weapons against his political opponents, and the powerful corrosive effect of corruption, continue to subvert the integrity of the legal system.

RUSSIA AND THE INTERNATIONAL COMMUNITY

Russia's thousand-year history of expansion, war, and state domination of society has left behind a legacy of autocratic rule and a preoccupation with defending national borders. The collapse of the Soviet regime required Russia to rebuild its political institutions, economic system, national identity, and relations with the outside world. During the Soviet period, state propaganda used the image of an international struggle between capitalism and socialism to justify its repressive control over society and its enormous military establishment. Now the country's leaders recognize that only through international integration can Russia hope to prosper. The return to authoritarian methods of rule, however, contradicts this aim.

Gorbachev, Yeltsin, and Putin all believed that integration of Russia into the community of developed democracies was strategically important for Russia. Gorbachev was willing to allow Communist regimes to fall throughout Eastern Europe for the sake of improved relations with the West. Yeltsin accepted the admission of East European states into NATO as a necessary condition for close relations

with the United States and Europe. Putin has repeatedly emphasized that he regarded Russia's admission to the World Trade Organization (WTO) as critical for Russia's long-term economic success. Following the September 11, 2001, terrorist attacks on the United States, Putin immediately telephoned President Bush to offer his support. Putin clearly saw an advantage for Russia in aligning itself with the United States against Islamic terrorism, which it identified as an immediate threat to its own security. Putin cited Russia's own war in Chechnia as part of the global struggle against Islamic terrorists.

Many elements of the political establishment criticized Gorbachev, Yeltsin, and Putin for making concessions to the United States and the West without receiving any benefits in return. Neither trade nor investment has blossomed as Russia had hoped, and Russia still depends on its raw materials exports to maintain a positive trade balance.

Russia has not fully embraced integration into the international community. It has expanded its military presence in several former Soviet republics, pressuring them to become satellites of Russia. In its brutal military campaigns in Chechnia, from 1994 to 1996, and then again from 1999 to the present, it has insisted that the war is a matter of domestic sovereignty and refused to allow international human rights organizations to monitor Russian practices. The regime has forced the mass media to report a sanitized picture of the situation. Corruption and inefficiency in government, both at the central level and in many regions, deter foreign investors from making a serious commitment of resources. Russian leaders constantly urge foreign business to invest in Russia. But, as many foreign investors point out, why should they take a greater risk than Russia's own business community, which has sent some $300 billion to off-shore havens?

Russia thus has some distance to go before it is fully integrated into the international community politically or economically. Yet it is far more open than it was under Soviet rule and its leaders recognize that they cannot retreat into isolation and autarky. Whether Putin is fully ready to embrace international standards of democracy, human rights, and the rule of law, however, is another matter.

Russia's post-Communist transition has been difficult and incomplete. Within Russia, many are disenchanted with the promise of democracy. At the same time, the end of communism has stimulated groups to

Boris Berezovsky was one of the most prominent oligarchs of the Yeltsin era. Today he lives in exile in Great Britain and faces criminal charges if he returns to Russia.

East News/Getty Images

organize for the protection of their interests. New institutions for articulating and aggregating these interests remain fragile. The spread of political and property rights has resulted in the emergence of a more pluralistic environment. Democratization in the post-Communist era succeeded in establishing some democratic institutions, such as competitive elections and a more open press. The accumulation of power by large financial-industrial conglomerates and by regional political bosses under Yeltsin, however, and the drive toward centralization of administrative and police power by Putin, have negated much of the progress Russia made in moving toward democracy. Russia's vast size and formidable climate have always challenged its rulers' ability to administer the state effectively. Throughout Russian history, rulers have relied on mobilization and centralization to accomplish their objectives. Today their challenge is to reconcile honest and efficient governance with democratic institutions for aggregating popular demands and making policy decisions.

KEY TERMS

bar
Chechnia
commercial courts
Communist Party of the
    Russian Federation
Constitutional Court
Federation Council
Federation of
    Independent Trade
    Unions of Russia
    (FITUR)

glasnost
Mikhail Gorbachev
governors
judiciary
law-governed state
League of Committees of
    Soldiers' Mothers
Vladimir Ilyich Lenin
loans for shares
nomenklatura

oligarchs
party of power
presidential decrees
privatization
procuracy
Vladimir Putin
Russian Union of
    Industrialists
    and Entrepreneurs
    (RUIE)

Security Council
shock therapy
single-member districts
Joseph Stalin
State Council
State Duma
United Russia
Boris Yeltsin
Yukos

SUGGESTED READINGS

Aslund, Anders. *Building Capitalism: The Transformation of the Former Soviet Bloc.* Cambridge, MA: Cambridge University Press, 2002.

Bahry, Donna. "Comrades into Citizens? Russian Political Culture and Public Support for the Transition." *Slavic Review* 58, No. 4 (1999): 841–53.

Breslauer, George W. *Gorbachev and Yeltsin as Leaders.* Cambridge, MA: Cambridge University Press, 2002.

Bunce, Valerie. *Subversive Institutions: The Design and the Destruction of Socialism and the State.* Cambridge, MA: Cambridge University Press, 1999.

Colton, Timothy J. *Transitional Citizens: Voters and What Influences Them in the New Russia.* Cambridge, MA: Harvard University Press, 2000.

Fish, M. Stephen. *Democracy from Scratch: Opposition and Regime in the New Russian Revolution.* Princeton, NJ: Princeton University Press, 1995.

Hellman, Joel S. "Winners Take All: The Politics of Partial Reform in Postcommunist Transitions." *World Politics* 50, No. 1 (1998): 203–34.

Hill, Fiona, and Clifford Gaddy. *The Siberian Curse: How Communist Planners Left Russia Out in the Cold.* Washington, DC, Brookings Institution, 2003.

Huskey, Eugene. *Presidential Power in Russia.* Armonk, NY: M. E. Sharpe, 1999.

McFaul, Michael. *Russia's Unfinished Revolution: Political Change from Gorbachev to Putin.* Ithaca, NY: Cornell University Press, 2001.

Rose, Richard, and Neil Munro. *Elections Without Order: Russia's Challenge to Vladimir Putin.* Cambridge: Cambridge University Press, 2002.

Sakwa, Richard. *Putin: Russia's Choice.* London: Rutledge, 2004.

Shleifer, Andrei, and Daniel Treisman. *Without a Map: Political Tactics and Economic Reform in Russia.* Cambridge, MA: MIT Press, 2000.

Sperling, Valerie. *Organizing Women in Contemporary Russia: Engendering Transition.* Cambridge, MA: Cambridge University Press, 1999.

Stoner-Weiss, Kathryn. *Local Heroes: The Political Economy of Russian Regional Governance.* Princeton, NJ: Princeton University Press, 1997.

White, Stephen, Richard Rose, and Ian McAllister. *How Russia Votes.* Chatham, NJ: Chatham House Publishers, Inc., 1997.

INTERNET SOURCES

An invaluable source for daily news about Russia and neighboring countries is the Radio Free Europe-Radio Liberty Newsline: www.rferl.org/newsline

A useful daily e-mail newsletter containing news stories and commentary is Johnson's Russia list: www.cdi.org/russia/johnson/

A portal to a wide range of political resources on the Web is: www.politicalresources.net/russia.htm

The University of Pittsburgh links to Web-based resources on Russia at: www.ucis.pitt.edu/reesweb

This is the home of "Friends and Partners," a joint Internet project by a team of Russians and Americans: www.friends-partners.org

The *Moscow Times* is an English-language daily newspaper published in Moscow, primarily for the expatriate community: www.themoscowtimes.com

The portal for the main institutions of the federal government—the president, the parliament, the government, and others—is: www.gov.ru/index.html

The University of Strathclyde's Center for the Study of Public Policy provides a wealth of public opinion and electoral information from Russia: www.RussiaVotes.org

ENDNOTES

1. Richard Pipes, *Russia Under the Old Regime,* 2nd ed. (New York: Penguin Books, 1995).

2. Archie Brown, *The Gorbachev Factor* (New York: Oxford University Press, 1996).

3. For a comparison of the leadership styles of Gorbachev and Yeltsin, see George W. Breslauer, *Gorbachev and Yeltsin as Leaders* (Cambridge, MA: Cambridge University Press, 2002); see also Archie Brown and Lilia Shevtsova, eds., *Gorbachev, Yeltsin, and Putin: Political Leadership in Russia's Transition* (Washington, DC: Carnegie Endowment for International Peace, 2001); Lilia Shevtsova, *Putin's Russia.* (Washington, DC: Carnegie Endowment for International Peace, 2003).

4. Konstantin Smirnov, "Vse pravitel'stvo: ekonomicheskii blok," *Vlast'.* 28 June 2004, pp. 63–78; World Bank. Russian Economic Report, June 2004. No. 8. From website: www.worldbank.org.ru

5. On the challenges of reconstructing national communities and loyalties in Russia and other post-Soviet successor states, see Ian Bremmer and Ray Taras, eds., *New States, New Politics: Building the Post-Soviet Nations* (Cambridge, MA: Cambridge University Press, 1997); Pal Kolsto, *Political Construction Sites: Nation Building in Russia and the Post-Soviet States* (Boulder, CO: Westview, 2000.)

6. J. Paul Goode, "The Push for Regional Enlargement in Putin's Russia," *Post-Soviet Affairs* 20, No. 3 (July–September 2004): 219–57.

7. Guillermo O'Donnell, "Delegative Democracy." *Journal of Democracy* 5, No. 1 (1994): 55–69.

8. For an alternative interpretation of Putin and his policies, see Richard Sakwa, *Putin: Russia's Choice* (London: Rutledge, 2004).

9. Quoted from text published on website Polit.ru, May 26, 2004.

10. Yuri Levada, "Svoboda ot vybora? Postelektoral'nye razmyshleniia," published on website Polit.ru, May 18, 2004. Levada heads a respected public opinion survey firm currently called the Levada Center. Until recently the center was called the All-Russian Center for Public Opinion Research (VTsIOM, according to its Russian language initials). However, the authorities maneuvered to take it over from Levada in 2003. Levada then founded his own firm under his own name.

11. Nationwide survey results conducted by the Public Opinion Foundation, reported by RFE/RL Newsline, December 10, 2001.

12. VTsIOM survey reported on website Polit.ru, May 16, 2002.

13. From a survey conducted by the Russian firm Ekspertiza, cited by Robert Coalson, "Russia's Evolving Liberalism," in RFE/RL Political Weekly, April 2, 2004.

14. From a national survey conducted by the Levada Center, "Sotsial'naia reforma dlia strany i naseleniia, September 22, 2004, Accessed September 30, 2004. http://www.levada.ru/press/2004092702.html.

15. James L. Gibson, "The Resilience of Support for Democratic Institutions and Processes in the Nascent Russian and Ukrainian Democracies," in Vladimir Tismaneanu, ed., *Political Culture and Civil Society in Russia and the New States of Eurasia* (Armonk, NY: M. E. Sharpe, 1995), p. 57.

16. L. Sedov, "Obshchestvenno-politicheskaia situatsiia v Rossii v iune 2004," from website of Levada Center http://www.levada.ru/press/2004071402.print.html.

17. Ibid.

18. Levada, "Svoboda ot vybora?

19. Ibid.

20. Ibid.

21. Sedov, "Obshchestvenno-politicheskaia situatsiia."

22. James R. Millar and Sharon L. Wolchik, "Introduction: The Social Legacies and the Aftermath of Communism," in James R. Millar and Sharon L. Wolchik, eds., *The Social Legacy of Communism* (Washington, DC and Cambridge: Woodrow Wilson Press and Cambridge University Press, 1994), p. 16.

23. Marcia A. Weigle, *Russia's Liberal Project: State-Society Relations in the Transition from Communism* (University Park, PA: Pennsylvania State University Press, 2000), pp. 432–41.

24. Richard Rose and Neil Munro, *Elections Without Order: Russia's Challenge to Vladimir Putin* (Cambridge: Cambridge University Press, 2002), p. 237.

25. Donna Bahry, "Society Transformed? Rethinking the Social Roots of Perestroika," *Slavic Review* 52, No. 3 (1993): 512–54.

26. William M. Reisinger, Arthur H. Miller, Vicki L. Hesli, and Kristen Hill Maher, "Political Values in Russia, Ukraine and Lithuania: Sources and Implications for Democracy," *British Journal of Political Science* 24 (1994): 200.

27. Lisovskaya, Elena and Vyacheslav Karpov, "New Ideologies in Postcommunist Russian Textbooks." *Comparative Education Review* 43, No. 4 (1999): 522–32.

28. RFE/RL Newsline, December 1, 2003.

29. For example, in July 2004 he warned that Russia must either work to strengthen the CIS or it will disappear. The fact that he made this statement at a meeting of the Security Council highlighted the strategic importance that he assigned to this task.

30. Reported on website www.russiavotes.org/ July 3, 2002.

31. Richard Rose, Neil Munro, and William Mishler, "Resigned Acceptance "Resigned Acceptance of an Incomplete Democracy: Russia's Political Equilibrium," *Post-Soviet Affairs* 20, No. 3 (2004): 195–218.

32. Sidney Verba, Norman H. Nie, and Jae-on Kim, *Participation and Political Equality: A Seven-Nation Comparison* (Cambridge, MA: Cambridge University Press, 1978).

33. Robert D. Putnam, *Making Democracy Work: Civic Traditions in Modern Italy* (Princeton, NJ: Princeton University Press, 1993).

34. Richard Rose and Neil Munro, *Elections Without Order: Russia's Challenge to Vladimir Putin* (Cambridge: Cambridge University Press, 2002), pp. 224–225; Richard Rose, *Getting Things Done with Social Capital: New Russia Barometer VII* (Glasgow, Centre for the Study of Public Policy, University of Strathclyde, 1998), pp. 32–33.

35. Rose, *Getting Things Done.*

36. Turnout in the December 2003 parliamentary elections was reported to be 55.45 percent and for the presidential election in March 2004, 64.4 percent. In the United States, turnout of the voting-age population for the closely contested presidential election in 2000 was 51.3 percent.

37. Rose and Munro, *Elections Without Order*, p. 66.

38. VTsIOM survey findings, as reported on Polit.ru website, January 10, 2001.

39. From a survey in *Novoe vremia,* No. 34, 2001, as reported in RFE/RL Newsline, September 4, 2001.

40. Eugene Huskey, "Nomenklatura Lite? The Cadres Reserve (*Kadrovyi reserv*) in Russian Public Administration," NCEEER Working Paper, October 24, 2003, Washington, DC, National Council for Eurasian and East European Research.

41. Olga Kryshtanovskaya and Stephen White, "Putin's Militocracy," *Post-Soviet Affairs* 19, No. 4 (2003): 289–306.

42. Igor M. Bunin, ed., *Biznesmeny Rossii: 40 istorii uspekha* (Moscow: OKO, 1994), p. 373.

43. Steven L. Solnick, *Stealing the State: Control and Collapse in Soviet Institutions* (Cambridge, MA: Harvard University Press, 1998), pp. 112–24.

44. Bunin, *Biznesmeny Rossii,* p. 366.

45. Jane I. Dawson, *Eco-Nationalism: Anti-Nuclear Activism and National Identity in Russia, Lithuania, and Ukraine* (Durham, NC: Duke University Press, 1996).

46. RFE/RL Newsline, June 13, 2001.

47. EastWest Institute, *Russian Regional Report,* Vol. 6, No. 42, November 28, 2001.

48. In a system where all prices were set by the state, there was no meaningful measure of profit in any case. Indeed, relative prices were profoundly distorted by the cumulative effect of decades of central planning. The absence of accurate measures of economic costs is one of the major reasons that Russia's economy continues to be so slow to restructure.

49. Article 59 of the 1993 constitution provides that young men of conscription age who are conscientious objectors to war may do alternative service rather than being called up to army service, but legislation that would specify how this right is to

be exercised still only passed in 2002, due to the strong opposition from the military itself. Thus would-be conscientious objectors and courts were in a legal limbo.

50. Several authors have examined the effect of Western aid on NGOs in Russia and other post-Communist countries. See Sarah L. Henderson, *Building Democracy in Contemporary Russia: Western Support for Grassroots Organizations* (Ithaca, NY: Cornell University Press, 2003); Thomas Carothers and Marina Ottaway, eds., *Funding Virtue: Civil Society Aid and Democracy* (Washington, DC, Carnegie Endowment for International Peace, 2000); Sarah E. Mendelson and John K. Glenn, eds., *The Power and Limits of NGOs: A Critical Look at Building Democracy in Eastern Europe and Eurasia* (New York: Columbia University Press, 2002.)

51. The FITUR reached a Faustian bargain with the government over the terms of a new Labor Relations Code which was adopted in 2001. Under the new legislation, employers no longer have to obtain the consent of the unions to lay off workers. But collective bargaining will be between the largest union at each enterprise and the management unless the workers have agreed on which union will represent them. Thus the new labor code favors the FITUR at the expense of the smaller independent unions.

52. Richard Rose, *New Russia Barometer VI: After the Presidential Election* (Glasgow: Centre for the Study of Public Policy, University of Strathclyde, Studies in Public Policy no. 272), p. 6; Richard Rose, *Getting Things Done*, p. 15. In 1996, the question was: At any point during the past 12 months, have you received your wages or pension late? In 1996, 78 percent responded yes, 21 percent no. In 1998, the question was: At any point during the past 12 months, have you received your wages late? 75 percent responded yes, 25 percent no.

53. RFE/RL Newsline, January 13, 1997; January 17, 1997; February 18, 1997; November 25, 1998; January 14, 1999; January 27, 1999; September 15, 1999; June 26, 2000.

54. Linda J. Cook, *Labor and Liberalization: Trade Unions in the New Russia* (New York: The Twentieth Century Fund Press, 1997), pp. 76–77.

55. Pauline Jones Luong and Erika Weinthal, "Contra Coercion: Russian Tax Reform, Exogenous Shocks, and Negotiated Institutional Change." *American Political Science Review* 98, No. 1 (2004): 139–52.

56. Stephen White, Richard Rose, and Ian McAllister, *How Russia Votes* (Chatham, NJ: Chatham House, 1997), p. 254.

57. White, Rose, and McAllister, *How Russia Votes,* pp. 241–70.

58. Quoted from a press release of the election observer mission of the Organization for Security and Cooperation in Europe posted to its website immediately following the election, as reported by RFE/RL Newsline, March 15, 2004.

59. Survey researchers have found that younger and better-educated voters are likelier to respond "yes" to the question, "Is there a party which represents your interests?" See Arthur H. Miller, Gwyn Erb, William M. Reisinger and Vicki L. Hesli, "Emerging Party Systems in Post-Soviet Societies: Fact or Fiction," *Journal of Politics* 62, No. 2 (May 2000): 464–66.

60. Henry Hale argues that "nonparty substitutes" such as governors' machines and big business began squeezing political parties out of the political arena in the mid-1990s, stunting the development of a party system. See Henry Hale, *Elections, Parties, and Democratization in Russia,* Cambridge, Cambridge University Press (forthcoming).

61. Joel S. Hellman, "Winners Take All: The Politics of Partial Reform in Postcommunist Transitions." *World Politics* 50, No. 1 (1998): 203–34.

62. Radio Free Europe/Radio Liberty Daily Report, July 1, 1994.

63. An excellent account of the "loans for shares" program, based on interviews with many of the participants, is Chrystia Freeland, *Sale of the Century: Russia's Wild Ride from Communism to Capitalism* (New York: Crown Publishers, 2000), pp. 169–89.

64. Joseph R. Blasi, Maya Kroumova, and Douglas Kruse, *Kremlin Capitalism: Privatizing the Russian Economy* (Ithaca, NY: Cornell University Press, 1997), p. 50.

65. Blasi, Kroumova, and Kruse, *Kremlin Capitalism;* Michael McFaul, "State Power, Institutional Change, and the Politics of Privatization in Russia," *World Politics* 47 (1995): 210–43.

66. Thane Gustafson, *Capitalism Russian-Style* (Cambridge, MA: Cambridge University Press, 1999), pp. 2–3, 94–95.

67. "OECD Economic Survey of the Russian Federation, 2004: The Challenge of Sustaining Growth" (Paris: OECD, 2004). From website: http://www.oecd.org/document/62/0,2340,en_2649_201185_32474302_1_1_1,00.html.

68. President's annual message to parliament, from Polit.ru, May 26, 2004.

69. OMRI Daily Digest, January 12, 1995.

70. The World Bank, *Transition: The First Ten Years: Analysis and Lessons for Eastern Europe and the Former Soviet Union* (Washington, DC: World Bank, 2002), p. 9.

71. RFE/RL Political Weekly, May 29, 2003.

72. RFE/RL Newsline, March 23, 2000; March 20, 2002.

73. Oksana Yablokova and Francesca Mereu, "Social Spending Takes a Back Seat," *Moscow Times,* June 21, 2004.

74. A seminal study of the influences on the development of law in the Soviet Union is Harold J. Berman, *Justice in the U.S.S.R.,* rev. ed. (Cambridge, MA: Harvard University Press, 1963).

75. G. A. Satarov, *Diagnostika rossiiskoi korruptsii: Sotsiologicheskii analiz* (Moscow: Fond INDEM, 2002).

76. Satarov, *Diagnostika,* pp. 16–17.

77. Ibid, p. 21.

78. Joel S. Hellman, Geraint Jones, and Daniel Kaufmann, "'Seize the State, Seize the Day': State Capture, Corruption, and Influence in Transition," Policy Research Working Paper, no. 2444 (Washington, DC: World Bank Institute, September 2000).

79. Susan Rose-Ackerman, *Corruption and Government: Causes, Consequences, and Reform* (Cambridge, MA: Cambridge University Press, 1999), pp. 159–74.

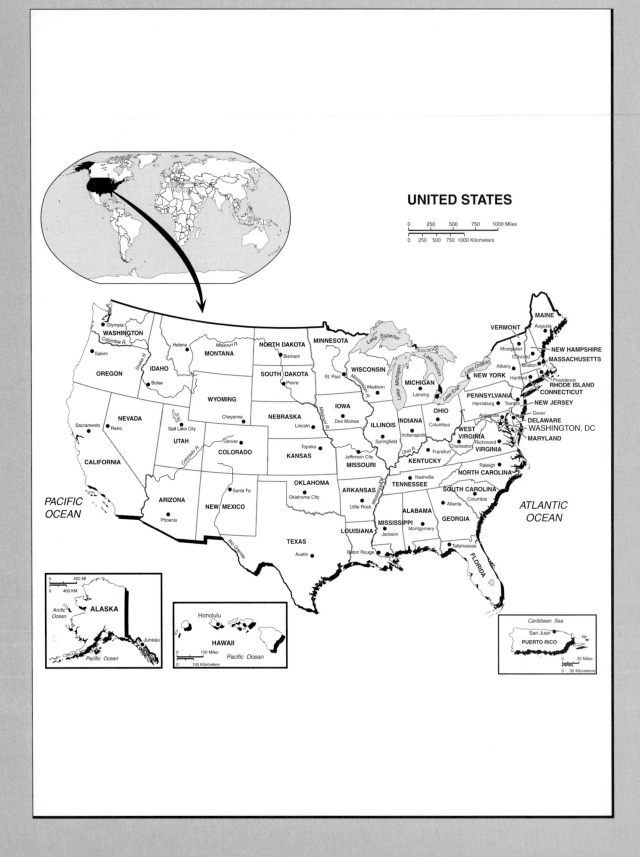

UNITED STATES

Scale in Miles: 0, 250, 500, 750, 1000 Miles
Scale in Kilometers: 0, 250, 500, 750, 1000 Kilometers

WASHINGTON — Olympia, Columbia R.
OREGON — Salem
IDAHO — Boise
NEVADA — Reno
Sacramento
CALIFORNIA
MONTANA — Helena, Missouri R.
WYOMING — Cheyenne
UTAH — Salt Lake City
Colorado R.
ARIZONA — Phoenix
NEW MEXICO — Santa Fe
NORTH DAKOTA — Bismark
SOUTH DAKOTA — Pierre
NEBRASKA — Lincoln
COLORADO — Denver
KANSAS — Topeka
OKLAHOMA — Oklahoma City
TEXAS — Austin
MINNESOTA — St. Paul
IOWA — Des Moines
MISSOURI — Jefferson City
ARKANSAS — Little Rock
LOUISIANA — Baton Rouge
WISCONSIN — Madison
ILLINOIS — Springfield
MICHIGAN — Lansing
INDIANA — Indianapolis
KENTUCKY — Frankfort
TENNESSEE — Nashville
MISSISSIPPI — Jackson
ALABAMA — Montgomery
GEORGIA — Atlanta
OHIO — Columbus
WEST VIRGINIA — Charleston
VIRGINIA — Richmond
NORTH CAROLINA — Raleigh
SOUTH CAROLINA — Columbia
FLORIDA — Tallahassee

MAINE — Augusta
VERMONT — Montpelier
NEW HAMPSHIRE — Concord
MASSACHUSETTS — Boston
NEW YORK — Albany
RHODE ISLAND — Providence
CONNECTICUT — Hartford
PENNSYLVANIA — Harrisburg
NEW JERSEY — Trenton
DELAWARE — Dover
MARYLAND — Annapolis
WASHINGTON, DC

Lake Superior, Lake Michigan, Lake Huron, Lake Erie, Lake Ontario

Missouri R.
Ohio R.
Mississippi R.
Rio Grande
Snake R.

PACIFIC OCEAN
ATLANTIC OCEAN

ALASKA — Juneau
Arctic Ocean, Pacific Ocean
0, 400 MI
0, 400 KM

HAWAII — Honolulu
Pacific Ocean
0, 100 Miles
0, 100 Kilometers

PUERTO RICO — San Juan
Caribbean Sea
0, 30 Miles
0, 30 Kilometers

CHAPTER 13

Politics in the United States

Austin Ranney

COUNTRY BIO—UNITED STATES			
Population	270.3 Million	**Head of Government**	President George W. Bush
Territory	3,475,031 sq. mi	**Languages**	English, Spanish (spoken by a sizeable minority)
Year of Independence	1776		
Year of Current Constitution	September 17, 1787 effective March 4, 1789	**Religion**	Protestant 56%, Roman Catholic 28%, Muslim 2%, Mormon 2%, Jewish 2%, none 10%
Head of State	President George W. Bush		

And what should they know of England
Who only England know?

Rudyard Kipling[1]

Why a chapter on the United States in a book on comparative politics? One reason is that most of its readers are Americans,[2] and politics in the United States affects our lives far more than politics in any other country. Moreover, however feeble we may feel is our personal power to influence the actions of our government, it is certainly greater than our personal power to influence the actions of other nations' governments.

The question Rudyard Kipling asked about the English in the quotation above can be asked with equal relevance about Americans. There are, of course, many excellent textbooks on the American political system written by American authors and intended for American students. But most of them make few references to, let alone systematic comparisons with, other political systems. Thus, viewing American politics with a special focus on how it resembles and differs from politics in other nations will help us better meet our version of Kipling's challenge. It may even give us some insight into how the distinctive ways of American politics are likely to af-

fect our country's ability to meet the enormous challenges it will face in the years ahead.

CURRENT POLICY CHALLENGES

The policy challenges facing the United States were radically altered by the events of September 11, 2001. The day after the terrorist attacks President George W. Bush announced that they had been planned and executed by members of Al Qaeda (The Base), an international terrorist organization of radical Muslim fundamentalists led by Osama bin Laden. Bush declared that the attacks "were more than acts of terror, they were acts of war." He added that the "war against terror" would be resolutely fought by the United States and its friends not only against Al Qaeda but also against any nation-state that sheltered terrorists, financed them, or supported them in any way.

The new war was unlike any other in American history. The enemy was not another nation-state, such as Nazi Germany or Imperial Japan in World War II, or even a seceding section of the U.S., like the Confederacy in the American Civil War.

At 8:45 A.M. on that fateful Tuesday, a hijacked American Airlines Boeing 767 was flown into the north tower of the World Trade Center in New York City, setting it on fire. At 9:03 A.M. a hijacked United Airlines Boeing 767 was flown into the Center's south tower, setting it on fire. At 9:43 A.M. a hijacked American Airlines Boeing 757 was flown into the west side of the Pentagon outside Washington, D.C. And at 10:10 A.M. a hijacked United Airlines Boeing 757 crashed in a rural area near Pittsburgh (it is believed that the plane was targeted on the White House or the Capitol, but that some passengers' efforts to re-

capture the plane deflected its course). At 10:05 A.M. the Trade Center's south tower, its structural steel fatally weakened by the fire's intense heat, collapsed from the top down, followed at 10:28 A.M. by the north tower.

The deaths totaled nearly 3,000, including the airplanes' hijackers, passengers, and crews, and the people caught in the burning buildings. This was the most killed in any peacetime disaster in the nation's history and far more than those slain in any other terrorist attack anywhere.

Consequently there were no organized armies to be defeated in battle by the U.S. armed forces, no enemy governments to acknowledge defeat and sign peace treaties, indeed, no way to tell when the war was over and whether the U.S. had won. Instead, the enemy was an unknown number of shadowy, hard-to-find secret cells of terrorists dedicated to destroying the U.S. and all it stands for, with no way of knowing what "victory" would be and how we would recognize it. So the United States now faces a long and difficult twilight struggle in which most of its other policy challenges will take second place.

Nevertheless, many such challenges will remain. In domestic affairs the problem of the economic and social status of African-Americans—some version of which has bedeviled the nation from its beginnings—remains high on the agenda. While African-Americans today are in many respects better off than they were a generation ago, they still lag behind whites in many areas, including family incomes, crime and imprisonment rates, formal education, housing quality, family stability, vulnerability to such diseases as AIDS and prostate cancer, and life expectancy. In the new millennium Hispanic-Americans in ever-growing numbers are joining in the demands for better status, and the national debate about whether compensatory racial preferences, sometimes called affirmative action, are constitutional and effective solutions will surely continue well into the twenty-first century.

Other, equally familiar domestic policy challenges will continue, including such diverse matters as the "war on drugs," national standards of educa-

tional achievement measured against national standards by national tests, reconciling environmental protection with economic growth, and addressing the bitter conflict over abortion between pro-choice and pro-life forces.

In the early years of the twenty-first century, the American economy, the largest in the world, was struggling with its deepest recession in a half-century, featuring such woes as increasing unemployment, a weakening dollar, and a stock market that from 2000 to 2003 lost over 40 percent of its value. In addition to coping with this slump, there are also a number of unsolved structural problems and other challenges. One is the longstanding problem of the complex, often incomprehensible, sometimes unfair national tax system, with proposed reforms ranging from a flat-rate income tax with a one-page Form 1040 to a national sales tax. Another problem is finding a politically acceptable structure for universal health care that will control costs and enable all Americans to get the care they need. Yet another is learning how to keep the federal budget balanced even when the economy is not booming and producing record tax revenues.

The unchallenged position of the United States as the world's most powerful nation and leader of the forces supporting democratic governments and free market economies will certainly continue in the early twenty-first century. But national hubris is not warranted, for such a position carries perils in foreign policy which, though different from what the U.S. faced during the cold war, are no easier.

At this writing, perhaps the biggest issue is whether the United States should conduct its foreign policy mainly or solely through the structures and procedures of the United Nations (UN) or do what the U.S. president thinks is imperative even if the UN votes against it, a policy choice that arose starkly in 2002–2003 in the debate over the Bush administration's intention to invade Iraq and remove its dictator, Saddam Hussein, without the clear authorization of a resolution by the United Nations, over the strong protests of public opinion in most nations, and over the determined opposition of such traditional allies as France and Germany.

The rationale underlying the Bush administration's choice is known as "the Bush doctrine." First enunciated by President George W. Bush after the Al Qaeda attacks of September 11, 2002, the doctrine declares that the United States should no longer wait to be attacked before it acts. It should, with the help of allies if possible but alone if necessary, take preemptive military action against any nation or terrorist group that possesses weapons of mass destruction that might be used against the U.S. It was intended to replace such earlier policies as the Truman doctrine (containment of hostile regimes), the Reagan doctrine (support all Freedom Fighters), and the Clinton doctrine (always act multilaterally).

The doctrine underlays the Bush administration's virtually unilateral decision in March 2003 to invade Iraq despite the U.S. failure to win endorsement from the UN Security Council. The war was quick, and Baghdad fell within weeks. However, this began an ongoing conflict with insurgents who oppose American presence in Iraq and the region (killing more than 1,300 American soldiers by the end of 2004). Even after the first democratic elections in January 2005, it appears that continued U.S. presence in Iraq is required to maintain order.

This brief sketch of some of the high priority domestic and foreign policy challenges facing the United States in the new century underlines the gravity, and in some cases the intractability, of its problems. Let us see how well or poorly its political system is equipped to deal with them.

THE UNITED STATES AMONG THE WORLD'S NATIONS

History

The world today is divided among more than 190 nations. The great majority of them are "new na-

tions," that is, nations that have recently broken away from older countries and become independent sovereign nations. Indeed, 73 percent of all modern nations have achieved their independence since the end of World War II in 1945.

Some of these nations have established political systems capable of meeting enough of their citizens' needs that their polities have remained relatively stable and peaceful. Unhappily, however, many of them have changed their political systems with some frequency since independence and have yet to find one that works well enough to stay in business very long (Cambodia, Ethiopia, Rwanda, Somalia, and Yugoslavia are among the sadder examples).

Seymour Martin Lipset has argued that the United States was the world's "first new nation," in the sense that the problems it faced in its efforts to establish a stable and principled political system after winning its independence from Great Britain in 1783 were in many respects similar to those faced by the nations created after 1945.[3] Thus the United States, which is so often described as a young nation, is actually an old one—not as old as, say, Great Britain, France, or Japan, but much older than most other modern nations. The U.S. has the world's oldest written constitution still in effect. It can fairly claim to have become a democracy well before any other large modern nation. In the 1790s it developed the world's first modern political parties, and today's Democratic party is generally recognized as the world's oldest active political party.

We will touch on several developments in American history throughout this chapter, but here we will emphasize only that the Civil War (1861–1865) is the United States' great historical watershed.[4] Before 1861 it was a much-disputed question whether the United States was merely a convenient alliance among independent sovereign states, which had every right to secede whenever they wished, or a indissoluble sovereign nation whose people chose to divide power between the national government and the state governments. After 1865, in both law and fact, it was established that the United States was, as every American schoolchild was drilled to know, "one nation, indivisible," and not a federation of sovereign states.

Before 1861 many Americans, especially those in the eleven Southern states that seceded to form the Confederacy, felt that they were first and foremost citizens of their states and derived their American citizenship from the membership of their states in the union. (The most famous example was Robert E. Lee: he strongly opposed both slavery and secession, and yet when Virginia seceded he refused command of the Union Army and cast his lot with Virginia because he felt he owed his primary loyalty to his state, not his nation.) The Fourteenth Amendment to the Constitution, ratified in 1868, removed all doubt by declaring that "All persons born or naturalized in the United States and subject to the jurisdiction thereof, are citizens of the United States and of the State wherein they reside." In short, all Americans are now primarily citizens of the United States, and derivatively become citizens of the state in which they reside.

Geography

The United States has jurisdiction over a territory totaling 3,475,031 square miles. This makes it geographically the fourth largest nation in the world, smaller only than Russia (6,592,800 square miles), Canada (3,849,674 square miles) and the People's Republic of China (3,696,100 square miles).[5] The U.S. is bounded by the Atlantic Ocean on the east, the Pacific Ocean on the west, Canada on the north, and Mexico on the south. This secure location—great oceans on two sides, militarily weak nations on the other two sides—made feasible the foreign policy of isolation from alliances and wars with foreign countries that the U.S. pursued until the end of the nineteenth century. In these days of intercontinental ballistic missiles, orbiting spy satellites, and international terrorism, however, no nation, including the United States, can count on its geographical location to keep it isolated from world politics.

Population

The U.S. Bureau of the Census estimated that in 2000 the United States had a total population of 270 million. This makes it the third most populous nation in the world, behind China with 1.2 billion and India with 1.0 billion. The U.S. rate of population increase has been impressive. The first census in 1790 reported a total population of 3.9 million, and so the 2000 figure represents a staggering increase of 665 percent in 224 years of nationhood. Over 50 million people have moved from other parts of the world to the United States—a phenomenon characterized by the British analyst H. G. Nicholas as "the

greatest movement of population in western history."[6] Accordingly, one of the most important facts to recognize about the United States is that, more than any other nation in history, it is a nation of immigrants. The census classifies only 2.6 percent of the population as being of Native American ancestry; the rest are immigrants or descendants of immigrants from all over the world.

According to the 2000 census, the main areas of Americans' ancestral origins are as shown in Figure 13.1

Most immigrants came in one or the other of three historic waves: (1) 1840–1860, mainly from Western Europe and Scandinavia; (2) 1870–1920, mainly from Asia and Eastern Europe; and (3) 1945–, mainly from Latin America. In the 1920s Congress imposed a ceiling on the number of immigrants allowed, and the immigration rate dropped sharply. Since the late 1970s the rate of immigration, mainly from Asia and Latin America, has increased, and about 730,000 *legal* immigrants continue to arrive in America every year. Thus, annually the United States adds populations greater than those of such cities as Denver, Milwaukee, or San Francisco.[7]

Thus, from its beginnings the United States has received far more immigrants than any other nation in history, and it has the most ethnically and culturally diverse population the world has ever seen (only India comes close). Later, we will consider some of the consequences for the American way of politics.

Economy

At the end of the 1990s the United States had the world's largest economy. In 2000 its gross national product (GNP), or the total value of all the goods and services it produced, was calculated at $9.9 trillion, compared with Japan's $4.1 trillion and Germany's $2.1 trillion.[8] The American dollar continues to be the world's basic monetary unit; the value of most nations' currencies is customarily measured by how many pounds, francs, euros, rubles, yen, and other units it takes to exchange for part or all of a dollar.

Some economists believe that American economic dominance has ended. The United States, which for many years was the world's greatest creditor nation, has become the world's greatest debtor nation, in part because Americans continue to buy billions of dollars more of foreign goods than for-

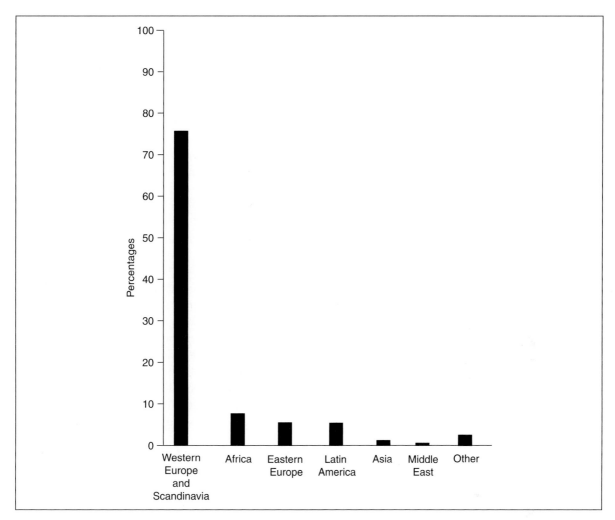

F I G U R E   1 3 . 1   Ancestral Origins of Americans, 1990

Source: Statistical Abstract of the United States 1990 (Washington: Bureau of the Census, 1990), table 48, p. 42.

eigners buy of American goods, and in part because of the longstanding enormous deficits in the federal government's budget. (From 1981 through 1996 the federal government spent a total of $3.7 trillion more than it took in.)[9] By 1997 the accumulated gross national debt was $5.2 trillion.

Most commentators saw no end to huge annual deficits and an ever-growing mountain of national debt passed on to future generations. Things changed briefly, beginning in 1997. Former Democratic President Bill Clinton and the Republican majorities of both houses of Congress actually adopted a new budgetary plan that aimed at an early end to annual deficits. Moreover, the booming economy produced tax revenues well above those expected and in 1998

Washington, D.C. was abuzz with talk about what should be done with the surplus (estimated to become $281 billion in 2001). However, all that ended in 2001 when a slumping economy yielded lower tax revenues, and increased war-related expenditures, combined with large tax cuts, again produced large deficits.

America has long been regarded as the citadel of capitalist economic ideas and institutions, and the main antagonist of people and nations who believe in socialism. If we measure the degree of capitalism in an economy by the proportion of economic enterprise that is privately owned and operated for profit, that characterization is correct. Even so, American economic institutions and practices have never come close to meeting the standards for completely free enterprise laid down by such laissez-faire economists as Adam Smith in the eighteenth century and Milton Friedman in the twentieth. These economists advocated the barest minimum of government interference in economic affairs, including no government regulation of the operations, profits, and wages paid by successful businesses and no government subsidies or "bailouts" for unsuccessful businesses.

Yet American governments have always subsidized American businesses in many ways. They do expensive research on materials, design, production, and marketing in a variety of areas and make their findings available to private businesses free of charge. Congress imposes tariffs and import quotas on certain foreign manufactured goods so as to prevent them from undercutting American manufacturers. Federal laws guarantee that all workers will be paid a certain minimum wage regardless of what they would get in a truly free market—and so on. Most of these goodies have come from political pressure by business associations, labor unions, and other pressure groups. Thus, it seems fair to say that, while most Americans say they believe in free enterprise, they prefer to practice safe enterprise.

America's Position in World Politics

Until the end of the nineteenth century the United States followed an isolationist foreign policy and was only a minor player in world politics. The changeover began with the Spanish-American War (1898), Theodore Roosevelt's mediation of the Russo-Japanese War (1905), and America's belated entry (1917) into World War I (1914–1918). Since 1918 America has been a leading player on the world stage.

From 1945 to 1989, world politics was dominated by the "cold war" between the two great superpowers and their allies: the United States, leading an alliance of Western capitalist/democratic nations; and the Soviet Union, leading an alliance of Eastern communist/authoritarian nations. The cold war came to an end in the early 1990s when the Soviet Union was formally dissolved (see Chapter 12) and Eastern European nations established their independence.

In the first years of the new millennium, the United States continues to be the world's most powerful nation, but a new international order is emerging. Whatever its final shape may be, the United States will continue to play a leading role, though

that role is bound to be different from what it was during the cold war.

THE CONSTITUTIONAL SYSTEM

As in most modern nations (Great Britain and Israel are two notable exceptions), the basic structure of the American system of government is set forth in a written constitution—the Constitution of the United States, a document drawn up in 1787, ratified in 1788, and inaugurated in 1789. It is the world's oldest written constitution still in force.

Of course, the Constitution of the 2000s differs from that of 1789 in a number of important ways. It has been formally amended twenty-seven times, the most recent being the 1992 amendment, which provided that no law changing the compensation for members of Congress shall take effect until an election of members of the House has been held.[10] Among the most important amendments are the following. The first ten, known collectively as the **Bill of Rights,** list the rights of individuals that the national government is forbidden to abridge (see Box 13.2).

The Fourteenth Amendment, ratified just after the Civil War, makes national citizenship legally superior to state citizenship, and prohibits the states from violating the "privileges and immunities" of U.S. citizens—which, by judicial interpretation, has come to mean nearly all the rights guaranteed against the national government by the first ten amendments (see Box 13.2). Other major amendments have outlawed slavery (the Thirteenth), guaranteed the right to vote to former slaves (the Fifteenth) and women (the Nineteenth), limited presidents to two elective terms (the Twenty-Second), and spelled out the conditions under which an incapacitated president can be replaced (the Twenty-Fifth). Even with these amendments, most of the basic elements of the 1789 Constitution have remained in force, whereas the written constitutions in many other countries and in most of the American states have been replaced altogether several times. Thus, if durability is a mark of constitutional strength, the Constitution of the United States is one of the strongest in history.

Yet the words in the Constitution do not tell all there is to be told about the basic structure of the American constitutional system. A number of customs, usages, and judicial decisions have significantly altered our way of governing without changing a

BOX 13.2   The U.S. Bill of Rights

1. Freedom of religion, speech, press.
2. Right to bear arms.
3. Freedom from quartering soldiers without owner's consent.
4. No unreasonable searches and seizures.
5. Trial of civilians only after indictment by a grand jury; no double jeopardy; prohibition against compelled self-incrimination; no deprivation of life, liberty, or property without due process of law; no taking of private property for public use without just compensation.
6. In criminal prosecutions, right to speedy and public trial by an impartial jury; defendant must be informed of the nature and cause of accusations; de-

fendant has power to compel testimony by witnesses in his or her favor; right to assistance of counsel.

7. Guarantee of trial by jury where the amount in controversy is over twenty dollars.
8. No excessive bail, no excessive fines, no cruel and unusual punishments.
9. Enumeration of certain rights in the Constitution shall not be construed to deny or diminish others retained by the people.
10. Powers not delegated to the national government nor prohibited to the states are reserved to the states or to the people.

---

word in the Constitution. Examples are the addition of judicial review, the development of political parties, and the conversion of the presidential selection process from a closed process by small cliques of insiders to popular elections open to all citizens. We will say more about each of these changes below.

Taken together, the provisions of the written Constitution of the United States and their associated customs and usages add up to a constitutional system that has three distinctive features: federalism, separation of powers, and judicial review.

Federalism

Federalism is a system in which governmental power is divided between a national government and several subnational governments, each of which is legally supreme in its assigned sphere. This system has some ancient precursors, notably the Achaean League of Greek city-states in the third century B.C. and the Swiss Confederation founded in the sixteenth century A.D. But the men who wrote the American Constitution established the first modern form of federalism. They did so because they had to. The 1787 convention in Philadelphia was called because its members felt that the new nation needed a much stronger national government than the Articles of Confederation provided, but the representatives from the small states refused to join any national government that did not preserve most of their established powers. The framers broke the resulting

stalemate by dividing power between the national and the state governments, and gave each state equal representation in the national Senate. Only thus could the large and small states agree on a new Constitution.

Even so, some of the framers regarded federalism as more than a political expedient. James Madison, for example, believed that the greatest threat to human rights in a popular government is the tyranny of popular majorities that results when one faction seizes control of the entire power of government and uses it to advance its own special interests at the expense of all other interests. He believed that division of power between the national and state governments, combined with separation of powers (see below), is the best way to prevent such a disaster.

Federalism has been widely praised as one of the greatest American contributions to the art of government. A number of nations have adopted it as a way of enabling different regions with sharply different cultures and interests to join together as one nation. The clearest examples of such nations today are Australia, Canada, Germany, and Switzerland, but significant elements of federalism are also found in systems as disparate as those of Brazil, India, and Mexico.

The American federal system divides government power in the following principal ways:

- Powers specifically assigned to the federal[11] government, such as the power to declare war, make treaties with foreign nations, coin money, and regulate commerce between the states.

- Powers reserved to the states by the Tenth Amendment. The main powers in this category are those over education, marriage and divorce, intrastate commerce, and regulation of motor vehicles. However, the federal government often grants money to the states to help them build and operate schools, construct and repair highways, make welfare payments to the poor and the sick, and so on. The states do not have to accept the money, but if they do they also have to accept federal standards governing how the money is to be spent and federal monitoring to make sure it is spent that way.

- Powers that can be exercised by both the federal government and the states, such as imposing taxes and defining and punishing crimes.

- Powers forbidden to the federal government, mainly those in the first eight amendments, such as abridging freedom of speech, press, and religion, and various guarantees of fair trials for persons accused of crimes.

- Powers forbidden to the state governments. Some of these are in the body of the Constitution, but the main ones are the Fourteenth Amendment's requirements that no state shall "abridge the privileges or immunities of citizens of the United States; nor shall any State deprive any person of life, liberty, or property without due process of law; nor Deny to any person within its jurisdiction the equal protection of the laws." A series of Supreme Court decisions have interpreted these phrases to mean that almost all the specific liberties guaranteed against the federal government in the first eight amendments are also guaranteed against the state governments by the Fourteenth Amendment.

When all is said and done, however, perhaps the most important single point to note about the nature of American federalism is made in Article VI of the Constitution:

> This Constitution, and the laws of the United States which shall be made in Pursuance thereof; and all Treaties made, or which shall be made, under the Authority of the United States, shall be the supreme Law of the Land; and the Judges in every State shall be bound thereby, any Thing in the Constitution or Laws of any State to the Contrary notwithstanding.

In short, while the federal government cannot constitutionally interfere with the powers assigned exclusively to the states, whenever a state constitution or law is inconsistent with a law or treaty the federal government has adopted in accordance with its proper powers, the conflicting state constitution and law must yield. Moreover, it is the Supreme Court of the United States, an organ of the federal government and not of the state governments, that decides which acts of the federal government and the state governments are within their respective powers. Thus, to the extent that the American federal system is a competition between the national government and the states, the chief umpire is a member of one of the two competing teams.

Separation of Powers

Since most analysts of the American system maintain that separation of powers is the most important single difference between the U.S. system (which is called a **presidential democracy**) and most other democratic systems (which are called *parliamentary democracies*),[12] let us be clear on the institution's main features.

Separation of powers means the constitutional division of government power among separate legislative, executive, and judicial branches (see Figure 13.2). The Constitution of the United States specifically vests the legislative power in the Congress (Article I), the executive power in the president (Article II), and the judicial power in the federal courts, headed by the Supreme Court (Article III).

The three branches are separated in several ways, the most important of which is the requirement in Article I, Section 6, that "No Person holding any Office under the United States, shall be a Member of either House during his Continuance in Office." This provision means that each branch is operated by persons entirely distinct from those operating the other two branches. Thus, for example, when Representative Norman Mineta was appointed Secretary of Transportation in 2001, he had to resign his seat in the House before he could take up his new post. This, of course, is the direct opposite of the fusion-of-powers rule in parliamentary democracies such as Great Britain and Germany, which require the head of the executive branch to be a member of Parliament.

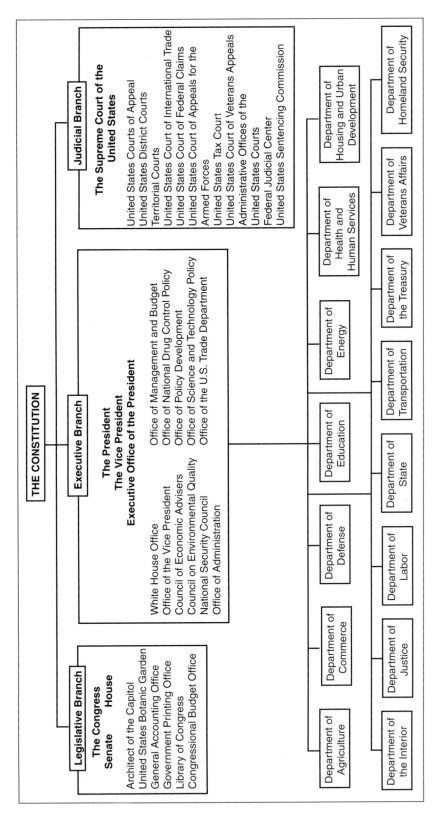

THE CONSTITUTION

Legislative Branch

The Congress
Senate   House

Architect of the Capitol
United States Botanic Garden
General Accounting Office
Government Printing Office
Library of Congress
Congressional Budget Office

Executive Branch

The President
The Vice President
Executive Office of the President

White House Office
Office of the Vice President
Council of Economic Advisers
Council on Environmental Quality
National Security Council
Office of Administration

Office of Management and Budget
Office of National Drug Control Policy
Office of Policy Development
Office of Science and Technology Policy
Office of the U.S. Trade Department

Judicial Branch

The Supreme Court of the United States

United States Courts of Appeal
United States District Courts
Territorial Courts
United States Court of International Trade
United States Court of Federal Claims
United States Court of Appeals for the Armed Forces
United States Tax Court
United States Court of Veterans Appeals
Administrative Offices of the United States Courts
Federal Judicial Center
United States Sentencing Commission

Department of Agriculture

Department of the Interior

Department of Commerce

Department of Justice

Department of Defense

Department of Labor

Department of Education

Department of State

Department of Energy

Department of Transportation

Department of Health and Human Services

Department of the Treasury

Department of Housing and Urban Development

Department of Veterans Affairs

Department of Homeland Security

F I G U R E   1 3 . 2   The Government of the United States

Source: The United States Government Manual 1997/1998 (Washington: U.S. Government Printing Office, 1997), p. 22.

The persons heading each branch of the U.S. government are selected by different procedures for different terms. Members of the House of Representatives are elected directly by the voters for two-year terms, with no limit on the number of terms they can serve. Members of the Senate are elected directly by the voters for six-year terms without term limits, and their terms are staggered so that one-third of the Senate comes up for election or reelection every two years.[13]

The president is elected indirectly by the **Electoral College** (though actually by direct popular election) for a four-year term, and is limited to two full elected terms. All federal judges, including the members of the Supreme Court, are appointed by the president with the approval of a majority of the Senate, and they hold office until death, resignation, or removal by Congress.

The other main devices ensuring the separation of powers are the **checks and balances** by which each branch can keep the other two branches from invading its constitutional powers. For example, the Senate can disapprove top-level presidential appointments and refuse to ratify treaties. The two chambers of Congress acting together can impeach, convict, and remove the president or federal judges from office. They can (and often do) deny the president the legislation, appropriations, and taxes he requests. The president, in turn, can veto any act of Congress, and the Constitution requires a two-thirds vote of both chambers to override the veto. The president also makes the initial appointments of all federal judges. Presidents have normally nominated judges who are likely to agree with their political philosophies and policy preferences, but once appointed and confirmed judges rule without political supervision.

The Supreme Court, through its power of judicial review, can declare any act of the president or Congress null and void on the ground that it violates the Constitution. Such a decision can be overturned only by a constitutional amendment or by the Court, usually with new members, changing its mind.

Some scholars believe that the American system is more accurately described as a system of "separated branches exercising shared powers," since getting government action usually requires some kind of joint action by the Congress and the president, with the acquiescence of the Supreme Court. Separation of powers is what most political scientists have called this feature of the system since the time of the *Federalist Papers*. Whatever it is called, this constitutional feature, more than any other, makes the American system different from most other democratic systems.[14]

Judicial Review

Judicial review can be defined as the power of a court to render a legislative or executive act null and void on the ground of unconstitutionality. All American courts, including the lower federal courts and all levels of the state courts, exercise this power on occasion. But the final word on all issues involving an interpretation of the national Constitution (which, as we have seen, is "the supreme law of the land") belongs to the U.S. Supreme Court.

Although every democracy has to determine who has the final word on what its constitution allows and prohibits, the United States is one of the few democracies in which that power is given to the top appellate court of the regular court system. Australia and Canada have similar systems, and some scholars say that as many as twelve other countries have some form of judicial review. However, some (e.g., Austria and Italy) give the final word to special tribunals rather than to bodies in their regular court systems, while in others (e.g., Mexico and Switzerland) the power includes only the "federal umpire" power, and not the power to override decisions of the national executive and legislature. Thus, judicial review is a prominent but not exclusive feature of the American constitutional system.

POLITICAL CULTURE AND SOCIALIZATION[15]

The American constitutional system, though important to how Americans make political decisions, is not the whole story. To a considerable degree, the American political system functions as it does because it is operated by Americans rather than by Britons, Italians, Mexicans, or Iraqis, and it does what it does because Americans have a distinctive political culture that underlies, animates, and shapes all of the formal institutions we have reviewed.

Two of this book's editors say that "a **political culture** is a particular distribution of political attitudes, values, feelings, information, and skills" that "affects the conduct of [a nation's] citizens and leaders throughout the political system."[16] Like most political scientists, they believe that political culture is one of the most important elements of any political system, for, in Alexis de Tocqueville's wise words, "There is no country in which everything can be provided for by the laws, or in which political institutions can prove a substitute for common sense and public morality."[17]

Melting Pot or Patchwork Quilt?

Most Americans are immigrants or descendants of immigrants who came from many different cultures in Africa, Asia, Western and Eastern Europe, and Latin America. Thus, throughout most of its history the U.S. has had to deal with how best to fit the immigrants and their different cultures into American economic, social, and political life.

During much of our history the prevailing policy has been that of the **"melting pot."** This policy sought to blend all the different cultures of immigrants into one uniquely American culture, which was to be expressed and passed on in one language, the American version of English. Some room was left for such special ethnic folkways as Polish weddings, Irish wakes, and Mexican food, but the paramount task given to the educational system was to turn everyone into an English-speaking American imbued with the main values and attitudes of the nation's political culture.

Since the 1960s, the melting pot policy has been increasingly challenged by a number of ethnic groups, especially African-Americans, Hispanics, and Asians. More and more spokespersons for these groups reject the idea that their ancient and distinct cultures should be homogenized into one prevailing national culture—a culture which, they say, is not truly a blend of all cultures but rather the culture of Western Europe, especially Great Britain, which has always been the culture of the dominant class and therefore an instrument for the oppression of minorities by the WASP (white Anglo-Saxon Protestant) majority. The only just policy, they say, is to make America a true cultural **"patchwork quilt"** (the phrase is Jesse Jackson's)—an array of the languages, history, customs, and values of each of the nation's major ethnic groups, each receiving the same attention, respect, and importance as every other, with none dominant.

Among the policies advocated by this new movement are bilingual education—educating minority-group children in their native languages rather than forcing them to learn English as their primary language; printing ballots and other official documents in Spanish as well as English; and broadening school curricula so as to give full and fair attention to the contributions of African, Asian, and Latin cultures as well as of British and Western European cultures.

Some backlash has set in against this movement. One manifestation is the laws adopted by several states declaring English to be the state's official language. We have yet to see whether the patchwork quilt ideal will replace the melting pot ideal, and, if so, what its impact will be on American political culture.

Main Elements of the Traditional American Political Culture

The first dimensions of political culture that political scientists usually consider are called trust in institutions, and trust in government and/or trust in leaders. How do Americans compare with other peoples on these dimensions? Some of the answers are presented in Table 13.1, which compares the levels of popular trust in government in the United States and four Western European nations.

Table 13.1 shows that significantly greater proportions of Americans than of British, West Germans,

T A B L E   1 3 . 1   Trust in Government in Five Western Nations (in percentages)

	United States	Great Britain	France	Germany	Italy
Most elected officials are trustworthy	44	39	30	32	26
Elected officials care what people like me think	41	43	26	20	15
Government is really run for the benefit of all the people	48	57	52	30	16
Trust the government	40	57	33	41	35
Average	43	49	35	31	23

Source: 1997 Deconstructing Distrust Survey, Pew Research Center for the People and the Press.

French, or Italians believe that most elected officials are trustworthy. On the other hand, higher proportions of Americans than Britons and French believe that government is really run for the benefit of all the people. Averaging the answers on all four trust-in-government questions shows that Americans rank above the French, Germans, and Italians, but below the British. These findings do not support the charge made by some commentators that Americans are exceptionally "alienated" from their government. Moreover, other studies have shown that more Americans say they are very proud of their country (80 percent) and willing to fight for it (71 percent) than the citizens of Great Britain, Spain, Italy, France, and Germany say about their countries (where the proportions range from 55 and 62 percent in Great Britain down to 21 percent and 35 percent in Germany.)[18]

Thus, while Americans may trust their governments to do what is right less than Western Europeans do, they are nevertheless more proud of being Americans and more willing to fight for America than the Western Europeans are for their countries. How can we explain this paradox?

The answer may lie in the fact that throughout history most Americans have strongly held two ideas that may be logically (but not emotionally) inconsistent. One is the idea that ordinary Americans are good, solid, reliable folks with plenty of common sense, and that America is a wonderful country. Conversely, they feel that the *government*, which is not the same thing as the country, is, as former President Ronald Reagan put it, "the problem, not the solution," and they feel that the professional politicians who fill its offices, lead its parties, and conduct its business are self-seeking lightweights more interested in winning votes and getting reelected than in making courageous and forward-looking policies to solve the nation's problems. Thus many Americans love their country but distrust the politicians who run its governments.

Another dimension of political culture is the degree to which ordinary people believe that their preferences significantly influence public officials. One of the findings of the first major comparative study of political cultures was that Americans score higher on this dimension than people in Great Britain, West Germany, Italy, and Mexico, and that in all five countries better educated people score higher than less educated people.[19] Subsequent studies have confirmed that Americans generally feel more "politically efficacious" in this sense than do the citizens of most other nations.

Political scientists usually think of ideology as a comprehensive and strongly-held set of convictions about how governments ought to make their decisions and/or what those decisions ought to be. The ideologies that receive the most attention in discussions of the political cultures of other nations are socialism and capitalism, with the Left (leaning more toward socialism) and the Right (leaning more toward capitalism). Considerable attention is also paid to democracy and authoritarianism, and constitutionalism and totalitarianism. Almost every comparative study of political cultures concludes that ideology plays a smaller role in American political culture than in many others, with only handfuls of Americans supporting such classically European ideologies as socialism, communism, or fascism.[20]

Many foreign commentators on America have been impressed by the depth of the conviction among most Americans—black and white, women and men, young and old—that they have certain basic rights and that often the best way to make sure they get their rights is not to wait for executives, legislatures, and bureaucrats to do the right thing but to file lawsuits to force public officials—and other private individuals—to honor their rights. For example, two recent British commentators on America were struck by the **litigiousness** of Americans—that is, by their tendency to file law suits against government officials and other private citizens for violating their rights, and by the consequent central role this tendency gives to the courts in America. They note that America has one lawyer for every 440 people, as compared with one lawyer for every 10,000 people in Japan. They cite the comments of Arthur Burns, the former chairman of the Federal Reserve Board, that if more talented Americans went into business and fewer into law, the country's economy would be a lot healthier. They conclude, however, that America has so many lawyers because so many Americans are insistent on demanding their rights.[21]

Political Socialization[22]

Political socialization is the process by which children are introduced to the values and attitudes of their society, shaping their notions of what the political world is like and which people, policies, and institutions are good and bad. That process in America is much the same as in every other modern populous industrialized democracy. Political socialization begins in children as young as age three or four and continues until old age and death. Children typically begin by perceiving some political figures, notably the president and the local policeman, as important persons outside their own families. As they grow older their perceptions broaden and deepen, and they learn about political parties, legislators, judges, and public policies and issues.

The main agencies shaping Americans' political socialization are their families (especially their parents), their schoolteachers, friends, schoolmates, work associates, and the mass communications media. Most recent studies agree that parents continue to have the most powerful impact on most people's political socialization, but as the influence of the mass communications media has increased in recent years parents' impact has lessened. This should not surprise us, for most analysts of political life in America and the other large-scale industrial democracies agree that the mass media, especially television, have become one of the most important forces—many would say *the* most important force—affecting people's political socialization, attitudes, and behavior.

THE MASS COMMUNICATIONS MEDIA

The term **mass communications media** includes all the devices used to transmit information, thought, or feeling to a mass audience that does not see the communicator face-to-face. They fall into two categories: the print media (newspapers, magazines, books, and pamphlets) and the electronic media (radio, broadcast television, and cable and satellite television).

The relative political importance of these media in America and three European democracies is shown in Table 13.2

Table 13.2 shows that television is the most important source of information about politics for most Americans as well as for most Britons, West Germans, and French, with newspapers a distant second in all four nations. In all four nations the other media, such as direct communications among people, are less important.

Ownership and Operation

The United States, like most other industrialized democracies, has a mixture of publicly owned and privately owned broadcast stations and networks, and satellite, and cable television broadcasters. The privately owned broadcast stations are businesses operated for profit, and they get most of their revenue from the sale of airtime to advertisers for broadcasting commercial messages. Cable and satellite television operators usually charge their subscribers monthly viewing fees, but a lot of their revenue comes from advertising. Most newspapers make small subscription charges to their readers, but their revenue comes mainly from the sale of space for advertisements. In most respects the privately owned media are much more important than the publicly owned in America: there are three times as many private as public broadcasting stations, and the public stations usually have only about 10 percent of the viewers.

T A B L E   1 3 . 2   Most Important Source of Political Information (in percentages)

	United States 1992	Great Britain 1989	West Germany 1989	France 1989
Television	69	53	56	44
Newspapers	43	30	37	24
Personal discussion	6	19	26	15
Radio	16	12	20	13
Other	4	5	18	7

Source: Russell J. Dalton, *Citizen Politics: Public Opinion and Political Parties in Advanced Industrial Democracies*, 2nd ed. (Chatham, NJ: Chatham House Publishers, 1996), Table 2.1, p. 24.

Regulation

In the United States, the political content of newspapers, books, magazines, and the other print media is almost entirely unregulated by government because of the First Amendment's protection of freedom of the press (see again Box 13.2). About the only restrictions on what is printed are libel and slander laws, but in the landmark case of *New York Times v. Sullivan* (1964) the Supreme Court held that public officials and public figures cannot collect damages for remarks made about them in the print media unless those comments are (1) knowingly false or made with a "reckless disregard" for their truth and (2) made with proved "malice" as a deliberate attempt to damage the victim's public reputation and standing—something that is very difficult to prove.[23]

Radio and television stations are much more closely regulated than the print media. They can broadcast only if they are granted a license by the Federal Communications Commission (FCC). That license, which must be renewed every five years, assigns broadcasting frequency, power of the transmitter, hours of broadcasting, and even the height of the transmitting antenna. It also requires that the political content of programs meet certain standards. For example, the stations must make available to all candidates for a particular political office an equal opportunity to make their appeals; they don't have to *give* any of them free time, but if they do give time to one candidate they must give it to all. If they sell time to one candidate they must sell it to all at the same rates and offer comparably desirable times. Even if they would rather not carry any political advertising at all (broadcasters believe it makes viewers tune out), they still must sell a reasonable amount of time for political advertisements to any candidate or party that wishes to buy. They cannot charge political advertisers higher rates than they charge commercial advertisers. If in the course of a broadcast someone makes a personal attack on the moral integrity of a political figure, that person must be given free time in which to reply to the charges.

The Supreme Court has consistently upheld the government's power to impose such restrictions on the electronic media while denying government any comparable power over the print media. The reasons have to do with what is generally called the **scarcity doctrine:** the Court has found that there is no limit,

other than economic, on the number of newspapers, books, magazines, or pamphlets that can be printed and circulated. But there is a physical limit on the number of broadcasting stations that can operate, because if two stations are broadcasting on the same frequency in the same viewing area, their signals will jam each other and no broadcasting will be possible. Accordingly, said the Court, in order to make possible the public good of broadcasting, the government must license stations and allocate particular frequencies to particular stations. Thus, broadcasting is a public resource, much like the national parks or navigable rivers; this gives the government the right not only to allocate frequencies, but also to set standards to ensure that their use will promote "the public convenience, interest, or necessity."[24]

POLITICAL PARTICIPATION AND RECRUITMENT

Participation by Voting

Ordinary citizens can participate in a nation's politics in various ways, but voting is widely regarded as the most important. Indeed, some analysts argue that having regular, free, and competitive elections for public office is the most important difference between democratic and nondemocratic systems.

Most political scientists believe that since voting in elections is the main way in which ordinary citizens in all democracies actually participate in their nations' governing processes, **voting turnout**—the percentage of all the people eligible to vote who actually do so—is one of the most important indicators of any democratic system's health. Studies of voting turnout in the world's democracies, like that in Table 13.3, usually find that the turnout is lower in the United States than in any other democracy except Switzerland.

Not only does Table 13.3 show that the U.S. has the next-to-lowest average voting turnout in the world, but it is also true that in U.S. presidential elections turnout has declined steadily since 1960, with the worst showing being 49 percent in 1996 (turnout is generally even lower in midterm congressional and state elections—it was 39 percent in 2002).

Many commentators view this finding as an alarming symptom of a deep sickness in America. They say it reflects a widespread popular feeling that election outcomes don't really matter, that the whole

T A B L E   1 3 . 3   Average Voting Turnout
in Elections to Lower House, 1961–1999

Nation	Average Turnout
Australia[†]	95
Belgium[†]	92
Italy[†]	90
Sweden	88
New Zealand	87
Germany	86
Canada	75
United Kingdom	75
France	75
Japan	69
India	59
United States	52*
Switzerland	52

[†]Compulsory voting law

*Presidential elections

Source: Adapted from Mark N. Franklin, "The Dynamics of Electoral
Participation," in Lawrence LeDuc, Richard G. Niemi, and Pippa Norris,
eds., *Comparing Democracies 2* (Thousand Oaks, CA: Sage Publications,
2002), Table 7.1, p. 150.

governmental system is rigged against ordinary people, and so there is no good reason why people
should bother with voting.

When voting turnout is calculated in exactly
the same way in the United States as it is in other
democracies—as a percentage of registered voters—
the American record looks much better. The point,
though technical, is important. In America, as in
most of the world's other democracies, citizens'
names must appear on voting registers before they
can legally vote. But the United States differs from
other nations in one important respect: in most other
countries, getting on the register requires no effort
by the voter. Public authorities take the initiative and
do the work to get all eligible citizens enrolled, and
as a result almost every citizen of voting age is on the
register. In the United States, by contrast, each state
regulates **voting registration,** and in most states
would-be voters must make an effort to get on the
register; no public official will do it for them. Moreover, in most democratic countries when voters
move from one part of the country to another, they
are automatically struck off the register in the place
they leave and are added to the register in the place
they move to, all with no effort on their part. In contrast, when people move from one U.S. state to another they are not automatically added to the register
in their new state.

In 1993 Congress passed the "Motor Voter" act,
which was intended to make registration much easier
and thereby increase voting turnout. The legislation
requires the states to allow citizens to register when
applying for a driver's license, to permit registrations
by mail, and to provide registration forms at public
assistance agencies such as those distributing unemployment compensation and welfare checks. Even
so, turnout in the 1996 presidential election *dropped*
to 49 percent. It rose to 52 percent in 2000, and then
to 57 percent in 2004.

Most political scientists applaud the new law,
and most were puzzled by the sharp decline in 1996.
Some, however, point out that America's status as a
low-turnout country is an artifact of the way turnout
is measured. They point out that turnout can be
measured in two ways that give markedly different
results. One is to take a percentage of all registered
voters, which, in most democracies, is nearly identical with the number of eligible persons. The other,
which is generally used in the United States, is to
take a percentage of all persons of voting age—
including not only unregistered persons and persons
who have moved but have not re-registered, but
even noncitizens of voting age.

One study has found that when turnout in the
U.S. is compared with that in 24 other democracies
and when the measure used is percent of persons of
voting age, the U.S., with an average turnout of
52.6 percent in presidential elections, ranks 23rd,
lower than in any other democracy except Switzerland. However, when the measure is percent of registered voters, the U.S. jumps to an average turnout of
86.8 percent, which makes it 11th highest.[25]

Another explanation for America's low voting
turnout arises from the fact that American voters are
called on to cast far more votes than the citizens of
any other country (only Switzerland comes close). In
the parliamentary democracies, the only national
elections are those for the national parliament, in
which voters normally vote for one candidate or for
one party. They also vote periodically for a candidate
or a party in the elections for the city or rural district
in which they live. In the federal systems, they also
vote for a member of their state or provincial parliament. Hence, in most democracies other than the

United States and Switzerland, the typical voter makes a total of only four or five voting decisions over a period of four or five years.[26]

In the United States, the combination of separation of powers, federalism, the direct primary, and, at the state and local level, the initiative and referendum means that citizens may be faced with several *hundred* electoral decisions in a period of four years. At the national level, voters are called on to vote in the presidential primaries of their parties, and in the general election to decide (mostly) between the Democratic and Republican candidates. They are also expected to vote in primary elections and general elections every two years for members of the House of Representatives and twice in every six years for members of the Senate. At the state and local level not only are the leading executive officials (governors and mayors) and members of the legislatures nominated in primary elections and elected in general elections, but in most states and localities a considerable number of other offices that are appointed positions in most other democracies—for example, state secretaries of state, attorneys general, treasurers, superintendents of education, judges, school superintendents, and members of local school boards, sanitary commissions, park commissions, and so on—are selected by much the same primary-plus-general election procedures. In addition, about half the states regularly hold elections on initiatives and referendums, in which the public votes directly on questions of public policy.[27]

Thus American citizens are called on to vote far more often than those of any other country except Switzerland. Surely the opportunity to vote in free, fair, and competitive elections is a sine qua non of democratic government, and therefore a good thing. Yet a familiar saying is that there can be too much of a good thing, and many Americans leaving their polling places after casting their ninetieth (or more) vote of the year are likely to conclude that the sheer number of voting decisions in America is a case in point.[28]

Participation by Other Means

Voting, of course, is only one of several ways citizens can participate in politics. They can also serve in office, work in political parties, donate money to candidates, parties, and causes, attend rallies, take part in street demonstrations, send letters, telegrams, faxes and e-mail messages to their elected representatives, write letters and op-ed pieces to newspapers, call radio and TV talk shows, try to persuade families and friends, file lawsuits against public officials, and so on. These other forms of participation have not been studied as extensively as voting, but Russell Dalton has collected some interesting comparative data on conventional and unconventional forms of participation in the United States and some Western European countries (see Table 13.4).

The responses in Table 13.4 show that citizens of France are more likely than citizens of the United States, Great Britain, or West Germany to participate in demonstrations and political strikes, whereas Americans are more likely than the others to persuade other people how to vote and to work with citizen groups.

Several other studies have found that the form of participation most frequently claimed by Americans is voting in elections (53 percent), followed by stating their political opinions to others (32 percent), contributing money to campaigns (12 percent), displaying political bumper-stickers and signs (9 percent), and attending political meetings or rallies (8 percent). Only 4 percent report belonging to a political club or working for a political party.[29]

In short, Americans participate in politics in ways other than voting in elections as much or more than the citizens of the other Western democracies for whom we have reliable information. These data certainly do not support the conclusion that Americans are in any way more alienated or lazier than the citizens of other democracies.

RECRUITMENT OF LEADERS

Leadership recruitment is the process whereby, out of the millions of a nation's citizens, emerge the few hundreds or thousands who hold elective and appointive public office, play leading roles in parties and pressure groups, decide how the mass communications media will portray politics, and, within the limits permitted by the general public, make public policy.

Many scholars have studied leadership recruitment in many countries and have found certain general tendencies that are also evident in American politics. For instance, American leaders, like leaders in other countries, are drawn disproportionately from the middle and upper ranges of wealth and status.

TABLE 13.4   Nonvoting Forms of Political Participation
in Four Democracies, 1990s (in percentages)

Activity	United States	Great Britain	West Germany	France
Voting				
Voted in last election	53	78	77	69
Campaign Activity				
Convince others how to vote	38	7	3	8
Attend meeting/rally	8	4	—	—
Work for party/candidate	3	2	—	—
Communal Activity				
Sign petitions	70	75	55	51
Work with citizens group	18	11	11	8
Protest Activity				
Participate in lawful demonstrations	15	13	25	31
Join in boycott	17	14	9	11
Participate in unofficial strike	4	8	2	9

Source: Russell J. Dalton, *Citizen Politics in Western Democracies,* 2nd ed. (Chatham, NJ: Chatham House Publishers, 1996), chapters 3 and 4.

The reason lies not in the existence of any conspiracy to oppress the lower classes but in the kinds of knowledge and skills a person must have to win the support needed for selection as a leader. These skills are more likely to be acquired and developed by well-educated rather than poorly educated people. For example, people's chances to climb in a political party or a pressure group, to be selected for public office, or to be appointed to higher administrative offices, are considerably enhanced if they have the ability to speak well in public, and, for elected officials increasingly, to look and sound good on television.

The federal and state governments choose most of their administrative employees by procedures and standards other than the unabashed political patronage that prevailed until the late nineteenth century. In today's system initial selection is made according to the applicants' abilities to score well on standardized examinations or possession of other abilities and experience desired by their employers, and salary increases and promotions depend on job performance rather than on party connections. Since the merit system was established in 1883, more and more federal positions have been placed under it or under the "general schedule" category, and today only about 1 percent are available for purely political appointments.

Accordingly, in most respects elite recruitment in the United States differs very little from its coun-terparts in other advanced industrialized democracies. But in one aspect of that process—the nomination of candidates for elective office—the United States is unlike any other nation in the world.

The Unique Direct Primary

We can divide the process of electing public officials into three parts: (1) *candidate selection,* the process by which political parties decide what persons to name as their standard-bearers and campaign for; (2) *nomination,* the process by which public authorities decide what persons' names will be printed on the official ballots; and (3) *election,* the process by which the voters register their choices among the nominees.

Many political scientists believe that candidate selection is the most important of the three processes. After all, the recruitment of public officials is essentially one of narrowing the choices from many to one. For example, in 2000 about 130 million Americans satisfied all the constitutional requirements for being elected president. Theoretically, all 130 million names could have been printed on the ballot and each voter could have had an absolutely free choice among them. But, of course, no voter can possibly make a meaningful choice among 130 million alternatives, and so a meaningful democratic election requires that the choices be narrowed down to a manageable number. The same is true for elections to office in all democratic countries.

In the United States, as in every other democracy, the narrowing process is accomplished mainly by the political parties. Each party chooses its candidates, gives their names to the election authorities, and those names appear on the ballot.[30] Accordingly, in 2000 the Republicans chose George W. Bush to be their presidential candidate over John McCain, Malcolm Forbes, Elizabeth Dole, and others. The Democrats chose Al Gore over Bill Bradley. These nominations made it relatively easy for the voters to make the final choice between Bush and Gore.

Given the crucial role of candidate selection in democratic elections, it is important to recognize that the United States is the only nation in the world that makes most of its nominations by direct primaries. In nearly all the parliamentary democracies, the parties' candidates for parliament are chosen by the parties' leaders or by small groups of card-carrying, dues-paying party members. A few countries, such as Belgium, Finland, and Germany, require the parties to choose their candidates by secret votes of local party members in procedures that resemble but, strictly speaking, are not direct primaries. Consequently, in every nation except the United States the candidates are selected by only a few hundred, or at most a few thousand, party insiders.[31]

In the United States, nominations for almost all major elective public offices are made by **direct primaries,** in which candidates are selected directly by the voters in government-conducted elections rather than indirectly by party leaders in caucuses and conventions. Moreover—and this is the key difference between America's direct primaries and the primary-like procedures in other countries mentioned above—public laws, not party rules, determine who is qualified to vote in a particular party's primary. Twenty-five states presently have **closed primaries,** in which only persons preregistered as members of a particular party can vote in that party's primary. Fourteen states have **crossover primaries,** which are the same as closed primaries except that voters do not have to make a public choice of the party primary in which they will vote until election day. Nine states have **open primaries,** in which there is no party registration of any kind, and voters can vote in whichever party primary they choose (they can, however, vote in only one party's

primary in any particular election) with no public disclosure of their choice; two states have **blanket primaries,** in which voters can switch back and forth between the parties in voting for nominees for particular offices, and do not disclose their switches or their choices.

Direct primaries make candidate selection in the United States by far the most open and participatory in the world. As noted above, in all other countries only a few thousand dues-paying party members at most participate in choosing candidates; in the United States they are chosen by any registered voter who wants to participate, and millions do in every election cycle. To give just one example: although American presidential candidates are formally selected by national nominating conventions, a great majority of the delegates to both conventions are chosen by direct primaries. In 2000, a grand total of 31,241,852 votes were cast in the Democratic and Republican presidential primaries.[32]

The American system for choosing its presidents may be wiser or more foolish than the ways other democracies select their top political leaders, but it is far more participatory.

INTEREST ARTICULATION: PRESSURE GROUPS AND PACS

As we have seen throughout this book, every society has a number of different and conflicting political interests,[33] and the more advanced the economy and the more heterogeneous the society the more individuals and groups there are with interests that to some degree conflict with other interests. The inevitable clash of these interests generates the political process, which consists of two main parts: (1) interest articulation, by which the persons and groups make known their desires for government action or inaction; and (2) interest aggregation, by which various demands are mobilized and combined to press for favorable government policies. That is why many political scientists agree with Harold D. Lasswell that the essence of government is deciding "who gets what, when, and how."[34]

In most democracies interests are articulated mainly by pressure groups and political parties, and the governing parties also aggregate interests in formulating and implementing their programs. In the

United States, however, the political parties are much weaker and less cohesive than those in most other democratic systems. Consequently, pressure groups play a major role in both interest articulation and aggregation in the United States.

Many foreign observers of America's peculiar politics have been especially struck by the great variety and power of our organized political groups.[35] Today they are even more numerous and important than in the past. They take two main forms, each of which specializes in a particular technique for influencing government: (1) political action committees and campaign contributions, and (2) pressure groups and lobbying.

PACs and Campaign Contributions

Strictly speaking, a **political action committee (PAC)** is any organization that is not formally affiliated with a particular party or candidate and spends money to influence the outcome of elections. PACs differ from political parties in two main respects: (1) unlike parties, they do not nominate candidates and put them on ballots with PAC labels; rather, they support or oppose candidates nominated by the parties; and (2) PACs are interested mainly in the policies public officials make, not in the party labels those officials bear. Hence, they often support candidates of both major parties who are sympathetic to the PACs' particular policy preferences.

Such organizations have operated in American politics at least since the Civil War, and some of them have had considerable success. For example, the Anti-Saloon League was founded in 1893 to support both Democratic and Republican candidates for Congress pledged to support a constitutional amendment outlawing the manufacture and sale of alcoholic beverages. Most historians believe that it deserves much of the credit (blame?) for the adoption of the Eighteenth Amendment (prohibition) in 1919. One of the most powerful organizations in the second half of the twentieth century has been the Committee on Political Education (COPE) of the AFL-CIO, which has supplied millions of dollars and thousands of election workers for candidates (mostly but not entirely Democrats) sympathetic to organized labor.

The greatest increase in the number and activity of PACs in American history has come since 1974 as an unanticipated (and, by many, unwanted) consequence of that year's amendments to the Federal Election Campaign Act. The amendments set low limits on the amount of money individuals could contribute to a candidate or a party, but considerably higher limits on what organizations could contribute. They also stipulated that although labor unions and business corporations could not directly

---

BOX 13.3   Top Ten PACs in Overall Spending, 1999–2000

Rank	PAC Name	Overall Spending	Rank	PAC Name	Overall Spending
1	National Rifle Association Political Victory Fund	$16,821,432	6	National Education Association Fund for Children and Public Education	6,108,964
2	Emily's List	14,746,248	7	Association of Trial Lawyers of America Pol. Action Committee	6,082,160
3	Democrat Republican Independent Voter Education Committee	9,000,564	8	Elect Life	4,882,154
4	American Federation of State County & Municipal Employees-PEOPLE, Qualified	8,557,040	9	New Republican Majority Fund	4,692.690
5	International Brotherhood of Electrical Workers Committee on Political Education	6,236,036	10	American Medical Association Political Action Committee	4,496,150

Source: Harold W. Stanley and Richard G. Niemi, eds, *Vital Statistics on American Politics,* 2001–2002 (Washington, DC: Congressional Quarterly, Inc., 2001), Table 2–15, pp. 105–106.

contribute money to election campaigns, they could sponsor PACs and their PACs could make campaign contributions as long as the funds came from voluntary contributions by sympathetic individuals rather than by direct levies on union and corporate funds.

In ruling on the constitutionality of these rules, the Supreme Court upheld the limits on direct contributions, but said that limiting the amounts of money that an individual or an organization can spend on behalf of a candidate (that is, by broadcasting or publishing ads *not* controlled by candidates or parties) was a violation of the First Amendment's guarantee of free speech.[36]

These changes in the substance and interpretation of the campaign finance laws led most politically active interests to conclude that forming a PAC was the best way to influence election outcomes, and that is just what they have done. In 1974 only 608 PACs operated in national elections; by 2001 the number had exploded to 3,907.

At present each PAC must register with the Federal Election Commission and periodically report its receipts (who contributed and how much) and its expenditures (to what candidates it gave contributions and how much, and how much it spent on its own independent campaigning). A PAC can contribute $5,000 to a particular candidate in a primary election and another $5,000 in the general election. However, there is no limit on the total amount it can contribute to all candidates and party committees. There is also no limit on the amount it can spend on behalf of a particular candidate or party as long as its beneficiaries have no say in how the money is spent. The enactment in 2002 of the McCain-Feingold bill prohibited all "soft money" contributions—formerly unlimited contributions that were made to federal, state, and local political parties.

Although many PACs take some part in presidential election campaigns, the federal government finances most of the costs of those campaigns. Thus, most PACs make most of their contributions to House and Senate campaigns. It is estimated that they now contribute about 30 percent of all the funds for those campaigns.[37]

The most important PACs can be classified in one of three main categories:

1. *Narrow material interest PACs.* These are PACs concerned mainly with backing candidates who will support legislation that favors a particular business or type of business: for example, Chrysler, Coca Cola, General Electric, General Motors, Texaco, and many other corporations have their own PACs, as do many labor unions, including the Air Line Pilots Association, the American Federation of State, County & Municipal Employees, and the American Federation of Teachers. In addition, a number of PACs represent the interests of whole industries, such as the Dallas Energy Political Action Committee (oil), Edison Electric Institute (electric power), and the National Association of Broadcasters (radio and television).

2. *Single, nonmaterial interest PACs.* These PACs promote candidates who favor their positions on a particular nonmaterial issue. For example, the National Abortion Rights Action League (pro-choice) and the National Right to Life Committee (anti-abortion) are concerned with the abortion issue and the National Rifle Association (anti-gun-control) and Handgun Control, Inc. (pro-control) focus on the gun control issue.

3. *Ideological PACs.* Finally, a number of PACs support candidates committed to strong liberal or conservative ideologies and issues. Liberal PACs include the National Committee for an Effective Congress and the Hollywood Women's Political Committee. Conservative PACs include the National Conservative Political Action Committee and the Conservative Victory Committee.

Pressure Groups and Lobbying

Another tactic that PACs use to advance their interests is lobbying through their Washington representatives. This stratagem concentrates on inducing public officials already in office to support government action (including administrative and judicial rulings as well as legislative acts) the groups favor and to block those the groups oppose.

In the bad old days, pressure groups often used straight bribes in the form of cash payments or guarantees of well-paid jobs after retirement. Sadly, bribes are still occasionally offered and accepted, but the laws against them are strict and the mass media's investigative reporters love to expose bribe-taking. Consequently, most interest groups and public officials have decided that giving and taking bribes is either too immoral or too risky or both, and bribery has become quite rare.

The main tactic of lobbyists is now *persuasion*—convincing members of Congress (and their staffs, who play key roles in making most members' decisions) that the legislation the lobbyist seeks is in the best interests of the nation and of the member's particular district or state. After all, almost all the members of Congress feel that their job is to do the best they can for the interests of their particular constituents. Since it is those constituents rather than the rest of the nation who determine whether or not the members will get re-elected, their likely reactions must be the members' first concern.

Accordingly, lobbyists for all interests use the most persuasive evidence and arguments they can to convince a particular member that the actions their groups want will be in everyone's best interest—the voters in the particular district or state, the member's, and the nation's. Lobbyists who work for interest groups that also have PACs sometimes say that if the member fails to see the light their PACs will contribute money to his or her challenger at the next election. Surprisingly, however, most lobbyists and PACs work quite independently of one another, and lobbyists concentrate mainly on persuading members already in office.

Although American interest groups most frequently employ electioneering and lobbying, they sometimes use tactics that are more widely used in other countries, such as mass political propaganda, demonstrations, strikes and boycotts, nonviolent civil disobedience, and sometimes even violence. There is one tactic, however, in which the United States leads the world: the use of **litigation** for political purposes. Tocqueville wrote in 1835, "Scarcely any political question arises in the United States that is not resolved, sooner or later, into a judicial question."[38] Political scientists Benjamin Ginsberg and Martin Shefter note that from 1955 to 1985 the number of civil cases brought in federal district courts increased from 50,000 a year to over 250,000 a year. One of several reasons for that enormous increase, they say, is the fact that a growing number of interest groups that have done poorly in both elections and lobbying have filed suits in the courts to reverse their losses in other arenas:

> Civil rights groups, through federal court suits, launched successful assaults on Southern school systems, state and local governments, and legislative dis-

tricting schemes. . . . Environmental groups used the courts to block the construction of highways, dams, and other public projects that not only threatened to damage the environment but also provided money and other resources to their political rivals. Women's groups were able to overturn state laws restricting abortion as well as statutes discriminating against women in the labor market.[39]

Conservative groups have countered by trying to ensure that conservatives rather than liberals or feminists are appointed to the Supreme Court and other federal judgeships. The fact that this tactic is used by interest groups far more in America than in any other democracy should not surprise us, because the popularity of pursuing one's individual rights through litigation is one way in which the political culture of America differs significantly from the political cultures of most other countries.

The most important special trait of interest articulation and aggregation in the United States, however, is the very different party environment in which they take place. In most of the democracies discussed in this book most interests operate closely within political parties. (Indeed, in several instances particular interest groups are formally associated with particular parties: the trade unions with the British Labour party and farmers' and business associations with the Austrian People's Party.) Their main tactic is to persuade the parties with which they are associated to give their demands prominent places in the parties' programs and actions in government.

In contrast, American political parties are so much weaker and so much less important players in the policymaking process that the interest groups operate largely outside the parties and are little concerned about whether they are helping or hurting the parties. In 1980, for example, the National Organization for Women (NOW) fought for a rule in the Democratic party to prevent the party from helping to elect any Democratic candidate who opposed the Equal Rights Amendment. In 1984 NOW said that it would refuse to support the party's national ticket unless a woman was nominated for the vice presidency (and, indeed, Geraldine Ferraro was nominated). In the 1996 election, Emily's List, a PAC supporting women candidates, contributed a total of $12,494,280 to women's campaigns, the largest amount spent by a single PAC.[40]

The same observation applies to the Republican party. For some time before 1994 many business PACs contributed much more campaign money to incumbent Democrats than to their Republican challengers even though the Republican political philosophy is much closer to that of business. The national leaders of the Republican party complained bitterly about what they regarded as treason to the party and to conservatism, but Doug Thompson, the leader of the National Association of Realtors, rejected the Republicans' complaints and has spelled out his PAC's political priorities:

> We are a special interest group. Our interest is real estate and housing issues; it is not Contra aid, it is not abortion, it is not the minimum wage. . . . Our members are demanding a lot more accountability. Gone are our free-spending days when we poured money into a black hole called "challenger candidates." Our marching orders on PAC contributions are very clear: Stop wasting money on losers.[41]

Since the Republicans won control of Congress in the 1994 election there have been more Republican than Democratic incumbents, and Republicans have received more PAC contributions than Democrats. In short, interest articulation and aggregation are in many respects different in the United States because its political parties are in most respects very different from those in any other democracy.

THE SPECIAL CHARACTERISTICS OF AMERICAN POLITICAL PARTIES

A Two-Party System

The American party system is usually a nearly-pure two-party system: that is, one in which two major parties are highly competitive with one another and taken together win almost all the votes and offices in elections.[42] As Figure 13.3 shows, the only notable exception since the 1930s came in 1992, when indepen-

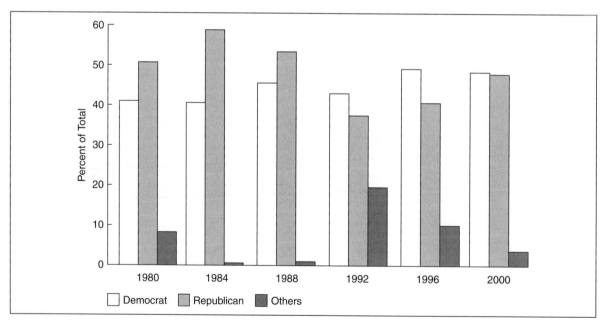

FIGURE 13.3   Party Shares of Presidential Votes, 1980–2000

Source: Statistical Abstract of the United States: 2001 (Washington, D.C.: Bureau of the Census, 2001), Table 378, p. 233.

dent H. Ross Perot won 19 percent of the popular votes for president (Democrat Bill Clinton won 43 percent and Republican incumbent George H. W. Bush won 38 percent). After the election Perot founded the Reform party and ran as its presidential candidate in 1996, but, as the figure shows, his vote share fell to 8.6 percent. He did not run in 2000, but his party's presidential candidate, Pat Buchanan, got less than 1 percent of the votes.[43]

In 2004, in addition to Republican George W. Bush and Democrat John Kerry, there were presidential candidates from a dozen other parties on the ballot in one or more states. However, all these other parties polled a few percent of the popular votes. In addition, nearly all the members of the House and Senate for the past several decades have been affiliated with one of the two major parties. The United States is one of the most distinctive two-party systems in the world.

The "Americanization" of Electioneering

Electioneering—what parties and candidates do in campaigns to maximize their votes in elections—has changed considerably in most democratic nations since the 1950s, and the United States is generally credited with (or blamed for) leading the way. Before the 1950s electioneering in democracies was conducted mainly by party leaders and workers. The party workers made direct contacts with their candidates' known and potential supporters, and used the mass media mainly to publish newspaper advertisements and to print pamphlets and flyers for the party workers to distribute.

Since the 1950s, American parties and candidates have replaced the old techniques. They now depend mainly on paid television advertisements and broadcasters' interviews and talk shows to showcase their candidates and policies to the voters. They employ experts to conduct frequent polls of the voters to test how well their strategies are working. They canvass voters by telephone rather than by ringing doorbells. They store and analyze information about the demographics and past electoral behavior of election districts in computerized databases. They also have transferred control of electioneering from party politicians to paid professional campaign consultants trained in advertising agencies rather than

party organizations. They have made televised debates among the candidates the most important events in campaigns.

Party leaders and candidates in other democracies have watched U.S. electioneering. Many have deplored it, and some have vowed never to "Americanize" (their term) their own campaigns. Nevertheless, campaigners in most democracies have adapted some or all of the high-tech American methods for their own uses. For example, the U.S. held its first nationally-televised debates between presidential candidates in 1960. Similar debates among leading parties and candidates are now regularly held also in Brazil, Chile, Denmark, France, Germany, Mexico, Norway, Sweden, and Venezuela. Most parties in most democracies now hire professional campaign consultants to plan their campaigns. They use private polls to assess the effectiveness of their campaigns, and they use the mass media, especially television, as their main device for soliciting the voters' support. In short, while the "Americanization" of electioneering may or may not be a healthy development, it has happened to some degree in all democracies and to a considerable degree in many.[44]

Differences Between the Major Parties

Many foreign observers (and not a few Americans) often ask just what are the differences between the Democratic and Republican parties? One well-known response is that there are no real differences—they are "like bottles with different labels but equally empty." A more accurate response is that while there is no philosophical principle or policy preference that all Democrats hold that is sharply different from what all Republicans hold, there are a number of respects in which most Democrats differ from most Republicans. Here we will note just two: the social composition of the parties' "identifiers" (that is, the people who say that to some degree they prefer one party to the other); and some issues on which most Democrats differ from most Republicans.

As is shown in Figure 13.4, Americans are almost evenly divided among Democrats (34 percent), Republicans (32 percent), and independents (34 percent). Democrats have greater support among women than men, among blacks than whites, and among people with lower incomes and educations than upper

BOX 13.4 The Presidential Election of 2000

Candidate	Popular Votes	Electoral Votes
George W. Bush, Republican	50,456,169	271
Al Gore, Democrat	50,996,064	266
Ralph Nader, Green	2,882,708	0

The presidential election of 2000 was not the closest in history or the first in which the candidate who received the most popular votes lost in the Electoral College. It was the first decided by the United States Supreme Court.

At the end of election night, Gore was ahead in twenty states and the District of Columbia, totaling 266 electoral votes; Bush was ahead in twenty-nine states, totaling 246 electoral votes. Thus whoever won Florida's 25 electoral votes would have a majority in the Electoral College.

Florida's preliminary official returns showed that Bush had 48.85 percent of the votes to Gore's 48.84 percent. After a recount, Bush's tiny margin—537 votes out of 5,963,110 cast—was reaffirmed. The Gore campaign, however, argued that there had been many errors in the casting and counting of the votes. They petitioned Florida Secretary of State Katherine Harris to hold up any certification of the winner until there had been a manual recount of the votes. But Ms. Harris (a Republican who had co-chaired Florida's Bush for President organization) rejected these requests.

A Gore legal team sued in the Florida courts to postpone the certification deadline and undertake manual recounts. The Florida Supreme Court (made up of Democrats appointed by previous Democratic governors), ruled that the certification deadline should be extended and that manual recounts should take place in several counties to discern in each ballot "the intent of the voter." The Bush team then petitioned the United States Supreme Court to overturn the Florida Court's ruling.

Many legal commentators' observed that the U.S. Supreme Court had almost never interfered in a state's election process (on the ground that such was an unjustified invasion of the states' constitutional prerogatives). While reviewing the case the Supreme Court ruled that the manual recounts be stopped until the legal issues were resolved (conservative Justice Antonin Scalia commented that allowing the manual count to continue "does, in my view, threaten irreparable harm to [Bush], and to the country, by casting a cloud upon what he claims to be the legitimacy of his election").[45] On December 12 the U.S. Supreme Court announced its decision in *Bush v. Gore* 121 S.Ct. 525 (2000). The Court held that in allowing election officials in each county to apply the standards they thought appropriate in recounting ballots, the Florida Court had violated the U.S. constitutional requirement of "equal protection of the laws." Since there was not enough time for the Florida Court to specify such standards for a recount, the recount was halted. Bush had won, and Gore conceded the next day.

Perhaps the clearest characteristic of the controversy was the partisan divide: almost everyone who favored the positions taken by the Gore team (e.g., the Democrats on the Florida Supreme Court and the liberal justices on the U.S. Supreme Court) wanted Gore to be president. Almost everyone who favored the positions taken by the Bush team wanted Bush to be president—for example, Katherine Harris, the Florida governor (Jeb Bush, the candidate's brother), the Republican majorities in Florida's legislature, and, above all, the conservative members of the U.S. Supreme Court. It appeared that decisions on the legal issues depended on where people stood politically, not on the law. Many Gore supporters thus believed Gore had been cheated, and questioned the legitimacy of Bush's presidency. But all that changed on September 11, 2001 (see Box 13.1).

BOX 13.5 2004 Election: Red and Blue States

The 2004 campaign between George W. Bush and John Kerry was an intensely fought election. Both sides felt the election would shape the future course of the nation, and the polarization over Iraq further divided the nation. young people were especially encouraged to vote, such as P. Diddy's "Vote or Die" project. As a result, turnout increased by about 5 percent over 2000.

However, the divisions in the nation followed the model of 2000. Two states switched to Bush, and only one shifted to Kerry. Bush received 286 electoral votes, Kerry garnered 252. The "red states" that went for Bush were located in the South, the Midwest and the Rocky Mountain states. The "blue states" that voted for Kerry were located in New England, the Eastern seaboard, and the West coast.

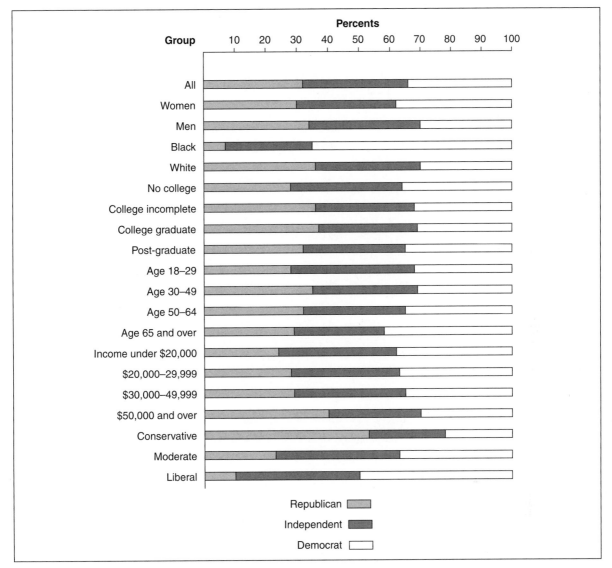

FIGURE 13.4   Social Composition of Major Party Identifiers, 2001

Source: Harold W. Stanley and Richard G. Niemi, *Vital Statistics on American Politics 2001–2002* (Washington, D.C.: CQ Press, 2001), Table 3–2, p. 117.

status people. Nevertheless, with the exception of the overwhelming rejection of the Republicans by African-Americans, both parties draw significant support from every major demographic group. Neither party, unlike some parties in some other countries, represents only farmers or industrial workers or members of a particular ethnic or linguistic interest.

In terms of political philosophy, both parties have the support of some liberals and some conservatives, although the Democrats have a higher proportion of liberals and the Republicans a higher proportion of conservatives. The same is true of the two

parties' members of Congress, as is illustrated by the roll call votes on some significant issues in both houses in 1993–2001 shown in Table 13.5).

Table 13.5 shows that there are significantly more liberals than conservatives among the Democrats in both houses of Congress and significantly more conservatives than liberals among the Republicans—although on most issues some Democrats vote for conservative positions and some Republicans vote for liberal positions.

Generally, Democrats tend to believe that government should take a major and active role in

T A B L E   1 3 . 5   Selected Votes in Congress, 1993–2001

	Republicans			Democrats		
	Liberal	Conservative	Cohesion Index*	Liberal	Conservative	Cohesion Index*
HOUSE						
Lift ban, leave gays-in-military issue to Clinton	101	157	22	163	11	88
Welfare reform	30	165	70	226	4	96
Override Clinton veto of bill outlawing partial-birth abortions	70	121	26	215	15	86
Balanced budget amendment to Constitution	99	151	20	172	1	98
Impeach President Clinton for perjury	5	223	98	200	5	98
Impeach President Clinton for obstruction of justice	12	216	95	199	5	98
Bush-proposed tax cut	0	219	100	197	10	91
SENATE						
"Brady bill" for handgun control	8	47	70	28	16	28
Reject House ban on funding abortions for poor women	21	34	24	38	6	72
Welfare reform	1	51	96	23	23	0
Bush-proposed tax cut	0	50	100	38	12	52
McCain-Feingold campaign finance reform	12	38	52	47	3	88

*The cohesion index is a measure of the extent to which members of a particular party in a legislature vote alike on matters of public policy. The percentages of the members voting each way are calculated, and the smaller percentage is subtracted from the larger. If they all vote alike the index is 100. If they split evenly the index is 0. If they split 75–25 the index is 50.

Source: Congressional Quarterly Reports, 1993–2002.

dealing with the nation's problems, while most Republicans tend to agree with Ronald Reagan that "big government *is* the problem." Thus, most Democrats favor higher levels of government spending than Republicans on aid for the poor and homeless, education, medical care, public housing, and the like. On the so-called social issues, Democrats tend to favor minimum government intervention in people's moral, religious, and intellectual lives, while Republicans favor greater government intervention in such matters as prohibiting the exhibition of obscene films and art, limiting or outlawing abortions, and encouraging prayer in the public schools.

Democrats also tend to be more egalitarian than Republicans. That is, Republicans tend to support measures for equal opportunity (giving every citizen an equal chance to engage in fair competition for material riches and the other good things in life), while Democrats tend to support measures for "equal conditions" (giving all citizens a guaranteed minimum of the good things in life even if they cannot earn them by their own efforts).

Although there are more differences in political philosophies and policy preferences *within* each of the major parties in the United States than in their counterparts in most other nations, there are still enough differences *between* most leaders and identifiers of the two parties to offer the voters meaningful choices in policies and candidates in most elections.

Decentralized Organization

Most political parties in most democracies are organized as **hierarchies,** with a national leader and national organization at the top holding the power to supervise the activities of local and regional party organizations. In sharp contrast, the American Democratic and Republican parties are organized, in Samuel Eldersveld's apt phrase, as "**stratarchies.**"[46] That is, their organizations at the national, state, and local levels have little power, legal or extralegal, over the organizations at the other levels. Moreover, within each level most parties have an executive organization and a legislative organization, and neither has any power over the other.

At the national level, for example, the Democrats and Republicans each have a **presidential party** and a **congressional party.** For the party that holds the presidency, the presidential party consists of the president, the national committee, the national chairman, and the national nominating conventions. The party that does not hold the presidency has no single person as its universally acknowledged leader.

Each party in each house of Congress has a caucus, consisting of all the party's members in the particular chamber (and thus equivalent to what in most democracies is called the parliamentary party). A floor leader is selected by the caucus to serve as the main coordinator of the party's legislative strategy and tactics. A policy committee, chosen by the caucus, advises the floor leader and the caucus on matters of substantive policy and legislative tactics. The whips are chosen by the caucus to serve as channels of communication between the leaders and the ordinary members. The campaign committees are chosen by the caucus to raise money and distribute it among the campaigns of selected candidates for the particular chamber.

We should emphasize, however, that the presidential party has little formal connection with the congressional party, and that any effort by the president (to say nothing of the national committee or the national chairman) to intervene in the congressional party's selection of its leaders or the determination of its policies or strategy is resented and rejected as "outside interference." On the other hand, in the 1998–1999 impeachment and trial of Democratic President Clinton, most Republican members sought his impeachment, conviction, and removal from office, while most Democrats supported him.

At the state level, both parties usually have a gubernatorial party and a legislative party. The gubernatorial party consists of the governor (the other party has no single, acknowledged leader), the state central committee, the state chair, and the state conventions. The legislative parties, like the congressional parties,

usually have caucuses, elected floor leaders, policy committees, and whips. But each state's gubernatorial and legislative parties have no power over one another, and the national parties have no power over any part of the state parties. The national and state parties are simply different strata, not higher and lower levels in a chain of command headed by the national agencies.

At the various local levels there are congressional district committees, county committees, city committees, ward and precinct committees, and others too numerous to list here. In most states the local party committees and conventions are, both in law and in fact, independent of the state and the national party agencies. Hence, they constitute a third stratum, which is just as independent from the state agencies as the state agencies are from the national agencies.

Far more than almost any major party in any other modern democratic nation, then, American party organizations are agglomerations of hundreds of different leaders and committees distributed among various organizational strata, each of which has little or no power to command or obligation to obey any other agency in its own stratum, let alone any agency in any other stratum.

Low Cohesion

The parliamentary parties in most modern democratic nations have high **party cohesion,** a term that denotes the degree to which the members of a legislative party vote together on issues of public policy. Abstentions and even votes against the party leaders' wishes are not unknown in those parties, and in some countries their frequency has increased, though very slowly, in recent years. But these are, at most, minor deviations from the norm that all the members of parliamentary parties in other countries vote solidly together in most parliamentary votes.

By sharp contrast, the only matters in either chamber of Congress on which all Democrats regularly vote one way and all Republicans vote the other way relate to "organizing" the chamber—that is, selecting the Speaker of the House, the President Pro Tem of the Senate, and the chairs of the leading standing committees. On all other issues they rarely vote unanimously.

On the issues shown in Table 13.5, party cohesion was generally higher among House Democrats than among Senate Democrats, and even higher among House Republicans than Senate Republicans. On some issues one party or the other approached the cohesion levels of most major parties in other democracies. For example, the House Democrats' opposition to President Clinton's impeachment was very high, while House Republicans had perfect cohesion for President George W. Bush's tax cut proposal in 2001. On the other hand, House Democrats split more evenly on gays in the military and Bush's tax cut.

Consequently, the congressional parties have some party cohesion. It is especially high on such issues as higher spending for social welfare measures and greater regulation of business—with the Democrats usually voting predominantly, but not unanimously, Yes, and the Republicans usually voting predominantly, but not unanimously, No. On the other hand, on issues that cut sharply across party lines, especially moral issues such as abortion, capital punishment, and the regulation of pornography, both parties regularly split relatively evenly. Thus in comparison with the major parliamentary parties in most other democratic nations, the American congressional Democrats and Republicans have low cohesion on most issues.

This situation has important consequences for the role of American parties in the policymaking process, which we will consider later. It also has several causes, the most important of which is the fact that, compared with most other democratic parties, the leaders of the Democrats and the Republicans have very weak disciplinary powers.

Weak Discipline

The leaders of most major parties in the world's democracies have a number of tools to ensure that the legislators bearing their parties' labels support the parties' policies in the national legislatures. For one, they can make sure that no unusually visible or persistent rebel against the party's positions is given a ministerial position or preferment of any kind. If that fails to bring the fractious member into line, they can expel him or her from the parliamentary party altogether. Many parties in many countries give their leaders the ultimate weapon: the power to deny the rebel reselection as an official party candidate at the next election.

In sharp contrast, in the United States any person who wins a party's primary for the House or Sen-

ate in any congressional district or state automatically becomes the party's legal candidate for that office, and no national party agency has the power to veto the nomination. On one notable occasion, called by historians "the purge of 1938," Franklin D. Roosevelt, an unusually popular and powerful national party leader, tried to intervene in the primary elections of several states to prevent the renomination of Democratic senators who had opposed his New Deal policies. He failed in twelve of thirteen attempts, and most people have since concluded that any effort by a national party leader to interfere in candidate selection at the state and local levels is bound to fail.

To be sure, presidents and their parties' leaders in Congress can and often do plead with their fellow partisans to support the president's policies for the sake of party loyalty and/or to increase the party's chances at the next election or to keep the party from looking foolish. Unless they have some strong reason to do otherwise, most members of Congress go along. However, unlike the leaders of most parties in most other countries, neither the president nor his party's congressional leaders have any effective disciplinary power to compel their members in Congress to vote in ways contrary to their consciences—or to what they perceive to be the interests and wishes of their constituents.

A Special Consequence: Divided Party Control of Government

In a pure parliamentary democracy one party cannot control the legislature while another party controls the executive. If the parliament refuses a cabinet request, the cabinet either resigns and a new cabinet acceptable to the parliament takes over, or the parliament is dissolved, new elections are held, and a new cabinet is formed that has the support of the new parliamentary majority. There can never be more than a short interim period in which the parliamentary majority and cabinet disagree on any major question of public policy.

In the United States, in contrast, separation of powers and the separate terms and constituencies for the president, the members of the House, and the members of the Senate make it possible for one party to win control of the presidency and the other party to win control of one or both houses of Congress. How often does it actually happen? From the election of 1832 (when most historians say the mod-

The election of 2000 produced unified Republican control, with President George W. Bush joining the Republican-controlled Congress. But it didn't last long: in 2001, Senator James Jeffords of Vermont announced that he was leaving the Republican party to become an Independent, and that he would vote with the Democrats. That gave the Democrats only a 50-49 margin, but with Jeffords's support they regained control of the Senate and once again became part of a divided government. In 2002, the voters restored control of both houses to the Republicans.

The most obvious cause for this situation, which is both unknown and impossible in parliamentary democracies, is the fact that the chief executive and the members of both houses of Congress are, as we have seen, elected separately by overlapping constituencies and with different terms. The constitutional structure thus makes it possible for American voters to do something that voters in most parliamentary democracies cannot do, namely, "split their tickets"—that is, vote for a member of one party for president and for a member of the other party for Congress.

Ticket-splitting explains the increasing frequency of divided party control. Figure 13.6 shows the changing percentages of respondents in the National Election Studies of all presidential elections from 1952 through 2000 who reported voting for the presidential candidate of one party and a candidate of another party for the House of Representatives. This figure shows that split-ticket voting has increased steadily and in 2000 it was noticeably higher than it was in 1952.

However, divided government apparently does not significantly weaken (or strengthen) the federal government's ability to make public policies. David Mayhew's careful study of the most important pieces of legislation passed from 1946 to 1990 shows that the rate of production was about the same in periods of divided party control as in periods of unified control.[47]

THE POLICYMAKING PROCESS IN AMERICA

When we consider the policymaking process in the United States, we must first understand that the constitutional framework within which the process operates was carefully designed to keep government from doing bad things, not to make it easier for it to do good things. To be sure, in writing the Constitution the men of Philadelphia hoped to get a more

Year	Congress	President
1948	Democrats	Harry S. Truman, Democrat
1950	Democrats	
1952	Republicans	Dwight D. Eisenhower, Republican
1954	Democrats	
1956	Democrats	
1958	Democrats	
1960	Democrats	John F. Kennedy, Democrat
1962	Democrats	
1963	Democrats	Lyndon B. Johnson, Democrat
1964	Democrats	
1966	Democrats	
1968	Democrats	Richard M. Nixon, Republican
1970	Democrats	
1972	Democrats	
1973	Democrats	Gerald R. Ford, Republican
1974	Democrats	
1976	Democrats	James E. Carter, Democrat
1978	Democrats	
1980	S–R, H–D	Ronald W. Reagan, Republican
1982	S–R, H–D	
1984	S–R, H–D	
1986	Democrats	
1988	Democrats	George H. W. Bush, Republican
1990	Democrats	
1992	Democrats	William J. Clinton, Democrat
1994	Republicans	
1996	Republicans	
1998	Republicans	
2000	S–D, H–R	George W. Bush, Republican
2002	Republicans	
2004	Republicans	

FIGURE 13.5   United/Split Party Control of the Presidency and Congress, 1948–2004

ern electoral and party systems began) through the election of 2000, there have been a total of 85 presidential and midterm elections. Each of these elections could have resulted in either divided party control or unified party control. In fact, 53 (61 percent) produced unified control, and 32 (39 percent) produced divided control.

Even more noteworthy is the fact that since the death of Franklin D. Roosevelt in 1945, **divided party control** has occurred so frequently that many observers feel it has become normal, not exceptional. In the period from 1946 through 2002 there have been 28 elections. Only 12 (43 percent) have produced unified control (10 with Democratic presidents and congresses, and 2 with a Republican president and congress), and sixteen (57 percent) have produced divided control (all but two with Republican presidents and Democratic congresses).

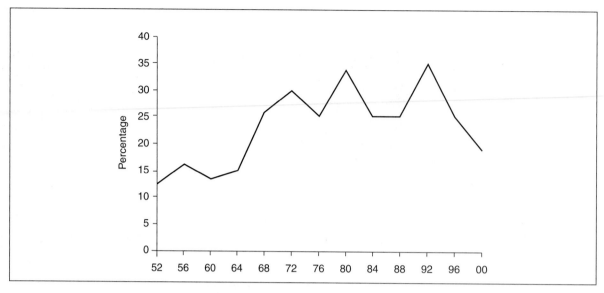

F I G U R E   1 3 . 6   Trend in Split-Ticket Voting, 1952–1996

Source: 1952–1996 American National Election Studies, Inter-University Consortium for Political and Social Research, University of Michigan. Data points are the percentage reporting a different vote for the presidential and House of Representatives elections; third party candidates are included in the calculations.

effective national government than that provided by the Articles of Confederation. But making and implementing effective, coherent, and forceful national policies was not their prime goal.

They believed that government should never be regarded as some kind of benevolent mother, doing whatever is necessary to keep all her children well fed and feeling good. We should never forget, they warned, that government is a powerful and dangerous institution created by fallible human beings. Its prime objective—indeed, its only legitimate reason for existing and being obeyed—is to secure every person's God-given right to life, liberty, and property. Anything that government does beyond that, they believed, is not only less important but not even acceptable if it in any way abridges those basic rights.

The best way to make a government strong enough to secure the rights of its citizens without becoming so powerful that it overrides them, they believed, is to disperse its power among many different agencies—among the federal and state governments by federalism, and within the federal government by separation of powers. The power should be so divided, they held, that no single faction would likely ever get control of the whole power of government and promote its interests at the expense of all the others.[48]

Accordingly, they did not think that policy deadlocks, in which the government cannot act because one of its parts blocks action by other parts, are some kind of terrible failure that should be avoided wherever possible and unblocked as soon as possible. Rather, they regarded such deadlocks as highly preferable to any government action that rides roughshod over the interests and objections of any significant part of the community. Consequently, whenever a deadlock blocks today's government from making effective policies to deal with budget deficits, mounting national debt, crime, health care, campaign finance, the war on terror, or any other public problem, the least we can say is that the policymaking process is operating as the framers intended.

Traditional Ways of Avoiding Deadlocks

Alexis de Tocqueville wrote: "I have never been more struck by the good sense and the practical judgment of the Americans than in the manner in which they elude the numberless difficulties resulting from their Federal Constitution."[49] He had a point. From the opening of the First Congress in 1789 to the twenty-first century, Americans have found that, however dangerous to human rights it may be, the government of the United States has to make and implement at least *some* policies. It has to regulate interstate and foreign commerce, increase or decrease the supply of money, conduct relations with foreign nations, levy taxes, make appropriations, and so on. As Tocqueville rightly observed, Americans have developed ways of getting policies made despite the constitutional system's many roadblocks and general tendency toward inertia. One set of ways has been traditionally used in ordinary times, and the other set has been called on in times of great crisis.

In ordinary times public policies in America have been made mainly by putting together ad hoc, issue-specific coalitions of interests by bargaining and cutting deals among their representatives. The main coalition builders have included public officials of all kinds, including presidents and their chief political aides in the Cabinet and the Executive Office of the President; members of Congress and their professional staffs; political heads and permanent civil servants in the executive departments and the independent agencies; and federal judges and their clerks. At least as active and often as powerful as these inside players are the outside players, especially the lobbyists representing the major organized interest groups that feel they have major stakes in the policy outcomes. The usual result is that, while each contest over each policy produces winners and losers, it never produces total victory or total defeat for any highly involved interest. Each contestant gets something of what it wants but never all; and each manages to stave off total disaster.[50]

Many commentators, past and present, have been highly critical of this process. They claim that it usually takes far too long to get anything done, and that what is done is usually messy, full of inconsistencies, self-defeating, and in constant need of repair. They are also struck by how difficult it is get closure on any major policy: typically, when a coalition loses in the presidency, it tries in the Congress; when it loses in the Congress, it tries in the bureaucracy; when it fails to persuade incumbent elected and appointed officials, it tries to replace them; and when it loses everywhere else, it turns to the courts to upset or water down policies made by the other agencies.

In recent years, for example, when the coalition that wanted to support the Contra rebels in Nicaragua failed to get enough support from Congress, they turned to secret machinations in the National Security Agency to provide the funds. As another example,

when civil rights advocates in the 1950s failed to get Congress to abolish racial segregation in the schools, they turned to the Supreme Court and won their victory in the landmark decision of *Brown v. Board of Education* (1954). In recent times the coalitions of feminists, gays, and lesbians, after losing in elections and among elected officials and bureaucrats, have often turned to the courts rather than give up.[51]

Without doubt the ordinary-times process falls far short of the neat, orderly, and swift policymaking process that parliamentary democracies usually enjoy because of their fusion of powers and the consequent impossibility of prolonged deadlock between the executive and the legislature. Yet the American process has undeniably produced a large number of major national policies, many of them quite successful: for example, the establishment of Alexander Hamilton's economic development program in the 1790s, the western expansion of the country in the nineteenth century, the absorption of millions of immigrants, the Progressive reforms of the early 1900s, the New Deal, the constant (though to some too slow) advance in the status of African-Americans since the end of slavery, the drastic overhaul of the tax system in 1986, and so on. Even at its best, however, the ordinary-times process has always taken a lot of time to produce results, and there have been occasions in American history when the danger that it would not work fast enough to meet the needs made the nation turn to another kind of policymaking process.

In 1889, the great English commentator on the American system, James Bryce, wrote:

> In troublous times . . . immense responsibility is thrown on one who is both the commander-in-chief and the head of the civil executive. Abraham Lincoln wielded more authority than any single Englishman has done since Oliver Cromwell. It is true that the ordinary law was for some purposes practically suspended during the War of Secession. But it will always have to be similarly suspended in similar crises, and the suspension enures to the benefit of the President, who becomes a sort of dictator.[52]

Bryce was right about Lincoln, who, when the Southern states started seceding in 1861, took a number of steps that were far outside the ordinary policymaking process. By executive proclamations he suspended the writ of habeas corpus, called for volunteers to join the Union Army, spent government money to buy them food, uniforms, and weapons, and made the fateful decision to provision Fort Sumter even though he expected the action would start a civil war. Then, after having done all this, he summoned Congress into session, told them what he had done, and asked for retroactive authority—which they had no choice but to give him.

Since then, presidents have often taken the view that when the national interest requires prompt action, they either should do it on their own, as Lincoln did, or persuade Congress to rush through their radical reform measures, as Franklin D. Roosevelt did in the 1930s when it seemed clear that in the absence of extraordinary measures the economy would collapse under the stress of the Great Depression.

Presidents usually exert these extraordinary powers in foreign rather than domestic crises, as when Truman ordered American troops into Korea in 1950, Kennedy and Johnson followed suit in Vietnam in the 1960s, the first Bush ordered troops to Panama, the Persian Gulf, and Somalia in the 1980s and early 1990s, Clinton sent troops to Haiti in 1994 and to Bosnia in 1995, and the second Bush in 2001–2002 sent American soldiers and airmen to Afghanistan to overthrow the terrorist-sheltering Taliban government; and in 2003, sent the armed forces to invade Iraq and depose Saddam Hussein. The War Powers Act of 1974 was designed to limit the president's power to take this kind of action without congressional approval, but in fact it has restrained presidents very little. No one doubts that in any future crisis, especially in foreign affairs, presidents will again bypass the ordinary policymaking process and do what they feel needs to be done.

The U.S. experience in Korea and Vietnam, however, makes it clear that the presidential-dictatorship escape valve does not stay open indefinitely. When the action accomplishes its mission quickly, there are few American casualties, and the troops get out in a few weeks, it works well. But when it drags on for months and years with huge expense, many casualties, and little hope of a clean-cut final victory—Korea and Vietnam are so far the leading examples—the president eventually loses popular and then congressional support, and the nation returns to the ordinary process. In any case, a leader who is held to account for his actions in free elections every four years is no dictator. How this will play out with the second Bush's war on Iraq remains to be seen.

POLICY PERFORMANCE

Tax Policies

When considering policy performance in the United States, it is important to remember that we are dealing with the outputs of many governments, not just the one in Washington, D.C.[53] In 1997 there were over 87,000 governmental units in America, including the federal government, 50 states, 3,043 counties, 19,372 municipalities, 16,629 townships, 13,726 local school districts, and 34,683 special districts—each of which had some constitutional or statutory power to make policies.[54]

Of these 87,504 authorities, the federal government extracts the greatest share of revenues: it collects 62 percent of all taxes and 57 percent of revenues from all sources. Its share is, of course, smaller than the shares taken by the national governments of unitary nations, such as Great Britain, Japan, and Sweden, but it is larger than those taken by the national governments in any of the federal systems except Austria.[55]

Table 13.6 displays the main types of taxes as percentages of total revenue in the United States and eight other industrialized nations in 1994. Table 13.6 shows that the United States relies more on personal income taxes than any other nation except Canada and Sweden. Social security taxes paid by both employees and employers in America are higher than average. The United States relies less on sales and other taxes on consumption than any other country except Japan. Part of the reason is that, unlike most European governments, the U.S. national government has never levied a sales tax or a value added tax, although most American states levy sales taxes as well as income taxes. Accordingly, the tax structure in the American federal system as a whole is more progressive (in the sense of placing the heaviest burden on people with the greatest ability to pay) than that in most but not all other nations.

Americans frequently complain about the heavy tax burden they bear, and Republican presidents Ronald Reagan, George H. W. Bush, and George W. Bush all made cutting taxes the cornerstones of their economic programs. Just how great is the tax burden of Americans compared with that borne by the residents of other industrialized democracies?

The answer depends on what measure is used. Expressed as a percentage of gross domestic product

T A B L E   1 3 . 6   Tax Sources as Percentages of Total Revenue, 1998

	Personal Income	Corporate Income	Employees' Social Sec.	Employers' Social Sec.	Sales and Consumption	Specific Goods
Great Britain	27.5	11.0	7.3	9.4	18.1	12.8
Canada	37.8	10.0	5.8	8.1	14.0	9.1
France	17.4	5.9	8.7	25.2	17.5	8.4
Germany	25.0	4.4	17.9	19.9	17.9	8.4
Italy	25.0	7.0	8.3	20.5	14.2	10.2
Japan	18.8	13.3	15.0	19.6	8.9	7.7
Netherlands	15.2	10.6	—	12.3	16.9	8.4
Sweden	35.0	5.7	5.8	22.5	13.8	7.3
United States	**40.5**	**9.0**	**10.2**	**12.2**	**7.6**	**6.5**

Source: Statistical Abstract of the United States: 2001 (Washington, DC: Bureau of the Census, 2001), Table 1348, p. 845.

(GDP), American taxes take a total of 29 percent, the lowest figure among the major industrialized nations (Sweden, at 56.9 percent, is the highest). Moreover, its take from GDP has increased at a slower rate than in any other industrialized democracy since 1980. (Again, Sweden leads with the highest rate of increase.)[56] In summary, compared with the tax systems of most other industrialized countries, the American system is one of the more progressive in its structure but takes a smaller proportion of the GDP than any of the others.

Distributive Performance

Of the total expenditures by all American governments in 1999, the federal government spent over half (56 percent), the states 19 percent, and local governments 25 percent. An overview of what they spent it on in 1999 is shown in Figure 13.7.

This Figure shows that in 2001 the federal government spent 58 percent of its budget on domestic welfare functions, 19 percent on defense-related functions, and 13 percent for interest on the national debt.

Among the world's other democratic governments, only Israel spends as high a proportion of its budget on defense as the United States. (Some Third World countries, such as Iraq, North Korea, Oman, and Saudi Arabia, spend even higher proportions.)[57] Some Americans argue that defense spending is far too high, especially now that the Cold War has ended. Others counter that the events of September 11, 2001 demonstrate that the world is still a dangerous place and America needs to spend whatever it takes to win the war on terror. Whatever the merits of these posi-

tions, the trend up to 2002 was toward lower proportions of federal spending on defense and higher proportions on domestic welfare programs.

Other international comparisons show that U.S. per capita expenditures on health care are by far the highest in the world, followed at some distance by Canada and Switzerland.[58] And in proportion of the gross domestic product spent on education, the U.S. (with 0.7 percent) ranks fifth behind Germany (1.9), Japan (1.2), Spain (1.1), and Canada (0.8).[59]

Regulatory Performance

Like all modern industrialized democracies, the United States is a welfare state in the sense that many of its policies proceed from the conviction that government has an obligation to guarantee certain minimum levels of life's basics to all its citizens, especially to those who cannot provide them for themselves. However, nations differ markedly both in the particular items of basic needs that government should provide and the levels at which they should be provided. In this section we will briefly review the major policies adopted by American governments in three main problem areas.

Social Insurance. The United States was among the last of the modern industrialized nations to embrace the goals of the welfare state, and today the proportion of the nation's GDP spent on public welfare programs is lower than that in most industrialized nations. Even so, the federal, state, and local governments together have a wide range of policies intended to put a floor beneath the income and living conditions

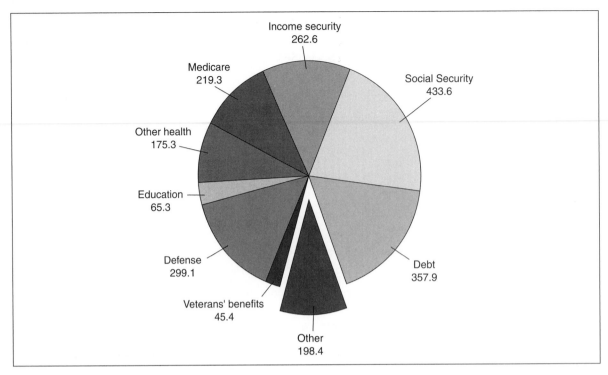

Income security
262.6

Social Security
433.6

Medicare
219.3

Other health
175.3

Education
65.3

Defense
299.1

Veterans' benefits
45.4

Debt
357.9

Other
198.4

FIGURE 13.7   Federal Spending by Function, 2001

Source: Statistical Abstract of the United States 2001 (Washington: Bureau of the Census, 2001), table 463, p. 307

of the poor. For that purpose they use two main instruments: social insurance and public assistance.

• *Social Insurance and Welfare.* This category includes programs to protect citizens against the risk of loss of income due to old age, retirement, sickness, industrial accidents, and unemployment. The basic federal legislation is the Social Security Act of 1935, which established a fund from mandatory contributions by employees and employers from which all wage-earners are entitled to receive cash payments at retirement or on reaching a certain age. Since the benefits are available to all who contribute, most Americans regard its benefits as entitlements, not handouts. No stigma attaches to receiving social security checks, and most Americans of all income levels approve of the program.

• *Public Assistance.* This category includes both direct cash and in-kind payments to poor people, such as cash aid to families with dependent children, food stamps, free milk for young children, and day care for children of working mothers with low incomes. Unlike Social Security, these programs are

noncontributory and thus constitute obvious income transfers from upper income people to lower income people. As a result, some social stigma does attach to receiving public assistance benefits, and these welfare programs are much more controversial than the social insurance programs.

For years there were many complaints that the welfare system, especially Aid for Families with Dependent Children (AFDC), was removing recipients' incentives to work and making them into lifelong dependents on government handouts. Then, in 1996, Congress passed and President Clinton signed a bill for **welfare reform.** The new law ended the federal guarantee of direct AFDC payments to all eligible families. Instead, the federal government gave $16.4 billion in block grants to the states to develop and fund their own new welfare programs, *provided* that the states impose work requirements for welfare recipients, develop job training programs for them, and put time limits on welfare benefits (thereby replacing welfare with "workfare" according to the new law's advocates).[60]

T A B L E 1 3 . 7   Educational Attainment, Ten Top Nations, 1998 (percent of persons 25- to 64-years-old)

Rank	Nation	Lower Secondary	Higher Secondary	Non-univ. Tertiary	University Education
1	United States	9	52	8	27
2	Netherlands	23	40	*	24
3	Norway	17	57	2	24
4	Canada	+	28	20	19
5	Japan	20	50	13	18
6	Australia	+	31	9	17
7	United Kingdom	19	57	8	15
8	Germany	14	56	9	14
9	Spain	22	13	6	14
10	Sweden	12	48	15	13

*Included in university education.

+Included in primary education

Source: Statistical Abstract of the United States 2001 (Washington, DC: Bureau of the Census, 2001), Table 1337, p. 839.

Education.   In the United States as in other industrialized nations, education is provided mainly by schools financed and operated by the government, although there are more privately owned and operated schools, especially universities (including such famous institutions as Columbia, Harvard, Princeton, Stanford, and Yale), in America than in most other countries (they are also important in Japan and Great Britain).

What sets the American school system apart from systems in other countries is its high degree of decentralization. Most schools, from kindergartens through universities, are locally financed and regulated, although the federal government provides considerable subsidies for many special programs, each of which carries restrictions on how the money is to be spent. For example, in awarding federally funded scholarships and other forms of financial aid for students, schools may not discriminate against applicants because of their race or gender. The local financing and regulation of schools has many consequences, not the least of which is the fact that schools in poor states and poor districts generally spend considerably less money per pupil than schools in richer states and districts.

Whatever the consequences of these differences, the United States, as Table 13.7 shows, still has a higher proportion of its youth enrolled in secondary schools and universities than any other na-

tion. It has the second highest proportion (after Japan) of seventeen-year-olds in secondary schools, the highest proportion of twenty-one-year-olds in colleges and universities, and the highest proportion of college graduates going on to graduate and professional schools.[61]

A number of industrialized nations operate on the theory that higher education should be reserved for only the most talented and accomplished students. They therefore require that only those students who do well in demanding nationally-administered tests after finishing one level may advance to a school at the next higher level. The United States, in contrast, operates on the theory that as many people as possible should be given a chance at a college education. As educational sociologist Martin Trow sums it up, "If Europe's slogan for higher education has been 'nothing if not the best,' America's has been 'something is better than nothing.'"[62] Consequently, it is much easier for American eighteen-year-olds to enter some kind of post-secondary education—a four-year college or university, or a two-year community college—than for their peers in any other country, and many more do so. In 1998, 27 percent of Americans between the ages of 25 and 64 had university educations—a higher proportion than in any other industrialized democracy. Only the Netherlands and Norway came close, with 24 percent each; the others ranged from 6 percent (Austria) to 19 percent (Canada).

What about the *quality* of American education? Many scholars, school administrators, and politicians in America have long and inconclusively debated that question, and the literature on the subject is far too vast and complicated to survey in detail here. We will note only that many commentators, both in America and abroad, have concluded that American pupils in primary and secondary schools (ages five to seventeen) do not score as well on cross-national standardized tests as their counterparts in Western Europe, Scandinavia, and Japan, nor are they as well equipped with such basic skills as reading and writing, foreign languages, mathematics, and science.

As we look higher on the educational pyramid, however, the performance and reputation of American schools get better. Undergraduate students in American colleges and universities come closer to matching the skills and performance of their counterparts in other countries, and the quality of graduate and professional programs in law, business, medicine, engineering, and perhaps even the humanities and social sciences are as good as any in the world and better than most. The proof is that many more foreign students come to America for advanced training than Americans go abroad for it.[63]

At present there is a widespread and growing feeling in the United States that American schools, especially at the primary and secondary levels, are doing an inadequate job of giving their pupils the kinds of basic skills the nation's labor force must have if its industries are to compete successfully with their competitors, especially those in Japan and the European Union. Since the late 1950s many special commissions have studied the schools and many reports have been issued recommending many reforms. Many of their recommendations have actually been put into practice; yet the pupils' skills do not seem to have improved very much.

Intensifying the turmoil surrounding the schools are the growing demands to increase the proportions of Americans of African, Hispanic, and Asian descent among the students and faculties at all levels of the system and to add more studies of non-Western cultures to the curriculum rather than perpetuate the traditional focus on Western, white

culture. Education policy has often been highly controversial in the United States, but seldom more so than at the beginning of the new millenium. The way the issue is resolved will, of course, have a profound effect on the nation's future.

Environmental Protection.   Of the policy areas considered here, environmental protection is the most recent to take center stage, not only in the United States but in most other industrialized nations as well. From the beginning of the Industrial Revolution in the late eighteenth century until well after World War II, one of the highest goals of every nation was economic growth—constantly increasing the nation's production of goods and services, both for home consumption and for sale abroad. Indeed, most political scientists during the 1950s and 1960s classified the world's nations as developed or developing, depending not only on the existing per capita size of their economies but also on their rates of economic growth.

For many purposes that goal remains highly desirable today. After all, economic growth is the best instrument nations have yet found for getting the resources their governments need to achieve most of their other policy goals. This holds whether the goals be increasing military strength and diplomatic clout, providing more food, shelter, and medical care for the poor, or increasing the coverage and improving the quality of health and education. Moreover, political scientists generally believe that many of the difficult problems involved in dividing a nation's economic "pie" fairly are much easier to handle when the total "pie" is steadily increasing than when it is constant or shrinking.

In recent years, however, policymakers in many nations, including the United States, have come to realize that economic growth, especially unrestrained and rapid growth, has great costs. Nowhere is this cost greater than in the area of toxic emissions and solid wastes that have been the byproducts of large-scale industrialization. Those wastes are contaminating the food we eat, the water we drink, and the very air we breathe. As a result, policymakers in the United States, Western Europe, Eastern Europe, and Japan—and even in industrializing nations such as Brazil, Nigeria, and the People's Republic of China—have become increasingly aware that they must grapple with environmental problems. These include regulating the emissions of cars and factories into the air and the discharges of factories and farms into rivers and lakes, disposing the growing mountains (or barge-loads) of solid waste, and determining how much economic growth they can afford to forego in order to protect and restore their environments.

Heidenheimer and his colleagues point out that some nations, especially Japan and Great Britain, have approached this problem less by relying on government regulations than on encouraging corporations and labor unions to work together to develop their own plans for dealing with pollution. The United States has taken a quite different approach. It has enacted a series of stringent laws, beginning with the Clean Air Act of 1970. These laws require manufacturers to reduce sharply their emissions that pollute the air and water by installing such expensive devices as smoke scrubbers and water purifiers, to recycle solid wastes, and to clean up, mostly at their own (and/or their insurance companies') expense, the toxic waste dumps they have previously created. The federal government has established a special agency, the Environmental Protection Agency (EPA), to make sure that these laws are strictly enforced.

The laws also provide that businesses that have been ordered to stop polluting and/or to clean up the results of past pollution can appeal those orders in the courts. As a result, many of the final decisions on environmental issues—especially those on who will pay for the cleanups—are being made, with little speed and great difficulty and expense, in extended litigation.

That should not surprise us, since we noted earlier that one of the strongest and most persistent strains in American political culture has been the conviction that one of the highest of all political values is to protect the rights of private individuals, political and religious minorities, and even corporations against the built-in tendencies of governments to abridge those rights. That idea has undoubtedly had great benefits in protecting those rights, but it has also had great costs in making and implementing effective public policies. The current conflict over how to preserve and renew the environment without causing too great a loss of the economic growth that supports so many other policies will continue to be one of the most difficult policy problems the nation faces in the years to come, not only in the United States but in all industrialized and industrializing nations.

AMERICAN EXCEPTIONALISM: MYTH OR REALITY?

The Idea in History

During much of its history, many of the United States' leaders and citizens—and some foreign commentators and many of the millions of immigrants who left their native countries to become Americans—have regarded the U.S. as not just another polity in a world of many polities, but as significantly different from other political systems. Some have viewed it as a great social experiment from which all political systems can and should learn lessons relevant to founding and reforming their own systems.

Thus in his first Inaugural Address, George Washington said, "The preservation of the sacred fire of liberty, and the destiny of the republican model of government, are justly considered as deeply, perhaps as finally staked, on the experiment intrusted to the hands of the American people."[64]

In December 1862, when the very existence of the American system was at stake in the Civil War, Abraham Lincoln said to the Congress, "We of this Congress and this administration, will be remembered in spite of ourselves. . . . The fiery trial through which we pass, will light us down, in honor or dishonor, to the latest generation. . . . We shall nobly save, or meanly lose, the last, best hope of earth."[65]

How True Is It?

It seems altogether fitting and proper that we should end this chapter by asking not whether the idea of **American exceptionalism** is noble or vainglorious, but rather how true it is. That is, in what respects and to what degree does the American system resemble and differ from the world's other political systems? Our conclusions are summarized in Table 13.8.

How the American System Closely Resembles Other Systems.   It is a government that has jurisdiction over a certain territory and peoples. It makes

TABLE 13.8   The U.S. Compared with Other Nations: A Summary

Characteristic	How the U.S. Is Like Other Nations	How the U.S. Resembles a Few Nations but Differs from Many	How the U.S. Is Unique or Nearly So
Society	Society composed of many different groups with different interests		
Political System	It has a government, which makes and enforces laws	It is a democracy	
Structure of Government		Based on principles of constitutionalism Federal system	Extensiveness of system of checks and balances
Executive Branch	It has a chief executive	Presidential system rather than parliamentary system Chief of state and head of government roles performed by same person President is directly elected through an electoral college	
Legislative Branch	It has a national legislature	Both houses of the legislature are directly elected	Truly bicameral national legislature Legislative committees play a critical role
Judicial Branch	Courts settle civil and criminal disputes	All national judges appointed; some state and local judges elected Most courts have power of judicial review	Many political issues settled by courts rather than by parties or legislatures
Parties and Elections	It has regular elections	Elections use single member districts and plurality decisions Elections are held on fixed dates; no power of dissolution Parties are closely regulated by law Party discipline weak in the legislature	It has a two-party system Candidates are selected by direct primaries Voter registration is decentralized and responsibility of voter Turnout in elections is low Voters have many elections and many choices at each Party leaders have no power to admit or expel party members Executive and legislative branches can be and often are controlled by different parties Parties are decentralized and largely undisciplined and un-cohesive

The new immigrants: Mexicans crossing the Rio Grande to enter the United States.

J.P. Laffont/Sygma

laws governing their behavior and enforces them with means up to and including capital punishment.

American society is composed of many different groups with different interests, and its political process is essentially a contest among them to advance their interests. Few if any policies benefit all groups and interests equally, and most political decisions have, relatively speaking, some winners and some losers.

In addition, this book's basic theoretical scheme for comparing governments is as applicable to the United States as to any other nation.

How the American System Resembles a Few Nations but Differs from Most. As Table 13.8 notes, The United States is a democracy along with other democracies. It is based on the principle of constitutionalism.

The United States is a presidential democracy rather than a parliamentary democracy, based on the separation of powers rather than on their fusion. The head of government is elected rather than hereditary. Furthermore, the roles of chief of

state and head of government are performed by the same official.

The United States is also unusual because it is a federal system rather than a unitary system.

The legislative system also displays differences to other systems. The presiding officers of its legislative chambers are partisan rather than neutral. Its legislative committees play a critical role in the legislative process. And American legislators are largely free of party discipline and control their own votes.

The U.S. legal system is based on the English Common Law rather than on the continental European Civil Law. Its highest court has the power to declare acts of other government officials and agencies unconstitutional and thereby render them null and void.

U.S. elections use the single-member, plurality system rather than proportional representation. Its elections are held on fixed dates, and there is no power of dissolution. The practice is well established by law and custom that members of the national legislature must live in the states and districts they represent. Particularly in some states and localities,

Congressional leaders: House Speaker Hastert, President Bush, Senate Majority Leader Frist.

AP/Wide World Photos

though not at the national level, there is extensive use of popular initiatives and referendums.

The United States has a great variety of ethnic groups, and ethnicity plays a major role in political conflict. Until recently it has followed a melting pot rather than a patchwork quilt policy toward the assimilation of immigrants.

How the United States Is Unique or Nearly So. Finally, Table 13.8 highlights many of the unique aspects of the American political system. For instance, it has a truly bicameral national legislature, in which on most matters the two chambers must act together.

The U.S. is closer to having its electoral politics dominated by two and only two political parties than almost any other country. Not only can different parties control different branches of government at the same time, but they often do. Its systems for registering voters also are largely decentralized and put most of the burden on the voters. By some measures, its voting turnout is among the lowest in the world.

American political parties choose most of their nominees for office by direct primaries conducted and regulated by public law, not by party rules. Many of its executive officers, particularly at the state and local levels, are directly elected and nominated by direct primaries; consequently, the U.S. voter faces more frequent elections and more decisions to make at each election than voters in any other democratic nation except Switzerland. In addi-

Republican leaders: Vice President Cheney, President Bush, House Speaker Hastert.

AP/Wide World Photos

tion, the political parties are closely regulated by law. But political parties do not control who can become and remain their members, and the parties are, compared with those in other democratic systems, uncohesive, undisciplined, and decentralized.

Because candidates run as individuals rather than as local representatives of national party teams, and because no publicly-financed free media time is given to parties or candidates, the raising and spending of large amounts of money is more important in American elections than in most other democracies.

The court system is also unusual. A higher proportion of political issues are settled in the courts than in any other democracy. Consequently, lawyers play a more important role in the American political system than in any other.

CONCLUSION

It seems fitting to end this chapter comparing the American political system to the world's other systems with a quotation from one of its greatest foreign observers, the English scholar and statesman, Lord Bryce:

> All governments are faulty; and an equally minute analysis of the constitutions of England, or France, or Germany would disclose mischiefs as serious . . . as those we have noted in the American system. To any one familiar with the practical working of free governments it is a standing wonder that they work at all. . . . What keeps a free government going is the good sense and patriotism of the people . . . and the United States, more than any other country, are governed by public opinion, that is to say, by the general sentiment of the mass of the nation, which all the organs of the national government and of the State governments look to and obey.[66]

KEY TERMS

American exceptionalism
Bill of Rights
blanket primaries
checks and balances
closed primaries
congressional parties
conservatives
crossover primaries
direct primaries
divided party control

Electoral College
federalism
hierarchies
impeachment
judicial review
liberals
litigation
litigiousness
lobbying

mass communications media
melting pot versus patchwork quilt
open primaries
party cohesion
political culture
political action committee (PAC)
presidential party

presidential democracy
presidential dictatorship
scarcity doctrine
separation of powers
stratarchies
ticket-splitting
voting registration
voting turnout
war on terror
welfare reform

INTERNET SOURCES

White House: **http://www.whitehouse.gov**

U.S. Senate: **http://www.senate.gov**

U.S. House of Representatives: **http://www.house.gov**

U.S. Courts: **http://www.uscourts.gov**

Library of Congress: **http://lcweb.loc.gov**

National Political Index: **http://politicalindex.com**

SUGGESTED READINGS

Abraham, Henry J. *The Judiciary: The Supreme Court in the Governmental Process,* 10th ed. New York: New York University Press, 1996.

Ansolabehere, Stephen, Roy Behr, and Shanto Iyengar. *The Media Game: American Politics in the Television Age.* New York: Macmillan, 1993.

Bryce, James. *The American Commonwealth,* 2nd ed. London: Macmillan and Co., 1889.

Davidson, Roger H. and Walter J. Oleszek. *Congress and Its Members,* 7th ed. Washington, DC: Congressional Quarterly Press, 2000.

Epstein, Leon D. *Political Parties in the American Mold.* Madison, WI: University of Wisconsin Press, 1986.

Ginsberg, Benjamin and Martin Shefter. *Politics by Other Means: The Declining Importance of Elections in America,* rev. ed. New York: Basic Books, Inc., 1999.

Hamilton, Alexander, James Madison, and John Jay. *The Federalist Papers,* ed. by Clinton Rossiter. New York: The New American Library, 1961.

Jones, Charles O. *Separate But Equal Branches: Congress and the Presidency.* Chatham, NJ: Chatham House Publishers, 1995.

King, Anthony S., ed. *The New American Political System.* Washington, DC: The American Enterprise Institute, 1978.

————. *Running Scared: Why American Politicians Campaign Too Much and Govern Too Little.* New York: Martin Kessler Books, 1997.

Mayhew, David R. *Divided We Govern: Party Control, Lawmaking, and Investigations, 1946–1988.* New Haven, CT: Yale University Press, 1991.

McClosky, Herbert and John Zaller. *The American Ethos: Public Attitudes Toward Capitalism and Democracy.* Cambridge, MA: Harvard University Press, 1984.

Neustadt, Richard E. *Presidential Power and the Modern Presidents: The Politics of Leadership from Roosevelt to Reagan.* New York: The Free Press, 1990.

Nicholas, Herbert G. *The Nature of American Politics,* 2nd ed. New York: Oxford University Press, 1986.

Peltason, Jack W. *Corwin & Peltason's Understanding the Constitution,* 14th ed. Fort Worth, TX: Harcourt Brace College Publishers, 1997.

Polsby, Nelson W. *Congress and the Presidency,* 4th ed. Englewood Cliffs NJ: Prentice Hall, 1986.

Robinson, Donald L., ed. *Reforming American Government: The Bicentennial Papers of the Committee on the Constitutional System.* Boulder, CO: Westview Press, 1985.

Rourke, Francis E. *Bureaucracy, Politics and Public Policy.* Boston, MA: Little, Brown and Co., 1984.

Schlozman, Kay Lehman and John T. Tierney, *Organized Interests and American Democracy.* New York: Harper & Row. 1986.

Tocqueville, Alexis de. *Democracy in America,* 2 volumes, the Henry Reeve text as revised by Francis Bowen and edited by Phillips Bradley. New York: Alfred A. Knopf, 1945.

Wildavsky, Aaron. *The New Politics of the Budgetary Process,* 2nd ed. New York: HarperCollins, 1992.

ENDNOTES

1. "The English Flag," in *Barrack-room Ballads and Other Verses* (London: Methuen, 1892), stanza 1.

2. Strictly speaking, "America" means all the nations located in North and South America, including Canada and the countries in Central America, the Caribbean, and South America. Yet, for better or worse, most people around the world use "American" to label anything connected with just one of those nations, the United States of America. With apologies to the citizens of other Western Hemisphere nations, I will follow this common, though technically incorrect, usage in this chapter.

3. Seymour Martin Lipset, *The First New Nation: The United States in Historical and Comparative Perspective* (New York: Basic Books, 1963).

4. There is a vast literature on the causes, conduct, and consequences of the Civil War. For a superbly written single-volume history, see James M. McPherson, *Battle Cry of Freedom: The Civil War Era* (New York: Oxford University Press, 1988).

5. *The World Almanac and Book of Facts 2002* (New York: World Almanac Books, 2002), pp. 782, 804.

6. H. G. Nicholas, *The Nature of American Politics,* 2d ed. (New York: Oxford University Press, 1986), p. 4.

7. For immigration rates from 1901 to 1998, see *Statistical Abstract of the United States, 2001,* (Washington, DC: U.S. Census Bureau, 2001), Table 5, p. 10.

8. *Statistical Abstract of the United States, 2001,* Table 1339, p. 840.

9. *Statistical Abstract of the United States, 2001,* Table 467, p. 310.

10. The Twenty-First Amendment repeals the Eighteenth (prohibition) Amendment, so there are, in effect, only twenty-five amendments.

11. A word about this usage: strictly speaking, the government in Washington is the "national" government, and the whole divided-powers system of government is the "federal" government. However, most Americans use the terms "national" and "federal" interchangeably to mean the government in Washington. I will do the same, but the reader should be aware of the ambiguity of this usage.

12. We should be clear that there are far more "parliamentary" than "presidential" democracies in the modern world. Presently about 110 nations have democratic systems, and of those only about 15—the United States, Finland, France, and a number of Latin American democracies—have "presidential" systems; all the rest are "parliamentary." Most of the 15 republics of the former Soviet Union are still working out the forms of their newly independent governments, and most appear to be working toward presidential systems closer to the French model than to the American: that is, directly-elected presidents with considerable independent powers as well as prime ministers chosen by the presidents but subject to the approval of the parliaments. Israel now directly elects its prime minister, and its system has been called "presidential parliamentarism."

13. As of 1998, twenty-one states have term limits for members of their legislatures. A number have also tried to impose similar limits on their members of Congress, but federal district judges in Washington state (1994) and Missouri (1998) have held that the states have no constitutional power to limit the terms of national legislators.

14. In recent years an old dispute has been revived by a number of political analysts who argue that presidential democracy is inherently inferior to parliamentary democracy, and the U.S. should convert to a system of parliamentary democracy similar to Great Britain's. Other analysts reply that, judging by

the results—effective policies, loyal citizens, and stability—the American system has done at least as well as the parliamentary systems. See Chapter 2 for a discussion of the issues and arguments in the dispute's current version.

15. The oldest, and in several ways still the most influential, study of American political culture is Alexis de Tocqueville, *Democracy in America,* (New York: Alfred A. Knopf, 1945). Two other classic commentaries by foreign observers are: James Bryce, *The American Commonwealth,* 2 vols. (London: Macmillan Co., 1889); and Gunnar Myrdal, *An American Dilemma: the Negro Problem and Modern Democracy* (New York: Harper, 1944). More recent studies include: Samuel P. Huntington, *American Politics: The Promise of Disharmony* (Cambridge, MA.: Harvard University Press, 1981); Herbert McClosky and Alida Brill, *Dimensions of Tolerance: What Americans Believe about Civil Liberties* (New York: Russell Sage Foundation, 1983); and Michael S. Delli Carpini and Scott Keeler, *What Americans Know about Politics and Why It Matters* (New Haven, CT: Yale University Press, 1996).

16. Gabriel A. Almond, G. Bingham Powell, Jr., and Robert J. Mundt, *Comparative Politics: A Theoretical Framework* (New York: HarperCollins, 1993), p. 55.

17. *Democracy in America,* vol I, p. 122.

18. James Q. Wilson and John J. DiIulio, *American Government,* 6th ed. (Lexington, MA.: D. C. Heath & Co., 1995), Table 4.3, p. 81.

19. Gabriel A. Almond and Sidney Verba, *The Civic Culture: Political Attitudes and Democracy in Five Nations* (Princeton, NJ: Princeton University Press, 1962), p. 186.

20. See, for example, Seymour Martin Lipset, *Political Man: the Social Bases of Politics,* 2nd ed. (London: Heineman, 1983); and Angus Campbell, Philip E. Converse, Warren E. Miller, and Donald E. Stokes, *The American Voter* (New York: John Wiley & Sons, 1960).

21. Edmund Fawcett and Tony Thomas, *America and the Americans* London: Fontana/Collins, 1983), pp. 333, 347, 351.

22. Classic studies of American political socialization include: David Easton and Jack Dennis, *Children in the Political System* (New York: McGraw-Hill, 1969); Fred I. Greenstein, *Children and Politics,* rev. ed. (New Haven, CT: Yale University Press, 1969); Richard E. Dawson and Kenneth Prewitt, *Political Socialization: an Analytic Study,* 2nd ed. (Boston, MA: Little, Brown, 1977); and M. Kent Jennings, *The Political Character of Adolescents: the Influence of Families* Princeton, NJ: Princeton University Press, 1974).

23. *New York Times v. Sullivan,* 376 U.S. 254 (1964).

24. The two key cases are: *National Broadcasting Company v. United States,* 319 U.S. 190 (1943) and *Red Lion Broadcasting Company v. Federal Communications Commission,* 395 U.S. 367 (1969).

25. David Glass, Peverill Squier, and Raymond E. Wolfinger, "Voter Turnout: An International Comparison," *Public Opinion* (December/January 1984), pp. 49–55.

26. Russell J. Dalton, *Citizen Politics,* 2nd ed. (Chatham, NJ: Chatham House, 1996), pp. 45–47.

27. The United States has never held an initiative or referendum election at the national level, but a majority of the states regularly have some initiative and referendum elections, and in about twelve states there are regularly anywhere from fifteen to thirty measures on the ballot in each election. For a full account of the conduct and impact of these "direct legisla-tion" elections, see: David B. Magleby, *Direct Legislation* (Baltimore, MD: Johns Hopkins University Press, (1984); and Thomas E. Cronin, *Direct Democracy* (Cambridge, MA: Harvard University Press, 1989). For a comparative study of direct legislation in many countries, see David Butler and Austin Ranney, *Referendums Around the World* (Washington, DC: The AEI Press, 1994). See also Lawrence LeDuc, "Referendums and Initiatives: The Politics of Direct Democracy," in *Comparing Democracies 2* (Thousand Oaks, CA: Sage Publications, 2002), Chapter 3.

28. One distinguished foreign observer of American politics argues persuasively that American public officials, such as members of the House of Representatives, face elections far more frequently than do their counterparts in other democracies. Consequently, he says, they have to spend large parts of their time in office raising money, touring their districts, appearing on television, and otherwise preparing for the next election. These necessities leave them less time than is needed for the careful study of public issues and the formulation of good public policy. See Anthony S. King, *Running Scared: Why America's Politicians Campaign Too Much and Govern Too Little* (New York: Martin Kessler Books, 1997).

29. Robert S. Erikson, Norman R. Luttbeg, and Kent L. Tedin, *American Public Opinion,* 4th ed. (New York: Macmillan, 1991), Table 1.2, p. 5.

30. Many democratic countries also allow the voters to write on the ballots names other than the parties' nominees, but few voters do so and write-in candidates almost never get more than a handful of votes.

31. See Reuven Y. Hazan, "Candidate Selection," in *Comparing Democracies 2,* Chapter 5.

32. Richard M. Scammon, Alice V. McGillivray, and Rhodes Cook, *America Votes 24* (Washington, DC: Congressional Quarterly, 2001), pp. 43, 45.

33. I take the term *political interest* to mean something of value to a person or group, to be gained or lost by what government does or does not do.

34. Harold D. Lasswell, *Politics: Who Gets What, When, How* (New York: Meridian Books, 1936).

35. See, for example, Alexis de Tocqueville, *Democracy in America,* Vol. I, pp. 191–193; and Michel Crozier, *The Trouble with America,* translated by Peter Heinegg (Berkeley: University of California Press, 1984), p. 81.

36. *Buckley v. Valeo,* 424 U.S. 1 (1976).

37. Frank J. Sorauf and Paul Allen Beck, *Party Politics in America,* 7th ed. (New York: HarperCollins, 1992), p. 377.

38. *Democracy in America,* Vol. I, p. 280.

39. Benjamin Ginsberg and Martin Shefter, *Politics by Other Means: The Declining Importance of Elections in America* (New York: Basic Books, 1990), pp. 151–152.

40. Harold W. Stanley and Richard G. Niemi, *Vital Statistics on American Politics,* 6th ed. (Washington, DC: Congressional Quarterly, 1998), Table 2–15, p. 99.

41. *New York Times,* November 21, 1988, p. A10.

42. Arend Lijphart puts the United States at the top of his list of democratic nations with the smallest number of effective legislative parties, closely followed by New Zealand, the United Kingdom, and Austria: *Democracies: Patterns of Majoritarian and Consensus Governments in Twenty-One Countries* (New Haven, CT: Yale University Press, 1984),

Table 7.3, p. 122. My own ranking of "two-partyness," based on the somewhat different measure of "party fractionalization," which includes both the number of effective parties and the closeness of electoral competition between them, ranks the U.S. parties second behind New Zealand (although in 1995 New Zealand adopted proportional representation, and since then it has had a multiparty system: *Governing: An Introduction to Political Science,* 8th ed. (Englewood Cliffs, NJ: Prentice Hall, 2001), Table 8.6, p. 181.

43. Richard Scammon, Alice McGillivray, and Rhodes Cook, *America Votes, 24* (Washington, DC: Congressional Quarterly Press, 2001), p. 8.

44. For a recent survey of changes in electioneering in the U.S. and other democratic nations, see David Butler and Austin Ranney, eds., *Electioneering: A Comparative Study of Continuity and Change* (New York: Oxford University Press, 1992).

45. Taken from http://www.cnn.com/2000/LAW/12/10/scalia.stevens/.

46. Samuel J. Eldersveld, *Political Parties in American Society* (New York: Basic Books, 1982), pp. 133–136.

47. David Mayhew, *Divided We Govern* (New Haven, CT: Yale University Press, 1991).

48. The fullest exposition of this philosophy is, of course, *The Federalist Papers,* especially the tenth paper, by James Madison. See Clinton Rossiter, ed., *The Federalist Papers* (New York: New American Library, 1961.)

49. *Democracy in America,* Vol. I, p. 167.

50. Political scientists Benjamin Ginsberg and Martin Shefter have suggested that in recent years America has changed its ordinary policymaking process to one in which the election outcomes play little or no role, and policymaking takes place almost entirely *between* elections in such arenas as congressional investigations, bargaining among nonelected presidential aides and congressional staff, revelations of wrongdoing in the mass media, and by civil suits and criminal prosecutions in the courts. They feel that the root cause of this change is the weakening of the voters' party loyalties and their apparently permanent tendency to elect a president of one party and a Congress of the other party. See *Politics by Other Means.*

51. Anthony King, a shrewd foreign observer of American government has asked "Why American politicians campaign so much and govern so little." Much of the answer, he argues, lies in the fact that American elected officials have short and fixed terms which force them to face elections far more of-

ten than their counterparts in other democracies except, perhaps. Switzerland. This forces them to devote a great deal of their time and energy to raising campaign money and campaigning—time that is subtracted from the time in which they can consider public policy. Moreover, he adds, they often feel compelled to vote in accordance with their constituents' preferences rather than their own conclusions about what would be best for the nation. See King's *Running Scared: Why America's Politicians Campaign Too Much and Govern Too Little* (New York: Martin Kessler Books, 1997).

52. *The American Commonwealth,* Vol. I, p. 61.

53. Hundreds of books have been written comparing American public policies with their counterparts in other nations. I have drawn heavily on two: Arnold J. Heidenheimer, Hugh Heclo, and Carolyn Teich Adams, *Comparative Public Policy,* 3rd ed. (New York: St. Martin's Press, 1990); and Harold Wilensky and Lowell Turner, *Democratic Corporatism and Policy Linkages* (Berkeley, CA: Institute of International Studies, University of California at Berkeley, 1987).

54. *Statistical Abstract of the United States, 2001,* Table 414, p. 259.

55. *Comparative Public Policy,* Table 6.5, p. 198.

56. *The American Almanac 1993–1994,* Table 1398, p. 857.

57. *The American Almanac, 1993–1994,* Table 1432, p. 875

58. *The American Almanac, 1993–1994,* Table 1383, p. 849.

59. *The American Almanac, 1993–1994,* Table 1384, p. 850.

60. For the law's details, see *Congressional Quarterly Almanac, 1996* (Washington, DC: Congressional Quarterly, Inc., 1997). pp. 6–13 to 6–24.

61. *Comparative Public Policy,* Table 2.1, p. 30.

62. Quoted in *Comparative Public Policy,* p. 29.

63. Cf. R. Burton Clark, ed., *The School and the University: An International Perspective* (Berkeley, CA: University of California Press, 1985). In 2000, a total of 515,000 foreign students were enrolled in American universities, most of them majoring in science, engineering, and business: *Statistical Abstract of the United States, 2001,* Table 269, p. 168.

64. *The Addresses and Messages of Presidents of the United States,* compiled by Edwin Williams (New York: Edward Walker, Publisher, 1846); vol. I, p. 32.

65. Address to Congress, December 1, 1862, in Roy P. Basler, ed., *The Collected Works of Abraham Lincoln* (New Brunswick, NJ: Rutgers University Press, 1953), vol. V, p. 537.

66. *The American Commonwealth,* Vol. I, pp. 300–301.

Politics in Iran

H.E. Chehabi and Arang Keshavarzian

COUNTRY BIO–IRAN			
Population	66.3 million	**Head of Government**	Mahmud Ahmadinejad
Territory	636 296 sq. mi	**Language**	Persian, regional languages
Year of Independence	550 BC	**Religion**	Twelver Shiite Muslim 90%, Sunni Muslim 10%, non-Muslims less than 1%
Year of Current Constitution	1979, amended in 1989		
Head of State	Ali Khamenei		

The Islamic Republic of Iran is the world's only **theocracy,** a form of government in which ideally all laws are grounded in religion and express the will of God, and a clergy exercises supreme power. While Islamic law has always been applied to varying degrees in Muslim states, it has almost always been complemented by some sort of nonreligious customary law. Moreover, various sultans, shahs, sheikhs, and, since the twentieth century, presidents or prime ministers have traditionally exercised political power in the Muslim world, and genuine theocracies have been very rare. Although the **ulema,** as religious scholars are called in the Muslim world, have at times been critical of rulers who strayed from the path of Islam, they almost never aspired to exercise power directly, which means that far from being a manifestation of Islamic conservatism, Iran's theocratic regime in fact constitutes a revolutionary break with Muslim tradition. The only other Muslim theocracy of the twentieth century was the short-lived regime of the Taliban in Afghanistan (1996–2001), a regime that, unlike that of Iran, never gained control over the entire country and was generally not recognized by the international community.

The Islamic Republic of Iran was established in 1979, a few months after a popular revolution uniting poor and middle-class, religious and secular people overthrew **Mohammad-Reza Shah Pahlavi** (r. 1941–1979), the last ruler of the country's ancient monarchy. The revolution was led by a charismatic clerical leader, **Ruhollah Khomeini,** who had authored a blueprint for theocratic government as early as 1970. In this blueprint, Khomeini made it quite clear that he opposed democracy on doctrinal grounds: sovereignty, he argued, belongs to God alone, and divine law, known as the ***shari'a,*** as interpreted and applied by the ulema, takes precedence over laws made by human legislators. In spite of its inauspicious beginnings as a clerical dictatorship, Iran developed a very lively political system after Khomeini's death in 1989, with presidential, parliamentary, and local elections offering the citizens a choice of candidates advocating differing policies. The appearance of limited democratic practices and institutions under a regime founded on the explicit negation of secular democracy is only one of many apparent paradoxes that can be discerned in Iran: in most other Third World dictatorships political leaders pay lip service to democracy while routinely violating its spirit and undermining its practices.

CURRENT POLICY CHALLENGES

As long as **Islamists,** by which we mean people who consider the religion of Islam a political ideology that addresses all issues of private and public life, are in opposition in a Muslim country, it is very easy for them to blame all shortcomings on the inadequate attention paid to the teachings of Islam by the ruling elites and their "blind following of Western models." Islamists promise a society characterized by social justice and moral propriety in which an "authentic" Muslim culture can flourish uncontaminated by Western "decadence." Iran is the first country in which Islamists have had to deliver on their promises. Therein lies the greatest challenge facing the regime.

During the first decade of the Islamic Republic a certain redistribution of wealth did indeed take place, as much of the property of the old prerevolutionary elite was expropriated. The new men of power came mostly from humble or middle-class backgrounds and adopted populist policies that somewhat bettered the lot of the poorest. For instance, despite the eight-year war with Iraq, the new regime invested heavily in rural development, including in health, women's education, and roads.

However, the postrevolutionary reality is far from ideal, with poverty, inequality, and underemployment continuing to be a major problem and publicly aired grievance. Like the monarchy in the 1960s and 1970s, the Islamic Republic is under pressure to improve the lot of ordinary Iranians and establish the basis for a long-term and sustainable development because it is blessed with the world's second largest oil and gas reserves. However, transforming natural wealth into income and long-term investment has proven difficult. In the ideological climate of the Islamic Republic, industrial entrepreneurs are seen as exploiters, and so private investment tends to go into speculation and rent-seeking rather than long-term industrial investment aimed at enhancing exports and creating sustainable development, resulting in very inadequate job creation.

The need to increase economic output is particularly important at this juncture, for providing employment for a very young labor force is perhaps the greatest challenge facing the government. Iran's population grows by about one million every year (see Figure 14.1), and although the government has been quite successful in bringing down the birth rate since the 1990s, the effects of the lower population growth rate will not make themselves felt for many years. In 2002, 59 percent of the total population was under the age of 25.[1] Even under the best of circumstances

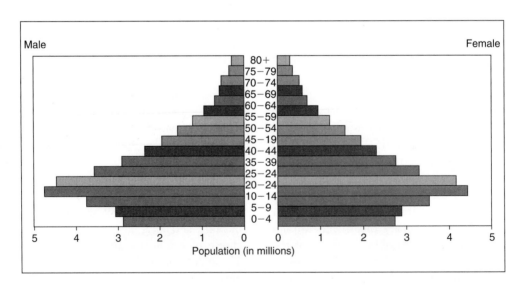

F I G U R E   1 4 . 1   Iran Population Pyramid for 2005

Source: U.S. Census Bureau, International Data Base.

it would be difficult to provide employment for the 800,000 men and women who enter the labor market every year, but Iran's anti-entrepreneurial economic outlook and its unattractiveness to foreign investment mean that the situation is even worse. Regional conflicts and the continuing tension between Iran and the United States make the short-term prospects for both foreign and domestic investment in the economy dire. At the same time, a vastly expanded educational system ensures that many of the young unemployed hold an academic degree, which adds to their frustration and discontent. One result has been massive migration. In recent years 200,000 Iranians have been leaving per year, causing one of the most massive brain-drains in the world: one in four Iranians with a higher education degree lives abroad.[2] The dominant ideology's anti-Western stance notwithstanding, millions of young Iranians dream of moving to the West.

The presence of a large Iranian diaspora in the United States, Canada, and Europe has rendered life in the West familiar for Iranians. Even poorer Iranians often have a relative in Los Angeles ("Tehrangeles") or Toronto ("Tehranto"), and thanks to cheap telephone cards and the Internet they are in daily touch with their relatives and friends abroad. They compare the opportunities Iran offers them not with those their parents had, but with those their cousins enjoy "on the other side," and find them terribly wanting.

Matters are made worse by widespread corruption, which increasingly is reported in the print media and is debated in parliament and by politicians. As many Iranians struggle to make ends meet and cannot find gainful employment, a new economic elite has emerged thanks to personalistic ties to officials who control access to hard currency, import licenses, and tax shelters. The relatives of former president **Ali-Akbar Hashemi Rafsanjani** are often cited as exemplifying this new elite nourished by privileged access and information.

For all these reasons, the promises of the Islamic revolutionaries concerning a more just and more moral society ring hollow with many Iranians, half of whom have no personal memory of the corruption, political repression, and inequality under the Shah. The result is a massive loss of legitimacy of the theocratic model of government. By and large people are still religious, but the ulema no longer command most believers' deference and respect, and Islam itself

is developing in new directions that questions the right of the ulema to rule.

Most recently a new challenge has arisen, namely dissatisfaction with the status quo among some of Iran's ethnic minorities, which live mostly in the country's peripheral areas: Azeris in the northwest, Kurds in the west, Arabs in the southwest, Turkomans in the northeast, and Baluchis in the southeast.[3] All these minorities have ethnic kin on the other side of the border, but until recently this did not matter much as they constituted minorities on the other side as well. With the break-up of the Soviet Union, however, independent Azerbaijan exerts a certain attraction for Azeris in Iran. The consolidation of a semi-independent Kurdish state in post-Saddam Iraq plays a similar role vis-à-vis Iran's (and Turkey's) Kurds, whereas Iran's Arabs, until now loyal to the Iranian state because they are mostly Shiites, may become less certain of their national affiliation if Shiites succeed in gaining the upper hand in neighboring Iraq. For the time being challenges to Iran's territorial integrity are relatively weak compared to neighboring states such as Iraq and Turkey, but they are growing partly because the government is perceived to have favored the economic development of the Persian-speaking core and partly because they are subtly encouraged by outside powers antagonized by Iran's ideologically driven foreign policy.

Like all Third World countries, Iran faces general challenges of community and development. Iran's leaders are confronted with the daunting tasks of integrating large groups of disaffected citizens (the young, the unemployed, and ethnic minorities) and fomenting enough economic development to improve living conditions for the poor and unemployed. The Islamic regime's failure so far to address these issues adequately has dented its legitimacy considerably.

HISTORICAL LEGACY

Iran, like China and Japan, is one of a handful of non-Western states that were never formally colonized by Europeans. Iran's borders were not drawn artificially by colonial powers and result from the balance of power between its shahs and their neighboring rulers. The Iranian state tradition is over twenty-five centuries old, but the current Iranian state was set up in the early sixteenth century by the Safavid dynasty, whose most lasting impact on Iranian society was the establishment of **Twelver Shiism** as the official religion of the state and the conversion of most Iranians, the vast majority of whom had been Sunnis, to that faith. Historically, the shrine cities of Iraq had been the cradle of this branch of Islam, but with the establishment of a powerful Shiite state in Iran, Iran became the political center of the Shiite world.

Twelver Shiism

The split between Sunnis, who constitute about 90 percent of all Muslims, and the Shiites came about after the death of the founder of Islam, the Prophet Muhammad. Muhammad was not only the founder of a new religion but also a political leader, and therefore the nascent Muslim community had to find a leader to succeed him in that capacity after he died in 628 C.E. A minority of believers, who later came to be known as Shiites, deemed the descendants of the Prophet to be his only rightful successors. Shiites call these hereditary successors to the Prophet *Imam*s, and of particular importance is the third Imam, Husayn, whose martyrdom in 680 C.E. symbolizes for Shiites the struggle of the just against the unjust and is still commemorated yearly in emotionally powerful processions that acquire a political dimension in times of political crisis.

While some small Shiite sects believe in an unbroken line of Imams all the way to the present, the vast majority believe that the twelfth was the last of the Imams, hence their name. According to these Shiites, the twelfth in the line of Imams disappeared from view as a child in 874 C.E., but did not die: in fact he is alive (rather like Elijah in the Jewish tradition) and will come forth and show himself to establish just rule at the end of times, when injustice and corruption will rule supreme. In other words, he is a messiah-like figure. From the moment the Twelfth Imam disappeared from public view, therefore, Twelver Shiite political thought faced a dilemma: the only figure who could exercise legitimate rule over the community of believers was not physically present, and no one knew when he would reveal himself. Most of the time this dilemma did not matter in practice, however, because Shiites were a minority lacking political power, making their political theology inconsequential in actual fact.

With the establishment of a Twelver Shiite state in sixteenth century Iran by the Safavid dynasty, the unavailability of the one truly legitimate ruler became an existential problem: in the absence of the Twelfth Imam, who had the right to rule in practice? Most ulema were willing to accord this right to the secular rulers, the shahs, so long as these ruled justly and in accordance with Islam. But by the end of the seventeenth century a minority of ulema argued that for the rule of a shah to be legitimate, he had to have the ulema's explicit endorsement. After the fall of the Safavids in 1722 Iran was in the grip of civil wars as various short-lived dynasties succeeded each other until the Qajar dynasty emerged victorious in 1796. During this troubled century the ulema established themselves as an institution independent of the state. The state being in disarray much of the time, believers' tithes were increasingly paid to the ulema directly, assuring them of financial independence. Moreover, the center of Twelver Shiism, the city of Najaf, lay in Ottoman Iraq, outside the control of Iran's worldly authorities. Beginning in the nineteenth century, therefore, the ulema had greater social, political, and religious prominence in Iran than in the Sunni world, as they were less dependent on the state and had their own sources of income. Their role and function in many ways came to resemble that of a clergy in Christian countries. Without this legacy the establishment of a theocracy would not even have been conceivable in the 1970s.

While the Shiite ulema form a loose hierarchy, they are not organized in a pyramidal structure like the Roman Catholic church. There is no equivalent of the pope, and no one leader can define dogma in a way that is binding for everyone else. Consequently the ulema have often disagreed among each other on political and even minor religious matters, a state of affairs that, as we will see, did not end with the creation of an Islamic state.

Constitutionalism in Iran

Iran's geographic location between the Russian empire in the north and the British empire in the south allowed it to survive the heyday of European imperialism as an independent state, as both empires tacitly agreed to keep it as a neutral buffer between their respective domains. But educated Iranians were aware of the fragility of their country's sovereignty, and as more and more of them gained personal knowledge of Europe in the nineteenth century, they became aware of their country's backwardness compared to Europe. As long as Iran was less developed than Europe, it would forever remain vulnerable to imperialist encroachments, and so "catching up with the West" became the major goal of its intellectual and political elite. The secret of Europe's superiority they saw in the fact that European states upheld the rule of law, whereas in Iran arbitrary rule prevailed. To strengthen the nation, they concluded, constitutional government had to be introduced. Japan's victory over Russia in the war of 1905 confirmed Iranian constitutionalists in their view. For the first time an Asian power had vanquished a European one, and Iranians argued that this reversal of fortunes was due to the fact that Japan was the only constitutional power in Asia, whereas Russia was the only autocracy among the major European powers.

In 1905 widespread dissatisfaction with the way the country was governed led to a popular movement that eventually succeeded in wresting a constitution from the shah in December 1906. Shiite ulema played a major role in the constitutionalist movement. Until a few years earlier the Iranian state had been characterized by an implicit contract between worldly and spiritual authorities: the shahs upheld the official religion, and the ulema legitimated their rule. But by the early twentieth century many politically active ulema supported the notions advocated by merchants and Western-educated intellectuals that the powers of the monarchy needed to be curtailed, that the citizenry had the right to elect a parliament to represent it, that the shah could name a prime minister only with the agreement of parliament, and that parliament could hold the government accountable. These very European institutional arrangements and ideas were criticized by conservative ulema for being alien to Islam, but in response constitutionalist ulema found ways to justify them in Islamic terms. Most famously, Ayatollah Muhammad-Husayn Na'ini argued that a despotic shah violated the rights of the Twelfth Imam and those of the people, whereas rule by the people violated only the rights of the Twelfth Imam, concluding that, while neither form of government was ideal, the latter was the lesser evil and thus preferable to the former.[4] Implied in this argument was the novel idea that as long as the Twelfth Imam chose to

remain in hiding, the believers themselves were his deputies. This elegant formulation reconciled Shiism's core beliefs with modern notions of constitutionalism and is a legacy that the revolutionaries of 1979 could not ignore as they set out to create an Islamic state.

The Pahlavi Monarchy

The constitution of 1906 did not bring the country the hoped-for progress. In 1907 Britain and Russia in a secret agreement divided Iran into two spheres of influence, and during World War I the belligerent powers repeatedly violated its neutrality and fought each other on Iranian territory, causing much hardship to the population. By the end of the war, local warlords were challenging the authority of the central government in peripheral regions. In 1921 a coup d'etat put an end to the rule of the old establishment. The commander of the troops, Reza Khan, lost no time in extending government control over rebellious provinces and began an ambitious modernization program to develop and centralize state authority. By 1925 he ousted the ruling Qajar dynasty and had parliament proclaim him new ruler as Reza Shah Pahlavi. From his coronation in 1926 until his ouster by the British in the wake of the Allies' occupation of Iran in 1941, he ruled as dictator, although he left the constitution formally in place. The new ruler initially enjoyed the support of most of the ulema, but in the 1930s relations between the government and the clergy deteriorated when he implemented a number of reforms that sharply reduced the social functions of the ulema or aimed at westernizing the daily culture of Iranians, such as prohibiting women's veiling. With his departure into exile politics opened up again, as his 21-year old son and successor, Mohammad-Reza Shah Pahlavi, did not have the authority yet to continue his father's ways. (See table on page 498.)

Between 1941 and 1953 Iran's political system more than ever approximated the ideals of the constitutional revolution. Three main political camps could be distinguished: the pro-Western conservative establishment, including the Shah and the landlords, which was supported tacitly by most of the ulema; the pro-Soviet communist **Tudeh party**; and the neutralist nationalists of the National Front who aimed at establishing the full rule of law within the country and consolidating its sovereignty on the international scene, which was compromised, as they saw it, by British control over Iran's oil resources and industry through the British-owned Anglo-Iranian Oil Company. The Iranian government had no say in the company, not even the right to see its books. The total net profits of the AIOC from 1945 to 1950 after deducting high British taxes, royalties, and exaggerated depreciation figures were £ 250 million, while royalties paid to Iran for its oil were £ 90 million.[5]

The leader of the National Front was **Mohammad Mossadegh,** who led the struggle for the nationalization of Iranian oil. This was accomplished in March 1951, and soon afterward Mossadegh was elected prime minister by parliament. Subsequent negotiations between the Iranian and British governments to resolve the oil dispute failed, and so the British began plotting Mossadegh's overthrow, which was accomplished with the help of the CIA in August 1953.[6] Iran's political system reverted to royal autocracy as the second ruler of the Pahlavi dynasty increasingly asserted himself, taking full command of the country in January 1963 when he launched a reform program that became known as the "White Revolution" and that included land reform and the granting of the suffrage to women. In the 1950s the Shah had enjoyed the support of the clerical hierarchy, but by the early 1960s his dictatorial methods and westernizing policies elicited the anger of religious traditionalists who rioted in June 1963 in support of a new oppositional member of the ulema, Ruhollah Khomeini. The riots were suppressed with bloodshed and Khomeini was arrested and exiled, finally settling in the Shiite shrine city of Najaf in Iraq, where he remained until October 1978, when he was expelled by Saddam Hussein and sought refuge in Paris, triumphantly returning to Iran on 1 February 1979.

Until 1963 opposition to royal autocracy had been carried out in the name of the constitution of 1906, which the two Pahlavi shahs were, rightly, accused of not respecting; free elections were the opposition's main demand. After 1963, however, opponents of the Shah, increasingly driven underground or abroad, despaired of ever attaining constitutional rule by peaceful means and became radicalized. Gradually the constitution itself suffered a loss of legitimacy, and opponents of the Shah began demanding the abolition of the monarchy and its replacement by a new regime. Given the Shah's suppression of civil society and of the secular opposition,

mosques and religious circles became the only places where one could speak one's mind, and so religion became more prominent in society again and a powerful political force, the state's secularist policies notwithstanding. By the 1970s Shiite activists, many of them students or followers of Khomeini, were arguing about the shape of the ideal Islamic state.

While the Shah's regime was increasingly contested at home, it continued to receive strong support from the West generally, and from the United States in particular. Since the Shah's autocratic rule had been made possible only through the direct intervention of the CIA, his opponents thought of him as an American puppet whose policies were designed to benefit the United States rather than Iran. Opposition to the Shah thus logically entailed opposition to the United States and Israel, with which the Shah had contracted a strategic alliance directed against radical Arab states such as Egypt, Iraq, and Syria. In recent years, evidence has appeared that at the height of his power in the early 1970s the Shah, far from being manipulated by the United States, in fact was quite successful in manipulating policymakers in Washington D.C. to achieve his ends.[7]

Ultimately Iran's first revolution failed to produce a constitutional state based on the rule of law, but during the seven decades of its life Iran acquired the trappings of a modern nation-state: the government acquired a monopoly of the use of legitimate force, unified legal codes were introduced, a functioning civil service was set up, including a territorial administration that extended the writ of the state into distant provinces, and externally the sanctity of the country's borders was secured. On the basis of these accomplishments, it was possible to give the new theocracy the form of an Islamic *republic* in the aftermath of the revolution of 1978–1979.

The Islamic Revolution

In 1977 Jimmy Carter became president of the United States and U.S. foreign policy began emphasizing respect for human rights by American allies.[8] Unbeknownst to the public, the Shah had terminal cancer, and to ensure a smooth transition to his heir at a time when U.S. support could no longer be taken for granted, he began liberalizing Iran's political system in 1977. Amir-Abbas Hoveyda, who had been prime minister since 1965 and embodied the cabinet's subservience to the Shah, was replaced with a techno-crat, former finance minister Jamshid Amuzegar. But this liberalization soon got out of control as various dissident and social groups with grievances took advantage of it to push for greater reforms. From late 1977 to early 1979 the calls for liberalization snowballed into a call for the abolition of the monarchy by a largely urban coalition consisting of intellectuals, university and high school students and teachers, bazaar merchants, politically active clerics and seminarians, industrial workers, and, in the final stage, state employees and white-collar workers.[9] The popular movement against the regime's despotism, corruption, and alliances with the United States and Israel united such diverse ideological factions as liberal adherents of the 1906 constitution, Marxist-Leninist leftists, and Islamists. The latter comprised democrats whose reading of Islam is decidedly liberal and non-coercive, leftists who stress the egalitarian aspects of Islam, and direct followers of Khomeini who championed an Islamic state supervised by clerics (see below). These men and women organized massive meetings, demonstrations and strikes, and distributed anti-regime pamphlets in a largely peaceful manner.[10] In his reaction, the Shah vacillated between repressing the movement militarily and making belated concessions to it, with the result that it became ever more radicalized during 1978, finally driving him and his family into exile in January 1979.[11]

In the course of the revolutionary uprising and immediately after the departure of the imperial family, it became evident that Khomeini's followers were the best organized and most united force, and so they were relatively quickly able to sideline the nonclerical currents in the revolutionary coalition. The organizational power of Khomeini and his followers was enhanced by their access to independent sources of revenue, as traditionally, observant Shiites pay their tithes directly to the ulema. In 1970 Khomeini had revived the strain in Twelver Shiite thought that called for clerical oversight of government and carried it to its logical conclusion. In a treatise titled "Islamic Government" he argued that God had not revealed his laws to humankind so that they would be ignored until the moment the Twelfth Imam chose to reveal himself, an event which may lie in the distant future, but in order that they be applied in the here and now. He then observed that the people most suited to rule in accordance with divine law are those who know it best, namely the ulema themselves. This principle came to be known as ***velayat-e faqih*** (pronounced roughly vella YATTay faKEEH), which can best be translated as "guardianship of the jurisprudent"[12] (see Box 14.1).

Given Khomeini's charismatic leadership of the revolution, his followers succeeded in late 1979 to enshrine this principle in the new Iranian constitution. However, in deference to the preexisting constitutional tradition and to placate the many non-Islamists and moderate Islamists who had participated in the revolution, a parliament elected by universal suffrage was maintained, while the shah was replaced with an elected president. The Islamic Republic was thus born with a mixed political system that is informed by both a version of Twelver Shiite political doctrine and Western notions of popular sovereignty and division of powers.[13]

BOX 14.1   Velayat-e Faqih

Velayat-e faqih: the lynchpin of Iran's theocratic constitution, it can best be translated as "guardianship of the jurisprudent." It was enunciated in its modern form in 1970 by Ayatollah Ruhollah Khomeini while he was in exile in Iraq. Khomeini argued that God having revealed the laws according to which Muslims should live and organize their community, Muslims should in fact apply these laws in practice rather than just debate them theoretically. The most qualified people to supervise the application of these laws in the state, he wrote, are those who know them best (i.e., the clerics who specialize in jurisprudence).

He concluded that such a cleric must therefore be the head of state. In 1979 this principle was enshrined in the constitution of the Islamic Republic of Iran, and Khomeini himself became the ruling jurisprudent, referred to henceforth as "Leader." For the first time in Iranian history, religious and worldly authorities were fused. *Velayat-e faqih* is not strongly grounded in scripture, and most other Twelver Shiite clerics disagree with the principle. They see the task of the Shiite clergy as being that of guiding the believers and advising rulers, as can be seen in post-Saddam Iraq.

From 1979 to June 1981 secular moderates, leftists, moderate Islamists, and radical Islamists inspired directly by Khomeini competed for power. As time went on, the confrontation between adherents of *velayat-e faqih* and their opponents became ever more implacable and violent. In fact, far more people were killed in confrontations among the revolutionaries than had died as a result of the Shah's half-hearted efforts to suppress the revolutionary mass movement. By the summer of 1981 the supporters of Khomeini gained the upper hand and began instituting Islamic law in all spheres of public life. Their suppression of all who opposed them was facilitated by the war that was now raging with neighboring Iraq.

Iran–Iraq War

Soon after the revolution, Khomeini, who had been expelled from Iraq by Saddam Hussein in October 1978, began calling for his overthrow. This provoked Saddam Hussein to attack Iran in September 1980. The war that ensued lasted until 1988 and ended in a stalemate.

Officially termed the "imposed war" or the "sacred defense" in Iran, the war was a major watershed. Over two million Iranians were mobilized, with over one million killed and injured, many due to Iraq's use of chemical weapons.[14] The war enabled the revolutionary regime to consolidate its hold on power by calling for national unity in the face of a foreign invasion; it became a means to suppress dissent and public debate. At the level of society, the conflict created a "war generation" of young men who were shaped as much by their experiences at the front as by the revolution. Now that many of these soldiers and officers are in their forties and fifties, those who have been politically inclined are demanding a bigger say in national and local politics. The tendency of these veterans has been to call for more "social order" and a greater state role in providing for the lower classes, disproportionately large numbers of whose members volunteered and perished in the war.

The Legacy of Oil Wealth: A Rentier State

The Iranian state, like other states that are endowed with large amounts of natural resources such as oil or diamonds, has particular characteristics that have shaped its relations with society. The export of petroleum products has made the Iranian state dependent on the world economy for the bulk of its budget. This revenue is rent, which is a windfall accruing directly to the treasury.

Since the 1960s, Iran's budget has not depended on domestic revenues (taxes or borrowing), which has made the state largely autonomous from society.[15] Unlike most states that must bargain with social groups to generate revenue for public projects, to pay public employees, and to fight wars, **rentier states** like Iran can sustain themselves independently of social pressures and powerful interest groups such as landlords, capitalists, or workers. At the same time, the state is particularly susceptible to fluctuations in the world oil market, making long-term planning more difficult. The massive revenue from petroleum exports has often been cited as a major reason for the Iranian state's unresponsiveness to social demands, and even its authoritarianism.[16] Thus, what was initially thought of as a blessing is now often seen as a curse (see section on interest aggregation for further discussion).

INSTITUTIONS OF THE ISLAMIC REPUBLIC

In the political system of the Islamic Republic of Iran two types of institutions coexist, namely appointed and elected offices, reflecting the attempted synthesis between divine and popular sovereignty enshrined in the constitution adopted in 1979 and amended in 1989. The institutional structure of Iran is further complicated by the existence of what has become known as **multiple power centers,** institutions created by the revolutionaries to supplement the activities of the traditional state institutions, with which they share overlapping responsibilities.

Leader

The highest authority in the Islamic Republic is the **Leader,** who combines religious and temporal authority in accordance with the theocratic principle of *velayat-e faqih*, as explained above. The position was tailor-made for Khomeini himself, who was both a high-level member of the ulema and a charismatic political leader. For his succession, the constitution provided for a popularly elected **Assembly of**

Experts consisting of ulema that would chose the Leader from among the most learned ulema. By 1989, however, none of those ulema who had the requisite learning shared his notions of theocratic rule, and so, in April 1989 Khomeini appointed an assembly to revise the constitution so as to relax the religious requirements of the office. Khomeini died on 3 June 1989 and the Assembly of Experts chose **Ali Khamenei,** who had been president for eight years but was a low-level cleric, to be the new Leader. Khamenei's religious authority was from the outset contested by much of the clerical hierarchy, reopening the split between state and "church" that the Islamic Republic had supposedly closed with its fusion of worldly and spiritual authorities.

The Leader sets the overall policies of the state and appoints some of its key figures, such as the head of the Judiciary, half the members of the **Council of Guardians,** the members of the **Expediency Council,** the director of the state radio and television broadcasting monopoly, and the commanders of the various military forces, such as the Islamic Revolutionary Guard Corps. He also oversees the numerous parastatal economic foundations and organizations that were formed after the revolution out of the expropriated companies belonging to the previous economic elite. These organizations are ostensibly oriented toward charity and bear names like Foundation of the Disinherited and War Injured and the Martyr's Foundation, but have in fact become major holding companies that benefit from state resources and subsidies without being accountable to and regulated by the elected government, and Khamenei has used these "nonprofit" organizations as a means to distribute patronage[17] (see Box 14.2).

In theory, the Assembly of Experts, which is elected every ten years by universal suffrage, is more powerful than the Leader; it elects him and can dismiss him if he can no longer assume the responsibilities of his office or proves unworthy of it. However, candidacies to the Assembly of Experts are subject to the approval of the Council of Guardians, whose members are chosen by the Leader, who thus maintains his supremacy in practice.

President

The president is elected by universal suffrage every four years. He has to be a Twelver Shiite and a man, although a number of women have tried, always

---

BOX 14.2 The Martyr's Foundation

Among the most powerful **parastatal foundations** is the Martyr's Foundation (*Bonyad-e Shahid*) established in 1979. Its original mandate was to provide for the needs of families of those who were martyred and the disabled in the Islamic Revolution and the Iran–Iraq war. It is estimated that the foundation provides support to 188,000 people by providing aid and priority admission for education, in-kind transfers, housing services to relatives of martyrs and disabled veterans, and other benefits. These services are funded by assets formerly belonging to supporters of the Shah that were expropriated, allocations from the state budget and the office of the Leader, and profits from the operation of various firms run by the foundation. In the mid-1980s it was reported that the Martyr's Foundation owned $3.3 billion in capital reserves including 68 industrial factories, 75 commercial firms, 21 construction companies, and many farms and pieces of urban property. To administer this large and diverse economic conglomerate, the Martyr's Foundation employs 30,000 people and has a whole host of subdivisions, such as the International Relations Office and the Marriage Bureau for Widows of Wartime Martyrs. The foundation also puts out a magazine that helps spread the early revolutionary ideology. In 1993, the foundation established the Shahid Investment Company in order to pool the savings of surviving relatives of the martyrs and invest them. By 2000 shareholders were complaining that the investment company never disclosed its accounts to the shareholders. Finally, Mehdi Karrubi was the president of the foundation from 1980 to 1992. Karrubi, who in the 1980s was identified as part of the radical foundation and in the 1990s was allied with the reformists, was speaker of the sixth parliament (2000–2004). He ran for president in 2005 on a pro-welfare and distribution platform and only narrowly came in third behind Hashemi-Rafsanjani and Ahmadinejad in the first round.

Sources: Ali A. Saeidi, "The Accountability of Para-governmental Organizations (*bonyad*s): The Case of Iranian Foundation," *Iranian Studies* 37, 3(September 2004), p. 488; Wilfred Buchta, *Who Rules Iran?*, p. 75.

unsuccessfully, to become presidential candidates. Until 1989 the office was largely ceremonial and the executive branch of government was headed by a prime minister chosen by parliament, but in the course of the constitutional revision mentioned earlier the office of prime minister was abolished and the presidency became an executive one. The president heads the executive except in matters reserved for the Leader, signs bills into law once they have been approved by the legislature, and appoints the members of the cabinet and provincial governors, subject to parliamentary approval. He can be impeached by parliament, at which point the Leader can dismiss him. The president does not have to be a cleric, but between 1981 and 2005 three members of the ulema each held the office for two consecutive terms, reflecting the hegemony of that group in the Islamic Republic. The June 2005 election of Mahmud Ahmadinejad, a lay (i.e., non-ulema) Islamist and a veteran of the Iran–Iraq war, may herald the partial replacement of the clergy by the "war generation," men who risked their lives in the revolution and the war and feel that it is time that they reap the benefits of their sacrifices.

Parliament

Iran's unicameral parliament, the **Majles,** comprises about 290 members elected by universal suffrage for four-year terms. Members have to be Muslims, but, like its predecessor, the constitution provides for five MPs to represent Christians (3), Jews (1), and Zoroastrians (1).

The Majles has law-making powers, but its legislative output must not contravene the constitution or Islam, as determined by the Council of Guardians (see below). It has the right to investigate affairs of state, to approve or reject the president' cabinet appointments, and to interpellate ministers and subject them to votes of no-confidence.

In his treatise on Islamic government, Khomeini assigned little importance to parliament, arguing that since Islam had already laid down laws for most matters, a legislative assembly's task was to draw up rules and regulations for minor issues not dealt with in Islamic jurisprudence. Since 1979, however, the Majles has shown remarkable dynamism and initiative. For one, as the leaders of the state themselves readily admitted, the traditional corpus of Islamic

law proved to be woefully inadequate for the purpose of governing a modern state, allowing parliament to fill some of the gaps. Furthermore, deputies have vigorously debated state business and held government officials accountable, the office of the Leader excepted.

In the first parliament of the Islamic Republic almost half of all deputies were clerics. Under the Shah no free elections had taken place, so few people had enough name recognition at the local level to get themselves elected to parliament, the result being that in many places voters chose the local cleric. But over time, the percentage of clerics in the Majles has declined, as can be seen in Table 14.1. Although the ulema had by and large opposed female suffrage in 1963, the founders of the Islamic republic maintained women's active and passive suffrage in spite of their patriarchal disposition, and since 1980 every legislature has included female deputies, who have often spoken out on women's rights. Table 14.1 shows the evolution of the number of women who have held seats in the parliament of the Islamic Republic.

The fact remains that the Majles's legislative role is seriously limited by two features of the political system. First, many policies, rules, and regulations are set by unelected specialized bodies, and, second, all its bills are subject to the veto of the Council of Guardians. Under the Islamic Republic the Majles has been above all a forum where policies are discussed and proposals aired, and where some state officials are taken to account.[18]

Council of Guardians

The constitution of 1906 provided for a committee of five Majles deputies who were members of the ulema to examine legislation for its compatibility

T A B L E   1 4 . 1   Women in Parliament

	Female MPs	Clerical MPs	Total MPs
First Majles (1980–84)	4	131	263
Second Majles (1984–88)	4	122	269
Third Majles (1988–92)	4	77	267
Fourth Majles (1992–96)	9	65	270
Fifth Majles (1996–2000)	10	53	274
Sixth Majles (2000–04)	13	35	278
Seventh Majles (2004–)	12	42	281

with Islam. This committee was never constituted, however, and in order to forestall any possibility for compromising the Islamic character of the state, the 1979 constitution instituted an altogether separate body for ensuring the conformity of legislation with Islam: the Council of Guardians.

The body consists of six members of the ulema and six lay but Muslim lawyers. The ulema are appointed by the Leader, the lawyers are nominated by the head of the Judiciary (who is himself appointed by the Leader) but must be approved by parliament. The compatibility of laws with Islam is determined by the six ulema members only; their compatibility with the constitution by the entire council. Through the years the Council of Guardians has rejected numerous bills because it interpreted them in violation of the constitution and/or Islamic law.

The Council of Guardians also "supervises" the elections to the Assembly of Experts, the presidency, and parliament. It has interpreted this provision of the constitution to signify that it can vet candidacies, and used this self-ascribed power to limit citizens' choice at elections by not allowing candidates of whose views it disapproves to run. When in 1991 the Majles passed a law stripping the council of these powers, the latter, unsurprisingly, declared the law to be contrary to the constitution.

Expediency Council

Disagreement between parliament and the Council of Guardians has been endemic in the Islamic Republic, resulting in legislative gridlock. As long as Khomeini was alive, he acted as the ultimate arbiter when a protracted stalemate arose, as all involved deferred to him. In early 1988 Khomeini set up a new collective body to arbitrate in such cases, and it was aptly called "Council for the determination of what is in the interest of the regime," an unwitting admission that conformity to the teachings of Islam now took a back seat to political expedience. Indeed, official Iranian documents render the name of this body in English as "Expediency Council." Its existence was anchored in the constitution when the latter was amended in 1989.

The over thirty members of this body are appointed directly by the Leader and chosen mainly from among top state and government officials such as the heads of the three branches of government,

key cabinet members and military leaders, the ulema members of the Council of Guardians, and ulema chosen for their personal prestige. In addition to arbitrating conflicts between the Majles and the Council of Guardians, the Expediency Council also has the constitutional mandate of advising the Leader in formulating overall state policy.

An Honestly Undemocratic Constitution

As the above discussion shows, the authority of the elective offices of the Islamic Republic, essentially the presidency and parliament, is systematically circumscribed by unelected bodies. To be sure, the Leader is in theory chosen by an elected body, the Assembly of Experts, but there is no limit on his term, making him for all intents and purposes an unremovable leader with vast powers. By appointing the head of the Judiciary and the commanders of the police, army, and **Islamic Revolutionary Guard Corps (*Pasdaran*),** he, rather than the president and the parliament, controls the coercive apparatus of the state.

The limited authority of president and parliament became startlingly blatant when reformists bent on liberalizing Iranian politics and society won a string of elections in the late 1990s, gaining control of the presidency in 1997 and 2001 with the (re)election of **Mohammad Khatami,** and of parliament in 2000. Unlike his predecessor, Leader Ali Khamenei did not remain above the fray and openly sided with the anti-reformist conservatives, from among whom he chose the head of the Judiciary and the members of the Council of Guardians. For example, when the lawyers proposed by the Judiciary to fill vacant seats on the Council of Guardians failed to gain the endorsement of parliament in 2001, the Leader simply refused to schedule the swearing-in ceremony of the reformist president, who had just been reelected with 77.9 percent of the popular vote. In the end, the lawyers took their seats without gaining majority support in parliament, after which the Leader consented to swear in the just-reelected president.

The reformists tried to bring about change by legal and constitutional means only, and the fact that they were ultimately stymied by the leader, the Council of Guardians, and the Judiciary, all using mostly the powers granted to them by the constitution, shows that this constitution is, if not liberal and democratic, at least honest: its provisions need not be violated to prevent democratic governance, as is the case in so many Third World nations where constitutional theory and practice diverge dramatically.

The same can be said for citizens' rights. Although freedom of speech and association and the safety of the person are guaranteed, these are usually qualified by the clause "within the criteria of Islam," leaving the authorities considerable leeway to abridge them. The same is true for the equality of citizens: although Christian, Jewish, and Zoroastrian Iranians are accorded some legal recognition and can practice their religion freely, Iran's largest non-Muslim minority, the adherents of the Baha'i faith, are considered heretics and systematically discriminated against; to this day they may not attend university, for instance. Even Sunni Muslims, representing about 10 percent of the total population, are systematically discriminated against in the civil service and are not allowed to maintain a mosque of their own in Tehran. In the words of a prominent exiled Iranian human rights lawyer, in the Islamic Republic "the rights of the clerics do not equal those of non-clerics, the rights of Twelver Shiites do not equal those of non-Twelver Shiites, the rights of Shiites do not equal those of Sunnis, the rights of Muslims do not equal those of non-Muslims, the rights of 'recognized religious minorities' do not equal those of other 'minorities,' and the rights of men do not equal the rights of women."[19] The explicit denial of legal equality to citizens found throughout Iran's constitution and legal system stands in sharp contrast to the universalist language of many other Third World regimes.

Multiple Power Centers

When the revolutionaries took over the state in 1979, they inherited an administrative personnel whose commitment to the new ideology they did not trust. Not content with purging state institutions of individuals they deemed counterrevolutionary, they built new ones whose competency overlapped with the old established ones. The idea was that the old institutions would more or less carry on with business as usual, while the new institutions would actively pursue the realization and defense of the new Islamic order (see Figure 14.2). Examples include the Construction Jihad which sent young people to the rural areas to help develop them parallel to the ministry of agriculture, the office of the

revolutionary prosecutor (paralleling the ministry of justice), the *komiteh*s (paralleling the police), and, most importantly, the Islamic Revolutionary Guard Corps, known in Persian as *Pasdaran*, whose original function was to safeguard the revolution but which in time developed into a parallel army and even acquired an air force and a navy. It was these revolutionary institutions that prevented the provisional government, which had taken over the Shah's administrative apparatus, from gaining control of the country.[20]

As hardliners consolidated their rule in the mid-1980s, attempts were made to merge state and revolutionary organizations, but these attempts were mostly unsuccessful and the revolutionary organizations are still active. In the late 1990s, as some state institutions came under the control of the reformists, conservatives created new parallel institutions under the aegis of the office of the Leader. Thus, when the ministry of information, as the secret police is called, came to be staffed mainly by reformists, the Judiciary, whose head is named by the Leader, proceeded to set up a parallel secret police which even maintains a prison system for political prisoners. These multiple power centers complicate policymaking considerably, as we shall see.

With these caveats about the relative importance of Iran's republican institutions in mind, let us now turn to elections and parties.

ELECTIONS AND PARTIES

The Prerevolutionary Legacy

With the brief exception of the 1940s, between 1906 and 1979 competitive elections were rarely held in Iran. In 1963 the Shah gave women the active and passive suffrage, and although this did not mean much in practice because there were no free elections for the remainder of his reign, it established standards that could not be undone. Although much of the ulema had vehemently opposed the extension of the suffrage to women in 1963, the mobilization of women in the course of the revolution was so important that it was simply not possible to deprive them of the right to vote again. In fact, the electorate was enlarged by fixing the minimum voting age at 15.

Under the monarchy political parties were mostly weak and ephemeral. After World War II,

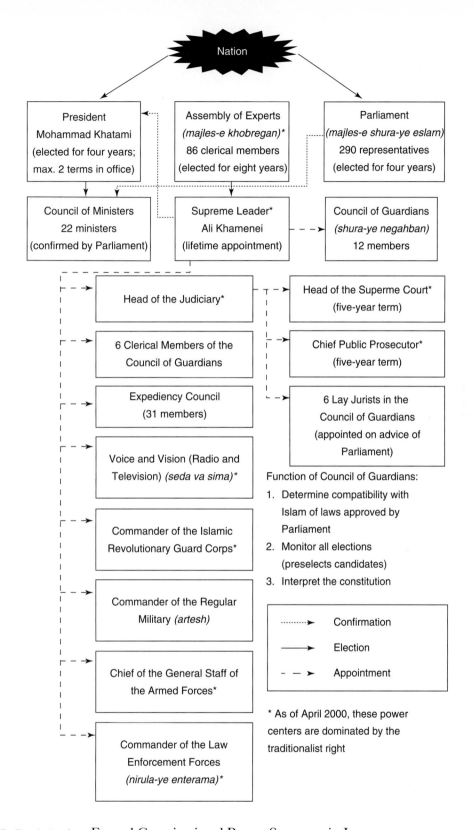

FIGURE 14.2 Formal Constitutional Power Structure in Iran

Source: Adapted from Wilfried Buchta, *Who Rules Iran?* (Washington, DC: Washington Institute for Near East Policy, 2000). © Wilfried Buchta, Rabat 2000.

two groupings succeeded in establishing a lasting societal presence: the Communist Tudeh party and the Nationalist National Front of Mohammad Mossadegh. Although the two were revived in the course of the revolution of 1978, they were overshadowed by more radical leftist or Islamist groups that had emerged from the armed struggle against the Shah, such as the Marxist-Leninist Fada'iyan-e Khalq and the leftist Islamist Mojahedin-e Khalq. Initially, the Liberation Movement of Iran (LMI), a moderate Islamist offshoot of the National Front founded in 1961, fared somewhat better. Its leaders largely staffed the provisional government of prime minister Mehdi Bazargan that administered the country from February to November 1979, when they resigned in protest over radical students' seizure of American diplomats as hostages. In 1981 the National Front, the Fada'iyan-e Khalq, and the Mojahedin-e Khalq were banned for advocating policies that contradicted the basic premise of the Islamic Republic, and in 1983 the Tudeh party was disbanded and its leaders jailed for having spied for the Soviet Union. The LMI, for its part, has managed to maintain a low-level activity within the country.

Postrevolutionary Parties

In early 1979 a group of loyal followers of Khomeini, including later president Rafsanjani and Leader Khamenei, founded a new party to work toward the realization of their version of an Islamic state: the Islamic Republican Party (IRP). Soon, however, different factions crystallized within the IRP around different economic, social, and foreign policy agendas. Factionalism having rendered the party dysfunctional, Rafsanjani and Khamenei wrote a letter to Khomeini in June 1987 in which they announced the dissolution of the IRP, justifying the move by saying that the party had achieved its goal, the establishment of *velayat-e faqih*, and had thus ceased to have a *raison d'etre*.

But the underlying reasons for the factionalism did not go away. Some regime figures advocated more state intervention in the economy on the grounds that Islam is the religion of social justice and that therefore an Islamic government has to look after the interests of the poor, whereas others argued that Islam protects the sanctity of private property, as a result of which more *laissez-faire* policies were in order

as long as everybody adhered to the many rules that Islamic jurisprudence has established for the conduct of economic activity. As the leaders of the Islamic Republic grappled with the problem of translating into practice the premise that Islam is a political ideology that provides guidance for the solution of all problems, it became clear that multiple policy options could be derived from Islamic principles. In 1987 the Speaker of Parliament Rafsanjani admitted that there were "two powerful wings" within the Islamic Republic, adding that "basically they represent two unorganized parties. Indeed when they describe the positions they hold, they are two parties, not two wings."[21] The tensions came out into the open in 1988 when the Society of Militant Clergy, a pro-*velayat-e faqih* group, split in two as some less conservative members, including future president Mohammad Khatami, left to form the Association of Militant Clerics.

As long as Khomeini was alive, he acted as the ultimate arbiter between the factions, as all deferred to him. When government figures turned to him to break a factional deadlock over a policy, he would normally urge all to cooperate, but when pressed more often than not came out against the conservatives. After Khomeini's death in 1989, the fact that the leadership of the Islamic Republic included no high-ranking ulema combined with the traditional pluralism of opinions among the ulema (a pluralism that was augmented by personal rivalries) to let many policy disagreements go largely unresolved. These disagreements were channeled into the political system and became the basis of electoral competition, as different candidates espoused opposing views on the basis of which they sought people's votes. This has given Iranian elections a poignancy they lack in other nondemocratic states.

These ideological differences were the basis of factional politics among three broad clusters in the political elite: conservatives, pragmatists, and radicals. The conservatives were clerics and lay politicians who argued in favor of stricter social rules (such as gender segregation in public places), simultaneously (and confusingly) supported market-oriented economic policies *and* the economic foundations mentioned above, and called for greater authority being given to the Leader at the expense of elected bodies. Pragmatists, including Rafsanjani and many technocrats who staffed the ministries in the 1990s, were more accommodating when it came to social issues and supported economic liberalization and the privatization of state-owned and parastatal companies. Moreover, they have toned down support for exporting the revolution and are somewhat more conciliatory regarding U.S.–Iranian relations. Finally, the radicals were the younger Islamist revolutionaries and clerics who were influenced by leftist and anti-imperialist politics. In the 1980s and the early 1990s they called for increased state control of the economy to ensure greater social justice and were active in supporting Islamist struggles in the Middle East. Beginning in the mid-1990s, these radicals modified their positions and became more liberal (more on this below).[22]

As a result of the political liberalization pursuant to the election of Mohammad Khatami, a number of political parties appeared on the scene. With the possible exception of the Islamic Iran Participation Front, the leading component of the reformist coalition that backed Khatami's policies, most are vehicles for one man's political ambitions and lack any grassroots organization. In the absence of strong parties, journals, newspapers, and increasingly websites play a key role as vehicles for discussing, formulating, and disseminating ideological alternatives.

Presidential Elections

In January 1980 Iran held its first ever presidential election, resulting in the victory of a lay Islamist, Abolhasan Banisadr. But Banisadr was impeached by parliament and deposed by Khomeini in June 1981, and his more pliant successor was killed two months later together with the prime minister by a bomb attack. The next four elections had predictable results, as close companions of Khomeini, Ali Khamenei in 1981 and 1985 and Ali-Akbar Hashemi Rafsanjani in 1989 and 1993, easily won contests in which the other candidates were minor figures. Consequently the participation rate went steadily down, as can be seen in Figure 14.3 on electoral participation.

The pattern seemed to repeat itself in 1997. Although Rafsanjani would have liked to run again, he could not because the constitution provides for only one immediate reelection: the mere fact that the term limit was respected shows to what an extent constitutional norms had finally come to govern Iranian politics. In the event the Speaker of Parliament, conservative cleric Ali-Akbar Nateq Nuri, was endorsed

by most of the government and the politically active ulema including the Leader, and most observers expected him to win. Instead Mohammad Khatami, a moderate cleric who had resigned as minister of culture in 1992 after conservatives gained control over parliament, ran a modern and effective campaign by reaching out to university students and active members of the nascent civil society, and won a landslide victory. As an "outsider," Khatami appealed to all those who had been humiliated by the regime: educated people who felt that the state discriminated against them in favor of less educated but ideologically reliable Islamic activists, women who resented the legal restrictions and discriminations to which they were subjected, and young people who were tired of being harassed on a daily basis by the guardians of public morality. To all these groups Khatami promised greater cultural openness and personal freedoms. Although his reforms petered out in 1999, he was easily reelected in 2001. In 2005 for the first time since 1981 there was no official candidate, as three allies of Khatami, four conservatives, and Rafsanjani ran for the highest elective office. No candidate having gained a majority, for the first time there was a second round pitting Rafsanjani against the arch-conservative mayor of Tehran, Mahmud Ahmadinejad. At around 60 percent, participation in the two rounds was lower than in the previous two elections, and Ahmadinejad won an upset victory amidst allegations that Islamic Revolutionary Guard Corps (IRGC) and *Basij* commanders had illegally urged troops to vote for him, and perhaps even engaged them in stuffing ballot boxes to increase his share of the vote in the first round, which allowed him to place second. Nonetheless, Ahmadinejad's message did appeal to the poor whose concerns had not been addressed by the cultural liberalization of the Khatami years (see Box 14.3).

Parliamentary Elections

For the purpose of parliamentary elections, Iran is divided into multimember constituencies, the largest being Tehran with thirty MPs. Each voter can write down the names of as many candidates as there are seats in a constituency. The top vote-getters in each constituency are elected provided they receive over 50 percent of the total vote. If a constituency has more seats than candidates who passed the 50 percent

PARLIAMENTARY ELECTIONS

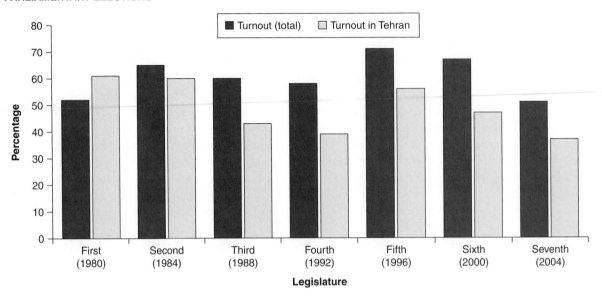

PRESIDENTIAL ELECTIONS

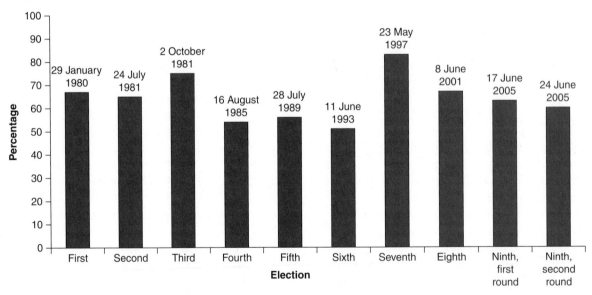

FIGURE   14.3   Electoral Participation

barrier, a second round is held to determine the remaining MPs from among the runners-up; this time the number of candidates is twice that of the seats that remain to be filled. In the absence of organized political parties, candidacies tend to be endorsed by a number of different political, religious, and cultural associations, making it difficult to deduce accurate figures about the relative popularity of different political groupings from the election results.

In the first legislative elections of 1980, a few National Front, LMI, and regionalist candidates were elected to parliament, but since 1984 only candidates unequivocally committed to *velayat-e faqih* have been allowed to run. Radicals formed the majority

BOX 14.3   Biography of Two Presidents and Two Generations

The biographies of Iran's last two presidents, Mohammad Khatami (1997–2005) and Mahmud Ahmadinejad (2005–present), illustrate the changing face of Iran's political elite from an older generation formed by the struggle against the Shah and the revolution to one that is largely shaped by events of the postrevolutionary era. Moreover, the socioeconomic differences between Khatami and Ahmadinejad are telling.

Khatami, born in 1943 into a family of notable clerics and landowners, is a cleric educated in the seminaries of Qom and holds a B.A. in philosophy from a secular university. He has authored several works on philosophy and is fluent in Arabic and knows some German and English. After the revolution, he became the Minister of Culture and Islamic Guidance (1982–1992), which regulates and censors all forms of media and publications, where he was known to be a supporter of freedom of speech and the press. Khatami was able to carve out some space for his cultural activities thanks to his close relationship with Khomeini and his son, as well as journalists and students who would later support his presidency. Nonetheless, after growing pressure from hard-line conservatives, Khatami was forced to resign in 1992 and became the director of the National Library until he successfully ran for president.

Ahmadinejad was born in 1956 to a blacksmith and moved to Tehran at a young age. He is a product of the prerevolutionary secular education system and studied engineering. He participated in the Iran–Iraq war as a member of the IRCG. He later performed very well during his three years as governor of the newly established Ardabil Province (1993–1996). In 1997 Ahmadinejad earned a Ph.D. from a technical university and continued to teach there. In 2003 he was part of the new conservative faction of younger politicians known as the Alliance of Builders of Islamic Iran, which swept the Tehran city council elections, and he was elected as mayor.

What brings these disparate profiles and outlooks together is that both were overwhelmingly elected President—against candidates favored by the establishment.

Sources: Buchta, p. 30. http://www.bbc.co.uk/persian/iran/story/2005/08/050801_pm-mv-khatami-profile.shtml
http://www.mardomyar.com/aspx2/aboutme.aspx

Photo courtesy of Getty Images

in the second (1984–1988) and third parliaments (1988–1992), but after Khomeini's death the conservative-dominated Council of Guardians arrogated to itself the right to vet candidacies, and proceeded to invalidate the candidacies of most radicals. Consequently the fourth and fifth parliaments (1992–2000) were dominated by conservatives, with pragmatist supporters of Rafsanjani forming the minority. In the wake of Mohammad Khatami's surprise victory in the presidential election of 1997, however, a record number of reformists became candidates, and being unknown to the Council of Guardians, were allowed to run for office in 2000. They swept the elections, gaining around 70 percent of the vote. But where did these reformists suddenly come from?

In the course of the 1990s many of the radicals of the 1980s had a change of heart and moderated their views. This evolution had a number of reasons. For one, the experience of spending time in the political wilderness after being barred from entering parliament in 1992 brought home the importance of fair elections and political pluralism. Furthermore, the collapse of Communism in the Soviet Union and Eastern Europe delegitimized the state-centric approach to social and political organization. At the same time, a group of Muslim intellectuals, some of them ulema themselves, began challenging both the traditional jurisprudential approach to religion that led to the preeminence of the ulema and the survival of obsolete rules and regulations, and the ideologization of religion that led to the loss of spirituality and totalitarian government. This more liberal approach to religion resulted in a tentative rapprochement between Islamic reformists and social groups who had hitherto not participated in politics, boosting participation rates at elections. For the parliamentary elections of 2004, however, the Council of Guardians disallowed about 2,000 reformist candidates, including about 80 sitting MPs, which was unprecedented. Thereupon many reformist personalities and associations called for a boycott of the elections. Although participation diminished, a respectable 50 percent of the population still went to the polls. The reason is that in many areas outside the main cities voters do not judge candidates by their ideology but by what they can do (or have done) to further the interests of their constituents. Figure 14.3 shows the evolution of electoral participation.

Local Elections

Although the constitution of 1906 provided for elected local government councils, these bodies were never actually constituted. The similar provisions of the 1979 constitution were first put into action in 1999, when Iranians for the first time went to the polls to elect city, town, and village councils.

Reformists won control over most councils, including Tehran. With the conservatives stymieing the reformist camp, apathy overtook voters in the new decade and voting came to be seen by many as a futile exercise since ultimately power rests with unelected bodies. And so it came to pass that in the second local elections in 2003 only 15 percent of the eligible voters in Tehran, mostly conservatives, bothered to vote, even though these were the freest elections in Iranian history: for the first time the Council of Guardians had not vetted candidates, and even avowed secularists were allowed to run. Consequently the nation's capital, home to about 15 percent of its total population, got a uniformly conservative city council, which proceeded to elect as mayor the man who would two years later use his position as springboard for a successful bid for the presidency. Elsewhere in the country, however, campaigns were more centered on concrete problems and participation was thus higher, testifying to a relatively high level of civic engagement of the citizenry.[23]

POLITICAL CULTURE

To a large extent Iran's political culture results from its place in the international system. Iran survived the age of imperialism as a formally sovereign state, but this continued independence did not prevent outside powers, mainly Great Britain and Russia, from meddling in Iran's domestic affairs and controlling its economy.[24] Their country having been a long-standing member of the international society of nations, Iranians have tended to compare themselves more readily with the dominant countries of the West than with other Third World nations, and transforming their country's formal independence into genuine sovereignty has always constituted a key concern of politically conscious Iranians.

One result of the continuous meddling of outside powers in Iranian affairs has been Iranians' propensity to believe in conspiracies and to interpret politics in the light of conspiracy theories (i.e., theories that purport to prove that politics is dominated by the ill-intentioned and conspiratorial machinations of small groups whose aims and values are profoundly opposed to those of the rest of society).[25] Belief in conspiracies as a motor force in history is common in the rest of the Middle East as well,[26] but in the Iranian case the plausibility of such theories is enhanced by the fact that Iran *has* indeed been the victim of conspiracies, most recently in 1953 when the U.S. and British governments conspired with Iranian conservatives to install the Shah as ruler of the country. The main reason why the seizure of the American hostages in November 1979 was so popular at the time was that it symbolically ended the era of foreign interference in Iranian affairs by allowing Iranians to occupy what most believed to be the epicenter of all conspiracies: the U.S. embassy.

System Level

Iran is not a country whose borders and statehood are a bequest of European colonialism, which helps explain why the modern polity enjoys considerable historic legitimacy among Iranians, in spite of their ethnic diversity: Iranians with different mother tongues have lived with each other for centuries. The Iranian nationalism propagated by the Pahlavi shahs included pride in the glories of ancient Persia and in a continuous "national" history of 2,500 years, a history that was interpreted as conferring upon Iranians an intrinsic nobility that neighboring peoples and states with a shorter history cannot match. This intense national pride survived the revolution but changed garb: while the glories of pre-Islamic Iran are now much less emphasized than before, the new authorities and their supporters considered Iran to be the vanguard of the Islamic world's struggle against Western domination, a position that fuses commitment to Islam with Iranian nationalism. However, in recent years Pahlavi-type ethnic Persian nationalism has been making a comeback among those very numerous Iranians who are disenchanted with theocratic rule. By the same token, ethnic nationalism has become stronger among Iran's non-Persian populations. This is particularly noticeable among the predominantly Sunni Kurds, who resent not only the poverty of the Kurdish areas but also discrimination on sectarian grounds. In the most recent presidential election, for instance, a candidate who expressly addressed Sunni grievances carried the largely Sunni province of Sistan and Baluchistan, whereas an Azeri who emphasized his ethnicity carried the three largely Azeri-speaking provinces of northwestern Iran. In theory there is no reason why this new ethnic assertiveness should not be compatible with a strong sense of Iranian civic nationalism, but that depends on how the central government will manage it: repressive measures are likely to erode the identification with the Iranian state in the ethnic periphery.

One time-honored way governments shore up their declining legitimacy is by appealing to feelings of patriotism. In Iran the issue around which the government has recently hoped to unite Iranians is the development of nuclear technology. The Iranian leaders' insistence that Iran has a "right" to develop nuclear energy has struck a sympathetic chord among ordinary Iranians, even among many of those who oppose Islamist rule. If Americans, Europeans, Chinese, and even Indians and Pakistanis have nuclear weapons, many people ask, why should Iranians not have them too?

Process Level

One indisputable result of the Islamic revolution was the dramatic increase in the number of citizens who participated in politics. The millions of Iranians who poured into the streets to demand the departure of the Shah throughout 1978 refused to become mere subjects of a theocratic state after the revolution was over. The same cannot be said for those who opposed either the revolution or the Islamic state to which it ultimately gave rise. Many emigrated, and those who remained behind tended to consider the "Association of Militant Clerics" and the "Society of Militant Clergy" little more than a tweedledum and tweedledee. It was these passive subjects of the Islamic Republic that Khatami had in mind when he repeatedly asserted that he wanted to be the president of *all* Iranians. They participated for the first time since the inception of the new regime, carrying electoral participation rates to new heights. In the elections of 2004 and 2005, however, many of them boycotted the elections, feeling that their participation had not brought the country nearer to a more republican and less theocratic form of government.

Another key feature of Iran's political culture is extreme individualism and lack of trust. Most observers impute this to the country's long history of despotism, which never allowed for the emergence of a state of law that would render life predictable and governed by rules rather than personal connections. The conspiracy belief mentioned earlier has added to this absence of trust. Political opponents have had a tendency to accuse each other of being in league with foreign powers, making compromise (necessary for deliberative politics) very difficult, for one cannot compromise or negotiate with a "traitor." In the Islamic Republic the fact that the revolutionary credentials of the leaders of the various factions are equally strong has led to a certain mutual tolerance among those political leaders who remain faithful to *velayat-e faqih*, but even now dissidents who question the system itself are invariably accused of doing the bidding of foreign (read: hostile) powers. The most consistent victims of this propensity to believe in conspiracies are religious minorities, especially Baha'is, who have been widely presented as agents of "Zionism," a charge motivated by the fact that the world center of the Baha'i faith is located in Israel, which is a historic accident.

Distrust is not something that only permeates the political elite, but is also evident among citizens.

Recent results of the World Value Survey suggest that Iranians, like Egyptians, do not trust government (see Figure 14.4).[27]

Since television channels are state-run and much of the press is owned by the state or heavily monitored by it, the low levels of trust in these institutions should be interpreted as also expressing a lack of trust in government. Meanwhile, the relatively high level of trust in the "mosque," should be interpreted with caution. As we will see below "the mosque" is far from a homogeneous entity and does not necessarily reflect a particular political agenda or culture.

This individualism and lack of trust is an underlying cause for the absence of true political parties and the constant splits that the few parties that did come into existence have undergone. While all Iranians bemoan their inability to cooperate, it is this very inability that saved Iran from becoming a totalitarian state in the 1980s, for had the ulema had the discipline and centralist organization of either the Roman Catholic church or a Communist party, their rule would have become far more totalitarian and monolithic, and factionalism would never have been institutionalized.

A final consequence of the individualism and conspiracy belief prevalent in Iran's political culture is the periodic appearance of charismatic leaders

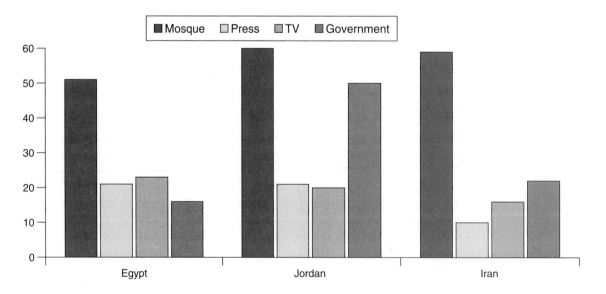

FIGURE 14.4 Percentage Expressing Very Great Trust

Source: Mansoor Moaddel and Taghi Azadarmaki, "The Worldviews of Islamic Publics: The Case of Egypt, Iran, and Jordan," In *Human Values and Social Change: Findings from the Values Survey.* Edited by Ronald Ingelhart (Leiden: Brill 2003): 81.

who embody the yearning of the citizenry for over-coming the current order and the source of all problems—imperialists and autocrats. Mohammad Mossadegh, Ayatollah Khomeini, and even, to a much lesser extent, Mohammad Khatami exemplify this tendency. Some have argued that Twelver Shiism, with its expectation of the Twelfth Imam, predisposes Iranians to put their hopes in a charismatic savior figure.

Policy Level

Given the fact that the Iranian state derives most of its income from oil, Iranians have tended to expect the state to provide welfare and material well-being for everybody and alleviate the gap between rich and poor. In other words, they want their share of the oil wealth. Part of the delegitimation of the Shah's regime derived from the perception that not enough wealth trickled down to the poorer strata.

Corruption has been endemic in Iran, and fighting it has been an aspiration of Iranians of all political persuasions. Its persistence has been blamed on the regime, which has thereby lost some legitimacy, just like the Pahlavi regime in the 1960s and 1970s.

A noteworthy feature of Iran's contemporary political culture is the suspicion of private enterprise in the industrial sector. Beginning under Reza Shah (r. 1925–1941), the state took a leading role in the development of industry. Under Reza Shah's son, this statism was supplemented by an emerging class of capitalists who contributed considerably to Iran's industrialization in the 1960s and 1970s. But they were closely connected to the Shah and his relatives, they cooperated with foreign companies whose activities were suspicious for the mere reason that they were foreign, and some of them were members of religious minorities. Consequently, both the Islamists and leftists who carried the revolutionary movement opposed them and the mode of economic development they represented, calling them exploiters. The legacy of this opposition is visible in Iran's constitution which puts heavy limits on foreign investment.

The populism propagated by the revolutionaries has intensified opposition to conspicuous consumption and privately owned large-scale economic activity. This has not affected rich bazaar merchants, who engage mostly in trade rather than production. Their activity is less immediately visible than that of an industrialist, as a merchant can deal in millions armed with nothing but a cell phone and sitting behind a desk in a small shop in the bazaar, whereas the factory and offices of an industrialist attract immediate attention.[28] The result of this general distrust of industrialists has been that citizens expect the state to be the main purveyor of development and increased living standards, and the election of Mahmud Ahmadinejad in 2005 is also due to some extent to the timid privatization carried out under his two predecessors, which aggravated income inequality.

While many Iranians thus expect the state to alleviate poverty and unemployment, others expect the state to provide an environment in which individual talent and creativity can flourish. Collectivism and individualism are both present in Iranian society, and there can be no doubt that Iran's political culture is highly conflictual. The citizenry is sharply divided over the very essence of the regime, with many, especially among the more educated, considering the Islamic theocracy, if not Islamic republic, to be a historically anachronistic form of government.

POLITICAL SOCIALIZATION

The political socialization of citizens is a process simultaneously driven from above by state institutions and from below by social practices. In Iran, state-controlled institutions such as the education system and the military have transmitted many of the basic political values and norms in society and also established the framework of political debate and contestation over their meaning. Meanwhile, Iranians have negotiated, challenged, and even undermined many of these through their everyday practices as members of their family, neighborhood, or social group.

As in many postrevolutionary and postcolonial regimes, state-sanctioned political socialization in Iran has aimed at generating national unity and masking political, ethnic, and socioeconomic cleavages. Under the Pahlavi monarchy national unity was championed in the mission of creating a modern, industrial, and Western society. Under this vision the nation was presented as secular, classless, and thoroughly Persian in identity. The schools, for instance, were the primary means to educate the entire Iranian population in the official language of Persian, a critical means to distance the significant numbers of Azeri (roughly 25%), Kurdish (8–10%), and Arabic

(2–5%) speakers from their local and ethnic loyalties. The calls for greater economic equality, ethnic inclusion, and religious observance during the Islamic revolution dramatically questioned both the notion of national homogeneity and the perception that the Iranian nation had accepted this image of itself. Under the Islamic republic, the content of the official discourse and normative agenda has changed, but the methods of socialization and overwhelming elite desire to limit input from citizens and ignore the pluralistic nature of society remains quite similar to the prerevolutionary regime.

Education System

The school system has been the principal "agent of socialization" for creating good Islamic citizens out of young Iranians. The school system was one of the first institutions to be Islamicized by the new regime. School curricula were changed to include a heavy dose of religious studies, yearly classes on the Islamic Revolution, and an increased number of mandatory Arabic language courses. Meanwhile, textbooks were rewritten to present a state-sanctioned history of Iran, which highlighted the role of the clergy in all "popular uprisings," erased or distorted any role played by nonreligious forces such as liberal nationalists or leftist parties, and presented the Pahlavi monarchy (and all monarchs) as equally and continually oppressive and immoral. Textbooks also depicted the state's image of the family. Unlike the prerevolutionary textbooks that showed Iranian women as unveiled, families eating around a table, and children with non-Arabic and nonreligious names, the postrevolutionary textbooks depicted all women as veiled (even inside the home), families sitting cross-legged around a simple spread on the floor, and children with Islamic names.[29] Schoolchildren also received revolutionary doctrine in the form of reciting chants and poems praising the greatness of Khomeini and the regime, while denouncing the Baathist regime in Iraq as well as "the imperialists," most commonly the United States.

The authorities initially emphasized the role of primary and secondary schools for creating loyal and mobilized supporters. However, a group of Islamist activists and scholars also led a charge to "cleanse" the universities of "counterrevolutionary" elements by reviewing both the faculty and the curriculum.

This "Cultural Revolution" was headed by what is now known as the Supreme Council for the Cultural Revolution. University campuses being the epicenter of anti-regime activism, the Cultural Revolution closed all universities for three years (1980–1983), and worked on ways to develop links between the universities and the religious seminaries. When the universities were re-opened, strict entrance requirements were established, including religious examinations, to give greater opportunities to those the regime suspected would be more supportive of its ambitions. In addition, war veterans and relatives of those killed in the revolution and the Iran–Iraq war were allotted special quotas in all universities. In the meantime, the regime established new institutions to create a new set of technocrats and teachers to staff the ministries and the universities. For instance, Imam Sadeq University (on the campus of a former business school affiliated with the Harvard Business School) was fashioned to produce technocrats. Another new aspect of the university system was the establishment of the "Islamic Open University," with autonomous campuses all over the country, including small towns, to provide higher education to Iranians living outside of the main population centers and providing opportunities for those students who fail to pass the highly competitive entrance examination for the elite national universities or whose families would not let them move to the larger cities. The very content of higher education itself was transformed by the Islamic Republic with the regime promoting and funding attempts to elaborate fields such as "Islamic Economics" and "Islamic Sciences" as ways to compete with what some intellectuals viewed as the fundamentally distorted and anti-Islamic nature of Western social and natural sciences. Over the years, the regime has also sponsored the establishment of pro-regime volunteer organizations (***Basij***) to monitor and contend with the political activities of students and faculty and mobilize students for pro-regime activities on the campuses.

Given the events of the last decade, it seems that the Islamic Republic's efforts to create obedient and loyal citizens out of the "children of the revolution" have been far from successful. Many of the investigative journalists exposing government abuses and incompetence or the staunchest supporters of reform and the burgeoning civil society (e.g., arts organizations and women's NGOs) are products of the state school system and its post-Cultural Revolution higher education establishments. In fact, the university that the state tried so hard to control in the wake of the revolution, is again full of students publishing political journals and declarations, organizing talks by intellectuals challenging the regime, and flaunting and mocking the social mores and the state's strict policies regarding gender relations. The large student demonstrations of 1999 and 2003 are indicative of the inability of the regime to fully manage this politicized space.

The Military

Military conscription has also been a fundamental mechanism for creating national unity, at least for young men. The shared experience of basic training and interacting with the military bureaucracy was augmented in the Iranian case by the experience of the long war with Iraq. As mentioned earlier, the war was a critical historical juncture that shaped a large number of Iranian men and their families. With approximately four to five million Iranians serving in the armed forces during the eight-year war, a very large percentage of Iranian families were directly affected by the war.[30] Various public commemorations, war murals, and a war cinema and fiction act to foster emotional bonds between the war generation and those who preceded and followed it.

Politically, however, the war has been divisive, with part of the ruling establishment questioning the policy to continue the war even after the Iraqi army was driven off Iranian soil in 1982.[31] Moreover, Iran's military includes the Islamic Revolutionary Guard Corps and the volunteer corps known as the *Basij* which have become distinct institutions with growing political influence: in the parliamentary election of 2004 over 100 former members of the Revolutionary Guards won seats, and in 2005 a former member won the presidency. These institutions are largely autonomous from the regular army and police force, are under the direct supervision of the Leader, and have acquired significant economic holdings.

Religion and Religious Institutions

It seems fair to state that most Iranians consider themselves as religious and consider religious matters and practices as important aspects of their lives.

Results from the 2000–2001 World Value Survey project, however, suggest a somewhat more complicated view.[32] Iranians seem to be quite religious, especially by Western European standards, although somewhat less so than Egyptians and Jordanians. Table 14.2 and Figure 14.5 show that many Iranians consider themselves as religious, believe religion is very important in life, and participate in religious services but at lower rates than Jordan and Egypt. Moreover, while surveyed Iranians tend more often characterize themselves as "above all a Muslim" than as "above all a nationalist," about a third put nationalism first, far more than in either Egypt or Jordan.

Notwithstanding these aggregate findings, it is interesting that under the Islamic Republic religion and religious practice have played a more divisive than unifying role. On the surface, religion permeates daily life. Official speeches and pronouncements are peppered with religious expressions and quotations, the calendar is full of religious holidays, and religious observance is often public and conspicuous. Shiite Islam plays a central role both in official discourse and as a means to regulate who can gain high office in the state. Friday congregational prayers and commemorations of religious anniversaries are state-regulated events that bring people from all walks of life together at neighborhood public spaces. As if to underline the emasculation of Tehran University as the center of secular opposition to the Islamic regime, Tehran's official Friday congregational prayers are held on what used to be the

TABLE 14.2 Percentage of People Describing Self as "a Religious Person"

Egypt	98
Nigeria	94
Jordan	85
Iran	82
USA	82
India	80
Turkey	75
Spain	75
Mexico	65
Russia	64
Germany	50
Sweden	33
Japan	24

Source: Moaddel and Azadarmaki, p. 75.

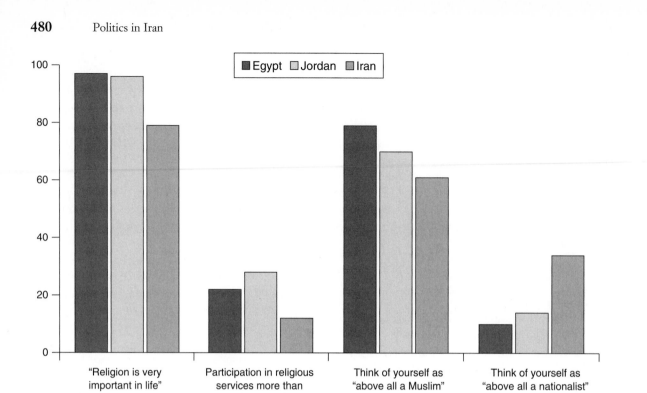

FIGURE 14.5   Religious Beliefs and Practice

campus's soccer field. On these occasions leading members of the government give sermons in which they passionately weave together religious and moral issues and the pressing political problems of the day. In staging these public and mass religious meetings, the state consciously attempts to mobilize citizens in support of the regime and also to transmit political messages. These events and state-owned radio and television are dominated by the well-versed and symbolic Shiite language of martyrdom and self-sacrifice, as exemplified by the third Imam, in the name of justice and standing up to the great powers who usurp the rights of the innocent and faithful.

However, it is notoriously difficult to monopolize the collection of symbols, interpretations, and ephemeral beliefs that make up all religions, and over the years the Islamic Republic has had difficulty maintaining tight control over members of the political elite and clergy, let alone the hearts and minds of its citizens. Given the absence of a Shiite "pope," Iran's theocratic state has never been able fully to impose its politicized vision of Shiite Islam within Iran, let alone across the Shiite world. With the death of Khomeini

and the appointment of the less religiously erudite and charismatic Khamenei, fundamental disagreements have emerged over the meaning of Islamic government and the role of religion in public life. For instance, the political faction commonly described as "reformists" has stressed the republican dimensions of the constitution and the revolution, whereas the conservatives have highlighted the centrality of clerical authority and its right of oversight over the popular will. Meanwhile, lay religious intellectuals, such as Abdol-Karim Soroush, and clerics, such as Hassan Eshkevari, have called for a reformulation of the relationships among God, the individual, and political authority that explicitly challenges the basic assumptions of the current interpretation of *velayat-e faqih*. These debates have not only percolated in the intellectual environments of the universities, seminaries, and magazines, but have begun to shape more public discussions regarding the relationship between religion and politics and resonate with the philosophical and political debates of ordinary Iranians too.[33]

Finally, in more organizational terms, religious observance has always had a localized flavor. Numerous neighborhood and guild-based Koranic reading groups and religious associations cater to the spiritual needs of men and women of different regional, ethnic, and class backgrounds. These informal meetings act as grassroots and independent forums for religious practice, which by definition escape the watchful eye of those clerics that are affiliated with the regime. Sometimes escaping the attention of observers is the tension between the clerical state and the seminaries in the cities of Qom and Mashhad. With the vast majority of clergy historically shying away from politics and the seminary system historically maintaining financial independence, Khomeini's political innovation of clerical-led government has reconfigured "church"-state relations. For instance, job opportunities and income are available for clerics in the judicial system and in the ministries, and as Friday prayer leaders, the last being appointed by the office of the Leader. While the ulema, especially former students of Khomeini, have been prominent in the higher reaches of the regime, the actual running of the state has never been dominated by seminary graduates and their presence has declined over the last quarter century. One indication is the decline in the number of clerics in the parliament; in the very first Majles almost half of the MPs were clerics, but by the late 1990s clerics constituted less than 20 percent of MPs.

For the vast majority of clerics, who remain in the seminaries to teach, study, and interpret religious texts, the regime has in fact been intrusive. The authorities in Tehran have tried to monitor teaching in the seminaries by dictating curricula and identifying texts to be taught in Qom, and the Leader has used his office and funds to support seminaries and teachers that are deemed to be "militant" and sympathetic to the regime's interpretations of Islam. The upshot has been that while in theory the mosque and state are perfectly aligned, in practice the state can never be sure that the seminaries are producing appropriate clergy for the government or to socialize Iranians in the official doctrine. Mosque and state have continued to be distinct entities despite the infusion of religion and seminarians into the constitution of the state.

Mass Media

The media play both a unifying and a divisive role in socializing Iranians. Radio and television are monopolized by the state and have been one of the major means to transmit the official doctrine and to mobilize Iranians for elections and rallies across the country. Since the head of the Radio and Television Organization is directly appointed by the Leader, in recent years it has also reflected the interests of the conservative wing of the regime. The strong bias of state TV was clearly demonstrated during the presidency of Mohammad Khatami (1997–2005), when news broadcasts either ignored or misrepresented many of the raging political debates. In recent years, as satellite TV has grown and the dishes have become less expensive, anti-regime Persian language programming from abroad and foreign news outlets (CNN and BBC) have provided greater diversity for the viewing public. In response, the state has repeatedly tried to outlaw private use of satellite dishes, although the law has not been applied consistently, and the dishes can be seen on roof tops in major cities and even small towns.

The printed press has been the most diverse and fascinating form of media in postrevolutionary Iran. In the first decade of the revolution, newspapers and journals became increasingly uniform in their coverage, but as the regime began to feel more consolidated and elite competition became more open after the passing away of Khomeini, a growing number of independent newspapers and magazines appeared on the scene. These newspapers and magazines reflected specific schools of thought and critical views from intellectuals on the right and left and the more republican and the more authoritarian wings of the regime. A flourishing nonstate press and burgeoning investigative journalism constituted the backbone of Khatami's surprising election victory in 1997 and underpinned the enormous popularity of the reformist movement in his first term. The critics of the government, many of whom were part of the revolutionary establishment, and the many young journalists writing critical articles and taking high-quality photos were able to present a new political language of accountability, civil society, and participation to the educated, urban, and young population of Iran as well as their parents, most of whom desired a change in their personal lives, if not in the regime. In doing so, these newspapers both reflected and produced deep cleavages among the ruling establishment. During the authoritarian backlash against the reformist movement since 2000, the conservative-controlled Judiciary has gone a long way in clamping down on the most vibrant aspects of this press. Currently, journalists have turned to the Internet to distribute their reports and publish their commentaries in online newspapers or in the mushrooming collection of weblogs: today Persian is the fourth most widely used language in terms of numbers of bloggers, after English, French, and Portuguese. In Iran today, journalists and newspaper editors, some of whom have been imprisoned or physically attacked, have become the new political heroes of many of the youth.

The Family and Social Groups

Political socialization takes place in the private sphere as well as the public sphere; this is particularly the case in more authoritarian contexts. In Iran, both under the monarchy and the Islamic Republic, the home has been a relatively free place to discuss politics by recounting the unofficial history of the country or debate current events with family members and friends. While patriarchy (and sometimes matriarchy) does prohibit unfettered debate in the family setting, the memory of key political episodes such as the 1953 coup or the events leading up to the overthrow of the Shah in 1979 are transmitted in these settings. By retelling stories from earlier eras or speculating about the conspiracies behind them, older family members indoctrinate the family's younger generation in a political memory and culture that have not been sanctioned by the state and that are at variance with the official story, as contained in school textbooks and official rhetoric.

But with greater numbers of Iranians completing high school and attending universities, the family dynamic appears to have changed. These new young men and women now have a certain authority as they are the first generation in their families to graduate from high school and university, and it is they who are interpreting politics for their relatives by explaining differences between political factions and bringing campus politics into their homes. Over the last ten years, greater political freedoms, or at least a less fearful setting, has allowed for many of these types of discussions to take place while one waits for oven-fresh bread outside the local bakery, peruses headlines at the newspaper kiosk, or shares a collective taxi with total strangers. These ritualistic acts of resistance prevent the state from fully dominating politics, but at the same time they do not challenge the bases of regime power.

In short, political socialization under the Islamic Republic has shifted from being solely the responsibility of the state to one that is contested by counterelite and popular voices. The early revolutionary message of unity and mobilization in the name of revolutionary Islam taught in school textbooks and recounted in unison in Friday sermons and newspaper pages has given way to greater pluralism and contestation, intriguingly by many of the same people who read those school texts and wrote those newspaper articles in the 1980s. Whether the regime will be able to accommodate and represent this cacophony or impose the single voice of unity is very much the question facing Iran's authorities. Their decision and capacity in this regard will determine whether Iran will move toward more democratic politics or an unstable authoritarianism.

RECRUITING THE POLITICAL ELITE

What kinds of people govern Iran? Under the Shah, the small class of educated and secular Iranians who could demonstrate personal loyalty to the monarch gained access to political offices. Many of the ministers came from land-owning families and attended Western high schools and universities.[34] The Shah, however, carefully monitored his court in order to prevent the rise of potential competitors with a strong personality or independent bases of support. For instance, highly competent policymakers and administrators, such the Abol-Hasan Ebtehaj, who headed the Plan and Budget Organization, were muscled out of office as soon as the Shah sensed they were growing in stature.[35] A consequence of this policy was a highly dependent inner circle, whose members were unwilling to challenge the Shah and preferred to censor information and opinions in order not to offend His Imperial Majesty. This passive and dependent nature of the political elite prevented the Shah from acting in a timely and decisive manner as the revolts and political challenges of 1977 and 1978 snowballed into the revolution.[36]

Under the Islamic Republic personalism has also played an important role, but in a broader sense. In the early years, political elites came from various backgrounds, but their most fundamental credentials are their revolutionary pedigree. Those who could point to active participation in the Islamic revolution, and in particular the various groups associated with

Khomeini and his students, leveraged this past experience into positions in ministries, the many parastatal economic foundations, the Islamic Revolutionary Guard Corps, and various other institutions with access to state revenue. Thus, the new political elite that came to power immediately after the revolution tended to be younger, less cosmopolitan, and from more middle-class and lower-middle-class backgrounds, often hailing from the provinces rather than the capital.

In general, the state has expanded since the revolution. From 1976 to 1986, the number of employees in the public sector more than doubled, reaching more than 30 percent of all employed Iranians. In the 1980s, four-fifths of all new jobs created were in the public sector, and by 1986 public sector employment accounted for 31 percent of total employment.[37] This expansion was due to a number of reasons, including the requisites of the war effort, the state-led economic development program, and the revolutionary agenda to restructure and Islamicize society from above.

Initially the clergy that were recruited into the state were trained in the seminaries in Najaf and Qom where Khomeini and his students taught during the 1960s and 1970s. The principal seminary that produced these new judges and ministers was the Fayziyeh Seminary in Qom. Over time, the Haqqani seminary in Qom has grown in importance, in part because many of its alumni include staunch conservatives who have dominated the Judiciary, the Council of Guardians, and the security apparatus. The so-called "Haqqani circle" have been important ideologues and figures in the conservative backlash against Khatami's attempts to institutionalize political reform and encourage active participation by civil society. In the recent parliamentary and presidential elections the Haqqani alumni in conjunction with some elements of the IRGC have both supported social conservatives and opposed moderate conservatives and reformists.

Nonclerical parliamentarians and ministers tend to emerge from educational and military institutions. First, many attend the newly Islamicized universities (see section on Socialization) such as Imam Sadeq University or Tarbiat Modarres University. In the 1990s, think tanks and research centers have also been important in recruiting and producing political elites. Many of the reformists who dominated the sixth parliament and supported President Khatami were based in the Center for Strategic Studies. These younger elites often are too young to have significant revolutionary

credentials, but their studies in these universities and institutes give them technical know-how, intellectual credentials, and the social networks to gain access to various government and state institutions. More recently, many of the new elite have come from the ranks of the Islamic Revolutionary Guard Corps and the *Basij*. The current president, Ahmadinejad, the mayor of Tehran, Mohammad-Baqer Qalibaf, and many of the ministers all were military figures from these corps or worked for the research institutes connected to the IRGC. It is worth noting that the regular army, navy, and air force have not had much of an influence in politics. This growing militarization of politics is a new phenomenon in modern Iranian history. Unlike neighboring Pakistan, Turkey, and Iraq, which have had numerous military coups and governments headed by generals, the Iranian political establishment was overwhelmingly civilian throughout the twentieth century.

Kinship ties are a commonly used means to gain political and economic power. Many of the sons and brothers, and on some rare occasions, daughters and sisters, of government officials for instance have used their family ties to gain access to the state. Often their contacts have been used as means for rent seeking (receiving subsidized hard currency, special import licenses, or securing subsidized loans) and personal enrichment. In addition, we see marriage used as a powerful way to cement political alliances and create bonds between prominent families. For instance, President Khatami's brother, Mohammad-Reza Khatami, who was a member of the sixth parliament and the secretary general of the reformist Islamic Iran Participation Front, is married to Zahra Eshraqi, a granddaughter of Khomeini. Meanwhile, the daughter of the current speaker of the Parliament, Gholam-Ali Haddad-Adel, is married to the son of Ali Khamenei, the Leader. These and other kinship relations have thus helped integrate the elite and distinguish them from ordinary citizens.

INTEREST ARTICULATION AND AGGREGATION

The mix of electoral politics and authoritarian powers has generated multiple and competing forms of interest articulation and aggregation under the Islamic Republic. The most institutionalized forms have been regular presidential, parliamentary, and local elections, as discussed above. The least institutionalized, but probably the most prevalent and effective, is the use of personalistic ties and patron-client relations. As a consequence, representation under the Islamic Republic has been highly fragmented, fluid, and contentious, although not fully pluralistic, competitive, and democratic.

Noninstitutional Forms of Interest Articulation and Aggregation

The principal means of interest aggregation in contemporary Iran is clientelism and the forging of relationships between political figures and citizens through patron-client networks. Given the state's access to external sources of revenue from the world oil market, Iranian political figures over the last four decades have exchanged political loyalty and support for access to resources such as subsidies, hard currency, subcontracts, and secure government jobs. This system of patronage can take a very direct form where parliamentarians, ministers, or bureaucrats dole out these resources to kin, schoolmates, and people from the same city or province. Special access to powerful figures in the office of the Leader, state-owned banks, and economic foundations have benefited these clients, while ensuring their dependence, if not loyalty, to the political system that plays more of a distributive, rather than extractive role. Since patron-client relations are based on the goods that the patron provides the client, if the patron loses power then so do his clients.

In a less targeted manner, the Islamic Republic has distributed large subsidies to ensure the loyalty of large portions of the population. Food and medicine are subsidized at a rate of about $2 billion and is in particular directed to the urban poor. By contrast, the annual $10 billion energy subsidy for gasoline and electricity is quite regressive in that it benefits the middle and upper classes that own automobiles, homes, and electrical equipment. Obviously, this form of political aggregation undermines pretensions of institutional impartiality and meritocracy that are essential principles behind equal citizenship and participation.

Institutionalized Forms of Interest Articulation and Aggregation: Voting

Elections, as discussed above, are regularized political events, but do not provide complete pluralism nor necessarily entail a shift in power and policies since the powers of the representative institutions are quite circumscribed. Elections have tended to function more as an act and measurement of regime legitimacy, and only secondarily as a means for citizens to express their interests by selecting among diverse sets of candidates with specified policy positions and constituents. Thus, except for the most recent elections there has been more discussion about election turnout than candidates. The turnout in the nine presidential elections has averaged around 63 percent (see Figure 14.3, presidential elections) and for the seven parliamentary elections has averaged about 60 percent.

Both the 1997 and 2005 presidential elections, however, indicated that under certain conditions elections can be moments of interest articulation and offer information regarding the preferences of citizens. In 1997, it was quite clear that regime candidate was Ali-Akbar Nateq-Nuri, the sitting speaker of the parliament and close confidant of the Leader. However, thanks in part to the burgeoning civil society and his low government profile, Mohammad Khatami, as "the outsider" and "non-regime" candidate, swept to victory with a surprising 70 percent of the vote. In somewhat similar fashion, although with very different political agenda and significance, Mahmud Ahmadinejad surprised many pundits by defeating Ali-Akbar Hashemi Rafsanjani, who has been one of the cornerstones of the Islamic Republic since its establishment. These surprising outcomes indicate in spite of the highly regulated and limited nature of elections in the Islamic Republic, voters do express their views, and these preferences do matter even when they go against the direct wishes of the ruling establishment and the expectations of political experts.

Given the weakness of party organizations mentioned earlier, political parties have played no major role. The factions that contend for power and influence in Iran have not formed a clearly defined party system that would act as a mechanism for representing and aggregating the interests of constituents. Parties and political associations, such as the Society of Combatant Clergy or the Islamic Iran Participation Front, are groupings of members of the political elite that become active during elections, yet until now they have been unable to maintain party discipline with direct and formalized links to the citizenry.

Institutional Groups and Professional Organizations

While political parties are less developed, groups based in state organizations have a more corporate identity and a greater ability to shape policy, in much the same manner as controlled interest group systems. The Islamic Revolutionary Guard Corps and the volunteer mobilization corps (*Basij*), consisting of 120,000, and 90,000 men, respectively,[38] are two of the most prominent arms of the state which directly represent their interests in various fields and policymaking areas, although they were initially established to mobilize support for the regime. These ostensibly military and security forces have also played a role in the economy through their business subsidiaries, which are involved in large-scale construction projects as well as allegedly importing consumer goods. Since the 2003 local council elections, the IRCG and *Basij* have taken a more visible role in politics with a number of their high-ranking figures running for local offices, parliament, and, most recently, the presidency. Finally, since they are in direct communication with the Leader, and not the president and parliament, they have the ability to influence policy.

Iran does have a host of associations representing the interests of labor, business, professional groups, and industrial sectors. However, the House of Labor or the Iranian Chamber of Commerce, Industries, and Mines and other such organizations have operated more as a means for state officials to manage these corporate entities rather than as vehicles to represent specific interest and shape policymaking. Only in very recent elections have professional organizations endorsed different candidates, which may signal the emergence of an independent role for these corporate groups in political competition.

In the course of the struggle against the Shah and in the years following his overthrow, neighborhood councils and guild associations sprang up all over the country as grassroots initiatives to address ordinary citizens' needs during the revolution and the war years, but over time they have become integrated into the patron-client system, and today they are either mere appendages of state officials or means for the state to penetrate society.[39] Hence, there is no clear separation between interest groups and government officials. Moreover, since the revolution the government has encouraged workers, merchants, and students to establish Islamic associations in universities, factories, and guilds as the principal means of aggregating the interests of these groups.

Nonetheless, in the 1990s and especially during the relatively less repressive administration of President Khatami, a large number of genuinely autonomous associations representing strata of society that had been largely sidelined by the revolutionary regime emerged. For instance, various women's organizations of both secular and reformist Islamist persuasion came into being and started initiatives seeking to change discriminatory laws, provide services, and raise general consciousness regarding women's issues. Most notably, the 2003 Nobel Peace Prize Winner, **Shirin Ebadi**, who had been the first women to become a judge under the Shah but lost her job when women were barred from that position following the revolution, was active in a host of legal organizations championing and defending the rights of women, children, and political dissidents. Simultaneously, students and secular intellectuals also took advantage of these opportunities to establish or reactivate associations and publications that were independently minded and represented alternative visions of politics.

Nonassociational Social Groups

As implied by the discussion, many strata in Iran exist without independent associations aggregating and representing their interests. Among the historically and politically important social groups without corporate representation, it is worth mentioning the bazaari merchants. Among the more recent social groups, the war veterans and the relatives of those killed in the war (referred to as "martyrs") stand out.

Bazaari merchants based in the historic covered bazaars of Iran, ranging from retailers and brokers to wholesalers and even international traders, have played a central role in various political episodes from the Constitutional Revolution (1905–1911) to the Oil Nationalization Movement (1951–1953) to the Islamic Revolution. Even though important differences have existed among these bazaaris in terms of socioeconomic status, political persuasion, and position in the international and national economy, they have developed a sense of solidarity because of the clearly defined and vibrant physical space of the bazaar, which ensures socially embedded and cross-cutting relations. Their political significance has historically been enhanced both by their economic power and their close relationship with the ulema. Since the revolution bazaari economic interests have been threatened by the state's domination of the economy and its homogeneity has been undermined by key pro-Khomeini bazaari families being co-opted by the new regime.

War veterans, the families of the martyrs, and those disabled in the Iran–Iraq war make up a large and politically important social group. They are ostensibly represented by various organizations and political groups such as the Martyr's Foundation, the Foundation of the Disinherited, the Society of the Devotees of the Islamic Republic, and the Headquarters of the POWs. But with time these organizations have proved unable to address the everyday demands of many of their constituents adequately, and have moved away from their original mandate of providing services to war veterans and their families. The state has also sought to provide for this important constituency by setting up all kinds of affirmative action schemes (ranging from easier access to higher education to priority in flight reservations) and subsidizing consumer goods for veterans and relatives of both veterans and "martyrs" in order to enhance their socioeconomic standing, yet these measures have not always worked adequately to address the needs of this social group and suppress challenges. Some prominent war veterans and former members of the IRGC have aligned themselves with the reformist faction, calling for greater political participation and freedoms, whereas others have accused the regime of turning its back on the wartime principles of self-sacrifice and justice. For much of the postwar era there have been growing complaints by some war veterans that the memory of the war and respect for the sacrifices of the war generation have faded, while the veterans and relatives of the martyrs have not been sufficiently provided for. This position was given voice by some ultra-conservative newspapers, certain filmmakers engaged in producing war films, and outspoken figures of a group called *Ansar-e Hezbollah* (Partisans of the Party of God) who have taken it upon themselves to combat moral, political, and economic corruption.

Demonstrations and Public Protests

Given the closed nature of institutional interest representation and aggregation, many social groups and political tendencies have turned to civil disobedience to express their grievances. The relatively fresh memory of the demonstrations and strikes that constituted the revolution of 1978–1979 act as a model for workers, students, activist women, and the urban poor to use public collective action as a means to make their claims. Throughout the 1990s, industrial workers, for instance, protested against privatization policies, the selling of state-owned factories, and nonpayment of their wages. One high-profile tactic has been workers blocking the main expressway connecting Tehran to the industrial satellite city of Karaj. These protesters have succeeded on several occasions to block the selling of state-owned factories to private business interests they suspected of planning to lay off workers. Teachers and government pensioners in recent years have protested in front of the parliament to draw attention to their inadequate income. On the eve of the 2005 presidential election, women's groups united to organize protests against the male bias enshrined in the constitution. Ethnic political groups, especially Kurdish and Arab activists on the Iran–Iraq border, have recently been quite vocal in calling for greater distribution of wealth and local authority in their provinces. In 2005, these tensions flared up with mysterious bombings taking place and the Iranian security forces and IRGC responding brutally.

The most dramatic protests, however, have been based in the universities and spearheaded by students. During the summers of 1999 and 2003, student organizations staged sit-ins and demonstrations to protest against authoritarian measures by the regime. In the first case they challenged the closure of a prominent reformist newspaper and in the second case the sentencing of an outspoken intellectual who had questioned clerical rule. These protests were originally based in Tehran University, but they spread to other cities and university campuses and persisted for several days. With little support or protection from reformist parties and other social groups (e.g., workers, bazaaris, and teachers), the volunteer forces (*Basij*) and police violently suppressed the demonstrators and prevented the movement from escalating out of hand.

Although these and other events demonstrate that Iranian society is not completely passive in the face of government policies, the inability for these disparate groups to unite or coordinate their localized organizational capabilities is an indication of the overwhelming social atomization in contemporary Iran. Given the pervasive use of patron-client relations and lack of trust among Iranians, collective action and alliance building is particularly difficult. Moreover, these noninstitutional forms of politics reflect the lack of efficacy of institutional politics and the belief on the part of many Iranians that their political voice cannot be heard unless it is in this form.

POLICY FORMULATION

In the Islamic Republic of Iran state policy is set by a number of bodies, some of them explicitly mentioned in the constitution, some not. Given the mixed nature of the political system, overlaps, duplications, and even contradictions abound, and it is not rare for different policymaking bodies to work at cross-purposes.

State Institutions Mentioned in the Constitution

As befits a theocracy in which, at least in theory, no state policy may contradict Islam, those who determine what contradicts Islam and what does not have a preponderant voice in setting policy. In the Islamic Republic this means first and foremost the Leader. The first Leader, Ruhollah Khomeini, on numerous occasions used his authority to determine state policy by issuing religious edicts (*fatwa*s). On a few occasions these edicts broke with established religious tradition, which is not astonishing given the charismatic nature of his leadership.[40] One of the earliest examples was his ruling on caviar. According to Shiite (and Jewish) dietary laws, a fish can be eaten only if it has scales. The sturgeon, however, has no scales and traditionally its meat and, by extension, its roe (caviar) were not deemed permissible. But caviar is one of Iran's main exports, and so the matter was revisited. A specially appointed state commission concluded that the sturgeon does indeed have scales, but that these are a peculiar shape. Taking note of this finding, in November 1983 Khomeini issued a *fatwa* declaring that caviar could be eaten. In 1988 he broke with other time-honored legal traditions by authorizing the

playing of chess, provided no bets were made on the outcome, betting and gambling being forbidden in Islam. He also liberalized the early republic's stifling cultural life by relaxing the rules pertaining to music and television programming.[41]

Khomeini's interventions in the state's policymaking were often made necessary by continued deadlock between parliament and the Council of Guardians, as discussed earlier. To avoid paralysis, in January 1988 Khomeini amended his doctrine of *velayat-e faqih*, guardianship of the jurisprudent, by issuing an edict that gave the state, as embodied by its Leader, authority to override religious law when that is expedient. This "absolute dominion of the jurisprudent" (*velayat-e motlaqe-ye faqih*), he averred, was the "most important of divine commandments and has priority over all derivative divine commandments . . . even over prayer, fasting, and the pilgrimage to Mecca."[42] This reinterpretation of the theocratic principle was enshrined in the constitution when that document was revised in 1989.

Needless to say, most traditional Muslims and most members of the ulema were horrified by this subordination of religion to reason of state, as the whole purpose of setting up an Islamic state had been the exact opposite. Moreover, no person other than Khomeini could conceivably get away with disregarding religion when it was expedient for the state to do so, and as a result shortly before his death Khomeini invested the newly established Expediency Council with the authority to advise the Leader on invoking the absolute authority. As president (1981–1989) Khamenei had been a member of the conservative faction, and in his first years as Leader he more or less tried to give the impression of remaining above the fray, but with the onset of the Khatami presidency in 1997 he abandoned all pretense of neutrality and became the *de facto* leader of the conservatives who did their best to stymie the reformist zeal of the elected officials.

The Expediency Council has emerged as the institution where the most vital policies of the nation are decided. For instance, in Iran's negotiations with Britain, France, Germany, and the International Atomic Energy Commission about its nuclear program, the top Iranian negotiator, Hassan Rowhani, did not come from the foreign ministry or the Atomic Energy Organization of Iran, but was an engineer-turned-cleric who was the secretary of the National

Security Council, where foreign policy is made, and as such a member of the Expediency Council. Politically identified with Hashemi Rafsanjani, he resigned from his position as chief negotiator after the election of Mahmud Ahmadinejad to the presidency in June 2005. With Ahmadinejad's election, the old establishment became apprehensive about the new president's ultraconservative and populist policies, policies that threaten not only the domestic status quo but also Iran's security.[43] And so in October 2005 the chairman of the Expediency Council since 1997, none other than Ali-Akbar Hashemi Rafsanjani, managed to extract a letter from the Leader that granted the Expediency Council broad supervisory powers over all three branches of government. Whether this move will have a moderating effect on the new administration's policymaking is impossible to tell at this point, but it shows that rivalries among institutions over policymaking powers have not disappeared now that both the presidency and parliament are dominated by conservatives.

In the course of the 1988 revision of the constitution, a body formed some years earlier was added to the official institutional structure: the National Security Council, whose members include the heads of the three branches of government, top military commanders, the foreign minister, the minister of information (i.e., intelligence), and a few other figures named by the Leader. It has emerged as the nation's highest policymaking body in matters of foreign and security policy, which, in the case of the Islamic Republic, includes the struggle against what is officially called "Western cultural aggression."

The Council of Guardians does not have a major policymaking role, but its six lay members are present in parliament when it is in session and have at times attempted to work with sympathetic MPs to introduce legislation. As for parliament itself, it has been largely emasculated as a policymaking body by the unelected bodies mentioned above. Legislative proposals in it come either from the cabinet or from a minimum of 25 MPs, and while successive parliaments have tried to create frameworks for conducting economic policies and changing the penal and civil codes, much of their activities have been stymied by the Council of Guardians.

Areas where the executive branch of government (prime minister until 1989, president since then) and parliament have had an impact on state policy include setting the state budget, the provision and regulation of social and welfare services, and territorial administration, which includes redrawing provincial borders. Beginning in the mid-1980s, for instance, the MPs of the northwestern city of Ardabil campaigned for the creation of a new province around their city. Young men from Ardabil having died in disproportionate numbers in the Iran–Iraq war, the people of the city used the moral leverage that their sacrifices gave them to renew their demands with greater fervor after the war ended in 1988. All sorts of civic associations mobilized for the demand, which was expressed inside parliament by the MPs. In the end the administration of President Hashemi Rafsanjani introduced a bill in parliament providing for the new province. The bill was hotly debated, and finally passed in a secret vote in early 1993.[44]

The extensive powers of the Leader and the existence of such unelected decision-making bodies as the Council of Guardians, the Expediency Council, and the National Security Council severely limit the policymaking role of the elected officials: the president, the individual cabinet members named by him and approved by parliament, and parliament itself. Popular sovereignty is thus severely undermined.

State Institutions Not Mentioned in the Constitution

The role of elected officials is further limited by councils that are not mentioned expressly in the constitution and that were established for the express purpose of formulating state policy in a particular field. The most prominent of these is the Supreme Council for the Cultural Revolution, which was set up by order of Khomeini in 1986 to perpetuate the policies unleashed during the Cultural Revolution of the early 1980s that purged universities of leftists and secularists. Its tasks include determining not only state policies in the realms of culture, education, and research, but also "the spread and reinforcement of the influence of Islamic culture in all areas of society." Its supremacy over parliament can be seen from the fact that in recent years the Council of Guardians has at times vetoed legislation on the grounds that it contradicted policies determined by the Supreme Council for the Cultural Revolution, the latter having the approval of the Leader.

Power Centers and the Difficulty of Policy Coordination

Given the existence of multiple power centers as discussed above, policies are often not coordinated, as some state institutions make and implement their own policies independently of the relevant ministries. This includes the Judiciary, which does not limit itself to implementing the law but in fact takes it into its own hands, and the Revolutionary Guards, who wage their own struggle against dissent and pursue a foreign policy independent of that of the foreign ministry and even the National Security Council.

The impact of these inconsistencies became particularly apparent under President Khatami, when the dispute between reformists and conservatives added an ideological dimension to the diffuse, ill-defined, and overlapping competencies of many state bodies. A few examples will illustrate this.

Under Khatami, who had been a liberalizing minister of culture between 1982 and 1992, the ministry of culture, which controls censorship and issues licenses for newspapers and journals, adopted more liberal policies, inaugurating a period of unprecedented press freedom and diversity. But the Judiciary, headed by a conservative ally of the Leader, used its powers to close down newspapers and indict and jail reformist journalists and editors who had incurred the displeasure of conservatives. For every newspaper that was closed down, the ministry of culture would issue a new license and the newspaper would appear under a new name.[45] But by 2000 the most critical voices had been silenced by the Judiciary and its allies in the armed forces.

Another example comes from the security apparatus. In late 1998, six months after the commander of the Revolutionary Guards had threatened violence against opponents of the regime, a number of opposition politicians, journalists, and writers were killed in what became known as the "chain murders." Khatami insisted on an investigation and persuaded Khamenei to give his consent. Soon it became clear that the murders had been carried out by members of the ministry of information. This led to a purge in the ministry, which operates under the authority of the president and of parliament.[46] It subsequently became more tolerant of dissent and respectful of the law, synergies with the rest of the Khatami administration being facilitated by the fact that some of the key strategists of the reformist camp had been information ministry officials. The result was that the Revolutionary Guards and the Judiciary proceeded to set up their own parallel intelligence organizations, replete with prosecutors and prisons, to pursue the conservatives' agenda of suppressing dissent.[47]

A final example is from foreign policy. Beginning at the end of the 1980s, a number of foreign ministry officials began calling for a policy that would privilege Iran's national interest in light of *realpolitik* rather than the pursuit of worldwide revolution. Tirelessly arguing their case and demonstrating the cost for Iran of remaining on the margins of world diplomacy, they managed to inflect foreign policy vis-à-vis a number of countries, except the United States and Israel. But while government officials engaged in diplomacy and denied that Iran meddled in the internal affairs of other countries, various state or parastatal institutions pursued their own activist foreign policy agendas. Thus, when in 1998 the ministry of foreign affairs reached an agreement with Britain to the effect that Iran would do nothing to carry out the death penalty imposed by Khomeini in 1988 on British author Salman Rushdie, the parastatal Second of Khordad Foundation immediately increased the $2 million bounty it had put on the author's head in 1989. Although the director of this foundation is appointed by the Leader, its administrative and financial autonomy from the government enabled the latter to claim that the foundation was not a state entity.[48] Likewise, while the foreign ministry under Khatami repeatedly stated that Iran would do nothing to impede the Arab-Israeli peace process, which the Iranian government deemed doomed in advance anyway, various organizations such as the IRGC channel funds to the Palestinian Islamic Jihad organization, which carries out suicide attacks on targets in Israel and the occupied territories. These inconsistencies have seriously damaged Iran's credibility on the international scene, as Iranian negotiators seem unable to deliver on their commitments.

Economic Policymaking

One of the most contentious topics in the post-revolutionary era was economic policymaking. From the very outset, the founders of the Islamic Republic and the new elite that staffed the ministries and parastatal organizations had fundamentally differing views on what was the best approach to foster economic development. Initially, those who favored a more state-centered approach to development dominated policymaking through the parliament, ministries, and such institutions as the Construction Jihad. In the 1980s the state played a critical role in rationing hard currency, setting prices for consumer goods, and using the public banking system to distribute loans to key sectors of the economy. The logic of state control found support at the time in large part due to the requirements of war, the political necessity of redistributing the assets of the numerous industrialists who had been forced into exile, and the fact that international investment had come to a standstill.

A liberal approach to development that placed greater emphasis on the private sector and market mechanisms began to dominate policymaking circles in the late 1980s thanks to the end of the Iran–Iraq war and the global rise of neo-liberal development agendas in the wake of the demise of the Soviet Union. The impetus to redirect economic policies,

however, was largely due to the general economic recession and poor performance of the economy, both in comparison to the 1960s and 1970s and in comparison to other late developers (see Figure 14.6 and discussion below). Thus, both the Rafsanjani and Khatami administrations endeavored to restructure Iran's economy by selling state-owned assets, lifting trade restrictions, and encouraging private and foreign investment. These policy initiatives have had mixed results. Iran's trade regime has been liberalized, with ministries and procurement boards now playing a less pronounced role. Furthermore, private banks and industries have begun to develop and take advantage of incentives to export goods. Nonetheless, the deregulation of the economy has also led to hardship, and has therefore faced opposition. On the one hand, many state employees and those who rely on state subsidies have been hurt by the economic insecurity and inflation that have resulted. Many of these Iranians were probably receptive to

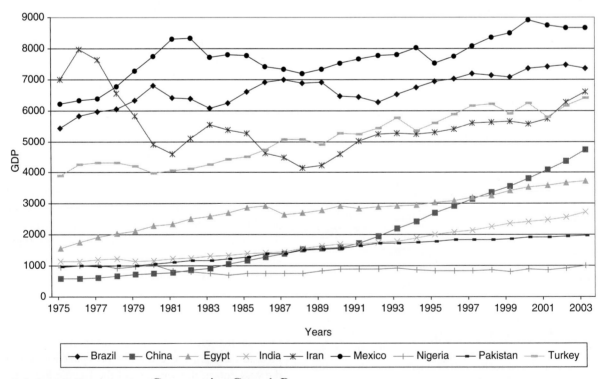

GDP per Capita in Constant PPP $: Selected Countries, 1975–2003

Brazil · China · Egypt · India · Iran · Mexico · Nigeria · Pakistan · Turkey

F I G U R E   1 4 . 6   Comparative Growth Rate

Source: Based on data from Massoud Karshenas and Hassan Hakimian, "Oil, Economic Diversification and the Democratic Process in Iran," *Iranian Studies* 38, 1(March 2055): 67–90.

Ahmadinejad's pro-welfare and anti-inequality message, a message that harkened back to the economic approaches of the 1980s. On the other hand, the government's attempt to reform the economy has challenged the economic powers and vested interests of the large economic foundations that control large portions of Iran's commercial, industrial, and agricultural sectors, and that are largely unaccountable to the parliament, the central bank, and development policymaking bodies.

Khatami's and the reformists' attempt to introduce greater transparency and competition into the economy was rendered largely mute due to the economic foundations' and parastatal organizations' autonomous and privileged access to resources and markets. Thus, any attempt to reform the economy to boost productivity and direct investment toward exports must address the inequality and inconsistencies borne out of the parallel economy largely controlled by these organizations. To date, those who favor liberalizing Iran's economy have been unable to limit the power of the parastatals or even persuade large numbers of Iranians that such an economic reform would benefit them, and this policy bottleneck thus remains unaddressed in practice.

POLICY OUTCOMES

Incoherent Policies

The result of the multiplicity of policymaking bodies has been frequent incoherence and sometimes paralysis. On a positive note, it is precisely this incoherence that has prevented the system from becoming totalitarian, as the overlapping spheres of activity of various state institutions have made centralized control of public life well nigh impossible. To illustrate this, let us look at one example from cultural policy, which is of supreme importance for a regime dedicated to changing the nation's culture.

Traditionally, the ulema have frowned on music, fearing that indulgence in it will whet listeners' appetites for illicit pleasures such as wine and fornication–an association not unknown in the West, as the triad "wine, women, and song" attests. After the revolution, most forms of music were officially banned in Iran, but given the impossibility of suppressing music in a modern society, Khomeini relaxed the prohibitions in a series of edicts, as we saw

earlier. Inside the ministry of culture, whose official name is "Ministry of Culture and Islamic Guidance," a general directorate for music has the task of defining guidelines for what musicians can do in public and what they cannot. Officially, for instance, the 6/8 rhythm, the basis of most Iranian dances, is outlawed; women may not sing solo in front of an audience that includes men; and certain poems by some of Iran's greatest poets, such as Hafez of Shiraz (1326–1390), that castigate the bigotry of the religious classes may not be sung at concerts. When musicians produce a tape, it is this directorate that has the task of granting or withholding a license to have it distributed commercially. This arrangement would seem to give the ministry total authority over musical life, except that another organization, the Islamic Propaganda Organization, which operates directly under the auspices of the Leader, has an arts section that contains a music department too, and this department issues licenses for recordings independently of the ministry of culture in addition to operating a state-of-the-art recording studio that musicians can rent for little money. Paradoxically, it is in fact more liberal than its ministerial counterpart, rumor having it that the Leader is secretly a lover and connoisseur of classical Persian music. Moreover, the state radio and television monopoly maintains its own music bureaucracy, which decides independently of the other two what can be broadcast and what cannot be. The result is that musicians can play one bureaucracy against the other, enhancing their chances of getting around restrictions.[49]

Spreading Progress and Prosperity

The chief complaint of the revolutionaries had been that the Shah's policies failed to benefit the majority of Iranians. And while succeeding administrations in the Islamic Republic have been on the whole indifferent to the interests of the educated upper middle class, they have tried to adopt policies that will improve the lot of the poor.

The state educational system is astonishingly good, given the limitations imposed by the political system. Iranian students regularly win medals at international science olympiads, and literacy rates have continued rising, reaching 84 percent for men and 70 percent for women by 2000, up from 48 percent and less than 25 percent, respectively, in 1970.[50]

After pro-natalist policies in the 1980s, the government realized that birth rates had to be brought down, and inaugurated a multifaceted policy of facilitating birth control. All forms of contraception are widely distributed and subsidized both in cities and in villages, everywhere clinics offer free sterilization to men and women, and the state actively encourages couples to have "only two children, be they boys or girls." All over Iran couples do indeed have fewer children than their parents' generation, but for the foreseeable future Iran's population will keep rising, as the very numerous Iranians born in the 1980s are beginning to have children of their own. The current growth rate of the Iranian population is 1.3 percent, one of the lowest in the Middle East.

Another area where much progress has been made is in health care. Many villages are served by small clinics staffed by paramedics, and there is no shortage of physicians. While the quality of medical care may not always be very high, the degree of its availability to the general population is respectable even when compared with rich Western countries. The success of these rural social and economic development programs has been partly because they have been spearheaded by young members of the

local communities rather than by experts from distant urban areas who typically are unaware of the local needs or social and cultural conditions.

Much effort has gone into improvements in the countryside. Paved roads now connect all towns and many villages, and many villages have been provided with clean water and electricity. But in spite of the state's efforts to create a welfare state financed by oil income, most Iranians struggle to make ends meet. To some extent this is because the middle class has grown tremendously. People whose parents were illiterate and poor peasants now aspire to a middle-class lifestyle; they expect to eat meat every day, send their children to good schools, and have decent housing. Table 14.3 compares some basic human development indicators for the year 2003 of Iran with those of a few comparable countries.[51]

As can be seen, the provision of basic services to the general population has been quite successful. Obviously, more than three decades of high oil income have made a difference, for in many ways the indicators for Iran are closer to those of Turkey than to those of Egypt or Pakistan. However, many Iranians are unwilling to credit the government for this, and impute it to the natural development of a country

TABLE 14.3   Comparison of Development Indicators, 2003

Country	Population	Pop. Growth	Life Expectancy	Infant Mortality (bef. age 1)	Access to Sanitation
Iran	66 million	1.3	69	33	84%
Turkey	70 million	1.5	69	33	83
Egypt	67 million	1.8	69	33	68
Pakistan	148 million	2.4	64	74	54
India	1 billion	1.5	63	63	30
China	1.3 billion	0.6	71	30	44
Mexico	102 million	1.4	74	23	77
Nigeria	136 million	2.4	45	98	38

Country	Literacy/men	Literacy/women	Edu. as part of GNP	GNP/ capita $	GNP/PPP $
Iran	84	70	4.9	2010	7000
Turkey	94	79	3.7	2240	6710
Egypt	67	44	?	1390	3940
Pakistan	57	28	1.8	520	2040
India	68	45	4.1	540	2880
China	95	87	?	1100	4980
Mexico	93	89	5.2	6230	8980
Nigeria	74	59	?	350	900

that disposes of a lot of oil income. It is often argued that with better planning, more competent management, and an acceptance of Saddam Hussein's offer to end the Iran–Iraq war in 1982, the situation might be much better still. Moreover, as Figure 14.6 reveals, over the last three decades Iran's overall macro-economic performance has fallen behind the newly developing countries in Latin America or East Asia and the per capita growth rates have not kept pace with the emerging economic powers of China and India.[52] In fact, Iran's growth indicators have been quite volatile, with a rather extended period of depression in the 1980s due to war, sanctions, high birth rates, and deficient economic policies. Even with the gradual improvement of in per capita GDP since the early 1990s, which was largely due to the rise in oil prices, unemployment remains the number-one worry for young people, and the growth rate of the economy is not nearly enough to absorb the growing population. In fact, youth unemployment increased from 14.8 percent in 1996 to 27.5 percent in 2001.[53]

Islamicization of Society

Another motivation of much policymaking has been the desire to roll back secularism and spread Islamic moral values among the population. Since the early 1980s alcohol consumption has been banned except for the non-Muslim minorities, veiling has been enforced in public spaces, the state has in theory been committed to minimizing contact between unrelated men and women so as to nip temptation in the bud, the religious content of education has been vastly expanded, and gruesome physical punishments have been introduced to chastise adulterers, homosexuals, and other offenders of religious morality.[54] Divine law, as interpreted by the state, also allows capital punishment, and in 2004 the number of death penalties carried out in Iran (159) was second only to China (3400), Iran coming before Vietnam (64) and the United States (59).[55]

Outwardly, the Islamicization of society has been a success. All women cover their hair in public, people are in general more familiar with religious doctrine than before the revolution, the country has more mosques, Friday congregational prayers have become routine in towns and cities, all flights of Iran Air (the national flag carrier) begin with a prayer, and even the best hotels serve no alcohol, even to foreign guests. Underneath the surface, the situation is more complicated, however. Prostitution is rife, driven by poverty. Over two million Iranians are drug addicts. Bootlegging flourishes, often with the connivance of the forces of order, who get a cut. As education has become longer and the marriage age has gone up, young people are much more likely to have premarital sex than their parents' generation, at least in Tehran. As for corruption, it operates at almost all levels, from the petty official who will only do his job if paid a bribe to the relatives of the top leaders who have enriched themselves by controlling economic life.

All of this should not be construed to mean that Iranians have become irreligious. But religious practice has become more private, as the influence of clerics over religious life has declined. One study, comparing data gathered in 1975 and in 2001, demonstrates that while levels of personal religiosity (e.g., frequency of prayer) have remained relatively constant, participation in organized religion (e.g., attendance of congregational Friday prayers) has declined, reflecting a growing ambivalence toward state-sponsored public religious practices.[56]

Iranian Islam has always contained a very anticlerical strain, as many believers have always criticized clerics for their greed and hypocrisy. The ulema's assumption of power in the Islamic Republic has given a new fillip to this tendency. Taxi drivers are known not to stop for clerics, many of whom have taken to wearing civilian clothes in public, and foreign observers are often astonished by how few turbaned clerics one sees in the streets of Tehran.

The rise of anticlericalism has led some of the more thoughtful members of the Shiite clergy to revisit the relations between "church" and state, and call for a separation of the two—not because they advocate secularism, but out of concern for the collective reputation of the ulema. In the Muslim world advocates of the separation of "church" and state had always been secularists; in Iran for the first time *religious* arguments are being made for that separation on the grounds that coercively imposed religion harms spirituality.[57] One may even wonder whether at least some of the pious people who voted for Mahmud Ahmadinejad in the last presidential election did not do so in order to rebuke the ulema, many of whom, such as the losing candidate, Hashemi Rafsanjani, have joined the country's ruling class and are seen to have been corrupted by power.

Gender Relations

One of the key reproaches that Islamists addressed to the Shah's regime before the revolution was that its promotion of Western lifestyles turned women into sex objects and was generally conducive to moral corruption and sexual depravity. Hence the effort to reorder gender relations and place them on an authentic Islamic footing.

Looked at from a Western, liberal perspective, the legal status of women improved dramatically under the Pahlavi monarchy, whereas society remained in its majority more conservative than the legislation governing it. After the revolution much of the legislation aimed at reducing the gender gap was repealed. According to the Islamic penal code introduced in 1981, the value of a woman's life is half of that of a man, in the sense that the law of the talion ("an eye for an eye") instituted by that code explicitly states that the blood-money of a woman is half of that of a man.[58] In practice, this means that if a man kills another man, the relatives of the victim can either ask for the execution of the murderer or accept a legally fixed blood-money, but if a man kills a woman, her relatives can ask for the murderer's execution only if they pay half a man's blood-money. By the same token, in courts of law the testimony of one man is worth that of two women; in some cases (e.g., adultery, murder), a woman's testimony does not count at all. A man can easily divorce his wife, whereas in principle a woman can initiate divorce proceedings only under exceptional circumstances determined by the law; polygamy is recognized under the law. To travel abroad, a wife needs the formal permission of her husband, but the latter can leave the country as he pleases. The foreign wife of an Iranian man can easily acquire Iranian citizenship, whereas an Iranian woman cannot obtain Iranian citizenship for her foreign husband and her children from that husband.[59]

In addition to these legally enshrined restrictions on women's rights, all sorts of *ad hoc* discriminations were instituted in the early years of the Islamic Republic. Many fields of study, such as agronomy and mining engineering, were closed to female students at the universities on the assumption that they were too rough for women, and women's sports were severely restricted because the attire worn by female athletes is incompatible with veiling. This differential treatment of men and women is in stark violation of the International Convention on Civil and Political Rights, an international treaty that prohibits discrimination on religious and gender grounds to which Iran acceded in 1975 and remained a party after its regime changed. But from the point of view of a theocracy, divine law obviously supercedes obligations incurred under international law.

In spite of these legal restrictions, Iranian women have continuously increased their participation in public life and their presence in the public sphere since strict Islamic law began to be enforced in the early 1980s, challenging at the same time the logic of patriarchy.[60] There are a number of reasons for this seemingly paradoxical development. The widespread participation of women in the mass anti-Shah demonstrations of 1978 made it unlikely that their interest in public affairs would end once the revolution was over. After the war against Iraq broke out in 1980, millions of men served at the front, forcing many women to do jobs hitherto performed by men, to the point where many had to become their families' main breadwinners. Furthermore, the aspiration to a middle-class existence awakened by the revolution, coupled with the slow growth of the economy, has meant that women have had increasingly to supplement their husbands' income by joining the labor force. And given the strictly enforced rules on veiling and gender interaction in the public sphere, more traditional women have felt more at ease entering the public sphere while, concomitantly, more traditional men have become less reluctant to let their wives, daughters, or sisters work outside the house. Restrictions that are deeply annoying to nontraditional women have thus had a liberating effect on religiously observant women—and these constitute, after all, a majority of the female population.

The relative strength of antitraditional attitude toward women's roles in society is reflected in the comparative results of the World Value Survey. For instance, while only 4 percent of Egyptians and 12 percent of Jordanians disagree with the statement that "Marriage has become an Outdated Institution," 17 percent of surveyed Iranians agree.[61] A plurality of surveyed Iranians disagree with the statement that "Women need to have children in order to feel satisfied," whereas only 12 percent of Egyptians and 9 percent of Jordanians disagree with it.[62] Finally, 40 percent of Iranians agreed with the statement that

"A working mother can develop intimate relationships with her children just like a non-working mother," a rate that is double that of surveyed Egyptians and Jordanians.[63] Thus, despite the regime initially attempting to inculcate a traditional image and role for women in the family and society, Iranian men and women seem to hold a less narrow view of women.

The visitor to today's Iran encounters women everywhere: they staff government agencies, work in offices, sell goods in shops, own and run businesses. Most dramatically, women now constitute over 60 percent of the student body at the universities, restrictions on what they can study having been gradually lifted throughout the 1990s to the point where none remain. In Persian literature, the traditional emphasis on poetry has given way to a boom in the writing of novels—and most novelists are women. In sports, a daughter of then president Hashemi Rafsanjani took over women's sports in the early 1990s and, using her father's clout, instituted a system whereby women compete under international rules and in normal athletic gear but at locations to which no men are admitted—leading, incidentally, to many more women than before becoming coaches, referees, paramedics, and state sports officials.[64] Even veiling is now enforced less strictly, and the partial covering of the head that hardliners call "mal-veiling" has spread. None other than Khomeini's granddaughter complained in an interview with an American journalist about the state's intrusiveness in this regard.[65]

The widening gap between women's growing participation in public life and the legal system governing their society, and the many-voiced debates to which this discrepancy has given rise, have had repercussions for Islam itself in Iran. Given the impossibility of criticizing any state of affairs from a secular perspective, feminists have had to couch their arguments in Islamic terms. This has led to the emergence of what has been called "Islamic feminism," which is espoused by both truly observant Muslim women and by secular women who have no other way of articulating their demands. Given the continued religiosity of Iranians in general, Islamic feminism has been arguably more effective in raising the gender consciousness of the average woman than secular feminism would have been. These Islamic feminists have been discreetly supported by a few sympathetic clerics who have helped them to contest discriminatory policies or laws by proposing ways to circumvent them or

even suggesting alternative readings of the relevant scriptural passages and legal principles. Small gains have thus been made. Take the issue of divorce. According to Islamic law, marriage is a contract whose clauses have to be agreed upon freely by both husband and wife. A woman has always had the right to ask that her marriage contract include a clause giving her the right to initiate divorce proceedings, but this clause had to be added on to the standard contract issued by the state, and very few bridegrooms consented to it. Since the early 1980s, however, the standard contract includes the clause, meaning that for the woman not to get the right to divorce, bride and bridegroom have to ask for its removal—to which nowadays few educated women consent.

The greater success of women in higher education and the fact that the vast majority of Iranian drug addicts are men, coupled with the continued existence of domestic violence perpetrated by men against women, have led Shirin Ebadi, the woman who, after winning the Nobel prize, more than any other personifies women's struggles and occasional successes, to quip that Iran does not have a "women's question" but a "men's question."

Foreign Policy

Under the Shah, Iran had been an ally of the United States, but the Islamic revolution dramatically changed the foreign policy orientation of the country. Like the French, Russian, Chinese, and Cuban revolutionaries before them, Iran's Islamic revolutionaries also saw themselves as the vanguard of a vast revolutionary wave that would encompass other countries as well. According to the preamble of the constitution of 1979, the role of the army and the IRGC is not limited to "securing the borders" of the country but includes "struggling to spread the rule of divine law in the world." As they took over the reins of government, they found themselves in a position where they had to defend the national interest of Iran vis-à-vis other countries. Managing the inherent tension between an ideological commitment to helping to overthrow or weaken other governments on the one hand, and dealing with these governments on a daily basis on the other, has posed a tremendous challenge. Beginning in the early 1990s, "national interest" rather than "export of the revolution" came to dominate the foreign policy agenda, the best example of this being the discreet support Iran gave to Christian Armenia in its conflict with Muslim (and predominantly Shiite) Azerbaijan in the war that opposed the two Caucasian successor republics of the Soviet Union after the break-up of the USSR in the mid-1990s. But, as elsewhere in the world, there is no consensus as to what actually is in Iran's national interest, and many in Iran argue that Iran's national interest demands the solidification of its ties with the rest of the Islamic world.

Ultimately, the foreign policy of the Islamic Republic has been driven by a "Third Worldist" desire to escape the hegemony of the Western world. In the parlance of Iran's leaders, Western hegemony is referred to as "world arrogance." In its struggle against "world arrogance," Iran has sought alliances, and these can be conceptualized in terms of three concentric circles. The outermost circle consists of Third World nations and in the beginning even included such groups as the Irish Republican Party (IRA) that fought British rule in Northern Ireland. The middle circle is made up of Muslim countries and movements, and the innermost one is constituted by the Shiites in West and South Asia (Lebanon, Iraq, Bahrain, Afghanistan, Pakistan).

In many Third World countries the revolution of 1979 was greeted with sympathy, but the subsequent triumph of hard-line Islamists put a damper on pro-Iranian sympathies in non-Muslim nations. For instance, then President Ali Khamenei's refusal to shake hands with female officials, as strict Islamic norms dictated, while on a state visit in Zimbabwe in 1986, caused a diplomatic incident. Sunni Islamists, for their part, were divided over support for revolutionary Iran. As the *Shiite* nature of the *Islamic* Republic became ever more apparent, and as Khomeini refused to accept Saddam Hussein's offer to end the Iran–Iraq war, thus causing continued intra-Muslim bloodshed, most Sunni Islamists turned away from Iran. This estrangement was encouraged by Saudi Arabia, because the Wahhabi version of Sunni Islam dominant in that country is, of all Sunnis, the most hostile to Shiism. With American connivance, Saudi money helped create a Sunni *cordon sanitaire* around Iran to contain the spread of revolutionary Shiism in such countries as Afghanistan and Pakistan, and so it came to pass that the second Islamic state in the region, that of the Taliban in Afghanistan, was implacably hostile to the Islamic Republic of Iran to the point where a number of Iranian diplomats in that country were actually killed.[66] Today Iran maintains very few

client movements among Sunnis, most notably the Palestinian Islamic Jihad.

This leaves Twelver Shiites as the only group among which Iranian efforts to spread the revolution have been somewhat successful. The founding of Lebanon's Hizballah in the early 1980s was facilitated by Iran, and Iran continues to support the party and its social welfare activities financially. Iran also sponsored formation in Iran of the Supreme Council for the Islamic Revolution of Iraq (SCIRI), a party that, ironically, has come to play a major role in Iraq thanks to the American intervention that led to the ouster of the Saddam Hussein regime.

In the aftermath of 9/11, Iran has found itself surrounded by American-installed governments in Afghanistan and Iraq and by U.S. troops and military bases in the countries to its north and south. At the same time, Al-Qaeda and other anti-Shiite groups pose a threat to the Islamic Republic's claim to constitute the vanguard of a worldwide Islamic revolution. Even within the world of Twelver Shiism, however, the Iranian theocracy may yet lose some influence. If Iraq stabilizes under Shiite hegemony, Najaf could conceivably regain its centrality and independence as a center of Shiite learning, thereby attracting Shiite scholars who do not share Khomeini's notion of *velayat-e faqih*, including even Iranians.

In its relations with the West and the Soviet bloc, the early Islamic Republic had as its motto "Neither East nor West." Iran had been an American ally under the Shah, but after the revolution it joined the Non-Aligned Movement. In practice, however, Iran's foreign policy, like that of many other Third World "non-aligned" countries, was far more anti-Western than anti-Soviet. In the case of the Islamic Republic, this stance reflected on the one hand the revolutionaries' mistrust of a West that had supported the hated Shah, and on the other hand the geographic proximity of the Soviet Union, whose invasion and occupation of neighboring Afghanistan in December 1979 were a constant reminder that greater caution was called for in dealing with this particular superpower. The Islamic Republic has maintained cordial relations with the Soviet Union and Russia, but has not had diplomatic relations with the United States ever since these were severed by the United States in response to the seizure of American diplomats as hostages in November 1979. Iranians have paid a heavy price for their government's hostility to the West. In the last stages of the war against Iraq, most

Western powers discreetly assisted the Iraqi side, and the United States has maintained an economic embargo on Iran, as a result of which, to give but one example, Iranian airlines have found it very difficult to purchase a sufficient number of modern passenger aircraft and adequate spare parts for the old ones, forcing them to keep flying old Russian planes or Boeing jets purchased before the revolution. As a result "Iran's civil aviation sector suffers from one of the world's highest rates of accidents and incidents."[67]

After Khomeini's death, presidents Hashemi Rafsanjani and Khatami tried to lessen Iran's diplomatic isolation. Relations with Arab countries, most of which had supported Iraq in the war, improved, and Iran made an effort to mend its ties with Europe and Japan. In the 1990s, the European Union embarked on a policy of "critical dialogue" with Iran, which offered Iran concessions in exchange for improvement in the field of human rights. During the Khatami years the policies of the government did indeed become less repressive, but given the overall control of unelected bodies none of these liberalizing measures could be institutionalized.

The main issue confronting Iranian diplomacy in its relations with the West is Iran's nuclear program. Since the days of the Shah, successive Iranian governments have declared that they are not interested in developing nuclear weapons, and the official line of the government of the Islamic Republic is that all weapons of mass destruction are contrary to Islamic ethics. Iran is a signatory of the Nuclear Non-Proliferation Treaty, whose article IV grants its signatories the "inalienable right" to "research, develop, produce, and utilize" nuclear technology for peaceful purposes. On that basis, the Iranian government has embarked on a vast program to develop a self-sufficient nuclear industry by mastering the fuel cycle in which uranium is enriched to produce the fuel needed for power reactors. Western countries worry that the know-how thus acquired would also allow Iran to produce highly enriched uranium or plutonium that could be used to manufacture nuclear weapons. What lends this worry a certain plausibility is Iran's development of long-distance missiles to which nuclear warheads could be fitted, and the fact that some nuclear facilities and experiments were kept secret for eighteen years until an exiled opposition group revealed their existence in 2002, at which point the Iranian government allowed IAEA inspectors to visit them. Britain, France, and Germany have negotiated with Iran in the hope of getting the government to suspend its enrichment program, while the IAEA has not declared Iran to be in violation of its treaty obligations. As of this writing, the negotiations were continuing.

CONCLUSION

Iranian politics in the twentieth century were tumultuous by most standards. The century started with a constitutionalist movement seeking to make a monarchy more accountable, and ended with a reformist movement striving to make a theocracy more republican. In between these two bookends, nationalist, religious, secular, and Marxist ideologies competed for followers, while social relations were restructured by deep processes associated with modernization. The Pahlavi monarchy promised to usher Iran into the industrial and modern age, and because of both its successes and failures in doing so, the Shah was overthrown by a mass revolution that established a republic, but one that, unlike other revolutionary regimes, incorporated the clergy.

To manage the many objectives of the revolutionaries, the Islamic Republic has created a bewildering set of institutions and organizations, many of which compete with one another and occasionally work at cross purposes. The regime has been in continuous conflict with the United States and some regional powers such as Israel. It has provided social welfare to many of its citizens, which has resulted in outcomes that were unintended by the establishment, whose authority has increasingly been challenged. By the admission of many of its own leaders, "the economy is sick" and "social pathologies" tarnish all layers of society. Unlike most other states in the region, which have almost completely muzzled dissent, contestation is pervasive and sometimes public even among state officials.

How has a regime that faces so many challenges survived for a quarter of a century, and what are the prospects for significant change? The irony is that the same institutions that have created contestation and allowed a degree of pluralism in Iran have also contributed to the regime's survival and ability to withstand opposition.[68] The fragmented nature of the state enables differences to emerge and persist, but it is this very fragmentation that prevents the aggregation of interests. Thus, even though many of the founders of the Islamic Republic have defected from the regime or called for quite fundamental changes, they have not had the leverage to restructure the regime. Elite politics in Iran today is factional politics, not party politics encompassing debates over specific policies and specified platforms and visions of the future. Factionalism is endemic to the system: although president and parliament have been controlled by the same party since June 2005, parliament refused to confirm the first three of the president's nominees for the important post of minister of oil.

Meanwhile, this fragmented state that spawns a myriad of patron-client networks, in conjunction with a robust coercive apparatus and an individualist political culture, creates divisions at all levels of society. Corporate and associational interests are ill defined and undermined by personalism, and even ideologically similar groups often battle with one another over access to assets. State-society relations as they are constituted now hinder coordination and alliance-building, which are essential for mass mobilization, and prevent the emergence of public deliberation and consensus building.

The multifarious problems faced by the Islamic Republic have reopened the debate on the proper relation between religion and politics in Iran. Going farther than revisiting Islamic law, some reformist Muslims have

begun questioning the very basis of the proposition that what is central to Islam is religious law rather than, say, ethics or personal experience of transcendence. These reformers impute the centrality of Islamic law in Muslim experience to the prominence of the ulema in Muslim society, pointing out that the ulema are, after all, above all legal scholars. This new tendency reconnects with other, nonclerical and nonlegalistic traditions within Islam, as exemplified by the aforementioned Persian poet Hafez of Shiraz, who wrote such verse as:

> Do what you want, but don't hurt anyone
> For that is the only sin in our *shari'a*

As we said at the beginning of this chapter, Iran was the first state in which Islamists got to exercise political power. The problems that they have faced, the forces they have unleashed, and the responses they have elicited from society, could have profound implications for political Islam in the rest of the world. In practice, however, Iran's experience remains of limited relevance to Islamists elsewhere, given the Shiite nature of the Iranian state, for Sunni Islamists can always brush aside the intellectual and social impasses encountered by Iran's regime in its effort to institute Islamic law in all spheres of social life by claiming that they are due to Iranians' sectarian deviation from "true" Islam.

Chronology of Major Events

Year	Important Events	Head of State	President	Prime Minister
1941	Allied invasion in WWII	Shah: Mohammad-Reza Pahlavi	—	Various cabinets
1951	Nationalization of oil			Mohammad Mossadegh
1953	Coup against Mossadegh			Various cabinets
1963	White Revolution and widespread riots in support of Khomeini			
1965				Amir-Abbas Hoveyda
1973	Quadrupling of the price of oil			
1977	Liberalization of regime			Jamshid Amuzegar
1978	Revolutionary mass mobilization			Various cabinets
1979	Revolution and abolition of monarchy	Leader: Ruhollah Khomeini		Mehdi Bazargan
1980	Start of Iran–Iraq war		Abolhasan Banisadr	Ali Rajai
1981	Fundamentalist victory in power struggle		Ali Khamenei	Mir-Hosein Musavi
1988	End of Iran–Iraq war			
1989	Constitutional revision	Ali Khamenei	Ali-Akbar Hashemi Rafsanjani	—
1997			Mohammad Khatami	
2005			Mahmud Ahmadinejad	

KEY TERMS

Assembly of Experts	Ali Khamenei	Mohammad-Reza Shah	Sunnism
Basij	Mohammad Khatami	Pahlavi	theocracy
Council of Guardians	Ruhollah Khomeini	parastatal foundations	Twelver Shiism
Shirin Ebadi	Leader	rentier state	Tudeh party
Expediency Council	*Majles*/Iranian	*Pasdaran*/Islamic	ulema
Islamist	parliament	Revolutionary Guard	*velayat-e faqih*
Ali-Akbar Hashemi	Mohammad Mossadegh	Corps	
Rafsanjani	multiple power centers	*shari'a*	

SUGGESTED READINGS

Abrahamian, Ervand. *Iran between Two Revolutions*. Princeton: Princeton University Press, 1982.

Adelkhah, Fariba. *Being Modern in Iran*. New York: Columbia University Press, 2000.

Amir Arjomand, Said. *The Turban for the Crown: The Islamic Revolution in Iran*. New York: Oxford University Amir Arjomand Press, 1987.

Amuzegar, Jahangir. *Iran's Economy under the Islamic Republic*. London: I.B. Tauris, 1997.

Ansari, Ali M. *Iran, Islam and Democracy: The Politics of Managing Change*. London: Royal Institute for International Affairs, 2000.

Ashraf, Ahmad and Ali Banuazizi. "The State, Classes and Modes of Mobilization in the Iranian Revolution." *State, Culture, and Society* 1, No. 3 (Spring 1985): 3–39.

Ashraf, Ahmad. "The Appeal of Conspiracy Theories to Persians." *Princeton Papers* No. 5 (Winter 1997): 57–88.

Atabaki, Touraj. *Azerbaijan: Ethnicity and Autonomy in Twentieth-Century Iran*. London: British Academic Press, 1993.

Azimi, Fakhreddin. *Iran: The Crisis of Democracy 1941–1953*. New York: St. Martin's, 1989.

Bakhash, Shaul. *The Reign of the Ayatollahs: Iran and the Islamic Revolution*. New York: Basic Books, 1984.

Bakhash, Shaul "The Politics of Land, Law, and Social Justice in Iran." *Middle East Journal* 43, No. 2 (1989).

Baktiari, Bahman. *Parliamentary Politics in Revolutionary Iran: The Institutionalization of Factional Politics*. Gainesville, FL: Florida University Press, 1996.

Bayat, Assef. *Street Politics: Poor People's Movements in Iran*. New York: Columbia University Press, 1997.

Bill, James A. *The Eagle and the Lion: The Tragedy of American-Iranian Relations*. New Haven: Yale University Press, 1988.

Binder, Leonard. *Iran: Political Development in a Changing Society*. Berkeley: University of California Press, 1964.

Buchta, Wilfried. *Who Rules Iran? The Structure of Power in the Islamic Republic*. Washington, DC: The Washington Institute, 1999.

Chehabi, H.E. "Religion and Politics in Iran: How Theocratic Is the Islamic Republic?" *Daedalus* 120, No. 1 (Summer 1991): 69–91.

Chehabi, H.E. "The Political Regime of the Islamic Republic of Iran in Comparative Perspective." *Government and Opposition* 36, No. 1 (Winter 2001): 48–70.

Gasiorowski, Mark J. *U.S. Foreign Policy and the Shah: Building a Client State in Iran*. Ithaca: Cornell University Press, 1991.

Hoogland, Eric, ed. *Twenty Years of Islamic Revolution: Political and Social Transformation in Iran since 1979*. Syracuse: Syracuse University Press, 2002.

Karshenas, Massoud. *Oil, State, and Industrialization in Iran*. Cambridge: Cambridge University Press, 1990.

Keddie, Nikki R. *Modern Iran: Roots and Results of Revolution*. New Haven: Yale University Press, 2003.

Keshavarzian, Arang. "Contestation without Democracy: Elite Fragmentation in Iran." In Marsha Pripstein Posusney and Michelle Penner Angrist, eds., *Authoritarianism in the Middle East: Regimes and Resistance*. Boulder: Lynne Rienner, 2005, pp. 63–88.

Kurzman, Charles. *The Unthinkable Revolution in Iran*. Cambridge, MA: Harvard University Press, 2004.

Maloney, Suzanne. "Agents or Obstacles? Parastatal Foundations and Challenges for Iranian Development." In Parvin Alizadeh, ed., *The Economy of Iran: Dilemmas of an Islamic State*. London: I.B. Tauris, 2000, pp. 145–176.

Martin, Vanessa. *Islam and Modernism: The Persian Revolution of 1906*. London: I.B. Tauris, 1988.

Menashri, David. *Post-Revolutionary Politics in Iran: Religion, Society, and Power*. Portland: Frank Cass, 2001.

Milani, Mohsen. *The Making of Iran's Islamic Revolution: From Monarchy to Islamic Republic*. 2nd ed. Boulder: Westview, 1994.

Moin, Baqer. *Khomeini: Life of the Ayatollah*. London: I.B. Tauris, 1999.

Moslem, Mehdi. *Factional Politics in Post-Revolutionary Iran*. Syracuse: Syracuse University Press, 2002.

Mottahedeh, Roy. *The Mantle of the Prophet: Religion and Politics in Iran*. 2nd ed. Oxford: Oneworld, 2000.

Paidar, Parvin. *Women and the Political Process in Twentieth-Century Iran*. Cambridge: Cambridge University Press, 1995.

Parsa, Misagh. *Social Origins of the Iranian Revolution*. New Brunswick, NJ: Rutgers University Press, 1989.

Sanasarian, Eliz. *Religious Minorities in Iran*. Cambridge: Cambridge University Press, 2000.

Schirazi, Asghar. *The Constitution of Iran: Politics and the State in the Islamic Republic*. London: I.B. Tauris, 1996.

Tajbakhsh, Kian. "Political Decentralization and the Creation of Local Government in Iran: Consolidation or Transformation of the Theocratic State?" *Social Research* 67, No. 2 (Summer 2000): 377–404.

Vahdat, Farzin. *God and Juggernaut: Iran's Intellectual Encounter with Modernity*. Syracuse: Syracuse University Press, 2002.

Zahedi, Dariush. *The Iranian Revolution Then and Now: Indicators of Regime Instability*. Boulder: Westview, 2000.

Zonis, Marvin. *The Political Elite of Iran*. Princeton: Princeton University Press, 1971.

ENDNOTES

1. From Population Action International: http://www.populationaction.org/news/press/ news_042302_Youth.htm
2. From the Washington Institute: http://washingtoninstitute.org/templateC05.php?CID=1556
3. All existing maps showing the linguistic and ethnic groups that make up Iran's population have to be used with caution. Census questions do not include ethnic or linguistic affiliation, and few areas have an ethnically or linguistically homogeneous population, as internal migrations and urbanization have uprooted many people from their original home area. Besides, ethnic self-identification is not equally important to all people. Among the Kurds, for instance, those who are Sunni are much more likely to identify subjectively as Kurds than those who are Shiites. We therefore dispense with a map here.
4. Abdul-Hadi Hairi, *Shiism and Constitutionalism in Iran* (Leiden: E.J. Brill, 1977).
5. Nikki R. Keddie, *Modern Iran: Roots and Results of Revolution* (New Haven: Yale University Press, 2003), p. 123.
6. Mark Gasiorowski, "The 1953 *Coup d'Etat* in Iran," *International Journal of Middle East Studies* 19 (1987): 261–86.
7. See James A. Bill, *The Eagle and the Lion: The Tragedy of American-Iranian Relations* (New Haven: Yale University Press, 1988), pp. 319–78.
8. Richard W. Cottam, *Iran and the United States: A Cold War Case Study* (Pittsburgh: University of Pittsburgh Press, 1988), pp. 156–69.
9. Ahmad Ashraf and Ali Banuazizi, "The State, Classes and Modes of Mobilization in the Iranian Revolution," *State, Culture, and Society* 1 (Spring 1985): 3–39.
10. Misagh Parsa, *Social Origins of the Iranian Revolution* (New Brunswick, NJ: Rutgers University Press, 1989).
11. Ironically, even the Shah himself believed in the omnipotence of the United States and Britain: after his ouster, he blamed these countries for having engineered his demise.
12. Ruhollah Khomeini, "Islamic Government," in *Islam and Revolution: Writings and Declarations of Imam Khomeini*, trans. and annotated by Hamid Algar (Berkeley, CA: Mizan, 1981).
13. See H.E. Chehabi, "The Political Regime of the Islamic Republic of Iran in Comparative Perspective," *Government and Opposition* 36 (Winter 2001): 48–70.
14. Kaveh Ehsani, "Islam, Modernity, and National Identity," *Middle East Insight* 11:5 (July–August 1995).
15. For the prerevolutionary period, see Hossein Mahdavy, "Patterns and Problems of Economic Development in Rentier States: The Case of Iran," in M.A. Cook, ed., *Studies in the Economic History of the Middle East: From the Rise of Islam to the Present Day* (London: Oxford University Press, 1970), pp. 428–67. For the Islamic Republic, see Hootan Shambayati, "The Rentier State, Interest Groups, and the Paradox of Autonomy: State and Business in Turkey and Iran," *Comparative Politics* 26 (April 1994): 307–31.
16. Homa Katouzian, *The Political Economy of Modern Iran* (New York: New York University Press, 1981).
17. On these parastatal foundations, see Suzanne Maloney, "Agents or Obstacles? Parastatal Foundations and Challenges for Iranian Development," in Parvin Alizadeh, ed., *The Economy of Iran: Dilemmas of an Islamic State* (London: I.B. Tauris, 2000), pp. 145–176.
18. Bahman Baktiari, *Parliamentary Politics in Revolutionary Iran: The Institutionalization of Factional Politics* (Gainesville, FL: Florida University Press, 1996).
19. Abdol-Karim Lahiji, "Moruri bar vaz'-e hoquqi-ye Iranian-e gheyr-e mosalman," *Iran Nameh* 19 (1379–80/2001): 19. On the legal discrimination of women, see section "Gender Relations" below.
20. Mehran Kamrava and Houchang Hassan-Yari, "Suspended Equilibrium in Iran's Political System," *The Muslim World* 94 (October 2004): 495–524.
21. Asghar Schirazi, *The Constitution of Iran: Politics and the State in the Islamic Republic* (London: I.B. Tauris, 1998), p. 134.
22. Mehdi Moslem, *Factional Politics in Post-Revolutionary Iran* (Syracuse: Syracuse University Press, 2002).
23. Kian Tajbakhsh, "Political Decentralization and the Creation of Local Government in Iran: Consolidation or Transformation of the Theocratic State?," *Social Research* 67:2 (Summer 2000): 377–404.
24. Before WWI, Westerners considered Iran and other non-Western but nominally sovereign countries such as China and Thailand as "semi-civilized" nations which had some but not all of the attributes of a full-fledged member of the international community. See Gerrit Gong, *The Standard of "Civilization" in International Society* (Cambridge: Cambridge University Press, 1984).
25. Ahmad Ashraf, "The Appeal of Conspiracy Theories to Persians," *Princeton Papers* 5 (Winter 1997): 57–88.
26. See L. Carl Brown, *International Politics and the Middle East* (Princeton: Princeton University Press, 1984), pp. 233–52.
27. Mansoor Moaddel and Taghi Azadarmaki, "The Worldviews of Islamic Publics: The Case of Egypt, Iran, and Jordan," in *Human Values and Social Change: Findings from the Values Survey*. Edited by Ronald Ingelhart (Leiden: Brill 2003): 81.
28. This line of reasoning is based on Azadeh Kian-Thiébaut, "Entrepreneurs privés: entre développement statocentrique et démocratisation politique," in *Les Cahiers de l'Orient* 60 (2000): 65–92.
29. Peter J. Chelkowski and Hamid Dabashi, *Staging a Revolution: The Art of Persuasion in the Islamic Republic of Iran* (New York: New York University Press, 1999), pp. 130–31.
30. Ehsani, "Islam, Modernity, and National Identity," p. 51.
31. Farideh Farahi, "The Antinomies of Iran's War Generation," in Lawrence C. Potter and Gary G. Sick, eds., *Iran, Iraq and the Legacies of War* (New York: PalgraveMacmillan, 2004), pp. 101–20.
32. Mansoor Moaddel and Taghi Azadarmaki, "The Worldviews of Islamic Publics: The Case of Egypt, Iran, and Jordan," in *Human Values and Social Change: Findings from the Values Survey*. Edited by Ronald Ingelhart (Leiden: Brill 2003).
33. Ahmad Sadri, "The Varieties of Religious Reform: Public Intelligentsia in Iran," in Ramin Jahanbegloo, ed., *Iran: Between Tradition and Modernity* (Lanham: Lexington Books, 2004), pp. 117–28.

34. Marvin Zonis, *The Political Elite of Iran* (Princeton: Princeton University Press, 1971).

35. Frances Bostock and Geoffrey Jones, *Planning and Power in Iran: Ebtehaj and Economic Development under the Shahs* (London: Frank Cass, 1989).

36. Khosrow Fatemi. "Leadership by Distrust: The Shah's *Modus Operandi*." *The Middle East Journal* 36 (Winter 1982): 48–61.

37. Mehran Kamrava, *The Modern Middle East: A Political History since the First World War* (Berkeley: University of California Press, 2005), p. 261.

38. Figures are from Wilfried Buchta, *Who Rules Iran? The Structure of Power in the Islamic Republic* (Washington, D.C.: The Washington Institute for Near East Policy and the Konrad Adenauer Stiftung, 2000), p. 68.

39. Assef Bayat, *Street Politics: Poor People's Movements in Iran* (New York: Columbia University Press, 1997).

40. In his discussion of charismatic authority, Max Weber points out that charismatic leaders oppose tradition, and summarizes this attitude in the famous statement ascribed to Jesus: "It has been written . . . , but *I* say unto you." *Economy and Society* (Berkeley: University of California Press, 1976), p. 1115.

41. Schirazi, *The Constitution of Iran*, pp. 67–68.

42. Quoted in Said Amir Arjomand, *The Turban for the Crown: The Islamic Revolution in Iran* (New York: Oxford University Press, 1987), p. 182.

43. In fact, Ahmadinejad belongs to a current of thought that considers the return of the Twelfth Imam imminent. This messianic expectation sets him apart from most other leaders of the Islamic Republic and may yet be the source of friction.

44. For details see H.E. Chehabi, "Ardabil Becomes a Province: Center-Periphery Relations in the Islamic Republic of Iran," *International Journal of Middle East Studies* 29 (Spring 1997): 235–53.

45. For an inside account see Elaine Sciolino, *Persian Mirrors: The Elusive Face of Iran* (New York: The Free Press, 2000), pp. 248–60.

46. For details see Buchta, *Who Rules Iran*, pp. 156–70.

47. How this multiplicity of power centers affects individuals is seen in the story of Dariush Zahedi, an Iranian-American political scientist who had met with dissidents while visiting Iran one recent summer for his research. He was arrested by the ministry of information and held prisoner for two months, before being told that, as far as the ministry was concerned, he was innocent. Except that upon leaving the prison he was immediately rearrested by the intelligence agency of the Revolutionary Guards, who held him for another two months in solitary confinement and subjected him to similar interrogations as his preceding jailers, only in a less respectful tone. He was finally released and returned to the United States through the intervention of a number of Iranian diplomats after academics in the United States had publicized his plight.

48. Maloney, "Agents or Obstacles," p. 149.

49. This is based on H.E. Chehabi's conversations with music officials and musicians in Iran.

50. From Earth Policy Institute: http://www.earth-policy.org/Updates/Update4ss.htm

51. The data are from the 2006 edition of *Der Fischer Weltalmanach* (Frankfurt/Main: Fischer, 2005), pp. 500–15. The source of most figures is the World Bank.

52. Massoud Karshenas and Hassan Hakimian, "Oil, Economic Diversification and the Democratic Process in Iran," *Iranian Studies* 38, 1(March 2055): 67–90.

53. "Youth Employment in Islamic Republic of Iran," report prepared by the Department of International Affairs of the National Youth Organization, October 2004.

54. Mehrangis Kar, "*Shari'a* Law in Iran," in Paul Marshall, ed., *Radical Islam's Rules: The Worldwide Spread of Extreme Sharia Law* (Freedom House's Center for Religious Freedom, 2005), pp. 41–64.

55. The numbers are from Amnesty International.

56. Abdolmohammad Kazemipur and Ali Rezaei, "Religious Life under Theocracy: The Case of Iran," *Journal for the Scientific Study of Religion* 42:3 (2003): 347–361.

57. See Mahmoud Sadri, "Sacral Defense of Secularism: Dissident Political Theology in Iran," in Negin Nabavi, ed., *Intellectual Trends in Twentieth-Century Iran* (Gainesville: University Press of Florida, 2003), pp. 180–92.

58. Mahmud Abbasi, *Qanun-e Mojazat-e Eslami* (Islamic Penal Code)(Tehran: Hoquqi, 2002), p. 108.

59. Following the victory of the Mujahidin in Afghanistan, as the Iranian government became keen on repatriating Afghan refugees to Afghanistan, tens of thousands of Iranian women who had married Afghan refugee men in Iran were told by the authorities that they faced the choice of either seeking a divorce from their husbands or following him to his country.

60. Mehrangiz Kar, "Women's Political Rights after the Islamic Revolution," in Lloyd Ridgeon, *Religion and Politics in Modern Iran: A Reader* (London: I.B. Tauris, 2005), pp. 253–278.

61. Mansoor Moaddel and Taghi Azadarmaki, "The Worldviews of Islamic Publics: The Case of Egypt, Iran, and Jordan," in *Human Values and Social Change: Findings from the Values Survey*. Edited by Ronald Ingelhart (Leiden: Brill 2003): 77.

62. Moaddel and Azadarmaki, "The Worldviews of Islamic Publics," 78. Forty-five percent of Iranians agree with this statement, while 88 and 89 percent Egyptians and Jordanians agree, respectively.

63. Moaddel and Azadarmaki, "The Worldviews of Islamic Publics," 79.

64. For details see *The International Encyclopedia of Women and Sport* (New York: Macmillan, 2001), s.v. "Iran," pp. 586–87. For an eyewitness account by a Western journalist, see Geraldine Brooks, *Nine Parts of Desire: The Hidden World of Islamic Women* (New York: Anchor Books, 1995), pp. 201–11, "Muslim Women's Games."

65. Asked whether she would ever "want to throw off the head scarf in public," she answered: "do you want to issue me my death sentence?" *International Herald Tribune*, 3 April 2003, p. 2.

66. On this point see Vali Nasr, "Regional Implications of Shi'a Revival in Iraq," *The Washington Quarterly* 27 (Summer 2004): 7–24.

67. Najmedin Meshkati, "Iran's Nuclear Brinkmanship, the U.S. Unilateralism, and a Mounting International Crisis: Can Civil Aviation Industry Provide a Breakthrough?" *Iran News*, 26 July 2004, p. 14. Available on the Internet at http://www.irannewsdaily.com/asp/iran_news.asp

68. Arang Keshavarzian, "Contestation without Democracy: Elite Fragmentation in Iran," in Marsha Pripstein Posusney and Michelle Penner Angrist, eds., *Authoritarianism in the Middle East: Regimes and Resistance* (Boulder: Lynne Rienner, 2005), pp. 63–88.

INDEX